Pre-Referral Intervention Manual

Fourth Edition

Stephen B. McCarney
Kathy Cummins Wunderlich

Edited by Samm N. House

Copyright © 2014 by Hawthorne Educational Services, Inc.

ISBN 978-0-578-99278-5

Printed in the
United States of America.
2/22

HAWTHORNE

Phone: (800) 542-1673   Fax: (800) 442-9509   Website: www.hawthorne-ed.com
800 Gray Oak Drive, Columbia, MO 65201

Table of Contents

D. Reading

Behavior
Number

E. Writing

Behavior
Number

I. Interpersonal Relationships

Behavior
Number

J. Depression/Motivation

Behavior
Number

K. Inappropriate Behavior Under Normal Circumstances

Behavior
Number

L. Rules and Expectations

Behavior Number

M. Group Behavior

Behavior Number

N. Social Skills/Communication

Behavior Number

I. Using the *Pre-Referral Intervention Manual*

Generally, the pre-referral process begins with a regular educator calling attention to a student with learning and/or behavior problems. A team of educators, typically composed of a special educator(s), a regular educator(s), and/or a counselor(s) from that building, meets with the educator identifying a student for pre-referral intervention. The team, along with input from the teacher calling attention to the student's needs, pinpoints the specific learning and/or behavior concerns for improvement. Goals and objectives for the student in the regular classroom are formally or informally determined, and intervention strategies for the school environment are agreed upon. With consultant assistance from the pre-referral team, the classroom teacher conducts adjusted behavior and teaching approaches for the student for a specific length of time, which may be for several weeks up to a few months. The student's progress is documented and communication continues between the pre-referral team and the classroom teacher. Based on student performance in response to pre-referral intervention strategies, decisions are made as to the student's ability to succeed in the regular classroom with adjustments in instruction, materials, testing, etc. If the student is successful with these adjustments, he/she remains in the regular classroom with continued support. If the student is not successful; formal referral, assessment, and special education services are likely to follow.

The following steps are recommended for using the *Pre-Referral Intervention Manual* in the pre-referral intervention process.

Step 1: The regular education teacher calls attention to the student with learning and/or behavior problems. The *Learning and Behavior Problem Checklist* is a valuable resource in pinpointing specific areas of concern.

Step 2: The pre-referral consultant team (e.g., special educator, regular educator, counselor) for the building meets with the regular education teacher to pinpoint specific learning and/or behavior problems the student exhibits.

Step 3: Goals and objectives for the student are determined. Specific intervention strategies from the *Pre-Referral Intervention Manual* are selected for the student from the learning and behavior problems which were pinpointed.

Step 4: With consultant assistance from the pre-referral team, the classroom teacher conducts adjusted behavior and teaching interventions for the student.

Step 5: The student's progress toward the goals and objectives are documented by the classroom teacher. Documenting may be done using the *Intervention Strategies Documentation Form.*

Step 6: The pre-referral team and the classroom teacher consult to determine the student's progress.

Step 7: If the student is progressing in the regular education classroom with interventions, the process is continued with consultant support for the classroom teacher and student.

Step 8: If the student's needs cannot be met in the regular classroom, with adjusted behavior and teaching interventions, formal documentation of the student's learning and behavior performance are used to make a formal referral for assessment and consideration for special services.

(Please note: A more detailed pre-referral model is provided by J.L. Graden, A. Casey, and S.L. Christenson, (1985). Implementing a pre-referral intervention system: Part I. The model. *Exceptional Children, 51(5),* 377-384.)

II. Interventions

A. Memory, Abstractions, Generalizations, and Organization

1. Model organization and appropriate use of work materials (e.g., putting materials away before getting others out, having a place for all materials, maintaining an organized desk area, following a schedule for the day, etc.).

2. Allow natural consequences to occur (e.g., work not done during work time must be made up during recreational time, materials not maintained will be lost or not serviceable, etc.) as the result of the student's inability to organize or use materials appropriately.

3. Allow the student to finish an activity unless it will be disruptive to the schedule.

4. Assess the quality and clarity of directions, explanations, and instructions given to the student.

5. Choose a peer to work with the student on specified activities to make sure the student has the materials necessary to do the activity.

6. Encourage the student to ask himself/herself each morning before leaving the house if he/she has everything.

7. Have the student leave necessary materials at specified activity areas.

8. Assist the student in finding a method of organization that works best for him/her (e.g., subject folders, tabbed binder, checklist, etc.).

9. Communicate with parents (e.g., notes home, phone calls, etc.) to share information about the student's progress. The parents may reinforce the student at home for being organized/prepared for specified activities at school.

10. Use monthly calendars to keep track of important events, due dates, assignments, etc.

11. Do not accept excuses. Regardless of the reasons, the student should take responsibility for not turning in a math assignment, losing pencils, etc.

12. Have the student chart the number of times he/she is organized/prepared for specified activities.

13. Help the student develop an awareness of himself/herself and the environment. Instruct the student to step back and ask himself/herself, "What materials do I need to complete this assignment?" "Have I put my assignment in the correct folder?"

14. Have the student list five qualities of an organized person. Have the student choose one of those qualities to work on each week for five weeks.

15. Encourage the student to keep necessary materials for specified activities together (e.g., gym clothes in a gym bag in the car, backpack with all school-related materials by the door, etc.).

16. Reduce distracting stimuli (e.g., place the student on the front row, provide a carrel or quiet place away from distractions, etc.). This is used as a means of reducing distracting stimuli and not as punishment.

17. Encourage the student to manage his/her daily performance as if he/she were self-employed. This should increase his/her motivation to be organized and fulfill his/her responsibilities.

18. Encourage the student to put items that should be taken to work/school in a designated place (e.g., in front of the door, at the bottom of the stairs, etc.).

19. Choose different people (e.g., counselor, paraprofessional, peer, etc.) to help the student maintain organization of assignments, materials, etc., at school.

20. Provide the student with an appropriate place to store/secure personal property (e.g., desk, locker, closet, etc.). Require the student to store all property when not in use.

21. Establish a routine to be followed for organization and appropriate use of school materials. Provide the routine for the student in written form and verbally review it often.

22. Assign the student organizational responsibilities in the classroom (e.g., equipment, software materials, etc.).

23. Establish classroom rules:
- Have necessary materials.
- Concentrate while working.
- Work quietly.
- Remain in your seat.
- Finish task.
- Meet task expectations.

Review rules often. Reinforce students for following the rules.

24. Evaluate the appropriateness of the task to determine (a) if the task is too easy, (b) if the task is too difficult, and (c) if the length of time scheduled to complete the task is adequate.

25. Assist the student in organizing materials. As the student demonstrates success, gradually decrease the assistance and require the student to independently assume more responsibility for organization.

26. Give the student one task to perform at a time. Introduce the next task after the student has successfully completed the previous task in an organized way.

27. Have the student assemble all the materials necessary to work on a project, assignment, etc., to reduce the need to search for materials.

28. Make the student aware that work not completed because necessary materials were not brought to the specified activity will need to be completed during recreational or break time.

29. Have the student discard items (e.g., paperwork) that have no future use.

30. Reduce the number of materials for which the student is responsible. As the student demonstrates appropriate responsibility for materials, increase the number of materials for which the student is responsible.

31. Do not replace materials when the student fails to appropriately care for them.

32. Have the student establish a routine to follow before coming to class (e.g., check which activity is next, determine what materials are necessary, collect materials, etc.).

33. Have the student choose a peer, friend, etc., who displays the ability to organize an assignment prior to beginning it. Have the student observe that person and try to model the behaviors which allow him/her to organize assignments.

34. Have the student label all personal property with his/her name.

35. Help the student develop an awareness of the consequences of his/her behavior by writing down or talking through problems which may occur due to disorganization (e.g., missed assignments, incomplete projects, misplaced textbooks, etc.).

36. Make sure that failure to have necessary materials results in loss of opportunity to participate in activities or a failing grade for that day's activity (e.g., art, home economics, industrial arts, physical education, etc.).

37. Have the student compile a list of materials (e.g., band instrument, gym clothes, calculator, etc.) necessary for each class.

38. Have the student organize major projects/assignments by dividing them into small segments. Set deadlines and provide the student with a reward after completing each segment of the assignment.

39. Have the student perform one task or step of a major project at a time.

40. Have the student ask questions about directions, expectations, instructions he/she does not understand.

41. Model being organized/prepared for specified activities.

42. Choose a peer to model being organized/prepared for specified activities for the student.

43. Instruct the student to carry needed items in a backpack or binder.

44. Have the student utilize a weekly schedule. Have the student develop an organizational checklist/chart for daily assignments to be completed during the week.

45. Interact frequently with the student to prompt organizational skills and appropriate use of materials.

46. Have the student establish a routine to follow before changing activities (e.g., put away materials, assemble materials for the next activity, make a list of what materials need to be replenished, etc.).

47. Limit the student's freedom to borrow school property if he/she is unable to remember to return borrowed items.

48. Limit the student's access to materials (i.e., provide the student with only those materials necessary at any given time).

49. Make sure that all personal property is labeled with the student's name.

50. Have the student organize his/her book bag/backpack every day before going home. Place paperwork in folders, prioritize the next day's assignments, and update his/her organizational calendar.

51. Make sure the student understands that he/she must replace things which are lost.

52. Minimize materials needed for specificd activities.

53. Monitor the student's performance in activities or tasks to make sure the student begins, works on, and completes an assignment in a timely manner so that he/she can go to the next activity in his/her routine.

54. Provide a color coded organizational system (e.g., notebook, folders, etc.).

55. Teach the student to maintain care of personal property and school materials (e.g., keep property with him/her, know where property is at all times, secure property in lockers, leave valuable property at home, etc.).

56. Provide adequate time for completion of activities.

57. Provide an organizer for materials inside the student's desk.

58. Require that lost or damaged property be replaced by the student. If the student cannot replace the property, restitution can be made by working at school.

59. Provide the student with a container in which to carry necessary materials for specified activities (e.g., backpack, book bag, briefcase, etc.).

60. Provide the student with a list of necessary materials for each activity of the day.

61. Remind the student at the end of the class period of materials required for specified activities the next day (e.g., note sent home, verbal reminder, etc.).

62. Provide the student with a schedule of daily events so that he/she knows exactly what and how much there is to do in a day.

63. Assign the student shorter tasks. As the student demonstrates success in organizing academic activities, gradually increase the length of tasks over time.

64. Assist the student in beginning each task to reduce impulsive behavior.

65. Provide the student with an organizational checklist (e.g., routine activities, materials needed, and steps to follow).

66. Provide the student with clearly stated criteria for acceptable work (e.g., neatness, etc.).

67. Reinforce those students in the classroom who are organized/prepared for specified activities.

68. Provide the student with more work space (e.g., a larger desk or table at which to work).

69. Provide the student with only those materials he/she needs to complete an assignment (e.g., pencil, paper, dictionary, handwriting sample, etc.). Be sure that the student has only these necessary materials on his/her desk.

70. Minimize materials needed to be kept inside the student's desk.

71. Provide the student with structure for all academic activities (e.g., specific directions, routine format for tasks, time limits, etc.).

72. Have the student maintain an assignment notebook which indicates those materials needed for each class.

73. Provide time at various points throughout the day for the student to organize his/her materials (e.g., before school, beginning of class period, break time, recess, lunch, end of the day, etc.).

74. Make sure that the student is not inadvertently reinforced for losing materials. Provide the student with used materials, copies of the materials, etc., rather than new materials if he/she fails to care for the materials in an appropriate manner.

75. Set aside time each week for the student to organize his/her locker.

76. Speak to the student to explain (a) what he/she is doing wrong (e.g., failing to bring necessary materials for specified activities) and (b) what he/she should be doing (e.g., having necessary materials for specified activities).

77. Require that assignments done incorrectly, for any reason, be redone.

78. Have the student use monthly calendars to keep track of important events, due dates, assignments, etc.

79. Supervise the student while he/she is performing school work to monitor quality.

80. Provide storage space for materials the student is not using.

81. Provide adequate transition time between activities for the student to organize his/her materials.

82. Teach the student time-management skills. Have the student make a daily plan and follow it. Encourage the student to avoid becoming distracted by events, impulses, and moods.

83. Provide the student with verbal reminders of necessary materials required for each activity.

84. Teach the student to prioritize assignments (e.g., according to importance, length, etc.).

85. Reinforce the student for having necessary materials for specified activities: (a) give the student a tangible reward (e.g., classroom privileges, line leading, passing out materials, five minutes free time, etc.) or (b) give the student an intangible reward (e.g., praise, fist bump, smile, etc.).

86. Teach the student how to conserve rather than waste materials (e.g., amount of glue, paper, tape, etc., to use; putting lids, caps, tops on such materials as markers, pens, bottles, jars, cans, etc.).

87. Write a contract with the student specifying what behavior is expected (e.g., having necessary materials for specified activities) and what reinforcement will be made available when the terms of the contract have been met.

88. Have the student develop and maintain one list of things to do to organize and focus on what needs to be accomplished for a specific task, day, etc.

2 Has limited memory skills

1. Have the student's hearing checked if it has not been recently checked.

2. Have the student ask questions about directions, explanations, and instructions he/she does not understand.

3. Have the student be a classroom messenger. Give the student a verbal message to deliver to another teacher, secretary, administrator, etc. As the student demonstrates success, increase the length of the messages.

4. Review the schedule of the morning and afternoon activities with the student and have him/her repeat the sequence. As the student is successful, increase the length of the sequence.

5. Have the student participate in concentration game activities with a limited number of symbols. As the student demonstrates success, gradually increase the number of symbols.

6. Reinforce the student for remembering to have such materials as pens, pencils, paper, textbooks, notebooks, etc.

7. At the end of the school day, have the student recall three activities in which he/she participated during the day. As the student demonstrates success, gradually increase the number of activities the student is required to recall.

8. After a field trip or special event, have the student sequence the activities which occurred.

9. After reading a short story, have the student identify the main characters, sequence the events, and report the outcome of the story.

10. Have the student deliver the schedule of daily events to other students.

11. Use multiple modalities (e.g., auditory, visual, tactile, etc.) when presenting directions, explanations, and instructional content.

12. Choose a peer tutor to participate in short-term memory activities with the student (e.g., concentration games, following directions, etc.).

13. Record a message. Have the student write down the message after he/she has heard it. As the student demonstrates success, increase the length of the message.

14. Involve the student in activities to facilitate short-term memory skills (e.g., deliver messages from one location to another; act as group leader, teacher assistant, etc.).

15. Have the student practice short-term memory skills by participating in activities which are purposeful (e.g., delivering messages, being in charge of room clean up, acting as custodian's helper, operating equipment, etc.).

16. Informally assess the student's auditory and visual short-term memory skills to determine which is stronger. Utilize the results when presenting directions, explanations, and instructional content.

17. Have the student practice repetition of information to increase short-term memory skills (e.g., repeating names, phone numbers, dates of events, etc.).

18. Teach the student how to organize information into smaller units (e.g., break the number sequence 132563 into units of 13, 25, 63).

19. Use sentence dictation to develop the student's short-term memory skills. Begin with sentences of three words. As the student demonstrates success, gradually increase the length of the sentences.

20. Show the student an object or a picture of an object for a few seconds. Ask the student to recall specific attributes of the object (e.g., color, size, shape, etc.) after it has been removed from sight.

21. Deliver directions, explanations, and instructional content in a clear manner and at an appropriate pace.

22. Have the student practice taking notes for specific information the student needs to remember.

23. Teach the student to recognize key words and phrases related to information to facilitate short-term or long-term memory skills.

24. Make sure the student is attending to the source of information (e.g., eye contact is being made, hands are free of materials, student is looking at assignment, etc.).

25. Reduce distracting stimuli when information is being presented, the student is studying, etc.

26. Stop at various points during the presentation of information to check the student's comprehension.

27. Give the student one task to perform at a time. Introduce the next task only when the student has successfully completed the previous task.

28. Have the student memorize the first sentence or line of poems, songs, etc. As the student experiences success, require more to be memorized.

29. Teach the student information-gathering skills (e.g., listen carefully, write down important points, ask for clarification, wait until all information is received before beginning, etc.).

30. Have the student repeat/paraphrase directions, explanations, and instructions.

31. Reduce the emphasis on competition. Competitive activities may cause the student to hurry and begin without listening carefully.

32. Provide the student with environmental cues and prompts designed to facilitate success in the classroom (e.g., posted rules, schedule of daily events, steps for performing tasks, etc.).

33. Provide the student with written lists of things to do, materials needed, etc.

34. Maintain consistency in sequential activities to facilitate the likelihood of student success (e.g., the student has math every day at one o'clock, recess at two o'clock, etc.).

35. Break sequences into units and have the student learn one unit at a time.

36. Establish a regular routine for the student to follow in performing activities, assignments, etc., (e.g., listen to the person speaking to you, wait until directions are completed, make sure you have all necessary materials, etc.).

37. Teach the student to use associative cues or mnemonic devices to remember sequences.

38. Actively involve the student in learning to remember sequences by having the student physically perform sequential activities (e.g., operating equipment, following recipes, solving math problems, etc.).

39. Have the student be responsible for helping a peer remember sequences.

40. Use concrete examples and experiences in sharing information with the student.

41. Teach the student to recognize main points, important facts, etc.

42. Teach the student to rely on resources in the environment to recall information (e.g., notes, textbooks, pictures, etc.).

43. When the student is required to recall information, provide auditory cues to help the student remember the information (e.g., key words, a brief verbal description to clue the student, etc.).

44. Assess the meaningfulness of the material to the student. Remembering is more likely to occur when the material is meaningful and the student can relate to real experiences.

45. Relate the information being presented to the student's previous experiences.

46. Give the student specific categories and have the student name as many items as possible within that category (e.g., objects, persons, places, etc.).

47. Give the student a series of words or pictures and have the student name the category to which they belong (e.g., objects, persons, places, etc.).

48. Help the student employ memory aids to recall words (e.g., a name might be linked to another word; for example, Mr. Green is a very colorful person.).

49. Give the student a series of words describing objects, persons, places, etc., and have the student identify the opposite of each word.

50. Encourage the student to play word games such as Hangman®, Scrabble®, Password™, etc.

51. Have the student complete fill-in-the-blank sentences with appropriate words (e.g., objects, persons, places, etc.).

52. Tell the student what to listen for when being given directions, receiving information, etc.

53. Evaluate the appropriateness of the memory activities to determine (a) if the task is too difficult and (b) if the length of time scheduled to complete the task is adequate.

54. Label objects, persons, places, etc., in the environment to help the student recall their names.

55. Make sure the student receives information from a variety of sources (e.g., texts, discussions, visual presentations, etc.) to facilitate memory/recall.

56. Teach the student listening skills (e.g., stop working, look at the person delivering questions and directions, have necessary note-taking materials, etc.).

57. Teach the student direction-following skills (e.g., stop doing other things, listen carefully, write down important points, wait until all directions are given, question any directions not understood, etc.).

58. Describe objects, persons, places, etc., and have the student name the items described.

59. Have the student audio record directions, explanations, instructions, lectures, etc. The student may replay the information as needed.

60. Highlight or underline important information the student reads (e.g., directions, reading assignments, math word problems, etc.).

61. Have the student outline, highlight, underline, or summarize information which should be remembered.

62. Have the student quietly repeat to himself/herself information just heard to help remember the information.

63. Make sure the student is not required to learn more information than he/she is capable of learning at any time.

64. Make sure the student has adequate opportunities for repetition of information through different experiences to facilitate memory.

65. Write a contract with the student specifying what behavior is expected (e.g., following one-step directions, two-step directions, etc.) and what reinforcement will be made available when the terms of the contract have been met.

66. Reinforce the student for demonstrating short-term or long-term memory skills based on the length of time the student can be successful. As the student demonstrates success, gradually increase the length of time required for reinforcement.

67. Reinforce the student for demonstrating short-term or long-term memory skills: (a) give the student a tangible reward (e.g., classroom privileges, line leading, passing out materials, five minutes free time, etc.) or (b) give the student an intangible reward (e.g., praise, fist bump, smile, etc.).

3 Has difficulty understanding abstract concepts

1. Use abstract concepts to describe tangible objects in the environment (e.g., larger, smaller, square, triangle, etc.).

2. Label tangible objects in the classroom with signs that convey abstract concepts (e.g., larger, smaller, square, triangle, etc.).

3. Use concrete examples when teaching abstract concepts (e.g., numbers of objects to convey "more than," "less than;" rulers and yardsticks to convey concepts of "height," "width," etc.).

4. Play *Simon Says* to facilitate the understanding of abstract concepts (e.g., "Find the largest desk." "Touch something that is a rectangle.").

5. Conduct a scavenger hunt. Have the student look for the smallest pencil, tallest boy, etc., in the classroom.

6. Teach shapes using common objects in the environment (e.g., round clocks, rectangular desks, square tiles on the floor, etc.).

7. Evaluate the appropriateness of having the student learn abstract concepts at this time.

8. Teach abstract concepts (e.g., dimensionality, size, shape, etc.) one at a time before pairing the concepts.

9. Provide repeated physical demonstrations of abstract concepts (e.g., identify things far away and close to the student, identify a small box in a large room, etc.).

10. Review daily abstract concepts which have been previously introduced. Introduce new abstract concepts only after the student has mastery of those previously presented.

11. Choose a peer to spend time each day with the student pointing out abstract concepts in the classroom (e.g., the rectangular light switch plate, the round light fixture, the tallest girl, etc.).

12. Rely on tangible objects (e.g., boxes for dimensionality, family members for size, distances in the classroom for space, cookie cutters for shape, etc.) when introducing abstract concepts. Do not introduce abstract concepts by using their descriptive titles such as square, rectangle, triangle, etc., without a tangible object.

13. Have the student match the names of abstract concepts (e.g., square, circle, etc.) with objects (e.g., floor tile, clock, etc.).

14. Give the student direction-following assignments (e.g., "Go to the swing which is the farthest away." "Go to the nearest sandbox.").

15. Have the student sort left and right gloves, shoes, hand and foot paper cut-outs, etc.

16. Have the student physically perform spatial relationships (e.g., have the student stand near the teacher, far from the teacher, on a table, under a table, etc.).

17. Have the student ask questions about directions, explanations, or instructions he/she does not understand.

18. Call attention to spatial relationships which occur naturally in the environment (e.g., a bird flying "over" a tree, a squirrel running "under" a bush, etc.).

19. Have the student follow simple map directions to practice more abstract concepts such as left and right; north, south, east, and west. Begin with a map of the school and progress to a map of the community, state, nation, etc., with more complex directions to follow.

20. Teach the student relationships of left and right by placing paper bands labeled "left" and "right" around his/her wrists. Discontinue the paper bands when the student can successfully identify left and right.

21. Use a scale, ruler, measuring cups, etc., to teach abstract measurement concepts.

22. Avoid the problem of mirror image by standing next to the student when giving right and left directions.

23. Do not require the student to learn more information than he/she is capable of learning at any time.

24. Use real coins and dollar bills, clocks, etc., to teach abstract concepts of money, telling time, etc.

25. Use the terms "right" and "left" as part of the directions you give to the student (e.g., refer to the windows on the left side of the room, the wall-mounted board on the right side of the room, etc.).

26. Have the student practice following directions on paper. Instruct the student to make marks or pictures on the right, left, middle, top, and bottom parts of the paper according to the directions given.

27. Relate what the student has learned in one setting or situation to other situations (e.g., vocabulary words learned should be pointed out in reading selections, math problems, story writing, etc.).

28. Make sure the student is attending to the source of information (e.g., eye contact is being made, hands are free of materials, etc.) when delivering directions that involve abstract concepts.

29. Label abstract concepts throughout the classroom (e.g., triangle shapes on the walls, left and right sides of a desk, compass directions on the walls, etc.) to help the student understand abstract concepts.

4 Fails to find locations in the building

1. Have the student ask questions about directions, explanations, and instructions he/she does not understand.

2. Have a peer accompany the student when attempting to find locations in the building.

3. Choose a peer to model finding locations in the building for the student.

4. Take the student on a personal tour of various locations in the building.

5. Limit the number of locations the student is required to find on his/her own. As the student demonstrates success, gradually increase the number of locations.

6. Develop clear, concise written directions or a map for the student to use to find locations in the building.

7. Color code locations in the building (e.g., boys' restroom doors painted red, girls' restroom doors painted yellow, names of locations, arrows, etc.).

8. Provide universal symbols at locations throughout the building (e.g., restroom, cafeteria, library, etc.).

9. Have the student run errands to specific locations in the building for practice in finding locations in the building.

10. Inform other personnel that the student has difficulty finding locations in the building so assistance and supervision may be provided.

11. Make sure the behavior demands are appropriate for the student's abilities (e.g., finding locations alone, finding locations with other students around, etc.).

12. Teach the student to ask for directions when he/she has difficulty finding locations in the building.

13. Be consistent in applying consequences for behavior (e.g., appropriate behavior receives positive consequences while inappropriate behavior receives negative consequences).

14. Identify regular routes the student is required to use to find locations in the building.

15. Have the student carry a map of locations in the building.

16. Have the student develop directions for finding locations in the building.

17. Allow the student to move from one location to another in the building only at specified times (e.g., if the student has difficulty finding locations in the building when other students are in the halls, allow the student to move from one location to another when others are not present).

18. Have the student move from one location to another with a group of students until he/she develops the ability to find the locations independently.

19. Have the student identify various landmarks throughout the building which can help in finding necessary locations in the building.

20. Make sure the student is attending to the source of information (e.g., eye contact is being made, hands are free of materials, etc.) when directions to specific locations in the school building are given.

21. Have the student review directions before leaving the classroom to find certain points throughout the building (e.g., have the student repeat directions back to you, have the student look at a map, etc.).

22. When giving the student directions to certain points throughout the building, use concrete clues such as the drinking fountain, restrooms, lunchroom, etc., (e.g., "Go to the room that is just past the lunchroom." "The bathroom is on the left side of the drinking fountain.").

23. Teach the student direction-following skills (e.g., stop doing other things, listen carefully, write down important points, wait until all directions are given, question any directions not understood, etc.).

24. Use pictures, diagrams, the wall-mounted board and gestures when delivering information.

25. When delivering directions, explanations, and information; be sure to use vocabulary that is within the student's level of comprehension.

26. Evaluate the appropriateness of the task to determine (a) if the task is too easy, (b) if the task is too difficult, and (c) if the length of time scheduled to complete the task is adequate.

27. Communicate with parents (e.g., notes home, phone calls, etc.) to share information about the student's progress. The parents may reinforce the student at home for finding necessary locations in the school.

28. Write a contract with the student specifying what behavior is expected (e.g., going to and from the restroom in a reasonable amount of time) and what reinforcement will be available when the terms of the contract have been met.

29. Reinforce those students in the classroom who demonstrate the ability to find necessary locations in the building.

30. Speak to the student to explain (a) what the student is doing wrong and (b) what the student should be doing.

31. Reinforce the student for demonstrating the ability to find necessary locations in the building: (a) give the student a tangible reward (e.g., classroom privileges, line leading, passing out materials, five minutes free time, etc.) or (b) give the student an intangible reward (e.g., praise, fist bump, smile, etc.).

5 Does not respond appropriately to environmental cues

1. Match the environmental cues to the student's ability to respond (e.g., visual cues are used for students who cannot hear, symbols or auditory cues are used for students who cannot read, etc.).

2. Have the student ask questions about environmental cues not understood.

3. Choose a peer to model appropriate responses to environmental cues for the student.

4. Provide supportive information to assist the student in responding appropriately to environmental cues (e.g., "When the bell rings, it is time for lunch.").

5. Provide repeated practice in responding appropriately to environmental cues.

6. Make the student responsible for identifying environmental cues for peers (e.g., bells, rules, reminders, etc.).

7. Provide the student with universal environmental cues (e.g., symbols for male and female, arrows, exit signs, danger symbols, etc.).

8. Pair environmental cues with verbal explanations and immediate reinforcement for appropriate responses.

9. Prepare the student in advance of the delivery of environmental cues to increase successful responding.

10. Make sure the same environmental cues are used throughout all locations in and outside of the building.

11. Establish environmental cues that the student is expected to follow (e.g., bells, rules, point cards, reminders, etc.).

12. Evaluate the appropriateness of the environmental cues the student is expected to follow to determine (a) if the cue is too difficult and (b) if the length of time required to respond to the cue is adequate.

13. Model appropriate responses to environmental cues for the student to imitate.

14. Have the student master appropriate responses to one environmental cue at a time, prioritizing environmental cues in order of importance for mastery, before introducing additional cues.

15. Have the student observe and imitate the responses of peers to environmental cues (e.g., as the student is learning to respond appropriately to doors identified as In and Out, the student can imitate the behavior of peers who use the appropriate doors to enter and leave areas of the educational environment) to increase success in learning environmental cues.

16. Reinforce the student for asking the meaning of environmental cues not understood (e.g., bells, signs, etc.).

17. Provide the student with simulation activities in the classroom to teach successful responses to environmental cues (e.g., responses to words, symbols, directions, etc.).

18. Choose a peer to accompany the student and act as a model in teaching appropriate responses to environmental cues as the student moves throughout the building.

19. Stop at various points throughout the day (e.g., when the lunch bell rings, when walking by restroom signs, etc.) to point out the different cues to the students.

20. Provide the student with verbal reminders or prompts when he/she misses an environmental cue.

21. Review daily the environmental cues that are important to the student (e.g., bells, signs, etc.).

22. Use vocabulary that is within the student's level of comprehension when delivering directions, explanations, and information.

23. Communicate with parents (e.g., notes home, phone calls, etc.) to share information about the student's progress. The parents may reinforce the student at home for responding appropriately to environmental cues at school.

24. Write a contract with the student specifying what behavior is expected (e.g., responding appropriately to bells, rules, point cards, reminders, etc.) and what reinforcement will be made available when the terms of the contract have been met.

25. Reinforce the student for responding appropriately to environmental cues based on the number of environmental cues the student can successfully follow. As the student demonstrates success, gradually increase the number of appropriate responses to environmental cues required for reinforcement.

26. Reinforce those students in the classroom who respond appropriately to environmental cues.

27. Speak to the student to explain (a) what the student is doing wrong (e.g., failing to respond appropriately to bells, signs indicating restroom directions, etc.) and (b) what the student should be doing (e.g., responding appropriately to bells, signs indicating restroom directions, etc.).

28. Reinforce the student for responding appropriately to environmental cues: (a) give the student a tangible reward (e.g., classroom privileges, line leading, passing out materials, five minutes free time, etc.) or (b) give the student an intangible reward (e.g., praise, fist bump, smile, etc.).

6 Does not stay in assigned areas for specified time

1. Reinforce the student for staying in an assigned area for the specified time period: (a) give the student a tangible reward (e.g., classroom privileges, line leading, passing out materials, five minutes free time, etc.) or (b) give the student an intangible reward (e.g., praise, fist bump, smile, etc.).

2. Speak to the student to explain (a) what he/she is doing wrong (e.g., leaving the assigned area) and (b) what he/she should be doing (e.g., staying in the assigned area for the specified time period).

3. Establish classroom rules:
- Concentrate while working.
- Work quietly.
- Remain in your seat.
- Finish task.
- Meet task expectations.

Review rules often. Reinforce students for following the rules.

4. Evaluate the appropriateness of the task to determine (a) if the task is too easy, (b) if the task is too difficult, and (c) if the length of time scheduled to complete the task is adequate.

5. Reinforce the student for staying in an assigned area for the specified time period based on the length of time the student can be successful. As the student demonstrates success, gradually increase the length of time required for reinforcement.

6. Write a contract with the student specifying what behavior is expected (e.g., staying in an assigned area for the specified time period) and what reinforcement will be made available when the terms of the contract have been met.

7. Communicate with parents (e.g., notes home, phone calls, etc.) to share information about the student's progress. The parents may reinforce the student at home for staying in an assigned area at school for the specified time period.

8. Reinforce those students in the classroom who stay in an assigned area for the specified time period.

9. Choose a peer to model staying in an assigned area for the specified time period for the student.

10. Have the student ask questions about directions, explanations, instructions he/she does not understand.

11. Evaluate the appropriateness of requiring the student to stay in an assigned area for the specified time period.

12. Establish rules for the school grounds (e.g., remain in assigned areas, share school equipment, use appropriate language, use school property with care, etc.).

13. Have the student ask questions about rules for the school grounds he/she does not understand.

14. Separate the student from the peer(s) who stimulates his/her inappropriate behavior in assigned areas.

15. Have the student carry a point card with him/her at all times so that he/she can be reinforced for staying in assigned areas in the building and on the school grounds.

16. Inform other school personnel of any behavior problems the student may have so that supervision and assistance may be provided in the assigned areas before, during, and after school.

17. Be consistent in applying consequences for behavior (i.e., appropriate behavior receives positive consequences while negative behavior receives negative consequences).

18. Provide organized activities in which to participate in assigned areas before, during, and after school (e.g., board games, softball, computer games, puzzles, checkers, flash cards, etc.).

19. Identify an area of the school grounds to be used as a time-out area when the student demonstrates inappropriate behavior on the school grounds.

20. Have the student take responsibility for a younger student in assigned areas.

21. Make sure the student knows where he/she is expected to be at all times.

22. Require the student to remain in assigned areas for short periods of time. As the student demonstrates success, gradually increase the length of time.

23. Make sure the student knows the location of all assigned areas.

24. Make sure the behavioral demands are appropriate for the student's abilities (e.g., ability to find locations of assigned areas, ability to tell time, ability to interact with peers appropriately, etc.).

25. Make sure the student is actively involved in an activity in the assigned area to facilitate his/her ability to stay in the assigned area for the specified time period.

26. Assign the student a responsibility to perform in an assigned area to keep him/her actively involved (e.g., supervision of others, responsibility for materials, group leader, etc.).

27. Provide the student with a timer to help him/her remain in the assigned area for the specified time period.

28. Post the times the student should enter and leave an assigned area (e.g., one clock face indicates time to enter, another clock face indicates time to leave, etc.).

29. Have the student carry a hall pass on which teachers will indicate arrival and departure times of assigned areas.

30. Deliver a predetermined signal (e.g., ring a bell, turn lights off and on, etc.) to indicate when to enter and leave assigned areas.

31. Set up physical barriers or boundary markings to help the student remain in an assigned area.

32. Identify areas that are off limits with signs such as *Danger, Keep Out,* etc.

33. Provide adequate supervision in assigned areas. As the student demonstrates success, gradually reduce the amount of supervision.

34. Provide the student with many opportunities for social and academic success in assigned areas.

35. Require time spent away from an assigned area to be made up during break time, lunch, free time, etc.

36. Choose a peer to remain in an assigned area with the student for the specified time period.

37. Make sure the student is able to tell time to increase the probability that he/she will know how long to remain in assigned areas.

38. Reduce stimuli in the assigned area which would cause the student to be unable to remain in the assigned area for the specified time period.

39. Reinforce the student for remaining in assigned areas (e.g., free time areas, student lounge, recreational areas, etc.).

40. Teach the student ways to deal with stimuli or problems in assigned areas which may cause the student to leave the area (e.g., talk to a teacher, move to a quiet place in the assigned area, avoid confrontations, etc.).

7 Needs verbal questions and directions frequently repeated

1. Instruct the student to carry a notepad with him/her at all times and to write information down to help him/her remember.

2. Assess the degree of task difficulty to determine if the student will require additional information, time, assistance, etc., before assigning a task.

3. Deliver verbal questions and directions that involve only one concept or step. As the student demonstrates success, gradually increase the number of concepts or steps.

4. Call the student by name to gain his/her attention prior to delivering verbal questions and directions.

5. Communicate with parents (e.g., notes home, phone calls, etc.) to share information about the student's progress. The parents may reinforce the student at home for responding to verbal questions and directions without requiring repetition at school.

6. Demonstrate the appropriate way to listen to verbal questions and directions (e.g., look at the person who is talking, ask questions, etc.).

7. Deliver directions and requests in a supportive rather than a threatening manner (e.g., "Please repeat the directions," rather than, "Tell me what I just said!").

8. Deliver directions, explanations, and information using vocabulary that is within the student's level of comprehension.

9. Deliver information to the student on a one-to-one basis or employ a peer tutor.

10. Deliver verbal directions prior to handing out materials.

11. Avoid placing the student in situations that require listening for an extended directions, announcements, seminars, etc. Provide the information for the student through a recording or lecture notes.

12. Deliver questions and directions in written form.

13. Demonstrate directions, explanations, and instructions as they are presented verbally (e.g., use the wall-mounted board to work a problem for the student, begin playing a game with the student, etc.).

14. Consider carefully the student's ability level when expecting him/her to respond to verbal questions and directions.

15. Determine if the student heard what was said by having him/her repeat it.

16. Discuss with the student the consequences of his/her behavior (e.g., if you begin a work assignment before all directions are understood, you may do things incorrectly).

17. Do not accept "forgetting" to listen as an excuse. Make the student accountable for missed information.

18. Encourage the student's parents to take advantage of dinner and other family-gathering times to talk and practice maintaining attention.

19. Do not punish the student for asking questions.

20. Write down important information for the student (e.g., the assembly begins today at 1:40, math test tomorrow, early dismissal on Friday, etc.).

21. Do not talk to the student from across the classroom. Go to the student, get his/her undivided attention, and then speak to him/her.

22. Encourage teachers, coaches, paraprofessionals, school officials, etc., to give the student written directions along with verbal directions.

23. Encourage the student to ask for clarification of any directions, explanations, and instructions before beginning a task to facilitate comprehension.

24. Encourage the student to avoid ingesting any substance (e.g., drugs, alcohol, cold remedies, etc.) that might further alter his/her ability to direct or maintain attention.

25. Provide recorded information from lectures and seminars. Develop questions from these recordings for the student.

26. Encourage the student to develop a 30 second definition of his/her goal to help himself/herself stay on task and focused (e.g., "I will listen carefully. The better I listen the better I will perform.").

27. Help the student develop an awareness of the consequences of his/her behavior by writing down or talking through problems which may occur due to his/her need to have verbal directions and questions frequently repeated (e.g., not focusing on directions may cause misunderstanding of an assignment which could lead to a lower grade and losing a place on the soccer team).

28. Choose a peer to model good communication skills for the student.

29. Encourage the student to recite a mantra to himself/herself when entering a situation where he/she will receive directions/instructions (e.g., listen carefully, listen carefully, listen carefully).

30. Do not criticize when correcting the student; be honest yet supportive. Never cause the student to feel negatively about himself/herself.

31. Establish classroom rules:
- Concentrate while working.
- Work quietly.
- Remain in your seat.
- Finish task.
- Meet task expectations.

Review rules often. Reinforce students for following the rules.

32. Establish rules for listening (e.g., listen to directions, ask questions about directions if they are not understood, follow the directions, etc.). These rules should be consistent and followed by everyone in the classroom. Talk about the rules often.

33. Evaluate the appropriateness of requiring the student to respond to verbal questions and directions without needing repetition.

34. Evaluate the visual and auditory stimuli in the classroom. Determine the amount of stimuli the student can tolerate. Remove the extraneous stimuli from the environment.

35. Give a signal to gain attention prior to delivering directions verbally to the student.

36. Give directions in a very simple, specific manner.

37. Give the student directions to follow with no more than two or three steps (e.g., "Please open your text and turn to page 28."). Directions that involve several steps can be confusing and cause the student to have difficulty following them.

38. Give the student one task to perform at a time. Introduce the next task after the student has followed directions and successfully completed the previous task.

39. Have a peer help the student follow verbal questions and directions.

40. Instruct the student to ask for clarification if he/she does not understand verbal or written directions.

41. Stand close to or directly in front of the student when delivering verbal questions and directions. Encourage the student to maintain written reminders of task sequences.

42. Have the student ask for help when he/she needs it.

43. Teach the student listening skills (e.g., stop working, clear desk of nonessential materials, attend to the source of information, write down important points, ask for clarification, and wait until all directions are received before beginning).

44. Have the student verbally repeat or paraphrase the directions to the teacher.

45. Have the student practice group listening skills (e.g., "Everyone take out a piece of paper. Write your name on the paper. Number your paper from 1 to 20.").

46. Seat the student close to the source of information to facilitate his/her ability to maintain attention.

47. Have the student ask questions about directions, explanations, and instructions he/she does not understand.

48. Have the student take notes relative to verbal questions and directions.

49. Help the student develop an awareness of himself/herself and the environment. Instruct the student to periodically, step back and ask himself/herself, "Am I listening and paying attention?" "What is the question?"

50. Have the student take notes when directions are being given following the "What, How, Materials, and When" format.

51. Choose a peer to model responding to verbal questions and directions without requiring repetition for the student.

52. Instruct the student to ask people to repeat parts of a conversation he/she was unable to follow.

53. Instruct the student to maintain attention to the source of information by maintaining eye contact, keeping hands free from other materials, and reducing other distractions.

54. Have the student do those things that need to be done when it is discussed instead of later (e.g., organize needed materials for an assignment to be completed later).

55. Interact frequently with the student to help the student follow directions for an activity.

56. Maintain a consistent manner in which verbal questions and directions are delivered.

57. Maintain mobility to provide assistance to the student.

58. Have the student practice listening skills by taking notes when directions, explanations, and instructions are presented.

59. Maintain visibility to and from the student to keep his/her attention when verbal questions/directions are being delivered. The teacher should be able to see the student and the student should be able to see the teacher. Make eye contact possible at all times.

60. Make sure that all directions, questions, explanations, and instructions are delivered in a clear, concise manner; at an appropriate pace; and loudly enough for the student to hear.

61. Make sure that eye contact is being made between you and the student when delivering verbal questions and directions.

62. Provide questions and directions in written form.

63. Provide opportunities for the student to talk to others on a one-to-one basis. As the student becomes more successful at listening and maintaining attention, gradually include more people in conversations.

64. Make sure that comments made to the student take the form of constructive criticism rather than perceived as personal, threatening, etc., (e.g., instead of saying, "You always make the same mistake," say, "A better way to do that might be . . .").

65. Reduce the number of auditory distractions around the student (e.g., seat the student away from doors, windows, pencil sharpener; move the student to a quiet area, etc.).

66. Make sure the student is attending when you deliver verbal questions and directions (e.g., making eye contact, hands free of writing materials, looking at assignment, etc.).

67. Have a peer, paraprofessional, etc., cue the student when he/she needs to maintain attention (e.g., the person can touch the student on the arm when it is time to listen).

68. Make sure the student is paying attention when he/she is told to do something. Have the student make eye contact and repeat the information to check for understanding.

69. Have the student's hearing checked if it has not been recently checked.

70. Present concepts following the outline of (1) Who, (2) What, (3) Where, (4) When, (5) How, and (6) Why.

71. Present verbal questions and directions in a clear and concise manner and at an appropriate pace for the student.

72. Present verbal questions and directions in a variety of ways to increase the probability of understanding (e.g., if the student does not understand verbal directions, present them in written form).

73. Provide information visually (e.g., written directions, instructions, etc.) to support the information the student receives auditorily.

74. Make sure that the expectations required of the student are appropriate for his/her level of development and ability.

75. Establish assignment rules (e.g., listen to directions, wait until all verbal directions have been given, ask questions about anything not understood, make sure you have all of the necessary materials, and begin the assignment when you are certain about what you are supposed to do, etc.).

76. Provide practice in listening for key information when directions are being given or information is being received (e.g., write down main points, ideas, step-by-step instructions, etc.).

77. Have the student verbally repeat directions, explanations, and instructions after they have been given to reinforce retention.

78. Choose a peer to deliver and/or repeat verbal questions and directions.

79. Provide visual information (e.g., written directions, instructions, etc.) to support the information the student receives auditorily.

80. Reduce distracting stimuli (e.g., place the student on or near the front row, provide a carrel or office space away from distractions, etc.). This is used as a form of reducing distracting stimuli and not as a form of punishment.

81. Make it pleasant and positive for the student to ask questions about things not understood. Reinforce the student by assisting, congratulating, praising, etc.

82. Reduce distractions to facilitate the student's ability to listen and follow directions.

83. Make instructions meaningful to the student. Attempt to relate instructions to past experiences.

84. Reinforce the student for responding to verbal questions and directions without requiring frequent repetition: (a) give the student a tangible reward (e.g., classroom privileges, line leading, passing out materials, five minutes free time, etc.) or (b) give the student an intangible reward (e.g., praise, fist bump, smile, etc.).

85. Reinforce those students in the classroom who respond to verbal questions and directions without requiring repetition.

86. Write down verbal directions. Instruct the student to cross each step off as it is completed.

87. Reward other students for listening, following directions, and answering verbal questions.

88. Provide directions/instructions that will accommodate different learning styles (e.g., visual, auditory, etc.).

89. Make a written list of procedures the student is to follow (e.g., how to label papers, format for mathematic assignments, etc.).

90. Reward the student (e.g., take a break, visit briefly with a peer, etc.) for maintaining eye contact and listening for a specific length of time.

91. Schedule important activities/assignments/lectures at times when the student is most likely to maintain attention (e.g., one hour after medication, 45 minutes after lunch, first thing in the morning, etc.).

92. Use pictures, diagrams, the wall-mounted board, and gestures when delivering information.

93. Speak to the student to explain (a) what he/she is doing wrong (e.g., needing verbal questions and directions repeated) and (b) what he/she should be doing (e.g., responding to verbal questions and directions without requiring repetition).

94. Tell the student what to listen for when being given directions, receiving information, etc.

95. Record the assignments and allow the student to listen to directions/instructions as often as necessary.

96. Teach and practice active listening skills. Instruct the student to listen to what another person is saying and respond based on information received.

97. Teach and practice effective communication skills. These skills include: listening, maintaining eye contact, and positive body language.

98. Tell the student that verbal questions and directions will be given only once.

99. Provide directions/instructions on a one-to-one basis before assigning a task.

100. Reinforce the student for responding to verbal questions and directions without requiring repetition based on the number of times the student can be successful. As the student demonstrates success, gradually increase the number of times required for reinforcement.

101. Teach the student direction-following skills (e.g., listen carefully, write down steps, etc.).

102. Stop at various points during the presentation of directions, explanations, or instructions to check the student's comprehension of the information given.

103. Use a timer to help the student monitor how much time he/she has to follow through with directions.

104. While concepts are presented, have the student listen and takes notes for "Who, What, Where, When, How, and Why."

105. Write a contract with the student specifying what behavior is expected (e.g., following directions with one cue) and what reinforcement will be made available when the terms of the contract have been met.

8 Demonstrates difficulty with visual memory

1. Have the student read and follow one-, two-, and three-step directions.

2. Have the student listen and take notes for "Who, What, Where, When, How, and Why" when concepts are presented.

3. Use multiple modalities (e.g., auditory, visual, tactile, etc.) when presenting directions, explanations, and instructional content.

4. Provide the student with auditory cues to help him/her remember the information previously presented (e.g., say key words, give a brief verbal description to clue the student, etc.).

5. Cut pictures from a cartoon strip. Show the pictures to the student in the correct sequence. Shuffle the pictures and ask the student to place them in the correct sequence.

6. Have the student play concentration games (e.g., matching numbers, words, symbols, etc., by turning them over and remembering their location).

7. Present directions following the outline of (1) What, (2) How, (3) Materials, and (4) When.

8. Reduce visual distractions (e.g., cover other information on the page, expose only a portion of a picture at a time, etc.) by isolating the information that is presented to the student.

9. Identify the student's most effective learning mode. Use it consistently to facilitate the student's understanding (e.g., if the student does not understand directions or information given verbally, present it in written form).

10. Record stories, directions, etc., so the student may listen to the information while reading along.

11. Highlight or underline important information the student reads (e.g., directions, reading assignments, math word problems, etc.).

12. Reduce the amount of information on a page (e.g., less print to read, fewer problems, isolate information this is presented to the student, etc.) if it is causing visual distractions for the student.

13. Provide the student with more than one exposure to the visual information prior to requiring him/her to remember it.

14. Teach the student to learn sequences and lists of information in segments (e.g., phone numbers are learned as 123, then 874, then 1710, etc.).

15. Have the student take notes when directions are being given following the "What, How, Materials, and When" format.

16. Present concepts following the outline of (1) Who, (2) What, (3) Where, (4) When, (5) How, and (6) Why.

17. Make it pleasant and positive for the student to ask questions about things not understood. Reinforce the student by assisting, congratulating, praising, etc.

18. Teach the student to recognize common visual symbols (e.g., a red octagon means stop, a skull and crossed bones represents poison, etc.).

19. Provide the student with written directions, rules, lists, etc. Reinforce the student for being able to recall the information given in written form.

20. Reinforce the student for remembering information received visually: (a) give the student a tangible reward (e.g., classroom privileges, line leading, five minutes free time, etc.) or (b) give the student an intangible reward (e.g., praise, fist bump, smile, etc.).

21. Evaluate the appropriateness of the task to determine if (a) the task is too easy, (b) the task is too difficult (e.g., too much information to remember) and (c) the length of time required for the student to remember is adequate (e.g., the presentation of information was too brief, time lapse between presentation of material and request for recall was too long, etc.).

22. Remind the student of the situation in which the material was originally presented to help him/her remember information (e.g., say, "Remember yesterday when we talked about . . . ?" "Remember when we were outside and we looked at the . . . ?" etc.).

23. Provide the student with visual cues to help him/her remember the information previously presented (e.g., using key words printed on the wall-mounted board, exposing part or all of a picture, etc.).

24. Draw the student's attention to key aspects of visual images (e.g., by highlighting, outlining, drawing arrows, etc.).

25. Provide auditory information (e.g., verbal directions or instructions, etc.) to support information the student receives visually.

26. Require the student to recall days of the week, months of the year, birth dates, addresses, phone numbers, etc., after seeing this information in written form.

9 Demonstrates difficulty with auditory memory

1. Have the student's hearing checked if it has not been recently checked.

2. Draw the student's attention to key aspects of auditory communications as they occur (e.g., repeat important points, call the student by name, tell the student which information is particularly important, etc.).

3. Evaluate the appropriateness of the task to determine (a) if the task is too difficult (e.g., too much information to remember) or (b) if the length of time required for the student to remember the information is too long (i.e., time lapse between presentation of material and request for recall is too long).

4. Provide the student with more than one source of directions, explanations, instructions, etc., before requiring him/her to remember information.

5. Provide the student with auditory cues when he/she is required to recall information to help him/her remember the information previously presented (e.g., say, "Remember yesterday when I said . . .," etc.).

6. Provide information visually to support information the student receives auditorily.

7. Teach the student to learn sequences and lists of information in segments (e.g., phone numbers are learned as 874, then 1710).

8. Gradually have the student follow verbal one-, two-, and three-step directions.

9. Provide the student with verbal directions, rules, lists, etc. Reinforce the student for being able to recall information which is presented in verbal form.

10. Provide stories, directions, etc., in a printed format so the student may read along as he/she listens.

11. Tell the student what to listen for before delivering auditory information.

12. Send the student to deliver verbal messages to other teachers in the building.

13. Present auditory information slowly enough for the student to comprehend the information being presented.

14. Have the student follow verbal one-, two-, and three-step directions.

15. While reading a story to the student, stop on occasion to ask questions about the plot, main characters, events in the story, etc.

16. Have the student pretend he/she is a waiter/waitress. Have him/her take an order and then repeat it.

17. Have the student paraphrase directions, explanations, and instructions soon after they have been given.

18. Use as much visual information as possible when teaching (e.g., wall-mounted board, overhead projections, pictures, etc.).

19. Have the student audio record directions, explanations, and instructions to replay as needed.

20. Use simple, concise sentences to convey information to the student.

21. Have the student recall names of friends, days of the week, months of the year, addresses, phone numbers, etc.

22. After listening to a recorded story, CD, etc., have the student recall characters, main events, sequence of events, etc.

23. Have the student read along while listening to a recorded story or book.

24. Present directions following the (1) What, (2) How, (3) Materials, and (4) When outline.

25. Have the student take notes following the "What, How, Materials, and When" format when directions are being given.

26. Reinforce the student for remembering information received auditorily: (a) give the student a tangible reward (e.g., special privileges, line leading, passing out materials, five minutes free time, etc.) or (b) give the student an intangible reward (e.g., praise, fist bump, smile, etc.).

27. Use pictures, diagrams, wall-mounted board, and gestures when presenting information.

28. Have the student prepare for tests using the "Who, What, Where, When, How, and Why" format.

29. Reduce distracting stimuli (e.g., noise and motion) around the student (e.g., place the student on the front row; provide a carrel or quiet place away from distractions; etc.). This is to be used as a means of reducing distracting stimuli and not as a form of punishment.

30. Use multiple modalities (e.g., auditory, visual, tactile, etc.) when presenting directions, explanations, and instructional content. Determine which modality is stronger and utilize that modality.

31. Present concepts following the (1) Who, (2) What, (3) Where, (4) When, (5) How, and (6) Why outline.

32. Make sure the student is attending to the source of information (e.g., eye contact is being made, hands are free of materials, student is looking at the assignment, etc.).

33. Stop at various points during a presentation of information to check the student's comprehension.

34. Provide the student with adequate opportunities for repetition of information through different experiences, to facilitate memory.

35. Provide information visually (e.g., written directions or instructions, etc.) to support information the student receives auditorily.

36. Deliver all directions, questions, explanations, and instructions in a clear, concise manner and at an appropriate rate for the student.

37. Use vocabulary that is on the student's level of comprehension when delivering directions, explanations, and information.

38. Have the student listen and take notes for "Who, What, Where, When, How, and Why" when concepts are presented.

10 Does not demonstrate an understanding of directionality

1. Teach "north," "south," "east," and "west" using the classroom, playground, school building, etc.

2. Use concrete examples when teaching concepts of "up-down," "high-low," "above-below," etc. Use books, balls, regular classroom materials, etc., when trying to convey these concepts.

3. Use the terms "right" and "left" as part of the directions you give to the student (e.g., refer to the windows on the left side of the room, the wall-mounted board on the right side of the room, etc.).

4. Identify directions in the classroom with signs (e.g., on the ceiling put "up," on the floor put "down," etc.).

5. Have the student practice following directions on paper. Instruct the student to make a mark or picture on the right, left, middle, top, and bottom parts of the paper according to the directions given.

6. Avoid the problem of mirror images by standing next to the student when giving "right" and "left" directions.

7. Design an obstacle course using materials in the room. Students can step "into" the box, crawl "over" the desk, walk "under" the coat rack, stand "on" the table, etc.

8. Hang directional signs in the room (e.g., "turn left," "games under cabinet," etc.).

9. Play *Simon Says* for practice with directions (e.g., "Raise your left hand." "Walk behind the chair.").

10. Conduct scavenger hunts. Have the student look for a pencil "in" the desk, a book "under" the table, a glass "on" the chair, etc.

11. Have the student sort "left" and "right" gloves, shoes, paper hand and foot cut-outs, etc.

12. Review daily the concepts of directionality.

13. Label strips of paper "left" and "right" and attach them around the student's wrists.

14. Have the student practice walking "forward" and "backward," moving toy cars and trucks "forward" and "backward," etc.

15. Have the student identify objects which move "up" and "down" (e.g., airplanes, teeter-totter, etc.).

16. Point out doors which are labeled push and "pull" and activities which require "pushing" and "pulling" (e.g., opening drawers, opening doors, etc.).

17. Use concrete examples and experiences in teaching directionality (e.g., "east-west" signs on the wall, "left-right" armbands, etc.).

18. Identify objects which represent "over" and "under" (e.g., a bridge is "over" water, people sleep "under" covers, birds fly "over" our heads, rugs are "under" our feet, etc.).

19. Teach the concept of "above" and "below" with examples in the classroom (e.g., the ceiling is "above" our heads and the floor "below" our feet, etc.).

20. Have the student find things that represent the concept of in and out (e.g., we pour milk "in" a glass and pour it "out," we walk "in" a room and walk "out," etc.).

21. Emphasize activities which require the action of "off" and "on" (e.g., we turn lights "on" for light and "off" when we do not need them, we turn the stove "on" to heat things and "off" when things are hot, we put clothes "on" to go to school, leaves fall "off" a tree in the fall, etc.).

22. Teach the concept of "before" and "after" with examples from the student's daily routine (e.g., we wake up "before" we eat breakfast, we go to school "after" we eat breakfast, we eat lunch "after" we have morning free time, etc.).

11   Has difficulty concentrating

1. Demonstrate when teaching new skills. Allow the student to practice hands-on learning of new skills to facilitate concentration.

2. Use pictures, diagrams, wall-mounted board, and gestures when delivering information to maintain the student's attention.

3. Use multiple modalities (e.g., auditory, visual, tactile, etc.) when presenting directions, explanations, and instructional content. By using multiple modalities, the information may hold the student's interest for a longer period of time.

4. Schedule important activities/assignments/meetings at times when the student is most likely to maintain attention (e.g., one hour after medication, 45 minutes after lunch, first thing in the morning, etc.).

5. Give an assignment that involves immediate, short-term tasks.

6. Highlight or underline important information the student reads (e.g., directions, reading assignments, math word problems, etc.).

7. Allow natural consequences to occur (e.g., work not done or completed inaccurately must be made up during recreational time, not concentrating while people are talking results in not knowing what to do, etc.) as a result of the student's inability to concentrate.

8. Teach time-management skills. Provide a daily plan and have the student follow it.

9. Establish classroom rules:
• Concentrate while working.
• Work quietly.
• Remain in your seat.
• Finish task.
• Meet task expectations.
Review rules often. Reinforce students for following the rules.

10. Organize assignments by dividing them into small segments. Set deadlines and provide the student with a reward after completing each segment of the assignment.

11. Present assignments in small amounts (e.g., assign 10 problems, use pages removed from workbooks, etc.).

12. Teach and practice information-gathering skills (e.g., listen carefully, write down important points, ask for clarification, wait until all information is presented before beginning a task, etc.).

13. Reinforce the student for beginning, attending to, and completing assignments.

14. Structure the environment to reduce distracting stimuli (e.g., place the student on the front row; provide a carrel or quiet place away from distractions; etc.). This is used as a means of reducing stimuli and not as a form of punishment.

15. Set time limits for completing assignments. Prompt the student as a reminder of time constraints when working on projects.

16. Use more interesting or stimulating activities as a reward for completing less interesting activities (e.g., the student must complete drill and practice before working on the computer).

17. Reinforce the student for concentrating: (a) give the student a tangible reward (e.g., classroom privileges, passing out materials, five minutes free time, etc.) or (b) give the student an intangible reward (e.g., praise, fist bump, smile, etc.).

18. Communicate clearly with the student the length of time he/she has to complete an assignment. The student may want to use a timer to complete the tasks within the given period of time.

19. Maintain physical contact with the student while talking to him/her (e.g., touch the student's hand or shoulder).

20. Provide clearly-stated directions, written or verbal. Make directions as simple and concrete as possible.

21. Establish an environmental setting for the classroom that promotes optimal individual performance (e.g., quiet room, background music, fresh air, etc.).

22. Provide clearly stated directions, written or verbal (e.g., make directions as simple and concrete as possible).

23. Choose different people (e.g., peer, counselor, paraprofessional, etc.) to help the student remain on task.

24. Have the student listen and take "Who, What, Where, When, How, and Why" notes when information is presented.

25. Present directions following the outline of (1) What, (2) How, (3) Materials, and (4) When.

26. Move objects used for tactile stimulation (e.g., pens, paper clips, loose change, etc.) away from the student's reach.

27. Provide the student with an individual assignment when the group setting is overly distracting.

28. Encourage the student to develop a 30 second definition of his/her goal to help him/her stay on task and focused (e.g., "I will listen carefully. The better I focus and stay on task, the better I will perform.").

29. Deliver information to the student on a one-to-one basis or use a peer tutor.

30. Provide an incentive statement along with a directive (e.g., "You can go to lunch after you complete 15 math problems.").

31. Reinforce the student for concentrating on a task for the length of time the student can be successful. As the student demonstrates success, gradually increase the length of time required for reinforcement.

32. Reduce the amount of information on a page (e.g., less print to read, fewer problems, isolate information that is presented to the student, etc.) if it is visually distracting for the student.

33. Follow a less desirable task with a more desirable task. Make completion of the first task necessary to perform the second.

34. Reward the student for concentrating on an assignment for a specific length of time (e.g., take a break, visit briefly with a peer, etc.).

35. Match the assignments with the student's activity level. When the student is feeling highly active, provide assignments which require a great degree of movement. When the student is most likely to maintain attention, provide assignments that require less movement and more sitting.

36. Encourage the student to avoid ingesting any substance (e.g., drugs, alcohol, cold remedies, etc.) that might further alter his/her ability to concentrate.

37. Assist the student in staying on task. As the student demonstrates success, gradually reduce the amount of assistance provided and require the student to independently remain on task.

38. Create an environment that is quiet and uncluttered (e.g., clean, well-lighted, fresh-smelling, and at a comfortable temperature).

39. Allow the student to occasionally take assignments home when the school setting is overly distracting.

40. Reward the student for completing an assignment within the amount of time allotted.

41. Help the student develop an awareness of himself/herself and the environment. Instruct the student to periodically step back and ask himself/herself, "Am I on task and paying attention?" "What should I be doing now?"

42. Help the student develop an awareness of the consequences of his/her behavior by writing down or talking through problems which may occur due to his/her inability to concentrate (e.g., not focusing on directions may cause misunderstanding of an assignment which could lead to a lower grade and losing a place on the soccer team).

43. Encourage the student to eat a balanced diet and get plenty of rest to facilitate his/her ability to concentrate.

44. Allow the student to take a break to regroup when he/she is no longer on task.

45. Have the student listen for key information when being given directions or receiving information (e.g., write down main points, ideas, step-by-step instructions, etc.).

46. Have the student develop a checklist/chart to follow which will allow him/her to record all assignments.

47. Encourage the student to ask for clarification of any directions, explanations, and instructions before beginning a task to facilitate comprehension.

48. Teach the student concentration and study skills (e.g., reading for the main idea, note-taking, highlighting, outlining, summarizing, studying in an appropriate environment, etc.).

49. Have the student make eye contact while delivering information to him/her.

50. Teach the student note-taking skills (e.g., copy main ideas from the wall-mounted board, identify main ideas from lectures, condense statements into a few key words, etc.).

51. Choose a peer, paraprofessional, friend, etc., to cue the student when he/she is off task (e.g., the person can touch the student's arm as a signal that he/she is not remaining on task).

52. Have the student take notes when directions are being given following the "What, How, Materials, and When" format.

53. Make sure the student knows that directions will only be given once.

54. Tell the student what to listen for when being given directions or receiving information, etc.

55. Assign one task at a time. Give the student a specific amount of time to complete it.

56. Have the student quietly repeat to himself/herself information just heard to help him/her remember the important facts.

57. Instruct the student to ask himself/herself questions (e.g., "What's next?") to keep himself/herself focused on assignments/projects.

58. Allow the student to underline or highlight important information he/she reads (e.g., directions, reading assignments, etc.) to facilitate concentration.

59. Evaluate the visual and auditory stimuli in the classroom. Determine the amount of stimuli the student can tolerate. Remove extraneous stimuli from the student's environment.

60. Set a timer for the student indicating a limited amount of time to finish a task or assignment.

61. Present concepts following the outline of (1) Who, (2) What, (3) Where, (4) When, (5) How, and (6) Why.

62. Allow the student to record information from lectures and assemblies and make notes from these recordings.

63. Write a contract with the student. It should be written within his/her ability level and focus on only one behavior at a time. Specify what behavior is expected (e.g., concentrating on a task) and what reinforcement will be made available when the terms of the contract have been met.

64. Provide the student with appropriate time limits for the completion of assignments.

65. Encourage the student to recite a mantra to himself/herself when entering a situation where he/she has to sit for an extended period of time (e.g., concentrate, concentrate, concentrate).

66. Do not assign the student too many things to do at once; provide more than enough time to complete tasks; and do not expect perfection.

67. Have the student assemble all the materials necessary to work on a project, assignment, etc., to reduce the need to search for materials.

68. Use a variety of high interest means to communicate with the student (e.g., auditory, visual, manipulatives, etc.).

69. Instruct the student to imagine the necessary steps required to complete a task before beginning that task.

70. Have the student maintain a list of things to do to organize and focus on what needs to be accomplished for a specific task, day, etc.

71. Have the student work with a peer who is calm and capable of concentrating on an assignment for an extended period of time.

72. Allow the student some movement while performing tasks. Monitor and limit the amount of movement.

73. Give the student one task to perform at a time. Introduce the next task after the student has successfully completed the previous task.

74. Stop at various points during a presentation of information to check the student's comprehension.

75. Establish a timeline for completing a project. Expect the student to meet each deadline to complete the project on time.

76. Make the subject matter meaningful to the student (e.g., explain the purpose of an assignment, relate the subject matter to the student's environment, etc.).

77. Make it a habit to periodically review with the student his/her notes, the daily calendar of events, or tasks that need to be completed.

78. Assess the quality and clarity of directions, explanations, and instructions given to the student.

79. Explain to the student when he/she does not stay on task, attend to a conversation, etc., exactly what he/she did wrong, what should have been done, and why.

80. Seat the student close to the source of information to facilitate his/her ability to maintain attention.

81. Teach the student listening skills (e.g., stop working, clear desk of nonessential materials, attend to the source of information, write down important points, ask for clarification, and wait until all directions are received before beginning).

82. While concepts are presented, have the student listen and take notes for "Who, What, Where, When, How, and Why."

83. Maintain visibility to and from the student at all times to monitor the student's concentration.

84. Give directions in steps. Give the student each additional step after the previous step has been completed.

85. Divide large tasks into smaller tasks (e.g., assign the student to write an outline for a book report, then the first rough draft, etc.).

86. Make sure that the student's academic tasks are on his/her ability level.

87. Avoid placing the student in situations that require listening for an extended directions, announcements, assemblies, seminars, etc. Provide the information for the student through a record or lecture notes.

88. Reduce distracting stimuli in and around the student's desk (e.g., materials in/on the desk, etc.).

89. Have the student participate in games requiring varying degrees of concentration (e.g., tic-tac-toe, checkers, chess, etc.).

90. Make sure the tasks required of the student are appropriate for his/her level of development and ability.

91. Make sure that the student understands the relationship between inappropriate behavior and the consequences which follow (e.g., failing to concentrate on schoolwork could result in low grades or incomplete work).

92. Assign the student fewer tasks. As the student demonstrates success, gradually increase the number of tasks over time.

93. Tell the student when it is time to begin an assignment, listen to others, etc.

94. Deliver one-, two-, and three-step directions to the student. As the student demonstrates success in concentrating, gradually increase the number of steps.

95. Assess the degree of task difficulty to determine whether or not the student will require additional information, time, assistance, etc., before beginning a task.

96. Make sure the student knows what to look for when reading (e.g., main characters, main ideas, sequence of events, etc.).

97. Choose a peer tutor to work with the student to model appropriate work habits.

98. Avoid seating the student near people with whom he/she may be tempted to talk during lectures, assemblies, group projects, etc.

99. Allow the student the option of working on the assignment at another time (e.g., earlier/later in the day, on another day, or at home) when he/she will be able to concentrate better.

100. Give directions in a variety of ways to facilitate the student's understanding (e.g., if the student does not understand verbal directions, present them in written form).

101. Designate a specific period of time (e.g., the last five minutes of each hour, transitioning from one task to another, after completing a task, etc.) when it is permissible for the student to talk with peers.

102. Provide simple, concrete directions.

103. Provide the student with a prompt when he/she is off task (e.g., move close to the student, speak to the student, etc.).

104. Have the student choose a peer who has the ability to remain on task. Instruct the student to observe that person and try to model the behaviors which allow him/her to maintain attention.

105. Separate the student from the peers who may be encouraging or stimulating the inappropriate behavior.

106. Make sure the student is attending to the source of information (e.g., eye contact is being made, hands are free of materials, student is looking at the assignment, etc.).

107. Try various groupings in the classroom to determine the situation in which the student is most successful concentrating.

108. Assign short-term projects that can be quickly completed.

1. Explain that the student should be satisfied with his/her best effort rather than insist on perfection.

2. Assign the student shorter activities. As the student demonstrates success, gradually increase the length of the activities.

3. Inform the student that work not completed in one sitting can be completed later. Provide the student with enough time to complete earlier assignments to guarantee closure.

4. Provide the student with more than enough time to finish an activity. As the student demonstrates success, gradually decrease the amount of time given to finish an activity.

5. Structure time limits so the student knows exactly how long he/she has to work and when work must be finished.

6. Provide a transition period between activities so the student can make adjustments in his/her behavior.

7. Employ a signal technique (e.g., turning lights off and on) to warn that the end of an activity is near.

8. Establish definite time limits and provide the student with this information before an activity begins.

9. Have the student time activities to monitor his/her own behavior and accept time limits.

10. Maintain a consistent daily routine.

11. Maintain consistent expectations within the ability level of the student.

12. Allow the student to finish the activity unless it will be disruptive to the schedule.

13. Provide the student with a list of materials needed for each activity (e.g., pencil, paper, textbook, workbook, etc.).

14. Present instructions/directions prior to handing out necessary materials.

15. Collect the student's materials (e.g., pencil, paper, textbook, workbook, etc.) when it is time to change from one activity to another.

16. Provide the student with clearly stated expectations for all situations.

17. Provide adequate transition time for the student to finish an activity and get ready for the next activity.

18. Prevent the student from becoming so stimulated by an event or activity that the student cannot control his/her behavior.

19. Identify expectations of different environments and help the student develop the skills to be successful in those environments.

20. In conjunction with other school personnel, develop as much consistency as possible in the school environment (e.g., rules, criteria for success, behavioral expectations, consequences, etc.).

21. Have the student practice transitional activities to reduce the effects of stimulating activities (e.g., put head on desk, listen to the teacher read a story, put headphones on and listen to relaxing music, etc.).

22. Provide the student with a schedule of daily events so the student knows exactly what is expected for the day.

23. Provide the student with verbal reminders or prompts when he/she perseverates.

24. Provide the student with increased opportunity for help or assistance on academic tasks (e.g., peer tutoring, directions for work sent home, frequent interactions, etc.).

25. Choose a peer to provide an appropriate model for changing from one activity to another.

26. Reinforce the student for changing from one activity to another without difficulty: (a) give the student a tangible reward (e.g., classroom privileges, line leading, passing out materials, five minutes free time, etc.) or (b) give the student an intangible reward (e.g., praise, fist bump, smile, etc.).

27. Have the student ask questions about directions, explanations, instructions he/she does not understand.

28. Evaluate the appropriateness of the task to determine (a) if the task is too easy, (b) if the task is too difficult, and (c) if the length of time scheduled to complete the task is adequate.

29. Write a contract with the student specifying what behavior is expected (e.g., put materials away and get ready for another activity) and what reinforcement will be made available when the terms of the contract have been met.

30. Reinforce those students in the classroom who change from one activity to another without difficulty.

31. Reinforce the student for demonstrating acceptable behavior based on the length of time the student can be successful. As the student demonstrates success, gradually increase the length of time required for reinforcement.

32. Establish classroom rules:
- Concentrate while working.
- Work quietly.
- Remain in your seat.
- Finish task.
- Meet task expectations.

Review rules often. Reinforce students for following the rules.

33. Speak to the student to explain (a) what he/she is doing wrong (e.g., failing to stop one activity and begin another) and (b) what he/she should be doing (e.g., changing from one activity to another).

34. Reduce distracting stimuli (noise and motion) around the student (e.g, place the student on the front row, provide a carrel or quiet place away from distractions, etc.). This is used as a means of reducing stimuli and not as a form of punishment.

13 Fails to demonstrate logical thinking

1. Give the student responsibilities that require logical thinking (e.g., assign the student to water plants and provide a watering can and a glass, telling the student to use the most appropriate container, etc.).

2. Each day provide the student with problem-solving situations which require logical thinking (e.g., "A stranger takes you by the arm in a department store. What do you do?" "You see smoke coming out of a neighbor's house and no one is home. What do you do?" etc.).

3. Make sure the student experiences the consequences of his/her behavior (e.g., appropriate behavior results in positive consequences while inappropriate behavior results in negative consequences).

4. Provide the student with a list of questions involving logic to answer verbally (e.g., "Why do we post 'wet' paint signs?" "Why do we have stop signs at intersections?" "Why do we wear seat belts?" etc.).

5. When something is broken, lost, etc., have the student identify what could have been done to prevent the situation. Discuss with the student the value of properly maintaining and organizing materials.

6. Have the student read stories involving a moral (e.g., *The Tortoise and the Hare, The Boy Who Cried Wolf,* etc.) and explain the reason for the outcome of the story.

7. Have the student read short stories without endings and Have the student develop logical endings for the stories.

8. Give the student situations/pictures and have him/her explain what variables are related (e.g., "Snow is falling, and the wind is blowing. Is the temperature hot or cold? What should you wear outdoors?").

9. Have the student sequence rearranged cartoon strips and explain the logic of the sequence he/she created.

10. Give the student fill-in-the-blank statements requiring an appropriate response from multiple-choice possibilities (e.g., The boy's dog was dirty so the boy decided to give his dog a _____ [dog biscuit, bath, toy].).

11. Show the student pictures of dangerous situations and have him/her explain why it is dangerous (e.g., a child running into the street from between parked cars, a child riding a bicycle without using his/her hands, etc.).

12. Use cause-and-effect relationships as they apply to nature and people. Discuss what led up to a specific situation in a story or a picture, what could happen next, etc.

13. Set aside time each day for a problem-solving game, analogies, decision making activities, assigned responsibilities, etc.

14. Make sure that the student can verbalize the reason for real-life outcomes of behavior (e.g., why the student had to leave the class line on the way to free time, why he/she earned the privilege of being line leader, etc.).

15. Have the student develop rules and explain why each rule is necessary.

16. Reinforce those students in the classroom who demonstrate logical thinking (e.g., making responsible decisions, solving problems, making references, etc.).

17. Have the student answer questions such as, "Why do we have rules?" "Why do you have to be a certain age before you can drive a car?" etc.

18. Have the student answer analogy situations (e.g., a garage is to a car as a house is to a _____).

19. Make sure the student is attending to the source of information (e.g., eye contact is being made, hands are free of materials, student is looking at the assignment, etc.).

20. Have the student identify appropriate consequences for rules (e.g., consequences for following rules and consequences for not following rules). Have the student explain the choice of consequences he/she identified.

21. Reinforce the student for appropriate decision making: (a) give the student a tangible reward (e.g., classroom privileges, line leading, passing out materials, five minutes free time, etc.) or (b) give the student an intangible reward (e.g., smile, fist bump, etc.).

22. Have the student ask questions about directions, explanations, and instructions he/she does not understand.

14 Has difficulty retrieving, recalling, or naming objects, persons, places, etc.

1. Have the student complete fill-in-the-blank sentences with appropriate words (e.g., objects, persons, places, etc.).

2. Present concepts following the (1) Who, (2) What, (3) Where, (4) When, (5) How, and (6) Why outline.

3. Have the student use a Schedule of Daily Events to recall assignments to be reviewed.

4. Have the student be a classroom messenger. Give the student a verbal message to deliver to another teacher, secretary, administrator, etc. As the student demonstrates success, gradually increase the length of the messages.

5. Reduce distracting stimuli (noise and motion) around the student (e.g., place the student on the front row; provide a carrel or quiet place away from distractions; etc.). This is used as a means of reducing distracting stimuli and not as a form of punishment.

6. Have the student compete against himself/herself by timing how fast he/she can name a series of pictured objects. The student tries to increase his/her speed each time.

7. Have the student listen and take notes following the "Who, What, Where, When, How, and Why" format when concepts are presented.

8. Have the student recall, at the end of the school day, three activities in which he/she participated during the day. As he/she demonstrates success, gradually increase the number of activities the student is required to recall.

9. Use multiple modalities (e.g., auditory, visual, tactile, etc.) when presenting instructional content.

10. Give the student specific categories and have him/her name as many items as possible within that category (e.g., objects, persons, places, etc.).

11. Give the student a choice of answers on worksheets (e.g., fill-in-the-blank, multiple-choice, etc.). This increases the student's opportunity for recognizing the correct answer.

12. Review daily those skills, concepts, tasks, etc., which have been previously introduced.

13. Reinforce the student for demonstrating accurate memory skills: (a) give the student a tangible reward (e.g., classroom privileges, line leading, passing out materials, five minutes free time, etc.) or (b) give the student an intangible reward (e.g., praise, fist bump, smile, etc.).

14. Reinforce the student for demonstrating accurate memory skills based on the length of time the student can be successful. As the student demonstrates success, gradually increase the length of time required for reinforcement.

15. When the student has difficulty with recalling information, remind the student that this can happen to everyone and not to be upset. Everyone has areas where they are weak and areas of strength as well.

16. Stop at various points during the presentation of information to check the student's comprehension.

17. Identify the student's most effective learning mode. Use it consistently to facilitate the student's understanding (e.g., if the student does not understand information verbally, present it in written form; if the student has difficulty understanding written information, present it verbally; etc.).

18. Describe objects, persons, places, etc., and have the student name the items described.

19. Label objects, persons, places, etc., in the environment to help the student recall their names.

20. Use concrete examples and experiences in sharing information with the student.

21. Make the material meaningful to the student. Remembering is more likely to occur when the material is meaningful and can be related to real-life experiences.

22. Have the student prepare for tests using the "Who, What, Where, When, How, and Why" format.

23. Make sure the student has repetition of information through different experiences to facilitate his/her memory.

24. Have the student outline, highlight, underline, or summarize information he/she needs to remember.

25. Make sure the student is attending to the source of information (e.g., eye contact is being made, hands are free of materials, student is looking at the assignment, etc.).

26. Teach concepts through associative learning (i.e., build new concepts based on previous learning).

27. Help the student use memory aids or mnemonic devices to recall words (e.g., a name might be linked to another word, for example, Mr. Green is a very colorful person.).

28. Have the student take notes from classes, presentations, lectures, etc., to help him/her facilitate recall.

29. Have the student make notes, lists, etc., of things he/she needs to be able to recall. The student should carry these reminders with him/her.

30. Show the student an object or a picture of an object for a few seconds and then remove it. Ask the student to recall specific attributes (e.g., color, size, shape, etc.) of the object.

31. After a field trip or special event, have the student recall the activities which occurred.

32. Choose a peer to participate in memory activities with the student (e.g., memory games, flash cards, math facts, etc.).

33. Make sure the student receives information from a variety of resources (e.g., texts, discussions, visual presentations, etc.) to facilitate his/her memory/recall.

34. Encourage the student to play word games such as Hangman®, Scrabble®, Password™, etc.

35. Develop tests and quizzes for the student using the "Who, What, Where, When, How, and Why" format.

36. Teach the student to recognize key words and phrases related to information to facilitate his/her memory skills.

37. Have the student practice repetition of information to facilitate memory skills (e.g., repeating names, phone numbers, dates of events, etc.).

38. When the student is required to recall information, remind him/her of the situation in which the material was originally presented (e.g., "Remember yesterday when we talked about . . . ?" "Remember when we were outside and I told you about the . . . ?" etc.).

39. Give the student a series of words describing objects, persons, places, etc., and have him/her identify the opposite of each word.

40. Give the student a series of words (e.g., objects, persons, places, etc.) and have the student list all the words he/she can think of with similar meanings (i.e., synonyms).

41. Give the student a series of words or pictures and have him/her name the category to which they belong (e.g., objects, persons, places, etc.).

42. After reading a short story, have the student recall the main characters, the sequence of events, and the outcome of the story.

43. Provide opportunities for the student to overlearn material presented to facilitate being able to recall the information.

44. Have the student memorize the first sentence or line of a poem, song, etc. As the student experiences success, require him/her to memorize more lines.

45. Teach the student how to organize information into smaller units (e.g., break a number sequence into small units - 132563 into 13, 25, 63).

46. Encourage the student to use semantic mapping techniques to facilitate visual memory.

47. Provide the student with verbal cues to stimulate recall of material previously presented (e.g., key words, a brief verbal description, etc.).

48. Evaluate the appropriateness of the information to be recalled to determine (a) if the task is too difficult and (b) if the length of time scheduled to complete the task is adequate.

49. Call on the student when he/she is most likely to be able to successfully respond.

50. Have the student record important information he/she should remember.

15 Demonstrates visual perception problems

1. Have the student's vision checked if it has not been recently checked.

2. Give the student the opportunity to find objects which are the same or different in size, shape, color, etc.

3. Have the student sort objects according to size, shape, color, etc.

4. Have the student use play equipment such as a ladder, jungle gym, teeter-totter, or balance beam to become more aware of body position in space.

5. Have the student complete partially drawn figures, words, numbers, etc.

6. Have the student use pictures from magazines, catalogs, etc., to assemble features and body parts.

7. Have the student build an object according to a pattern (e.g., construction toys, blocks, etc.).

8. Have the student participate in sequencing activities (e.g., put numbers in order, place pictures in correct order, etc.).

9. Have the student pick out specific objects from pictures, around the classroom, in the environment, while on the playground, etc.

10. Have the student perform a variety of activities such as tracing, cutting, coloring, pasting, etc.

11. Have the student complete jigsaw puzzles, beginning with simple self-made puzzles and progressing to more complex puzzles.

12. Develop a variety of activities for the student using a pegboard.

13. Provide the student with a variety of classifying activities (e.g., from simple classifying of types of clothes, cars, etc., to more complex classifying of which items would be located at certain stores, etc.).

14. Have the student find specific shapes in the room (e.g., the door is a rectangle, the clock is a circle, etc.).

15. Provide the student with simple designs to be reproduced with blocks, sticks, paper, etc.

16. Have the student identify objects by looking at the outline of objects on a cardboard silhouette, etc.

17. Reduce visual stimuli on a worksheet or in a book by covering all of the page except the activity on which the student is working.

18. Have the student repeat the names of objects, shapes, numbers, or words presented to him/her for a limited time period.

19. Provide the student with a variety of exercises in which he/she must identify the missing parts, common objects, etc.

20. Provide the student with a variety of visual recall tasks (e.g., the student writes numbers, shapes, and words he/she was shown for a specific time, etc.).

21. Use a variety of colored tiles to make a pattern. Have the student duplicate the pattern while looking at the model, then complete the design from memory without using the model.

22. Place several items on a tray, such as a pencil, a flower, a penny, and a piece of gum. Allow the student to study the items, then take the items away and have the student identify what was on the tray.

23. Have the student practice tracing outlines of pictures. Worksheets with dotted lines of pictures, letters, numbers, etc., can be used to develop eye-hand coordination.

24. Play a matching game in which hidden pictures, numbers, or shapes are turned over one at a time and the student must remember where the matching picture is located.

25. Using pictures from magazines, remove an important part of the picture and ask the student to identify the missing part.

26. Read directions to the student before he/she is asked to begin a workbook page. Work the first problem with the student so he/she understands what is expected.

27. Reduce the amount of information on a page for the student (e.g., less print, fewer problems, etc.).

28. Provide math problems on graph paper so the numbers are in columns in the ones, tens, and hundreds places.

29. Have writing paper color-coded so the student knows where to start and stop on the page.

30. Highlight or underline important words, phrases, etc., in the student's assignments that require reading.

31. Allow the student to use a typewriter to facilitate skills and reinforce word recognition.

32. Provide the student with shorter tasks, but provide more of them. As the student demonstrates success, increase the length and decrease the number of the tasks.

33. Reduce distracting stimuli on or near the student's desk (e.g., materials on the desk, things inside the desk, etc.).

34. Provide the student with a quiet place to work (e.g., carrel, office, etc.). This is used as a means of reducing distracting stimuli and not as a form of punishment.

35. Identify the student's most effective learning mode and use it consistently to increase the probability of understanding (e.g., if the student has difficulty understanding written information or directions, present it verbally).

1. Make sure the student understands that all objects, people, ideas, actions, etc., can be grouped based on how they are alike. Provide the student with concrete examples.

2. Give the student pairs of objects and have the student name all the ways in which they are alike and then the ways in which they are different. Proceed from simple things which can be seen and touched to more abstract ideas which cannot be seen or touched.

3. Explain that each new word which is learned is an example of some category. When defining a word, it should first be put into a category (e.g., a hammer is a tool, anger is an emotion, etc.).

4. Present a series of objects and have the student create a category into which they fit.

5. Present a series of objects and have the student tell which ones do not belong in the same category as the others.

6. Give the student a list of words or pictures and have him/her identify the categories to which they belong. (Love and hate are both emotions. Love fits into the specific category of good feelings, and hate fits into the specific category of negative or unhappy feelings.)

7. Explain that words can be categorized according to many different attributes, such as size, function, texture, etc.

8. Ask the student to help make lists of some categories which fit inside larger categories (e.g., flowers, trees, and bushes are all categories which can be included in the plant category).

9. Name a category or group and ask the student to identify as many things as possible which belong in the group. Begin with large categories (e.g., living things) and move to smaller categories (e.g., living things which are green).

10. Play a game such as "I'm thinking of an object" in which an object is described and the student must guess the object based on questions he/she has asked.

11. Suggest that parents ask for the student's help when grocery shopping by having him/her make a list of items needed in a particular food group (e.g., dairy products, meats, etc.).

12. Have the student cut out pictures for a notebook of favorite foods, television shows, or other categories. The student can then group the pictures in accurate categories.

13. Use pictures, diagrams, the wall-mounted board, and gestures when delivering information verbally.

14. Give the student specific categories and have him/her name as many items as possible within the categories (e.g., objects, persons, places, etc.).

15. Give the student a word and ask the student to list as many words as possible which have similar meanings (i.e., synonyms).

16. Make the subject matter meaningful to the student (e.g., explain the purpose of an assignment, relate the subject matter to the student's environment, etc.).

17. Stop at various points during the presentation of information to check the student's comprehension.

17 Fails to generalize knowledge from one situation to another

1. Make sure the student understands that all objects, people, ideas, actions, etc., can be grouped based on how they are alike. Provide the student with concrete examples (e.g., dogs, cats, cows, and horses are all mammals).

2. Give the student pairs of objects, and have the student name the ways in which they are alike and the ways they are different. Proceed from simple things which can be seen and touched to more abstract ideas which cannot be seen or touched.

3. Name a category or group and ask the student to identify as many things as possible which belong in the group. Begin with large categories (e.g., living things) and move to more specific categories (e.g., living things which are green).

4. Ask the student to help in making lists of some categories which fit inside larger categories (e.g., flowers, trees, and bushes are all categories which can be included in the plant category).

5. Identify related concepts and explain to the student how we can generalize from one to another (e.g., numbers to money, fuel to energy, words to sentences, etc.).

6. Have the student play analogy games involving multiple-choice possibilities (e.g., food is to a person as gasoline is to _____ [a skateboard, an automobile, a house]).

7. Deliver instructions by using examples of relationships (e.g., rely on what has already been learned, use examples from the student's environment, etc.).

8. Call attention to situations in the classroom which generalize to more global situations (e.g., being on time for class is the same as being on time for work; schoolwork not done during work time has to be made up before school, after school, or during recreational time, just as responsibilities at places of employment have to be completed at night or on weekends if not completed on the job; etc.).

9. Have the student explain outcomes, consequences, etc., (e.g., when the student earns a reward or privilege, make sure he/she can explain that the reward was the result of hard work and accomplishment; etc.).

10. Have the student respond to statements that begin with "What if" (e.g., "What if it rained for forty days and forty nights?" "What if there were no rules and laws?" etc.).

11. Be sure to relate what the student has learned in one setting or situation to other situations (e.g., vocabulary words learned should be pointed out in reading selections, math word problems, story writing, etc.).

12. Have the student write letters, complete applications, etc., to demonstrate the generalization of handwriting, spelling, grammar, sentence structure, etc., to real-life situations.

13. Provide the student with situations in which he/she can generalize skills learned in mathematics to simulations of the use of money (e.g., making change, financing a car, computing interest earned from savings, etc.).

14. Make sure that the student is provided with an explanation of "why" he/she is learning particular information or skills (e.g., we learn to spell, read, and write to communicate; we learn to solve math problems to make purchases, use a checking account, measure, and cook; etc.).

15. Have the student develop a series of responses representing his/her ability to generalize from common situations in the environment (e.g., "We should drive no more than the posted speed limit on the highway because . . . ." Appropriate responses concern safety, conservation of fuel, care of vehicle, fines for speeding, etc.).

16. Use pictures, diagrams, the wall-mounted board, and gestures when delivering information.

17. When delivering explanations and information, be sure to use vocabulary that is within the student's level of comprehension.

18. When the student is required to generalize knowledge from one situation to another, provide visual and/or auditory cues to help him/her remember the information previously presented (e.g., provide key words, expose part of a picture, etc.).

19. Use multiple modalities (e.g., auditory, visual, tactile, etc.) when presenting instructional material that requires the student to generalize knowledge. Use the modality that is stronger to present instructional material.

20. As soon as the student learns a skill, make sure that he/she applies it to a real-life situation (e.g., when the student learns to count by fives, have him/her practice adding nickels).

21. Use concrete examples and experiences when teaching concepts and sharing information with the student.

22. Use daily drill activities to help the student memorize math facts, sight words, etc.

23. Use a variety of instructional approaches to help the student generalize knowledge gained to real-life situations (e.g., after studying the judicial system, provide a simulated courtroom trial, etc.).

18 Demonstrates confusion

1. Have the student's vision checked if it has not been recently checked.

2. Make sure that all directions, explanations, and instructions are delivered in a clear and concise manner.

3. Teach the student direction-following skills (e.g., stop doing other things; listen to what is being said; do not begin until all information is delivered; question any directions, explanations, and instructions you do not understand).

4. Teach the student to rely on environmental cues when moving about the school and related areas (e.g., look for signs, room numbers, familiar surroundings, etc.).

5. Make sure the student knows how to ask questions, ask for directions, etc.

6. Teach the student a basic survival/directional word vocabulary (e.g., *ladies, gentlemen, push, pull, left, right,* etc.).

7. Have the student verbally repeat/paraphrase instructions and information given so that the instructor can provide a means of clarification and redirection of the given information.

8. Have the student practice finding various locations in the building before or after school or during classes when few other students are in the halls.

9. Have the student practice finding locations in the building by following verbal directions, written directions, directions from teachers or other students, etc.

10. Have the student follow a schedule of daily events as he/she moves from place to place in the school.

11. Pair the student with a classmate who has a similar class schedule to have a peer who can direct the student if he/she gets lost or confused.

12. Have the student learn to use a floor plan to find specific rooms, hallways, and areas while following his/her daily class or work schedule.

13. Make sure the student has designated instructors or peers who act as a source of information within the school.

14. Choose a peer to accompany the student to locations in the building until the student develops familiarity with his/her surroundings.

15. Make sure the student has been provided with an adequate orientation to all areas of the school environment he/she will be using.

16. Have the student practice problem-solving skills if he/she should become lost or confused in the school environment (e.g., ask directions, return to where you started, look for familiar surroundings, read signs, etc.).

17. Make sure the school environment is conducive to finding locations the student uses (e.g., posting signs, posting directions, color-coding pods and similar areas, etc.).

18. Before leaving the classroom have the student review directions to locate certain points throughout the building (e.g., have the student repeat directions back to you, have the student look at a map, etc.).

19. When giving the student directions to certain points throughout the building, use landmarks such as the drinking fountain, restroom, lunchroom, etc., (e.g., "Go to the room that is just past the lunchroom." "The bathroom is on the left side of the drinking fountain.").

20. Use vocabulary that is within the student's level of comprehension when delivering directions, explanations, and information.

21. Make sure the student is attending when directions are being given (e.g., eye contact is being made, hands are free of materials, etc.).

22. Reduce or remove those stimuli from the environment which are distracting to the student and interfering with his/her ability to listen successfully.

23. Have the student be a peer tutor to teach a concept he/she has mastered to another student. This can serve as reinforcement for the student.

24. Call on the student when he/she is most likely to be able to respond successfully.

25. Provide the student with shorter tasks, but more of them, throughout the day (e.g., four assignments of five problems each rather than one assignment of 20 problems).

26. Review, on a daily basis, those skills, concepts, tasks, etc., which have been previously introduced.

27. Give the student one task to perform at a time. Introduce the next task only when the student has successfully completed the previous task.

28. Stop at various points during the presentation of information to check the student's comprehension.

29. Make sure the student is attending to the source of information (e.g., eye contact is being made, hands are free of materials, student is looking at the assignment, etc.).

30. Provide the student with environmental cues and prompts designed to facilitate his/her success in the classroom (e.g., posted rules, schedule of daily events, steps for performing a task, etc.).

31. Use pictures, diagrams, the wall-mounted board, and gestures when delivering information.

32. Reduce the amount of information on a page (e.g., have less print to read, have fewer problems, isolate information that is presented to the student) if it causes visual distractions for the student.

33. Assign the student shorter tasks. As the student demonstrates success, gradually increase the length of tasks.

34. Identify the student's most effective learning mode. Use it consistently to increase the student's understanding (e.g., if the student fails to understand directions or information given verbally, present it in written form; if the student has difficulty understanding written information or directions, present it verbally).

35. Make sure that verbal directions are delivered in a nonthreatening and supportive manner (e.g., positive voice, facial expressions and language such as "Will you please . . ." or "You need . . ." rather than "You better . . ." or "If you don't . . .").

36. Make sure the student has mastery of concepts at one level before introducing a new skill level.

37. Use vocabulary that is within the student's level of comprehension when delivering directions, explanations, and information.

38. Deliver information to the student on a one-to-one basis or employ a peer tutor.

1. Have the student record important information that he/she should remember.

2. Present information verbally if the student has difficulty remembering written information.

3. Have the student outline, highlight, underline, or summarize information that should be remembered.

4. Use concrete examples and experiences in sharing information with the student.

5. Teach the student to recognize main points, important facts, etc.

6. Make sure the student has adequate opportunities for repetition of information through different experiences to facilitate memory.

7. Present information to the student in the most clear and concise manner possible.

8. Reduce distracting stimuli when the student is attempting to recall important information.

9. Teach the student to rely on resources in the environment to recall information (e.g., notes, textbooks, pictures, etc.).

10. Provide auditory cues to help the student recall information (e.g., key words, a brief verbal description to clue the student, etc.).

11. Have the student make notes, lists, etc., of important information to carry with him/her at all times.

12. When the student is required to recall information, remind him/her of the situation in which the material was originally presented (e.g., "Remember yesterday when we talked about . . ." "Remember when we were outside and I told you about the . . .").

13. Make the material meaningful to the student. Remembering is more likely to occur when the material is meaningful and the student can relate the material to real experiences.

14. Relate the information being presented to the student's previous experiences.

15. Have the student follow a regular routine of daily events to establish consistency in his/her behavior pattern.

16. Have the student quietly repeat to himself/herself information just heard to help him/her remember the important facts.

17. Do not require the student to learn more information than he/she is capable of remembering at any time.

18. Give the student a choice of answers (e.g., more than one possible answer, multiple-choice on a worksheet, etc.) to facilitate his/her ability to recognize the correct answer.

19. Provide reminders throughout the educational environment to help the student be more successful in remembering information (e.g., rules, lists, schedules, etc.).

20. Help the student employ memory aids to recall words (e.g., a name might be linked to another word, for example, Mr. Green is a very colorful person.).

21. Provide the student with adequate opportunities for repetition of information through different experiences to facilitate his/her memory.

22. Review daily those skills, concepts, tasks, etc., which have been previously introduced to help the student remember information previously presented.

23. Have the student take notes when directions are being given following the "What, How, Materials, and When" format.

24. Use daily drill activities to help the student memorize math facts, vocabulary words, etc.

25. Identify the student's most effective learning mode. Use it consistently to facilitate the student's understanding (e.g., if the student does not understand directions or information given verbally, present it in written form; if the student has difficulty understanding written information or directions, present it verbally; etc.).

26. Provide the student opportunities to apply new skills or information to other situations (e.g., when he/she learns to count by fives, have him/her practice adding nickels; vocabulary words learned should be pointed out in reading selections; etc.).

27. Present directions following the outline of (1) What, (2) How, (3) Materials, and (4) When.

28. Have the student listen and take notes for "Who, What, Where, When, How, and Why" while concepts are presented.

29. Present concepts following the outline of (1) Who, (2) What, (3) Where, (4) When, (5) How, and (6) Why.

30. Call on the student when he/she is most likely to be able to successfully respond.

1. Use multiple modalities (e.g., auditory, visual, tactile, etc.) when presenting directions, explanations, and instructional content. Determine which modality is stronger and utilize that modality.

2. Use concrete examples of experiences in teaching concepts and sharing information with the students.

3. Review daily those skills, concepts, tasks, etc., which have been previously introduced.

4. Use pictures, diagrams, the wall-mounted board, and gestures when delivering information verbally.

5. Reinforce the student for listening to what is said: (a) give the student a tangible reward (e.g., classroom privileges, line leading, five minutes free time, passing out materials, etc.) or (b) give the student an intangible reward (e.g., praise, fist bump, smile, etc.).

6. Have the student repeat or paraphrase what is said to him/her to determine what he/she heard.

7. Reinforce the student for listening carefully based on the length of time the student can be successful. As the student demonstrates success, gradually increase the length of time required for reinforcement.

8. Speak to the student to explain (a) what he/she is doing wrong (e.g., failing to listen carefully) and (b) what the student should be doing (e.g., listening carefully).

9. Evaluate the difficulty level of information verbally delivered to the student (i.e., information should be communicated on the student's ability level).

10. Have the student ask questions about directions, explanations, instructions, etc., he/she does not understand.

11. Give the student short directions, explanations, or presentations of concepts. As the student demonstrates success, gradually increase the length of the directions, explanations, or presentations of concepts.

12. Maintain a consistent format for the delivery of verbal instructions.

13. Make sure the student is attending to the source of information (e.g., making eye contact, hands free of writing materials, looking at the assignment, etc.).

14. Provide the student with written directions and instructions to supplement verbal directions and instructions.

15. Emphasize or repeat word endings, key words, etc.

16. Speak clearly and concisely when delivering directions, explanations, and instructions.

17. Place the student near the source of information.

18. Reduce distracting stimuli (e.g., noise and motion in the classroom) to facilitate the student's ability to listen successfully.

19. Stop at key points when delivering directions, explanations, and instructions to determine the student's comprehension.

20. Deliver directions, explanations, and instructions at an appropriate rate.

21. Identify a list of word endings, key words, etc., that the student will practice listening for when someone is speaking.

22. Deliver verbal questions and directions that involve only one concept or step. As the student demonstrates success, gradually increase the number of concepts or steps presented in verbal questions and directions.

23. Move the student away from other students who may interfere with his/her ability to attend to directions, explanations, and instructions.

24. Teach the student listening skills (e.g., listen carefully, write down important points, ask for clarification, wait until all directions are received before beginning, etc.).

25. Use demonstrations along with the presentation of information.

26. Scan all materials for new words. Use simple terms when possible. Teach new vocabulary and provide practice through application.

27. Give concrete examples and hands-on experiences to reduce abstractions.

28. Present a new concept by relating it to previously presented information.

29. Prepare or obtain manuals with simple definitions of technical vocabulary, simple vocabulary and sentence structure, step-by-step instructions, and diagrams or pictures.

30. Sequence known concepts with skills or concepts not mastered to facilitate the recognition of relationships to new skills and concepts.

31. Highlight or underline the important facts in reading material.

32. Rewrite instructions at an appropriate reading level for the student.

33. Present concepts using the student's most effective learning mode.

34. Provide the student with a written copy of material presented verbally.

35. Provide the student with a verbal presentation of material if he/she has difficulty with the written presentation of concepts.

36. Record the presentation of new concepts. Allow the student to listen to it as often as necessary.

37. Choose a peer to repeat the presentation of concepts to the student when he/she does not understand.

38. Have the student be a peer tutor to teach units of information he/she has mastered to another student.

39. Develop tests and quizzes for the student using the "Who, What, Where, When, How, and Why" format.

40. Have the student listen and take notes for "Who, What, Where, When, How, and Why" when concepts are presented.

41. Have the student take notes using semantic mapping techniques.

42. Provide the student with the information he/she needs (e.g., list of facts, a summary of important points, outline of important events, etc.) to facilitate learning.

43. Present concepts following the (1) Who, (2) What, (3) Where, (4) When, (5) How, and (6) Why outline.

21 Fails to remember sequences

1. Have the student maintain a notebook in which he/she keeps notes regarding necessary sequential information (e.g., lists of things to do, schedule of events, days of the week, months of the year, etc.).

2. Provide the student with a schedule of daily events for each day's activities at school.

3. Use multiple modalities to accommodate more than one learning style (e.g., visual, auditory, tactile, etc.) when presenting directions/instructions, explanations, and instructional content.

4. Involve the student in activities in which he/she can be successful and which will help him/her feel good about himself/herself. Repeated failures result in frustration and impatience.

5. Assign the student additional activities which require the use of sequences to facilitate his/her ability to remember sequences.

6. Clarify instructions/directions/expectations before assigning a task.

7. Have the student ask questions about directions, explanations, or instructions he/she does understand.

8. Consider carefully the student's age and experience before expecting him/her to remember lengthy sequences of activities.

9. Encourage the student to ask people to repeat parts of a conversation he/she was unable to follow.

10. Instruct the student to ask himself/herself questions (e.g., "What's next?") to keep himself/herself focused on assignments/projects.

11. Encourage the student to avoid ingesting any substance (e.g., drugs, alcohol, cold remedies, etc.) that might further alter his/her ability to remember.

12. Instruct the student to carry a notepad with him/her at all times and to write information down to help him/her remember.

13. Make sure that comments made to the student take the form of constructive criticism rather than perceived as personal, threatening, etc., (e.g., instead of saying, "You always make the same mistake," say, "A better way to do that might be . . . .").

14. Have the student ask for help when he/she needs it.

15. Reduce the emphasis on competition. Competitive activities may cause the student to omit necessary steps in a task.

16. Establish a timeline for completing a project. Expect the student to meet each deadline to complete the project on time.

17. Write down verbal directions. Cross each step off as it is completed.

18. Practice sequential memory activities daily. Practice those sequences which the student needs to memorize (e.g., important phone numbers, addresses, etc.).

19. Help the student develop an awareness of himself/herself and the environment. Instruct the student to periodically step back and ask himself/herself, "Am I on task and following the necessary steps?" "What should I be doing now?"

20. Assist the student in developing a flow chart of the steps necessary to complete a task.

21. Assist the student in developing a checklist/chart to follow which will allow him/her to complete all assignments.

22. Stop at various points during the presentation of information to check the student's comprehension.

23. Encourage the student to eat a balanced diet and get plenty of rest to facilitate his/her memory.

24. Have the student use electronic reminders to assist him/her in following a routine (e.g., a programmable watch, computer programs, voice mail, etc.).

25. Provide the student with environmental cues and prompts (e.g., lists of jobs to perform, schedule of daily events, bell, timer, etc.).

26. Maintain a consistent sequence of activities to facilitate the student's success (e.g, the student has math every day at one o'clock, recess at two o'clock, etc.).

27. Encourage the student to establish a routine for himself/herself by developing a weekly schedule and a weekend schedule. Assist the student in developing a checklist/chart for daily assignments to be completed.

28. Provide the student with frequent opportunities to recite sequences throughout the day to facilitate memory skills.

29. Allow the student to highlight sequential information in written materials.

30. Instruct the student to imagine the steps required to complete a task before beginning that task.

31. Make sure the activities in which the student engages are not too difficult for him/her.

32. Assign a task that involves immediate, short-term steps.

33. Teach the student to make reminders for himself/herself (e.g., notes, lists, etc.).

34. Help the student employ memory aids.

35. Have the student maintain notes, written reminders, etc., to remember sequences.

36. Choose different people (e.g., peer, counselor, paraprofessional, etc.) to help the student improve his/her memory skills.

37. Make it pleasant and positive for the student to ask questions about things he/she does not understand. Reinforce the student by assisting, congratulating, praising, etc.

38. Instruct the student to post needed sequential information in a readily accessible location (e.g., folder, on desktop, in front of text book, etc.).

39. Encourage the student to practice patience and follow the necessary steps in tasks. If the student is impatient, he/she is more likely to omit necessary steps in a sequence.

40. Have the student practice remembering sequences by engaging in sequential activities which are purposeful to him/her (e.g., operating equipment, following recipes, opening a combination lock, etc.).

41. Reinforce the student for remembering sequences based on the number of times he/she can be successful. As the student demonstrates success, gradually increase the length of the sequence required for reinforcement.

42. Reinforce the student for remembering sequences: (a) give the student a tangible reward (e.g., classroom privileges, line leading, passing out materials, five minutes free time, etc.) or (b) give the student an intangible reward (e.g., praise, fist bump, smile, etc.).

43. Have the student verbally repeat directions, explanations, and instructions after they have been given to reinforce retention.

44. Have the student be responsible for helping a peer remember sequences.

45. Maintain a consistent daily routine in the classroom.

46. Give the student short sequences (e.g., two components, three components, etc.) to remember. As the student demonstrates success, gradually increase the length of the sequence.

47. Prevent frustrating or anxiety-producing situations from occurring (e.g., do not place the student in a competitive situation which requires sequencing skills).

48. Teach and practice different strategies to remember steps in a task:
- repetition,
- mnemonic,
- acronym, and
- association.

49. Do not require the student to learn more information than he/she is capable of remembering at any time.

50. Teach and have the student practice listening for key information when he/she is being given directions or receiving information (e.g., write down main points, ideas, step-by-step instructions; etc.).

51. Deliver information to the student on a one-to-one basis or use a peer tutor.

52. Establish a rule (e.g., take your time and follow sequential directions). This rule should be consistent and followed by everyone in the classroom. Talk about the rule often and reward the student for following the rule.

53. Allow the student to record information from lectures and seminars and make notes from these recordings.

54. Provide written reminders of task sequences.

55. Assess the degree of task difficulty to determine whether or not the student will require additional information, sequencing models, time, assistance, etc., before beginning a task.

56. Have the student identify the main characters, sequence the events, and report the outcome of a short story he/she has just read.

57. Demonstrate new skills. Allow the student to practice hands-on learning of new skills.

58. Make instructions meaningful to the student. Attempt to relate instructions to past experiences.

59. Have the student sequence the activities which occurred during a field trip or special event.

60. Reinforce those students in the classroom who remember sequences.

61. Reward other students in the classroom for following necessary steps in tasks.

62. Evaluate the appropriateness of the task to determine (a) if the task is too easy, (b) if the task is too difficult, and (c) if the length of time scheduled to complete the task is adequate.

63. Use written/verbal repetition to aid retention of information.

64. Tell the student what to listen for when being given directions or receiving information, etc.

65. Break a sequence into units and have the student learn one unit at a time.

66. Teach the student to use environmental resources to remember sequences (e.g., calendar, dictionary, etc.).

67. Teach the student to use associative cues or mnemonic devices to remember sequences.

68. Have the student quietly repeat to himself/herself information just heard to help him/her remember the important facts.

69. Encourage the student to use an electronic pocket organizer for phone numbers, reminders, and messages.

70. Encourage the student to use visual reminders (e.g., attach a note to a backpack, place a self-adhesive note on the inside of his/her locker, etc.).

71. Have the student work with a peer who is able to successfully follow the necessary steps in tasks.

B. Listening

1. Maintain visibility to and from the student. The teacher should be able to see the student, and the student should be able to see the teacher. Make eye contact possible at all times when giving verbal directions.

2. Assess the quality and clarity of verbal directions, explanations, and instructions given to the student.

3. Choose a peer to work with the student to help him/her follow verbal directions.

4. Deliver directions, explanations, and information using vocabulary that is within the student's level of comprehension.

5. Avoid placing the student in situations that require listening for an extended directions, announcements, seminars, etc. Provide the information for the student through a recordimg or lecture notes.

6. Be consistent in expecting the student to listen to and follow directions. Do not allow the student to fail to follow directions one time and expect directions to be followed the next time.

7. Be sure the student has heard what was said by having him/her give acknowledgment (e.g., by saying, "Okay!" "Will do!" etc.).

8. Clarify for the student that it is his/her behavior which determines whether consequences are positive or negative.

9. Communicate clearly to the student when it is time to listen to verbal directions.

10. Assist the student in performing his/her responsibilities. As he/she demonstrates success following verbal directions, gradually decrease the assistance and require the student to independently assume more responsibility.

11. Deliver a predetermined signal (e.g., clapping hands, turning lights off and on, etc.) before giving verbal directions.

12. Communicate with parents (e.g., notes home, phone calls, etc.) to share information about the student's progress. The parents may reinforce the student at home for following verbal directions at school.

13. Demonstrate directions, explanations, and instructions as they are presented verbally (e.g., use the wall-mounted board to work a problem for the student, begin playing a game with the student, etc.).

14. Demonstrate the steps of verbal directions as they are delivered to facilitate the likelihood that the student will follow the directions accurately.

15. Develop direction-following assignments/activities (e.g., informal activities designed to have the student carry out verbal directions in steps with increasing degrees of difficulty).

16. Evaluate the visual and auditory stimuli in the environment. Determine the amount of stimuli the student can tolerate. Remove the extraneous stimuli from the environment.

17. Do not criticize when correcting the student; be honest yet supportive. Never cause the student to feel negatively about himself/herself.

18. Do not give directions to the student from across the classroom. Go to the student, get his/her undivided attention, and tell the student what he/she is to do. As the student's ability to follow verbal directions increases, gradually increase the distance of communication.

19. Give verbal directions before handing out materials.

20. Give the student short directions, explanations, and instructions to follow. As the student demonstrates success, gradually increase the length of the directions, explanations, and instructions.

21. Encourage the student to recite a mantra to himself/herself when entering a situation where the student will receive directions/instructions (e.g., listen carefully, listen carefully, listen carefully).

22. Help the student develop an awareness of the consequences of his/her behavior by writing down or talking through problems which may occur due to his/her need to have verbal directions and questions frequently repeated (e.g., If you do not focus on the directions, you may not complete assignments correctly. Then, you may not pass the class and earn the credit needed for graduation.).

23. Establish classroom rules:
- Concentrate while working.
- Work quietly.
- Remain in your seat.
- Finish task.
- Meet task requirements.

Review rules often. Reinforce the student for following the rules.

24. Establish rules for listening to and following directions (e.g., listen when someone is giving directions, ask questions about directions if they are not understood, etc.). These rules should be consistent and followed by everyone in the class. Talk about the rules often.

25. Evaluate the appropriateness of the task to determine (a) if the task is too easy, (b) if the task is too difficult, and (c) if the length of time scheduled to complete the task is adequate.

26. Facilitate the student's ability to follow verbal directions by communicating with the student's cooperative work experience/vocational education teacher to provide appropriate strategies and interventions at the student's job site.

27. Follow a less desirable task with a highly desirable task. Make the following of verbal directions and completion of the first task necessary to perform the second task.

28. Give directions in a variety of ways to facilitate the student's understanding (e.g., if the student does not understand verbal directions, present them in written form).

29. Give the student one task to perform at a time. Introduce the next task only when the student has successfully completed the previous task.

30. Encourage the student to avoid ingesting any substance (e.g., drugs, alcohol, cold remedies, etc.) that might further alter his/her ability to listen to or follow verbal directions.

31. Encourage the student to ask for clarification of any directions, explanations, and instructions before beginning a task to facilitate comprehension.

32. Have a designated person be the only individual to deliver verbal directions to the student.

33. Have a peer help the student with any verbal directions he/she does not understand.

34. Instruct the student to periodically, step back and ask himself/herself, "Am I on task and paying attention?" "What should I be doing now?"

35. Have the student attend to the source of information by maintaining eye contact, keeping hands free from other materials, and reducing other distractions.

36. Require that assignments done incorrectly, for any reason, be redone.

37. Have the student maintain a record (e.g., chart or graph) of his/her performance in following verbal directions.

38. Reduce verbal directions to steps (e.g., give the student each additional step after completion of the previous step).

39. Have the student practice group listening skills (e.g., "Everyone take out a piece of paper. Write your name on the paper. Number your paper from 1 to 20.").

40. Make sure the student is attending (e.g., making eye contact, hands free of writing materials, looking at assignment, etc.) before verbal directions are given.

41. Have the student ask questions about verbal directions, explanations, and instructions he/she does not understand.

42. Provide constant, positive reinforcement for appropriate behavior. Ignore as many inappropriate behaviors as possible.

43. Have the student audio record directions, explanations, and instructions. Allow him/her to replay information as often as needed.

44. Have the student's hearing checked if it has not been recently checked.

45. Make sure that the student understands the relationship between inappropriate behavior and the consequences which follow (e.g., failing to listen to and follow directions during football practice may result in being benched for a game).

46. Have the student verbally repeat directions, explanations, and instructions after they have been given to reinforce retention.

47. Let the student know that directions will only be given once and that he/she will not be reminded to follow the directions.

48. Maintain a consistent format for verbal directions.

49. Allow natural consequences to occur (e.g., school or class detention, missed assignment, etc.) due to the student's failure to listen to and follow directions.

50. Make sure that all directions, questions, explanations, and instructions are delivered in a clear, concise manner; at an appropriate pace; and loudly enough for the student to hear.

51. Present directions in both written and verbal form.

52. Make sure that verbal directions are delivered in a supportive rather than threatening manner (e.g., "Will you please . . ." or "You need . . ." rather than "You better . . ." or "If you don't . . .").

53. Make sure the student achieves success when following verbal directions.

54. Make sure the student has all the materials needed to complete the assignment/activity.

55. Have the student practice verbal direction-following on nonacademic tasks (e.g., recipes, games, etc.).

56. Provide alternatives for the traditional format of presenting verbal directions (e.g., record directions, summarize directions, directions given by peers, etc.).

57. Have the student repeat directions or give an interpretation after receiving verbal directions.

58. Make sure the student knows that you expect him/her to listen to you (e.g., by saying, "William, it is important that you listen carefully to what I have to say. The book report is due on Monday.").

59. Interact frequently with the student to help him/her follow verbal directions for the activity.

60. Make instructions meaningful to the student. Attempt to relate instructions to past experiences.

61. Choose a peer to model appropriate listening to and following of verbal directions for the student.

62. Make sure the student is paying attention when he/she is told to do something. Have the student make eye contact and repeat the information to check for understanding.

63. Prevent the student from becoming overstimulated by an activity (e.g., frustrated, angry, etc.).

64. Provide clearly stated verbal directions (e.g., make the directions as simple and concrete as possible).

65. Make sure that verbal directions are given at the level at which the student can be successful (e.g., two-step or three-step directions are not given to students who can only successfully follow one-step directions).

66. Provide directions on a one-to-one basis before assigning a task.

67. Provide supplemental directions/instructions in the student's preferred learning style (e.g., visual, auditory, etc.).

68. Work the first problem or problems with the student to make sure that he/she follows the verbal directions accurately.

69. Provide the student with a written copy of verbal directions.

70. Speak to the student to explain (a) what he/she is doing wrong (e.g., ignoring verbal directions) and (b) what he/she should be doing (e.g., listening to and following through when given verbal directions).

71. Reduce distracting stimuli to increase the student's ability to follow verbal directions (e.g., place the student on the front row, provide a carrel or office space away from distractions, etc.). This is used as a means of reducing distracting stimuli and not as a form of punishment.

72. Make sure that verbal directions are delivered in a nonthreatening manner (e.g., positive voice, facial expression, language used, etc.).

73. Reduce the emphasis on competition. Competitive activities may cause the student to hurry to begin the task without verbal directions.

74. Reduce the emphasis on early completion. Hurrying to complete assignments may cause the student to fail to follow directions.

75. Reinforce the student for following verbal directions: (a) give the student a tangible reward (e.g., classroom privileges, line leading, passing out materials, five minutes free time, etc.) or (b) give the student an intangible reward (e.g., praise, fist bump, smile, etc.).

76. Have the student carry out one step of the verbal directions at a time. After each step, have him/her check with the teacher to make sure that each step is successfully followed before attempting the next.

77. Reinforce the student for following verbal directions based on the length of time he/she can be successful. As the student demonstrates success, gradually increase the length of time required for reinforcement.

78. Reinforce those students in the classroom who follow verbal directions.

79. Stand next to the student when giving verbal directions.

80. Require the student to wait until the teacher gives him/her a signal to begin a task (e.g., give a hand signal, ring a bell, etc.).

81. Teach the student skills for following verbal directions (e.g., listen carefully, write down important points, use environmental cues, wait until all directions are received before beginning, etc.).

82. Reward the student (e.g., take a break, visit briefly with a peer, etc.) for maintaining eye contact and listening for a specific length of time.

83. Structure the environment to provide the student with increased opportunities for help or assistance on academic tasks (e.g., peer tutoring, directions for work sent home, frequent interactions, etc.).

84. Record directions for the student to listen to and replay as necessary.

85. Teach and have the student practice listening for key information when he/she is being given directions or receiving information (e.g., write down main points, ideas, step-by-step instructions, etc.).

86. Teach and practice effective communication skills. These skills include: listening, maintaining eye contact, and positive body language.

87. Work through the steps of the verbal directions as they are delivered to make sure the student follows the directions accurately.

88. Teach and provide practice in information-gathering skills (e.g., listen carefully, write down important points, ask for clarification, wait until all information is presented before beginning a task, etc.).

89. Teach the student listening skills (e.g., stop working, clear desk of nonessential materials, attend to the source of information, write down important points, ask for clarification, and wait until all directions are received before beginning).

90. Seat the student close to the source of the verbal directions (e.g., teacher, aide, peer, etc.).

91. Provide the student with a predetermined signal (e.g., lights turned off and on, hand signals, etc.) when he/she is not following verbal directions.

92. Seat the student far enough away from peers to ensure increased opportunities for attending to verbal directions.

93. Provide the student with a clearly understood list of consequences for inappropriate behavior.

94. Use vocabulary that is within the student's level of comprehension when delivering directions, explanations, and information.

95. Write a contract with the student specifying what behavior is expected (e.g., following verbal directions) and what reinforcement will be made available when the terms of the contract have been met.

96. Teach and provide practice in active listening skills. Have the student listen to what another person is saying and respond based on information received.

97. Write down verbal directions. Instruct the student to cross each step off as it is completed.

23 Does not hear word endings, does not hear key words such as "do not," etc.

1. Play games that teach listening skills.

2. Deliver directives in a supportive rather than a threatening manner (e.g., "Please listen to the directions," rather than, "You had better listen!").

3. Talk to the student before going into an assembly or group activity and remind him/her of the importance of listening to and following directions.

4. Have the student ask questions about directions, explanations, and instructions, etc., he/she does not understand.

5. Deliver all directions, questions, explanations, and instructions in a clear, concise manner and at an appropriate rate for the student.

6. Demonstrate the appropriate way to listen to and follow directions.

7. Encourage parents to take advantage of dinner and other family-gathering times to talk and practice maintaining attention.

8. Remove the student from the situation (e.g., school assembly, school play, guest speaker, etc.) when he/she has difficulty listening until he/she can demonstrate self-control.

9. Instruct the student to carry a notepad with him/her at all times. Encourage him/her to write information down to help him/her maintain attention.

10. Make sure you have the student's undivided attention when you are talking to him/her. Stand close to the student, maintain eye contact, and have the student repeat the information.

11. Do not reinforce the student's inappropriate behavior by laughing when he/she has not listened to directions.

12. Determine if the student heard a direction by having the student repeat it.

13. Teach and practice information-gathering skills (e.g., listen carefully, write down important points, ask for clarification, wait until all information is presented before beginning a task, etc.).

14. Reduce the emphasis on competition in the classroom. Competition may cause the student to begin an activity before hearing all of what is said.

15. Establish rules for listening to and following directions (e.g., listen when someone is giving directions, ask questions about directions if they are not understood, etc.). These rules should be consistent and followed by everyone in the classroom. Talk about the rules often.

16. Help the student listen to and follow directions by reducing distractions.

17. Reduce distracting stimuli (e.g., noise and motion in the classroom) to facilitate the student's ability to listen successfully.

18. Encourage the student to write down verbal directions.

19. Emphasize or repeat key words, due dates, quantity, etc.

20. Use multiple modalities to accommodate more than one learning style (e.g., visual, auditory, tactile, etc.) when presenting directions/instructions, explanations, and instructional content.

21. Make sure the student knows that you expect him/her to listen to you (e.g., by saying, "William, it is important that you listen carefully to what I have to say. Your rough draft is due on Wednesday.").

22. Reward the student's peers in the classroom for listening to and following directions.

23. Encourage the student to ask for clarification of any directions, explanations, and instructions before beginning a task to ensure all needed information was heard.

24. Choose different people (e.g., peers, paraprofessionals, counselors, family members, etc.) to help the student improve his/her listening skills.

25. Do not give directions to the student from across the room. Go to the student, get his/her undivided attention, and explain the directions to him/her.

26. Have the student's hearing checked if it has not been recently checked.

27. Have the student rehearse in his/her head information just heard to help him/her remember the important facts.

28. Be positive. When correcting the student, be honest yet supportive. Never cause the student to feel negatively about himself/herself.

29. Maintain a consistent format in the verbal delivery of information.

30. Encourage the student to ask for clarification if he/she does not understand directions that are given verbally or in writing.

31. Give the student short directions, explanations, and instructions to follow. As the student demonstrates success, gradually increase the length of the directions, explanations, and instructions.

32. Allow natural consequences to occur (e.g., miss instructions for assignment, miss information on school activities, etc.) due to the student failing to listen to and follow directions.

33. Have the student repeat or paraphrase what is said to him/her to determine what he/she heard.

34. Be consistent in expecting the student to listen to and follow directions. Do not allow the student to fail to listen without accepting natural consequences.

35. Reinforce the student for listening (e.g., making eye contact, hands free of writing materials, looking at assignment, etc.) to what is said: (a) give the student a tangible reward (e.g., classroom privileges, five minutes free time, etc.) or (b) give the student an intangible reward (e.g., praise, fist bump, smile, etc.).

36. Give the student directions with no more than two or three steps (e.g., "Please open your text and turn to page 28."). Directions that involve several steps can be confusing and cause the student to have difficulty following them.

37. Place the student near the source of information.

38. Stop at key points when delivering directions, explanations, and instructions to check the student's comprehension.

39. Help the student develop an awareness of himself/herself and those around him/her. Instruct the student to periodically, step back and ask himself/herself, "Am I listening and paying attention?" "What should I be doing now?"

40. Help the student develop an awareness of the consequences of not listening by writing down or talking through problems which may occur due to his/her need to have verbal directions and questions frequently repeated (e.g., if you do not focus on the directions, you may miss information and produce poor quality work).

41. Reinforce the student for listening carefully based on the length of time the student can be successful. As the student demonstrates success, gradually increase the length of time the student is required to listen.

42. Provide the student with directions on a one-to-one basis before he/she begins a task.

43. Have the student ask for help when he/she needs it.

44. Teach the student the relationship between inappropriate behavior and the consequences which follow (e.g., failing to listen to and follow directions may result in reduced grades, etc.).

45. Instruct the student to ask people to repeat parts of a conversation he/she was unable to follow.

46. Avoid placing the student in situations that require listening for an extended directions, announcements, seminars, etc. Provide the information for the student through a recording or lecture notes.

47. Encourage the student to develop a 30 second definition of his/her goal to help stay on task and focus (e.g., "I will listen carefully. The better I focus and stay on task, the better I will hear what is said.").

48. Write a contract with the student. It should be written within his/her ability level and focus on only one behavior at a time. Specify what behavior is expected and what reinforcement will be made available when the terms of the contract have been met.

49. Deliver directions, explanations, and instructions at an appropriate rate.

50. Teach and practice effective communication skills. These skills include: listening, maintaining eye contact, and positive body language.

51. Identify a classmate who has good communication skills. Encourage the student to observe that classmate and model his/her behaviors which promote good communication.

52. Instruct the student to maintain attention to the source of information by maintaining eye contact, keeping hands free from other materials, and reducing other distractions.

53. Choose a peer, paraprofessional, etc., to cue the student when he/she needs to maintain attention (e.g., the person can touch the student on the arm when it is time to listen).

54. Encourage the student to avoid ingesting any substance (e.g., drugs, alcohol, cold remedies, etc.) that might further alter his/her ability to direct or maintain attention.

55. Make sure the student is attending to the source of information (e.g., making eye contact, hands free of writing materials, looking at the assignment, etc.).

56. Allow natural consequences to occur (e.g., schoolwork not done on time, homework done incorrectly, etc.) due to the student's failure to follow verbal directions.

57. Evaluate the difficulty level of information verbally delivered to the student (e.g., information should be communicated on the student's ability level).

58. Encourage the student to recite a mantra to himself/herself when entering a situation where he/she will receive directions/instructions (e.g., listen carefully, listen carefully, listen carefully).

59. Teach active listening skills. Encourage the student to listen to what another person is saying and respond based on information received.

60. Have a peer provide the information the student does not hear.

61. Teach and have the student practice how to listen for key information when he/she is being given directions or receiving information (e.g., write down main points, ideas, step-by-step instructions; etc.).

62. Provide the student with written directions and instructions to supplement verbal directions and instructions.

63. Provide opportunities for the student to talk to others on a one-to-one basis. As the student becomes more successful at listening and maintaining attention, gradually include more people in conversations.

64. Give simple, specific directions to the student.

65. Speak to the student to explain (a) what he/she is doing wrong (e.g., failing to listen for key words, etc.) and (b) what he/she should be doing (e.g., listening for key words, etc.).

66. Consider carefully the student's age and experience when expecting him/her to listen to and follow directions.

67. Identify a list of word endings, key words, etc., that the student will practice listening for when someone is speaking.

68. Present directions following the (1) What, (2) How, (3) Materials, and (4) When outline.

69. Teach the student listening skills:
- Stop working.
- Clear desk of nonessential materials.
- Attend to the source of information.
- Write down important points.
- Ask for clarification.
- Wait until all directions are received before beginning.

70. Be sure the student has heard what was said by having him/her give acknowledgment (e.g., by saying, "Okay!" "Will do!" etc.).

71. Tell the student what to listen for when being given directions or receiving information, etc.

72. Evaluate the visual and auditory stimuli in the classroom and remove or reduce the extraneous environmental stimuli.

73. Speak clearly and concisely when delivering directions, explanations, and instructions.

74. Have the student take notes following the "What, How, Materials, and When" format when directions are being given.

75. Have the student listen and take notes for "Who, What, Where, When, How, and Why" when concepts are presented.

76. Present concepts following the (1) Who, (2) What, (3) Where, (4) When, (5) How, and (6) Why outline.

77. Have the student prepare for tests using the "Who, What, Where, When, How, and Why" format.

1. Interact frequently with the student to help him/her follow directions for an activity.

2. Allow the student to record information from lectures and seminars and make notes from these recordings.

3. Avoid placing the student in situations that require listening for an extended directions, announcements, seminars, etc. Provide the information for the student through a recordimg or lecture notes.

4. Avoid seating the student near people with whom he/she may be tempted to talk during lectures, assemblies, seminars, projects, etc.

5. Be consistent in expecting the student to listen to and follow directions. Do not allow the student to fail to follow directions one time and expect directions to be followed the next time.

6. Be sure the student has heard what was said by having him/her give acknowledgment (e.g., by saying, "Okay!" "Will do!" etc.).

7. Call the student by name to gain his/her attention prior to delivering directions, explanations, or instructions.

8. Consider carefully the student's age and experience before expecting him/her to be successful in activities that require listening.

9. Deliver verbal questions and directions that involve only one step. As the student demonstrates success, gradually increase the number of concepts or steps.

10. Determine if the student heard a direction by having him/her repeat it.

11. Create an environment that is quiet and uncluttered (e.g., clean, well-lighted, fresh-smelling, and at a comfortable temperature).

12. Do not criticize when correcting the student; be honest yet supportive. Never cause the student to feel negatively about himself/herself.

13. Do not give directions to the student from across the classroom. Go to the student, get his/her undivided attention, and tell him/her what to do.

14. Encourage the parents to take advantage of dinner and other family-gathering times for their student to talk and practice maintaining attention.

15. Encourage the student to ask for clarification of any directions, explanations, and instructions before beginning a task to facilitate comprehension.

16. Instruct the student to ask for clarification if he/she does not understand information given verbally.

17. Help the student develop an awareness of the consequences of his/her behavior by writing down or talking through problems which may occur due to his/her inability to maintain attention (e.g., not focusing on directions may cause misunderstanding of an assignment which could lead to a lower grade and losing a place on the soccer team).

18. Choose different people (e.g., peer, paraprofessional, counselor, etc.) to help the student improve his/her listening skills.

19. Establish assignment rules (e.g., listen carefully, wait until all verbal directions have been given, ask questions about anything you do not understand, begin the assignment only when you are certain about what you are to do, make sure you have all the necessary materials, etc.).

20. Give a signal to gain the student's attention before delivering directions, explanations, or instructions (e.g., clap hands, turn lights off and on, etc.).

21. Let the student know that directions will only be given once and that he/she will not be reminded to follow the directions.

22. Give simple, specific directions as to what the student is to do.

23. Interact frequently with the student to help him/her attend to a source of sound.

24. Have the student verbally repeat directions, explanations, and instructions after they have been given to reinforce retention.

25. Have a peer, paraprofessional, friend, etc., cue the student when he/she needs to maintain attention. (e.g., the person can touch the student on the arm when it is time to listen).

26. Have the student's hearing checked if it has not been recently checked.

27. Choose a peer to model responding to information from any location in the classroom for the student.

28. Identify the student's preferred learning style and use it consistently to increase the probability of understanding and remaining on task for longer periods of time.

29. Encourage the student to avoid ingesting any substance (e.g., drugs, alcohol, cold remedies, etc.) that might further alter his/her ability to direct or maintain attention.

30. Instruct the student to ask people to repeat parts of a conversation he/she was unable to follow.

31. Instruct the student to carry a notepad with him/her at all times and to write information down to help him/her remember.

32. Instruct the student to listen for key information when being given directions or receiving information from a distance (e.g., write down main points, ideas, step-by-step instructions, etc.).

33. Instruct the student to maintain attention to the source of information by maintaining eye contact, keeping hands free from other materials, and reducing other distractions.

34. Instruct the student to write down verbal directions and cross each one off as it is completed.

35. Allow natural consequences to occur due to the student's failure to follow verbal directions or attend to information given in public places.

36. Have the student take notes when directions are being given following the "What, How, Materials, and When" format.

37. Establish rules for listening (e.g., listen to directions, ask questions about directions if they are not understood, follow the directions, etc.). These rules should be consistent and followed by everyone in the classroom. Talk about the rules often.

38. Maintain consistency in the manner in which verbal questions are asked and directions are given.

39. Reinforce the student for attending to information presented from any location in the classroom: (a) give the student a tangible reward (e.g., classroom privileges, line leading, passing out materials, five minutes free time, etc.) or (b) give the student an intangible reward (e.g., praise, fist bump, smile, etc.).

40. Make sure that directions, explanations, or instructions are delivered loudly enough to be heard by the student.

41. Reduce distracting stimuli (e.g., make sure the classroom is quiet, reduce movement in the classroom, etc.).

42. Make sure that the student has adequate opportunities for repetition of information through different experiences.

43. Reward the student (e.g., take a break, visit briefly with a peer, etc.) for maintaining eye contact and listening for a specific length of time.

44. Make sure the student is attending before delivering directions, explanations or instructions (e.g., maintaining eye contact, hands free of writing materials, looking at the assignment, etc.).

45. Move objects used for tactile stimulation (e.g., pens, paper clips, loose change, etc.) away from the student's reach.

46. Present concepts following the outline of (1) Who, (2) What, (3) Where, (4) When, (5) How, and (6) Why.

47. Present directions, explanations, or instructions as simply and clearly as possible (e.g., "Get your book. Turn to page 29. Do problems 1 through 5.").

48. Stand close to or directly in front of the student when delivering verbal questions and directions.

49. Stop at various points during the presentation of directions, explanations, or instructions to check the student's comprehension of the information given.

50. Present verbal questions and directions in a clear and concise manner.

51. Provide directions on a one-to-one basis before assigning a task.

52. Maintain mobility to provide assistance to the student, frequently be near the student, etc.

53. Make sure that all directions, questions, explanations, and instructions are delivered at an appropriate pace for the student.

54. Reinforce those students who attend to information from any location in the classroom.

55. Remove the student from the situation until he/she can demonstrate self-control and follow directions when he/she has difficulty attending to and following directions in the presence of others (e.g., at an assembly, on a field trip, playing a game with peers, etc.).

56. Maintain visibility to and from the student to keep his/her attention when verbal questions/directions are being delivered. The teacher should be able to see the student and the student should be able to see the teacher. Make eye contact possible at all times.

57. Schedule important activities/assignments/meetings at times when the student is most likely to maintain attention (e.g., one hour after medication, 45 minutes after lunch, first thing in the morning, etc.).

58. Make sure you have the student's undivided attention when you are talking to him/her. Stand close to the student, maintain eye contact, and have him/her repeat the information.

59. Seat the student close to the source of information in the classroom. As the student demonstrates success, gradually move him/her away from the source of information.

60. Present directions following the outline of (1) What, (2) How, (3) Materials, and (4) When.

61. Teach the student direction-following skills (e.g., listen carefully, write down important points, etc.).

62. Teach and practice active listening skills. Encourage the student to listen to what another person is saying and respond based on information received.

63. While concepts are presented, have the student listen and takes notes for "Who, What, Where, When, How, and Why."

64. Teach and practice effective communication skills. These skills include: listening, maintaining eye contact, and positive body language.

65. Move the student away from other students who may interfere with his/her ability to attend to directions, explanations, or instructions.

66. Teach the student listening skills (e.g., stop working, clear desk of nonessential materials, attend to the source of information, write down important points, ask for clarification, and wait until all directions are received before beginning).

67. Teach and practice information-gathering skills (e.g., listen carefully, write down important points, ask for clarification, wait until all information is presented before beginning a task, etc.).

68. Write a contract with the student specifying what behavior is expected (e.g., attending to information presented from any location in the classroom) and what reinforcement will be made available when the terms of the contract have been met.

1. Have the student's hearing checked if it has not been recently checked.

2. Evaluate the level of difficulty of the information to which the student is expected to listen (e.g., /ch/ and /sh/ blends, similar consonant sounds, rhyming words, etc.).

3. Have the student repeat or paraphrase what is said to him/her to determine what was heard.

4. Make sure the student is attending to the source of information (e.g., making eye contact, hands free of writing materials, looking at assignments, etc.).

5. Emphasize or repeat /ch/ or /sh/ blends, similar vowel sounds, similar consonant sounds, rhyming words, etc.

6. Speak clearly and concisely when communicating with the student.

7. Place the student in the location most appropriate for him/her to hear what is being said.

8. Reduce distracting stimuli (e.g., noise and motion in the classroom) to facilitate the student's ability to listen successfully.

9. Have the student keep a notebook with pictures of words that rhyme.

10. Stop at key points when delivering directions, explanations, and instructions to determine student comprehension.

11. Identify a list of words with /ch/ and /sh/ blends, similar vowel sounds, similar consonant sounds, rhyming words, etc., that the student will practice listening for when someone else is speaking.

12. Stand directly in front of the student when delivering information.

13. Play a game in which the student tries to imitate the sounds made by the teacher or other students (e.g., *Simon Says*).

14. Use pictures of similar words to help the student recognize their differences (e.g., if the student has trouble differentiating /ch/ and /sh/ blends, use pictures of /ch/ and /sh/ words such as chips and ships).

15. Give the student simple words and ask him/her to rhyme them verbally with as many other words as possible.

16. Use fill-in-the-blank sentences and have the student pick the correct word from a group of similar words (e.g., I _____ (wonder, wander) what's in the box, etc.).

17. Have the student make up poems and tongue twisters using /ch/ and /sh/ blends, similar vowel sounds, similar consonant sounds, and rhyming words.

18. Present pairs of words and have the student tell if the words rhyme.

19. Explain and demonstrate how similar sounds are made (e.g., where the tongue is placed, how the mouth is shaped, etc.).

20. Have the student listen to a series of directions and act out the ones that make sense (e.g., bake your head, rake your bread, shake your head).

21. Identify the speech sounds the student has difficulty differentiating. Spend time each day having the student listen to sounds and have the student use the sounds in conversation.

22. Teach the student listening skills:
- Stop working.
- Clear desk of nonessential materials.
- Attend to the source of information.
- Write down important points.
- Ask for clarification.
- Wait until all directions are received before beginning.

23. Encourage the student to watch the lips of the person speaking to him/her.

26   Is unsuccessful in activities requiring listening

1. Have the student audio record directions, explanations, and instructions so that he/she may replay information as often as needed.

2. Allow the student to record information from lectures and seminars and make notes from these recordings.

3. Deliver a predetermined signal (e.g., hand signal, turning off and on lights, etc.) prior to bells ringing, announcements being made, etc.

4. Consider carefully the student's ability level and experience before expecting the student to be successful in activities that require listening.

5. Avoid placing the student in situations which require listening for an extended period of time, such as lectures, seminars, etc. Provide supplemental information through a recordimg or lecture notes.

6. Avoid seating the student near people with whom he/she may be tempted to talk during lectures, guest speakers, group projects, etc.

7. Be consistent in expecting the student to listen. Hold the student accountable for not listening to important information.

8. Call the student by name prior to bells ringing, announcements being made, directions being given, etc.

9. Ask the student for immediate repetition of directions.

10. Reduce the number of visual distractions around the student (e.g., move the student's work area away from windows, doors, computer area, etc.).

11. Arrange for individual assignments when the group setting is overly distracting.

12. Deliver directions to the student individually.

13. Make sure that competing sounds (e.g., talking, movement, noises, etc.) are silenced when directions are being given, public address announcements are being made, etc.

14. Deliver directives in a supportive rather than a threatening manner (e.g., "Please repeat the directions given," rather than, "Tell me what I just said!").

15. Deliver verbal directions prior to handing out materials.

16. Deliver information slowly to the student.

17. Demonstrate appropriate listening behavior (e.g., sit up straight, eyes on speaker, etc.).

18. Demonstrate directions, explanations, and instructions as they are presented verbally (e.g., use the wall-mounted board to work a problem for the student, begin playing a game with the student, etc.).

19. Allow natural consequences to occur (e.g., miss assignments, miss information regarding a school event, etc.) due to the student's failure to follow directions.

20. Provide activities designed to teach listening skills.

21. Create an environment that is quiet and uncluttered (e.g., clean, well-lighted, fresh-smelling, and at a comfortable temperature).

22. Talk to the student before beginning an activity and remind him/her of the importance of listening to others.

23. Give the student directions to follow with no more than two or three steps (e.g., "Please open your text and turn to page 28."). Directions that involve several steps can be confusing and cause the student to have difficulty following them.

24. Do not criticize when correcting the student; be honest yet supportive. Never cause the student to feel negatively about himself/herself.

25. Establish rules for listening (e.g., listen to directions, ask questions about directions if they are not understood, follow the directions, etc.). These rules should be consistent and followed by everyone in the class. Talk about the rules often.

26. Deliver information in a variety of ways (e.g., pictures, diagrams, gestures, etc.) to facilitate the student's ability to attend.

27. Do not give directions to the student from across the room. Go to the student, get his/her undivided attention, and explain the directions to him/her.

28. Encourage the student to ask for clarification of any directions, explanations, and instructions before beginning a task to facilitate comprehension.

29. Have the student ask for help when he/she needs it.

30. Help the student develop an awareness of himself/herself and the environment. Instruct the student to periodically step back and ask himself/herself, "Am I listening and paying attention?" "What should I be doing now?"

31. Help the student develop an awareness of the consequences of his/her behavior by writing down or talking through problems which may occur due to his/her inability to listen for sustained periods of time (e.g., not focusing on directions may cause misunderstanding of an assignment which could lead to a lower grade and losing a place on the soccer team).

32. Encourage the student to recite a mantra to himself/herself when entering a situation where he/she will receive directions/instructions (e.g., listen carefully, listen carefully, listen carefully).

33. Teach the student listening skills:
- Stop working.
- Clear desk of nonessential materials.
- Attend to the source of information.
- Write down important points.
- Ask for clarification.
- Wait until all directions are received before beginning.

34. Evaluate the difficulty level of information to which the student is expected to listen (e.g., information communicated on the student's ability level).

35. Give directions in a variety of ways to facilitate the student's ability to attend.

36. Allow the student to occasionally take assignments home when the class setting is overly distracting.

37. Choose a peer, paraprofessional, etc., to cue the student when he/she is not listening (e.g., the person can touch the student's arm as a signal that he/she is not focused on the speaker).

38. Evaluate the visual and auditory stimuli in the classroom and remove or reduce the extraneous environmental stimuli.

39. Have a peer provide the information the student does not hear.

40. Have the student participate in activities designed to develop his/her listening skills (e.g., following one-, two-, or three-step directions; listening for the main point; etc.).

41. Choose a peer to model good listening skills for the student.

42. Have the student practice group listening skills (e.g., "Everyone take out a piece of paper. Write your name on the paper. Number your paper from 1 to 20.").

43. Make sure that comments made to the student take the form of constructive criticism rather than perceived as personal, threatening, etc., (e.g., instead of saying, "You always make the same mistake," say, "A better way to do that might be . . .").

44. Have the student practice listening to what other students are saying (e.g., following simple instructions, sharing information, etc.).

45. Ask the student to repeat parts of a conversation as the discussion is taking place.

46. Have the student ask questions about directions, explanations, and instructions he/she does not understand.

47. Provide the student with public announcements, directions, and instructions in written form while presenting them verbally.

48. Have the student rehearse in his/her head information just heard to help him/her remember the important facts.

49. Have the student take notes when directions are being given following the "What, How, Materials, and When" format.

50. Have the student's hearing checked if it has not been recently checked.

51. Have the student verbally repeat directions, explanations, and instructions after they have been given to facilitate retention.

52. Identify the student's most effective learning mode. Use it consistently to facilitate the student's understanding (e.g., if the student does not understand directions or information given verbally, present it in written form).

53. Instruct the student to maintain attention to the source of information by maintaining eye contact, keeping hands free from other materials, and reducing other distractions.

54. Interact frequently with the student. Make sure that eye contact is being made to ensure that the student is attending.

55. Let the student know that directions will only be given once and that he/she will not be reminded to follow the directions.

56. Maintain visibility to and from the student at all times to ensure he/she is attending.

57. Write a contract with the student specifying what behavior is expected (e.g., listening to directions, explanations, and instructions) and what reinforcement will be made available when the terms of the contract have been met.

58. Make sure the student is attending (e.g., making eye contact, hands free of writing materials, etc.) before delivering directions, explanations, and instructions.

59. Make sure the student understands that if he/she does not listen to and follow directions when working in a group, participating in activities, etc., others may not want to work with him/her.

60. Gain the student's attention before giving him/her directions. Have the student make eye contact and repeat the information to check for understanding.

61. Play games designed to teach listening skills (e.g., *Simon Says, Red Light-Green Light, Mother May I?*).

62. Instruct the student to carry a notepad with him/her at all times and write information down to help him/her remember.

63. Have the student participate in activities designed to develop his/her listening skills (e.g., following one-, two-, or three-step directions; listening for the main point; etc.).

64. Present one concept at a time. Make sure the student understands each concept before presenting the next.

65. Provide directions on a one-to-one basis.

66. Speak to the student when he/she does not listen to explain (a) what he/she is doing wrong (e.g., not listening to directions, explanations, and instructions) and (b) what he/she should be doing (e.g., listening to directions, explanations, and instructions) and why.

67. Have the student practice listening skills by taking notes when directions, explanations, and instructions are presented.

68. Reduce visual and auditory stimuli in and around the classroom which interfere with the student's ability to listen successfully (e.g., close the classroom door and windows, draw the shades, etc.).

69. Present directions, explanations, and instructions as simply and clearly as possible (e.g., "Get your book. Turn to page 29. Do problems 1 through 5.").

70. Provide the student with public announcements, directions, and instructions in written form.

71. Reduce distracting stimuli in the immediate environment (e.g., place the student on or near the front row, provide the student with a carrel or office space away from distractions, etc.). This is used as a form of reducing distracting stimuli and not as a form of punishment.

72. Reinforce the student for listening: (a) give the student a tangible reward (e.g., classroom privileges, five minutes free time, etc.) or (b) give the student an intangible reward (e.g., praise, fist bump, smile, etc.).

73. Reinforce those students in the classroom who listen to directions, explanations, and instructions.

74. Teach information-gathering skills (e.g., listen carefully, write down important points, ask for clarification, wait until all information is presented before beginning a task, etc.).

75. Rephrase directions, explanations, and instructions to facilitate the student's understanding of what is being presented.

76. Reward the student for listening. Possible rewards include verbal praise (e.g., "You did a great job listening to every step of the directions!" "You were able to tell me five details.").

77. Schedule important activities/assignments/lectures at times when the student is most likely to maintain attention (e.g., one hour after medication, 45 minutes after lunch, first thing in the morning, etc.).

78. Teach the student direction-following skills (e.g., stop doing other things, listen carefully, write down important points, wait until all directions are given, question any directions not understood, etc.).

79. Present concepts following the outline of (1) Who, (2) What, (3) Where, (4) When, (5) How, and (6) Why.

80. Stand directly in front of the student when delivering directions, explanations, and instructions.

81. Stop at various points when delivering directions, announcements, etc., to ensure that the student is attending.

82. Present directions following the outline of (1) What, (2) How, (3) Materials, and (4) When.

83. Teach and have the student practice how to listen for key information when he/she is being given directions or receiving information (e.g., write down main points, ideas, step-by-step instructions, etc.).

84. Evaluate the difficulty level of information presented to the student to determine if the information is at a level the student can understand.

85. Remove the student from the situation (e.g., school assembly, school play, guest speaker, etc.) when he/she has difficulty listening until he/she can demonstrate self-control.

86. Use multiple modalities (e.g., auditory, visual, tactile, etc.) when presenting directions, explanations, and instructional content. Utilize the modality which is stronger for the student.

87. When concepts are presented, have the student listen and takes notes for "Who, What, Where, When, How, and Why."

88. Teach the student when to ask questions, how to ask questions, and what types of questions obtain what types of information.

89. Deliver directions, explanations, and information using vocabulary that is within the student's level of comprehension.

90. Have the student repeat or paraphrase information presented to determine if the student correctly heard what was said.

91. Seat the student close to the source of directions, explanations, and instructions to facilitate his/her ability to maintain attention.

92. Use pictures, diagrams, wall-mounted board, and gestures when presenting information.

1. Maintain a consistent manner in which verbal questions are asked and directions are given.

2. Have the student take notes when directions are being given following the "What, How, Materials, and When" format.

3. Interact frequently with the student to help him/her attend to a source of sound.

4. Reinforce the student for attending to information presented from any location in the classroom: (a) give the student a tangible reward (e.g., classroom privileges, line leading, passing out materials, five minutes free time, etc.) or (b) give the student an intangible reward (e.g., praise, fist bump, smile, etc.).

5. Provide directions on a one-to-one basis before assigning a task.

6. Call the student by name to gain his/her attention prior to delivering directions, explanations, or instructions.

7. Reinforce those students who attend to information from any location in the classroom.

8. Maintain mobility to provide assistance to the student, frequently be near the student, etc.

9. Deliver all directions, questions, explanations, and instructions at an appropriate rate for the student.

10. Give simple, specific directions as to what the student is to do.

11. Do not criticize when correcting the student; be honest yet supportive. Never cause the student to feel negatively about himself/herself.

12. Interact frequently with the student to help him/her follow directions for an activity.

13. Maintain visibility to and from the student to keep his/her attention when verbal questions/directions are being delivered. The teacher should be able to see the student and the student should be able to see the teacher. Make eye contact possible at all times.

14. Do not give directions to the student from across the classroom. Go to the student, get his/her undivided attention, and explain the directions to him/her.

15. Stop at various points during the presentation of directions, explanations, or instructions to check the student's comprehension of the information presented.

16. Give a signal to gain the student's attention before delivering directions, explanations, or instructions (e.g., clap hands, turn lights off and on, etc.).

17. Seat the student close to the source of information in the classroom. As the student demonstrates success, gradually move him/her away from the source of information.

18. Present directions following the outline of (1) What, (2) How, (3) Materials, and (4) When.

19. Have the student listen and takes notes for "Who, What, Where, When, How, and Why" while concepts are presented.

20. Deliver verbal questions and directions that involve only one step. As the student demonstrates success, gradually increase the number of concepts or steps.

21. Make sure you have the student's undivided attention when you are talking to him/her. Stand close to the student, maintain eye contact, and have him/her repeat the information.

22. Be consistent in expecting the student to listen to and follow directions. Do not allow the student to fail to follow directions one time and expect directions to be followed the next time.

23. Write a contract with the student specifying what behavior is expected (e.g., attending to information presented from any location in the classroom) and what reinforcement will be made available when the terms of the contract have been met.

24. Avoid placing the student in situations that require listening for an extended directions, announcements, seminars, etc. Provide the information for the student through a recordimg or lecture notes.

25. Move objects used for tactile stimulation (e.g., pens, paper clips, loose change, etc.) away from the student's reach.

26. Teach and practice effective communication skills. These skills include: listening, maintaining eye contact, and positive body language.

27. Remove the student from the situation until he/she can demonstrate self-control and follow directions when he/she has difficulty attending to and following directions in the presence of others (e.g., at an assembly, on a field trip, playing a game with peers, etc.).

28. Choose a peer to model responding to information from any location in the classroom for the student.

29. Allow the student to record information from lectures and seminars and make notes from these recordings.

30. Create an environment that is quiet and uncluttered (e.g., clean, well-lighted, fresh-smelling, and at a comfortable temperature).

31. Avoid seating the student near people with whom he/she may be tempted to talk during lectures, assemblies, seminars, projects, etc.

32. Choose different people (e.g., peer, para-professional, counselor, etc.) to help the student improve his/her listening skills.

33. Move the student away from other students who may interfere with his/her ability to attend to directions, explanations, or instructions.

34. Provide the student with adequate opportunities for repetition of information through different experiences.

35. Deliver directions, explanations, or instructions loudly enough to be heard by the student.

36. Be sure the student has heard what was said by having him/her give acknowledgment (e.g., by saying, "Okay!" "Will do!" etc.).

37. Establish rules for listening (e.g., listen to directions, ask questions about directions if they are not understood, follow the directions, etc.). These rules should be consistent and followed by everyone in the classroom. Talk about the rules often.

38. Present concepts following the outline of (1) Who, (2) What, (3) Where, (4) When, (5) How, and (6) Why.

39. Identify the student's most effective learning mode. Use it consistently to facilitate the student's understanding and remaining on task for longer periods of time.

40. Encourage the student to avoid ingesting any substance (e.g., drugs, alcohol, cold remedies, etc.) that might further alter his/her ability to direct or maintain attention.

41. Stand close to or directly in front of the student when delivering verbal questions and directions.

42. Present verbal questions and directions in a clear and concise manner.

43. Instruct the student to listen for key information when being given directions or receiving information from a distance (e.g., write down main points, ideas, step-by-step instructions; etc.).

44. Have the student's hearing checked if it has not been recently checked.

45. Instruct the student to ask for clarification if he/she does not understand information presented verbally.

46. Encourage the student to ask for clarification of any directions, explanations, and instructions before beginning a task to facilitate comprehension.

47. Instruct the student to write down verbal directions and mark each one off as it is completed.

48. Choose a peer, paraprofessional, friend, etc., to cue the student when he/she needs to maintain attention (e.g., the person can touch the student on the arm when it is time to listen).

49. Allow natural consequences to occur due to the student's failure to follow verbal directions or attend to information presented in public places.

50. Have the student verbally repeat directions, explanations, and instructions after they have been given to facilitate retention.

51. Let the student know that directions will only be given once and that he/she will not be reminded to follow the directions.

52. Reduce distracting stimuli in the environment (e.g., make sure the classroom is quiet, reduce movement in the classroom, etc.).

53. Establish assignment rules (e.g., listen carefully, wait until all verbal directions have been given, ask questions about anything you do not understand, begin the assignment only when you are certain about what you are to do, make sure you have all the materials necessary, etc.).

54. Instruct the student to maintain attention to the source of information by maintaining eye contact, keeping hands free from other materials, and reducing other distractions.

55. Make sure the student is attending before delivering directions, explanations, or instructions (e.g., maintaining eye contact, hands free of writing materials, looking at the assignment, etc.).

56. Instruct the student to ask people to repeat parts of a conversation he/she was unable to follow.

57. Schedule important activities/assignments/meetings at times when the student is most likely to maintain attention (e.g., one hour after medication, 45 minutes after lunch, first thing in the morning, etc.).

58. Present directions, explanations, or instructions as simply and clearly as possible (e.g., "Get your book. Turn to page 29. Do problems 1 through 5.").

59. Consider carefully the student's age and experience before expecting him/her to be successful in activities that require listening.

60. Help the student develop an awareness of the consequences of his/her behavior by writing down or talking through problems which may occur due to his/her inability to maintain attention (e.g., not focusing on directions may cause misunderstanding of an assignment which could lead to a lower grade and losing a place on the soccer team).

61. Encourage the parents to take advantage of dinner and other family-gathering times for their student to talk and practice maintaining attention.

62. Instruct the student to carry a notepad with him/her at all times and write information down to help him/her remember.

63. Teach and practice active listening skills. Encourage the student to listen to what another person is saying and respond based on information received.

64. Reward the student (e.g., take a break, visit briefly with a peer, etc.) for maintaining eye contact and listening for a specific length of time.

65. Determine if the student heard a direction by having him/her repeat it.

66. Teach and practice information-gathering skills (e.g., listen carefully, write down important points, ask for clarification, wait until all information is presented before beginning a task, etc.).

67. Teach the student direction-following skills (e.g., listen carefully, write down important points, etc.).

68. Teach the student listening skills:
- Stop working.
- Clear desk of nonessential materials.
- Attend to the source of information.
- Write down important points.
- Ask for clarification.
- Wait until all directions are received before beginning.

1. Make sure that the student is seated close enough to make eye contact with and hear the teacher when information is being delivered.

2. Encourage the student to ask for clarification of any directions, explanations, and instructions before beginning a task to facilitate comprehension.

3. Avoid placing the student in situations that require listening for an extended directions, announcements, seminars, assemblies, etc. Provide the information for the student through a recordimg or lecture notes.

4. Encourage the parents to take advantage of dinner and other family-gathering times for their child to talk and practice maintaining eye contact.

5. Deliver information in a clear, concise manner.

6. Make sure information is delivered loudly enough to be heard by the student.

7. Deliver information to the student on a one-to-one basis. As the student demonstrates the ability to listen successfully, gradually include more students in the group with him/her.

8. Determine which stimuli in the environment interfere with the student's ability to listen successfully. Reduce or remove those stimuli from the environment.

9. Teach the student listening skills:
- Stop working.
- Clear dcsk of nonessential materials.
- Attend to the source of information.
- Write down important points.
- Ask for clarification.
- Wait until all directions are received before beginning.

10. Encourage the student to ask people to repeat parts of a conversation he/she was unable to follow.

11. Deliver a predetermined signal (e.g., hand signal, turn lights off and on, etc.) to the student prior to delivering information.

12. Make sure the student is not engaged in activities that interfere with directions, explanations, and instructions (e.g., looking at other materials, putting away materials, talking to others, etc.).

13. Choose a peer to model good attending skills for the student.

14. Call the student by name to gain his/her attention prior to delivering information.

15. Reinforce the student for listening based on the length of time the student can be successful. As the student demonstrates success, gradually increase the length of time required for reinforcement.

16. Encourage the student to recite a mantra to himself/herself when entering a situation where he/she will receive directions/instructions (e.g., maintain eye contact, maintain eye contact, maintain eye contact).

17. Choose different people (e.g., peer, paraprofessional, counselor, friend, etc.) to help the student maintain eye contact.

18. Evaluate the difficulty level of information presented to the student. Determine if the information is presented at a level the student can understand.

19. Deliver information in both verbal and written form.

20. Choose a peer, paraprofessional, friend, etc., to cue the student when he/she needs to maintain eye contact (e.g., the person can touch the student on the arm when it is time to attend to a speaker).

21. Reinforce the student for listening based on the length of time the student can be successful. As the student demonstrates success, gradually increase the length of time required for reinforcement.

22. Have the student verbally repeat directions, explanations, and instructions after they have been given to facilitate retention.

23. Have the student take notes when directions are being given following the "What, How, Materials, and When" format.

24. Have the student take notes when information is verbally presented.

25. Have the student listen and takes notes for "Who, What, Where, When, How, and Why" while concepts are presented.

26. Have the student's hearing checked if it has not been recently checked.

27. Present directions following the outline of (1) What, (2) How, (3) Materials, and (4) When.

28. Instruct the student to maintain attention to the source of information by maintaining eye contact, keeping hands free from other materials, and reducing other distractions.

29. Maintain a consistent format in which information is verbally presented.

30. Maintain visibility to and from the student at all times to ensure that the student is attending.

31. Allow natural consequences to occur as a result of the student's failure to listen (e.g., the inability to respond correctly, a failing grade, etc.).

32. Evaluate the visual and auditory stimuli in the classroom and remove or reduce the extraneous environmental stimuli.

33. Make the subject matter meaningful to the student (e.g., explain the purpose of an assignment, relate the subject matter to the student's environment, etc.).

34. Move objects used for tactile stimulation (e.g., pens, paper clips, loose change, etc.) away from the student's reach.

35. Have the student ask questions about directions, explanations, or instructions he/she does not understand.

36. Help the student develop an awareness of himself/herself and the environment. Instruct the student to periodically step back and ask himself/herself, "Am I maintaining eye contact?" "What should I be doing now?"

37. Schedule important activities/assignments/ lectures at times when the student is most likely to maintain attention (e.g., one hour after medication, 45 minutes after lunch, first thing in the morning, etc.). Tell the student what to listen for when being given directions or receiving information, etc.

38. Present concepts following the outline of (1) Who, (2) What, (3) Where, (4) When, (5) How, and (6) Why.

39. Provide opportunities for the student to talk to others on a one-to-one basis. As the student becomes more successful at maintaining attention and eye contact, gradually include more people in conversations.

40. Reduce visual and auditory stimuli in and around the classroom which interfere with the student's ability to listen successfully (e.g., close the classroom door and windows, draw the shades, etc.).

41. Stop at various points during the presentation of information to check the student's comprehension.

42. Reinforce the student for attending to the source of information. Continuous eye contact is not necessary for reinforcement.

43. Teach and practice information-gathering skills (e.g., listen carefully, write down important points, ask for clarification, wait until all information is presented before beginning a task, etc.).

44. Reinforce the student for maintaining eye contact: (a) give the student a tangible reward (e.g., classroom privileges, five minutes free time, etc.) or (b) give the student an intangible reward (e.g., praise, fist bump, smile, etc.).

45. Provide directions on a one-to-one basis before assigning a task.

46. Teach and practice effective communication skills. These skills include: listening, maintaining eye contact, and positive body language.

47. Use multiple modalities (e.g., auditory, visual, tactile, etc.) when presenting directions, explanations, and instructional content. Utilize the modality which is stronger for the student.

48. Reinforce those students in the classroom who focus visual attention on the speaker.

49. Ask the student to repeat or paraphrase information heard to determine successful listening.

50. Seat the student close to the source of information in the classroom. As the student demonstrates success, gradually move him/her farther away from the source of information.

51. Speak to the student to explain (a) what he/she is doing wrong (e.g., failing to listen to directions, explanations, and instructions) and (b) what he/she should be doing (e.g., listening to directions, explanations, and instructions).

52. Teach and practice active listening skills. Instruct the student to listen to what another person is saying and respond based on information received.

53. Reinforce the student for listening: (a) give the student a tangible reward (e.g., classroom privileges, line leading, passing out materials, five minutes free time, etc.) or (b) give the student an intangible reward (e.g., praise, fist bump, smile, etc.).

54. Tell the student what to listen for when being given directions, receiving information, etc.

55. Verbally present information that is necessary for the student to know to perform a task successfully.

56. Maintain eye contact when delivering information to the student. As the student demonstrates the ability to listen successfully, gradually decrease the amount of eye contact.

57. Write a contract with the student specifying what behavior is expected (e.g., listening to directions, maintaining eye contact) and what reinforcement will be made available when the terms of the contract have been met.

58. Stop at various points during the presentation of information to ensure the student is attending and maintaining eye contact.

59. Help the student develop an awareness of the consequences of his/her behavior by writing down or talking through problems which may occur due to his/her inability to maintain attention (e.g., not focusing on directions may cause misunderstanding of an assignment which could lead to a lower grade and losing a place on the soccer team).

60. Remove distracting stimuli in the student's immediate environment (e.g., books, writing materials, personal property, etc.).

1. Instruct the student to maintain attention to the source of information by maintaining eye contact, keeping hands free from other materials, and reducing other distractions.

2. Do not force the student to interact with someone when he/she is not completely comfortable.

3. Have the student work with a peer and the teacher. The first student will dictate a short paragraph to be typed by the teacher and will also compose a comprehension question. The second student, after listening to the process, will read the story verbally and point out the answer. Then student roles can be reversed.

4. Be consistent in expecting the student to listen to what others are saying. Do not provide missed information if the student fails to listen.

5. Consider carefully the student's ability level and experience when expecting him/her to be a good listener.

6. Have the student's hearing checked if it has not been recently checked.

7. Demonstrate the appropriate way to listen by listening to the student when he/she talks.

8. Allow the student some movement while listening to other students. Monitor and limit the amount of movement.

9. Encourage the student to develop a 30 second definition of his/her goal to help stay on task and focus on the speaker (e.g., "I will listen carefully. The better I focus and stay on task, the better I will listen.").

10. Determine if the student heard what was said by having him/her repeat it.

11. Make sure the student is near the students who are speaking.

12. Develop the student's awareness of the consequences of his/her behavior by writing down or talking through problems which may occur due to his/her inability to maintain attention (e.g., not focusing on directions may cause misunderstanding of an assignment which could lead to a lower grade and losing a place on the soccer team).

13. Do not criticize when correcting the student; be honest yet supportive. Never cause the student to feel negatively about himself/herself.

14. Do not ignore the student when he/she wants to tell you something. When you ignore the student, he/she may learn that it is acceptable to be inattentive.

15. Encourage parents to take advantage of dinner and other family-gathering times to talk and practice maintaining attention.

16. Identify a classmate who has good communication skills. Encourage the student to observe that classmate and model his/her behaviors which promote good communication.

17. Help the student develop an awareness of himself/herself and those around him/her. Instruct the student to periodically step back and ask himself/herself, "Am I on task and paying attention?" "What should I be doing now?"

18. Encourage the student to interact with others.

19. Establish rules for listening (e.g., listen when others are talking, ask questions if you do not understand, etc.). These rules should be consistent and followed by everyone in the class. Talk about the rules often.

20. Evaluate the visual and auditory stimuli in the classroom and remove or reduce the extraneous environmental stimuli.

21. Make sure that other students speak clearly and concisely when speaking to the student.

22. Teach and have the student practice listening for key information when he/she is being given directions or receiving information (e.g., write down main points, ideas, step-by-step instructions, etc.).

23. Choose a peer, paraprofessional, student, etc., to cue the student when he/she needs to maintain attention (e.g., the person can touch the student on the arm when it is time to listen).

24. Write a contract with the student. It should be written within his/her ability level and focus on only one behavior at a time. Specify what behavior is expected and what reinforcement will be made available when the terms of the contract have been met.

25. Have other students stand directly in front of the student when speaking to him/her so the student will be more likely to listen to what others are saying.

26. Provide opportunities for the student to talk to others on a one-to-one basis. As the student becomes more successful at listening and maintaining attention, gradually include more people in conversations.

27. Reduce the emphasis on competition in the classroom. Competition may cause the student to become excited or distracted and fail to listen to what other students are saying.

28. Have the student rehearse in his/her head information just heard from other students to facilitate remembering important information.

29. Instruct the student to ask for clarification if he/she does not understand information presented verbally.

30. Instruct the student to ask people to repeat parts of a conversation he/she was unable to follow.

31. Allow natural consequences to occur (e.g., miss information, miss a school activity, etc.) due to the student failing to listen to others.

32. Instruct the student's peers to preface statements with the student's name to gain his/her attention before speaking.

33. Make sure that competing sounds (e.g., talking, noises, motion in the classroom, etc.) are silenced when other students are talking, to facilitate the student's ability to listen to what others are saying.

34. Encourage the student to recite a mantra to himself/herself when entering a situation where he/she will receive directions/instructions (e.g., listen carefully, listen carefully, listen carefully).

35. Have the student repeat or paraphrase what other students have said to him/her to determine what the student heard.

36. Choose different people (e.g., peers, paraprofessionals, counselors, etc.) to help the student maintain attention to conversations.

37. Provide group settings that are quiet, well-lighted, and at a comfortable temperature.

38. Talk to the student before beginning an activity and remind him/her of the importance of listening to others.

39. Have the student practice listening to what other students are saying (e.g., following simple instructions, sharing information, etc.).

40. Reduce the number of visual distractions in the classroom when listening is required (e.g., move the student's work area away from windows, doors, etc.).

41. Teach and practice information-gathering skills (e.g., listen carefully, write down important points, ask for clarification, wait until all information is presented before beginning a task, etc.).

42. Reduce the occurrence of situations that may contribute to difficulty maintaining attention (e.g., timed activities, competition, long meetings, etc.).

43. Provide the student with frequent opportunities to meet new people.

44. Reinforce the students in the classroom who listen to what other students are saying.

45. Remove the student from the situation (e.g., school assembly, school play, guest speaker, etc.) when he/she has difficulty listening until he/she can demonstrate self-control.

46. Schedule opportunities for peer interaction at times when the student is most likely to maintain attention (e.g., one hour after medication, 45 minutes after lunch, first thing in the morning, etc.).

47. Model respecting others and what they are saying by respecting the student and what he/she says.

48. Reinforce the student for listening to what other students are saying based on the length of time the student can be successful. As the student demonstrates success, gradually increase the number of times or length of time required to listen.

49. Instruct the student to sit close to the source of information to facilitate his/her ability to maintain attention.

50. Make sure the student is attending to what other students are saying (e.g., making eye contact, stopping other activities, responding appropriately, etc.).

51. Talk to the student before going to an activity (e.g., assembly, school play, field trip, etc.) and remind him/her of the importance of listening to what others are saying.

52. Teach active listening skills. Provide opportunities for the student to listen to what another person is saying and respond based on information received.

53. Teach and practice effective communication skills. These skills include: listening, maintaining eye contact, and positive body language.

54. Reinforce the student for listening (e.g., making eye contact, putting aside materials, etc.) to what is said to him/her by other students: (a) give the student a tangible reward (e.g., classroom privileges, passing out materials, five minutes free time, etc.) or (b) give the student an intangible reward (e.g., praise, fist bump, smile, etc.).

55. Teach the student listening skills:
- Stop working.
- Clear desk of nonessential materials.
- Attend to the source of information.
- Write down important points.
- Ask for clarification.
- Wait until all directions are received before beginning.

56. Treat the student with respect. Talk in an objective manner at all times.

57. Speak to the student to explain (a) what he/she is doing wrong (e.g., failing to listen to what other students are saying) and (b) what he/she should be doing (e.g., listening to other students when they speak to him/her, listening to other students when they speak to a group, etc.).

C. Speaking

1. Be sure that the student can hear the difference between the target sound the way it should be made and the way it sounds when incorrectly produced.

2. Have the student keep a list of all the words he/she can think of which contain sounds he/she has difficulty producing accurately.

3. During verbal reading, underline words containing the target sound and reinforce the student for correct productions.

4. Evaluate the appropriateness of requiring the student to accurately produce certain sounds (e.g., developmentally, certain sounds may not be produced accurately until the age of 8 or 9).

5. Have the student cut out pictures of items depicting words containing the target sound. Display them where they can be practiced each day.

6. Make cards with the target sound and cards with vowels. Have the student combine a target sound card with a vowel card to make a syllable that he/she can produce (e.g., *ra, re, ro,* and *ar, er, or*).

7. Have the student keep a notebook of difficult words encountered each day. These can be practiced by the student with teacher or peer assistance.

8. Have the student read simple passages and record them. Have him/her listen to the recording and mark error and/or correct productions.

9. Use a board game that requires the student to label pictures containing the target sound. The student needs to produce the target sound correctly before he/she can move on the game board. (This activity can be simplified or expanded based on the level of expertise of the student.)

10. Have the student's hearing checked if it has not been recently checked.

11. Use a schematic drawing as a visual aid to show the student how the mouth looks during production of the target sound.

12. Have the student stand up each time he/she hears the target sound produced accurately as contrasted with inaccurate productions (e.g., /s/, /th/, /s/, /s/, /th/, etc.).

13. Provide the student with a list of words containing the target sound. Have him/her practice the words daily. As the student masters the word list, add more words. (Using words from the student's everyday vocabulary, reading lists, spelling lists, etc., will facilitate transfer of correct production of the target sound into everyday speech.)

14. Have the student tally the number of correct productions of the targeted sound when the teacher or a peer reads a list of words.

15. Have the student use phonics "fun" sheets to practice his/her sound verbally. These are also good for home practice.

16. Tell the student what to listen for when requiring him/her to imitate speech sounds.

17. Have the student write sentences using words containing the target sound.

18. Choose a peer to model correctly producing targeted words for the student.

19. Initially, each correct production may need reinforcement. As the student progresses, random reinforcement may be adequate.

20. Show the student a labeled picture and have the student show thumbs up each time the target sound is produced accurately and thumbs down if the target sound is produced inaccurately.

21. Have the student make up sentences using words containing the target sound.

22. Involve parents by asking them to rate their child's speech for a specific length of time (e.g., during dinner count no errors, a few errors, or many errors).

23. Make sure the student is attending to the source of information (e.g., eye contact is being made, hands are free of materials, etc.).

24. Play a game such as *Simon Says* in which the student tries to imitate correct productions of targeted words.

25. Provide the student with verbal reminders or prompts when he/she requires help imitating speech sounds.

26. Reinforce the student for correct productions of the target sound: (a) give the student a tangible reward (e.g., classroom privileges, line leading, passing out materials, five minutes free time, etc.) or (b) give the student an intangible reward (e.g., praise, fist bump, smile, etc.).

27. Have the student read a list of words and rate his/her production after each word.

28. Have the student use a carrier phrase combined with a word containing the target sound (e.g., "I like _____. "I see a _____.").

29. Record a spontaneous monologue given by the student. Have him/her listen to the recording and tally errors and/or correct productions. The teacher should also listen to the recordimg. The teacher and the student should compare their analyses of the productions.

30. Have the student raise a hand or clap hands when he/she hears the target sound produced during a series of isolated sound productions (e.g., /s/, /sh/,/r/, /m/, /r/, /t/, /k/, /r/, /z/, /w/, /n/, /r/, etc.).

31. Use a puppet to produce the target sound correctly and incorrectly. The student earns a sticker for correctly distinguishing a set number of correct/incorrect productions the puppet makes.

32. Present the student with a list of topics. Have the student select a topic and then give a spontaneous speech for a specific length of time. Count errors and suggest ways for him/her to improve.

33. Use pictures of similar sounding words (e.g., if the student says /sh/ for /ch/, use pictures of /sh/ and /ch/ words such as *ships* and *chips*). As the teacher says the words, the student points to the appropriate picture, then the student takes a turn saying the words as the teacher points.

34. Speak to the student to explain what he/she needs to do differently (e.g., make the sound like you do). The teacher should be careful to use the sound that is being targeted and not the letter name (e.g., /s/ not "s").

31 Omits, adds, substitutes, or rearranges sounds or words when speaking

1. Using pictures of similar sounding words, say each word and have the student point to the appropriate picture (e.g., *run* and *one*, or *bat* and *back*).

2. Provide the student with a word list containing the target words. Have the student practice the words daily. As the student masters the word list, add more words. (Using words from the student's everyday vocabulary, reading lists, spelling lists, etc., will facilitate transfer of correct production of the target word into everyday speech.)

3. Have the student write sentences using the target sound or words.

4. Have the student show thumbs up each time the target sound is produced accurately when a picture is labeled and thumbs down if the target sound is produced inaccurately.

5. Involve parents by asking them to rate their child's speech for a specific length of time (e.g., during dinner count no errors, a few errors, or many errors).

6. Play a game such as *Simon Says* in which the student tries to imitate the target sound or words when produced by the teacher or peers.

7. Evaluate the appropriateness of requiring the student to accurately produce certain sounds (e.g., developmentally, certain sounds may not be produced accurately until the age of 8 or 9).

8. During verbal reading, underline targeted sounds or words and reinforce the student for correct production.

9. Reinforce the student for correct productions of the target sound: (a) give the student a tangible reward (e.g., classroom privileges, line leading, passing out materials, five minutes free time, etc.) or (b) give the student an intangible reward (e.g., praise, fist bump, smile, etc.).

10. Make cards with the target sound and cards with vowels. Have the student combine a target sound card with a vowel card to make a syllable that he/she can produce (e.g., *ra, re, ro,* and *ar, er, or*).

11. Use a board game that requires the student to label pictures containing the target sound or words. The student needs to produce the target sound or words correctly before he/she can move on the game board. (This activity can be simplified or expanded based on the level of expertise of the student.)

12. Use a puppet to produce targeted words correctly and incorrectly. The student earns a sticker for correctly distinguishing a set number of correct/incorrect productions the puppet makes.

13. Have the student cut out pictures of items containing the target sound or words and display them where they can be practiced each day.

14. Have the student read simple passages and record them. Then have him/her listen to the recording and mark error and/or correct productions.

15. Have the student tally the number of correct productions of the target sound when the teacher or a peer reads a list of words.

16. Have the student keep a notebook of difficult words encountered each day. These can be practiced by the student with teacher or peer assistance.

17. Provide the student with a list of words containing the target sound. (The student will probably be able to produce the target sound more easily at the beginning or end of a word than in the middle.) Have the student practice the words daily. As the student masters the word list, add more words. (Using words from the student's everyday vocabulary, reading lists, spelling lists, etc., will facilitate transfer of correct production of the target sound into everyday speech.)

18. Have the student keep a list of all the words he/she can think of which contain sounds that are difficult for him/her to produce accurately.

19. Have the student read a list of words and rate his/her production of the target sound or target word after each production.

20. Present the student with a list of topics. Have the student select a topic and then give a spontaneous speech for a specific length of time. Count errors and suggest ways for him/her to improve.

21. Have the student use a carrier phrase combined with a word containing the target sound (e.g., "I like _____. "I see _____.").

22. Be sure that the student can hear the difference between the sound as it should be made (target sound) and the way he/she is producing it incorrectly (error sound).

23. Have the student raise a hand or clap hands when he/she hears the target sound produced during a series of isolated sound productions (e.g., /s/, /sh/, /r/, /m/, /r/, /t/, /k/, /r/, /z/, /w/, /n/, /r/, etc.).

24. Record a spontaneous monologue given by the student. Have him/her listen to the recording and tally error and/or correct productions. The teacher should also listen to the recording, and the teacher and the student should compare their analyses of the productions.

25. Speak to the student to explain what he/she needs to do differently (e.g., use the /r/ sound instead of the /w/ sound). The teacher should be careful to use the <u>sound</u> that is being targeted and not the letter name (e.g., /r/ not "r").

26. Have the student stand up each time he/she hears the target sound produced accurately in contrast to the error sound (e.g., /w/, /r/, /r/, /w/, /w/, /w/, /r/, /r/, etc.).

27. Have the student stand up each time he/she hears targeted words produced accurately when contrasted with inaccurate productions (e.g., "*play, pay, pay, play,*" etc.).

28. Be sure that the student can hear the difference between words as they should be made and the way the words sound when incorrectly produced (e.g., sounds added or omitted).

29. Have the student's hearing checked if it has not been recently checked.

30. Choose a peer who correctly produces the target sound or word to model for the student.

31. Use a schematic drawing as a visual aid to show the student how the mouth looks during production of the target sound.

32. Have the student use phonics "fun" sheets to verbally practice his/her sound. These are also good for home practice.

1. Have the student's hearing checked if it has not been recently checked.

2. Be sure that the student can hear the difference between words as they should be made and the way the words sound when incorrectly produced (sounds distorted).

3. Have the student raise a hand or clap hands when he/she hears the target sound produced during a series of isolated sound productions (e.g., /s/, /sh/, /r/, /m/, /r/, /t/, /k/, /r/, /z/, /w/, /n/, /r/, etc.).

4. Use a puppet to produce targeted words correctly and incorrectly. The student earns a sticker for correctly distinguishing a set number of correct/incorrect productions the puppet makes.

5. Have the student stand up each time he/she hears targeted words produced accurately as contrasted with inaccurate productions (e.g., *shoup, soup, soup, shoup, soup,* etc.).

6. Have the student show thumbs up each time targeted words are produced accurately when pictures are labeled and thumbs down if targeted words are produced inaccurately.

7. Using pictures of similar sounding words, say each word and have the student point to the appropriate picture (e.g., *run* and *one*, *bat* and *back*).

8. Have the student tally the number of correct productions of targeted words when the teacher or a peer reads a list of words.

9. Have the student read simple passages and record them. Then have the student listen to the recording and mark error and/or correct productions.

10. Have the student cut out pictures of items depicting the targeted words and display them where they can be practiced each day.

11. Record a spontaneous monologue given by the student. Have him/her listen to the recording and tally error and/or correct productions. The teacher should also listen to the recording. The teacher and the student should compare their analyses of the productions.

12. Have the student read a list of words and rate his/her production after each word.

13. Choose a peer to model correctly producing targeted words for the student.

14. Play a game such as *Simon Says* in which the student tries to imitate the targeted words when produced by the teacher or peers.

15. Using pictures of similar sounding words, have the student say each word as the teacher points to a picture (e.g., *run* and *one*, *bat* and *back*).

16. Use a schematic drawing as a visual aid to show the student how the mouth looks during production of the target sound.

17. Make cards with the target sound and cards with vowels. Have the student combine a target sound card with a vowel card to make a syllable that he/she can produce (e.g., *ra, re, ro,* and *ar, er, or*).

18. Use a board game that requires the student to label pictures of the targeted words. The student needs to produce the targeted words correctly before he/she can move on the game board. (This activity can be simplified or expanded based on the level of expertise of the student.)

19. Provide the student with a list of the targeted words. Have the student practice the words daily. As the student masters the word list, add more words. (Using words from the student's everyday vocabulary, reading lists, spelling lists, etc., will facilitate transfer of correct production of the target sound into everyday speech.)

20. Have the student use phonics "fun" sheets to practice his/her sound verbally. These are also good for home practice.

21. Have the student keep a notebook of difficult words encountered each day. These can be practiced by the student with teacher or peer assistance.

22. Have the student use a carrier phrase combined with a word containing the target sound (e.g., "I like _____." "I see a _____.").

23. Have the student keep a list of all the words he/she can think of which contain sounds the student can produce accurately.

24. During verbal reading, underline targeted words and reinforce the student for correct productions.

25. Involve parents by asking them to rate their child's speech for a specific length of time (e.g., during dinner count no errors, a few errors, or many errors).

26. Present the student with a list of topics. Have the student select a topic and then give a spontaneous speech for a specific length of time. Count errors and suggest ways for him/her to improve.

27. Reinforce the student for correct production of the target sound or words: (a) give the student a tangible reward (e.g., classroom privileges, line leading, passing out materials, five minutes free time, etc.) or (b) give the student an intangible reward (e.g., praise, fist bump, smile, etc.).

28. Speak to the student to explain what he/she needs to do differently (e.g., make sounds more precisely). The teacher should be careful to use the <u>sound</u> that is being targeted and not the letter name (e.g., /s/ not "s").

29. Evaluate the appropriateness of requiring the student to accurately produce certain sounds (e.g., developmentally, certain sounds may not be produced accurately until the age of 8 or 9).

30. Have the student write sentences using targeted words.

1. After recording the student's speech, have him/her identify incorrect subject-verb agreement and make appropriate corrections.

2. Determine the type of grammatical model to which the student is exposed at home. Without placing negative connotations on his/her parents' grammatical style, explain the difference between standard and nonstandard grammar.

3. Ask the parents to encourage the student's correct use of grammar at home by praising him/her when correct subject-verb agreement is used.

4. Choose a peer to model appropriate subject-verb agreement for the student.

5. Determine if the student's errors are the result of dialectical differences (the pattern of subject-verb agreement may not be atypical within his/her social group).

6. During the day, write down specific subject-verb errors produced by the student. Read the sentences to the student and have him/her make appropriate corrections verbally.

7. Evaluate the appropriateness of requiring the student to speak with subject-verb agreement (e.g., developmentally, a child may not utilize appropriate subject-verb agreement until the age of 6 or 7).

8. Explain that certain forms of verbs go with certain subjects and that correct subject-verb agreement requires the appropriate match of subject and verb. Be sure that the student knows the various possibilities of subject-verb agreement and how to select the correct one.

9. Give the student a series of sentences, both written and verbal, and have him/her identify which are grammatically correct and incorrect.

10. Have the student complete written worksheets in which he/she must choose the correct verb forms to go with specific subjects (e.g., "I _____ [saw, seen] a new car.").

11. Have the student complete written worksheets in which he/she must choose the correct subject forms to go with specific verbs (e.g., "[I, She] _____ eats.").

12. Have the student select a verb to master using correctly as a goal. As the student masters the correct use of the verb, he/she puts it on a list with a star and selects another verb to master.

13. Have the student verbally construct sentences with specific verb forms and subjects.

14. Increase the student's awareness of the problem by recording the student when speaking with another student who exhibits appropriate subject-verb agreement. Play back the recording for the student to analyze and see if he/she can identify correct/incorrect subject-verb forms.

15. Make a list of those verbs the student most commonly uses incorrectly. This list will become the guide for learning activities in subject-verb agreement.

16. Have the student's hearing checked if it has not been recently checked.

17. Make sure the student understands that sentences express thoughts about a subject and what that subject is or does.

18. Make sure the student understands the concept of subject and verb by demonstrating through the use of objects, pictures, and/or written sentences (depending on the student's abilities).

19. Make sure the student understands the concept of plurality (e.g., have the student point to a picture of a cat and point to a picture of cats).

20. Provide the student with correct examples of subject-verb agreement for those combinations he/she most commonly uses incorrectly.

21. Reinforce the student for appropriate use of subject-verb agreement: (a) give the student a tangible reward (e.g., classroom privileges, line leading, passing out materials, five minutes free time, etc.) or (b) give the student an intangible reward (e.g., praise, fist bump, smile, etc.).

22. Routinely record the student's speech and point out errors in subject-verb agreement. With each successive taping, reinforce the student as his/her use of grammar improves.

23. Speak to the student to explain that he/she is using inappropriate subject-verb agreement and emphasize the importance of speaking in grammatically correct sentences.

24. Use a private signal (e.g., touching earlobe, raising index finger, etc.) to remind the student to use correct subject-verb agreement.

25. When speaking privately with the student, restate his/her subject-verb error with a rising inflection (e.g., "He done it?") to assess if the student recognizes errors and spontaneously makes appropriate corrections.

26. Write down specific subject-verb errors made by the student during the day. Give the written sentences to the student and have him/her make appropriate corrections. (At first, mark the errors for the student to correct. As the student becomes more proficient with this task, have him/her find and correct the errors independently.)

1. Have the student sequence the activities which occurred on a field trip or special event with an emphasis on vocabulary.

2. During conversation, repeat phrases used by the student, revising the vocabulary to include additional words (e.g., The students says, "The TV show was good." Repeat by saying, "I'm glad the TV show was so entertaining.").

3. Have the student write sentences or stories using new words he/she has learned.

4. Allow the student to speak without being interrupted or hurried.

5. Determine the type of language model the student has at home. Without placing negative connotations on the language model in his/her home, explain the difference between language which is rich in meaning and that which includes a limited repertoire of vocabulary.

6. Encourage the student to use gestures when necessary to clarify his/her message. Gestures may also facilitate recall of vocabulary the student is having difficulty retrieving.

7. Ask questions which stimulate language. Avoid those which can be answered by "yes/no" or a nod of the head (e.g., "What did you do at recess?" rather than "Did you play on the slide?" or "Tell me about your vacation." rather than "Did you stay home over the holidays?" etc.).

8. Describe objects, persons, places, etc., to the student and have him/her name the items described.

9. Select relevant and appropriate reading material and have the student underline each unfamiliar word. Make a list of these words and review their meanings with the student until he/she can use them when speaking.

10. Give the student a list of words and ask him/her to tell the opposite of each word.

11. Have the student paste a picture from a magazine on one side of a piece of paper and list all of the vocabulary that could be associated with it on the other side (including verbs). Have the student dictate or write a story about the picture using the vocabulary.

12. Explain the importance of expanding one's vocabulary (i.e., comprehension and communication are based on the knowledge and use of appropriate/accurate vocabulary).

13. Discuss with the student's parents the ways in which they can help their child develop an expanded speaking vocabulary (e.g., encouraging the student to read the newspaper, novels, magazines, or other materials for enjoyment). Emphasize to parents that they can set a good example by reading with the student.

14. Explain to the student where he/she can go to find word meanings in the classroom library (e.g., dictionary, thesaurus, encyclopedia, etc.).

15. Have the student list all the vocabulary he/she can think of that goes with a specific word (e.g., "space" - astronaut, lunar rover, rocket, shuttle, launch, etc.).

16. Refer to previously presented information that is related to the topic when presenting new vocabulary.

17. Explain to the student how to classify new words as to category, function, antonym, synonym, etc., so the student will have a way of "filing" the words to memory.

18. Give the student or let the student choose a "word of the day" which is to be incorporated into conversations. Reinforce the student each time he/she uses the word.

19. Encourage the student to apply new vocabulary to personal experiences in written and verbal work (e.g., "Can you think of another word to use for sleep?").

20. Have the student act out verbs and label actions performed by classmates.

21. Have the student demonstrate and identify different verbs of the same category (e.g., walk, creep, slither, saunter, march, etc.).

22. Record the student's spontaneous speech, noting specific words. Have the student list other words which could be substituted for the identified words (synonyms).

23. Place interesting pictures or objects on a table and have the student describe them in detail. Provide assistance in formulating appropriate vocabulary to use when describing the object.

24. Have the student make up sentences or stories using new words he/she has learned.

25. Review daily new vocabulary words and their meanings. Have the student use the words daily.

26. Have the student provide as many adjectives as possible to go with a given noun (e.g., "lady" - pretty, tall, nice, etc.).

27. Give the student a picture of a specific location (e.g., grocery store) and have the student name as many objects, actions, persons, etc., as he/she can think of that can be found there.

28. Have the student provide associations for given words (e.g., "circus" - clown, elephant, trapeze, tent, lion tamer, etc.).

29. Use a multisensory approach to facilitate retention when teaching new vocabulary (e.g., use the scent of fragrant flowers or freshly baked spice cake to facilitate retention of the vocabulary word "aroma").

30. Encourage verbal output. Increase the student's opportunities to communicate verbally to provide him/her with necessary practice in using vocabulary.

31. Include new vocabulary in daily conversation as often as possible.

32. Have the student role-play various situations in which good vocabulary skills are important (e.g., during a job interview, talking to a group of people, etc.).

33. Choose a peer to model comprehension and use of an expanded vocabulary for the student.

34. Use new words in a sentence completion activity. Have the student explain how the use of different words changes the meaning of the sentence (e.g., I like Jerry because he is _____ [sincere, humorous, competitive], etc.).

35. In addition to identifying objects, persons, actions, etc.; have the student provide places where each could be seen (e.g., "actor" - TV, theater, stage, etc.).

36. Attach labels to items in the student's environment (e.g., wall-mounted board, window, desk, doorway, etc.) for the student to make visual associations with the vocabulary words.

37. Make sure the student has mastery of vocabulary words at each level before introducing new words.

38. Do not require the student to learn more vocabulary words and meanings than he/she is capable of comprehending.

39. In addition to labeling objects, persons, places, etc.; have the student provide verbs that could be used with each (e.g., "book" - read, browse through, skim, etc.).

40. Have the student's hearing checked if it has not been recently checked.

41. Use pictures to help the student understand the meanings of new vocabulary words.

42. Explain to the student how to use context clues to determine the meanings of words he/she hears or sees (e.g., listening to or looking at the surrounding words and determining what type of word would be appropriate).

43. Use games to teach comprehension and expression of new vocabulary. (Research has shown that novel situations help students to learn new information.)

44. When the student is asked to recall new vocabulary, give him/her clues about the word (e.g., "Remember when we talked about the animal that walks on all fours, barks, and people keep as pets?" etc.).

45. Teach new vocabulary within the context of known information (e.g., category, associations, etc.).

46. Have the student divide cards that label objects, persons, places, etc., in the environment into difference categories (e.g., function, color, size, use, composition, etc.). Point out the similarities and differences between items as they change categories (e.g., a ball and an apple may be red, round, and smooth; but you can only eat the apple, etc.).

47. Name a category and have the student identify things within the category. Introduce new words which belong in the same group.

48. Point out words that have a variety of meanings and use them appropriately in different contexts.

49. Have the student maintain a vocabulary notebook (picture or word) with definitions of words whose meanings he/she does not know.

50. Prepare a list of new words which the student will encounter while reading a given assignment. Help the student (or choose a peer to help the student) look up each word and practice saying it and using it in a sentence before reading the given assignment.

51. Provide the student with fewer weekly vocabulary words. As the student demonstrates success, gradually increase the number of vocabulary words from week to week.

52. Have the student provide as many adverbs as possible to go with a given verb (e.g., "run" - slow, fast, crooked, etc.).

53. Reinforce the student for using an expanded speaking vocabulary: (a) give the student a tangible reward (e.g., classroom privileges, line leading, passing out materials, five minutes free time, etc.) or (b) give the student an intangible reward (e.g., praise, fist bump, smile, etc.).

54. Have the student participate in role-playing to foster the use of new vocabulary (e.g., set up an imaginary restaurant and have the student and peers play the various roles of customers, waiter/waitress, cook, etc., varying the time of day and the occasion).

55. Send home new vocabulary words and encourage parents to use them in activities and general conversation.

56. Take advantage of unusual or unique situations to teach new vocabulary. Typically, a student will retain information learned in a novel situation better than information learned during a regular routine. The uniqueness of the situation will also facilitate the student's memory skills when you provide a reminder to help the student recall the vocabulary (e.g., "Remember yesterday during the fire drill when we talked about _____?").

57. Prompt the student to help him/her respond with adequate vocabulary (e.g., Student says "that thing." Teacher responds, "What thing, what is it doing?" etc.).

58. Review daily previously learned vocabulary words and their meanings. Have the student incorporate previously learned vocabulary words into daily conversation and activities.

59. To reinforce new vocabulary, write the new word on an envelope and put pictures inside that do and do not go with it (e.g., "arctic" - polar bears, snow, parrots, palm trees, etc.). Have the student remove the inappropriate picture and explain why it doesn't belong.

60. Use a large purse, box, bag, etc., with objects inside (e.g., different shaped blocks, pieces of fruit, school supplies, etc.). Have the student reach into the container and try to determine what each item is by describing how it feels before seeing it.

61. Have the student maintain a notebook of all new vocabulary words to call upon for daily conversation and activities.

62. Use hands-on activities to teach vocabulary by constructing objects and/or organizing manipulatives (e.g., under the heading "fruit" provide actual pieces of fruit, under the heading "school supplies" provide actual school materials, etc.).

63. When teaching new vocabulary and engaging in conversation, be sure to use vocabulary that is within the student's level of comprehension.

64. Use visual aids whenever possible when introducing new vocabulary.

65. Have the student label all the objects, persons, places, etc., in the environment that he/she can. Then have the student point to the item in the environment as you label the ones he/she was unable to name. The items the student was unable to label will comprise a foundation for <u>new</u> vocabulary to be learned. Activities to foster expansion of expressive vocabulary should focus on the items the student pointed to but could not label.

66. Give the student a series of words or pictures and have him/her name the category in which they belong (e.g., objects, persons, places, etc.).

67. Reinforce those students in the classroom who use an expanded speaking vocabulary.

1. After recording the student's speech, have him/her identify the incorrect verb tenses and make appropriate corrections.

2. Determine the type of grammatical model to which the student is exposed at home. Without placing negative connotations on the parents' grammatical style, explain the difference between standard and nonstandard grammar.

3. Have the student select a verb to master using correctly as a goal. As the student masters the correct use of the verb, he/she puts it on a list with a star and selects another verb to master.

4. Ask the parents to encourage the student's correct use of verb tenses at home by praising him/her when appropriate verb tenses are used.

5. Copy a simple paragraph which is in the present tense. Highlight the verbs and have the student change all the verbs to past and/or future tense. This activity could be completed verbally or in written form.

6. Determine if the student's errors are the result of dialectical differences (i.e., the pattern of verb tense usage may not be atypical within his/her social group).

7. Reinforce those students in the classroom who use verb tenses correctly.

8. Use a private signal (e.g., hand over shoulder/past tense, pointing forward/future tense, etc.) to remind the student to use correct verb tense.

9. During the day, write down specific verb tense errors produced by the student. Read the sentences to the student and have him/her make appropriate corrections verbally.

10. Explain that changes must be made in a verb to indicate when an event happened (e.g., past, present, future).

11. Give the student a sentence and have him/her change it from present to past, past to present, future to past, etc.

12. While the class is engaged in various activities, describe your observations using present tense. Have students do likewise. Expand this activity to include past and future tenses by asking appropriate questions (e.g., "What just happened?" "What were you doing?" "What will you do next?").

13. Choose a peer to practice verb tenses with the student. Each tense should be used in a sentence rather than only conjugating the verbs.

14. Have the student assist in correcting other students' written work, looking for errors in verb tenses.

15. Determine whether the student has appropriate sequencing skills. The concept of sequencing influences comprehension of verb tensing (e.g., Can the student answer questions using first, next, then, etc.? Does he/she use such vocabulary when speaking even though verb tenses are incorrect?).

16. Have the student make corrections for incorrect verb tenses on written worksheets.

17. When speaking privately with the student, restate his/her verb tense error with a rising inflection (e.g., "Yesterday he <u>plays</u>?") to assess if the student recognizes errors and spontaneously makes appropriate corrections.

18. Choose a peer to model correct verb tenses for the student.

19. Increase the student's awareness of the problem by recording the student while he/she is speaking with another student who uses verb tenses correctly. Play the recording back for the student to see if he/she can identify correct/incorrect verb tensing.

20. Make a list of those verb tenses the student most commonly uses incorrectly. This list will become the guide for identifying the verb tenses which the student should practice each day.

21. Have the student's hearing checked if it has not been recently checked.

22. Make headings entitled "yesterday," "today," and "tomorrow" under which the class can list activities they "were doing," "are doing," or "will do." The following day, change the "today" heading to "yesterday" and the "tomorrow" heading to "today." Emphasize appropriate verb tenses throughout this activity.

23. Have the student make up sentences with given verbs in the past, present, and future tenses.

24. Make sure the student understands the concept of verb tenses by demonstrating what "is happening," what "already happened," and what "will happen" through the use of objects, pictures, and/or written sentences (depending on the student's abilities).

25. Reinforce the student for using verb tenses correctly: (a) give the student a tangible reward (e.g., classroom privileges, line leading, passing out materials, five minutes free time, etc.) or (b) give the student an intangible reward (e.g., praise, fist bump, smile, etc.).

26. Give the student a series of sentences, both written and verbal, and have him/her identify the ones which demonstrate appropriate verb tensing. Have him/her make appropriate modifications for those sentences which demonstrate inappropriate verb tensing.

27. Have the student complete worksheets in which he/she must supply the correct verb tenses to go with the sentences (e.g., "Yesterday I _____ to school.").

28. Record the student's speech to point out errors in verb tenses. With each successive taping, reinforce the student as his/her use of verb tenses improves.

29. Determine whether the student understands the concept of time which influences comprehension of verb tensing (e.g., Can he/she answer questions using "yesterday," "today," "tomorrow," "before," "later," etc.? Does he/she use such vocabulary when speaking even though the verb tense is incorrect?).

30. Video the student and his/her classmates performing various actions. Play back the recording without the sound and have the student narrate what is happening in present tense, what happened in past tense, and/or what will happen in future tense. (This activity could be modified by using a prerecorded video.)

31. Write down specific verb tense errors made by the student during the day. Give the written sentences to the student and have him/her make appropriate corrections. (At first, mark the errors for him/her to correct. As the student becomes more proficient with this task, have him/her find and correct the errors independently.)

32. Make the conjugation of verbs a daily activity.

33. Have the student list activities he/she did when little, activities the student can do now, and things he/she will be able to do when grown up. Emphasize appropriate verb tenses throughout this activity.

1. As the student is able to speak fluently in more situations (e.g., delivering messages to the office, speaking with the counselor, etc.), gradually increase those experiences as long as the student continues to be successful.

2. Determine whether or not the student avoids certain situations because of his/her perception of increased dysfluency. Discuss with the student the aspects of those situations that seem to cause increased anxiety. Examine possible modifications that could be implemented in the classroom to facilitate frustration tolerance (e.g., if speaking in front of the whole class causes stress, reduce the number of listeners and gradually increase the size of the group as the student's frustration tolerance increases).

3. Have the student keep a list of times and/or situations in which speech is difficult (e.g., times when he/she is nervous, embarrassed, etc.). Discuss the reasons for this and consider possible solutions to the difficulty experienced.

4. Discuss and role-play with the entire class different kinds of disabilities and the accompanying frustrations they might feel if they were experiencing similar difficulties. Include speech problems in this discussion.

5. Do not interrupt or finish the student's sentences even if you think you can anticipate what the student is going to say. This can be extremely frustrating and may decrease the student's willingness to participate in future communicative interactions.

6. During conversations, calmly delay your verbal responses by one or two seconds.

7. If the student is speaking too rapidly, remind him/her to slow down. Develop a private signal (e.g., raising one finger, touching earlobe, etc.) to avoid calling too much attention to the student's speech in front of the whole class.

8. During verbal reading, underline or highlight words which are difficult for the student to say and provide reinforcement when he/she says them fluently.

9. Empathize with feelings of anger which the student may be experiencing due to speaking dysfluently.

10. Encourage the student to maintain eye contact during all speaking situations. If the student is noticeably more fluent when eye contact is averted, attempt to facilitate eye contact on a gradual basis.

11. When the student is speaking fluently, try to extend the positive experience by allowing him/her to continue speaking.

12. Evaluate the appropriateness of requiring the student to speak without dysfluency (e.g., developmentally, young children experience normal dysfluency in their speech and all persons are occasionally dysfluent).

13. Develop a list of the attributes which are likely to help a person become a good speaker. Have the student practice each attribute.

14. Familiarize yourself and the student with the terms fluency, dysfluency, stuttering, easy speech, etc. Keep these words as neutral as possible, without negative connotations.

15. Have the student identify a good speaker and give the reasons that make that person a good speaker.

16. If the student is more dysfluent when involved in another activity at the same time he/she is talking, encourage the student to stop the other activity.

17. Have the student identify the specific words or phrases on which he/she becomes dysfluent and practice those particular words or phrases.

18. When the student seems extremely frustrated by a stuttering episode, react calmly with a reassuring statement (e.g., "Sometimes words do not come out easily, do they?" or "You worked hard on that word.").

19. Have the student speak in unison with you while you are modeling slow, easy speech.

20. Do not require the student to speak in front of other students if he/she is uncomfortable doing so. Have the student speak to the teacher or another student privately if the student would be more comfortable doing so.

21. Provide the student with many opportunities for social and academic successes.

22. Help the student learn to identify periods of dysfluency and periods of slow, easy speech.

23. Choose a peer to model appropriate speech for the student. Pair the students to sit together, perform assignments together, etc.

24. If the student is highly excited, wait until he/she is calmer before requiring any verbal explanations or interactions. A high level of excitement often precipitates an anxiety level that interferes with fluency.

25. During moments of dysfluency, use nonverbal activities to relax the student.

26. Reinforce the student for speaking fluently: (a) give the student a tangible reward (e.g., classroom privileges, line leading, passing out materials, five minutes free time, etc.) or (b) give the student an intangible reward (e.g., praise, fist bump, smile, etc.).

27. Have the student's hearing checked if it has not been recently checked.

28. Meet with the student's parents to determine the level of dysfluency at home, parental reactions to the dysfluency, and successful strategies the parents have employed when dealing with the dysfluent speech.

29. Help the student learn to identify situations in which he/she is more fluent or less fluent. Determine the aspects of the fluent situations that seem to facilitate fluency and try to transfer those features to the less fluent situations.

30. Model slow, easy speech for the student and encourage him/her to speak at a similar rate. Practice with the student for a short time each day until he/she is able to match the rate.

31. Have the student make a list of his/her strong points or the things he/she does well to improve his/her overall level of confidence.

32. Point out to the student that he/she is capable of fluent speech and is in control of speech in many situations.

33. Reduce the emphasis on competition. Competitive activities may increase the student's anxiety and cause him/her to speak more dysfluently.

34. Prepare simple verbal reading passages in written form in which phrases are separated by large spaces (indicating a pause). Have the student practice reading the passages aloud.

35. Use a private cue (e.g., raise a finger, touch earlobe, etc.) to encourage the student to answer questions at a slow rate of speech.

36. Provide the student with an appropriate model of slow, easy speech. Lengthen the pauses between words, phrases, and sentences.

37. Reinforce the student each time he/she answers a question or makes a spontaneous comment in class.

38. Take time to listen to the student when he/she displays frustration/anger. Talk to the student about appropriate ways of dealing with these feelings.

39. Teach the student ways to restate or rephrase a misunderstood message rather than continuing to repeat the original message with the same error patterns.

40. Provide the student with a list of sentences and encourage him/her to read these at a slow rate.

41. Try to give the student your undivided attention so he/she will not feel a need to hurry or compete with others for attention.

42. When the student is dysfluent during conversation, explain that this happens to everyone at times.

43. Reinforce the student's moments of relative fluency and emphasize that these occurred during moments when he/she was speaking slowly and easily.

44. Use a private cue (e.g., raise a finger, touch earlobe, etc.) to encourage the student to use a slow speaking rate during classroom activities.

45. Record the student so he/she may listen to and evaluate his/her own speech.

46. Empathize with the student and explain that he/she is not less valuable as a person because of his/her dysfluency. Emphasize the student's positive attributes.

47. Have the student practice techniques for relaxing (e.g., deep breathing, tensing and relaxing muscles, etc.) which can be employed when he/she starts to speak dysfluently.

48. When the student experiences a severe episode of dysfluency, respond by paraphrasing/repeating the content of his/her message to communicate that the message has been understood.

1. Allow the student to speak without being interrupted or hurried.

2. Use a private signal (e.g., touching earlobe, raising index finger, etc.) to remind the student to speak in complete sentences and use specific terminology.

3. Provide the student with a topic (e.g., rules to follow when riding your bike) and have him/her write complete sentences about it.

4. When the student is required to recall information, remind him/her of the situation in which the material was originally presented (e.g., "Remember yesterday when we talked about . . ." "Remember when we were outside and I told you about the . . .").

5. When the student is required to recall information, provide visual and/or auditory cues to help him/her remember the information (e.g., mention key words, expose part of a picture, etc.).

6. Ask the student leading questions to facilitate the process of speaking in complete sentences and using specific vocabulary.

7. Ask the parents to encourage the student's use of complete sentences and thoughts at home by praising him/her when these are used.

8. Provide frequent interactions and encouragement to support the student's confidence (e.g., make statements such as "You're doing great." "Keep up the good work." "I really am proud of you.").

9. Increase the student's awareness of the problem by recording the student while he/she is speaking with another student who uses complete sentences. Replay the recording for the student to see if he/she can identify incomplete sentences and nondescript terminology. Have the student make appropriate modifications.

10. Teach the student the components of a complete sentence (i.e., subject, verb, and an object). Point out the components using objects, pictures, sentences, etc., depending on the student's abilities.

11. Make sure the student understands that a complete sentence has to express a complete thought about a subject and what that subject is or does, and that use of specific vs. nondescriptive vocabulary is important to clarify the message.

12. Make a list of the student's most common incomplete statements and uses of nondescriptive terminology. Spend time with the student practicing how to make these statements or thoughts complete and making appropriate replacements for nondescriptive vocabulary.

13. List the qualities a good speaker possesses (e.g., rate, diction, volume, vocabulary, etc.) and have the student evaluate himself/herself on each characteristic. Set a goal for improvement in only one or two areas at a time.

14. Make groups of cards containing subjects, verbs, adjectives, etc. Have the student combine the cards in various ways to construct complete sentences.

15. Encourage verbal output. Increase the student's opportunities to communicate verbally to provide him/her with necessary practice.

16. Focus on completeness of the student's thought and not the grammatical accuracy of the statement. Reinforce complete thoughts that include specific vocabulary.

17. When speaking privately with the student, restate his/her incomplete sentences and/or nondescriptive vocabulary with a rising inflection to indicate the need for more information (e.g., "You saw the <u>stuff</u> in the sky?" or "Your brown dog . . .?") to see if the student recognizes the problem and spontaneously makes appropriate corrections.

18. Have the student give process statements to sequence an activity (e.g., how to make a peanut butter and jelly sandwich). Have the student focus on making each statement a complete thought with specific vs. nondescriptive vocabulary.

19. Give the student a factual statement (e.g., Some animals are dangerous.) and have him/her provide several complete sentences relating to that topic.

20. Provide the student with sentence starters (e.g., Go _____. Run _____. Today I _____. Anyone can _____. etc.) and have him/her write complete sentences.

21. Routinely record the student's speech and point out incomplete statements and nondescript terminology. With each successive taping, reinforce the student as his/her use of complete sentences and specific vocabulary improves.

22. After a field trip or special event, have the student retell the activities which occurred with an emphasis on using descriptive vocabulary and complete sentences.

23. Choose a peer to model speaking in complete sentences for the student. Assign the students to work together, perform assignments together, etc.

24. Have the student role-play various situations in which speaking well is important (e.g., during a job interview).

25. Have the student correct a series of phrases by making each a complete sentence.

26. Give the student several short sentences and have him/her combine them to produce one longer sentence (e.g., "The dog is big." "The dog is brown." "The dog is mine." becomes "The big, brown dog is mine.").

27. When the student uses incomplete sentences or nondescriptive terminology, provide the student with models of expansion and specific vocabulary using his/her statements as a foundation.

28. Have the student complete fill-in-the-blank sentences with appropriate words (e.g., objects, persons, places, etc.).

29. Video the student and classmates performing various actions. Play back the recording without sound and have the student narrate observations in complete sentences with descriptive vocabulary. (This activity could be modified by using a prerecorded video.)

30. Choose a topic for a paragraph or story and alternate making up sentences with the student to provide a model of the components of a complete sentence.

31. Ask questions which stimulate language. Avoid those which can be answered by yes/no or a nod of the head (e.g., "What did you do at recess?" instead of "Did you play on the slide?" or "Tell me about your vacation." instead of "Did you stay home over the holidays?").

32. Show the student an object or a picture of an object for a few seconds. Ask the student to recall specific attributes of the object (e.g., color, size, shape, etc.).

33. Give the student a series of words (e.g., objects, persons, places, etc.) and have the student list all the words he/she can think of with similar meanings (i.e., synonyms).

34. Give the student a series of words or pictures and have him/her name as many items as possible within that category (e.g., objects, persons, places, things that are hot, etc.).

35. Give the student a series of words describing objects, persons, places, etc., and have him/her identify the opposite of each word.

36. Give the student a series of complete and incomplete sentences, both written and verbal, and ask him/her to identify which are correct and incorrect and make appropriate modifications.

37. Give the student a group of related words (e.g., *baseball, fans, glove, strikeout,* etc.) and have him/her write a paragraph that includes each word.

38. Give the student a list of transition words (e.g., *therefore, although, because,* etc.) and have him/her write sentences using each word.

39. Have the student make notes, lists, etc., of vocabulary that is needed to be recalled and have the student carry these reminders for reference.

40. Have the student keep a list of times and/or situations in which he/she is nervous, anxious, etc., and has more trouble than usual with speech. Help the student identify ways to feel more successful in those situations.

41. Teach the student to recognize key words and phrases related to information to facilitate his/her recall.

42. Have the student identify a good speaker and give the reasons that make that person a good speaker.

43. Make sure the student receives information from a variety of sources (e.g., textbooks, like presentations, discussions, etc.) to facilitate memory/recall.

44. Have the student complete worksheets in which he/she must replace nondescriptive or inaccurate vocabulary with specific and appropriate terminology (e.g., "The thing tastes good." could be changed to "The cake (meal, soda, etc.) tastes good." or "He used the digger to make the hole." could be changed to "He used the shovel (backhoe, spade, etc.) to make the hole.").

45. Label objects, persons, places, etc., in the environment to help the student be able to recall names.

46. Have the student's hearing checked if it has not been recently checked.

47. Have the student compete against himself/herself by timing how fast he/she can name a series of pictured objects. Each time, the student tries to improve his/her speed.

48. Have the student describe himself/herself and/or classmates in complete sentences with emphasis on specific vocabulary to differentiate one student from another.

49. Call on the student when he/she is most likely to be able to successfully respond.

50. Using a wordless picture book, have the student tell the story using descriptive vocabulary and complete sentences. Record the story and replay it for the student. Have the student listen for complete/incomplete sentences and specific/nondescriptive terminology and make appropriate corrections.

51. After reading a short story, have the student recall the main characters, sequence the events, and retell the outcome of the story.

52. Encourage the student to use gestures when necessary to clarify his/her message. Gestures may also facilitate recall of vocabulary the student is having difficulty retrieving.

53. Provide the student with the first sound of a word he/she is having difficulty retrieving to facilitate recall.

54. Speak to the student to explain that he/she is using incomplete sentences or thoughts when speaking and explain the importance of speaking in complete sentences and choosing specific words to express ideas.

55. When the student has difficulty during a conversation, remind him/her that this occasionally happens to everyone.

56. Reinforce the student for using complete sentences or thoughts when speaking: (a) give the student a tangible reward (e.g., classroom privileges, line leading, passing out materials, five minutes free time, etc.) or (b) give the student an intangible reward (e.g., praise, fist bump, smile, etc.).

57. Reinforce the students in the classroom who use complete sentences or thoughts when speaking.

58. Have a number of students build a sentence together (e.g., The first one starts with a word (e.g., I). The next student adds the second word (e.g., like). This process continues as long as possible to create one long, complete sentence. Do not accept nondescriptive terminology.).

59. Make a list of the attributes which are likely to help a person become a good speaker (e.g., takes his/her time, thinks of what to say before starting, etc.).

60. Provide the student with an appropriate model to imitate speaking in complete sentences or thoughts (e.g., speak clearly, slowly, concisely, and in complete sentences, statements, and thoughts).

61. Describe objects, persons, places, etc., and have the student name the items described.

62. Give the student specific categories and have him/her name as many items as possible within that category (e.g., things that are cold, objects, persons, places, etc.).

63. Give the student a subject and have him/her write as many complete sentences about it as possible, emphasizing the use of specific vocabulary.

64. Give the student scrambled words and have him/her put them in the correct order to form a complete sentence.

65. Teach the concept of verb and noun phrases as soon as possible so the student has a means of checking to see if a sentence is complete.

66. Encourage the student to use an appropriate synonym when experiencing difficulty retrieving the exact word he/she wants to say.

67. Help the student employ memory aids to recall words (e.g., a name might be linked to another word; for example, Mr. Green is a very colorful person.).

68. Demonstrate acceptable and unacceptable speech (including incomplete thoughts and non-descriptive terminology such as thing or stuff, etc.) and have the student critique each example making suggestions for improvement.

69. Have the student complete associations (e.g., knife, fork, and _____; men, women, and _____; etc.).

70. Reduce the emphasis on competition. Competitive activities may cause the student to hurry and not speak in complete sentences.

D. Reading

Behavior Number

1. Have the student prepare test questions based on information that has been read to facilitate the ability to focus on key elements of the reading material.

2. Have the student read a story. Provide statements out of sequence which reflect the main points of the story. Have the student arrange the statements in the correct order to demonstrate comprehension.

3. Have the student read a short paragraph which contains one or more errors which make comprehension difficult. If the student does not recognize the errors, encourage the student to stop frequently while reading to ask himself/herself, "Does this make sense?"

4. When the student encounters a new word or one whose meaning is not understood, have the student construct sentences in which the word is used in the correct context.

5. Have the student maintain a vocabulary notebook with definitions of words whose meanings he/she did not know.

6. Pair the student with a peer to summarize material to answer the questions "Who, What, Where, When, How, and Why."

7. Have the student use a highlighter pen to highlight the facts requested by the teacher.

8. Provide the student with a quiet place (e.g., carrel, study booth, etc.) where he/she may go to participate in reading activities.

9. Have the student read ahead on a subject to be discussed in class so that he/she is familiar with new vocabulary and concepts that will be used during instructional periods.

10. Have the student write and answer the questions "Who, What, Where, When, How, and Why" using the Flash Card Study Aid.

11. Have the student's hearing checked if it has not been recently checked.

12. Maintain mobility in the classroom to be frequently near the student to provide reading assistance.

13. Reduce the emphasis on competition. Competitive activities may increase the student's anxiety and reduce the student's ability to comprehend information.

14. Choose a peer who demonstrates good comprehension skills to read with the student and help him/her with the meanings of words not understood.

15. Reinforce the student for demonstrating comprehension of reading material: (a) give the student a tangible reward (e.g., classroom privileges, line leading, passing out materials, five minutes free time, etc.) or (b) give the student an intangible reward (e.g., praise, fist bump, smile, etc.).

16. Teach the student to draw from personal learning experiences to facilitate comprehension of reading material. Provide a variety of learning experiences at school to expand the student's background of knowledge.

17. Have the student look for story elements when reading a selection (e.g., setting, characters, plot, ending).

18. Have the student look for key words (e.g., Christopher Columbus, Spain, New World, etc.).

19. Have the student look for direction words (e.g., circle, underline, choose, list, etc.).

20. Have the student look for action words (e.g., sailed, discovered, founded).

21. Have the student look for the key words and main ideas when reading that will answer "Who, What, Where, When, How, and Why" (e.g., "Christopher Columbus sailed from Spain to discover the New World during the year 1492.").

22. After reading a selection, have the student complete a semantic map answering the questions "Who, What, Where, When, How, and Why."

23. Have the student read high-interest signs, advertisements, notices, etc., from newspapers, magazines, movie promotions, etc., placing an emphasis on comprehension skills.

24. Teach the student to identify main points in material to facilitate his/her comprehension.

25. Avoid placing the student in uncomfortable reading situations (e.g., reading aloud in a group, reading with time limits, etc.).

26. Have the student read independently each day to practice reading skills.

27. Highlight or underline important information the student should pay close attention to when reading.

28. Reduce the amount of information on a page (e.g., less print to read, fewer pictures, etc.) if it is visually distracting for the student.

29. Make sure the student is practicing comprehension skills which are directly related to high-interest reading activities (e.g., adventure, romance, mystery, sports, etc.).

30. Make sure the student is reading material on his/her ability level. If not, modify or adjust reading material to the student's ability level.

31. Make sure the student learns the meanings of all commonly used prefixes and suffixes.

32. Make sure the student learns dictionary skills to independently find the meaning of words.

33. Cut out pictures from magazines and newspapers and have the student match captions to them. This activity could be varied by having one student write the caption while another student determines if it is appropriate.

34. Make a list of main points from the student's reading material, written on the student's reading level.

35. Have the student take notes while reading to facilitate comprehension.

36. Reduce the amount of material the student reads at one time (e.g., reduce reading material to single sentences on a page, a single paragraph, etc.). As the student demonstrates success, gradually increase the amount of material to be read at one time.

37. Have the student supply missing words in sentences provided by classmates and/or the teacher to facilitate comprehension skills.

38. Have the student list new or difficult words in categories such as people, food, animals, things that are hot, etc.

39. Teach the student meanings of abbreviations to assist in comprehending material read.

40. Include frequent written assignments on topics which are of interest to the student to reinforce the correlation between writing and reading ability.

41. Have the student identify one word each day that he/she does not understand. Have the student define the word and then require him/her to use that word throughout the day in various situations.

42. Find the central word or phrase around which the story is constructed. Check for pinpoint words that relate back to the central word/phrase and determine the number of times they are used and how this helps to develop the story.

43. Have the student verbally paraphrase material just read to assess his/her comprehension.

44. Underline or highlight important points before the student reads the material silently.

45. Make it pleasant and positive for the student to ask questions about things not understood.

46. Teach new vocabulary words prior to having the student read the material.

47. Record the student's reading material and have him/her listen to the recording while simultaneously reading the material.

48. Have the student read progressively longer segments of reading material to build comprehension skills (e.g., begin with a single paragraph and progress to several paragraphs, chapters, short stories, etc.).

49. Record lectures to provide an additional source of information for the student.

50. Have the student outline reading material using the Outline Form.

51. Give the student high-interest reading material on his/her ability level (e.g., comic books, adventure stories, etc.) requiring him/her to answer the questions "Who, What, Where, When, How, and Why."

52. Have the student record what he/she reads to facilitate comprehension by replaying and listening to the material read.

53. Prior to reading a selection, familiarize the student with the general content of the story (e.g., when reading a selection about birds, have the students brainstorm and discuss birds to develop a point of reference).

54. Have the student dictate stories which are then put in print for him/her to read, placing an emphasis on comprehension skills.

55. Write paragraphs and short stories requiring skills the student is currently developing. These passages should be of high interest to the student using his/her name, family members, friends, pets, and interesting experiences.

56. Make available for the student a learning center area where a variety of information is available for him/her in content areas (e.g., the library may have a section with visuals, videos and recorded lectures, on such subjects as pilgrims, the Civil War, the judicial system, etc.).

57. Use lower grade-level texts as alternative reading material in subject areas.

58. Outline reading material for the student using words and phrases on his/her ability level.

59. Reduce distracting stimuli in the environment to facilitate the student's ability to concentrate on what he/she is reading (e.g., place the student on the front row, provide a carrel or office space away from distractions, etc.). This should be used as a means of reducing distracting stimuli and not as punishment.

60. Determine whether or not the student can make inferences, predictions, determine cause-effect, etc., in everyday experiences. Teach these skills in contexts that are meaningful to the student to facilitate the ability to employ these concepts when reading.

61. Introduce new words and their meanings to the student before reading new material.

62. Teach the student to think about the reading selection and predict what will happen prior to reading the selection.

63. Choose a peer tutor to study with the student for quizzes, tests, etc.

64. Give the student time to read a selection more than once. Emphasize accuracy not speed.

65. Write notes and letters to the student to provide reading material which he/she will want to read for comprehension. Students may be encouraged to write notes and letters to classmates at a time set aside each day, once a week, etc.

66. Have the student outline, underline, or highlight important points in written material.

67. Teach the student to use context clues to identify the meanings of words and phrases not known.

68. Teach the student to use related learning experiences in his/her classes (e.g., DVDs, movies, recordings, demonstrations, discussions, lectures, videos, etc.). Encourage teachers to provide alternative learning experiences for the student.

69. Stop the student at various points throughout a reading selection to check for comprehension.

70. Use a sight-word vocabulary approach to teach the student key words (e.g., circle, underline, match, etc.) and phrases when reading directions and instructions.

71. Have the student identify words he/she does not comprehend. Have him/her find the definitions of these words in the dictionary.

72. Have the student work with a peer and teacher. The first student will dictate a short paragraph to be typed by the teacher and will also compose a comprehension question. The second student, after listening to the process, will read the story verbally and point out the answer. Then student roles can be reversed.

73. Have the student match vocabulary words with pictures representing the words.

74. Provide the student with written direction-following activities that target concrete experiences (e.g., following a recipe, following directions to put a model together, etc.) to facilitate comprehension.

75. Provide the student with written one-step, two-step, and three-step direction-following activities (e.g., sharpen your pencil, open your text to page 121, etc.).

76. Use reading series material with high interest, low vocabulary for the older student.

39 Fails to finish assignments because of reading difficulties

1. Make sure that the reading demands of the assignment are within the ability level of the student.

2. Record directions, explanations, and instructions to facilitate the student's success.

3. Choose a peer to read directions, explanations, and instructions to the student to facilitate success.

4. Require the student to verbally repeat directions, explanations, and instructions.

5. Read directions, explanations, and instructions to the student when necessary.

6. Use a sight word-vocabulary approach to teach the student key words (e.g., circle, underline, match, etc.) and phrases when reading directions and instructions.

7. Deliver all directions, explanations, and instructions verbally.

8. Reduce all directions, explanations, and instructions to a minimum.

9. Shorten the length of assignments that require reading so the student can complete assignments in the same length of time as the other students.

10. Provide the student with additional time to complete the assignment.

11. Deliver directions, explanations, and instructions prior to handing out materials.

12. Make sure that the student's knowledge of a particular skill is being assessed rather than the student's ability to read directions, instructions, and content.

13. Maintain mobility to provide assistance to the student.

14. Maintain a consistent format in which written directions, explanations, and instructions are delivered.

15. Have the student practice timed drills consisting of reading directions, explanations, content, etc., to reduce reading time.

16. Provide more than enough time for the student to complete an assignment.

17. Assess the quality and clarity of written directions, explanations, instructions, content, etc.

18. Keep written directions as simple and concrete as possible.

19. Reduce distracting stimuli in the environment to facilitate the student's ability to follow written directions (e.g., place the student on the front row; provide a carrel or office space away from distractions; etc.). This is used as a means of reducing distracting stimuli and not as a form of punishment.

20. Reduce written directions to individual steps. Give the student an additional step after completion of the previous step.

21. Make sure the student achieves success when following written directions.

22. Prevent the student from becoming over-stimulated (e.g., frustrated, angry, etc.) by an activity.

23. Provide the student with a copy of written directions at his/her desk in addition to on the wall-mounted board, posted in the classroom, etc.

24. Seat the student close to the source of the written information (e.g., wall-mounted board, projector, etc.).

25. Make sure the print is bold and large enough to facilitate the student's success in following written directions.

26. Transfer directions from texts and workbooks when pictures or other stimuli make it difficult to attend to or follow written directions.

27. Provide the student a quiet place (e.g., carrel, study booth, etc.) where he/she may go to participate in activities which require following written directions.

28. Work the first problem or problems with the student to make sure that he/she follows written directions.

29. Have the student carry out written directions one step at a time and then check with the teacher to make sure that each step is successfully completed before attempting the next.

30. As the student demonstrates success, gradually increase the level of difficulty or complexity of written directions, explanations, instructions, content, etc.

31. Modify or adjust the reading level of material presented to the student to facilitate success.

32. Reduce the emphasis on competition. Competitive activities may make it difficult for the student to finish assignments because of frustration with reading difficulties.

33. Introduce new words and their meanings to the student before he/she reads new materials. These may be entered in a vocabulary notebook kept by the student as a reference for new vocabulary words.

34. Avoid placing the student in uncomfortable reading situations (e.g., reading aloud in a group, identifying that the student's reading group is the lowest level, etc.).

35. Record difficult reading material for the student to listen to as he/she reads along.

36. Give the student time to read a selection more than once. Emphasize comprehension rather than speed.

37. Use reading series material with high interest (e.g., adventure, romance, mystery, sports, etc.) and low vocabulary.

38. Reduce the amount of material the student reads at one time (e.g., reduce reading material to single sentences on a page, a single paragraph, etc.). As the student demonstrates success, gradually increase the amount of material to be read at one time.

39. Make the subject matter meaningful to the student (e.g., explain the purpose of an assignment, relate the subject matter to the student's environment, etc.).

40. Give the student one task to complete at a time. Introduce the next task only when the student has successfully completed the previous task.

41. Reduce the amount of information on a page (e.g., less print to read, fewer pictures on the page, isolate information that is presented to the student) if it is visually distracting for the student.

42. Have the student read material to the teacher to determine if it is on his/her reading level.

43. Have the student use his/her finger to point to words that are being read. The teacher should observe as the student points to the words while reading. This would help to determine the causes of slow reading.

44. Reduce the student's anxiety level by not requiring the student to finish a reading assignment within a specified time period.

45. Teach the student that work not done during work time must be completed at other times such as free time, recess, after school, etc.

46. Have the student ask questions about directions, explanations, instructions he/she does not understand.

47. Choose a peer to model how to complete assignments for the student.

48. Evaluate the appropriateness of the task to determine (a) if the task is too easy, (b) if the task is too difficult, and (c) if the length of time scheduled to complete the task is adequate.

49. Communicate with parents (e.g., notes home, phone calls, etc.) to share information about the student's progress. The parents may reinforce the student at home for finishing assignments at school.

50. Write a contract with the student specifying what behavior is expected (e.g., finishing assignments) and what reinforcement will be made available when the terms of the contract have been met.

51. Reinforce the student for finishing assignments based on the number of times he/she can be successful. As the student demonstrates success, gradually increase the number of times required for reinforcement.

52. Reinforce the student for finishing assignments: (a) give the student a tangible reward (e.g., classroom privileges, line leading, passing out materials, five minutes free time, etc.) or (b) give the student an intangible reward (e.g., praise, fist bump, smile, etc.).

53. Establish classroom rules:
- Concentrate while working.
- Work quietly.
- Remain in your seat.
- Finish task.
- Meet task requirements.

Review rules often. Reinforce the student for following the rules.

54. Reinforce those students in the classroom who finish assignments.

55. Speak to the student to explain (a) what he/she is doing wrong (e.g., failing to finish assignments) and (b) what he/she should be doing (e.g., finishing assignments).

1. Prepare a list of words and phrases from the student's reading material which he/she does not recognize. Have the student practice using phonics skills, context clues, picture clues, etc., to decode these words.

2. Have the student identify words and phrases that he/she does not recognize. Make these words the student's word list to be learned.

3. Teach the student word attack skills using a root word sight vocabulary to which various prefixes and suffixes may be added.

4. Reinforce the student each time he/she makes an attempt to sound out a word. As the student demonstrates success, gradually increase the number of attempts required for reinforcement.

5. Use a peer tutor to review word attack skills previously learned utilizing games and activities.

6. Make sure the student uses a sight vocabulary to support weaknesses in phonics skills.

7. Make sure the student develops an awareness of hearing word sounds (e.g., say, "Listen to these words, each of them begins with a /bl/ sound: blue, black, block, blast.").

8. Make sure the student develops an awareness of seeing letter combinations that make the sounds (e.g., have the student circle all of the words in a reading passage that begin with the /bl/ blend).

9. Provide practice with reading /bl/ words, /pl/ words, /pr/ words, etc., by presenting a high-interest paragraph or story that contains these words.

10. Demonstrate skills in decoding words (e.g., using contractions from conversation, write the abbreviated form of the word and the two complete words to show how to recognize the contraction).

11. Encourage the student to try several sounds to arrive at the correct answer (e.g., omit letters from a word used in context and give several choices to be filled in).

12. Write paragraphs and short stories requiring word attack skills the student is currently learning. These passages should be of high interest to the student using his/her name, family members, friends, pets, and interesting experiences.

13. Have the student dictate stories which are then put in print for him/her to read. Require the student to place an emphasis on word attack skills.

14. Have the student read high-interest signs, advertisements, notices, etc., from newspapers, magazines, movie promotions, etc., placing emphasis on word attack skills.

15. Make sure the student is practicing word attack skills which are directly related to high-interest reading activities (e.g., adventure, romance, mystery, sports, etc.).

16. Encourage the student to scan the newspapers, magazines, etc., and underline words he/she can decode using word attack skills (e.g., phonics, context clues, picture clues, etc.).

17. Require the student to verbally explain context clues in sentences to identify words not known.

18. Have the student use related pictures to help identify words in sentences not known.

19. Teach the student the most common prefixes and suffixes to add to root words he/she can identify.

20. When the student has difficulty with word attack skills, encourage him/her to continue working on developing word attack skills. Everyone has areas of weakness that require extra work.

21. Have the student be a peer tutor to teach a concept he/she has mastered to another student. This can serve as a reinforcement for the student.

22. Avoid placing the student in uncomfortable reading situations (e.g., reading aloud in a group, identifying that the student's reading group is the lowest level, etc.).

23. Record difficult reading material for the student to listen to as he/she reads along.

24. Use reading material with pictures and predictable reading to help the student master word attack skills.

25. Have the student read aloud to the teacher each day to provide evaluative feedback.

26. Introduce new words and their meanings to the student before he/she reads new materials. These may be entered in a vocabulary notebook kept by the student as a reference for new vocabulary words.

27. Teach the foundation for reading and writing in a sequential, systematic method with much positive reinforcement.

28. Allow the student to use the wall-mounted board so that teaching and learning become active. The student hears, writes, and sees the sounds in isolation and then joins them together to make words.

29. The student should practice vocabulary words from required reading material by writing them while saying the sounds.

30. Teach the student pronunciation rules (e.g., vowel sounds, blends, etc.). Start with simple words and sounds where the student achieves 95%-100% accuracy. Do not move on to more difficult words until practice, drill, and review of preceding lessons produces accuracy.

31. Use D'Nealian® handwriting when teaching sounds by hearing, writing, and saying. This eliminates many potential reversal problems.

32. Have the student memorize word meanings and practice spotting the most common prefixes and suffixes. Using a sheet of paper with a window cut in it, target the base word.

33. Play alphabet bingo with the student using phonics instead of letter names.

34. Teach the student individual consonant and vowel sounds.

1. Provide the student with a computer software program or a hand-held educational device to practice sight words he/she is learning. Drill and repetition is often necessary to commit words to memory.

2. Provide the student with a quiet area (e.g., carrel, study booth, etc.) where he/she may go to practice sight words.

3. Have the student read aloud to the teacher each day to provide evaluative feedback.

4. Start with simple words and sounds where the student achieves 95%-100% accuracy. Do not move on to more difficult words until practice, drill, and review of preceding lessons produces accuracy.

5. Teach the student word attack skills using a root word sight vocabulary to which various prefixes and suffixes may be added.

6. Reduce the emphasis on competition. Competitive activities may cause the student to hurry and make errors.

7. Teach the student individual consonant and vowel sounds.

8. When the student has difficulty with reading words on grade level, encourage him/her to continue working. Everyone has areas of weakness that require extra work.

9. Maintain mobility to be frequently near the student to provide reading assistance.

10. Have the student read high-interest signs, advertisements, notices, etc., from newspapers, movie promotions, magazines, etc.; placing an emphasis on reading skills.

11. Encourage classroom teachers to include more alternative learning experiences in their classrooms (e.g., lectures, demonstrations, guest speakers, field trips, discussions, visuals, DVDs, videos, etc.).

12. Provide the student with increased opportunity for help or assistance on academic tasks (e.g., peer tutoring, directions for work sent home, frequent interactions, etc.).

13. Make sure the student is practicing reading skills which are directly related to high-interest reading activities (e.g., adventure, romance, mystery, sports, etc.).

14. Make a list of main points from the student's reading material, written on the student's reading level.

15. Provide the student with many high-interest reading materials (e.g., comic books, magazines, etc.) to practice sight words.

16. Reduce the amount of material the student reads at one time (e.g., reduce reading material to single sentences on a page, a single paragraph, etc.). As the student demonstrates success, gradually increase the amount of material to be read at one time.

17. Record difficult reading material for the student to listen to as he/she reads along.

18. Modify or adjust reading materials to the student's ability level.

19. Set up a system of reinforcers, either tangible (e.g., computer time, helper for the day, etc.) or intangible (e.g., smile, praise, fist bump, etc.) to encourage the student to be more successful in reading.

20. Record lectures to provide an additional source of information for the student.

21. Encourage the student to read material with many illustrations and context clues to support learning new sight words.

22. Make sure that the reading demands of all subjects and assignments are within the ability level of the student. If they are not, modify or adjust the reading material to the student's ability level. A lower grade-level text may be an alternative.

23. Have the student dictate stories which are then put in print for him/her to read, placing an emphasis on reading skills.

24. Write paragraphs and short stories requiring skills the student is currently developing. These passages should be of high interest to the student using his/her name, family members, friends, pets, and interesting experiences.

25. Make available for the student a learning center area where a variety of information is available in content areas (e.g., the library may have a section with visuals, videos, recorded lectures, etc.; on such subjects as Pilgrims, the Civil War, the judicial system, etc.).

26. Make sure that the student's knowledge of a particular skill is being assessed rather than the student's ability to read directions, instructions, etc. Reading directions to the student may facilitate success.

27. Use D'Nealian® handwriting when teaching sounds by hearing, writing, and saying. This eliminates many potential reversal problems.

28. Use lower grade-level texts as alternative reading material in subject areas.

29. Outline reading material for the student using words and phrases on his/her reading level.

30. Allow students to use the wall-mounted board so that teaching and learning become active. The student hears, writes, and sees the sounds in isolation.

31. Choose a peer tutor to study with the student for quizzes, tests, etc.

32. Use a highlight marker to identify key words and phrases for the student. These words and phrases become the student's sight-word vocabulary.

33. Choose a peer tutor to practice sight words with the student to reinforce words learned.

34. Teach the student to use related learning experiences in his/her classes (e.g., DVDs, movies, recordings, demonstrations, discussions, videos, lectures, etc.). Encourage teachers to provide a variety of learning experiences for the student to facilitate learning grade level sight words.

35. Teach the student to use context clues to identify words and phrases he/she does not know.

36. Teach the student to use context clues to identify sight words the student is learning.

37. Use a sight-word vocabulary approach to teach the student key words (e.g., circle, underline, match, etc.) and phrases when reading directions and instructions.

38. Have the student practice vocabulary words from required reading material by writing the words while saying the sounds.

39. Use reading series material with high interest (e.g., adventure, romance, mystery, sports, etc.) and low vocabulary.

40. Have the student identify words and phrases that he/she does not recognize. Make these words the student's list of words to be learned.

41. Create a list of words and phrases from the student's reading material which he/she will not recognize (e.g., have the science teacher identify the words the student will not recognize in the following week's assignment). These words and phrases will become the student's list of reading words for the following week.

42 Loses place when reading

1. Have the student use a paper strip to move down the page as he/she reads each line.

2. Have the student place a ruler or paper strip under each line as he/she reads it. The student then moves the ruler or paper strip under the next line and so on.

3. Consider carefully the student's ability level and experience when expecting him/her to read large amounts of written information independently.

4. Have the student read aloud to maintain his/her place.

5. Have the student read aloud to the teacher each day. Provide evaluative feedback relative to maintaining his/her place while reading.

6. Have the student read aloud to the teacher each day to provide evaluative feedback relative to omissions.

7. Give written directions that are specific and simple to understand.

8. Choose a peer to assist the student in maintaining his/her place during reading activities.

9. Encourage the student to avoid ingesting any substance (e.g., drugs, alcohol, cold remedies, etc.) that might further alter his/her ability to track when reading.

10. Have the student's vision checked if it has not been recently checked.

11. Reduce the emphasis on competition. Competitive activities may cause the student to hurry and omit words or loose his/her place when reading.

12. Modify or adjust reading materials to the student's ability level.

13. Do not criticize when correcting the student; be honest yet supportive. Never cause the student to feel negatively about himself/herself.

14. Have the student read directions aloud to aid comprehension.

15. Help the student read directions and review what to do when he/she has difficulty following written directions.

16. Establish an environmental setting for the classroom that promotes optimal individual performance (e.g., quiet room, background music, fresh air, etc.).

17. Make a reading window for each textbook the student uses. The student moves the reading window down and across the page as he/she reads.

18. Provide a quiet place for the student to work (e.g., office space, a study carrel, etc.).

19. Avoid placing the student in uncomfortable reading situations (e.g., reading aloud in a group, identifying that the student's reading group is the lowest level, etc.).

20. Reduce the amount of information on a page (e.g., less print to read, fewer problems, isolate information that is presented to the student, etc.) if it is visually distracting for the student.

21. Make sure the student is paying attention when he/she is reading directions. Have him/her repeat the directions to check for understanding.

22. Reduce the amount of material the student reads at one time (e.g., reduce reading material to single sentences on a page, a single paragraph, etc.).

23. Verbally correct the student's omissions as often as possible so he/she correctly reads the reading material.

24. Have the student highlight or underline the material as he/she reads.

25. Have the student read verbally and strive for 95%-100% accuracy in maintaining his/her place.

26. Have the student read verbally, working for 95%-100% accuracy with no omissions.

27. Record the student's reading so he/she can hear omissions.

28. Record the student reading aloud. Play it back so that he/she can hear how successfully he/she maintained his/her place when reading.

29. Make sure that the reading demands of all subjects and assignments are within the ability level of the student. If they are not, modify or adjust the reading material to the student's ability level.

30. Assist the student in reading directions. As the student demonstrates success, gradually reduce the assistance and require the student to independently assume more responsibility.

31. In a small group setting, have the students point to all words as they are read verbally. Have a student read just one sentence, then move automatically to the next student without a break for discussion.

32. Enlarge the print the student is reading.

33. Make sure that the student's knowledge of a particular skill is being assessed rather than the student's ability to read directions, etc.

34. Provide extra time for the student to read directions.

35. Make a list of those words in which the student makes omissions. Have the student practice reading these words.

36. Give the student extra time to read a selection more than once. Emphasize comprehension rather than speed.

37. Have the student point to every word read to hold his/her place.

38. Have the student point to syllables, words, etc., while reading to recognize omissions.

39. Have the student point to syllables, words, etc., as he/she reads them to maintain his/her place.

40. Use a highlight marker to identify key syllables, words, etc., for the student. These words and phrases become the student's sight-word vocabulary.

41. Have the student outline, underline, or highlight important information in printed materials.

42. Correct the student's omissions verbally as often as possible so that he/she hears the correct version of the reading material.

43. Explain to the student when he/she does not maintain his/her place when reading exactly what he/she did wrong, what should have been done, and why.

1. Have the student's hearing checked if it has not been recently checked.

2. Have the student read and write friends' first names which include the sound-symbol relationships that he/she does not recognize.

3. Have the student say the sounds that consonants make as he/she points to them (e.g., "d" makes the /d/ sound, etc.).

4. Present the alphabet to the student on flash cards and have him/her make the sounds as the letters are flashed (e.g., "d" makes the /d/ sound, etc.). This is an appropriate activity for a peer tutor to conduct with the student each day.

5. Identify a sound the student does not know. Have the student circle all the words containing that sound in a paragraph or a page of a book.

6. Put each letter of the alphabet on an individual card. Have the student collect all the letters for which he/she knows the sound. The goal is to collect all the letters of the alphabet.

7. Provide the student with sounds (e.g., /d/, /b/, /p/, etc.) and have him/her write or otherwise identify the letters that make the sounds.

8. Start by teaching the student sounds in the student's first name only. When the student has mastered the sounds in his/her first name, go on to the last name, parents' names, etc.

9. Take every opportunity throughout the day to emphasize a designated sound for that day (e.g., identify the sound when speaking, writing, reading, etc.).

10. Identify a letter for the day. Have the student listen for the sound made by that letter and identify the sound-symbol relationship each time the sound is heard.

11. Practice, drill, and review every day.

12. Assign the student a sound-symbol relationship. Have the student use a highlight marker to identify each word in a passage in which the sound-symbol relationship appears.

13. Use an audio card reader to pair the sounds of letters with the symbols of letters.

14. Do not require the student to learn more information than he/she is capable of learning at any time.

15. Have the student be a peer tutor to teach a concept he/she has mastered to another student. This can serve as reinforcement for the student.

16. Review daily those skills previously introduced.

17. Use both auditory and visual cues to help the student master sound-symbol relationships (i.e., the letter "a," a picture of an apple, and the sound the letter "a" makes).

18. Have the student make the sounds of letters as he/she writes words containing the letters (e.g., /d/ /a/ /d/).

19. Provide the student with a desktop chart of sounds. The student should be instructed to point to and say the sound the teacher says.

20. Have the student make sentences with words that begin with only one target letter sound (e.g., Tongue twisters tease Tootsie's tonsils.).

21. Teach intensive phonics as a foundation for reading, spelling, and handwriting.

22. Have the student practice daily those sound-symbol relationships he/she does not know.

1. Set up a system of motivators, either tangible (e.g., extra computer time, free time, etc.) or intangible (e.g., smile, fist bump, praise, etc.), to encourage the student to be more successful in reading.

2. Prepare a list of words and phrases from the student's reading material which he/she does not recognize. Have the student practice phonics skills using these words.

3. Have the student identify words and phrases that he/she does not recognize. Make these words the student's word list to be learned.

4. Teach the student word attack skills using a root word sight vocabulary to which various prefixes and suffixes may be added.

5. Reinforce the student each time he/she makes an attempt to sound out a word. As the student demonstrates success, gradually increase the number of attempts required for reinforcement.

6. Use a peer tutor to review phonics concepts previously instructed, by utilizing games and activities.

7. Teach the student to use context clues to identify words and phrases he/she does not know.

8. Make sure the student uses a sight vocabulary to support weaknesses in phonics skills.

9. Make sure the student develops an awareness of hearing word sounds (e.g., say, "Listen to these words. Each of them begins with a /bl/ blend: *blue, black, block, blast*.").

10. Make sure the student develops an awareness of seeing letter combinations that produce sounds (e.g., have the student circle all of the words in a reading passage that begin with the /bl/ blend).

11. Provide practice with reading /bl/ words, /pl/ words, /pr/ words, etc., by presenting a high-interest paragraph or story that contains these words.

12. Demonstrate skills in decoding words (e.g., using contractions from conversation, write the abbreviated form of the word and the two complete words to show how to recognize the contraction, etc.).

13. Encourage the student to try several sounds to arrive at a correct answer (e.g., omit letters from a word used in context and give several choices to be filled in).

14. Encourage the student to scan newspapers, magazines, etc., and underline learned phonics elements.

15. Develop a list of phonics sounds the student needs to master. Remove sounds from the list as the student demonstrates mastery of phonics skills.

16. Write paragraphs and short stories requiring phonics skills the student is currently learning. These passages should be of high interest to the student using his/her name, family members, friends, pets, and interesting experiences.

17. Have the student dictate stories which are then put in print for him/her to read, placing an emphasis on reading skills.

18. Have the student read high-interest signs, advertisements, notices, etc., from newspapers, magazines, movie promotions, etc., placing an emphasis on phonics skills.

19. Make sure the student is practicing phonics skills which are directly related to high-interest reading activities (e.g., adventure, romance, mystery, sports, etc.).

20. Have the student make a list of phonics skills that have been mastered (e.g., words he/she can identify by sounding out). The student continues to add to the list as he/she identifies more and more words.

21. Teach the student all beginning sounds before expecting him/her to blend sounds into words.

22. Record difficult reading material for the student to listen to as he/she reads along.

23. Make sure that the reading demands of all subjects and assignments are within the ability level of the student. If they are not, modify or adjust the reading material to the student's ability level.

24. Make sure that the student's knowledge of a particular skill is being assessed rather than the student's ability to read directions, instructions, etc. Reading directions to the student may facilitate success.

25. Provide the student with verbal reminders or prompts when he/she is unsure of sounds that letters make when blended together.

26. Reduce the amount of information on a page (e.g., less print to read, fewer pictures to look at, etc.) if it is visually distracting for the student.

27. Avoid placing the student in uncomfortable reading situations (e.g., reading aloud in a group, identifying that the student's reading group is the lowest level, etc.).

28. Determine if the student has instant recall of all consonant and vowel sounds and combinations.

29. Practice active learning at the wall-mounted board by having students hear, write, and read words.

30. Practice, drill, and review every day.

31. Have students say sounds as they write them.

32. Allow students to write a story, paragraph, or sentence using phonetic shorthand. This narrowing of sounds helps the student to identify the sounds with letters used to construct words.

1. Require all students in a small group to point, look, and listen when other group members read verbally.

2. Have the student develop a sight vocabulary of root words to be able to decode words with prefixes and suffixes and increase his/her word attack skills.

3. Have the student place a ruler or paper strip under each line as he/she reads it. The student then moves the ruler or paper strip under the next line and so on.

4. Correct the student's omissions, additions, substitutions, and reversals verbally as often as possible so that he/she correctly reads the reading material.

5. Have the student read aloud to the teacher each day. Provide evaluative feedback relative to his/her omissions, additions, substitutions, and reversals while reading.

6. Provide the student with an alphabet strip on his/her desk to use as a reference for correct letter formation to reduce reversal-related errors when reading.

7. Have the student use an electronic speaking dictionary to find word definitions and pronunciations.

8. Use a sight-word vocabulary approach to teach the student key words (e.g., circle, underline, match, etc.) and phrases when reading directions and instructions.

9. Instruct the student to ask for clarification if he/she does not understand written directions.

10. Teach the student word attack skills using a root word sight vocabulary to which various prefixes and suffixes may be added.

11. Encourage the student to avoid ingesting any substance (e.g., drugs, alcohol, cold remedies, etc.) that might further alter his/her ability to read material accurately.

12. Use a kinesthetic approach by having the child point to every word as he/she reads verbally. Stop the student for immediate correction if necessary, while continuing with ample praise for hard work and success.

13. Have the student's vision checked if it has not been recently checked.

14. Reduce the emphasis on competition. Competitive activities may cause the student to omit, add, substitute, or reverse letters, words, or sounds when reading.

15. Do not criticize when correcting the student; be honest yet supportive. Never cause the student to feel negatively about himself/herself.

16. Have the student ask for help when he/she needs it.

17. Establish an environmental setting for the classroom that promotes optimal individual performance (e.g., quiet room, background music, fresh air, etc.).

18. Teach reading, spelling, and handwriting simultaneously.

19. Reduce the amount of information on a page (e.g., less print to read, fewer problems, isolate information that is presented to the student, etc.) if it is visually distracting for the student.

20. Make sure the student is learning basic word lists to assist in reading.

21. Record difficult reading material for the student to listen to while he/she reads along.

22. Reduce the amount of material the student reads at one time (e.g., reduce reading material to single sentences on a page, a single paragraph, etc.). As the student demonstrates success, gradually increase the amount of material to be read at one time.

23. Modify or adjust reading materials to the student's ability level.

24. Set up a system of reinforcers, either tangible (e.g., extra computer time, helper for the day, etc.) or intangible (e.g., smile, fist bump, praise, etc.), to encourage the student to be more successful in reading.

25. Keep a simple picture-coded phonics chart available at all times for the student to use when decoding words.

26. Record the student reading aloud. Play it back so that he/she can hear omissions, additions, substitutions, or reversals.

27. Assist the student in reading written information. As the student demonstrates success, gradually decrease the assistance and require the student to independently assume more responsibility.

28. Make sure that the reading demands of all subjects and assignments are within the ability level of the student. If they are not, modify or adjust the reading material to the student's ability level.

29. Make sure that the student's knowledge of a particular skill is being assessed rather than the student's ability to read directions, instructions, etc. Reading directions, instructions, etc., to the student can facilitate success.

30. Have the student write those words in which he/she omits, adds, substitutes, or reverses letters or sounds. Have the student practice reading those words.

31. Make a list of those words which the student has made omission, addition, substitution, or reversal errors when reading. Have the student practice reading those words.

32. Use a highlight marker to identify key syllables, words, etc., for the student. These words and phrases become the student's sight-word vocabulary.

33. Use a cardboard window to focus attention on a single line as you read.

34. Have the student point to syllables, words, etc., as he/she reads them to help him/her recognize omissions, additions, substitutions, or reversals.

35. Teach the student to use context clues when reading to aid word recognition and meaning. These skills will be particularly helpful when he/she is experiencing difficulty with reversals.

36. Teach the student basic word lists (e.g., Dolch) to assist in reading.

37. Make a list of words and phrases from the student's reading material which he/she will not recognize (e.g., have the science teacher identify the words and phrases the student will not recognize in the following week's assignment). These words and phrases will become the student's list for reading activities for the following week.

38. Have the student identify words and phrases that he/she does not recognize. Make these words part of the student's sight word list to be learned.

39. Record pronunciations of words which the student commonly mispronounces so that he/she can hear the correct pronunciation.

40. Have the student read written information more than once. Emphasize accuracy not speed.

41. Provide extra time for the student to read directions.

1. Have the student make a list of new words he/she has learned. The student can add words to the list at his/her own rate.

2. Provide the student with a quiet place (e.g., carrel, study booth, etc.) where he/she may go to participate in reading activities.

3. When the student encounters a new word or one whose meaning he/she does not know, have the student construct sentences in which the word is used in the correct context.

4. Provide the student with a variety of visual teaching materials to support word comprehension (e.g., DVDs, pictures, charts, etc.).

5. Have the student identify a word a day that he/she does not understand. Have the student define the word and require him/her to use that word throughout the day in various situations.

6. Have the student maintain a vocabulary notebook with definitions of words whose meanings he/she does not know.

7. Have the student develop a picture dictionary representing those words which are difficult for him/her to recognize.

8. Anticipate new vocabulary words and teach them in advance of reading a selection.

9. Teach the student synonyms and antonyms of familiar words to strengthen his/her vocabulary.

10. Teach new vocabulary words and concepts prior to reading a selection.

11. Reinforce the student for asking the meanings of words he/she does not understand.

12. Reduce the emphasis on competition. Competitive activities may make it difficult for the student to comprehend what he/she reads.

13. Have the student look for vocabulary definitions within the material read (e.g., The long house, an Indian dwelling, was used by Eastern Indians.).

14. Have the student look for vocabulary words in italics, boldface, headings, and captions.

15. Choose a peer to help the student, when needed, with the meanings of words not understood.

16. Have the student read high-interest signs, advertisements, notices, etc., from newspapers, magazines, movie promotions, etc.; placing an emphasis on vocabulary skills.

17. Avoid placing the student in uncomfortable reading situations (e.g., reading aloud in a group, identifying that the student's reading group is the lowest level, etc.).

18. Label objects and activities in the classroom to help the student associate words with tangible aspects of the environment.

19. Reduce the amount of information on a page (e.g., less print to read, fewer pictures, etc.) if it is visually distracting for the student.

20. Make sure the student is developing a sight-word vocabulary of the most commonly used words in his/her reading material.

21. Make sure the student is reading material on his/her ability level.

22. Design classroom games (e.g., *Jeopardy!*, *Pictionary*, etc.) to review vocabulary words periodically.

23. Make sure the student learns dictionary skills to independently find meanings of words.

24. Make sure the student learns the meaning of all commonly used prefixes and suffixes.

25. Reinforce the student for looking up the definitions of words he/she does not understand.

26. Make a list of main points from the student's reading material, written on the student's reading level.

27. Modify or adjust reading material to the student's ability level.

28. Have the student list new or difficult words in categories such as people, food, animals, etc.

29. Have the student teach new vocabulary to his/her peers (e.g., require the student to be creative by showing, acting out, drawing or making an example of the word).

30. Have the student match objects or pictures with sounds produced by that object (e.g., phone ring, vacuum cleaner, etc.).

31. Set up a system of reinforcers either tangible (e.g., extra computer time, helper for the day, etc.) or intangible (e.g., smile, fist bump, praise, etc.) to encourage the student to be more successful in reading.

32. Prepare a written list of vocabulary words. Verbally present a sentence with a blank and have the student determine which vocabulary word should be used.

33. Have the student verbally paraphrase material that has just been read to assess comprehension.

34. Review new vocabulary words periodically with the student (e.g., weekly or bi-weekly).

35. Make it pleasant and positive for the student to ask the meanings or look up words he/she does not understand. Reinforce the student by assisting him/her, congratulating, praising, etc.

36. Teach the student to predict what will happen in the story based on new vocabulary words and the title page.

37. Teach the student to read for the main point in sentences, paragraphs, etc.

38. Make sure that the reading demands of all subjects and assignments are within the ability level of the student. If they are not, modify or adjust the reading material to the student's ability level.

39. Have the student record what he/she reads to facilitate comprehension by replaying and listening to the material.

40. Prior to reading a selection, familiarize the student with the general content of the story to develop a point of reference. Through this approach, introduce new vocabulary words.

41. Have the student dictate stories which are put in print for him/her to read, placing an emphasis on comprehension skills.

42. Write paragraphs and short stories requiring skills the student is currently developing. These paragraphs should be of high interest to the student using his/her name, family members, friends, pets, and interesting experiences.

43. Before reading, tell the student what he/she is to find in the story (e.g., who are the main characters, what are the main events, etc.).

44. Do not require the student to learn more information than he/she is capable of learning at any time.

45. Make sure that the student's knowledge of a particular skill is being assessed rather than the student's ability to read directions, instructions, etc. Reading directions, instructions, etc., to the student can facilitate success.

46. Use a lower grade-level text as alternative reading material in subject areas.

47. Reduce distracting stimuli in the environment to facilitate the student's ability to concentrate on what he/she is reading (e.g., place the student on the front row, provide a carrel or office space away from distractions). This is used as a means of reducing distracting stimuli and not as a form of punishment.

48. Outline reading material for the student using words and phrases on his/her reading level.

49. Introduce new words and their meanings to the student before he/she reads new material.

50. Give the student time to read a selection more than once. Emphasize comprehension rather than speed.

51. Write notes and letters to the student to provide reading material which he/she will want to read for comprehension. Students may be encouraged to write each other notes and letters at a time set aside each day, week, etc.

52. Have the student outline, underline, or highlight important vocabulary in reading material.

53. Make sure the student underlines or circles words not understood. These words will become the student's vocabulary assignment for the week.

54. Use the current vocabulary words being studied by the student in daily classroom conversation.

55. Teach the student to use context clues to identify words not understood.

56. Use a sight-word vocabulary approach to teach the student key words (e.g., circle, underline, match, etc.) and phrases when reading directions and instructions.

57. Have the student match vocabulary words with pictures representing the words.

58. Have the student review vocabulary words by providing related clues. The student then identifies the vocabulary word.

59. Use reading series material with high interest (e.g., adventure, romance, mystery, sports, etc.) and low vocabulary.

60. Have the student identify words he/she does not comprehend. Have him/her find the definitions of these words in the dictionary.

61. Require the student to use new vocabulary words in follow-up assignments (e.g., have the student use these words on written assignments, crossword puzzles, etc.).

1. Provide the student with a dictionary and require him/her to find the definitions of those words he/she did not recognize.

2. Have the student maintain a list with definitions of those words he/she most frequently fails to recognize in different contexts.

3. Provide the student with a quiet place (e.g., carrel, study booth, etc.) where he/she may go to participate in reading activities.

4. Have the student read aloud to the teacher each day to provide evaluative feedback.

5. Reduce the emphasis on competition. Competitive activities may cause the student to hurry and not recognize words in a particular context.

6. Identify words the student does not recognize in different contexts and put these words on flash cards. Have the student match these words to the same words in sentences, paragraphs, short stories, etc.

7. Make a reading window for the student. The student moves the reading window down and across the page as he/she reads.

8. Avoid placing the student in uncomfortable reading situations (e.g., reading aloud in a group, identifying that the student's reading group is the lowest level, etc.).

9. Reduce the amount of information on a page (e.g., less print to read, fewer pictures to look at, etc.) if it is causing visual distractions for the student.

10. Make sure the student is reading material on his/her ability level.

11. Provide the student with large-print reading material to facilitate the student's success in recognizing words in different contexts.

12. Record difficult reading material for the student to listen to as he/she reads along.

13. Require the student to read a selection each day which includes the vocabulary currently being studied.

14. Have the student read short sentences to make it easier to recognize words in different contexts. As the student demonstrates success, present longer sentences.

15. Write paragraphs and short stories using those words the student most frequently fails to recognize in different contexts. These paragraphs should be of high interest to the student using his/her name, family members, friends, pets, and interesting experiences.

16. Use a lower grade-level text as alternative reading material in subject areas.

17. Reduce distracting stimuli in the environment to facilitate the student's ability to concentrate on what he/she is reading (e.g., place the student on the front row, provide a carrel or office space away from distractions). This is used as a means of reducing distracting stimuli and not as a form of punishment.

18. Have the student list those words he/she most frequently fails to recognize into categories such as people, food, animals, etc., to help the student recognize those words in different contexts.

19. Write notes and letters to the student to provide reading material which includes words the student frequently has difficulty with.

20. Use daily drill activities to help the student memorize vocabulary words.

21. Teach the student to use context clues to identify words not understood.

22. Highlight or underline those words the student most frequently fails to recognize in different contexts.

23. Highlight or underline those words in reading material the student is unable to recognize. Have the student identify those words as he/she reads them.

1. Have the student be a peer tutor to teach younger students reading or to read verbally to younger students.

2. Pair the class with a lower grade-level class on a weekly basis. Let each student read to a younger child.

3. Make reading materials easily accessible to the student in the classroom.

4. Make visiting the library an enjoyable weekly experience.

5. Incorporate listening skills/techniques as part of the daily routine in reading class (e.g., listening center where the student reads along as a recording plays, teacher reads to the student, students read to each other, etc.).

6. Offer memberships in paperback book clubs to the student.

7. Encourage interest in reading by having students share interesting things they have read. This should be informal sharing in a group and not necessarily a book report.

8. Find a book series by an author that the student finds enjoyable. Make these books available for the student to read.

9. To encourage reading, make sure that the student knows he/she is not reading for assessment purposes but for enjoyment.

10. Read excerpts of your favorite children's books to entice the student to read the same book.

11. Encourage the student to find books about different subjects being taught or discussed (e.g., when studying electricity, encourage the student to read a book about Thomas Edison, etc.).

12. Assist the student in finding reading material which fits his/her interests and reading level. The student may not be comfortable or able to find books by himself/herself in the library.

13. Record reading material for the student to listen to as he/she reads along.

14. Provide the student with high-interest reading material that is also short in length so the student can finish reading the material without difficulty.

15. Have the student read high-interest signs, advertisements, notices, etc., from newspapers, magazines, movie promotions, etc.

16. Encourage interesting reading by highlighting an author a month. The teacher should share information about an author, read books by the author and have additional titles by the author available for independent reading.

17. Develop a reading area in the classroom that is appealing to the student (e.g., tent, bean bag chair, carpeted area, etc.).

18. While teaching a unit in a content area, bring in related fiction or nonfiction books to share with your students to spark interest in reading.

19. Avoid placing the student in uncomfortable reading situations (e.g., reading aloud in a group, identifying that the student's reading group is the lowest level, etc.).

20. Include predictable reading books in the class library. Predictability can make books more appealing to beginning readers and build confidence.

21. Make sure the student is reading material on his/her ability level.

22. Have the student read lower grade-level stories to younger children to build his/her feelings of confidence relative to reading.

23. Provide the student with many high-interest reading materials (e.g., comic books, magazines relating to sports, fashion, etc.).

24. Expose the student to materials with large print. Large print can appear less intimidating to the student who does not choose to read.

25. Modify or adjust reading materials to the student's ability level.

26. Write periodic letters or notes to the student to encourage him/her to write back.

27. Set up a system of reinforcers, either tangible (e.g., extra computer time, helper for the day, etc.) or intangible (e.g., smile, fist bump, praise, etc.), to encourage the student to be more successful in reading.

28. Have the student dictate stories which are then put in print for him/her to read.

29. Provide the student a quiet place (e.g., carrel, study booth, office, etc.) where he/she may go to participate in reading activities.

30. Read, or have someone read, high-interest material to the student to promote his/her interest in reading.

31. Encourage the student to read material with many illustrations and a limited amount of print. As the student demonstrates success, gradually decrease the number of pictures and increase the amount of print.

32. Encourage parents to make reading material on the student's interest and reading level available to the student at home.

33. Teach the student necessary reading skills before expecting him/her to read independently.

34. Write paragraphs and short stories for the student. These passages should be of high interest to the student using his/her name, family members, friends, pets, and interesting experiences.

35. Set aside a fixed or random time (e.g., a half-hour daily, an hour a week, etc.) for reading. Everyone, teacher included, chooses a book that he/she likes and reads it for pleasure.

36. Conduct a survey of the student's interests to provide reading material in those interest areas.

37. Encourage parents to read to their child at home and to have their child read to them. Encourage parents to read for their own enjoyment to serve as a model for their child.

38. Have the student write to the author of material he/she reads to encourage an interest in reading more by the same author.

39. Provide reading material in various settings (e.g., art books in the art center, science books in the science center, weather books in the weather center, etc.).

49   Does not discriminate between similar letters and words

1. Have the student's hearing checked if it has not been recently checked.

2. Each day have the student practice those letters and words he/she cannot discriminate.

3. Take every opportunity throughout the day to emphasize a designated letter or word the student cannot discriminate (e.g., identify the sound when speaking, writing, reading, etc.).

4. Make sure the student looks closely at word endings and beginnings to discriminate similar words (e.g., cap and cat).

5. Make a list of words the student cannot discriminate. Have the student and a peer work together with flash cards to develop the student's ability to recognize the differences in the letters and words.

6. Record stories and paragraphs the student can listen to while reading along.

7. Have the student read aloud to the teacher each day to provide evaluative feedback relative to his/her ability to discriminate letters and words.

8. Verbally correct the student as often as possible when he/she does not discriminate between letters and words so he/she hears the correct version of the reading material.

9. Have the student write those letters and words he/she has trouble discriminating so he/she has a greater opportunity to conceptualize the correct version.

10. Teach the student to use context clues in reading. These skills will be particularly helpful when he/she is unable to discriminate between letters and words.

11. Identify a letter or word each day which the student has difficulty discriminating. Have the student underline or highlight that letter or word each time he/she reads it that day.

12. Use highlight markers (e.g., pink and yellow) to have the student mark the letters and words in a passage he/she does not discriminate (e.g., all "m"s marked with the pink marker and all "n"s marked with the yellow marker).

13. Provide the student with an alphabet strip at his/her desk to use as a reference when reading or performing assignments.

14. Reduce the emphasis on competition. Competitive activities may cause the student to hurry and not discriminate between similar letters and words.

15. Have the student cut letters out of magazines or newspapers and glue the letters in sequence to make words, sentences, etc.

16. Make sure that the student's knowledge of a particular skill is being assessed rather than the student's ability to read directions, instructions, etc.

17. Make sure that the reading demands of all subjects and assignments are within the ability level of the student. If they are not, modify or adjust the reading material to the student's ability level.

1. Set up a system of reinforcers, either tangible (e.g., computer time, helper for the day, etc.) or intangible (e.g., praise, fist bump, smile, etc.), to encourage the student to learn the letters of the alphabet.

2. Provide the student with an alphabet strip at his/her desk to use as a reference when reading or performing assignments.

3. Each day have the student print those letters of the alphabet he/she does not know.

4. Choose a peer to work with the student on one letter of the alphabet each day (e.g., tracing the letter, printing the letter, recognizing the letter in words in a paragraph, etc.).

5. Have the student read and write friends' first names which include letters the student does not recognize.

6. Introduce letters to the student as partners (e.g., Aa, Bb, Cc, Dd, etc.).

7. Have the student say the letters of the alphabet in sequence. Repeat by rote several times a day.

8. Present the alphabet to the student on flash cards. This is an appropriate activity for a peer tutor to conduct with the student each day.

9. Identify a letter the student does not know. Have the student find the letter in all the words in a paragraph or on a page of a book.

10. Put each letter of the alphabet on an individual card. Have the student collect and keep the letters he/she knows with the goal to collect all the letters of the alphabet.

11. Start by teaching the names of letters in the student's first name only. When the student has mastered the letters in his/her first name, go on to the last name, parents' names, etc.

12. Give the student a word which begins with each letter of the alphabet (e.g., apple, bad, cat, etc.). Go over several of the words each day, stressing the alphabet letters being learned.

13. Take every opportunity throughout the day to emphasize a designated letter for that day (e.g., identify the letter when speaking, writing, reading, etc.).

14. Use daily drills to help the student memorize the alphabet.

15. Avoid placing the student in uncomfortable reading situations (e.g., reading aloud in a group, identifying that the student's reading group is the lowest level, etc.).

51 Understands what is read to him/her but not what he/she reads silently

1. Pair the student with a peer to summarize material read to answer the questions "Who, What, Where, When, How, and Why."

2. Have the student read aloud when reading to himself/herself.

3. Use a sight-word vocabulary approach to teach the student key words (e.g., circle, underline, match, etc.) and phrases when reading directions and instructions.

4. Use lower grade-level texts as alternative reading material in subject areas.

5. Have the student practice comprehension skills which are directly related to high-interest reading activities (e.g., adventure, romance, mystery, sports, etc.).

6. Have the student look for action words (e.g., sailed, discovered, founded, etc.).

7. Have the student look for direction words (e.g., circle, underline, choose, list, etc.).

8. Have the student look for key words (e.g., Christopher Columbus, Spain, New World, etc.).

9. After reading a selection, have the student complete a semantic map answering the questions "Who, What, Where, When, How, and Why."

10. Have the student read high-interest signs, advertisements, notices, etc., from newspapers, magazines, movie promotions, etc., placing emphasis on comprehension skills.

11. Teach the student to identify main points in material he/she has read to assess comprehension.

12. Have the student answer in writing the questions "Who, What, Where, When, How, and Why" using the Flash Card Study Aid.

13. Have the student read independently each day to practice reading skills.

14. Reduce the amount of information on a page (e.g., less print to read, fewer pictures to look at, etc.) if it is causing visual distractions for the student.

15. Make sure the student is reading material on his/her ability level.

16. Make sure the student is practicing comprehension skills which are directly related to high-interest reading activities (e.g., adventure, romance, mystery, sports, etc.).

17. Make a list of main points from the student's reading material, written on the student's reading level.

18. Modify or adjust reading material to the student's ability level.

19. Record difficult reading material for the student to listen to as he/she reads along.

20. Have the student take notes while reading to facilitate comprehension.

21. Teach the student meanings of abbreviations to assist in comprehending material read.

22. Have the student underline or highlight important points in reading material.

23. Have the student verbally paraphrase material he/she has just read to assess his/her comprehension.

24. Underline or highlight important points before the student reads the assigned material silently.

25. Teach new vocabulary words prior to having the student read the material.

26. Have the student read progressively longer segments of reading material to build comprehension skills (e.g., begin with a single paragraph and progress to several paragraphs, short stories, chapters, etc.).

27. Provide the student a quiet place (e.g., carrel, study booth, etc.) where he/she may go to participate in reading activities.

28. Make sure that the reading demands of all subjects and assignments are within the ability level of the student. If they are not, modify or adjust the reading material to the student's ability level.

29. Teach the student when reading to look for key words and main ideas that answer "Who, What, Where, When, How, and Why" (e.g., "Christopher Columbus sailed from Spain to discover the New World during the year 1492.").

30. Give the student high-interest reading material on his/her ability level (e.g., comic books, adventure stories, etc.) requiring him/her to answer the questions "Who, What, Where, When, How, and Why."

31. Have the student outline reading material using the Outline Form.

32. Have the student practice reading and following written directions to facilitate comprehension (e.g., following a recipe, following directions to put together a model, etc.).

33. Have the student record what he/she reads to facilitate comprehension by replaying and listening to the material read.

34. Prior to reading a selection, familiarize the student with the general content of the story (e.g., if the selection is about elephants, brainstorm and discuss elephants to develop a point of reference).

35. Have the student dictate stories which are then put in print for him/her to read, placing emphasis on comprehension skills.

36. Write paragraphs and short stories requiring reading skills the student is currently developing. These passages should be of high interest to the student using his/her name, family members, friends, pets, and interesting experiences.

37. Do not require the student to learn more information than he/she is capable of learning at any time.

38. Outline reading material the student reads silently using words and phrases on his/her reading level.

39. Make available for the student a learning center where a variety of information is available in content areas (e.g., the library may have a selection of visuals, videos, recorded lectures, etc.).

40. Make sure that the student's knowledge of a particular skill is being assessed rather than the student's ability to read directions, instructions, etc. Reading directions, instructions, etc., to the student may facilitate his/her success.

41. Reduce distracting stimuli in the environment to facilitate the student's ability to concentrate on what he/she is reading (e.g., place the student in the front row, provide a carrel or office space away from distractions, etc.). This is used as a means of reducing distracting stimuli and not as a form of punishment.

42. When reading verbally with the student, pause at various points to discuss material read up to that point. Have the student predict what will happen next before proceeding.

43. Write notes and letters to the student to provide reading material which he/she will want to read for comprehension. Students may be encouraged to write each other notes and letters at a time set aside each day, once a week, etc.

44. Give the student time to read a selection more than once. Emphasize comprehension rather than speed.

45. Teach the student to think about the reading selection and predict what will happen next, prior to completing the selection.

46. Have the student outline, underline, or highlight important points in reading material.

47. Teach the student to use context clues to identify words and phrases he/she does not know.

48. Stop at various points while the student is reading silently to check for comprehension.

49. Use reading series materials with high-interest (e.g., adventure, romance, mystery, sports, etc.) and low vocabulary.

52   Has difficulty recalling the sequence of events in stories read

1. Check the student's understanding of first, next, and last by having the student tell what happens during daily events in first, next, and last order.

2. Provide the student with a recording of the story to listen to as he/she reads along.

3. Have the student write the main events of stories as he/she reads them.

4. Have the student read one paragraph of a new story and make notes on the events, then read the next paragraph and make notes, etc.

5. Model making notes of the sequence of events as a you read selections with the student.

6. Have the student paraphrase the sequence of events in each paragraph read. The teacher can transcribe the paraphrased sequence or the student can record it.

7. Informally assess the student's auditory and visual short-term memory skills to determine which is the stronger. Use the student's stronger mode to facilitate the retention of sequential information.

8. Give the student one task to perform at a time. Introduce the next task only when the student has successfully completed the previous task.

9. Teach the student to visualize information as if it were a movie, then play it back mentally when he/she needs to verbalize it.

10. Have the student practice repetition of information to increase short-term memory skills (e.g., repeating names, phone numbers, dates of events, etc.).

11. Teach the student to identify the main idea of a story and causal relationships within the story to facilitate the recall of information in the correct order.

12. Have the student practice remembering sequences by engaging in sequential activities which are purposeful to him/her (e.g., operating equipment, following recipes, opening a combination lock, etc.).

13. Use a flannel board or Colorforms® to practice sequencing a familiar story or a familiar action.

14. Have the student be a peer tutor to teach another student a concept he/she has mastered.

15. Provide practice in sequencing using a computer software program that gives the student immediate feedback.

16. Make sure the student has mastery of reading concepts at each level before introducing a new skill level.

17. Make sure the student is not required to learn more information than he/she is capable of learning at any time.

18. Reduce the emphasis on competition. Competitive activities may cause the student to hurry and commit errors.

19. Reduce the amount of information on a page if it is causing visual distractions for the student (e.g., have less print to read, isolate information that is presented to the student, etc.).

20. Identify the student's most effective learning mode and use it consistently to increase the probability of understanding (e.g., If the student does not understand information presented verbally, present it in written form. If the student has difficulty understanding written information, present it verbally.).

21. Give the student time to read a selection more than once, emphasizing comprehension rather than speed.

22. Use reading series materials with high interest (e.g., adventures, romances, mysteries, athletics, etc.).

23. Write notes and letters to the student to provide reading material which he/she will want to read for comprehension. Students may be encouraged to write each other notes and letters at a time set aside each day, week, etc.

24. Write paragraphs and short stories requiring skills the student is currently developing. These passages should be of high interest to the student using his/her name, family members, friends, pets, and interesting experiences.

25. Make sure that the reading demands of all subjects and assignments are within the ability level of the student. If not, modify or adjust the reading material to the student's ability level. A lower-level text may be an alternative.

26. Have the student practice a new skill or assignment alone or with an aide, the teacher, or a peer before the entire group attempts the activity or before performing for a grade.

27. Speak to the student to explain (a) what the student is doing wrong and (b) what the student should be doing.

28. Reinforce the student for sequencing: (a) give the student a tangible reward (e.g., classroom privileges, line leading, passing out materials, five minutes free time, etc.) or (b) give the student an intangible reward (e.g., praise, fist bump, smile, etc.) for accurately demonstrating correct sequencing activities.

29. Communicate with parents (e.g., notes home, phone calls, etc.) to share information about the student's progress. Parents may reinforce the student at home for improvements in sequencing events at school.

30. Evaluate the appropriateness of the task to determine (a) if the task is too difficult and (b) if the length of time scheduled to complete the task is adequate.

31. Choose a peer to model sequencing of events for the student and also to assist the student with directions.

32. Allow the student to perform alternative versions of the assignments. As the student demonstrates success, gradually introduce more components of the regular assignments until those can be performed successfully.

53 Does not demonstrate an understanding of alphabetical order

1. When lining up or dismissing the students, ask each student to tell the letter that comes next in alphabetical order. The students are dismissed as they correctly name each letter.

2. After students are proficient at naming succeeding letters, have students name preceding letters.

3. Using a small group, have one student begin saying the alphabet. When the teacher points to another student, the first student becomes quiet and the second student begins saying the alphabet where the first student stopped.

4. Provide the student with an alphabet strip at his/her desk to use as a reference.

5. Have the student say the alphabet as he/she points to each letter in alphabetical order.

6. Have the student alphabetize 26 words, each beginning with a different letter of the alphabet.

7. After the student has mastered alphabetizing by the first letter of words, have the student alphabetize 26 words which begin with the same first letter but have each letter of the alphabet represented as the second letter (e.g., Aaron, able, acid, adapt, etc.).

8. Have the student begin alphabetizing with only two words. Add a third word and so on as the student further develops an understanding of alphabetical order.

9. Have the student be a peer tutor to teach another student a concept he/she has mastered.

10. Provide practice in alphabetizing by using a computer software program that gives the student immediate feedback.

11. Make sure the student has mastery of alphabetizing concepts at each level before introducing a new skill level (e.g., alphabetizing to the first letter, second letter, third letter, etc.).

12. Make sure that the student is not required to learn more information than he/she is capable of learning at any time.

13. Reduce the emphasis on competition. Competitive activities may cause the student to hurry and commit errors.

14. Review, on a daily basis, those skills, concepts, tasks, etc., which have been previously introduced.

15. Reinforce the student for alphabetizing: (a) give the student a tangible reward (e.g., classroom privileges, line leading, passing out materials, five minutes free time, etc.) or (b) give the student an intangible reward (e.g., praise, fist bump, smile, etc.) for demonstrating an understanding of alphabetizing.

16. Speak to the student to explain (a) what he/she is doing wrong and (b) what he/she should be doing.

17. Evaluate the appropriateness of the task to determine (a) if the task is too difficult and (b) if the length of time scheduled to complete the task is adequate.

18. Choose a peer to model alphabetizing for the student and also to assist the student with directions.

19. Have the student practice a new skill or assignment alone, with an aide, the teacher, or a peer before the entire group attempts the activity or before performing for a grade.

1. Make sure the student understands that the first sentence of a paragraph should always be considered as a possible topic sentence and main idea.

2. Make sure the student understands that a topic sentence or main idea for a paragraph will always contain one or more of the following, which will be the whole idea of the paragraph: *Who, What, Where, When, How.*

3. Make sure the student understands that the topic sentence or main idea can be determined by choosing the one sentence in a paragraph that makes sense when it stands alone (e.g., in the process of elimination, isolate each sentence and decide if it tells what the whole paragraph is about).

4. Have the student write a paragraph about a favorite topic and use a triangle to determine the hierarchy of sentences:
- (1) Most important (topic),
- (2) Most important detail,
- (3) Less important detail, and
- (4) Incidental detail (e.g., could be left out without changing the paragraph meaning).

5. Have the student employ the satellite system to identify the main idea of a paragraph. The student should choose the one word or phrase around which the entire paragraph is built. Then the student should name the other details that describe that word or phrase. This allows the student to focus on the <u>subject</u> to spot the main idea.

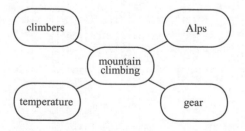

6. Reinforce the student for identifying the topic sentence and/or main idea: (a) give the student a tangible reward (e.g., classroom privileges, line leading, passing out materials, five minutes free time, etc.) or (b) give the student an intangible reward (e.g., praise, fist bump, smile, etc.).

7. Speak to the student to explain (a) what the student is doing wrong and (b) what the student should be doing.

8. Write a contract with the student specifying what behavior is expected and what reinforcement will be made available when the terms of the contract have been met.

9. Have the student ask questions about directions, explanations, and instructions not understood.

10. Communicate with parents (e.g., notes home, phone calls, etc.) to share information about the student's progress. The parents may reinforce the student at home for correctly identifying topic sentences at school.

11. Evaluate the appropriateness of the task to determine (a) if the task is too difficult and (b) if the length of time scheduled to complete the task is adequate.

12. Choose a peer to model identifying topic sentences for the student and also to assist the student with directions, etc.

13. Specify exactly what is to be done for the completion of a task (e.g., indicate definite starting and stopping points, indicate a minimum requirement, etc.).

14. Have the student be a peer tutor to teach another student a concept he/she has mastered. This can serve as reinforcement for the student.

15. Provide practice in identifying the topic sentence and/or main idea using a computer software program that gives the student immediate feedback.

16. Make sure the student has mastery of reading concepts at each level before introducing a new skill level.

17. Make sure the student is not required to learn more information than he/she is capable of learning at any time.

18. Reduce the emphasis on competition. Competitive activities may cause the student to hurry and commit errors.

19. Reduce the amount of information on a page if it is causing visual distractions for the student (e.g., have less print to read, isolate information that is presented to the student).

20. Highlight or underline important information the student reads (e.g., directions, assignments, etc.).

21. Give the student time to read a selection more than once, emphasizing comprehension rather than speed.

22. Stop at various points during the presentation of information to check the student's comprehension.

23. Use reading series materials with high interest (e.g., adventures, romances, mysteries, athletics, etc.) and low vocabulary.

24. Write paragraphs and short stories requiring skills the student is currently developing. These passages should be of high interest to the student using his/her name, family members, friends, pets, and interesting experiences.

25. Make sure that the reading demands of all subjects and assignments are within the ability level of the student. If not, modify or adjust the reading material to the student's ability level. A lower grade-level text may be an alternative.

26. Reduce the amount of material the student reads at one time (e.g., reduce reading material to single sentences on a page, a single paragraph, etc.). As the student demonstrates success, gradually increase the amount of material.

1. Have the student identify the words which are used to make the most common contractions he/she uses (e.g., *can't, won't, wouldn't,* etc.).

2. Provide the student with a list of the most common contractions and compound words with the corresponding words from which they are created. Allow the student to keep the list at his/her desk as a reference.

3. Have the student make his/her own dictionary of contractions and compound words with the corresponding words from which they are created.

4. Include a contraction and/or compound word in each week's spelling list for the student to learn.

5. Show the student how compound words are made by writing two words on construction paper and sliding them together.

6. Have the student be a peer tutor to teach another student a concept he/she has mastered. This can serve as reinforcement for the student.

7. Provide practice in compound words and contractions by using a computer program that gives the student immediate feedback.

8. Make sure the student is not required to learn more information than he/she is capable of learning at any time.

9. Reduce the emphasis on competition. Competitive activities may cause the student to hurry and commit errors.

10. Have the student ask questions about directions, explanations, and instructions not understood.

11. Provide the student with increased opportunity for help or assistance on academic tasks (e.g., peer tutoring, directions for work sent home, frequent interactions, etc.).

12. Reinforce the student for beginning, staying on, and completing assignments.

13. Have the student practice a new skill or assignment alone or with an aide, the teacher, or a peer before the entire group attempts the activity or before performing for a grade.

14. Introduce compound words and contractions and their meanings to the student before he/she reads new material. These may be entered in a vocabulary notebook kept by the student.

15. Reinforce the student for demonstrating a knowledge of compound words and contractions: (a) give the student a tangible reward (e.g., classroom privileges, line leading, passing out materials, five minutes free time, etc.) or (b) give the student an intangible reward (e.g., praise, fist bump, smile, etc.).

16. Communicate with parents (e.g., notes home, phone calls, etc.) to share information about the student's progress. The parents may reinforce the student at home for improved understanding of contractions and compound words at school.

17. Evaluate the appropriateness of the task to determine (a) if the task is too difficult and (b) if the length of time scheduled to complete the task is adequate.

18. Choose a peer to model understanding contractions and compound words for the student and to assist the student with directions, etc.

1. Provide the student with a dictionary. Name a word and have the student look up the word in the dictionary using the guide words at the top of each page. Time the student and see if his/her best time can be beaten.

2. Make sure the student has an understanding of how to use guide words at the top of the dictionary page.

3. Make sure the student knows how to alphabetize words to the first, second, third, etc., letter.

4. Make sure the student knows the reasons for using a dictionary or glossary (e.g., to look up the meanings of words, to look up how to spell words, to look up the correct pronunciation of words, etc.).

5. Make sure the student knows that the glossary is located in the back of the book.

6. Make sure the student is using a dictionary that is on his/her reading level.

7. Make sure the student knows how to alphabetize.

8. Assign the student words to look up in his/her textbook glossary. Begin with easier words, and add words with more difficult spellings and definitions as the student demonstrates success.

9. Have the student find the target word of a paragraph, sentence, story, etc., and look it up in the glossary of the book.

10. Have the student select words from a spelling list and write a story using those words. Then have the student make a glossary to attach to the end of the story with word meanings shown in pictures.

11. Have the student compare a glossary from a textbook with a student-level thesaurus for building a glossary of his/her own vocabulary.

12. Have the student ask questions about directions, explanations, or instructions not understood.

13. Have the student review the words in a textbook glossary and determine why those particular words were selected to be in the glossary and more commonly used words were not selected.

14. Reinforce the student for demonstrating knowledge of glossary and/or dictionary skills: (a) give the student a tangible reward (e.g., classroom privileges, line leading, passing out materials, five minutes free time, etc.) or (b) give the student an intangible reward (e.g., praise, fist bump, smile, etc.).

15. Speak to the student to explain (a) what the student is doing wrong and (b) what the student should be doing.

16. Reinforce the student for demonstrating knowledge of glossary skills and/or dictionary skills based on the number of times the student can be successful. As the student demonstrates success, gradually increase the number of times required for reinforcement.

17. Communicate with parents (e.g., notes home, phone calls, etc.) to share information about the student's progress. The parents may reinforce the student at home for demonstrating glossary and dictionary skills at school.

18. Evaluate the appropriateness of the task to determine (a) if the task is too difficult and (b) if the length of time scheduled to complete the task is adequate.

19. Choose a peer to model glossary and dictionary skills for the student and to assist the student with directions, etc.

20. Have the student be a peer tutor to teach another student a concept he/she has mastered.

21. Provide practice in glossary and/or dictionary skills by using a computer software program that gives the student immediate feedback.

22. Make sure the student has mastery of concepts at each level before introducing a new skill level.

23. Make sure the student is not required to learn more information than he/she is capable of learning at any one time.

24. Reduce the emphasis on competition. Competitive activities may cause the student to hurry and commit errors.

25. Provide the student with increased opportunity for help or assistance on academic tasks (e.g., peer tutoring, directions for work sent home, frequent interactions, etc.).

26. Review, on a daily basis, those skills, concepts, tasks, etc., which have been previously introduced.

57 Has difficulty finding supporting details when reading

1. Have the student identify the main idea of each paragraph. Then have the student list all information from the paragraph which relates to the main idea.

2. Teach the student mapping techniques to identify supporting details.

3. Provide the student with a diagram in which supporting details are like the legs of a bug. The student can learn to make "bug notes" in this way: An oval shape is the bug's body on which the teacher writes the main idea of a paragraph. Each supporting detail is written on a line coming out from the oval which represent the bug's legs. The number of legs each bug note has depends on the number of supporting details there are for a given topic.

4. Have the student pretend to be a detective and play the game *Prove It*. After reading a selection, the main idea is determined and written on the wall-mounted board. The student must prove it by telling the supporting details that were discovered in the reading selection.

5. Reinforce the student for identifying supporting details: (a) give the student a tangible reward (e.g., classroom privileges, line leading, passing out materials, five minutes free time, etc.) or (b) give the student an intangible reward (e.g., praise, fist bump, smile, etc.).

6. Speak to the student to explain (a) what the student is doing wrong and (b) what the student should be doing.

7. Communicate with parents (e.g., notes home, phone calls, etc.) to share information about the student's progress. The parents may reinforce the student at home for finding supporting details at school.

8. Have the student ask questions about directions, explanations, and instructions not understood.

9. Evaluate the appropriateness of the task to determine (a) if the task is too difficult and (b) if the length of time scheduled to complete the task is adequate.

10. Choose a peer to model finding supporting details for the student and to assist the student with directions, etc.

11. Specify exactly what is to be done for the completion of a task (e.g., indicate definite starting and stopping points, indicate minimum requirements, etc.).

12. Have the student be a peer tutor to teach another student a concept he/she has mastered.

13. Provide practice in identifying the supporting details by using a computer software program that gives the student immediate feedback.

14. Make sure the student has mastery of reading concepts at each level before introducing a new skill level.

15. Make sure the student is not required to learn more information than he/she is capable of learning at any time.

16. Reduce the emphasis on competition. Competitive activities may cause the student to hurry and commit errors.

17. Reduce the amount of information on a page if it is causing visual distractions for the student (e.g., have less print to read, isolate information that is presented to the student, etc.).

18. Highlight or underline important information the student reads (e.g., directions, assignments, etc.).

19. Stop at various points during the presentation of information to check the student's comprehension.

20. Reduce the amount of material the student reads at one time (e.g., reduce reading material to single sentences on a page, a single paragraph, etc.). As the student experiences success, gradually increase the amount of material.

21. Write paragraphs and short stories requiring skills the student is currently developing. These passages should be of high interest to the student using his/her name, family members, friends, pets, and interesting experiences.

22. Make sure that the reading demands of all subjects and assignments are within the ability level of the student. If not, modify or adjust the reading material to the student's ability level. A lower grade-level text may be an alternative.

23. Use reading series materials with high interest (e.g., adventure, romances, mysteries, athletics, etc.) and low vocabulary.

24. Give the student time to read a selection more than once, emphasizing comprehension rather than speed.

E. Writing

1. Allow the student to perform schoolwork in a quiet place (e.g., study carrel, library, resource room, etc.) to reduce distractions.

2. Assign the student shorter tasks while increasing the quality of expectations.

3. Supervise the student while he/she is performing schoolwork to monitor handwriting quality.

4. Provide the student with clearly stated criteria for acceptable work.

5. Have the student read/go over schoolwork with the teacher so that the student can become aware of the quality of his/her work.

6. Provide the student with samples of work to serve as models for acceptable quality (e.g., the student is to match the quality of the sample before turning in the assignment).

7. Provide the student with additional time to perform schoolwork to achieve quality.

8. Teach the student procedures for doing quality work (e.g., listen to directions, make sure directions are understood, work at an acceptable pace, check for errors, correct for neatness, copy the work over, etc.).

9. Acknowledge quality work (e.g., display the student's work, congratulate the student, etc.).

10. Conduct a preliminary evaluation of the student's assignment. Require him/her to make necessary corrections before final grading.

11. Establish levels of expectations for quality handwriting performance. Require the student to correct or repeat assignments until the expectations are met.

12. Provide the student with materials (e.g., pencil with eraser, paper, dictionary, handwriting sample, etc.) to neatly perform assignments.

13. Provide the student with ample opportunity to master handwriting skills (e.g., instruction in letter positioning, direction, spacing, etc.).

14. Provide the student with an appropriate model of handwriting (e.g., other students' work, teacher samples, commercial samples, etc.) to use at his/her desk.

15. Model appropriate handwriting at all times.

16. Provide a variety of opportunities for the student to practice handwriting skills (e.g., writing letters to sports and entertainment figures, relatives, or friends; writing for free information on a topic in which the student is interested, etc.).

17. Have the student trace handwriting models. Fade the models as the student develops the skill.

18. Gradually reduce the space between lines as the student's handwriting improves.

19. Use primary paper to assist the student in sizing uppercase and lowercase letters. Use standard-lined paper when the student's skills improve.

20. Use horizontally and vertically lined paper (e.g., | | | |) to teach the student appropriate spacing skills (e.g., K|a|t|h|y).

21. Use adhesive material (e.g., tape, rubber cement, etc.) to keep paper positioned appropriately for handwriting.

22. Have the student use a pencil grip (e.g., three-sided, foam rubber, etc.) to help him/her appropriately position the pencil or pen.

23. Use handwriting models with arrows that indicate the direction in which the student should correctly form the letters.

24. Provide older students with functional handwriting opportunities (e.g., job application forms, reinforcer surveys, order forms, checks to write, etc.).

25. Make sure that all educators who work with the student maintain consistent expectations of handwriting quality.

26. Make sure the student has a number line and alphabet strip on his/her desk to use as a reference for the correct formation of letters and numbers to reduce errors.

27. Make sure the student understands that work not done neatly must be redone.

28. Provide the student with shorter tasks, but more of them throughout the day (e.g., four assignments of five problems each rather than one assignment of 20 problems).

29. Reduce the emphasis on competition. Competitive activities may cause the student to rush and perform work in a careless manner.

30. Work not completed according to teacher directions and expectations, must be completed during recreational or break time.

31. Have the student chart the number of times his/her handwriting is acceptable during a given week.

32. Use a pencil grip or different-sized pencil to assist the student with fine motor skills to produce acceptable handwriting.

33. Check the student's grip on the pencil to make sure that he/she is holding the pencil correctly.

34. Choose a peer to model acceptable work for the student to imitate.

35. Evaluate the appropriateness of the task to determine (a) if the task is too easy, (b) if the task is too difficult, and (c) if the length of time scheduled to complete the task is adequate.

36. Communicate with the parents (e.g., notes home, phone calls, etc.) to share information about the student's progress. The parents may reinforce the student at home for improving the quality of his/her handwriting at school.

37. Write a contract with the student specifying what behavior is expected (e.g., improving the quality of his/her handwriting) and what reinforcement will be made available when the terms of the contract have been met.

38. Reinforce the student for improving the quality of handwriting based on ability. As the student demonstrates success, gradually increase the amount of improvement expected for reinforcement.

39. Reinforce those students in the classroom who turn in assignments which are legible.

40. Establish classroom rules:
• Concentrate while working.
• Work quietly.
• Remain in your seat.
• Finish task.
• Meet task expectations.
Review rules often. Reinforce students for following the rules.

41. Speak with the student to explain (a) what the student is doing wrong (e.g., turning in work which has spelling errors or spacing errors, work that is illegible, etc.) and (b) what he/she should be doing (e.g., taking time to check for spelling, spacing errors, etc.).

42. Reinforce efforts to improve handwriting (e.g., double-checking spelling, proper positioning of letters, correct spacing, etc.): (a) give the student a tangible reward (e.g., classroom privileges, line leading, passing out materials, five minutes free time, etc.) or (b) give the student an intangible reward (e.g., praise, fist bump, smile, etc.).

59   Fails to copy letters, words, sentences, and numbers from a model at a close proximity

1. Allow the student periods of rest to avoid eye fatigue.

2. Assess the appropriateness of giving the student assignments which require copying at a close proximity if the student's ability makes it impossible to complete the assignments.

3. Assign short-term tasks that can be quickly and accurately copied. As the student demonstrates success, gradually increase the length of tasks.

4. Assist the student in copying information. As the student demonstrates success, gradually decrease the assistance and require the student to assume more responsibility.

5. Explain to the student exactly what he/she is doing wrong (e.g., hurrying just to get things done), and what he/she should be doing (e.g., carefully completing work). For example: The student is hurrying through copying assignments. Tell him/her that he/she is hurrying and needs to slow down and carefully copy the material to complete the assignments correctly.

6. Have the student copy small amounts of material (e.g., a sentence or line) at a time.

7. Change the format of the materials from which the student copies (e.g., have less material on a page, remove or cover pictures on pages, enlarge the print, etc.).

8. Check what the student has copied from the wall-mounted board, textbook, etc., for accuracy. Working quickly is acceptable if the student performs the task accurately.

9. Evaluate the appropriateness of the task to determine (a) if the task is too easy, (b) if the task is too difficult, and (c) if the length of time scheduled to complete the task is adequate.

10. Consider carefully the student's ability level and experience before expecting him/her to complete copying tasks on his/her own.

11. Encourage the student to monitor his/her neatness. Awareness should reduce production of poor quality work.

12. Encourage the student to develop a 30 second definition of his/her goal to help him/her stay on task and focus (e.g., "I will copy this sentence perfectly. The better I focus and stay on task, the better I will perform.").

13. Make sure that the student has only those materials necessary for copying (e.g., pencil, pen, paper, etc.) on his/her desk.

14. Establish a timeline for completing a project. Expect the student to meet each deadline to complete the project on time.

15. Establish rules for completing tasks (e.g., have the student take his/her time, ask for help when necessary, proofread material copied from the board, textbook, etc.). These rules should be consistent and followed by everyone in the classroom. Talk about the rules often.

16. Assess the level of task difficulty to determine whether or not the student will require additional time, assistance, etc., to copy written information.

17. Evaluate the visual and auditory stimuli in the classroom and remove or reduce the extraneous environmental stimuli.

18. Give recognition for quality work (e.g., display the student's work, congratulate the student, etc.).

19. Employ a variety of ways for the student to obtain information without copying it (e.g., teacher made material, commercially produced material, photocopy of the material, etc.).

20. Give the student a short break while he/she is working on monotonous assignments to relieve restlessness and improve concentration.

21. Choose a peer to assist the student in copying material (e.g., read the material aloud as the student copies it, copy the material for the student, etc.).

22. Have the student ask for help when he/she needs it.

23. Provide the student with the necessary materials to complete assignments (e.g., pencil with eraser, paper, dictionary, handwriting sample, etc.). Be sure that the student has only the necessary materials on the desk.

24. Maintain a consistent format from which the student copies.

25. Have the student read his/her written work out loud when proofing.

26. Establish an environmental setting for the classroom that promotes optimal individual performance (e.g., quiet room, background music, fresh air, etc.).

27. Have the student ask questions about directions, explanations, or instructions he/she does not understand.

28. Place the material from which the student is to copy at a distance to him/her. As the student demonstrates success, gradually move the material closer to the student.

29. Have the student work on the assignment at another time (e.g., later in the day, during lunch, etc.) when he/she should be able to concentrate better.

30. Reinforce the student for copying letters, words, sentences, and numbers from a model at a close proximity: (a) give the student a tangible reward (e.g., classroom privileges, line leading, passing out materials, five minutes free time, etc.) or (b) give the student an intangible reward (e.g., praise, fist bump, smile, etc.).

31. Help the student complete writing tasks so he/she will not have to hurry.

32. Highlight or underline the material the student is to copy.

33. Enlarge the print from which the student is copying.

34. Choose a peer to proofread all of the student's work before it is submitted.

35. Identify any particular letters or numbers the student has difficulty copying and have him/her practice copying those letters or numbers.

36. Have the student's vision checked if it has not been recently checked.

37. Increase supervision (e.g., by teacher, peer, paraprofessional, etc.) of the student while he/she is performing assignments which require copying.

38. Instruct the student to list five qualities of a peer who produces neat work. Have him/her choose one of those qualities to work on each week for five weeks.

39. Have the student practice writing letters, words, and sentences by tracing over a series of dots.

40. Maintain consistent expectations for the student to complete a task neatly and accurately.

41. Make sure that the material to be copied has a sharp contrast with the background/foreground to maximize visibility (e.g., black on white projections, white marker on green wall-mounted board, etc.).

42. Use an overhead projector to enlarge the material to be copied.

43. Have the student proofread all of his/her work before submitting it.

44. If the student wears glasses, encourage him/her to wear them if needed while working.

45. Provide the student with a number line and alphabet strip on his/her desk to use as a reference for correct form of letters and numbers to reduce errors.

46. Make sure there is no glare on the material to be copied from a distance.

47. Teach the student that work not done accurately will be redone, corrected, etc., during his/her recreation time.

48. Make sure the student's desk is free of all material except that from which he/she is copying.

49. Make sure the student has all the materials necessary prior to beginning an assignment to reduce unnecessary distractions while copying.

50. Match the student's assignments with his/her activity level. When the student is feeling highly active, assign tasks which require a great level of movement. When the student is most likely to maintain attention, assign more sedentary tasks (e.g., copying from textbook, wall-mounted board, etc.).

51. Provide an incentive statement along with a directive (e.g., "When you have copied the work correctly, you can work on computer.").

52. Provide more hands-on activities instead of copying materials from books.

53. Modify the material from which the student is to copy (e.g., reduce the amount of material to be copied, enlarge the print, etc.).

54. Set aside time at the end of each class period for the student to complete unfinished assignments.

55. Use a frame or window to cover all material except that which the student is to copy.

56. Provide the student with the material to be copied at his/her desk if he/she is unable to copy it from a distance.

57. Teach the student the relationship between inappropriate behavior and the consequences which follow (e.g., failing to copy the directions will result in homework assignments being done incorrectly).

58. Recognize quality work (e.g., display student's work, congratulate the student, etc.).

59. Reduce distracting stimuli (e.g., noise and motion in the classroom) to facilitate the student's ability to copy letters, words, sentences, and numbers from a model.

60. Reduce the emphasis on competition. Competitive activities may cause the student to hurry and be careless when copying.

61. Have the student use word processing on the computer as an alternative to using pencil and paper.

62. Use the computer and monitor as an alternative writing tool.

63. Require the student to proofread all written work. Reinforce the student for each correction made.

64. Seat the student closer to the material being copied.

65. Require the student to complete a task again if it has been done incorrectly due to his/her hurrying just to get things done.

66. Provide the student with a private place to work (e.g., study carrel, private office, etc.). This is used to reduce distracting stimuli and not as a form of punishment.

60 Fails to copy letters, words, sentences, and numbers from a model at a distance

1. Have the student's vision checked if it has not been recently checked.

2. Enlarge the print from which the student is copying.

3. Change the format of the material from which the student copies (e.g., less material to be copied, enlarge the print, etc.).

4. Seat the student closer to the material being copied.

5. Highlight or underline the material the student is copying.

6. Have the student copy small amounts of material (e.g., a sentence or line) at a time.

7. Make sure that the student has only those materials necessary for copying (e.g., pencil, pen, paper, etc.) on his/her desk.

8. Provide the student with a private place to work (e.g., study carrel, office, etc.). This is used to reduce distracting stimuli and not as a form of punishment.

9. Use a variety of ways for the student to obtain information without copying it (e.g., teacher-made material, commercially produced material, photocopy of the material, etc.).

10. Choose a peer to assist the student in copying the material (e.g., read the material aloud as the student copies it, copy the material for the student, etc.).

11. Maintain a consistent format from which the student copies.

12. Make sure that the material to be copied has a sharp contrast with the background/foreground to maximize visibility (e.g., black on white projections, white marker on green wall-mounted board, etc.).

13. Make sure there is no glare on the material to be copied from a distance.

14. Place the material from which the student is to copy close to him/her. As the student demonstrates success, gradually move the material away from him/her.

15. Provide the student with material to copy at his/her desk if he/she is unable to copy it from a distance.

16. Identify any particular letters or numbers the student has difficulty copying and have him/her practice copying those letters and numbers.

17. Have the student practice writing letters, words, and sentences by tracing over a series of dots.

18. Provide the student with a number line and alphabet strip on his/her desk to use as a reference for the correct form of letters and numbers to reduce errors.

19. Require the student to proofread all written work. Reinforce the student for each correction made.

20. Recognize quality work (e.g., display student's work, congratulate the student, etc.).

21. Provide the student with the necessary materials to complete assignments (e.g., pencil with eraser, paper, dictionary, handwriting sample, etc.). Be sure that the student has only the necessary materials on the desk.

22. Assess the appropriateness of giving the student assignments which require copying at a distance if the student's ability makes it impossible to complete the assignment.

23. Reduce the emphasis on competition. Competitive activities may cause the student to hurry and commit errors.

24. If the student wears glasses, encourage him/her to wear them for board work.

25. Reduce distracting stimuli (e.g., noise and motion in the classroom) to facilitate the student's ability to copy letters, words, sentences, and numbers from a model at a distance.

26. Have the student ask questions about directions, explanations, or instructions not understood.

27. Use the computer and monitor as an alternative writing tool.

28. Evaluate the appropriateness of the task to determine (a) if the task is too easy, (b) if the task is too difficult, and (c) if the length of time scheduled to complete the task is adequate.

29. Reinforce the student for copying letters, words, sentences, and numbers from a model at a distance: (a) give the student a tangible reward (e.g., classroom privileges, line leading, passing out materials, five minutes free time, etc.) or (b) give the student an intangible reward (e.g., praise, fist bump, smile, etc.).

61   Fails to use capitalization correctly when writing

1. After checking the student's work, require him/her to make all necessary corrections in capitalization.

2. Check the student's work at various points throughout an assignment to make sure the student is capitalizing where needed.

3. Display a capitalization rules chart in the front of the classroom.

4. Emphasize one rule of capitalization until the student masters that rule, then move on to another rule (e.g., proper names, cities, states, streets, etc.).

5. Find names, cities, states, etc., on a newspaper page and underline them.

6. Give the student a series of sentences representing all the capitalization rules. Have the student identify the rules for each capitalization. Remove each sentence from the assignment when the student can explain the rules for the capitalization in the sentence.

7. Have the student participate in writing activities which should cause him/her to do as well as possible in capitalization and other writing skills (e.g., writing letters to a friend, rock star, famous athlete, etc.).

8. Have the student practice writing words which are always capitalized (e.g., countries, bodies of water, nationalities, languages, capitols, days of the week, months of the year, etc.).

9. Highlight or underline all the capitalized letters in a passage or paragraph and have the student explain why each is capitalized.

10. Make a notebook of rules for capitalization to be used to proofread work.

11. Provide the student with a list of rules for capitalization at his/her desk to use as a reference.

12. Teach the student capitalization at each level before introducing a new skill level.

13. Have the student practice correct capitalization by providing the student with several sentences with errors on the wall-mounted board or overhead projector. The student is then expected to correct the capitalization errors and discuss them with the teacher.

14. Do not require the student to learn more information than he/she is capable of learning at any time.

15. Teach the student how to form all the capital letters of the alphabet.

16. Make sure the student proofreads his/her work for correct capitalization. Reinforce the student for each correction made in capitalization.

17. Review with the student common capitalization rules before starting a creative writing activity.

18. Make sure the student receives instruction in the rules of capitalization (e.g., first word of a sentence, the pronoun I, proper names, cities, states, streets, months, days of the week, dates, holidays, titles of movies, books, newspapers, magazines, etc.).

19. Model appropriate capitalization of sentences when assigning creative writing activities. This could be done on the wall-mounted board, an overhead projector or in chart form.

20. Reinforce the student for capitalizing correctly: (a) give the student a tangible reward (e.g., classroom privileges, line leading, five minutes free time, etc.) or (b) give the student an intangible reward (e.g., praise, fist bump, smile, etc.).

21. Write a contract with the student specifying what behavior is expected (e.g., using capitalization correctly) and what reinforcement will be made available when the terms of the contract have been met.

22. Provide practice with capitalization using a computer software program or a hand-held educational device that gives the student immediate feedback.

23. Provide the student with the necessary materials to complete the assignment (e.g., pencil with eraser, paper, dictionary, handwriting sample, etc.). Be sure that the student has only the necessary materials on the desk.

24. Provide the student with a list of examples of capitalization (e.g., proper names, cities, streets, holidays, etc.) that the student keeps at his/her desk to refer to when writing.

25. Reduce the emphasis on competition. Competitive activities may cause the student to hurry and make mistakes in capitalization.

26. Provide the student with computer software that provides practice and reinforcement in capitalizing words.

27. Recognize quality work (e.g., display student's work, congratulate the student, etc.).

28. Provide the student with lists of words and have him/her indicate which should be capitalized (e.g., water, new york, mississippi, etc.).

62 Uses inappropriate spacing between words or sentences when writing

1. Have the student's vision checked if it has not been recently checked.

2. Have the student sit in an appropriately sized chair with feet touching the floor, his/her back pressed against the back of the chair, shoulders slightly inclined, arms resting on the desk, and elbows just off the lower edge of the desk.

3. Check the student's paper position. A right-handed person writing in cursive should tilt the paper to the left so the lower left-hand corner points toward the person's midsection and as writing progresses, the paper should shift, not the writing arm.

4. Place dots between letters and have the student use fingers as a spacer between words.

5. Make sure the student is shifting his/her paper when writing.

6. Using appropriate spacing, print or write words or sentences. Have the student trace what was written.

7. Reduce the emphasis on competition. Competitive activities may cause the student to hurry and not use correct spacing when writing words and sentences.

8. Provide the student with samples of handwritten words and sentences he/she can use as a reference for correct spacing.

9. Have the student leave a finger space between each word he/she writes.

10. Draw vertical lines for the student to use to space letters and words (e.g., | | | |).

11. Provide the student with the necessary materials to complete the assignment (e.g., pencil with eraser, paper, dictionary, handwriting sample, etc.). Be sure that the student has only necessary materials on his/her desk.

12. Teach the student to always look at the next word to determine if there is enough space before the margin.

13. Provide the student with graph paper, instructing him/her to write letters in each block, while skipping a block between words and sentences.

14. Recognize quality work (e.g., display student's work, congratulate the student, etc.).

15. Check the student's work at various points throughout an assignment to make sure the student is using appropriate spacing.

16. Give the student one handwriting task to complete at a time. Introduce the next task only when the student has successfully completed the previous task.

17. Assign the student fewer tasks. As the student demonstrates success, gradually increase the number of tasks over time.

18. Have the student practice writing letters, words, and sentences by tracing over a series of dots.

19. Use vertical lines or graph paper to help the student space letters correctly.

20. Have the student participate in writing activities designed to cause the student to want to be successful in writing (e.g., writing a letter to a friend, rock star, famous athlete, etc.).

21. Have the student look at correctly spaced written material to serve as a model.

22. Reinforce the student for each word and/or sentence that is appropriately spaced: (a) give the student a tangible reward (e.g., classroom privileges, line leading, five minutes free time, etc.) or (b) give the student an intangible reward (e.g., praise, fist bump, smile, etc.).

23. Have the student perform a practice page before turning in the actual assignment.

1. Have the student's vision checked if it has not been recently checked.

2. Use board activities (e.g., drawing lines, circles, etc.) to teach the student proper directionality for each letter or number.

3. Physically guide the student's hand, providing the feeling of directionality.

4. Place letters on transparencies and project them on the wall-mounted board or paper. Have the student trace the letters.

5. Have the student trace letters and numbers in magazines, newspapers, etc., which he/she typically reverses when writing.

6. When correcting papers with reversed letters, use direction arrows to remind the student of correct directionality.

7. Identify the letters and numbers the student reverses and have him/her practice making one or more of the letters correctly each day.

8. Teach the student to recognize the correct form of the letters and numbers when he/she sees them (e.g., *b, d, 2, 5,* etc.).

9. Teach the student to check all work for those letters and numbers he/she typically reverses. Reinforce the student for correcting any reversed letters and numbers.

10. Provide the student with visual cues to aid in making letters and numbers (e.g., arrows indicating strokes).

11. Provide the student with large letters and numbers to trace which he/she typically reverses.

12. Make sure that the student's formation of letters is appropriate and consistently correct.

13. Given letters and numbers on separate cards, have the student match the letters and numbers that are the same.

14. Have the student keep a card with the word *bed* at his/her desk to help remember the correct form of *b* and *d* in a word he/she knows.

15. Have the student keep a list of the most commonly used words which contain letters he/she reverses. This list can be used as a reference when the student is writing.

16. After identifying those letters and numbers the student reverses, have him/her highlight or underline those letters and numbers found in a magazine, newspaper, etc.

17. Point out the subtle differences between letters and numbers that the student reverses. Have the student scan five typewritten lines containing only the letters or numbers that are confusing (e.g., *nnhnhhnn*). Have the student circle the "n"s and the "h"s with different colors.

18. Cursive handwriting may prevent reversals and may be used by some students as an alternative to manuscript.

19. Recognize quality work (e.g., display the student's work, congratulate the student, etc.).

20. Provide the student with a number line and alphabet strip on his/her desk to use as a reference to make the correct forms of letters and numbers.

21. Reduce the emphasis on competition. Competitive activities may cause the student to hurry and reverse numbers and letters when writing.

22. Have the student participate in writing activities designed to cause the student to want to be successful in writing (e.g., writing a letter to a friend, rock star, famous athlete, etc.).

23. Reinforce the student for making letters and numbers correctly when writing: (a) give the student a tangible reward (e.g., classroom privileges, line leading, passing out materials, five minutes free time, etc.) or (b) give the student an intangible reward (e.g., smile, fist bump, praise, etc.).

24. Have the student practice writing letters, words, and sentences by tracing over a series of dots.

25. Require the student to proofread all written work. Reinforce the student for each correction made.

1. Have the student's vision checked if it has not been recently checked.

2. Check the student's work at various points throughout the assignment to make sure that the student is writing within a given space.

3. Check the student's paper position. A right-handed person writing in cursive should tilt the paper to the left so the lower left-hand corner points toward the person's midsection and as writing progresses, the paper should shift, not the writing arm.

4. Check the student's pencil grasp. The pencil should be held between the thumb and first two fingers, holding the instrument one inch from its tip.

5. Make sure the student is shifting his/her paper as writing progresses.

6. Draw a margin on the right side of the student's paper as a reminder for him/her to write within a given space.

7. Place a ruler or construction paper on the baseline, making certain the student touches the line for each letter.

8. Use a ruled paper with a midline, explaining to the student that minimum letters (*a, b, c, d, e, g, h,* etc.) touch the midline.

9. Highlight lines on the paper for the student to use as a prompt.

10. Reinforce the student for each word or letter correctly spaced.

11. Have the student look at correctly written material to serve as a model for him/her to imitate.

12. Darken the lines on the paper so the student can more easily use them to write within the given space.

13. Allow the student to draw his/her own lines on paper for writing activities.

14. Allow the student to use a ruler as a guide or bottom line.

15. Provide the student with a physical prompt by guiding his/her hand as he/she writes.

16. Have the student correct his/her own writing errors.

17. Have the student perform a practice page before turning in the actual assignment.

18. Have the student practice writing letters, words, and sentences by tracing over a series of dots.

19. Provide the student with extra large sheets of paper on which to write. As the student demonstrates success, gradually reduce the size of the paper to standard size.

20. Recognize quality work (e.g., display student's work, congratulate the student, etc.).

21. Provide the student with the necessary materials to complete the assignment (e.g., pencil with eraser, paper, dictionary, handwriting sample, etc.). Be sure that the student has only the necessary materials on the desk.

22. Use vertical lines or graph paper to help the student space letters correctly.

23. Make a border so the student knows when he/she has written to the edge of the writing space.

24. Evaluate the appropriateness of the task to determine (a) if the task is too easy, (b) if the task is too difficult, and (c) if the length of time scheduled to complete the task is adequate.

25. Assign the student shorter writing assignments. As the student demonstrates success, gradually increase the number of writing assignments over time.

26. Give the student one handwriting task to complete at a time. Introduce the next task only when the student has successfully completed the previous task.

27. Have the student participate in writing activities designed to cause the student to want to be successful in writing (e.g., writing a letter to a friend, rock star, famous athlete, etc.).

65   Fails to punctuate correctly when writing

1. After checking the student's work, require him/her to make all necessary corrections in punctuation.

2. Check the student's work at various points throughout an assignment to make sure the student is using punctuation when appropriate.

3. Display a chart of punctuation rules in the front of the classroom.

4. Give the student a list of sentences in which the punctuation has been omitted. Have the student supply the correct punctuation with colored pencils.

5. Review with the student common punctuation rules before starting a creative writing activity.

6. Give the student a series of sentences representing all the punctuation rules. Have the student identify the rules for each punctuation. Remove each sentence from the assignment when the student can explain the rules for punctuation in the sentence.

7. Provide the student with computer software which provides practice and reinforcement in punctuating sentences and other creative writing assignments (e.g., addresses, letters, etc.).

8. Give the student sentences requiring him/her to fill in specific punctuation he/she is learning to use (e.g., periods, commas, question marks, etc.).

9. Make sure the student receives instruction in the rules of punctuation (e.g., periods belong at the end of sentences, question marks are used when a question is asked, etc.).

10. Have the student participate in writing activities which should cause him/her to do as well as possible on punctuation and other writing skills (e.g., writing letters to a friend, rock star, famous athlete, etc.).

11. Teach the student what all punctuation marks look like and their uses.

12. Have the student keep a list of basic rules of punctuation at his/her desk to use as a reference when writing (e.g., use a period at the end of a sentence, etc.).

13. Give the student a set of three cards; one with a period, one with a question mark, and one with an exclamation point. As you read a sentence to the student, have him/her hold up the appropriate punctuation card.

14. Have the student practice correct punctuation by providing the student with several sentences with errors on the wall-mounted board. The student is then expected to correct the punctuation errors and discuss them with the teacher.

15. Write a contract with the student specifying what behavior is expected (e.g., using punctuation correctly) and what reinforcement will be made available when the terms of the contract have been met.

16. Have the student practice using one form of punctuation at a time before going on to another (e.g., period, question mark, etc.).

17. Highlight or underline punctuation in passages from the student's reading assignment. Have the student explain why each form of punctuation is used.

18. Do not require the student to learn more information than he/she is capable of learning at any time.

19. Use a newspaper to locate different types of punctuation. Have the student circle periods in red, commas in blue, etc.

20. Require the student to proofread all written work for correct punctuation. Reinforce the student for each correction he/she makes on punctuation.

21. Model appropriate punctuation through charts and overheads for student reference during all creative writing activities.

22. Provide practice with punctuation using a computer program or hand-held educational device that gives the student immediate feedback.

23. Provide the student with the necessary materials to complete the assignment (e.g., pencil with eraser, paper, dictionary, handwriting sample, etc.). Be sure that the student has only the necessary materials on the desk.

24. Make a notebook for punctuation rules to be used to help with proofreading work.

25. Recognize quality work (e.g., display student's work, congratulate the student, etc.).

26. Reduce the emphasis on competition. Competitive activities may cause the student to hurry and make errors in punctuation.

27. Provide the student with a list of examples of the forms of punctuation he/she is expected to use (e.g., periods, commas, question marks, exclamation points, etc.). The student keeps the examples at his/her desk and refers to them when writing.

28. Teach the student punctuation at each level before introducing a new skill level.

29. Reinforce the student for using correct punctuation when writing: (a) give the student a tangible reward (e.g., classroom privileges, line leading, five minutes free time, etc.) or (b) give the student an intangible reward (e.g., praise, fist bump, smile, etc.).

1. After checking the student's written work, make sure he/she makes all necessary corrections in subject-verb agreement.

2. Assess the type of grammatical model to which the student is exposed at home. Without placing negative connotations on his/her parents' grammatical style, explain the difference between standard and nonstandard grammar.

3. Correct the student each time he/she uses subject-verb agreement incorrectly when speaking.

4. Have the student make up sentences with given verbs and subjects.

5. Explain that certain forms of verbs go with certain subjects and that correct subject-verb agreement requires the appropriate match of subject and verb. Teach the student the various possibilities of subject-verb agreement and how to select the correct one.

6. Give the student a choice of answers (e.g., more than one possible answer, multiple-choice on a worksheet, etc.) to facility his/her ability to recognize the correct answer.

7. Have the student pick out the correct verb when given choices on fill-in-the-blank worksheets (e.g., "They _____ (have, has) a new dog.").

8. Provide the student with a computer software program or a hand-held educational device that gives practice and reinforcement in subject-verb agreement.

9. Give the student a series of sentences with both incorrect and correct usage of verbs and ask the student to identify which are correct and incorrect.

10. Have the student find examples of correct subject-verb agreement in his/her favorite books or magazines.

11. Give the student a series of sentences, both written and verbal, and have him/her identify which are grammatically correct and incorrect.

12. Have the student practice correct subject-verb agreement by providing the student with several sentences with errors on the wall-mounted board or overhead projector. The student is then expected to correct the subject-verb errors and discuss them with the teacher.

13. Speak to the student to explain that he/she is using inappropriate subject-verb agreement and emphasize the importance of writing grammatically correct sentences.

14. Have the student read the written work of peers in which subject-verb agreement is used correctly.

15. Highlight or underline subject-verb agreements in the student's reading to call attention to the appropriate combinations.

16. Have the student write sentences with given verbs and subjects.

17. Play *Concentration* to match subject-verb agreement.

18. Have the student help correct other students' written work by checking subject-verb agreement and correcting the assignment.

19. Identify the most common errors the student makes in subject-verb agreement. Have the student spend time each day writing one or more of these subject-verb combinations in correct form.

20. Make a list of the correct forms of subject-verbs the student has difficulty writing correctly. Have the student keep the list at his/her desk for a reference when writing.

21. Make a list of those verbs the student most commonly uses incorrectly. This list will become the guide for learning activities in subject-verb agreement.

22. Have the student complete written worksheets on which he/she must supply the correct verb forms to go with specific subjects (e.g., "He _____ the dishes.").

23. Teach the student that different forms of verbs go with different subjects and that correct subject-verb agreement requires the appropriate verb form. Have the student practice matching verb forms to lists of subjects.

24. Make sure the student receives instruction in subject-verb agreement for those subject-verb combinations he/she commonly has difficulty writing correctly.

25. Review daily those skills, concepts, tasks, etc., which have been previously introduced.

26. Teach the student the concept of subject and verb by demonstrating through the use of objects, pictures, and/or written sentences (depending on the student's abilities).

27. Recognize quality work (e.g., display the student's work, congratulate the student, etc.).

28. Model appropriate subject-verb agreement when speaking so the student learns appropriate subject-verb agreement through verbal channels.

29. Have the student be a peer tutor to teach a concept he/she has mastered to another student as reinforcement.

30. Provide a review of standard subject-verb agreement rules through a chart posted in the classroom (e.g., cows run, a cow runs, etc.).

31. Provide the student with increased opportunity for help or assistance on academic tasks (e.g., peer tutoring, directions for work sent home, frequent interactions, etc.).

32. Teach the student the concept of plurality (e.g., have the student point to a picture of a cat and point to a picture of cats).

33. Reduce the emphasis on competition. Competitive activities may cause the student to hurry and make errors in subject-verb agreement.

34. Do not require the student to learn more information than he/she is capable of learning at any time.

35. Reinforce the student for using appropriate subject-verb agreement when writing: (a) give the student a tangible reward (e.g., classroom privileges, line leading, passing out materials, five minutes free time, etc.) or (b) give the student an intangible reward (e.g., praise, fist bump, smile, etc.).

36. Require the student to proofread his/her written work for subject-verb agreement. Reinforce the student for correcting all errors.

37. Teach the student that sentences express thoughts about a subject and what that subject is or does.

38. Give the student specific verb forms and have him/her supply appropriate subjects to go with each (e.g., "_____ runs.").

39. Show the student pictures of people, places, or things. Ask him/her to make a statement about each picture. Have the student identify the subject and verb of the verbal sentence and tell whether or not they agree.

67 Does not compose complete sentences or express complete thoughts when writing

1. Model writing in complete sentences or thoughts in legible handwriting for the student to imitate.

2. After the student proofreads his/her written work, have him/her explain why specific sentences do or do not express complete thoughts.

3. Assess whether or not the student uses complete sentences or expresses complete thoughts when speaking. Proficiency in spoken language typically precedes and influences the type of language used in written work.

4. Ask questions which stimulate language. Avoid those which can be answered by yes/no or a nod of the head (e.g., "What did you do at recess?" instead of "Did you play on the slide?" or "Tell me about your vacation." instead of "Did you stay home over the holidays?").

5. Assign the student shorter tasks while increasing the quality of expectations.

6. Check the student's written work at various points throughout the assignment to make sure the student is using complete sentences and thoughts in legible handwriting.

7. Provide exercises for making sentences out of non-sentence groups of words.

8. Give the student a group of related words (e.g., author, read, love, best-seller, etc.) and have him/her make up a paragraph including all the words. Emphasize the use of complete sentences or thoughts in legible handwriting.

9. Choose a topic for a paragraph or story and alternate writing sentences with the student to provide a regular model of the components of a complete sentence.

10. Provide the student with clearly stated criteria for acceptable work (e.g., neatness, complete sentences, legible handwriting, etc.).

11. Ask the parents to encourage the student's use of complete sentences and thoughts, both verbal and written, by praising him/her when these are used at home.

12. Encourage the student to read written work aloud to help identify incomplete sentences and thoughts.

13. Establish levels of expectations for quality handwriting performance, and require the student to correct or repeat assignments until the expectations are met.

14. Give the student a factual statement (e.g., some animals are dangerous) and have him/her compose several complete sentences relating to that concept.

15. Make sure the student is aware of the types of errors made when writing (e.g., not completing sentences or thoughts, writing too big or small, etc.).

16. Give the student a note card to keep at his/her desk to serve as a reminder that all sentences must have a subject and a verb.

17. Give the student scrambled words and have him/her put them in the correct order to form a complete sentence.

18. Give the student several short sentences and have him/her combine them to make one longer complete sentence (e.g., "The dog is big. The dog is brown. The dog is mine." becomes "The big, brown dog is mine.").

19. Have a number of students build a sentence while someone writes it down (e.g., The first one starts with a word (e.g., I). The next student adds the second word (e.g., like). This process continues as long as possible to create one long, complete sentence.).

20. Choose a peer to model writing in complete sentences or thoughts for the student. Assign the students to work together, perform assignments together, etc.

21. Provide older students with functional writing opportunities (e.g., job application forms, reinforcer surveys, order forms, checks to write, customer surveys, etc.).

22. Choose a peer to read the student's written work aloud to help him/her identify incomplete sentences.

23. Have the student assist in grading or proofreading other students' written work to make him/her more aware of incomplete sentences or thoughts.

24. Have the student give verbal or written process statements to sequence an activity (e.g., how to make a peanut butter and jelly sandwich). Have him/her focus on making each statement a complete thought.

25. Have the student identify who he/she thinks is a good writer and why.

26. Give the student a list of conjunction words (e.g., therefore, although, because, etc.) and have him/her make sentences using each word.

27. Have the student read/go over schoolwork with the teacher so the student can become aware of the quality of his/her work.

28. Have the student read/go over written communication so the student can become aware of the quality of his/her work.

29. Have the student write a daily log, expressing his/her thoughts in complete sentences.

30. Choose a peer to model writing and speaking in complete sentences or thoughts for the student.

31. Make sure that parents and all educators who work with the student maintain consistent expectations of writing quality.

32. Identify the qualities a good writer possesses (e.g., writing in complete sentences or thoughts, using appropriate vocabulary, etc.) and have the student evaluate himself/herself on each characteristic. Set a goal for improvement in only one or two areas at a time.

33. If the student's errors reflect the lack of a language-enriching home environment, explain to the student that language can be fun and that you and he/she will work together to help him/her discover this.

34. Give the student a series of written phrases and have him/her indicate which ones express a complete thought.

35. Make sure the student has the necessary materials to write with legible handwriting (e.g., pen with ink, sharpened pencil, lined paper, etc.).

36. Reduce the emphasis on competition. Competitive activities may cause the student to hurry and not write in complete sentences or thoughts.

37. Teach the concept of verb and noun phrases as soon as possible so the student has a means of checking to see if a sentence is complete.

38. Have the student's hearing checked if it has not been recently checked.

39. Use a pencil grip (e.g., three sided, foam, rubber, etc.) to provide the student assistance in appropriate positioning of the pencil or pen.

40. Make groups of cards containing subjects, verbs, adjectives, etc. Have the student combine the cards in various ways to construct complete sentences.

41. Teach the student the concept of a complete sentence by pointing out the subject/verb/object components through the use of objects, pictures, and/or written sentences (depending on the student's abilities).

42. Reinforce the students in the classroom who use complete sentences or thoughts when writing.

43. Give the student a series of complete and incomplete sentences, both written and verbal, and ask him/her to identify which are correct and incorrect and make appropriate modifications.

44. Teach the student that a complete sentence has to express a complete thought about a subject and what that subject is or does.

45. Play a game by providing students with a box labeled *Trash*. Provide sentence strips with complete and incomplete sentences. Instruct students to throw incomplete sentences in the trash.

46. Have the student write letters to friends, relatives, etc., to create additional ways he/she can practice writing complete sentences and thoughts in legible handwriting.

47. Provide a multitude of writing opportunities for the student to practice expressing complete sentences and thoughts in legible handwriting (e.g., writing letters to sports and entertainment figures, relatives, or friends; writing for free information on a topic in which the student is interested).

48. Provide the student with a topic (e.g., rules to follow when riding your bike) and have him/her write complete sentences about it.

49. Provide the student with additional time to complete schoolwork to achieve quality.

50. When correcting/grading the student's writing, provide specific evaluative feedback which will assist the student in constructing complete sentences (e.g., Student writes: "Going to the show." Teacher comments: "Who is going?" or "Subject is missing."). After checking the student's written work, make sure he/she makes all necessary corrections.

51. Provide the student with ample opportunity to master handwriting skills (e.g., instruction in letter positioning, directions, spacing, etc.).

52. Provide the student with examples of subjects and verbs on a classroom chart.

53. Read verbally to the student to stimulate the student's thought and writing processes.

54. Give the student a subject and have him/her write as many complete sentences in legible handwriting as possible about the subject.

55. Recognize quality work (e.g., display the student's work, congratulate the student, etc.).

56. Reinforce the student for using complete sentences or thoughts when writing: (a) give the student a tangible reward (e.g., classroom privileges, line leading, passing out materials, five minutes free time, etc.) or (b) give the student an intangible reward (e.g., praise, fist bump, smile, etc.).

57. Require the student to proofread all written work and reinforce him/her for completing sentences or thoughts in legible handwriting.

58. Speak to the student and explain that he/she is using incomplete sentences or thoughts when writing and explain the importance of expressing complete thoughts in written work.

59. Teach the student the difference between communicating verbally and in written form. When speaking, using incomplete or run-on sentences, pronouns without referents, etc., is more acceptable because nonverbal cues can be used to clarify the message. However, such cues are not available in written work.

60. When correcting the student's written work, be sure to provide written and verbal evaluative feedback which is designed to be instructional (e.g., help the student rewrite for better completion of sentence or thoughts, rewrite legibly for student, etc.).

61. Provide the student, both verbally and in written form, with sentence starters (e.g., Go _____, Run _____, Today I _____, Anyone can _____, etc.) and have him/her write complete sentences.

62. Use a different size pencil or pencil grip to assist the student with fine motor skills to produce acceptable writing.

63. Have the student correct a series of phrases by making each a complete sentence.

64. Teach the student to proofread each sentence in isolation to check for a complete thought.

65. Provide the student with appropriate time limits for the completion of written assignments.

66. Teach the student to use a typewriter or computer if inadequate fine motor skills make handwriting skills difficult for him/her.

67. Use adhesive material (e.g., tape, Dycem® material, etc.) to keep paper positioned appropriately for handwriting.

1. At the top of a piece of paper, write five or six sentences out of sequence about a story the student has read. Have the student cut the sentences apart and paste them in the proper order on the bottom of the paper.

2. Check the student's work frequently to make sure that the student is organizing the writing activity appropriately.

3. Give the student a group of related words (e.g., *author, read, love, bestseller*, etc.) and have him/her write an appropriately organized paragraph that includes each word.

4. Give the student several short sentences and have him/her combine them to make one longer complete sentence (e.g., "The dog is big. The dog is brown. The dog is mine." becomes "The big, brown dog is mine.").

5. Have the student arrange a series of statements on a topic in an appropriate order so that they make sense in a paragraph.

6. Have the student begin to practice organizational writing skills by writing simple sentences with subjects and verbs. Have the student then expound the sentences by adding adjectives, adverbs and prepositional phrases.

7. Have the student create stories about topics which are of interest. The student is more likely to try to be successful if he/she is writing about something of interest.

8. Have the student develop an outline or skeleton of what he/she is going to write. From the outline, the student can then practice organizational skills in writing.

9. Have the student develop organizational skills in writing simple sentences. As the student demonstrates success, gradually increase the complexity of sentence structure required and move on to paragraphs, short stories, etc.

10. Have the student read a short story and then list the events of the story. From that list, have the student construct a paragraph using the correct sequence of events.

11. Reduce distracting stimuli by placing the student in a study carrel or office when engaged in writing activities. This is used as a means of reducing distracting stimuli and not as a form of punishment.

12. Have the student read his/her own written work aloud to help him/her identify errors in organization.

13. Provide practice organizing writing activities using a computer software program or a hand-held educational device that gives the student immediate feedback.

14. Have the student write a paragraph describing the events of a daily comic strip.

15. Using a written essay that the student has not seen, cut the paragraphs apart and ask him/her to reconstruct the essay by putting the paragraphs in an appropriate order.

16. Have the student write step-by-step directions (e.g., steps in making a cake) so he/she can practice sequencing events.

17. Help the student brainstorm ideas about a topic and then show him/her how to put these ideas into outline form by combining some ideas and discarding others.

18. Teach the student writing concepts at each level before introducing a new skill level.

19. Have the student practice writing paragraphs according to "Who, What, Where, When, How, and Why."

20. Make sure the student is not interrupted or hurried when engaging in writing activities.

21. Have the student write a daily log, expressing his/her thoughts in complete sentences.

22. Do not require the student to learn more information than he/she is capable of learning at any time.

23. Teach the student that paragraphs, essays, etc., need an introduction, a middle section where information is contained, and a conclusion or ending.

24. Have the student read sentences, paragraphs, stories, etc., written by peers who demonstrate good organizational skills in writing.

25. Provide the student with a paragraph in which a statement does not belong. Have the student find the inappropriate statement.

26. Provide the student with appropriate time limits for the completion of assignments.

27. Recognize quality work (e.g., display student's work, congratulate the student, etc.).

28. Have the student practice organizational skills in writing activities by having him/her participate in writing activities designed to cause the student to want to be successful (e.g., writing a letter to a friend, rock star, famous athlete, etc.).

29. Reduce the emphasis on competition. Competitive activities may cause the student to hurry and not correctly organize his/her writing activities.

30. Reinforce the student for correctly organizing writing activities: (a) give the student a tangible reward (e.g., classroom privileges, line leading, passing out materials, etc.) or (b) give the student an intangible reward (e.g., praise, fist bump, smile, etc.).

31. Require the student to proofread all written work. Reinforce all corrections in organization.

32. Teach outlining principles to the student so he/she understands the difference between main ideas and supporting details.

33. Have the student write a weekly account of the previous week, past weekend, etc., with primary attention given to organization (e.g., sequencing events, developing a paragraph, using correct word order, etc.).

34. When correcting the student's organizational skills in writing, be sure to provide evaluative feedback which is designed to be instructional (e.g., help the student rewrite for better organization, rewrite passages for the student, etc.).

1. Assess the level of task difficulty to determine whether or not the student will require additional information, time, assistance, etc., before assigning a task.

2. Assist the student in writing information. As the student demonstrates success, gradually decrease the assistance and require the student to assume more responsibility.

3. Check the student's performance for accuracy when writing. Working quickly is acceptable if the student performs the task accurately.

4. Check the student's work at various points throughout a writing assignment to detect any omissions, additions, or substitutions.

5. Consider carefully the student's ability level and experience before expecting the student to complete tasks independently.

6. Dictate sentences to the student so he/she can practice writing simple sentences accurately.

7. Encourage the student to create stories about topics which interest him/her to provide more experiences in writing.

8. Have the student practice writing simple sentences successfully without omissions, additions, and substitutions.

9. Give the student a group of related words (e.g., baseball, fans, glove, strikeout, etc.) and have him/her make up a paragraph that includes each word.

10. Establish an environmental setting for the classroom that promotes optimal individual performance (e.g., quiet room, background music, fresh air, etc.).

11. Give the student a list of transition words (e.g., therefore, although, because, etc.) and have him/her make sentences using each word.

12. Require the student to proofread all written work. Reinforce the student for each correction made.

13. Evaluate the visual and auditory stimuli in the environment and remove or reduce the extraneous environmental stimuli.

14. Explain to the student exactly what he/she is doing wrong (hurrying just to get things done) and, what he/she should be doing (working slowly and carefully). For example: The student is hurrying through writing assignments. Tell him/her that he/she is hurrying and needs to slow down and write carefully so the assignments will be correct.

15. Make sure the student is not interrupted or hurried when engaged in writing activities.

16. Have the student assist in grading or proofreading other students' written work to become more aware of omissions, additions, and substitutions.

17. Give dictation sentences to the student to encourage successful writing of simple sentences.

18. Encourage the student to read all written work aloud to detect omissions, additions, or substitutions.

19. Give the student scrambled words from a sentence and have him/her put them in the correct order to form the sentence.

20. Have the student ask for help when he/she needs it.

21. Have the student write a daily log or diary expressing thoughts in complete sentences.

22. Make a list of the student's most common omissions, additions, and substitutions and have him/her refer to the list when engaged in writing activities to check for errors.

23. Increase supervision (e.g., by a paraprofessional, peer, etc.) of the student while he/she is writing.

24. Maintain consistent expectations for the student to write information without omitting, adding, or substituting words.

25. Teach the student the relationship between inappropriate behavior and the consequences which follow (e.g., omitting, adding, or substituting words when writing directions down will result in homework assignments being done incorrectly).

26. Make sure that the writing assignments given to the student are appropriate for his/her level of development and ability.

27. Teach the student to use context clues when reading to aid word recognition and meaning.

28. Make sure the student has written work proofread by someone (e.g., aide, peer, etc.) for omissions, additions, and substitutions before turning in the completed assignment.

29. Have the student participate in writing activities designed to cause him/her to want to be successful in writing (e.g., writing a letter to a friend, rock star, famous athlete, etc.).

30. Make sure you are not requiring too much of the student at one time and causing him/her to hurry to get things done.

31. Reduce distracting stimuli when the student is engaged in writing activities by placing the student in a carrel or office space. This is used as a means of reducing the distracting stimuli and not as a form of punishment.

32. Have the student read simple passages and record them. Then have the student underline passages that were omitted.

33. Reduce the emphasis on competition. Competitive activities may cause the student to hurry and omit, add, or substitute words when writing.

34. Require the student to rewrite a selection if it has been done incorrectly due to his/her hurrying just to get things done.

35. Have the student complete fill-in-the-blank stories and sentences and then read them aloud.

36. Speak to the student to explain what he/she is doing wrong (e.g., substituting words, leaving words out, etc.) and what he/she should be doing (e.g., writing each word carefully, rereading written work, etc.).

37. Make sure the student is aware of the types of errors made (e.g., omits words, substitutes words, etc.) to be more conscious of them when writing.

38. Have the student proofread all written work for omissions, additions, or substitutions. Reinforce the student for correcting omissions, additions, or substitutions.

39. When correcting the student's written work, provide evaluative feedback which is constructive (e.g., point out omissions, additions, and substitutions; explain to the student the effect these mistakes have on content and meaning; have the student rewrite his/her work to correct the omissions, additions, and substitutions; etc.).

40. Structure the environment to reduce distracting stimuli (e.g., place the student on or near the front row, provide a carrel or quiet place away from distractions, etc.). This is to be used as a means of reducing distracting stimuli and not as a form of punishment.

41. Recognize quality work (e.g., display the student's work, congratulate the student, etc.).

1. Make sure the student is instructed in each letter formation, giving the student verbal as well as physical descriptions and demonstrations.

2. Provide the student with physical prompts by moving the student's hand, giving him/her a feeling of directionality.

3. Use arrows to show the student directionality when tracing or using dot-to-dot to form letters.

4. Check the student's writing position. A right-handed person writing in cursive should tilt the paper to the left so the lower left-hand corner points toward the person's midsection. As writing progresses, the paper should shift, not the writing arm.

5. Use color cues for lines (e.g., red for the top line, yellow for the middle line, green for the bottom line) to indicate where letters are to be made.

6. Draw simple shapes and lines for the student to practice forming on lined paper.

7. Highlight the base line or top line on the paper to help the student stay within the given spaces.

8. Make sure the student sits in an appropriate size chair with feet touching the floor, his/her back pressed against the back of the chair, shoulders slightly inclined, arms resting on the desk, and elbows just off the lower edge of the desk.

9. Have the student practice tracing letters at his/her desk.

10. Have the student practice tracing letters on the wall-mounted board.

11. Have the student practice forming letters correctly by tracing over a series of dots.

12. Check the student's pencil grasp. The pencil should be held between the thumb and the first two fingers, one inch from its tip, with the top pointing toward the right shoulder (if right-handed).

13. Have the student practice tracing with reduced cues. Write the complete letter and have the student trace it. As the student demonstrates success, gradually provide less of the letter for him/her to trace (e.g., dashes, then dots).

14. Identify those letters the student does not form correctly. Have him/her practice the correct form of one or more of the letters each day.

15. To facilitate appropriate holding of a pencil, put colored tape on parts of the pencil to correspond to finger positions. Then put colored tape on the student's fingernails and have the student match colors.

16. Provide the student with an alphabet strip attached to his/her desk in either printed or written form to serve as a model for correct letter formations.

17. Reinforce the student for making correct letters: (a) give the student a tangible reward (e.g., classroom privileges, line leading, passing out materials, five minutes free time, etc.) or (b) give the student an intangible reward (e.g., praise, fist bump, smile, etc.).

18. Have the student practice forming letters correctly by using writing activities which are most likely to cause the student to want to be successful (e.g., writing a letter to a friend, rock star, famous athlete; filling out a job application, contest form, etc.).

19. Check the student's handwritten work at various points throughout a handwriting activity to make sure that the student is forming letters correctly.

20. Recognize quality work (e.g., display the student's work, congratulate the student, etc.).

21. Provide the student with the necessary materials to complete the assignment (e.g., pencil with eraser, paper, handwriting sample, etc.). Be sure that the student has only those necessary materials on the desk.

22. Do not require the student to learn more information than he/she is capable of learning at any time.

23. Require the student to proofread all written work. Reinforce the student for each correction made.

24. Teach the student handwriting skills at each level before introducing a new skill level.

25. Reduce the emphasis on competition. Competitive activities may cause the student to hurry and not form letters correctly.

26. Provide tactile stimulation for the child (e.g., sand, fur, clay, wood, etc.).

27. Use specific manipulatives (strings, toothpicks, etc.) to form letters for visual models.

28. Choose a peer to model working daily on drills involving letter formation, ending and connecting strokes, spacing, and slant for the student.

1. Provide the student with examples of verb tenses for those verbs most commonly used incorrectly and have the student keep the examples for reference.

2. Make a list of those verbs the student most commonly uses incorrectly. This list will become the guide for learning activities in verb tenses.

3. Write a contract with the student specifying what behavior is expected (e.g., using correct verb tenses) and what reinforcement will be made available when the terms of the contract have been met.

4. Choose a peer to model the correct use of verb tenses for the student.

5. Teach the student that changes must be made in a verb to indicate when an event happened (e.g., past, present, future).

6. Have the student complete written worksheets in which he/she must supply the correct verb tense to go in the sentence (e.g., "Yesterday I _____ to my house.").

7. Have the student pick out the correct verb tense on multiple-choice worksheets (e.g., "Tomorrow she _____ [ate, eat, will eat] her supper.").

8. Give the student specific verb tenses and have him/her supply appropriate sentences to go with each (e.g., played: "John played at my house last night.").

9. Have the student write sentences with given verbs in past, present, and future tenses.

10. Have the student listen to examples of incorrect verb tenses and then identify each error and correct it.

11. Provide the student with the necessary materials to complete the assignment (e.g., pencil with eraser, paper, dictionary, handwriting sample, etc.). Be sure the student has only those necessary materials on the desk.

12. Present a series of sentences and ask the student to change the tense from past to present, present to future, etc.

13. Give the student a series of sentences (both verbal and written) and ask him/her to indicate if each is grammatically correct.

14. Ask the parents to encourage the student's correct use of verb tenses by praising him/her when grammar is appropriate.

15. Explain the importance of correct written communication and what would happen if the verb tenses were used incorrectly (e.g., confusion as to when an event took place).

16. Make sure the student proofreads all written work and makes corrections in verb tenses. Reinforce the student for each correction.

17. Allow the student to assist in proofreading or grading other students' papers to facilitate awareness of correct verb tense usage.

18. Encourage the student to read written work aloud to find errors in verb tenses.

19. Read a series of sentences to the student and have him/her identify if each one is in the past, present, or future tense.

20. Provide the student with a list of all tenses of verbs most commonly used. Have him/her keep this list at his/her desk.

21. Choose a peer to practice verb tenses with the student. Each tense is used in a sentence rather than only conjugating verbs.

22. Make conjugating of verb tenses a daily activity.

23. Give the student a choice of answers (e.g., more than one possible answer, multiple-choice on a worksheet, etc.) to facility his/her ability to recognize the correct answer.

24. Recognize quality work (e.g., display the student's work, congratulate the student, etc.).

25. Do not require the student to learn more information than he/she is capable of learning at any time.

26. Teach the student writing concepts at each level before introducing a new skill level.

27. Check the student's work at various points throughout the assignment to make sure the student is using appropriate verb tenses.

28. Have the student participate in writing activities designed to cause him/her to want to be successful in writing (e.g., writing a letter to a friend, rock star, famous athlete, etc.).

29. Reinforce those students in the classroom who use correct verb tenses when writing.

30. Reinforce the student for using appropriate verb tenses when writing: (a) give the student a tangible reward (e.g., classroom privileges, line leading, passing out materials, five minutes free time, etc.) or (b) give the student an intangible reward (e.g., praise, fist bump, smile, etc.).

1. Check the student's posture. Have the student sit in an appropriately sized chair with feet touching the floor, his/her back pressed against the back of the chair, shoulders slightly inclined, arms resting comfortably on the desk, and elbows just off the edge of the desk.

2. Check the student's paper position. A right-handed person writing in cursive should tilt the paper to the left so the lower left-hand corner points toward the person's midsection and as writing progresses the paper should shift, not the writing arm.

3. Check the student's pencil grasp. The pencil should be between the thumb and first two fingers, holding the instrument one inch from its tip.

4. Use paper that has a midline and a descender space.

5. Have the student identify maximum (*b, d, f, h, k, l*), intermediate (*t*), and minimum (*a, c, e, g, i, j, m, n, o, p, q, r, s, u, v, w, x, y, z*) letters to help him/her locate the correct placement of each group.

6. Make sure the student is shifting his/her paper as writing progresses.

7. Evaluate writing alignment by drawing a horizontal line across the tops of the letters that are to be of the same size.

8. Highlight lines on the paper as a reminder for the student to make correct letter size.

9. Choose a peer to model making letters the appropriate size when writing for the student.

10. Provide the student with samples of letters of the appropriate size for activities that require writing.

11. Provide the student with an alphabet strip at his/her desk with letters the size he/she is to form.

12. Write letters on the student's paper and have him/her trace them.

13. Write letters on the student's paper in a broken line and have the student connect the lines.

14. Using examples written on grid paper, have the student copy the examples beneath them.

15. Darken the lines on the student's paper which are used for correct letter size.

16. Have the student correct his/her mistakes in letter size.

17. Draw boxes to indicate the size of specific letters in relationship to the lines on the paper.

18. Using tracing paper, have the student trace over specific letters or words.

19. Provide the student with clearly stated criteria for acceptable work (e.g., neatness, etc.).

20. Recognize quality work (e.g., display the student's work, congratulate the student, etc.).

21. Provide the student with the necessary materials to complete the assignment (e.g., pencil with eraser, paper, dictionary, handwriting sample, etc.). Be sure that the student has only those necessary materials on the desk.

22. Teach the student handwriting skills at each level before introducing a new skill level.

23. Check the student's work at various points throughout the assignment to make sure that the student is making letters the appropriate size.

24. Using a series of dots, have the student trace words or sentences.

25. Provide the student with a number line and alphabet strip on the desk to use as a reference for correct form of letters and numbers to reduce errors.

26. Provide the student with a different size pencil or pencil grip.

27. Evaluate the appropriateness of the task to determine (a) if the task is too easy, (b) if the task is too difficult, and (c) if the length of time scheduled to complete the task is adequate.

28. Using an original story by the student, prepare a transparency to use on an overhead projector. Project the story onto a paper on the wall that the student will trace. This is particularly appropriate for those students who tend to write too small.

29. Reinforce the student for using appropriate letter size when writing: (a) give the student a tangible reward (e.g., classroom privileges, line leading, passing out materials, five minutes free time, etc.) or (b) give the student an intangible reward (e.g., praise, fist bump, smile, etc.).

30. Have the student's vision checked if it has not been recently checked.

31. Use vertical lines or graph paper to help the student space letters correctly.

F. Spelling

1. Attach a list of word endings (e.g., *-ed, -ing, -ly, -er,* etc.) and sample words to the student's desk for use as a reference when writing.

2. Do not require the student to learn more information than he/she is capable of learning at any time.

3. Choose a peer to practice the use of spelling rules when writing words, sentences, etc., each day with the student.

4. Cut a spelling word apart letter by letter to make a puzzle. Have the student scramble the letters and then arrange them to spell the word.

5. Do not require the student to learn too many spelling words at one time.

6. Give the student a magazine or newspaper. Have him/her highlight words which follow the spelling rule he/she is learning.

7. Have the student identify a list of words (e.g., 5, 10, or 15 words) each week which he/she wants to learn to spell. Teach the student to spell these words using the spelling rules.

8. Post a chart in the classroom with a list of words which represent the spelling rules. The student can refer to the list when completing written assignments (e.g., *hoping* represents dropping the silent *e* when adding *ing*, *hopping* represents doubling the final consonant when adding *ing*, etc.).

9. Have the student keep a copy of the rules for word endings at his/her desk.

10. Make sure the student has had adequate practice using the spelling rules in writing words, sentences, etc.

11. Integrate spelling rules with the total language arts program (e.g., activities, methods, and materials related to the teaching of spelling, reading, and language as a whole rather than separately).

12. Have the student practice a new spelling skill alone, with an aide, the teacher, or a peer before attempting it with the entire group or before being graded on it.

13. Provide a computer software program or a hand-held educational device which gives practice and reinforcement for correctly spelling words.

14. Have the student consistently practice a spelling rule until that rule is mastered (e.g., "*i* before *e* except after *c*," etc.). When one rule is mastered, a new one is introduced.

15. Reduce the emphasis on competition. Competitive activities may cause the student to hurry and make mistakes.

16. Have the student spend time each day practicing the use of a single word ending (e.g., *-ed*). When the student demonstrates mastery of a word ending, introduce a new one.

17. Teach the student spelling concepts at each level before introducing a new skill level.

18. Have the student type his/her list of spelling words.

19. Have the student use current spelling words in a meaningful manner (e.g., writing a letter to a friend, rock star, famous athlete, etc.) to facilitate his/her desire to improve.

20. Highlight or underline word endings (e.g., *-ed, -ing, -ly, -er,* etc.) in the student's reading assignments to call attention to the appropriate use of word endings.

21. Keep a salt (or sand) box in which the student can trace spelling words.

22. Have the student be a peer tutor to teach a spelling concept he/she has mastered to another student. This can serve as reinforcement for the student.

23. Make sure the student has adequate time to complete written assignments to facilitate the student's improvement in using spelling rules.

24. Have the student write current spelling words in different locations (e.g., wall-mounted board, transparencies, on a posted list at his/her desk, etc.) throughout the classroom as he/she is learning them.

25. Use daily drills to help the student memorize spelling rules.

26. Provide the student with adequate opportunities for repetition of information through different experiences to improve his/her memory.

27. Have the student keep a dictionary of frequently misspelled words at his/her desk. Require the student to check the spelling of all words he/she is not sure are spelled correctly.

28. Create and perform a rap using the spelling rule.

29. Pair the student with a peer to proofread each other's work.

30. Have the student start a personal dictionary of misspelled words at his/her desk. Require him/her to check the spelling of all words he/she is not sure are spelled correctly.

31. Post a chart with a list of spelling rules so the student can refer to it when completing written assignments.

32. Provide the student with a list of words which represent the spelling rules to keep at his/her desk for reference (e.g., "hoping" represents dropping the silent *e* when adding *ing*, "hopping" represents doubling the final consonant when adding *ing*, etc.).

33. Have the student practice basic spelling rules daily.

34. Provide the student with self-checking materials. Require corrections to be made before turning in assignments.

35. Recognize quality work (e.g., display the student's work, congratulate the student, etc.).

36. Reduce distracting stimuli in the classroom when the student is working on spelling and related activities (e.g., place the student in a carrel or office space).

37. Have the student practice using spelling rules in words, sentences, etc., which are written every day.

38. Provide the student with commercial or teacher-made games which provide practice using spelling rules.

39. Require the student to proofread his/her written assignments using spelling rules. Reinforce the student for each correction he/she makes when using spelling rules.

40. Review daily those spelling skills which have been previously introduced.

41. Teach the student to use spelling rules to spell words correctly rather than simply memorizing the spelling of words for testing purposes (e.g., dropping the silent e when adding ing, etc.).

42. Require the student to use the dictionary to find the correct spelling of any words he/she cannot spell correctly. Emphasize spelling accurately.

43. Review daily those spelling skills which have been previously introduced.

44. Teach the student why he/she is learning spelling rules (e.g., provide the student with a concrete example of how each word can be used in his/her life).

45. Provide the student with a list of spelling rules to keep at his/her desk. Require the student to refer to the rules when writing words, sentences, etc.

46. Review daily those spelling skills which have been previously introduced.

47. Use wall charts showing word endings (e.g., *-ed, -ing, -ly, -er,* etc.) and sample words for the student to use as a reference when writing.

48. Require the student to verbally explain how he/she spells words using spelling rules (e.g., "*i* before *e* except after *c*," etc.).

1. Choose a peer to model spelling words phonetically. Have the student read what a peer writes phonetically.

2. Cut a word apart letter by letter to make a puzzle. Have the student scramble the letters and then arrange them to spell the word.

3. Dictate one sound at a time for the student to write.

4. Do not require the student to learn more information than he/she is capable of learning at any time.

5. Have the student identify a list of words each week which he/she wants to learn to use in writing activities. Teach the student phonetic approaches to spelling these words.

6. Provide spelling practice using a computer software program or a hand-held educational device that gives the student immediate feedback.

7. Do not require the student to learn too many spelling words at one time.

8. Give the student fewer words to learn to spell at one time. Spend extra time on each word until he/she can spell it correctly.

9. Let the student dictate sounds for you to write.

10. Choose a peer to participate in daily drills spelling words phonetically with the student.

11. Have the student be a peer tutor to teach a spelling concept he/she has mastered to another student. This can serve as reinforcement for the student.

12. Reduce distracting stimuli in the classroom when the student is working on spelling and related activities (e.g., place the student in a carrel or office space).

13. Have the student practice a new spelling lesson or assignment alone, with an aide, the teacher, or a peer before attempting it with the entire group or before being graded on it.

14. Use flash cards to teach the words. Have students look at the word, say the word, then spell the word aloud as they are looking at the word.

15. Try various activities to help strengthen and reinforce the phonetic spelling of words (e.g., writing his/her own story, sentences, etc.).

16. Have the student practice spelling phonetically the words most commonly used in everyday speech and writing.

17. Provide the student with a list of words he/she is required to spell phonetically. Provide the student with evaluative feedback indicating how the words can be spelled phonetically.

18. Have the student use a phonetic approach to spelling words in sentences written each day.

19. Teach the student spelling concepts at each level before introducing a new skill level.

20. Help the student separate his/her spelling list into those words which are spelled phonetically and those which are not.

21. Integrate spelling with the total language arts program (e.g., activities, methods, and materials are related to the teaching of reading and language as a whole rather than separately).

22. Make sure the student correctly hears the sounds in the words he/she misspells. Have the student say the words aloud to determine if he/she is aware of the letters or sound units in the words.

23. Give the student short drills in spelling each day which require a selected phonetic sound. As the student demonstrates success, increase the number of phonetic sounds.

24. Provide the student with an example of phonetic spelling for those words he/she fails to attempt to spell phonetically.

25. Have the student keep a dictionary of "most misspelled words." Require the student to check the spelling of all words he/she is not sure are spelled correctly.

26. Reinforce the student for spelling words phonetically: (a) give the student a tangible reward (e.g., classroom privileges, line leading, passing out materials, five minutes free time, etc.) or (b) give the student an intangible reward (e.g., praise, fist bump, smile, etc.).

27. Require the student to use a phonetic approach to spelling any word he/she does not know how to spell.

28. Have the student write sentences, paragraphs, or a story each day about a favorite subject. Encourage the student to use a phonetic approach to spelling the words he/she uses.

29. Teach the student the sound each letter makes. Have the student practice making letter sounds as he/she sees the letters on flash cards.

30. Recognize quality work (e.g., display the student's work, congratulate the student, etc.).

1. Choose a peer to participate in daily spelling word drills with the student.

2. Have the student type his/her list of spelling words.

3. Cut a word apart letter by letter to make a puzzle. Have the student scramble the letters and then arrange them to spell the word.

4. Have the student keep a dictionary of "most misspelled words." Require the student to check the spelling of all words he/she is not sure are spelled correctly.

5. Do not require the student to learn too many words at one time.

6. Give the student fewer words to learn to spell at one time. Spend extra time on each word until the student can spell it correctly.

7. Have the student be a peer tutor to teach a spelling concept he/she has mastered to another student. This can serve as reinforcement for the student.

8. Teach the student why he/she needs to spell words correctly (e.g., provide the student with a concrete example of how each word can be used in his/her life).

9. Have the student proofread all written work for omissions, substitutions, additions, or rearranged letters or sound units. Reinforce the student for each correction made.

10. Provide opportunities for the student to read often so he/she sees in print those words he/she needs to learn to spell.

11. Make sure that the student's spelling words are those which he/she sees on a routine basis, rather than infrequently, to facilitate correct spelling and use of the words.

12. Recognize quality work (e.g., display the student's work, congratulate the student, etc.).

13. Highlight or underline in the student's reading assignments those letters or sound units the student omits, substitutes, adds, or rearranges to direct the student's attention to the correct spelling of words.

14. Identify those words the student misspells by omitting, substituting, adding, or rearranging letters or sound units. Have the student practice spelling the words correctly in sentences written each day.

15. Provide magnetic or felt letters for the student to correctly sequence into spelling words.

16. Teach the student spelling concepts at each level before introducing a new skill level.

17. Make a list of the words the student misspells by omitting, substituting, adding, or rearranging letters or sound units. Have the student practice spelling the words correctly. Remove each word from the list as the student demonstrates mastery.

18. Provide commercial or teacher-made games which provide practice spelling. The student should have a personalized list of words for this practice.

19. Require the student to use the dictionary to find the correct spelling of any words he/she cannot spell correctly. Emphasize spelling accurately.

20. Have the student identify a list of words (e.g., 5, 10, or 15 words) each week to learn to spell (e.g., if the student is interested in cars, identify words from automotive magazines, advertisements, etc.).

21. Use daily drills to help the student memorize spelling words.

22. Identify those words the student misspells by omitting, substituting, adding, or rearranging letters or sound units. Have the student start and frequently update a personalized dictionary with the words he/she misspells to use as a reference.

23. Reinforce the student for spelling words correctly: (a) give the student a tangible reward (e.g., classroom privileges, line leading, five minutes free time, etc.) or (b) give the student an intangible reward (e.g., praise, fist bump, smile, etc.).

24. Make sure the student correctly hears those letters or sound units omitted, substituted, added, or rearranged when spelling words. Have the student say the words aloud to determine if the student is aware of the letters or sound units in the words.

25. Have the student use current spelling words in a meaningful manner (e.g., writing a letter to a friend, rock star, famous athlete, etc.) to facilitate his/her desire to improve.

26. Provide spelling practice using a computer software program or a hand-held educational device that gives the student immediate feedback.

27. Reduce the emphasis on competition. Competitive activities may cause the student to hurry and misspell words.

28. Provide personalized computer software which will allow the student to practice his/her personal word list.

76 Has difficulty spelling words that do not follow the spelling rules

1. Choose a peer to spend time each day having the student practice spelling words which do not use spelling rules.

2. Cut a spelling word apart letter by letter to make a puzzle. Have the student scramble the letters and then arrange them to spell the word.

3. Do not require the student to learn more information than he/she is capable of learning at any time.

4. Give the student fewer words to learn to spell at one time. Spend extra time on each word until the student can spell it correctly.

5. Have the student be a peer tutor to teach a spelling concept he/she has mastered to another student.

6. Have the student keep a dictionary of "most misspelled words." Require the student to check the spelling of all words he/she is not sure are spelled correctly.

7. Make a list of the words the student most commonly misspells. Keep a copy of the list of correctly spelled words at his/her desk to use as a reference when writing.

8. Have the student make a song or chant of the word (e.g., L-A-UGH, L-A-UGH).

9. Require the student to proofread his/her written assignments for spelling errors. Reinforce the student for each correction he/she makes.

10. Provide opportunities for the student to read often so he/she sees in print those words he/she needs to learn to spell.

11. Have the student practice a new skill or assignment alone, with an aide, the teacher, or a peer before attempting it with the entire group or before being graded on it.

12. Teach the student spelling concepts at each level before introducing a new skill level.

13. Have the student type his/her list of spelling words.

14. Try various activities to help strengthen and reinforce the phonetic spelling of words (e.g., writing his/her own story, sentences, etc.).

15. Have the student use current spelling words in a meaningful manner (e.g., writing a letter to a friend, rock star, famous athlete, etc.) to facilitate his/her desire to improve.

16. Reduce distracting stimuli in the classroom when the student is working on spelling and related activities (e.g., place the student in a carrel or office space).

17. Have the student write current spelling words in different locations throughout the classroom (e.g., wall-mounted board, transparencies, on a posted list at his/her desk, etc.) as he/she is learning them.

18. Identify the most common words the student uses which do not follow spelling rules. Teach the student to spell these words as a sight-word vocabulary.

19. Have the student write sentences, paragraphs, or a story each day about a favorite subject. Encourage the student to use available references (e.g., dictionary, lists of words, etc.) to facilitate correct spelling.

20. Integrate spelling with the total language arts program (e.g., activities, methods, and materials are related to the teaching of reading and language as a whole rather than separately).

21. Provide computer software that provides practice and reinforcement in spelling words correctly.

22. Make a list of frequently seen words which do not follow spelling rules for the student to keep at his/her desk.

23. Have the student identify a list of words (e.g., 5, 10, or 15 words) each week which he/she wants to learn to spell. These words become the student's spelling words for the week.

24. Make sure the student has adequate time to complete written assignments so that he/she will be more likely to spell words correctly.

25. Teach the student the sounds that letters and letter combinations make. Have the student practice making letter sounds as he/she sees the letters on flash cards.

26. Provide the student with a spelling list of words he/she uses which do not follow the spelling rules. Add new words to the list as the student demonstrates mastery of any of the words.

27. Recognize quality work (e.g., display the student's work, congratulate the student, etc.).

28. Review daily those spelling words which have been previously introduced.

29. Reinforce the student for spelling words that do not follow spelling rules: (a) give the student a tangible reward (e.g., classroom privileges, line leading, passing out materials, five minutes free time, etc.) or (b) give the student an intangible reward (e.g., praise, fist bump, smile, etc.).

30. Require the student to use the dictionary to find the correct spelling of any words he/she cannot spell correctly. Emphasize spelling accurately.

31. Make sure the student hears the sounds in the words misspelled. Have the student say the words aloud to determine if the student is aware of the letters or sound units in the words.

32. Use daily drills to help the student memorize spelling words (e.g., flash cards, writing the spelling words three times, etc.).

33. Make sure the student does not have too many words to learn to spell at one time.

34. Provide commercial or teacher-made games which provide practice spelling words which do not follow the spelling rules.

1. Attach a list of word endings (e.g., *-ed, -ing, -ly, -er,* etc.) and sample words to the student's desk for him/her to use as a reference when writing.

2. Choose a peer to participate in daily word-ending drill activities with the student.

3. Make sure the student correctly hears the misspelled sounds. Have the student say the words aloud to determine if the student is aware of the letters or sound units in the words.

4. Do not require the student to learn more information than he/she is capable of learning at any time.

5. Give the student a few words to learn to spell at one time. Spend extra time on each word until the student can spell it correctly.

6. Have the student keep a copy of the rules for word endings at his/her desk.

7. Recognize quality work (e.g., display the student's work, congratulate the student, etc.).

8. Have the student keep a dictionary of "most misspelled words." Require the student to check the spelling of all words he/she is not sure are spelled correctly.

9. Highlight or underline word endings (e.g., *-ed, -ing, -ly, -er,* etc.) in the student's reading assignments to call attention to the appropriate use of word endings.

10. Identify a list of words the student has difficulty spelling correctly. Use this list as ongoing spelling words for the student.

11. Have the student practice a new skill or assignment alone, with an aide, the teacher, or a peer before attempting it with the entire group or before being graded on it.

12. Teach the student spelling concepts at each level before introducing a new skill level.

13. Have the student spend time each day practicing the use of a single word ending (e.g., *-ing*). When the student demonstrates mastery of the word ending, introduce a new one.

14. Require the student to use the dictionary to find the correct spelling of any words he/she cannot spell correctly. Emphasize spelling accurately.

15. Reduce the emphasis on competition. Competitive activities may cause the student to hurry and make mistakes using word endings.

16. Have the student use current spelling words in a meaningful manner (e.g., writing a letter to a friend, rock star, famous athlete, etc.) to facilitate his/her desire to improve.

17. Make sure the student has received instruction in using word endings (e.g., *-ed, -ing, -ly, -er,* etc.).

18. Provide practice with word endings using a computer software program or a hand-held educational device that gives the student immediate feedback.

19. Require the student to proofread all written work for spelling errors. Reinforce the student for correcting each spelling error.

20. Use wall charts showing word endings (e.g., *-ed, -ing, -ly, -er,* etc.) and sample words for the student to use as a reference when writing.

21. Reinforce the student for using word endings correctly when spelling: (a) give the student a tangible reward (e.g., classroom privileges, line leading, passing out materials, five minutes free time, etc.) or (b) give the student an intangible reward (e.g., praise, fist bump, smile, etc.).

22. Have the student be a peer tutor to teach a spelling concept he/she has mastered to another student. This can serve as reinforcement for the student.

78 Spells words correctly in one context but not in another

1. Choose a peer to participate in daily spelling word drills with the student.

2. Require the student to write his/her spelling words frequently over a period of time, to facilitate the student's visual memory of the spelling words.

3. Have the student identify a list of words (e.g., 5, 10, or 15) each week from an area of interest to learn to spell. If the student is interested in cars, he/she can identify words from automotive magazines, advertisements, etc.

4. Do not require the student to learn too many spelling words at one time.

5. Reinforce the student for practicing the writing of the spelling words within sentences and paragraphs.

6. Teach the student why he/she is learning each spelling word (e.g., provide the student with a concrete example of how each word can be used in his/her life).

7. Give tests and quizzes when the student is certain to succeed (e.g., after he/she has had adequate time to learn the information).

8. Have the student keep a dictionary of "most misspelled words." Require the student to check the spelling of all words he/she is not sure are spelled correctly.

9. Require the student to proofread his/her written work, circling any words which he/she thinks are misspelled. The student then checks with the teacher or the dictionary to correct those misspellings.

10. Give the student fewer words to learn to spell at one time. Spend extra time on each word until the student can spell it correctly.

11. Make sure the student has adequate time to complete written assignments.

12. Have the student use current spelling words in a meaningful manner (e.g., writing a letter to a friend, rock star, famous athlete, etc.) to facilitate his/her desire to improve.

13. Provide opportunities for the student to read often so he/she sees in print those words he/she needs to learn to spell.

14. Integrate spelling with the total language arts program (e.g., activities, methods, and materials are related to the teaching of reading and language as a whole rather than separately).

15. Tape a list of the student's current spelling words on his/her desk. Have the student practice them frequently.

16. Require the student to proofread all of his/her written work for spelling errors. Reinforce him/her for correcting each spelling error.

17. Have the student write current spelling words in different locations (e.g., wall-mounted board, transparencies, on a posted list at his/her desk, etc.) throughout the classroom as he/she is learning them.

18. Write sentences, paragraphs, etc., for the student to read which repeat the student's spelling words throughout the written material.

19. Make sure that the student's spelling words are those which he/she sees on a routine basis, rather than infrequently, to facilitate correct spelling and use of the words.

20. Reduce the emphasis on competition. Competitive activities may cause the student to hurry and make spelling mistakes.

21. Provide the student with self-checking materials. Require corrections to be made before turning in assignments.

22. Have the student maintain a folder of all of his/her spelling words. Require the student to refer to the list when he/she is engaged in writing activities to check spelling.

23. Make sure the student has had adequate the spelling words (e.g., drills, sentence activities, etc.).

24. Recognize quality work (e.g., display the student's work, congratulate the student, etc.).

25. Provide opportunities for the student to use computer software to write stories. He/she should check the spelling of words with the computer's spell check.

26. Require the student to use the dictionary to find the correct spelling of any words he/she cannot spell correctly. Emphasize spelling accurately.

27. Reduce distracting stimuli in the classroom when the student is working on spelling and related activities (e.g., place the student in a carrel or office space).

28. Have the student write a sentence daily for each spelling word.

29. Teach the student to use spelling words rather than simply memorizing the spelling of the words for testing purposes (e.g., have the student use the words in writing activities each day).

30. Reinforce the student for spelling the word correctly in all contexts: (a) give the student a tangible reward (e.g., classroom privileges, line leading, passing out materials, five minutes free time, etc.) or (b) give the student an intangible reward (e.g., praise, fist bump, smile, etc.).

31. Try various activities to help strengthen and reinforce the visual memory of the spelling words (e.g., flash cards, word lists on the wall-mounted board, a list on the student's desk, etc.).

1. Choose a peer to participate in daily spelling word drills with the student.

2. Develop crossword puzzles which contain only the student's spelling words and have him/her complete them.

3. Have the student indicate when he/she has learned one of his/her spelling words. When the student demonstrates he/she can spell the word, remove it from his/her current spelling list.

4. Give the student fewer words to learn to spell at one time. Spend extra time on each word until the student can spell it correctly.

5. Do not require the student to learn more information than he/she is capable of learning at any time.

6. Evaluate the appropriateness of the task to determine (a) if the task is too easy, (b) if the task is too difficult, and (c) if the length of time scheduled to complete the task is adequate.

7. Have the student highlight or underline spelling words in passages from reading assignments, newspapers, magazines, etc.

8. Provide spelling practice using a computer software program or a hand-held educational device that gives the student immediate feedback.

9. Have the student identify a list of words (e.g., 5, 10, or 15 words) each week to learn to spell (e.g., if the student is interested in cars, identify words from automotive magazines, advertisements, etc.).

10. Reduce the emphasis on competition. Competitive activities may cause the student to hurry and make spelling errors.

11. Have the student quiz others over spelling words (e.g., teacher, aide, peers, etc.).

12. Write sentences, passages, paragraphs, etc., for the student to read which repeat the student's spelling words throughout the written material.

13. Have the student use current spelling words in sentences written each day.

14. Make sure that the student's spelling instruction is on a level where success can be met. As the student demonstrates success, gradually increase the level of difficulty.

15. Teach the student why he/she is learning each spelling word (e.g., provide the student with a concrete example of how each word can be used in his/her life).

16. Have the student write current spelling words in different locations (e.g., wall-mounted board, transparencies, on a posted list at his/her desk, etc.) throughout the classroom as he/she is learning them.

17. Initiate a "Learn to Spell a Word a Day" program with the student.

18. Have the student be a peer tutor to teach spelling words to another student.

19. Recognize quality work (e.g., display the student's work, congratulate the student, etc.).

20. Have the student use current spelling words in a meaningful manner (e.g., writing a letter to a friend, rock star, famous athlete, etc.) to facilitate his/her desire to improve.

21. Have the student review spelling words each day for a short period of time rather than two or three times per week for longer periods of time.

22. Have the student practice a list of new spelling words alone, with an aide, the teacher, or a peer before attempting it with the entire group or before being graded on it.

23. Use words for the student's spelling list which are commonly found in his/her daily surroundings (e.g., commercials, hazard signs, directions, lunch menu, etc.).

24. Integrate spelling with the total language arts program (e.g., activities, methods, and materials are related to the teaching of reading and language as a whole rather than separately).

25. Require the student to use the dictionary to find the correct spelling of any words he/she cannot spell correctly. Emphasize spelling accurately.

26. Reinforce the student for practicing the writing of the spelling words.

27. Reinforce the student for learning to spell words correctly: (a) give the student a tangible reward (e.g., classroom privileges, line leading, passing out materials, five minutes free time, etc.) or (b) give the student an intangible reward (e.g., praise, fist bump, smile, etc.).

28. Require the student to proofread all written work for spelling errors. Reinforce the student for correcting each spelling error.

29. Have the student's current spelling words listed on the wall-mounted board at all times.

30. Tape a list of the student's current spelling words on his/her desk. Have the student practice them frequently.

G. Mathematical Calculations

1. Make sure that it is not an inability to read that is the cause of the student's difficulty solving math word problems.

2. Have the student read the word problem silently and then aloud. Have him/her identify the mathematical operation required.

3. Provide short and concise word problems that require a one-step process.

4. Teach the student clue or key words to look for in word problems that indicate mathematical operations.

5. Have the student verbally analyze the steps that are required to solve word problems (e.g., "What is given?" "What is asked?" "What operation(s) is used?" etc.).

6. Represent the numerical amounts presented in the word problems in concrete forms (e.g., problems involving money can be represented by providing the student with the appropriate amount of real or play money).

7. Have the student write a number sentence after reading a math word problem. (This process will help the student see the numerical relationship prior to finding the answer.)

8. Have the student create word problems for number sentences. Place the number sentences on the wall-mounted board and have the student tell or write word problems that could be solved by the number sentence.

9. Have the student restate math word problems in his/her own words.

10. Ask the student to identify the primary question that must be answered to solve a given word problem. Continue this activity using more difficult word problems containing two or more questions. Make sure the student understands that questions are often implied rather than directly asked.

11. Have the student write word problems involving specific operations. Have other students in the classroom solve these problems.

12. Supplement textbook problems with teacher-made problems that deal with classroom experiences and include students' names to make them more realistic and meaningful to the student.

13. Use word problems that are related to the student's experiences and are of interest to him/her.

14. Make sure the student reads through the entire word problem before attempting to solve it.

15. Teach the student to break down each word problem into specific steps.

16. Have the student make notes to set the word problem up in written form as he/she reads it.

17. Have the student simulate situations which relate to math word problems (e.g., trading, selling, buying, etc.).

18. Have the student solve word problems by manipulating objects and by stating the process(es) used.

19. Help the student recognize common patterns in word problems (e.g., how many, add or subtract, etc.).

20. Discuss words and phrases which usually indicate an addition operation (e.g., together, altogether, sum, in all, both, gained, received, total, won, saved, etc.). Provide the student with a list of those words and phrases.

21. Discuss words and phrases which usually indicate a subtraction operation (e.g., difference between, from, left, how many [more, less], how much [taller, farther, heavier], withdrawal, spend, lost, remain, more, etc.). Provide the student with a list of those words and phrases.

22. Allow the student to use a calculator when solving word problems.

23. Discuss words and phrases which usually indicate a multiplication operation (e.g., area, each, times, product, double, triple, twice, etc.). Provide the student with a list of those words and phrases.

24. Discuss words and phrases which usually indicate a division operation (e.g., into, share, each, average, monthly, daily, weekly, yearly, quotient, half as many, etc.). Provide the student with a list of those words and phrases.

25. Teach the student to convert words into their numerical equivalents to solve word problems (e.g., two weeks = 14 days, one-third = 1/3, one year = 12 months, one quarter = 25 cents, one yard = 36 inches, etc.).

26. Teach the student math vocabulary often found in word problems (e.g., dozen, amount, triple, twice, etc.).

27. Require the student to read math word problems at least twice before beginning to solve the problem.

28. Have the student begin solving simple word problems which combine a single operation with words such as:

$$7 \text{ apples}$$
$$\text{and} \quad \underline{3 \text{ apples}}$$
$$\text{equals} \quad 10 \text{ apples}$$

As the student demonstrates success, gradually change the problems to a math word problem.

29. Present the student with phrases to be translated into number sentences (e.g., six less than ten equals or 10 - 6 =) before introducing word problems.

30. Choose a peer to model solving math word problems for the student.

31. Reduce the number of problems assigned to the student at one time (e.g., 5 problems instead of 10).

32. Demonstrate for the student how to solve math word problems by reading the problem and solving the problem on paper step-by-step.

33. Provide the student with a number line on his/her desk to use as a reference.

34. Speak with the student to explain (a) what he/she is doing wrong (e.g., using the wrong operation, failing to read the problem carefully, etc.) and (b) what the student should be doing (e.g., using the appropriate operation, reading the problem carefully, etc.).

35. Evaluate the appropriateness of the tasks to determine (a) if the task is too easy, (b) if the task is too difficult, and (c) if the length of time scheduled to complete the task is adequate.

36. Correlate word problems with computation procedures just learned in the classroom (e.g., multiplication, operations with multiplication word problems, etc.).

37. Teach the student the meaning of mathematical terms (e.g., sum, dividend, etc.). Frequently review terms and their meanings.

38. Highlight or underline key words in math problems (i.e., reference to the operation involved, etc.).

39. Provide the student with a checklist to follow in solving math word problems (e.g., what information is given, what question is asked, what operation(s) is used).

40. Teach the student why he/she is learning to solve math word problems. Provide the student with concrete examples and opportunities to apply these concepts in real-life situations.

41. Have the student talk through math word problems as he/she is solving them to identify errors the student is making.

42. Provide the student with a math reference sheet to keep at his/her desk (e.g., steps used in doing subtraction, multiplication, addition, and division problems).

43. Have the student check his/her word problems using a calculator to reinforce the learning of math facts.

44. Teach the student the concepts of more than, less than, equal to, and zero. The use of tangible objects should facilitate the learning process.

45. Do not require the student to learn more information than he/she is capable of learning at any time.

46. Have the student be a peer tutor and teach a concept the he/she has mastered to another student. This can serve as reinforcement for the student.

47. Provide practice solving math word problems using a computer software program or a hand-held educational device that gives immediate feedback to the student.

48. Make sure the student has mastery of math concepts at each level before introducing a new skill level.

49. Have the student manipulate objects (e.g., apples, oranges, toy cars, toy airplanes, etc.) as the operation is described.

50. Reduce the emphasis on competition. Competitive activities may cause the student to hurry and solve math word problems incorrectly.

51. Provide the student with a quiet place to work (e.g., office or study carrel, etc.). This is used as a means of reducing distracting stimuli and not as a form of punishment.

52. Have the student ask questions about directions, explanations, or instructions he/she does not understand.

53. Reinforce the student for correctly solving math word problems: (a) give the student a tangible reward (e.g., classroom privileges, line leading, passing out materials, five minutes free time, etc.) or (b) give the student an intangible reward (e.g., praise, fist bump, smile, etc.).

54. Recognize quality work (e.g., display the student's work, congratulate the student, etc.).

81 Fails to change from one math operation to another

1. Assess the quality and clarity of directions, explanations, and instructions given to the student.

2. Develop a math reference sheet for the student to keep at his/her desk (e.g., steps used in doing subtraction, multiplication, addition, and division problems).

3. Evaluate the appropriateness of the task to determine (a) if the task is too easy, (b) if the task is too difficult, and (c) if the length of time scheduled for the task is adequate.

4. Have the student check his/her math assignments using a calculator to reinforce the learning of math facts.

5. Have the student estimate math solutions before solving a problem as a tool for self-checking.

6. Have the student verbally explain the problem to a teacher, assistant, or peer before solving the problem.

7. Have the student practice recognizing series of math symbols (e.g., +, -, ÷, x).

8. Have the student solve math problems using a calculator.

9. Do not require the student to learn more information than he/she is capable of learning at any time.

10. Teach the student why he/she is learning a math concept. Provide the student with concrete examples and opportunities for him/her to apply those concepts in real-life situations.

11. Have the student talk through math problems as he/she solves them to identify errors he/she is making.

12. Make sure the student recognizes all math operation symbols (e.g., +, -, ÷, x).

13. Enlarge the math operation symbols so the student will be more likely to observe the symbols.

14. Provide math practice using a computer software program or a hand-held educational device that gives immediate feedback to the student.

15. Choose a peer to help the student solve math problems.

16. Provide the student with computer software or a hand-held educational device that requires him/her to solve a variety of math problems.

17. Provide the student with self-checking materials to reinforce solving problems correctly.

18. Recognize quality work (e.g., display the student's work, congratulate the student, etc.).

19. Reduce the amount of information on a page (e.g., fewer problems, less print, etc.) if it is causing visual distractions for the student.

20. Reduce the number of problems on a page (e.g., five problems to a page with the student required to do four pages of problems throughout the day).

21. Reinforce the student for correctly changing from one math operation to another: (a) give the student a tangible reward (e.g., classroom privileges, line leading, passing out materials, five minutes free time, etc.) or (b) give the student an intangible reward (e.g., praise, fist bump, smile, etc.).

22. Require the student to go through math assignments and highlight or otherwise mark the operation of each problem before beginning to solve the math problems.

23. Work the first problem or two of a math assignment for the student so he/she knows which operation to use.

24. Speak to the student to explain (a) what he/she is doing wrong (e.g., adding instead of subtracting) and (b) what he/she should be doing (e.g., adding addition problems, subtracting subtraction problems, etc.).

25. Teach the student direction-following skills: (a) listen carefully, (b) ask questions, (c) use environmental cues, (d) rely on examples provided, and (e) wait until all directions have been given before beginning.

26. Use a separate piece of paper for each math operation (i.e., place problems with the same operation on the same piece of paper). As the student demonstrates success, gradually introduce problems with different operations on the same page.

27. Use a written reminder beside each math problem to indicate which operation is to be used (e.g., division, addition, subtraction, etc.). As the student demonstrates success, gradually reduce the use of reminders.

28. Color-code the operation symbol for each math problem (e.g., make addition signs green, subtraction signs red, etc.). As the student demonstrates success, gradually reduce the use of color-coding.

29. Use visual cues (e.g., stop signs or red dots) on the student's paper when he/she must change operations. Have the student raise his/her hand when reaching stop signs and provide the student with instructions for the next problem.

82 Does not understand abstract math concepts without concrete examples

1. Choose a peer to provide concrete examples associated with each math problem (e.g., 9 minus 7 becomes 9 apples minus 7 apples) and assist the student in solving the math problems.

2. Evaluate the appropriateness of having the student learn abstract concepts at this time (i.e., Is it too difficult for the student?).

3. Have the student be a peer tutor and teach a concept he/she has mastered to another student. This can serve as reinforcement for the student.

4. Have the student draw pictures to illustrate math problems.

5. Have the student play games with colored chips with values assigned to each color to learn the concept of one, tens, etc.

6. Have the student practice the concept of regrouping by borrowing and carrying from manipulatives arranged in columns set up like math problems.

7. Have the student use sets of objects from the environment to practice addition, subtraction, multiplication, and division problems.

8. Have the student use concrete manipulatives in real-life situations (e.g., use measuring cups to prepare a recipe, use money to purchase items from the store).

9. Introduce abstract math concepts with a concrete example (e.g., use a liquid and measuring cups with ounces indicated to introduce liquid measurement).

10. Make sure all of the student's math problems have concrete examples associated with them (e.g., 9 minus 7 becomes 9 apples minus 7 apples, etc.).

11. Make sure the student has mastery of math concepts at each level before introducing a new skill level.

12. Do not require the student to learn more information than he/she is capable of learning at any time.

13. Teach the student why he/she is learning a math concept. Provide the student with concrete examples and opportunities for him/her to apply those concepts in real-life situations.

14. Use abstract concepts to describe tangible objects in the environment (e.g., larger, smaller, square, triangle, etc.).

15. Make it pleasant and positive for the student to ask questions about things he/she does not understand. Reinforce the student by assisting the student, congratulating, praising, etc.

16. Teach the student concepts such as square and cube separately. It may be confusing to introduce both concepts at the same time.

17. Introduce abstract symbols and terms after the student has worked with concrete manipulatives and mastered the concept (e.g., ounce, oz.; cup, c.; pint, pt.).

18. Provide physical objects to teach math concepts (e.g., provide the student with a yardstick when referring to a yard, etc.).

19. Provide repeated physical demonstrations of abstract concepts (e.g., identify things far away and close to the student, a small box in a large room, etc.).

20. Provide the student with clock stamps that he/she completes when practicing the concept of telling time.

21. Provide the student with computer software which uses graphics associated with math problems.

22. Use a scale, ruler, measuring cups, etc., to teach math concepts using measurement.

23. Work the first problem or two with the student explaining how to associate concrete examples with each problem (e.g., 9 minus 7 becomes 9 apples minus 7 apples).

24. Review daily previously introduced abstract concepts. Introduce new abstract concepts only after the student has mastery of those concepts previously presented.

25. Teach shapes using common objects in the environment (e.g., round clocks, rectangular desks, square tiles on the floor, etc.).

26. Teach the student abstract concepts (e.g., dimensionality, size, space, shape, etc.) one at a time before pairing the concepts.

27. Use actual coins and dollar bills, clocks, etc., to teach concepts of money, telling time, etc.

28. Use concrete examples when teaching abstract concepts (e.g., objects to convey more than, less than; rulers and yardsticks to convey height, width, etc.).

29. Have the student follow a recipe to make a treat for the class using measuring cups, teaspoons, etc.

30. Use the following steps when introducing an abstract concept:
- concrete - cups and liquid,
- practice - use cups to solve problems,
- abstract - word problems with cups,
- practice - prepare a recipe,
- review,
- test.

31. Provide the student with money stamps to solve money problems (e.g., penny, nickel, dime, etc.).

83 Fails to correctly solve math problems requiring regrouping (i.e., borrowing and carrying)

1. Choose a peer to model how to correctly solve math problems that require regrouping for the student.

2. Develop a math reference sheet for the student to keep at his/her desk (e.g., steps used in solving subtraction problems, addition problems, etc.).

3. Develop a regrouping reference sheet for the student to use at his/her desk when solving math problems which require regrouping.

4. Evaluate the appropriateness of the task to determine if the student has mastered the skills needed for regrouping.

5. Provide opportunities for the student to apply regrouping in real-life situations (e.g., getting change in the cafeteria, figuring how much items cost when added together while shopping, etc.).

6. Have the student check his/her math assignments using a calculator to reinforce the learning of math facts.

7. Have the student independently solve half of his/her math problems each day. Allow him/her to use a calculator to solve the other half of the assignment as reinforcement.

8. Have the student perform timed drills to reinforce regrouping. The student competes against his/her own best time and score.

9. Have the student play games using colored chips. Assign a value to each color to teach that a ten chip is equal to ten chips with a value of one.

10. Have the student practice the concepts of borrowing and carrying from graphic representations of sets.

11. Have the student practice the concept of regrouping by borrowing and carrying objects set up in columns like math problems.

12. Have the student raise his/her hand after completing several problems so the teacher can check his/her work before continuing.

13. Have the student solve math problems by manipulating objects to practice regrouping.

14. Have the student solve money math problems using pennies and dimes to practice regrouping.

15. Have the student talk through math problems as he/she solves them to identify errors he/she is making.

16. Have the student use Cuisenaire® rods when solving borrowing and carrying math problems.

17. Make sure that the language used to communicate with the student about regrouping is consistent (e.g., borrow, carry, etc.).

18. Provide the student with a number line on his/her desk to use as a reference.

19. Make sure the student has mastery of math concepts at each level before introducing a new skill level.

20. Do not require the student to learn more information than he/she is capable of learning at any time.

21. Teach the student the concepts of more than, less than, equal, and zero. The use of tangible objects should facilitate the learning process.

22. Teach the student number concepts and the relationship of number symbols to numbers of objects before requiring him/her to solve math problems involving regrouping.

23. Make sure the student understands the concept of place value and that problems are solved beginning with the ones column on the right and moving to the left.

24. Provide regrouping practice using a computer software program or a hand-held educational device that gives immediate feedback to the student.

25. Provide the student with learning experiences in grouping tangible objects into groups of ones, tens, hundreds, etc.

26. Provide the student with many concrete experiences to help him/her learn and remember regrouping skills. Use popsicle sticks, tongue depressors, paper clips, buttons, base ten blocks, etc., to form groupings to teach regrouping.

27. Provide the student with shorter math assignments, but give more of them throughout the day (e.g., four assignments of five problems each rather than one assignment of twenty problems).

28. Reduce the emphasis on competition. Competitive activities may cause the student to hurry and make mistakes when regrouping.

29. Reinforce the student for attempting and completing work. Emphasize the number of problems correctly solved. Encourage the student to see how many more he/she can correctly solve without help. Have the student maintain a private chart of his/her math performance.

30. Reinforce the student for correctly solving math problems that require regrouping: (a) give the student a tangible reward (e.g., classroom privileges, line leading, five minutes free time, etc.) or (b) give the student an intangible reward (e.g., praise, fist bump, smile, etc.).

31. Require the student to check addition problems using subtraction.

32. Require the student to check subtraction problems using addition (e.g., difference plus the subtrahend equals the minuend). Reinforce the student for each error he/she corrects.

33. Use daily drill activities to help the student with regrouping (e.g., written problems, flash cards, etc.).

34. Use manipulative objects (e.g., base ten blocks) to teach the student regrouping.

35. Work the first problem or two of the math assignment with the student to make sure that he/she understands directions and the operation necessary to solve the problems.

36. Provide the student with opportunities for tutoring by peers or teachers. Allow the student to tutor others when he/she has mastered a concept.

84 Works math problems from left to right instead of right to left

1. Choose a peer to model working math problems from right to left for the student.

2. Develop a math reference sheet for the student to keep at his/her desk (e.g., steps used in doing addition, subtraction, multiplication, and division problems).

3. Display a large poster-board sign or use the wall-mounted board to create a message that indicates reading begins to the left and math problems begin to the right (e.g., READING BEGINS ON THE LEFT. MATH BEGINS ON THE RIGHT.).

4. Have the student check his/her math assignments using a calculator.

5. Have the student talk through math problems as he/she is solving them to identify errors the student is making.

6. Have the student use a calculator to solve math problems.

7. Have the student verbally explain steps to the teacher for solving a math problem to check the student's thinking processes.

8. Provide the student with a number line on his/her desk to use as a reference.

9. Teach the student why he/she is learning a math concept. Provide the student with concrete examples and opportunities for him/her to apply those concepts in real-life situations.

10. Make sure the student has mastered place value concepts and understands that columns to the left are higher values than those to the right.

11. Make sure the student has mastery of math concepts at each level before introducing a new skill level.

12. Make sure the student understands place value and can explain the concept of the ones column, the tens column, etc.

13. Model proper right-to-left solving of math problems on the wall-mounted board or overhead projector before the student begins a new assignment.

14. Pair the student with another student to solve math problems on the wall-mounted board.

15. Provide math practice using a computer software program or a hand-held educational device that gives immediate feedback to the student.

16. Provide the student practice solving math problems on the computer, which will automatically solve problems right to left.

17. Put the student's math problems on graph paper or vertically lined paper to align columns. Include a reminder to begin each problem at the right.

18. Recognize quality work (e.g., display the student's work, congratulate the student, etc.).

19. Reduce the amount of information on a page (e.g., fewer math problems, less print, etc.) if it is visually distracting for the student.

20. Reduce the emphasis on competition. Competitive activities may cause the student to hurry and make mistakes in math problems.

21. Reinforce proper right-to-left problem solving through the use of math games.

22. Reinforce the student for doing math problems from right to left: (a) give the student a tangible reward (e.g., classroom privileges, line leading, passing out materials, five minutes free time, etc.) or (b) give the student an intangible reward (e.g., praise, fist bump, smile, etc.).

23. Require the student to work each math problem using a bookmark/strip of paper to cover all columns except the one on the right. Move the marker to the left as he/she moves from the ones column to the tens columns to the hundreds column, etc.

24. Require the student to solve math problems by place value (e.g., begin with the ones column, then the tens column, hundreds column, etc.).

25. Write the place value above each math problem to remind the student to begin with the ones column to solve the problems.

26. Speak to the student to explain (a) what he/she is doing wrong (e.g., working math problems from left to right) and (b) what he/she should be doing (e.g., working math problems from right to left).

27. Use a marker to highlight the ones column to show the student where to begin to work math problems.

28. Use large colored arrows to indicate where the student begins to work math problems (e.g., right to left).

29. Work the first problems for the student as he/she watches to provide a demonstration and an example.

1. Allow the student to use a calculator for math computation and emphasize the math process.

2. Assess the degree of task difficulty to determine whether or not the student will require additional information, time, assistance, etc., before beginning a math assignment.

3. Assign math problems which require the same operation to make it easier for the student to follow steps in solving the problems. As the student demonstrates success, introduce problems with a different operation.

4. Have the student circle each math problem's operation symbol before he/she solves any math problems.

5. Have the student ask for help when needed.

6. Use demonstration and hands-on learning when teaching new math skills.

7. Have the student write the name of the operation beside each word problem before he/she solves any math word problems. Check the student's choice of operations before he/she begins to solve the problems.

8. Color-code math operation symbols next to math problems so the student will be more likely to observe the symbol.

9. Develop a math reference sheet for the student to keep at his/her desk (e.g., steps used in doing subtraction, multiplication, addition, and division problems).

10. Have the student check his/her answers to math problems on a calculator.

11. Have the student tutor another student who is learning new math concepts. Explaining the steps in basic math problems will help the student reinforce his/her own skills.

12. Have the student ask himself/herself questions (e.g., "What is next?") to keep himself/herself focused on solving a problem.

13. Have the student verbally repeat directions, explanations, and instructions after they have been given to reinforce retention.

14. Have the student ask questions about directions, explanations, or instructions before beginning a task to reinforce comprehension.

15. Have the student raise his/her hand after completing several problems so the teacher can check his/her work before continuing.

16. Have the student relate math problems to real-life situations so that he/she will better understand the steps involved in solving the problem (e.g., "If I work 6 hours at $4.35 an hour, will I earn enough to buy 2 movie tickets which cost $12.99 each?").

17. Have the student talk through math problems as he/she is solving them to identify errors he/she is making.

18. Have the student verbally explain steps to the teacher for solving a math problem to check proper sequence of steps.

19. Have the student verbally state the steps required to complete a specific math operation (e.g., the steps in long division are $\div$, $\times$, -, bring down, etc.).

20. Have the student work math problems at the board so the teacher can see the steps being performed.

21. Have the student write down directions, explanations, and instructions after they have been given to reinforce retention.

22. Highlight the math symbol for each math problem using a highlight marker.

23. List the steps in solving math problems on the wall-mounted board, bulletin board, etc.

24. Provide sample problems, formulas, formats, etc., as references for solving math problems.

25. Use constructive criticism rather than comments that could be perceived as negative, personal, threatening, etc., (e.g., instead of saying, "You always make the same mistake," say, "A better way to do that might be . . .").

26. Provide the student with a number line on his/her desk to use as a reference.

27. Make sure the student has mastery of math concepts at each level before introducing a new skill level.

28. Do not require the student to learn more information than he/she is capable of learning at any time.

29. Make sure the student recognizes all math operation symbols (e.g., x, -, +, ÷).

30. Teach the student the definitions of specific math vocabulary (e.g., sum, difference, quotient, product, etc.).

31. Enlarge the math operation symbols next to the problems so the student will be more likely to observe the symbol.

32. Use an overhead projector or wall-mounted board to model all steps required when solving a math problem.

33. Model the proper sequence of steps when solving math problems on the wall-mounted board or overhead projector before the student begins a new assignment.

34. Observe the student as he/she solves a math problem to identify and correct error patterns.

35. Pair the student with another student to solve math problems on the wall-mounted board and reinforce the proper sequence of steps.

36. Post necessary sequential information in a readily accessible location (e.g., bulletin board, desktop, inside the student's math folder, etc.).

37. Provide math activities that require active learning rather than memorization.

38. Provide math practice using a computer software program or a hand-held educational device that gives immediate feedback to the student.

39. Provide the student with a list to keep at his/her desk of the steps necessary for the problems he/she is attempting to solve.

40. Provide the student with a computer software program or a hand-held educational device that reinforces the correct sequence of steps in solving math problems.

41. Provide the student with written reminders of task sequences.

42. Place all math problems involving the same steps together on a single line, separate sheet of paper, etc.

43. Reduce the emphasis on competition. Competitive activities may cause the student to hurry and not follow the necessary steps in math problems.

44. Work the first problem or two of a math assignment with the student so he/she will know which steps to use.

45. Reinforce the student for following the necessary steps in math problems: (a) give the student a tangible reward (e.g., classroom privileges, free homework pass, passing out materials, five minutes free time, etc.) or (b) give the student an intangible reward (e.g., fist bump, praise, smile, etc.).

46. Choose a peer to work with the student while he/she learns to follow the steps in solving math problems.

47. Teach and provide practice with different strategies to remember steps in a task:
- repetition,
- mnemonic,
- acronym, and
- association.

48. Use a separate piece of paper for each type (e.g., addition, subtraction, etc.) of math problem. As the student demonstrates success, gradually introduce different types of problems on the same page.

49. Use large colored arrows to indicate where the student should begin to work problems.

50. Use written/verbal repetition to aid the retention of information.

51. Use visual cues (e.g., stop signs, red dots, etc.) to signal when the student must change operations while solving a multi-step math problem.

52. Use written reminders next to math problems to indicate which step is to be done. As the student demonstrates success, gradually reduce the use of reminders.

53. Evaluate the appropriateness of the task to determine (a) if the task is too easy, (b) if the task is too difficult, and (c) if the length of time scheduled for the task is adequate.

54. Have the student use vertical lines or graph paper to help him/her keep math problems in the correct columns.

1. Teach the student that 8/8 equals a whole, 10/10 equals a whole, etc.

2. Choose a peer to work with the student on problems involving fractions or decimals.

3. Provide a variety of restaurant menus for the student to select items from for a meal. Have him/her compute the cost of the items (each involving a decimal point).

4. Cut pieces of paper into equal numbers (e.g., fourths, sixths, tenths, etc.); have the student add fractions together, subtract fractions, etc.

5. Develop a reference sheet for fractions and decimals for the student to keep at his/her desk.

6. For math problems involving fractions with unlike denominators, have the student use a tangible object such as a ruler to help him/her solve the problem (e.g., compare 3/4 to 7/8).

7. Have the student do rote counting by decimals (e.g., .2, .4, .6, .8, etc.).

8. Have the student do rote counting by fractions (e.g., 2/8, 4/8, 6/8, etc.).

9. Have the student earn a hypothetical income and solve money-related math problems using decimals (e.g., taxes, social security, savings, rent, food, clothing, auto payments, recreation, etc.). Match the level of difficulty to the student's ability level.

10. Have the student use a calculator when learning to solve problems involving decimals.

11. Have the student solve fraction problems using real-life measurement such as ounces, inches, pounds, etc., to determine weight, length, volume, etc.

12. Have the student solve math problems involving decimals using tangible objects (e.g., two dollar bills and one fifty cent piece equals $2.50, etc.).

13. Have the student solve math problems involving fractions and decimals using tangible objects (e.g., pennies which are one-tenth of a dime, inch cubes which are one-twelfth of a foot, etc.).

14. Have the student solve money problems to practice decimal problems.

15. Have the student practice solving problems involving fractions and decimals using computer software.

16. Provide the student with a newspaper or catalog. Have him/her make a list of things advertised which he/she would like to purchase and then determine the total cost of the items he/she selected.

17. Do not require the student to learn more information than he/she is capable of learning at any time.

18. Teach the student why he/she is learning the concepts of factions and decimals. Provide the student with concrete examples and opportunities for him/her to apply these concepts in real-life situations.

19. Teach the student number concepts and the relationships of number symbols to numbers of objects before requiring him/her to solve math problems involving fractions and decimals.

20. Teach the student the concept of regrouping (e.g., changing mixed numerals into improper fractions, etc.).

21. Provide practice with fractions and decimals using a computer software program or a hand-held educational device that gives immediate feedback to the student.

22. Provide the student daily with a shopping list of items and a corresponding list with the cost of each item (each involving a decimal point). Have the student determine the total cost of his/her purchase.

23. Provide the student with manipulatives which represent the fractions involved in solving a problem.

24. Reinforce the student for correctly solving problems involving fractions or decimals: (a) give the student a tangible reward (e.g., classroom privileges, line leading, passing out materials, five minutes free time, etc.) or (b) give the student an intangible reward (e.g., praise, fist bump, smile, etc.).

25. Provide the student with many concrete experiences to help him/her learn to use fractions and decimals (e.g., exchanging money, cutting pie-shaped pieces, measuring, weighing, telling time, etc.).

26. Provide the student with paper which has blank boxes and decimal points to guide the student to proper placement of decimal numbers when solving problems involving decimals.

27. Work the first few problems of the math assignment with the student to make sure that he/she understands/follows the directions and the operations necessary to solve the problems.

28. Provide the student with enjoyable math activities involving fractions and decimals which he/she can perform for drill and practice either alone or with a peer (e.g., computer games, math games, manipulatives, etc.).

1. Develop a math reference sheet for the student to keep at his/her desk (e.g., steps used in doing subtraction, multiplication, addition, and division problems).

2. Have the student check his/her math assignments using a calculator to reinforce learning math facts.

3. Have the student practice regrouping a number in different positions and determining its value (e.g., 372, 627, 721).

4. Have the student talk through math problems as he/she is solving them to identify place value errors the student is making.

5. Have the student use a calculator to reinforce learning math facts. Have the student solve several problems each day using a calculator.

6. Make sure the student has mastery of math concepts at each level before introducing a new skill level.

7. Make sure the student has the prerequisite skills to learn place value (e.g., counting, writing numbers to 100, etc.).

8. Do not require the student to learn more information than he/she is capable of learning at any time.

9. Teach the student the concepts and terminology necessary to learn place value (e.g., set, column, middle, left, digit, etc.).

10. Use manipulative objects (e.g., base ten blocks, connecting links, etc.) to teach the student place value and to provide a visual image.

11. Use vertical lines or graph paper to help the student visualize columns and put a single digit in a column.

12. Teach the student that addition, subtraction, and multiplication problems are worked from right to left beginning with the ones column.

13. Teach the student that the collective value of ten *ones* is equal to one *ten* and that ten *tens* is equal to one hundred.

14. Teach the student the zero concept in place value (e.g., there are no tens in the number 207 so a zero is put in the tens column).

15. Money concepts will help the student learn place value association (e.g., $1.26 is the same as six pennies or six ones; two dimes or two tens; one dollar or one hundred).

16. Provide practice with place value using a computer software program or a hand-held educational device that gives immediate feedback to the student.

17. Provide the student with concrete experiences to help him/her learn and remember math facts.

18. Provide the student with learning experiences in grouping tangible objects into groups of *tens, hundreds,* etc., (e.g., popsicle sticks, tongue depressors, paper clips, buttons, etc.).

19. Reduce the emphasis on competition. Competitive activities may cause the student to hurry and make mistakes solving math problems.

20. Have the student practice labeling columns to represent ones, tens, hundreds, etc.

21. Choose a peer to work with the student each day on place value activities (e.g., flash cards).

22. Teach the student why he/she is learning a math concept. Provide the student with concrete examples and opportunities for him/her to apply those concepts in real-life situations.

88 Confuses operational signs when working math problems

1. Evaluate the appropriateness of the task to determine (a) if the task is too easy, (b) if the task is too difficult, and (c) if the length of time scheduled for the task is adequate.

2. Have the student practice recognizing operational symbols (e.g., flash cards of ÷, +, -, x).

3. Use a written reminder beside math problems to indicate which math operation is to be used (e.g., addition, subtraction, multiplication, division). As the student demonstrates success, gradually reduce the use of reminders.

4. Enlarge the math operation symbols next to the problems so the student will be more likely to observe the symbol.

5. Color-code math operation symbols next to math problems so the student will be more likely to observe the symbol.

6. Require the student to go through the math problems on each daily assignment highlighting or otherwise marking the operation of each problem before he/she begins to solve them.

7. Work the first problem or two of the math assignment for the student so he/she knows what operation to use.

8. Use a separate piece of paper for each type of math problem. As the student demonstrates success, gradually introduce different types of math problems on the same page.

9. Place the math operation symbols randomly around the room and have the student practice identifying the operation involved as he/she points to the symbol.

10. Have the student solve his/her math problems using a calculator.

11. Provide the student with a math operation symbol reference sheet to keep and use at his/her desk (e.g., + means add, - means subtract, x means multiply, ÷ means divide).

12. At the top of each sheet of math problems, provide a math operational symbol reminder for the student (e.g., + means add, - means subtract, x means multiply, ÷ means divide).

13. Have the student practice matching math operation symbols to the word identifying the operation using flash cards (e.g., +, -, x, ÷; add, subtract, multiply, divide).

14. Choose a peer to work with the student to provide reminders as the student solves his/her math problems.

15. Make sure the student knows why he/she is learning a math concept. Provide the student with concrete examples and opportunities for him/her to apply those concepts in real-life situations.

16. Have the student check his/her math assignments using a calculator to reinforce the memorization of math facts.

17. Do not require the student to learn more information than he/she is capable of learning at any time.

18. Provide operational sign practice using a computer software program or a hand-held educational device that gives immediate feedback to the student.

19. Make sure the student has mastery of math concepts at each level before introducing a new skill level.

20. Highlight operational signs to draw the student's attention to the signs before beginning the operation.

1. Separate the basic addition and subtraction facts into sets to be memorized by the student.

2. Provide a variety of restaurant menus for the student to select items from for a meal. Have him/her compute the cost of the items.

3. Choose a peer to work with the student every day practicing coin values, paper money values, money combinations, etc.

4. Have the student use a calculator to reinforce solving problems involving money. Have the student solve several money problems each day using the calculator.

5. Have the student earn a hypothetical income and solve money-related math problems. The difficulty level of the problems should match the student's ability level (e.g., taxes, social security, savings, rent, food, clothing, auto payments, recreation, etc.).

6. Have the student match equal values of bills (e.g., five one-dollar bills to a five-dollar bill, two five-dollar bills to a ten-dollar bill, etc.).

7. Have the student match equal values of coins (e.g., two nickels to a dime, two dimes and a nickel to a quarter, five nickels to a quarter, etc.).

8. Have the student talk through money math problems as he/she solves them to identify errors he/she is making.

9. Have the student use a calculator to reinforce solving problems involving money. Have the student solve several money problems each day using a calculator.

10. Provide the student with a newspaper or a catalog. Have him/her make a list of items advertised which he/she would like to purchase and then determine the total cost of the items he/she selected.

11. Provide the student with real money to simulate transactions in the classroom (e.g., purchasing lunch, groceries, snacks, clothing, etc.). Have the student practice acting as both a customer and a clerk.

12. Teach the student to count by ones, fives, tens, and twenties.

13. Teach the student to count by pennies, nickels, dimes, quarters, and half-dollars.

14. Teach the student to recognize all of the coins (e.g., penny, nickel, dime, quarter, half-dollar).

15. Make sure the student knows all the processes necessary to solve problems involving the use of money (e.g., the student can solve math problems of the same difficulty as those involving money).

16. Do not require the student to learn more information than he/she is capable of learning at any time.

17. Teach the student why he/she is learning the concept of money. Provide the student with concrete examples and opportunities for him/her to apply the concept in real-life situations.

18. Teach the student to recognize common denominations of paper money (e.g., one dollar bill, five dollar bill, ten dollar bill, twenty dollar bill, etc.).

19. Make sure the student understands all math operations involved in using money (e.g., addition, subtraction, multiplication, division, decimals, etc.).

20. Provide practice solving money problems using a computer software program or a hand-held educational device that gives immediate feedback to the student.

21. Review daily those skills, concepts, tasks, etc., which have been previously introduced.

22. Provide the student with math word problems involving the use of money. Make sure the appropriate operation is clearly stated.

23. Reduce the emphasis on competition. Competitive activities may cause the student to hurry and make mistakes solving problems involving money.

24. Provide the student with a daily shopping list of items and a corresponding list of the cost of each item. Have the student determine the total cost of his/her purchase.

25. Reinforce the student for correctly solving problems involving money: (a) give the student a tangible reward (e.g., classroom privileges, line leading, passing out materials, five minutes free time, etc.) or (b) give the student an intangible reward (e.g., praise, fist bump, smile, etc.).

26. Use real coins when teaching the student coin recognition and values (e.g., count by ones, fives, tens, etc.; matching combinations of coins; etc.).

27. Provide real-life situations for the student to practice using money (e.g., paying for lunch in the cafeteria line, making purchases from book order clubs, purchasing a soft drink, etc.).

90 Fails to correctly solve problems using measurement

1. Choose a peer to model solving measurement problems for the student.

2. Assign the student measurement activities that he/she will want to perform successfully (e.g., following a cooking recipe, building a model, etc.).

3. Call on the student when he/she is most likely to be able to successfully respond.

4. Develop a measurement reference sheet for the student to use at his/her desk when solving math problems involving measurement.

5. Discuss and provide the student with a list of words and phrases which usually indicate a measurement problem (e.g., pound, inches, millimeter, kilogram, etc.).

6. Evaluate the appropriateness of the task to determine (a) if the task is too easy, (b) if the task is too difficult, and (c) if the length of time scheduled for the task is adequate.

7. Provide opportunities for the student to apply measurement skills in real-life situations (e.g., cooking, measuring the length of objects, etc.).

8. Have the student begin solving problems using same and whole units of measurement (e.g., 10 pounds minus 8 pounds, 24 inches plus 12 inches, etc.). Introduce fractions and mixed units (e.g., pounds and ounces, etc.) only after the student has demonstrated success with same and whole units.

9. Have the student participate in a hands-on experience by following a simple recipe (e.g., gelatin, peanut butter cookies, etc.).

10. Have the student practice basic measurement skills (e.g., pound, ounce, inch, foot, etc.) using everyday measurement devices in the environment (e.g., scale, measuring cup, ruler, etc.).

11. Have the student practice measurement skills in the environment to find an item's length, weight, etc.

12. Have the student practice using smaller units of measurement to create larger units of measurement (e.g., twelve inches to make one foot, three feet to make one yard, eight ounces to make one cup, four cups to make one quart, etc.).

13. Have the student solve simple measurement problems using measurement devices before solving the problems on paper (e.g., five inches plus four inches using a ruler; three liquid ounces plus five liquid ounces using a measuring cup, etc.).

14. Have the student use a calculator to solve measurement problems, check the accuracy of problems worked, etc.

15. Let students use dry ingredients such as macaroni, beans, rice, etc., to measure fractions of a cup.

16. Make sure the language used to communicate with the student about measurement is consistent (e.g., meters, grams, etc.).

17. Make sure the student has mastery of math concepts at each level before introducing a new skill.

18. Do not require the student to learn more information than he/she is capable of learning at any time.

19. Make sure the student knows the basic concepts of fractions before requiring him/her to solve problems involving fractional measurement (e.g., ¼ inch, 1-½ feet, etc.).

20. Teach the student why he/she is learning measuring concepts. Provide the student with concrete examples and opportunities for him/her to apply the concepts in real-life situations.

21. Provide practice solving measurement problems using a computer software program or a hand-held educational device that gives immediate feedback to the student.

22. Work the first problem or two of the math assignment with the student to make sure that he/she understands directions and the operation necessary to solve the problem.

23. Reduce the emphasis on competition. Competitive activities may cause the student to hurry and make mistakes solving measurement problems.

24. Reinforce the student for correctly solving problems involving measurement: (a) give the student a tangible reward (e.g., classroom privileges, line leading, passing out materials, five minutes free time, etc.) or (b) give the student an intangible reward (e.g., praise, fist bump, smile, etc.).

25. Review daily those skills, concepts, tasks, etc., which have been previously introduced.

26. Provide the student with enjoyable measurement activities during free time in the classroom (e.g., computer games, math games, etc.).

1. Have the student count the value of nickels, dimes, quarters, etc., by adding repeated, equal increments.

2. Provide the student with a number line on his/her desk to use as a reference for skip counting.

3. Have the student use a number line when counting by 2s, 5s, 10s, etc., so he/she can see that the increments are being added.

4. Have the student count by 2s, 5s, 10s, etc., and write the numbers as he/she counts. The student can then go back to the numbers he/she has written and see that the increment used (e.g., 2, 5, 10, etc.) is added to each number.

5. Have the student use tangible objects (pennies, paper clips, etc.) when counting by 2s, 5s, 10s, etc., to see that the total number is increasing in equal increments.

6. Have the student use a calculator to do skip counting, adding 2, 5, 10, etc., to each successive number to see that skip counting increases by the increment used in counting.

7. Have the student use a clock in the classroom to count by 2s, 5s, 10s, etc.

8. Teach the student number concepts and the relationship of number symbols to number of objects before requiring him/her to solve math problems involving addition.

9. Choose a peer to work with the student to help him/her understand the concept of skip counting.

10. Teach the student why he/she is learning the concept. Provide the student with concrete examples and opportunities for him/her to apply the concept in real-life situations.

11. Use manipulative objects (e.g., abacus, base ten blocks, etc.) to provide a visual image when teaching the student the concept of skip counting.

12. Do not require the student to learn more information than he/she is capable of learning at any time.

13. Have the student practice a new skill or assignment alone or with an aide, the teacher, or a peer before attempting it with the entire group or before being graded on it.

14. Have the student be a peer tutor and teach a concept he/she has mastered to another student. This can serve as reinforcement for the student.

15. Provide skip counting practice using a computer software program or a hand-held educational device that gives immediate feedback to the student.

16. Make sure the student has mastery of math concepts at each level before introducing a new skill level.

1. Make sure the student understands all concepts involved in telling time (e.g., counting by 15s, 10s, 5s; the big hand and the little hand; etc.).

2. Make sure the student understands the concepts of morning, afternoon, evening, and night.

3. Make sure the student understands which seasons come before and after other seasons.

4. Make sure the student understands the concept of length of a minute, five minutes, ten minutes, fifteen minutes, one hour, ninety minutes, twenty-four hours, etc.

5. Make sure the student has a standard clock in the classroom to use as a visual reference.

6. Make sure the student knows the number of hours in a day, days in a week, weeks in a year, etc.

7. Make sure the student understands the terms used in telling time (e.g., *a quarter 'til, half past, ten 'til, a quarter after,* etc.).

8. Make sure the student can count by common divisors of time (e.g., one minute, five minutes, ten minutes, thirty minutes, an hour, etc.).

9. Have the student recognize when events occur in the daily routine (e.g., recess at 10:15, lunch at 11:45, dismissal at 3:20, etc.).

10. Have the student indicate when the clock in the classroom is on the hour.

11. Have the student indicate when the clock in the classroom is on the half hour.

12. Have the student indicate when the clock in the classroom is on the quarter hour.

13. Have the student set the hands on a clock as the teacher/tutor indicates times of the day.

14. Give the student time word problems involving math concepts on his/her ability level (e.g., "At 10 minutes after 9 o'clock you will begin walking to school. It takes 10 minutes to walk to school. What time will it be when you arrive?").

15. Make sure the student has a clock face with hands to manipulate when learning to tell time.

16. Using a large clock face, set the hands and have the student indicate the time. Begin with the hours, the half hours, the quarter hours, etc.

17. Make sure the student can read a digital clock or watch.

18. Have watches in the classroom which the student can borrow to wear during the school day while he/she is learning to tell time.

19. Make sure the student knows why he/she is learning to tell time. Provide the student with concrete examples and opportunities to apply those concepts in real-life situations.

20. Make sure the student is not required to learn more information than he/she is capable of learning at any time.

21. Have the student learn to recognize one specific important time and let the teacher know when the clock has reached that specific time.

22. Have the student work with a peer each day practicing skills required for telling time.

23. Provide practice in telling time by using computer software programs that give immediate feedback to the student.

24. Reinforce the student for telling time correctly: (a) give the student a tangible reward (e.g., classroom privileges, line leading, five minutes free time, passing out materials, etc.) or (b) give the student an intangible reward (e.g., praise, fist bump, smile, etc.).

1. Give the student alternative math assignments. As the student demonstrates success, gradually introduce more components of the regular assignments.

2. Call on the student when he/she is most likely to be able to successfully respond.

3. Choose a peer to model how to solve addition problems for the student.

4. Deliver information to the student on a one-to-one basis or use a peer tutor.

5. Develop a math facts reference sheet for addition for the student to use at his/her desk when solving math problems.

6. Discuss and provide the student with a list of words and phrases which indicate an addition operation in word problems (e.g., together, altogether, sum, in all, both, gained, received, total, saved, etc.).

7. Evaluate the appropriateness of the task to determine (a) if the task is too easy, (b) if the task is too difficult, and (c) if the length of time scheduled for the task is adequate.

8. Provide opportunities for the student to apply addition facts in real-life situations (e.g., getting change in the cafeteria, measuring the length of objects in industrial arts, etc.).

9. Have the student be a tutor and teach a concept he/she has mastered to another student.

10. Have the student add numbers of objects. Have him/her then pair number symbols with the correct number of objects while he/she solves simple addition problems. As the student demonstrates success in solving simple addition problems, gradually reduce pairing objects with the number symbols until only number symbols are used.

11. Have the student check all math work. Reinforce the student for each error he/she corrects.

12. Have the student independently solve half of his/her addition facts/problems each day. Allow him/her to use a calculator to solve the rest of the problems as reinforcement.

13. Have the student group objects into sets and then add the sets together to obtain a sum.

14. Have the student perform timed drills with addition math facts. The student competes against his/her own best time.

15. Have the student solve addition problems by manipulating objects and stating the process(es) involved.

16. Have the student talk through the math problems as he/she solves them to identify errors he/she is making.

17. Have the student use a calculator for drill of basic addition facts.

18. Have the student use a calculator to reinforce the process of addition. Have the student solve several addition problems each day using a calculator.

19. Provide the student with a number line attached to his/her desk to help solve addition problems.

20. Deliver all directions, questions, explanations, and instructions in a clear, concise manner and at an appropriate rate for the student.

21. Make sure that the language used to communicate with the student about addition is consistent (e.g., "Add the numbers." "What is the total?" or "Find the sum.").

22. Make sure the student has mastery of math concepts at each level before introducing a new skill level.

23. Do not require the student to learn more information than he/she is capable of learning at any time.

24. Teach the student the concepts of more than, less than, equal, and zero. The use of tangible objects should facilitate the learning process.

25. Teach the student why he/she is learning the concept of addition. Provide the student with concrete examples and opportunities for him/her to apply the concept in real-life situations.

26. Teach the student number concepts and the relationship of number symbols to numbers of objects before requiring him/her to solve math problems involving addition.

27. Provide practice of addition facts using a computer software program or a hand-held educational device that gives immediate feedback to the student.

28. Provide the student with a quiet place to work (e.g., office, study carrel, etc.). This is used as a means of reducing distracting stimuli and not as a form of punishment.

29. Provide the student with enjoyable math activities during free time in the classroom (e.g., computer games, math games, manipulatives, etc.).

30. Provide the student with increased opportunity for help or assistance on academic tasks (e.g., peer tutoring, directions for assignments sent home, frequent interactions, etc.).

31. Require the student to use graph paper to line up the numbers correctly in columns.

32. Provide the student with opportunities for tutoring by peers or teachers. Allow the student to tutor others when he/she has mastered a concept.

33. Provide the student with self-checking materials. Require corrections to be made before turning in assignments.

34. Provide the student with shorter math tasks, but give more of them throughout the day (e.g., four assignments of five problems each rather than one assignment of twenty problems).

35. Reduce the emphasis on competition. Competitive activities may cause the student to hurry and solve addition problems incorrectly.

36. Reinforce the student for attempting and completing work. Emphasize the number or problems correctly solved. Encourage the student to see how many more he/she can correctly solve without help. Have the student maintain a private chart of his/her math performance.

37. Reinforce the student for correctly solving addition problems: (a) give the student a tangible reward (e.g., classroom privileges, line leading, passing out materials, five minutes free time, etc.) or (b) give the student an intangible reward (e.g., praise, fist bump, smile, etc.).

38. Teach the student to use resources in the environment to help him/her solve math problems (e.g., counting figures, counting numbers of objects, using a calculator, etc.).

39. Use daily drill activities to help the student memorize addition facts (e.g., written problems, flash cards, etc.).

40. Work the first problem or two of the math assignment with the student to make sure that he/she understands the directions and the operation necessary to solve the problems.

41. Provide the student with many concrete experiences to help him/her learn and remember math facts. Use popsicle sticks, tongue depressors, paper clips, buttons, fingers, etc., to form groupings to teach addition facts.

1. Give the student alternative math assignments. As the student demonstrates success, gradually introduce more components of the regular assignments.

2. Choose a peer to model how to solve subtraction problems for the student.

3. Call on the student when he/she is most likely to be able to successfully respond.

4. Deliver information to the student on a one-to-one basis or use a peer tutor.

5. Develop a math facts reference sheet for subtraction for the student to use at his/her desk when solving math problems.

6. Discuss and provide the student with a list of words and phrases which usually indicate subtraction operations (e.g., difference between, from, left, how many less, how much taller, how much farther, etc.).

7. Evaluate the appropriateness of the task to determine (a) if the task is too easy, (b) if the task is too difficult, and (c) if the length of time scheduled for the task is adequate.

8. Provide opportunities for the student to apply subtraction facts in real-life situations (e.g., getting change in the cafeteria, measuring the length of objects in industrial arts, etc.).

9. Have the student be a tutor and teach a concept he/she has mastered to another student.

10. Have the student check all math work. Reinforce the student for each error he/she corrects.

11. Have the student independently solve half of his/her subtraction problems each day. Allow him/her to use a calculator to solve the other half of the assignment as reinforcement.

12. Have the student subtract a certain number of objects from a group, then pair number symbols with the objects while the student solves the subtraction problem. In the last step, the student subtracts the number symbols without using objects.

13. Have the student perform timed drills with subtraction facts as reinforcement. The student competes against his/her own best times.

14. Have the student solve subtraction problems by manipulating objects and stating the process(es) involved.

15. Have the student talk through math problems as he/she solves them to identify errors he/she is making.

16. Have the student use a calculator for drill of basic subtraction facts.

17. Have the student use a calculator to reinforce the process of subtraction. Have the student solve several problems each day using a calculator.

18. Provide the student with a number line attached to his/her desk to help solve subtraction problems.

19. Deliver all directions, questions, explanations, and instructions in a clear, concise manner and at an appropriate rate for the student.

20. Make sure that the language used to communicate with the student about subtraction is consistent (e.g., "Subtract the numbers." "What is the difference?" etc.).

21. Make sure the student has mastery of math concepts at each level before introducing a new skill level.

22. Require the student to use graph paper to line up the numbers correctly in columns.

23. Teach the student the concepts of more than, less than, equal, and zero. The use of tangible objects should facilitate the learning process.

24. Teach the student why he/she is learning a math concept. Provide the student with concrete examples and opportunities for him/her to apply those concepts in real-life situations.

25. Teach the student the concept of subtraction (e.g., "You have three toys and I take away two of them. How many do you have left?").

26. Teach the student number concepts and the relationship of number symbols to numbers of objects before requiring him/her to solve math problems involving subtraction.

27. Provide subtraction practice using a computer software program or a hand-held educational device that gives immediate feedback to the student.

28. Provide the student with a quiet place to work (e.g., office, study carrel, etc.). This is used as a means of reducing distracting stimuli and not as a form of punishment.

29. Provide the student with enjoyable math activities during free time in the classroom (e.g., computer games, math games, manipulatives, etc.).

30. Do not require the student to learn more information than he/she is capable of learning at any time.

31. Reduce the emphasis on competition. Competitive activities may cause the student to hurry and solve subtraction problems incorrectly.

32. Provide the student with opportunities for tutoring by peers and teachers. Allow the student to tutor others when he/she has mastered a concept.

33. Use daily drill activities to help the student memorize subtraction facts (e.g., written problems, flash cards, etc.).

34. Provide the student with self-checking materials. Require corrections to be made before turning in assignments.

35. Provide the student with shorter math tasks, but give more of them throughout the day (e.g., four assignments of five problems each rather than one assignment of twenty problems).

36. Provide the student with increased opportunity for help or assistance on academic tasks (e.g., peer tutoring, directions for assignments sent home, frequent interactions, etc.).

37. Reinforce the student for attempting and completing work. Emphasize the number of problems correctly solved. Encourage the student to see how many more he/she can correctly solve without help. Have the student maintain a private chart of his/her math performance.

38. Reinforce the student for correctly solving subtraction problems: (a) give the student a tangible reward (e.g., class privileges, line leading, passing out materials, five minutes free time, etc.) or (b) give the student an intangible reward (e.g., praise, fist bump, smile, etc.).

39. Require the student to check subtraction problems using addition (i.e., the difference plus the subtrahend equals the minuend). Reinforce the student for each error he/she corrects.

40. Teach the student to use resources in the environment to help him/her solve math problems (e.g., counting figures, counting numbers of objects, using a calculator, etc.).

41. Work the first problem or two of the math assignment with the student to make sure that he/she understands the directions and the operation necessary to solve the problems.

42. Provide the student with many concrete experiences to help him/her learn and remember subtraction facts. Use popsicle sticks, paper clips, fingers, etc., to form groupings to teach subtraction facts.

95 Fails to correctly solve math problems requiring multiplication

1. Give the student alternative math assignments. As the student demonstrates success, gradually introduce more components of the regular assignments.

2. Choose a peer to model how to solve multiplication problems for the student.

3. Call on the student when he/she is most likely to be able to successfully respond.

4. Deliver information to the student on a one-to-one basis or use a peer tutor.

5. Develop a math facts reference sheet for multiplication for the student to use at his/her desk when solving math problems.

6. Discuss and provide the student with a list of words and phrases which usually indicate a multiplication operation (e.g., area, each, times, product, double, triple, twice, etc.).

7. Evaluate the appropriateness of the task to determine (a) if the task is too easy, (b) if the task is too difficult, and (c) if the length of time scheduled for the task is adequate.

8. Have the student use a calculator for drill of basic multiplication facts.

9. Have the student check all math work. Reinforce the student for each error he/she corrects.

10. Have the student practice the multiplication tables each day with a peer using flash cards.

11. Have the student be a tutor and teach a concept he/she has mastered to another student.

12. Have the student count by equal distances on a number line. Demonstrate that the equal distances represent skip counting, which is the concept of multiplication.

13. Have the student independently solve half of his/her multiplication problems each day. Allow him/her to use a calculator to solve the other half of the assignment as reinforcement.

14. Have the student perform timed drills with multiplication facts as reinforcement. The student competes against his/her own best time.

15. Have the student solve multiplication problems by manipulating objects and stating the process(es) involved.

16. Have the student talk through math problems as he/she solves them to identify errors he/she is making.

17. Have the student use a calculator to reinforce the process of multiplication. Have the student solve several multiplication problems each day using a calculator.

18. Identify specific multiplication problems the student fails to correctly solve. Target those problems for additional instruction, tutoring, and drill activities.

19. Deliver all directions, questions, explanations, and instructions in a clear, concise manner and at an appropriate rate for the student.

20. Make sure the student has mastery of math concepts at each level before introducing a new skill level.

21. Do not require the student to learn more information than he/she is capable of learning at any time.

22. Teach the student why he/she is learning multiplication. Provide the student with concrete examples and opportunities for him/her to apply those concepts in real-life situations.

23. Practice skip counting by 2s, 3s, and 5s.

24. Teach the student number concepts and the relationship of number symbols to numbers of objects before requiring him/her to solve math problems involving multiplication.

25. Teach the student that multiplication is a way of adding that takes less time. Give examples of how much longer it takes to add than to multiply.

26. Provide practice of multiplication facts using a computer software program or a hand-held educational device that gives immediate feedback to the student.

27. Provide the student with a quiet place to work (e.g., office, study carrel, etc.). This is used as a means of reducing distracting stimuli and not as a form of punishment.

28. Provide the student with enjoyable math activities during free time in the classroom (e.g., computer games, math games, manipulatives, etc.).

29. Provide the student with increased opportunity for help or assistance on academic tasks (e.g., peer tutoring, directions for assignments sent home, frequent interactions, etc.).

30. Teach the student that any number times zero will be zero.

31. Provide the student with opportunities for tutoring by peers or teachers. Allow the student to tutor others when he/she has mastered a concept.

32. Provide the student with self-checking materials. Require corrections to be made before turning in assignments.

33. Provide the student with shorter math tasks, but give more of them throughout the day (e.g., four assignments of five problems each rather than one assignment of twenty problems).

34. Reduce the emphasis on competition. Competitive activities may cause the student to hurry and solve multiplication problems incorrectly.

35. Reinforce the student for attempting and completing work. Emphasize the number of problems correctly solved. Encourage the student to see how many more he/she can correctly solve without help. Have the student maintain a private chart of his/her math performance.

36. Reinforce the student for correctly solving multiplication problems: (a) give the student a tangible reward (e.g., classroom privileges, line leading, passing out materials, five minutes free time, etc.) or (b) give the student an intangible reward (e.g., praise, fist bump, smile, etc.).

37. Require the student to use graph paper to line up the numbers correctly in columns.

38. Teach the student that any number times one remains that number.

39. Teach the student to use resources in the environment to help him/her solve math problems (e.g., counting figures, counting numbers of objects, using a calculator, etc.).

40. Use daily drill activities to help the student memorize multiplication facts (e.g., written problems, flash cards, etc.).

41. Work the first problem or two of the math assignment with the student to make sure that he/she understands the directions and the operation necessary to solve the problems.

42. Provide the student with many concrete experiences to help him/her learn and remember math facts. Use popsicle sticks, tongue depressors, paper clips, buttons, fingers, etc., to form groupings to teach multiplication facts.

1. Give the student alternative math assignments. As the student demonstrates success, gradually introduce more components of the regular assignments.

2. Call on the student when he/she is most likely to be able to successfully respond.

3. Choose a peer to model how to solve division problems for the student.

4. Deliver information to the student on a one-to-one basis or use a peer tutor.

5. Develop a math fact reference sheet for division for the student to use at his/her desk when solving math problems.

6. Discuss and provide the student with a list of words and phrases which usually indicate a division operation in word problems (e.g., into, share, each, average, quotient, half as many, etc.).

7. Evaluate the appropriateness of the task to determine (a) if the task is too easy, (b) if the task is too difficult, and (c) if the length of time scheduled for the task is adequate.

8. Provide opportunities for the student to apply division facts in real-life situations (e.g., money, average length of time it takes to do a job, etc.).

9. Give the student several objects (e.g., one inch cubes, plastic links, etc.) and have him/her divide them into groups.

10. Have the student be a tutor and teach a concept he/she has mastered to another student.

11. Identify specific division problems the student fails to correctly solve. Target those problems for additional instruction, tutoring, and drill activities.

12. Have the student check all math work. Reinforce the student for each error he/she corrects.

13. Have the student independently solve half of his/her math problems each day. Allow him/her to use a calculator to solve the other half of the assignment as reinforcement.

14. Teach the student to divide numbers of objects. Then have the student pair number symbols with the number of objects while solving the division problem. In the last step, the student divides without using objects.

15. Have the student list all the skills necessary to work a division problem (e.g., subtraction, multiplication, etc.).

16. Have the student perform timed drills with division facts as reinforcement. The student competes against his/her own best time.

17. Have the student practice the division tables each day with a peer using flash cards.

18. Have the student solve math problems by manipulating objects and stating the process(es) involved.

19. Have the student talk through math problems as he/she solves them to identify errors he/she is making.

20. Have the student use a calculator for drill of basic division facts.

21. Have the student use a calculator to reinforce the process of division. Have the student solve several division problems each day using a calculator.

22. Teach the student that any number divided by one remains that number.

23. Deliver all directions, questions, explanations, and instructions in a clear, concise manner and at an appropriate rate for the student.

24. Make sure that the language used to communicate with the student about division is consistent (e.g., "Divide the numbers." "What is the divisor?" "What is the dividend?" etc.).

25. Make sure the student has mastery of math concepts at each level before introducing a new skill level.

26. Teach the student the concept of sets. Have the student practice dividing sets into two subsets, etc., to reinforce the concept of division.

27. Do not require the student to learn more information than he/she is capable of learning at any time.

28. Teach the student the concepts of more than, less than, equal, and zero. The use of tangible objects should facilitate the learning process.

29. Teach the student why he/she is learning the concept of division. Provide the student with concrete examples and opportunities for him/her to apply the concept in real-life situations.

30. Teach the student number concepts and the relationship of number symbols to numbers of objects before requiring him/her to solve math problems involving division.

31. Provide practice of division facts using a computer software program or a hand-held educational device that gives immediate feedback to the student.

32. Provide the student with a quiet place to work (e.g., office, study carrel, etc.). This is used as a means of reducing distracting stimuli and not as a form of punishment.

33. Provide the student with enjoyable math activities during free time in the classroom (e.g., computer games, math games, manipulatives, etc.).

34. Provide the student with increased opportunity for help or assistance on academic tasks (e.g., peer tutoring, directions for assignments sent home, frequent interactions, etc.).

35. Provide the student with many concrete experiences to help him/her learn and remember math facts. Use popsicle sticks, tongue depressors, paper clips, buttons, fingers, etc., to form groupings to teach division facts.

36. Provide the student with opportunities for tutoring by peers or teachers. Allow the student to tutor others when he/she has mastered a concept.

37. Provide the student with self-checking materials. Require corrections to be made before turning in assignments.

38. Provide the student with shorter math tasks, but give more of them throughout the day (e.g., four assignments of five problems each rather than one assignment of twenty problems).

39. Reduce the emphasis on competition. Competitive activities may cause the student to hurry and solve division problems incorrectly.

40. Reinforce the student for attempting and completing work. Emphasize the number of problems correctly solved. Encourage the student to see how many more he/she can correctly solve without help. Have the student maintain a private chart of his/her math performance.

41. Reinforce the student for correctly solving division problems: (a) give the student a tangible reward (e.g., classroom privileges, line leading, passing out materials, five minutes free time, etc.) or (b) give the student an intangible reward (e.g., praise, fist bump, smile, etc.).

42. Use practical applications of division. Have each student bring something that must be divided among the whole class.

43. Teach the student to use resources in the environment to help him/her solve math problems (e.g., counting figures, counting numbers of objects, using a calculator, etc.).

44. Use daily drill activities to help the student memorize division facts (e.g., written problems, flash cards, etc.).

45. Use task analysis on each problem to determine the point at which the student is unable to complete the calculations correctly.

46. Work the first problem or two of the assignment with the student to make sure that he/she understands the directions and the operation necessary to solve the problems.

1. Be sure addition and subtraction facts have been mastered before introducing multiplication and division facts.

2. Separate the basic addition and subtraction facts into sets. Require the student to memorize each set in succession.

3. Build upon and reinforce math facts the student has mastered. As the student demonstrates success, add one new fact at a time.

4. Choose a peer to drill the student each day on math facts (e.g., flash cards).

5. Choose one fact the student has not mastered. Make it the student's fact of the day, and review it several times throughout the day.

6. Develop a math facts reference sheet for addition, subtraction, multiplication, or division for the student to use at his/her desk when solving math problems.

7. Develop and post basic addition, subtraction, multiplication, and division charts which the student can use in solving math problems.

8. Provide opportunities for the student to apply math facts in real-life situations (e.g., getting change in the cafeteria, measuring the length of objects in industrial arts, etc.).

9. Have students complete a math facts quiz sheet as they arrive each morning.

10. Have the student complete a math facts worksheet and use a calculator to check and correct the answers.

11. Have the student independently solve half of his/her math problems each day. Allow him/her to use a calculator to solve the other half of the assignment as reinforcement.

12. Have the student use a number line attached to his/her desk to add and subtract.

13. Have the student perform timed drills to reinforce with basic math facts as reinforcement. The student competes against his/her own best times.

14. Have the student play a math facts game with other students. Let each student take turns answering and checking facts.

15. Have the student practice skip counting to reinforce multiplication facts (e.g., 5s: 5, 10, 15, 20, 25, 30, etc.).

16. Have the student use a calculator for drill activities of basic math facts.

17. Have the student use a calculator to reinforce memorization of math facts. Have the student solve several problems each day using a calculator.

18. Have the student use math facts CDs and DVDs for drill activities.

19. If a student has difficulty memorizing facts, allow him/her to keep a chart of facts at his/her desk to use as a reference.

20. Provide practice and reinforcement of math facts using computer software programs that provide game-like activities.

21. Provide practice of math facts using a computer software program or a hand-held educational device that gives immediate feedback to the student.

22. Provide the student with many concrete experiences to help learn and remember math facts. Use popsicle sticks, tongue depressors, paper clips, buttons, etc., to form groupings to teach math facts.

23. Using the tracking technique to help the student learn math facts, present a few facts at a time. As the student demonstrates success, gradually increase the number of facts the student must memorize.

24. Review daily those skills, concepts, tasks, etc., which have been previously introduced.

25. Reinforce the student for improving retention of math facts: (a) give the student a tangible reward (e.g., classroom privileges, line leading, passing out materials, five minutes free time, etc.) or (b) give the student an intangible reward (e.g., praise, fist bump, smile, etc.).

26. Have the student practice facts at home with flash cards, computer programs, or hand-held games.

27. Play class games to reinforce math facts (e.g., bingo, *Jeopardy!*, teacher-made games, etc.).

28. Teach the student that subtraction facts are the inverse of addition facts. The same concept holds true for multiplication and division.

29. Use daily drill activities to help the student memorize math facts (e.g., written problems, flash cards, etc.).

30. Use fingers to teach the student to form addition and subtraction combinations. Have the student hold up fingers and add or subtract other fingers to find the correct answer.

31. Do not require the student to learn more information than he/she is capable of learning at any time.

32. Use manipulative objects (e.g., peg board, abacus, base ten blocks, etc.) to provide a visual image when teaching the student basic math facts.

33. Reduce the emphasis on competition. Competitive activities may cause the student to hurry and make mistakes when solving math problems.

1. Choose a peer to model the use of columns when working math problems for the student.

2. Develop a marked column format (e.g., /thousands/hundreds/tens/ones/) which can be copied from an original for the student to use in solving all assigned math problems.

3. Have the student exchange 10 pennies for a dime and correlate that activity with grouping ten ones and placing a 1 in the tens column and a 0 in the ones column.

4. Have the student practice labeling columns to represent ones, tens, hundreds, etc.

5. Have the student practice regrouping a number in different positions and determining its value (e.g., 372, 723, 237).

6. Have the student practice using columns when solving math problems by using a computer program which automatically chooses the correct column at input.

7. Have the student talk through math problems as he/she is solving them to identify errors hc/she is making.

8. Have the student use a calculator to solve math problems involving the use of columns.

9. Make sure the student has the prerequisite skills to learn place value (e.g., counting verbally, understanding sets, writing numbers to 100, etc.).

10. Teach the student the concepts and terminology necessary to learn place value (e.g., set, column, middle, left, digit, etc.).

11. Teach the student why he/she is learning a math concept. Provide the student with concrete examples and opportunities for him/her to apply the concept in real-life situations.

12. Teach the student that math problems of addition, subtraction, and multiplication move from right to left beginning with the ones column.

13. Teach the student that the collective value of ten *ones* is equal to one *ten* and that ten *tens* is equal to one hundred.

14. Teach the student the zero concept in place value (e.g., there are no tens in the number *207* so a zero is put in the tens column).

15. Use money concepts to help the student learn place value by association (e.g., $1.26 is the same as six pennies or six ones, two dimes or two tens, one dollar or one hundred).

16. Provide practice with a computer software program or a hand-held educational device that gives immediate feedback to the student.

17. Provide the student with a masked window to help the student use columns accurately.

18. Provide the student with learning experiences in grouping tangible objects into groups of ones, tens, hundreds, etc.

19. Use vertical lines on graph paper to help the student visualize columns and put a single digit in each column.

20. Teach the student to place a number in the ones column and move to the left to the next column from ones to tens, hundreds, thousands, etc.

21. Use manipulative objects (e.g., base ten blocks, connecting links, etc.) to provide a visual image when teaching the student place value.

22. Provide the student with many opportunities to indicate the value of columns in multiple-digit numbers (e.g., 56 = ( ) tens and ( ) ones; 329 = ( ) hundreds, ( ) tens, and ( ) ones; etc.).

23. Provide the student with color-coded columns to help the student use columns accurately.

24. Reinforce the student for accurately using columns when solving math problems: (a) give the student a tangible reward (e.g., classroom privileges, line leading, passing out materials, five minutes free time, etc.) or (b) give the student an intangible reward (e.g., praise, fist bump, smile, etc.).

25. Require the student to check all his/her math assignments for accuracy. Reinforce the student for each correction made in the use of columns.

26. Provide the student with self-checking materials to reinforce the use of columns.

H. Academic Performance

99 Does not perform or complete classroom assignments during class time

1. Teach the student direction-following skills (e.g., listen carefully, write down important points, ask for clarification, wait until all directions are received before beginning, etc.).

2. Practice direction-following skills on nonacademic tasks.

3. Establish assignment rules:
- Listen to directions.
- Wait until all directions have been given.
- Ask questions about anything you do not understand.
- Begin the assignment only when you are certain about what you are supposed to do.
- Make sure you have all the necessary materials, etc.

4. Deliver directions/instructions before handing out materials.

5. Maintain consistency in the classroom's daily routine.

6. Allow natural consequences to occur (e.g., may not participate in extracurricular sports, may not earn graduation credit, etc.) due to the student's failure to complete classwork.

7. Assign the student shorter tasks (e.g., modify a 20-problem math activity to 4 activities of 5 problems each to be done at various times during the day). As the student demonstrates success, gradually increase the length of each task and decrease the number of tasks.

8. Communicate with the student's parents (e.g., notes home, phone calls, etc.) to share information about their child's progress. The parents may reinforce the student at home for completing assignments at school.

9. Specify exactly what is to be done for the completion of an assignment or task (e.g., indicate definite starting and stopping points, indicate the minimum requirements, etc.).

10. Assign one task/assignment at a time. Give the student enough time to complete it.

11. Assist the student in writing a contract for himself/herself designating a time to complete an assignment and avoid procrastination.

12. Establish a timeline for completing a project. Expect the student to meet each deadline to complete the project on time.

13. Maintain consistent expectations within the ability level of the student.

14. Deliver reinforcement for any and all measures of improvement.

15. Help the student develop an awareness of the consequences of his/her behavior by writing down or talking through problems which may occur due to his/her not completing assignments (e.g., if the student does not focus on assignments in class, he/she may not pass the class. If he/she does not pass the class, he/she will not earn a credit, etc.).

16. Help the student develop an awareness of himself/herself and the environment. Instruct the student to step back and ask himself/herself, "Am I on task and completing my assignments?" "What should I be doing now?"

17. Choose a peer to model appropriate completion of the assignments or tasks during the time provided for the student.

18. Supervise the student during class assignments to maintain on-task behavior.

19. Reinforce the student for completing assignments or tasks based on the amount of work he/she can successfully complete in a given period of time. As the student demonstrates success, gradually increase the duration of assignments or tasks.

20. Provide the student with shorter assignments or tasks given more frequently.

21. Reinforce the student for completing assignments or tasks during the time provided based on the length of time the student can be successful (e.g., every 5 minutes, 10 minutes, etc.). As the student demonstrates success, gradually increase the length of time required for reinforcement.

22. Schedule important activities/assignments/meetings at times when the student is most likely to maintain attention (e.g., one hour after medication, 45 minutes after lunch, first thing in the morning, etc.).

23. Have the student keep a chart/graph representing the number of class assignments completed.

24. Have the student develop a checklist/chart to follow which will allow him/her to complete all assignments.

25. Have the student and a classmate who has the same assignment do their classwork together.

26. Reinforce those students in the classroom who complete assignments or tasks during the time provided.

27. Set time limits for completing classroom assignments so that the student knows exactly how long he/she has to work and when to be finished. Encourage the student to be aware of time constraints when working on projects.

28. Allow some free time between classwork assignments if the student appears to need a break.

29. Assess the degree of task difficulty to determine whether or not the student will require additional information, time, assistance, etc., before beginning a task.

30. Assess the degree of task difficulty in comparison with the student's ability to perform the task.

31. Have the student ask questions about directions, explanations, and instructions he/she does not understand.

32. Establish classroom rules:
- Concentrate while working.
- Work quietly.
- Remain in your seat.
- Finish task.
- Meet task requirements.

Review rules often. Reinforce students for following the rules.

33. Have the student repeat the directions verbally to the teacher.

34. Require the student to begin each assignment or task within a specified period of time (e.g., three minutes, five minutes, etc.).

35. Speak with the student to explain (a) what he/she is doing wrong (e.g., not completing assignments) and (b) what he/she should be doing (e.g., completing assignments during class).

36. Provide the student with structure for all academic activities (e.g., specific directions, routine format for tasks, time limits, etc.).

37. Make it pleasant and positive for the student to ask questions about things he/she does not understand. Reinforce the student by assisting, congratulating, praising, etc.

38. Encourage the student to ask for clarification of directions for classroom assignments.

39. Provide alternatives to the traditional format of directions (e.g., record directions, summarize directions, peers give directions, etc.).

40. Give directions in steps (e.g., give the student each additional step after completion of the previous step).

41. Teach the student time management skills. Have the student make a daily plan and follow it. Encourage the student to avoid becoming distracted by events, impulses, and moods.

42. Interact frequently with the student to help him/her follow directions for the assignments.

43. Explain to the student, when he/she does not complete an assignment correctly, what he/she is doing wrong, what he/she is supposed to be doing, and why.

44. Have the student ask for help when he/she needs it.

45. Have the student schedule his/her own time for assignments or tasks (e.g., 20 minutes for each of 3 assignments, 15 minutes for each of 4 assignments, etc.) to pace himself/herself.

46. Encourage the student to manage his/her daily performance as if he/she were self-employed. This should increase his/her motivation to successfully complete assignments.

47. Assist the student in performing his/her classwork. As the student demonstrates success, gradually decrease the assistance and require the student to independently assume more responsibility.

48. Interact frequently with the student to maintain involvement with class assignments (e.g., ask the student questions, ask the student's opinion, stand close to the student, seat the student near the teacher's desk, etc.).

49. Provide simple, concrete, clearly-stated directions in written or verbal form.

50. Present the assignment or task in the most attractive and interesting manner possible.

51. Have the student complete assignments in a private place (e.g., carrel, office, quiet study area, etc.) to reduce the anxiety of public failure.

52. Repeat directions to facilitate the probability of the student's understanding.

53. Organize assignments by dividing them into small segments. Set deadlines and provide the student with a reward after completing each segment of the assignment.

54. Do not require the student to learn more information than he/she is capable of learning at any time.

55. Make sure that the student is attending to the teacher when directions are given (e.g., making eye contact, hands free of writing materials, looking at assignment, etc.).

56. Remind the student when it is time to do classwork.

57. Consider carefully the student's ability level and experience before assigning tasks to him/her.

58. Provide the student with quality material to complete the assignment (e.g., pencil with eraser, paper, dictionary, handwriting sample, etc.). Be sure that the student has only the necessary material on his/her desk.

59. Complete the first few items of an assignment or task with the student to serve as a model and start the student on the assignment or task.

60. Assess the quality and clarity of directions, explanations, and instructions given to the student.

61. Allow the student the option of performing the assignment or task at another time (e.g., earlier in the day, later, on another day, or at home).

62. Give directions in a variety of ways to facilitate the student's understanding (e.g., if the student does not understand verbal directions, present them in written form).

63. Reward the student for concentrating on an assignment for a specific length of time (e.g., smile, verbal praise, a note acknowledging his/her effort, etc.).

64. Reduce the amount of information on a page (e.g., less print to read, fewer problems, isolate information that is presented to the student, etc.) if it is visually distracting for the student.

65. Reduce emphasis on academic and social competition. Fear of failure may cause the student to not want to complete assignments or tasks during the time provided.

66. Reinforce the student for the steps of beginning, working on, and completing each individual assignment or task during the time provided.

67. Provide the student with the opportunity to perform assignments/activities in a variety of ways (e.g., recorded, with a calculator, verbally, etc.).

68. Have the student time assignments or tasks to monitor his/her own behavior and accept time limits.

69. Maintain consistency in the assignments or tasks to be completed within the time provided.

70. Prevent the student from becoming over-stimulated by an activity (e.g., frustrated, angry, excited, etc.).

71. Have the student choose a peer who has the ability to complete work assignments. Instruct the student to observe that person and try to model the behaviors which allow him/her to complete assignments.

72. Allow the student access to pencils, pens, etc., only after directions have been given.

73. Encourage the parents to make positive comments about school and the importance of completing classwork.

74. Provide the student with a schedule of activities so that he/she knows exactly what and how much there is to do in a given period of time.

75. Provide the student with a variety of assignments. Have him/her to choose a minimum number from the total to complete (e.g., present the student with 10 academic tasks from which 6 must be completed that day).

76. Ask the student why he/she is not completing assignments or tasks in the time provided. The student may have the most accurate perception as to why he/she is not completing the required assignments or tasks during the time provided.

77. Allow the student more decision-making opportunities relative to class activities and assignments.

78. Provide the student with increased opportunities for help or assistance on academic assignments or tasks (e.g., peer tutoring, directions for work sent home, frequent interactions, etc.).

79. Evaluate the visual and auditory stimuli in the classroom. Determine the amount of stimuli the student can tolerate. Remove the extraneous stimuli from the environment.

80. Write a contract with the student specifying what behavior is expected (e.g., completing assignments or tasks during the time provided) and what reinforcement will be made available when the terms of the contract have been met.

81. Structure time limits so the student knows exactly how long he/she has to work and when to be finished.

82. Make sure the student achieves success when following directions.

83. Prioritize tasks by importance (e.g., task A must be done today, task B can be done today, and task C can wait until tomorrow).

84. Teach the student organizational and task completion skills (e.g., begin with a clean desk, read directions carefully, collect all the necessary materials, ask for assistance if needed, look for the main idea, follow examples provided, answer questions you know first and leave those you are unsure of for last, etc.).

85. Evaluate the appropriateness of the task to determine (a) if the task is too easy, (b) if the task is too difficult, and (c) if the length of time scheduled to complete the task is adequate.

86. Provide the student with more than enough time to finish an activity. As the student demonstrates success, gradually decrease the amount of time provided to finish an activity.

87. Make sure the student understands that classwork not completed and turned in on time must still be completed and turned in at a later time.

88. Encourage the student to realize that all behavior has negative or positive consequences. Encourage the student to practice behaviors that will lead to positive consequences.

89. Have the student verbally repeat the directions to the teacher.

90. Have the student explain to the teacher what he/she should do to complete the assignment or task.

91. Communicate clearly with the student the length of time he/she has to complete an assignment. The student may want to use a timer to complete the tasks within the given period of time.

92. Reinforce the student for completing the assignments or tasks during the time provided: (a) give the student a tangible reward (e.g., classroom privileges, line leading, passing out materials, five minutes free time, etc.) or (b) give the student an intangible reward (e.g., praise, fist bump, smile, etc.).

93. Deliver directions verbally to increase the probability of the student's understanding of class assignments.

94. Make sure the student understands the natural consequences for failing to complete assignments or tasks during the time provided (e.g., students who do not finish their work are not allowed to do more desirable activities).

95. Discuss the student's responsibilities at the beginning of each class period so he/she knows what is expected.

96. Maintain visibility to and from the student. The teacher should be able to see the student and the student should be able to see the teacher. Make eye contact possible at all times.

97. Reduce distracting stimuli (e.g., place the student on the front row, provide a carrel or office space away from distractions, etc.). This is used as a means of reducing stimuli and not as a form of punishment.

98. Have the student assemble all the materials necessary to work on a project, assignment, etc., to reduce the need to search for materials and unnecessary distractions.

99. Work a few problems of the assignment with the student to serve as a model and start the student on the assignment.

100. Choose a peer to help the student with class assignments or tasks.

101. Structure the environment to provide the student with increased opportunity for help or assistance on assignments (e.g., peer tutoring, directions for work sent home, frequent interactions, etc.).

102. Along with the student, chart those assignments that have been completed within the time provided.

103. Have the student record the time it took him/her to complete each assignment or task to accurately determine how much time is spent on each assignment or task.

104. Present one assignment at a time. As each assignment is completed, deliver reinforcement along with the presentation of the next assignment.

105. Have the student use a timer to complete tasks within a given period of time.

106. Create challenges in assigned tasks to increase interest and motivation (e.g., cooperative learning strategies, etc.).

107. Provide an incentive statement along with a directive (e.g., "When you finish your classwork, you may go to lunch.").

108. Establish assignment rules (e.g., listen to directions, wait until all verbal directions have been given, ask questions about anything not understood, make sure you have all of the necessary materials, and begin the assignment when you are certain about what you are supposed to do, etc.).

109. Make sure that the student understands the relationship between inappropriate behavior and the consequences which follow (e.g., failure to perform or complete classroom assignments will result in a low grade).

110. Check over the student's classwork when he/she is finished so you can be sure that everything is completed.

111. Reinforce the student for beginning, working on, and completing assignments.

112. Take proactive steps to deal with a student's refusal to perform an assignment to prevent contagion in the classroom (e.g., refrain from arguing with the student, place the student at a carrel or other quiet place to work, remove the student from the group or classroom, etc.).

113. Allow the student additional time to complete class assignments or homework.

114. Explain to the student that work not done during class/work time will have to be done during other times (e.g., recess, break time, recreational time, before/after school, lunchtime, etc.).

115. Follow a less desirable assignment with a highly desirable assignment. Require the student to complete the first in order to begin the second.

116. Provide the student with step-by-step written directions for completing class assignments or tasks.

1. Chart homework assignments completed.

2. Speak to the student to explain (a) what the student is doing wrong (e.g., not turning in homework assignments) and (b) what the student should be doing (i.e., completing homework assignments and returning them to school).

3. Encourage the student to reduce distractions (e.g., turn off the music and/or TV, ask people to talk quietly, etc.) to complete homework.

4. Take proactive steps to deal with a student's refusal to perform a homework assignment to prevent contagion in the classroom (e.g., refrain from arguing with the student, place the student at a carrel or other quiet place to work, remove the student from the group or classroom, etc.).

5. Choose a peer to model completing homework assignments and returning them to school for the student.

6. Encourage the student to realize that all behavior has negative or positive consequences. Encourage the student to practice behaviors that will lead to positive consequences.

7. Encourage the student to set up an office at home where homework can be completed.

8. Have the student evaluate the visual and auditory stimuli in his/her designated work space at home to determine the amount of stimuli he/she can tolerate.

9. Develop a contract with the student and his/her parents requiring that homework be done before more desirable activities take place at home (e.g., playing, watching television, going out for the evening, etc.).

10. Assign homework that provides drill and practice rather than introducing new concepts or information.

11. Assign small amounts of homework. As the student demonstrates success, gradually increase the amount of homework (e.g., one or two problems to complete may be sufficient to begin the homework process).

12. Maintain consistency in assigning homework (i.e., assign the same amount of homework each day).

13. Make sure the amount of homework assigned is not excessive and can be completed within a reasonable amount of time. Remember, secondary students may have six or seven teachers assigning homework each day.

14. Evaluate the appropriateness of the homework assignment to determine (a) if the task is too easy, (b) if the task is too difficult, and (c) if the length of time scheduled to complete the task is adequate.

15. Reinforce the student for completing homework assignments and returning them to school: (a) give the student a tangible reward (e.g., classroom privileges, five minutes free time, etc.) or (b) give the student an intangible reward (e.g., praise, fist bump, smile, etc.).

16. Reinforce the student for completing homework assignments based on the number of assignments the student can successfully complete. As the student demonstrates success, gradually increase the number of assignments required for reinforcement.

17. Reinforce those students who complete their assignments at school during the time provided.

18. Send home one homework assignment at a time. As the student demonstrates success completing assignments at home, gradually increase the number of homework assignments sent home.

19. Present the tasks in the most attractive and interesting manner possible.

20. Identify the materials the student consistently fails to take home. Provide a set of those materials for the student to keep at home.

21. Help the student develop an awareness of the consequences of his/her behavior by writing down or talking through problems which may occur due to his/her not completing homework assignments (e.g., if he/she does not complete the homework assignment, his/her grade may drop then he/she may not be able to participate in extracurricular activities).

22. Provide the student with a book bag, backpack, etc., to take homework assignments and materials to and from home.

23. Provide a reinforcing activity at the beginning of the day/class period contingent upon the completion and return of homework assignments.

24. Have the student organize assignments by dividing them into small segments. Have the student set deadlines and provide himself/herself with a reward after completing each segment of the assignment.

25. Have the student develop a checklist/chart to follow which will allow him/her to complete all assignments.

26. Establish an environmental setting for the classroom that promotes optimal individual performance (e.g., quiet room, background music, fresh air, etc.).

27. Encourage the parents to make positive comments about school and the importance of completing homework.

28. Provide time at school for homework completion when the student cannot be successful completing assignments at home.

29. Specify exactly what is to be done for the completion of the homework task (e.g., indicate definite starting and stopping points, indicate the minimum requirements, etc.).

30. Have the student ask questions about directions, explanations, or instructions not understood.

31. Allow natural consequences to occur for failure to complete homework assignments (e.g., students who do not finish their homework do not get to participate in more desirable activities).

32. Provide the student with written directions for doing homework assignments.

33. Provide the parents with information necessary for them to help the student with homework (e.g., what the assignments are and how to help with the assignments).

34. Encourage the student to reward himself/herself (e.g., take a ten minute break, speak briefly with a relative, phone a friend, etc.) for concentrating on an assignment for a specific length of time.

35. Allow the student to perform a highly desirable task when homework has been turned in to the teacher.

36. Have the student place notes in highly visible areas (e.g., refrigerator door, bathroom door, front door, etc.) to remind the student to take homework assignments to school.

37. Allow the student to perform alternative homework assignments. As the student demonstrates success, gradually introduce more components of the regular homework assignment until the assignments are routinely performed and returned to school.

38. Make sure the student understands that homework assignments not completed and turned in to the teacher will have to be completed during other times (e.g., break time, recreational time, before/after school, etc.).

39. Work a few problems of the homework assignment with the student to start the student on the assignment.

40. Have the student enlist the help of a relative, friend, etc., to remind him/her of homework assignments.

41. Make sure the student understands that homework not completed and turned in on time must still be completed and turned in.

42. Have the student verbally repeat the homework assignment to reinforce the student's awareness of the assignment.

43. Have the student prioritize tasks by importance (e.g., task A must be done today, task B can be done today, and task C can wait until tomorrow).

44. Find a tutor (e.g., a volunteer in the community, one of the student's classmates, etc.) to help the student complete homework.

45. Have the student set a timer to complete assignments in a reasonable period of time.

46. Deliver directions verbally to the student to facilitate the probability of this/her understanding of homework assignments.

47. Encourage the student to follow a less desirable task with a more desirable task. Make completion of the first task necessary to perform the second.

48. Maintain consistent expectations within the ability level of the student.

49. Encourage the student to set time limits for completing homework assignments. Encourage the student to be aware of time constraints when working on projects.

50. Encourage the student to recite a mantra to himself/herself when he/she brings work home (e.g., I will finish, I will finish, I will finish).

51. Deliver reinforcement for any and all measures of homework improvement.

52. Communicate with the student's parents the need to establish homework rules at home (e.g., start homework upon arriving home from school, finish homework before watching TV or talking on the phone, ask for help when necessary, etc.).

53. Encourage the student to reduce the number of visual distractions around him/her (e.g., move his/her work area away from windows, doors, kitchen, TV, etc.).

54. Encourage the student to put completed homework assignments in a designated place to be taken to school (e.g., in front of the door, at the bottom of the stairs, etc.).

55. Establish homework assignment rules:
- Concentrate while working.
- Finish task.
- Meet task expectations.

Review rules often. Reinforce students for following the rules.

56. Encourage the student to choose interesting or stimulating activities as a reward for completing less interesting activities (e.g., complete homework before going to the mall).

57. Have the student keep a chart or graph representing the number of homework assignments completed and returned to school.

58. Encourage the student's parents to check over their child's homework when he/she is finished to make sure that everything is completed.

59. Introduce the student to other resource persons who may be of help in completing homework assignments (e.g., librarian, special education teacher, other personnel with expertise or time to help, etc.).

60. Communicate with parents (e.g., notes home, phone calls, etc.) to share information about the student's progress. The parents may reinforce the student at home for returning completed homework to school.

61. Arrange with the student's parents to pick up homework each day if the student has difficulty remembering to take it home.

62. Establish a timeline for completing a project. Expect the student to meet each deadline to complete the project on time.

63. Do not use homework as a punishment (i.e., additional work should not be assigned as a consequence for inappropriate behavior at school or as a consequence for not preparing for school assignments).

64. Encourage the parents to set aside quiet time each night when the family turns off the TV, music, etc., to read, do homework, write letters, etc.

65. Have the student maintain sample letters, reports, forms, etc., as references for completing homework assignments.

66. Encourage the student to establish a routine for himself/herself. Have the student develop a weekly schedule and a weekend schedule. Have the student develop a checklist/chart for daily homework assignments to be completed.

67. Communicate with the student's parents by sending home explanations of how to help their child with homework if it is necessary for the student to receive help.

68. Have the student develop problem-solving skills:
- Identify the problem (e.g., not completing homework, not returning completed homework to school).
- Identify the goals and objectives.
- Develop a strategy/plan for action.
- Carry out the plan.
- Evaluate the results.

69. Schedule the student's time at school so that homework will not be absolutely necessary if he/she takes advantage of the school time provided to complete assignments.

70. Write a contract with the student specifying what behavior is expected (e.g., completing homework assignments and returning them to school) and what reinforcement will be made available when the terms of the contract have been met.

71. Assess the appropriateness of giving the student assignments which require copying if the student's ability level makes it impossible for him/her to complete the assignment.

72. Meet with parents to discuss appropriate ways to help the student with homework.

73. Encourage the parents to provide the student with a quiet, comfortable place and adequate time to do homework.

74. Encourage the parents to reward the student for following homework rules. Possible rewards include verbal praise (e.g., "Thank you for finishing your homework before going to the mall."), a kiss on the cheek, a hug, staying up past bedtime, watching a favorite TV show, renting a video, etc.

75. Choose a peer to help the student with homework.

76. Assess the appropriateness of assigning the student homework if his/her ability level or circumstances at home make it impossible for him/her to complete and return the assignments.

77. Develop an assignment sheet for the student. Talk with the student's parents so they are aware of the assignment sheet and the work that should be completed each night. Ask the parents to sign the assignment sheet to indicate that they have reviewed it.

78. Ask the parents to review with the student his/her homework responsibilities after school so he/she knows what he/she is expected to do that evening.

79. Make sure the student has all the materials necessary prior to beginning an assignment to reduce unnecessary distractions.

80. Have the student ask for help when he/she needs it.

81. Set up a homework system for the student (e.g., 2 days a week drill with flash cards, 3 days a week work from a workbook or textbook, etc.). This will add some variety to the student's homework.

82. Make sure that the student understands the relationship between inappropriate behavior and the consequences which follow (e.g., forgetting to complete homework will result in a low grade).

83. Repeat directions to facilitate the student's probability of understanding.

84. Make sure the student has mastered the concepts presented at school. Homework should be a form of practice for what has been learned at school.

85. Have the student establish a specific time each evening to work on homework assignments.

86. Assess the degree of task difficulty to determine whether or not the student will require additional information, time, assistance, etc., to complete a task at home.

87. Have the student ask a friend to call him/her at night or in the morning to remind him/her to bring assignments to school.

88. Give directions in a variety of ways to facilitate the student's understanding (e.g., if the student does not understand verbal directions, present them in written form).

89. Teach the student time-management skills. Have the student make a daily plan and follow it. Encourage the student to avoid becoming distracted by events, impulses, and moods.

90. Allow the student additional time to turn in homework assignments.

91. Create a learning center at school where professional educators are available to help with homework assignments before school begins, the last hour of each school day, etc.

92. Have the student and a classmate who has the same assignment do their homework together (e.g., right after school at one home or the other, during study hall, etc.).

93. Reinforce those students in the classroom who complete their homework assignments and return them to school.

94. Send homework assignments and materials home with someone other than the student (e.g., brother, sister, neighbor, etc.).

95. Provide the student with a variety of assignments, requiring him/her to choose a minimum number from the total to complete (e.g., present the student with 10 academic tasks from which he/she must finish 6 that day).

101 Fails to perform tasks or assignments independently

1. Establish classroom rules:
   - Concentrate while working.
   - Work quietly.
   - Request assistance when needed.
   - Remain in your seat.
   - Finish task.
   - Meet task expectations.

   Review rules often. Reinforce students for following the rules.

2. Set time limits for completing assignments.

3. Reinforce the student for performing assignments independently.

4. Have the student prioritize tasks by importance (e.g., task A must be done today, task B can be done today, and task C can wait until tomorrow).

5. Structure the environment to facilitate task completion (i.e. Make sure the student's tasks are on his/her ability level, be sure that instructions are clear, and maintain frequent interactions with the student to facilitate success).

6. Encourage parents to set aside and enforce a consistent time period at home for the student to complete homework. All family members should work on tasks (e.g., correspondence, balancing accounts, reading, etc.) during this time.

7. Provide the student with structure for all academic activities (e.g., specific directions, routine format for tasks, time limits, etc.).

8. Reinforce the student for beginning, working on, and completing assignments.

9. Make sure that directions, explanations, and instructions are delivered on the student's ability level.

10. Assess the appropriateness of giving the student assignments which require copying if the student's ability level makes it impossible for him/her to complete the assignment.

11. Allow the student additional time to complete assignments when working independently.

12. Provide the student with a variety of assignments and require him/her to choose a minimum number of assignments to perform independently (e.g., present the student with 10 academic tasks from which six must be completed that day).

13. Communicate expectations to the student for the successful completion of assignments.

14. Provide a written list of directions for a long-term assignment.

15. Schedule recreational activities at the end of the day. Make participation in these activities dependent upon completion of assignments.

16. Communicate with the student's parents (e.g., notes home, phone calls, etc.) to share information about their child's progress. The parents may reinforce the student at home for completing assignments independently.

17. Assess the degree of task difficulty in relation to the student's ability to perform the task.

18. Be consistent in expecting the student to complete assignments. Do not allow the student to not complete assigned tasks one time and expect tasks to be completed the next time.

19. Reinforce those students in the classroom who complete assignments independently.

20. Encourage the student to follow a less desirable task with a more desirable task. Make completion of the first task necessary to perform the second.

21. Assess the degree of task difficulty to determine whether or not the student will require additional information, time, assistance, etc., before beginning a task.

22. Instruct the student in thinking through instructions/directions before beginning a task.

23. Instruct the student on ways to reduce distracting activities which interfere with his/her responsibilities (e.g., turn off the TV when it is time to complete tasks, do not allow friends to come over when it is time to do homework, etc.).

24. Explain to the student that work not done during work time will have to be done during other times (e.g., break time, recreational time, after school, etc.).

25. Assist the student in writing a contract for himself/herself designating a time to complete an assignment and avoid procrastination.

26. Encourage the student to reward himself/herself (e.g., take a ten minute break, speak briefly with a relative, phone a friend, etc.) for concentrating on an assignment for a specific length of time.

27. Provide the student with step-by-step written directions for assignments.

28. Specify exactly what is to be done for the completion of an assignment (e.g., indicate definite starting and stopping points, indicate the minimum requirements, etc.).

29. Do not give directions to the student from across the room. Go to student, get his/her undivided attention, and tell him/her what to do.

30. Reinforce the student for completing assignments independently: (a) give the student a tangible reward (e.g., classroom privileges, free homework pass, five minutes free time, etc.) or (b) give the student an intangible reward (e.g., praise, fist bump, smile, etc.).

31. Allow the student to perform alternative assignments. As the student demonstrates success, gradually introduce more components of the regular assignments until those assignments are routinely performed.

32. Have the student keep a chart/graph representing the number of assignments performed independently.

33. Communicate to the student an interest in his her success.

34. Have the student review and update his/her assignment calendar daily. Encourage the student to prepare in advance for assignments, due dates, etc.

35. Communicate with parents, agencies, or the appropriate parties, to inform them of the problem, determine the cause of the problem, and consider possible solutions to the problem.

36. Reduce distracting stimuli (e.g., place the student in the front row, provide a carrel or quiet place away from distractions, etc.). This is to be used as a means of reducing stimuli and not as a form of punishment.

37. Allow the student to set a timer to complete assignments in a reasonable period of time.

38. Create challenges in assignments to increase interest and motivation (e.g., stress problem solving and creative/critical thinking rather than drill/repetition, etc.).

39. Communicate to the student that he/she is a worthwhile individual.

40. Present assignments in the most interesting manner possible.

41. Communicate clearly with the student the length of time he/she has to complete an assignment. The student may want to use a timer to complete the tasks within the given period of time.

42. Reinforce the student for completing assignments independently based on the number of times he/she can be successful. As the student demonstrates success, gradually increase the number of times required for reinforcement.

43. Encourage the student to ask for clarification of any directions, explanations, and instructions before beginning a task to reinforce comprehension.

44. Maintain mobility throughout the classroom to determine the student's attention to task.

45. Call on the student often to encourage communication.

46. Have the student assemble all materials necessary to work on a project, assignment, etc., to reduce the need to search for materials.

47. Make sure that the student understands the relationship between inappropriate behavior and the consequences which follow (e.g., not completing assignments independently results in lower grades, less responsibility, etc.).

48. Make sure that assignments given to the student are appropriate for his/her level of development and ability.

49. Establish an environmental setting for the classroom that promotes optimal individual performance (e.g., quiet room, background music, fresh air, etc.).

50. Maintain consistent expectations within the ability level of the student.

51. Choose a peer, friend, etc., who displays the ability to organize an assignment prior to beginning it. Have the student observe that person and try to model the behaviors which allow him/her to organize assignments.

52. Discuss with the student the expectation at the beginning of each period so he/she knows what is required.

53. Work a few problems of the assignment with the student to serve as a model and start the student on the assignment.

54. Assign the student shorter tasks. As the student demonstrates success, gradually increase the length of the tasks.

55. Organize assignments by dividing them into small segments. Set deadlines and provide the student with a reward after completing each segment of the assignment.

56. Develop a checklist/chart for daily assignments to be completed by the student.

57. Teach the student time-management skills. Have the student make a daily plan and follow it. Encourage the student to avoid becoming distracted by events, impulses, and moods.

58. Enlist the help of a peer, paraprofessional, parent, etc., to remind the student of assignments.

59. Have the student use a daily calendar to write down assignments, projects, due dates, etc. Use the calendar to develop the student's time-management skills.

60. Have the student schedule independent working times when he/she is most likely to maintain attention (e.g., one hour after medication, 45 minutes after dinner, first thing in the morning, etc.).

61. Allow the student more decision-making opportunities relative to class activities and assignments.

62. Have the student use electronic reminders to assist him/her in completion of assignments (e.g., programmable watch, computer programs, voice mail, etc.).

63. Speak to the student to explain (a) what he/she is doing wrong (e.g., off task, failing to complete assignments) and (b) what he/she should be doing (e.g., attending to task, completing assignments sequentially, completing tasks).

64. Write a contract with the student specifying what behavior is expected (e.g., complete assigned project by due date) and what reinforcement will be made available when the terms of the contract have been met.

65. Have the student develop a checklist/chart to follow which will allow him/her to complete all assignments.

66. Make sure the student is paying attention when he/she is told to do something. Have the student make eye contact and repeat the information to check for understanding.

67. Encourage the student to take a break while working on monotonous assignments to relieve restlessness and improve concentration. Set a definite time limit for breaks.

68. Create an environment that is quiet and uncluttered (e.g., clean, well-lighted, fresh-smelling, and at a comfortable temperature).

1. Teach and encourage the student to practice basic study skills (e.g., reading for the main point, note taking, summarizing, highlighting, studying in an appropriate environment, using time wisely, etc.) before taking tests or quizzes.

2. Assess student performance in a variety of ways (e.g., have the student give verbal explanations, simulations, physical demonstrations of a skill, etc.).

3. Give shorter tests or quizzes, but give them more frequently. As the student demonstrates success, gradually increase the length of tests or quizzes over time.

4. Have tests or quizzes read to the student.

5. Have the student verbally answer tests or quizzes.

6. Record the tests or quizzes and allow the student to listen to questions as often as necessary.

7. Arrange a time for the student to study with a peer tutor before taking tests or quizzes.

8. Have the student take tests or quizzes in the resource room where the resource teacher can clarify questions, offer explanations, etc.

9. Provide the student with opportunities for review before taking tests or quizzes.

10. Have the student ask questions about things he/she does not understand while taking tests or quizzes.

11. Make sure that the tests or quizzes measure knowledge of content and not related skills, such as reading or writing.

12. Teach the student test-taking strategies (e.g., answer questions you are sure of first, learn to summarize, check each answer, etc.).

13. Have the student maintain a performance record for each subject in which he/she is experiencing difficulty.

14. Allow the student to take tests or quizzes in a quiet place to reduce distractions (e.g., study carrel, library, etc.).

15. Provide a variety of opportunities for the student to learn the information covered by tests or quizzes (e.g., visuals, visitors, community resources, etc.).

16. Allow the student to respond to alternative test or quiz questions (e.g., more generalized questions which represent global understanding).

17. Provide the opportunity for the student to study daily assignments with a peer.

18. Have the student take a sample test or quiz before the actual test.

19. Remove the threat of public knowledge of failure (e.g., test or quiz results are not read aloud or posted, test ranges are not made public, etc.).

20. Reduce the emphasis on formal testing by grading the student on daily performance.

21. Provide parents with information on test or quiz content (e.g., which material will be covered by the test or quiz, format, types of questions, etc.).

22. Modify instructions to include more concrete examples to facilitate student learning.

23. Monitor student performance to detect errors and determine where learning problems exist.

24. Reduce the emphasis on competition. Students who compete academically and fail may cease to try to succeed and do far less than they are capable of achieving.

25. Only give tests and quizzes to the student when he/she is certain to succeed (e.g., after determining that the student has learned the information).

26. Make sure the student has mastery of skills at each level before testing a concept.

27. Reinforce those students who demonstrate improved test or quiz scores. (It may be best to reinforce privately rather than publicly.)

28. Make sure that all directions, questions, explanations, and instructions are delivered in a clear, concise manner and at an appropriate rate for the student.

29. Identify the student's most effective learning mode. Use it when giving tests or quizzes to facilitate the student's understanding.

30. Evaluate the appropriateness of the task to determine (a) if the task is too easy, (b) if the task is too difficult, and (c) if the length of time scheduled for the task is adequate.

31. Communicate with the parents (e.g., notes home, phone calls, etc.) to share information about the student's progress. The parents may reinforce the student at home for improved test or quiz scores.

32. Write a contract with the student specifying what behavior is expected (e.g., improved test or quiz scores) and what reinforcement will be made available when the terms of the contract have been met.

33. Provide the student with increased opportunities for help or assistance on academic tasks (e.g., peer tutoring, directions for work sent home, frequent interactions, etc.).

34. Establish classroom rules:
- Concentrate while working.
- Work quietly.
- Remain in your seat.
- Finish task.
- Meet task requirements.

Review rules often. Reinforce the student for following the rules.

35. Speak with the student to explain (a) what the student is doing wrong (e.g., not attending during class, not using study time, etc.) and (b) what the student should be doing (e.g., attending during class, asking questions, using study time, etc.).

36. Reinforce improved test or quiz scores: (a) give the student a tangible reward (e.g., classroom privileges, line leading, passing out materials, five minutes free time, etc.) or (b) give the student an intangible reward (e.g., praise, fist bump, smile, etc.).

103 Does not prepare for assigned activities or daily routines

1. Have the student verbally repeat the school assignment to reinforce the student's awareness of the assignment.

2. Allow natural consequences to occur (e.g., receiving low grades, being excluded from extracurricular activities, not earning course credit, etc.) due to the student's failure to complete his/her school assignments.

3. Help the student develop an awareness of the consequences of his/her behavior by writing down or talking through problems which may occur due to his/her inability to complete assignments (e.g., if you do not return the assignment to school, you are in danger of failing the class then you may not get the credit you need for graduation).

4. Allow natural consequences to occur for failure to turn in homework assignments (e.g., students who do not finish their homework do not get to participate in more desirable activities).

5. Allow the student to perform a highly desirable task when assignments have been turned in.

6. Provide the student with adequate time at school to prepare for assigned activities (e.g., supervised study time).

7. Have the student make it a habit to periodically review notes, daily calendar of events, or tasks that need to be completed.

8. Allow the student to perform alternative homework assignments. As the student demonstrates success, gradually introduce more components of the regular homework assignment until the assignments are routinely performed and returned to school.

9. Arrange with the student's parents to pick up homework each day if the student has difficulty remembering to take it home.

10. Ask the student why he/she is unprepared for assigned activities. The student may have the most accurate perception.

11. Have the student chart his/her completed assignments.

12. Assess the quality and clarity of directions, explanations, and instructions given to the student.

13. Choose a peer to accompany the student to specified activities to make sure the student has the necessary materials.

14. Have the student find a method of organization that works best for him/her (e.g., daily list, weekly list, etc.) and use that method consistently. Delete accomplished tasks to keep an up-to-date list.

15. Choose a peer to help the student with homework.

16. Choose a peer tutor to work with the student to prepare for assigned activities.

17. Assign short-term tasks that can be quickly and accurately completed. As the student demonstrates success, gradually increase the length of assignments.

18. Assign small amounts of homework initially, gradually increasing the amount as the student demonstrates success (e.g., one or two problems may be sufficient to begin the homework process).

19. Assist the student in performing his/her school assignments. As the student demonstrates success, gradually decrease the assistance and require the student to independently assume more responsibility.

20. At the end of the day, remind the student when materials are required for specified activities for the next day (e.g., send a note home, give a verbal reminder, etc.).

21. Find a tutor (e.g., peer, volunteer, etc.) to work with the student at home.

22. Chart homework assignments completed.

23. Communicate with parents (e.g., notes home, phone calls, etc.) to share information about the student's progress. The parents may reinforce the student at home for being prepared for assigned activities at school.

24. Communicate with parents or guardians to inform them of the student's homework assignments and what they can do to help him/her prepare for assigned activities.

25. Consider carefully the student's ability level when expecting him/her to be able to study for a specific amount of time.

26. Create a learning center at school, open the last hour of each school day, where professional educators are available to help with homework.

27. Deliver directions verbally and in written format to increase the probability of the student's understanding of school assignments.

28. Allow natural consequences to occur when the student is unprepared for assigned activities (e.g., the student will fail a test or quiz, work not done during work time must be completed during recreational time, etc.).

29. Deliver reinforcement for any and all measures of improvement.

30. Develop a contract with the student and his/her parents requiring that homework be done before more desirable activities take place at home (e.g., playing, watching television, going out for the evening, etc.).

31. Do not use homework as a punishment (i.e., homework should not be assigned as a consequence for inappropriate behavior at school).

32. Choose a peer to help the student review information needed to successfully complete a school assignment.

33. Encourage the parents to provide the student with a quiet, comfortable place and adequate time to study and prepare for school assignments.

34. Encourage the parents to set aside quiet time each night when the family turns off the TV, music, etc.; to read, do homework, write letters, etc.

35. Encourage the student to put completed homework assignments in a designated place to be taken to school (e.g., in front of the door, at the bottom of the stairs, etc.).

36. Establish a time line for completing a school assignment. Expect the student to meet each deadline to complete the project on time.

37. Have the student leave necessary materials at specified activity areas.

38. Establish school assignment rules:
  • Concentrate while working.
  • Work quietly.
  • Finish task.
  • Meet task expectations.
  • Turn in task.
Review rules often. Reinforce students for following the rules.

39. Make sure the student has mastered the concepts presented at school. All homework should be a form of practice for what has been learned at school.

40. Evaluate the appropriateness of the assignment to determine (a) if the task is too easy, (b) if the task is too difficult, and (c) if the length of time scheduled to complete the task is adequate.

41. Find a tutor (e.g., a volunteer in the community, peer, etc.) to help the student complete his/her school assignments.

42. Assess the appropriateness of assigning the student homework if his/her ability level or circumstances at home make it impossible for him/her to complete and return the assignments.

43. Follow a less desirable task with a more desirable task. Make completion of the first task necessary to perform the second.

44. Maintain consistent expectations within the ability level of the student.

45. Give directions in a variety of ways to facilitate the student's understanding (e.g., if the student does not understand verbal directions, present them in written form).

46. Have the student anticipate future tasks/ assignments and develop plans for addressing them.

47. Have the student develop a checklist/chart to follow which will allow him/her to self monitor all assignments.

48. Have the student establish a routine to follow before coming to class (e.g., check which activity is next, determine what materials are necessary, collect materials, etc.)

49. Assess the degree of task difficulty to determine whether or not the student will require additional information, time, assistance, etc., before beginning a task.

50. Have the student keep a chart/graph of the number of assignments turned in to the teacher.

51. Model being prepared for assigned activities.

52. Have the student ask questions about directions, explanations, and instructions not understood.

53. Choose a peer to model turning in school assignments for the student.

54. Develop a school/home assignment sheet to be reviewed and signed by the parents each evening. Communicate with the parents and student to establish clear expectations and positive consequences for completing and returning the assignment sheet.

55. Have the student time activities to monitor personal behavior and accept time limits.

56. Choose a peer to model being prepared for assigned activities for the student.

57. Have the student set a timer to complete assignments in a reasonable period of time.

58. Provide the student with a written list of assignments to be completed each day and have him/her check each assignment as it is completed.

59. Identify the materials the student consistently fails to take home. Provide a set of those materials for the student to keep at home.

60. Maintain consistency in assigning homework (i.e., assign the same amount of homework each day).

61. Reinforce those students who complete their assignments at school during the time provided.

62. Make sure that failure to be prepared for assigned activities results in losing the opportunity to participate in activities or a failing grade for that day's activity.

63. Have the student establish a routine and utilize a weekly schedule. Have the student develop a checklist/chart for daily school assignments to be completed.

64. Make sure that homework is designed to provide drill activities rather than introduce new information.

65. Provide the student with a book bag, backpack, etc., to take homework assignments and materials to and from home.

66. Do not require the student to learn more information than he/she is capable of learning at any time.

67. Identify resource personnel from whom the student may receive additional assistance (e.g., librarian, special education teacher, other personnel with expertise or time to help, etc.).

68. Make sure the student understands that assignments not completed and turned in on time must still be completed and turned in late.

69. Provide the student with written directions to follow in preparing for all assigned activities.

70. Make positive comments about school and the importance of completing assignments.

71. Schedule the student's time at school so homework will not be absolutely necessary if he/she takes advantage of the school time provided to complete assignments.

72. Make sure the student has all the materials necessary to complete school assignments (e.g., pencils, paper, erasers, etc.).

73. Meet with the student's parents to discuss with them appropriate ways to help their child with school assignments.

74. Minimize materials needed.

75. Introduce the student to other resource persons who may be of help in doing homework (e.g., other teachers, the librarian, etc.).

76. Present assignments/tasks in the most attractive and interesting manner possible.

77. Provide individual assistance to the student to help him/her prepare for assigned activities (e.g., time set aside during the day, study hall, after school, etc.).

78. Provide the student with a list of necessary materials for each activity of the day.

79. Provide the student with structure for all academic activities (e.g., specific directions, routine format for tasks, time limits, etc.).

80. Make sure the student understands the relationship between behavior and the consequences which follow (e.g., forgetting to complete his/her school assignments will result in a low grade).

81. Provide the student with verbal reminders of materials required for each activity.

82. Reinforce those students in the classroom who are prepared for assigned activities.

83. Provide time at school for homework completion when the student cannot be successful completing assignments at home.

84. Reduce the number/length of assignments. As the student demonstrates success, gradually increase the number/length of assignments.

85. Provide time each day for the student to organize his/her materials (e.g., before school, break time, at lunch, at the end of the day, etc.).

86. Repeat directions to increase the student's probability of understanding.

87. Work a few problems of the school assignment with the student to serve as a model and start the student on the assignment.

88. Speak to the student to explain (a) what he/she is doing wrong (e.g., not turning in assignments) and (b) what he/she should be doing (e.g., completing homework/school assignments and returning them to school).

89. Review on a daily basis, those skills, concepts, tasks, etc., which have been previously introduced.

90. Send home explanations each day so the student's parents may help their child with his/her school assignments if necessary.

91. Write a contract with the student specifying what behavior is expected (e.g., studying for tests or quizzes) and what reinforcement will be made available when the terms of the contract have been met.

92. Send homework assignments and materials home with someone other than the student (e.g., brother, sister, neighbor, etc.).

93. Set aside time at the end of the day for the student to complete unfinished assignments.

94. Set up a homework system for the student (e.g., two days a week work with drill flash cards, three days a week work on book work sent home, etc.). This will add some variety to homework.

95. Send home one homework assignment at a time. As the student demonstrates success completing assignments at home, gradually increase the number of homework assignments sent home.

96. Reinforce the student for being prepared for assigned activities based on the number of times he/she can be successful. As the student demonstrates success, gradually increase the number of times required for reinforcement.

97. Take proactive steps to deal with a student's refusal to perform a school assignment to prevent contagion in the classroom (e.g., refrain from arguing with the student, place the student in a carrel or other quiet place to work, remove the student from the group or classroom, etc.).

98. Teach the student time-management skills. Have the student make a daily plan and follow it. Encourage the student to avoid becoming distracted by events, impulses, and moods.

99. Reinforce the student for being prepared for assigned activities: (a) give the student a tangible reward (e.g., classroom privileges, line leading, passing out materials, five minutes free time, etc.) or (b) give the student an intangible reward (e.g., praise, fist bump, smile, etc.).

100. Specify exactly what is to be done for the completion of assignments (e.g., make definite starting and stopping points, determine a minimum requirement, etc.).

104 Does not remain on task for the required length of time

1. Establish classroom rules:
   - Concentrate while working.
   - Work quietly.
   - Remain in your seat.
   - Finish task.
   - Meet task requirements.

   Review rules often. Reinforce the student for following the rules.

2. Set time limits for completing assignments.

3. Speak to the student to explain (a) what the student is doing wrong (e.g., not attending to tasks) and (b) what the student should be doing (e.g., attending to tasks).

4. Choose a peer to model on-task behavior for the student.

5. Encourage the student to develop a 30 second definition of his/her goal to help him/her stay on task and focused (e.g., "I will complete ten math problems without a reminder from the teacher to stay on task. The better I focus and stay on task, the better I will perform.").

6. Move objects used for tactile stimulation (e.g., pens, paper clips, loose change, etc.) away from the student's reach.

7. Follow a less desirable task with a more desirable task. Make completion of the first task necessary to perform the second.

8. Reinforce the student for attending to a task based on the length of time he/she can be successful. As the student demonstrates success, gradually increase the length of time required for reinforcement.

9. Provide an incentive statement along with a directive (e.g., "When you complete this assignment, you may earn a pass to the water fountain.").

10. Present tasks in the most attractive and interesting manner possible.

11. Reduce auditory and visual stimuli to a level at which the student can successfully function. As the student demonstrates that he/she can successfully tolerate increased levels of stimuli, gradually allow auditory and visual stimuli to increase.

12. Reward the student for concentrating on an assignment for a specific length of time (e.g., take a break, get a drink of water, talk briefly with a peer, etc.).

13. Position the student's desk or work area so that he/she is not visually distracted by others (e.g., turn the student's desk away from other students, etc.).

14. Use more interesting or stimulating activities as a reward for completing less interesting activities (e.g., after completing a rough draft on paper, the student can choose graphics available on the computer).

15. Reward the student for completing an assignment within the amount of time allotted.

16. Assist the student in completing class assignments. As the student demonstrates success, gradually decrease assistance and require the student to independently remain on task.

17. Have the student define a goal. Assist the student in developing specific strategies to achieve his/her goal and following through on those strategies.

18. Help the student develop an awareness of himself/herself and the environment. Have the student periodically, step back and ask himself/herself, "Am I on task and paying attention?" "What should I be doing now?"

19. Help the student develop attention-maintaining behaviors (e.g., maintain eye contact, take notes on the subject, ask questions related to the subject, etc.).

20. Allow the student to take a break while working on monotonous assignments to relieve restlessness and improve concentration.

21. Have the student organize assignments by dividing them into small segments. Set deadlines and provide the student with a reward after completing each segment of the assignment.

22. Reduce the number of current assignments by adding new assignments when previous assignments have been completed.

23. Allow the student to close the classroom door or windows to reduce auditory and visual distractions from outside of the classroom.

24. Create a quiet area in the classroom where absolute silence must be observed.

25. Schedule a fun educational activity (e.g., computer game) during the day to provide incentive for the student to stay on task and behave appropriately.

26. Assist the student in writing a contract for himself/herself designating a time to complete an assignment and avoid procrastination.

27. Be proactive. Work with the school counselor to create a schedule to facilitate the student's success (e.g., physical education scheduled the last period of the day, intersperse electives which allow greater freedom of movement with classes requiring extended periods of concentration, etc.).

28. Make participation in extracurricular activities dependent upon completion of class assignments.

29. Specify exactly what is to be done for the completion of a task (e.g., indicate definite starting and stopping points, indicate the minimum requirements, etc.).

30. Remove any peer from the immediate environment who may be interfering with the student's ability to remain on task.

31. Have the student ask questions about directions, explanations, and instructions not understood.

32. Reduce the emphasis on competition. Repeated failure may cause the student to remove himself/herself from competition by not remaining on task.

33. Provide the student with increased opportunities for help or assistance on academic tasks (e.g., peer tutoring, directions for work, frequent interactions, etc.).

34. Provide activities which increase the opportunities for active participation.

35. Make sure only those materials necessary for performing the task are on the student's desk (i.e., pencil, textbook, paper, etc.). Additional materials may distract the student (e.g., crayons, library book, etc.).

36. Have the student participate in small group activities (e.g., free time, math, reading, etc.). As the student demonstrates success, gradually increase the size of the group.

37. Position the student's seat so that he/she experiences the least amount of auditory and visual distractions.

38. Assess the degree of task difficulty in relation to the student's ability to successfully perform the task.

39. Evaluate the auditory and visual stimuli in the classroom to determine what level of stimuli the student can respond to in an appropriate manner.

40. Model for the student appropriate behavior in the presence of auditory and visual stimuli in the classroom (e.g., continuing to work, asking for quiet, moving to a quieter part of the classroom, etc.).

41. Set aside time at the end of each class period to complete assignments.

42. Set clear expectations for the completion of tasks. Consistently deliver reinforcement and consequences to all students.

43. Provide the student with a variety of assignments. Have him/her to choose a minimum number from the total to complete (e.g., present the student with 10 academic tasks from which he/she must finish 6 that day).

44. Communicate clearly with the student the length of time he/she has to complete an assignment. The student may want to use a timer to complete the tasks within the given period of time.

45. Encourage the student to manage his/her class performance as if he/she were self-employed. This should increase his/her motivation to be organized and fulfill his/her responsibilities.

46. Deliver reinforcement for any and all measures of improvement.

47. Identify the student's most effective learning mode. Use it consistently to facilitate the student's understanding and remaining on task for longer periods of time.

48. Assign the student shorter tasks but more of them (e.g., modify a 20-problem math activity to 4 activities of 5 problems each, to be performed at various times during the day). As the student demonstrates success, gradually increase the number of problems for each activity and decrease the number of activities.

49. Make sure the student has all the necessary materials to perform assignments.

50. Have the student assemble all materials needed prior to beginning a task to reduce interruptions.

51. Reward the student for being productive in the presence of auditory and visual stimuli for short periods of time. As the student demonstrates success, gradually increase the length of time the student is required to be productive.

52. Make sure the student understands the instructions/directions for the task (e.g., present instructions in a variety of ways; have the student verbalize what he/she is to do to perform the activity; etc.).

53. Provide the student with a list of assignments for the day and Have the student choose the order of the activities. The student may be in the best position to identify the order of tasks he/she will be able to perform successfully.

54. Provide a routine that will minimize off-task behavior which may result in negative consequences.

55. Structure the environment to reduce the opportunity for off-task behavior. Reduce lag time by providing the student with enough activities to maintain productivity.

56. Monitor the student's performance in activities or tasks to make sure the student begins, works on, and completes an assignment to be ready to move to the next activity in his/her routine.

57. Provide the student with a carrel or divider at his/her desk to reduce auditory and visual distractions.

58. Have the student time activities to monitor his/her behavior and time limits.

59. Interact frequently with the student to maintain involvement in the activity (e.g., ask the student questions, ask the student's opinion, stand close to the student, seat the student near the teacher's desk, etc.).

60. Have the student chart his/her on-task behavior. Reinforce the student for increasing the amount of time spent on task.

61. Have the student work with a peer tutor to maintain his/her attention to tasks.

62. Have the student work with a peer who manages time well.

63. Position the student away from those peers who create the most auditory and visual stimulation in the classroom.

64. Give the student one task to perform at a time. Introduce the next task only when the student has successfully completed the previous task.

65. Allow the student some movement while performing tasks. Monitor and limit the amount of movement.

66. Have the student communicate with appropriate personnel (e.g., counselor, nurse, administrator, etc.) about concerns (e.g., home, peer, personal problems, etc.) which interfere with his/her ability to stay on task.

67. Communicate with parents (e.g., notes home, phone calls, etc.) to share information about the student's progress. The parents may reinforce the student at home for staying on task in the classroom.

68. Provide the student with a quiet place in which to work where auditory and visual stimuli are reduced. This is used to reduce distracting stimuli and not as punishment.

69. Have the student ask himself/herself questions (e.g., "What's next?") to keep himself/herself focused on assignments/projects.

70. Develop a classroom environment that is quiet and uncluttered (e.g., clean, well-lighted, fresh-smelling, and at a comfortable temperature).

71. Have the student maintain a chart representing the amount of time spent on task.

72. Teach the student appropriate ways to respond to visual and auditory stimuli in the classroom (e.g., moving to another part of the room, asking others to be quiet, leaving the group, etc.).

73. Help the student learn to be satisfied with his/her best effort rather than some arbitrary measure of success. Success is measured individually according to ability levels and progress of any kind is a measure of success.

74. Seat the student so that he/she experiences the least amount of auditory and visual stimuli.

75. Provide the student with a predetermined signal (e.g., hand signal, verbal cue, etc.) when he/she begins to display off-task behaviors.

76. Have the student ask for help when he/she needs it.

77. Write a contract with the student specifying what behavior is expected (establish a reasonable length of time to stay on task) and what reinforcement will be made available when the terms of the contract have been met.

78. Schedule highly desirable activities contingent upon staying on task a required amount of time (i.e., staying on task for a required amount of time earns the student the opportunity to participate in a desirable activity).

79. Provide flexibility in scheduling so the student may perform alternative activities which result in more successful on-task behavior.

80. Maintain visibility to and from the student. The teacher should be able to see the student and the student should be able to see the teacher. Make eye contact possible at all times.

81. Minimize stimulation which interferes with the student's ability to remain on task (e.g., maintain a routine schedule of events, schedule special activities for the end of the day, etc.).

82. Allow the student to leave the task and return to it at a later time when he/she should be more successful remaining on task.

83. Reinforce the student for staying on task in the classroom: (a) give the student a tangible reward (e.g., classroom privileges, line leading, passing out materials, five minutes free time, etc.) or (b) give the student an intangible reward (e.g., praise, fist bump, smile, etc.).

84. Allow the student to take assignments/tasks to other areas of the school where he/she is most likely to be able to demonstrate on-task behavior (e.g., library, study hall, learning center, etc.).

85. Provide the student with alternative ways to perform an assignment and have the student choose the most desirable.

86. Use multiple modalities to accommodate more than one learning style (e.g., visual, auditory, tactile, etc.) when presenting directions/instructions, explanations, and instructional content.

87. Choose a peer, paraprofessional, etc., to cue the student when he/she is off task (e.g., the person can touch the student's arm as a signal that he/she is not remaining on task).

88. Make sure that the student understands the relationship between inappropriate behavior and the consequences which follow (e.g., failure to remain on task will result in incomplete assignments).

89. Provide the student with assistance for those activities which he/she has the most difficulty attending to for the required amount of time.

90. Provide the student with adequate transition time between activities to increase on-task behavior after activities have begun (e.g., after break time, lunch, special activities, etc.).

91. Teach the student how to manage time until the teacher can provide assistance (e.g., try the problem again, go on to the next problem, wait quietly, etc.).

92. Provide the student with a timer to be used to increase the amount of time during which he/she maintains attention (e.g., have the student work on the activity until the timer goes off).

93. Provide assignments that involve immediate, short-term tasks.

94. Make sure the student knows what to do when he/she cannot successfully perform assignments (e.g., raise hand, ask for assistance, go to the teacher, etc.).

95. Provide the student with the opportunity to move to a quiet place in the classroom when auditory and visual distractions interfere with his/her ability to function successfully.

96. Assess the degree of task difficulty to determine whether or not the student will require additional information, time, assistance, etc., before beginning a task.

97. Remove the student from an activity until he/she can demonstrate appropriate on-task behavior.

98. Make sure that all auditory and visual stimuli in the classroom are reduced as much as possible for all learners.

99. Have the student's cooperative work experience/vocational education teacher provide him/her with interventions to assist in remaining on task at his/her job.

100. Provide the student with headphones to wear if auditory stimuli interfere with his/her ability to function. As the student functions more successfully in the presence of auditory stimuli, gradually reduce the amount of time the headphones are worn.

101. Designate a specific period of time (e.g., each hour on the hour, last five minutes of class, after completing a task, etc.) when it is permissible for the student to talk with his/her peers.

102. Acknowledge the student when his/her hand is raised to let him/her know assistance will be provided as soon as possible.

103. Make sure the student has enough work area to perform the task.

104. Provide the student with shorter tasks which do not require extended attention to be successful. As the student demonstrates success, gradually increase the length of the tasks.

105. Reinforce those students in the classroom who demonstrate on-task behavior.

106. Place the student with peers who will be appropriate role models and facilitate his/her academic and behavioral success.

107. Reduce distracting stimuli which could interfere with the student's ability to remain on task (e.g., provide enough room for him/her to move without physical contact; keep noise level to a minimum; keep movement in the environment to a minimum; etc.).

108. Consider individual needs of the student (e.g., hunger, need for rest, comfort level, etc.) which may be interfering with his/her on-task behavior. Intervene to correct the situation or change the expectations.

109. Make sure the student understands that work not done during work time must be completed at other times (e.g., lunch, during assemblies, after school, etc.).

1. Establish classroom rules:
- Concentrate while working.
- Work quietly.
- Remain in your seat.
- Finish task.
- Meet task expectations.

Review rules often. Reinforce students for following the rules.

2. Present concepts following the (1) Who, (2) What, (3) Where, (4) When, (5) How, and (6) Why outline.

3. Have the student teach a concept he/she has mastered to another student as reinforcement.

4. Provide the student with a variety of assignments. Require him/her to select a minimum number from the total amount to complete (e.g., present the student with ten academic tasks from which he/she must complete six that day).

5. Assess student performance in a variety of ways (e.g., have the student give verbal explanations, simulations, physical demonstrations, etc.).

6. Have the student develop a flow chart of the steps necessary to complete a task.

7. Have the student maintain a chart representing the number of tasks he/she has completed and the neatness rate of each task.

8. Record assignments and allow the student to replay questions as often as necessary.

9. Have the student practice an assignment with the teacher, aide, or a peer before completing the assignment independently for a grade.

10. Record the assignments and allow the student to listen to directions/instructions as often as necessary.

11. Maintain a consistent format and expectation for assignments.

12. Have the student listen and take notes following the "Who, What, Where, When, How, and Why" format when concepts are presented.

13. Deliver reinforcement for any and all measures of improvement.

14. Have the student ask questions about directions, explanations, or instructions not understood before beginning a task to reinforce comprehension.

15. Assess the appropriateness of assigning homework to the student.

16. Do not grade every assignment completed by the student. Assignments may be used to evaluate student ability or knowledge and provide feedback. Grades may not need to be assigned until mastery/minimal accuracy has been attained.

17. Provide frequent interactions and encouragement to build the student's confidence and optimism for success (e.g., make statements such as "You're doing great," "Keep up the good work," "I'm really proud of you," etc.).

18. Make sure that homework assignments do not introduce new concepts but relate to concepts already taught.

19. Give the student alternative assignments. As the student demonstrates success, gradually introduce more components of the regular assignments.

20. Have reference materials readily available in the classroom (e.g., dictionary, thesaurus, list of frequently misspelled words, etc.).

21. Encourage the student to avoid ingesting any substance (e.g., drugs, alcohol, cold remedies, etc.) that might further alter his/her ability to perform up to his/her ability level.

22. Assess the quality and clarity of directions, explanations, and instructions given to the student.

23. Provide the student with clearly stated step-by-step directions for homework so that someone at home may be able to provide assistance.

24. Make sure that comments made to the student take the form of constructive criticism rather than perceived as personal, threatening, etc., (e.g., instead of saying, "You always make the same mistake," say, "A better way to do that might be . . .").

25. Reduce the emphasis on competition. Students who compete academically and fail to succeed may cease to try to do well and do far less than they are able.

26. Monitor student performance to detect errors and determine where learning problems exist.

27. Have the student perform difficult assignments in the resource room where the resource teacher can answer questions.

28. Build varying degrees of difficulty into assignments to build the student's self-confidence and provide a challenge (e.g., easier problems are intermingled with problems designed to measure knowledge gained).

29. Provide the student with evaluative feedback for assignments completed (i.e., identify what the student did successfully, what errors were made, and what should be done to correct the errors).

30. Have the student prepare for tests using the "Who, What, Where, When, How, and Why" format.

31. Develop tests and quizzes for the student using the "Who, What, Where, When, How, and Why" format.

32. Assess the appropriateness of giving the student assignments which require copying if the student's ability level makes it impossible for him/her to complete the assignment.

33. Provide time at school for homework to be completed or redone if assigned homework has not been completed or has resulted in failure. (The student's failure to complete homework assignments may be the result of variables in the home over which he/she has no control.)

34. Modify academic tasks (e.g., format, requirements, length, etc.).

35. Provide instruction and task format in a variety of ways (e.g., verbal instructions, written instructions, demonstrations, simulations, manipulatives, drill activities with peers, etc.).

36. Provide a variety of formats for the student to learn information (e.g., videos, visitors, community resources, etc.).

37. Give shorter assignments more frequently. As the student demonstrates success, increase the length of the assignments and decrease the frequency.

38. Make sure the student has mastery of the concepts at each level before introducing a new skill level.

39. Allow the student to highlight important information in written materials.

40. Have the student read his/her written work out loud when proofing.

41. Reinforce the student for improving academic task and homework performance: (a) give the student a tangible reward (e.g., classroom privileges, free homework pass, five minutes free time, etc.) or (b) give the student an intangible reward (e.g., praise, fist bump, smile, etc.).

42. Assess the student's performance in a variety of ways (e.g., have the student give verbal explanations, simulations, physical demonstrations, etc.).

43. Identify the student's preferred learning style (e.g., visual, auditory, etc.) and use it consistently to facilitate the student's understanding.

44. Identify resource personnel (e.g., librarian, special education teacher, other personnel with expertise or time to help, etc.) from whom the student may receive additional assistance.

45. Require the student to make corrections after assignments have been checked by the teacher.

46. Make sure the assignments measure knowledge of content and not related skills such as reading or writing.

47. Modify instruction to include more concrete examples to facilitate student learning.

48. Communicate with parents (e.g., notes home, phone calls, etc.) to share information about the student's progress. The parents may reinforce the student at home for improving his/her academic task and homework performance.

49. Provide adequate repetition/drill of concepts/skills to help the student achieve minimal accuracy on assignments (i.e., require mastery/minimal accuracy before moving to the next skill level).

50. Require the student to redo assignments of poor quality if you are certain the task is within the student's ability level.

51. Establish a minimum level of accuracy which will be accepted as a level of mastery.

52. Monitor the student's performance of the first problem or part of the assignment to make sure the student knows what is expected.

53. Give directions on a one-to-one basis before assigning a task.

54. Choose different people (e.g., peer, paraprofessional, tutor, counselor, etc.) to help the student improve work performance.

55. Reduce distracting stimuli (e.g., place the student in the front row, provide a carrel or office space away from distractions, etc.). This is used as a means of reducing distracting stimuli and not as a form of punishment.

56. Teach the student to practice basic study skills (e.g., reading for the main idea, note taking, summarizing, highlighting, studying in a good environment, using time wisely, etc.).

57. Work the first few problems of an assignment with the student to make sure that he/she knows what to do, how to complete the assignment, etc.

58. Structure the environment (e.g., provide a peer tutor, seat the student near the teacher or aide, etc.) to provide the student with increased opportunity for help or assistance on academic or homework tasks.

59. Have the student verbally repeat directions, explanations, and instructions after they have been given to reinforce retention.

60. Allow the student to put an assignment away and return to it at a later time when he/she might be more successful.

61. Provide parents with information regarding appropriate ways in which to help their child with homework (e.g., read directions with the student, work a few problems together, answer questions, check the completed assignment, etc.).

62. Modify homework assignments to provide practice/reinforcement of skills presented in class.

63. Have the student verbally respond to tasks.

64. Allow the student to respond to alternative assignment questions (e.g., general questions that represent global understanding).

65. Provide the student with sample letters, reports, forms, etc., as references for written communication.

66. Provide the student with self-checking materials. Require the student to make corrections before turning in assignments.

67. Teach the student direction-following skills: (a) listen carefully, (b) ask questions, (c) use environmental cues, and (d) rely on examples provided, etc.

68. Teach the student direction-following skills (e.g., listen carefully, write down steps, etc.).

69. Teach the student test-taking skills (e.g., organization, test-taking skills, etc.).

70. Teach the student information-gathering skills (e.g., listen carefully, write down important points, ask for clarification, wait until all information is presented before beginning a task, etc.).

71. Teach the student note-taking skills. Emphasize noting main concepts rather than details and data.

72. Interact frequently with the student to monitor his/her task performance.

73. Do not require the student to learn more information than he/she is capable of remembering at any time.

74. Provide the student with supplemental activities which offer review and repetition of skills presented to the general class population.

75. Provide the student with the opportunity to review assignments prior to them being graded.

76. Allow the student to record information from lectures and seminars and make notes from these recordings.

77. Assess the degree of task difficulty to determine whether or not the student will require additional information, time, assistance, etc., before beginning a task.

78. Evaluate the appropriateness of tasks assigned if the student consistently fails to complete assignments with minimal accuracy.

79. Set aside time at the end of each class period for the student to complete unfinished assignments.

80. Evaluate the appropriateness of the task to determine (a) if the task is too easy, (b) if the task is too difficult, and (c) if the length of time scheduled to complete the task is adequate.

81. Present directions/instructions in the student's preferred learning style (e.g., visual, auditory, etc.).

82. Have assignments read to the student.

83. Arrange a time for the student to study with a peer tutor before completing an assignment to be graded.

84. Reinforce those students in the classroom who show improvement on academic task and homework performance.

85. Write a contract with the student specifying what behavior is expected (e.g., completing an assignment with _____% accuracy) and what reinforcement will be made available when the terms of the contract have been met.

86. Provide a time during the day when the student can receive assistance at school if he/she has difficulty completing homework assignments with minimal accuracy.

87. Seat the student close to the source of information to maintain his/her attention (e.g., in the front row or near the speaker during a lecture).

88. Monitor the student's performance to detect errors and determine where learning problems exist.

89. Organize assignments by dividing them into small segments. Assign a deadline for each segment and provide the student with a reward after completing each segment of the assignment.

90. Speak to the student to explain (a) what he/she is doing wrong (e.g., performing below his/her ability level, failing assignments, etc.) and (b) what he/she should be doing (e.g., improving his/her academic task and homework performance).

91. Provide repetition and drill to ensure that the student achieves minimal accuracy on assignments (i.e., require mastery/minimal accuracy before moving to the next skill level).

92. Choose a peer to work a few problems with the student to serve as a model and help the student begin an assignment.

93. Do not expect mastery too soon after introducing new information, skills, etc.

94. Provide the student with written reminders of task sequences.

95. Give the student written/verbal repetition to aid retention of information.

96. Arrange for individual assignments when the group setting is overly distracting.

97. Allow the student to use educational aids to assist in the completion of assignments (e.g., calculator, dictionary, models of tasks, etc.).

98. Have the student use word processing programs that check spelling, grammar, etc.

99. Allow/require the student to correct assignments after they have been checked the first time.

106 Does not read or follow written directions

1. Establish classroom rules:
   • Concentrate while working.
   • Work quietly.
   • Remain in your seat.
   • Finish task.
   • Meet task requirements.
Review rules often. Reinforce the student for following the rules.

2. Deliver a predetermined signal (e.g., clapping hands, turning lights off and on, etc.) before giving written directions.

3. Have the student maintain a record (e.g., chart or graph) of his/her performance in following written directions.

4. Provide the student with a copy of written directions at his/her desk in addition to on the wall-mounted board, posted in the classroom, etc.

5. Provide the student with a recorded copy of written directions.

6. Make sure the student achieves success when following written directions.

7. Transfer directions from texts and workbooks when pictures or other stimuli make it difficult to attend to or follow written directions.

8. Have the student ask questions about written directions, explanations, or instructions he/she does not understand.

9. Make sure that directions are given at a level at which the student can be successful (e.g., two-step or three-step directions should not be given to students who can only successfully follow one-step directions).

10. Prevent the student from becoming over stimulated (e.g., frustrated, angry, etc.) by an activity.

11. Make sure that written directions are presented on the student's reading level.

12. Assess the quality and clarity of written directions, explanations, and instructions given to the student.

13. Reduce the emphasis on competition. Competitive activities may cause the student to hurry to begin the task without following written directions.

14. Teach the student written direction-following skills (e.g., read carefully, write down important points, ask for clarification, wait until all directions are received before beginning, etc.).

15. Provide clearly stated written directions (i.e., make the directions as simple and concrete as possible).

16. Seat the student far enough away from peers to facilitate attending to written directions.

17. Deliver all directions, questions, explanations, and instructions in a clear and concise manner and at an appropriate rate for the student.

18. Reinforce the student for following written directions based on the length of time the student can be successful. As the student demonstrates success, gradually increase the length of time required for reinforcement.

19. Reinforce the student for following written directions: (a) give the student a tangible reward (e.g., classroom privileges, line leading, passing out materials, five minutes free time, etc.) or (b) give the student an intangible reward (e.g., praise, fist bump, smile, etc.).

20. Have the student practice following written directions on nonacademic tasks (e.g., recipes, games, etc.).

21. Maintain a consistent format for written directions.

22. Deliver written directions before handing out materials.

23. Maintain visibility to and from the student. The teacher should be able to see the student and the student should be able to see the teacher. Make eye contact possible at all times.

24. Work the first few problems of an assignment with the student to make sure that he/she accurately follows the written directions

25. Choose a peer to help the student with any written directions not understood.

26. Require that assignments done incorrectly, for any reason, be redone.

27. Reduce written directions to individual steps (e.g., give the student each additional step after completion of the previous step).

28. Highlight, circle, or underline key words (e.g., match, circle, underline, etc.) in written directions.

29. Choose a peer to model how to appropriately follow written directions for the student.

30. As the student becomes more successful in following directions, gradually increase the level of difficulty or complexity of written directions.

31. Communicate with parents (e.g., notes home, phone calls, etc.) to share information about the student's progress. The parents may reinforce the student at home for following written directions at school.

32. Practice following written directions on nonacademic tasks (e.g., recipes, games, etc.).

33. Have the student carry out written directions one step at a time and check with the teacher to make sure that each step is successfully completed before attempting the next.

34. Structure the environment (e.g., peer tutoring, directions for work sent home, frequent interactions, etc.) to provide the student with increased opportunities for help or assistance on academic tasks.

35. Make sure that the print is bold and large enough to facilitate the student's success in following written directions.

36. Make sure the student has all the materials needed to complete the assignment or activity.

37. Provide the student a quiet place (e.g., carrel, study booth, etc.) where he/she may go to participate in activities which require following written directions.

38. Interact frequently with the student to help him/her follow written directions.

39. Make sure that the student is attending to the teacher (e.g., eye contact, hands free of writing materials, looking at assignment, etc.) before giving written directions.

40. Give the student one task to complete at a time. Introduce the next task only when the student has successfully completed the previous task.

41. Follow a less desirable task with a highly desirable task. Make completion of the first task necessary to complete the second task.

42. Reduce distracting stimuli in the environment to facilitate the student's ability to follow written directions (e.g., place the student on the front row, provide a carrel or office space away from distractions, etc.). This is used as a means of reducing distracting stimuli and not as a form of punishment.

43. Reinforce those students in the classroom who follow written directions.

44. Develop assignments/activities for the following of written directions (e.g., informal activities designed to have the student carry out directions in steps, increasing the level of difficulty).

45. Record directions for the student to listen to individually and replay as necessary.

46. Use visual cues in written directions (e.g., green dot to start, red dot to stop, arrows, etc.).

47. Evaluate the appropriateness of the task to determine (a) if the task is too easy, (b) if the task is too difficult, and (c) if the length of time scheduled to complete the task is adequate.

48. Present directions in both written and verbal form.

49. Have the student read written directions to his/her teacher.

50. Give directions in a variety of ways to facilitate the student's understanding (e.g., if the student does not understand written directions, present them verbally).

51. Speak to the student to explain (a) what he/she is doing wrong (e.g., not following written directions) and (b) what he/she should be doing (e.g., following written directions).

52. Seat the student close to the source of the written directions (e.g., teacher, aide, peer, wall-mounted board, projector, etc.).

53. Require the student to wait until the teacher gives him/her a signal to begin the task (e.g., hand signal, ring bell, etc.).

54. Use vocabulary that is within the student's level of comprehension when delivering directions, explanations, and information.

55. Have the student quietly repeat to himself/herself information just read to help remember the important facts.

56. Write a contract with the student specifying what behavior is expected (e.g., following written directions) and what reinforcement will be made available when the terms of the contract have been met.

1. Present the task in the most interesting and attractive manner possible.

2. Maintain mobility to provide assistance for the student.

3. Structure time limits so that the student knows exactly how long he/she has to work and when the work must be finished.

4. Provide the student with more than enough time to finish an activity. As the student demonstrates success, gradually decrease the amount of time provided to finish an activity.

5. Give directions in a variety of ways to facilitate the student's understanding (e.g., if the student does not understand verbal directions, present them in written form).

6. Have the student repeat the directions verbally to the teacher.

7. Give a signal (e.g., clapping hands, turning lights off and on, etc.) before giving verbal directions.

8. Provide the student with a predetermined signal (e.g., verbal cue, hand signal, etc.) when he/she is not beginning a task.

9. Tell the student that directions will only be given once.

10. Rewrite directions at a lower reading level.

11. Deliver verbal directions in a simple, concrete manner.

12. Help the student with the first few items on a task. As the student demonstrates success, gradually reduce the amount of help over time.

13. Follow a less desirable task with a highly desirable task, making the completion of the first necessary to perform the second.

14. Provide the student with shorter tasks given more frequently.

15. Provide the student with a schedule of daily events so that he/she knows exactly what and how much there is to do in a day.

16. Prevent the student from becoming overstimulated by an activity (e.g., frustrated, angry, etc.).

17. Specify exactly what is to be done for the completion of a task (e.g., make definite starting and stopping points, a minimum requirement, etc.).

18. Require the student to begin each assignment within a specified period of time (e.g., three minutes, five minutes, etc.).

19. Provide the student with a variety of assignments, requiring him/her to choose a minimum number from the total to complete (e.g., present the student with ten academic tasks from which six must be finished that day).

20. Start with a single problem and add more problems to the task over time.

21. Reduce emphasis on competition (e.g., academic or social). Fear of failure may cause the student to refuse to attempt new assignments or tasks.

22. Provide the student with self-checking materials so he/she may check work privately, thus reducing the fear of public failure.

23. Have the student attempt the new assignment/task in a private place (e.g., carrel, office, quiet study area, etc.).

24. Have the student practice a new skill (e.g., jumping rope, dribbling a basketball, etc.) alone or with a peer or the teacher before the entire group attempts the activity.

25. Provide the student with the opportunity to complete the assignment/task in a variety of ways (e.g., recorded, with a calculator, verbally, etc.).

26. Allow the student to perform a new assignment/task in a variety of places in the building (e.g., resource room, library, learning center, etc.).

27. Provide the student with a sample of the assignment/task which has been partially completed by a peer or teacher (e.g., book report, project, etc.).

28. Have the student maintain a record (e.g., chart or graph) of his/her performance in attempting new assignments/tasks.

29. Allow the student the option of performing the assignment/task at another time (e.g., earlier in the day, later, on another day, etc.).

30. Make sure that the student has all the materials needed to complete the assignment/task.

31. Have the student paraphrase to the teacher what should be done to complete the assignment/task.

32. Explain to the student that work not done during work time will have to be made up at other times (e.g., at break time, before school, after school, during lunchtime, etc.).

33. Teach the student direction-following skills: (a) listen carefully, (b) ask questions, (c) use environmental cues, (d) rely on examples provided, and (e) wait until directions are given before beginning.

34. Provide the student with optional courses of action to prevent total refusal to obey teacher directives.

35. Allow the student to perform alternative versions of a new assignment. As the student demonstrates success, gradually introduce more components of the regular assignments until they can be performed successfully.

36. Have the student teach a concept he/she has mastered to another student.

37. Provide practice for new assignments or tasks using a computer software program that gives the student immediate feedback.

38. Make sure the student has mastery of concepts at each level before introducing a new skill level.

39. Have the student time activities to monitor his/her own behavior and accept time limits.

40. Communicate clearly to the student when it is time to begin.

41. Do not require the student to complete the assignment/task in one sitting.

42. Reduce distracting stimuli (e.g., place the student on the front row, provide a carrel or office space away from distractions, etc.). This is used as a means of reducing distracting stimuli and not as punishment.

43. Structure the environment to provide the student with increased opportunity for help or assistance.

44. Choose a peer or volunteer to help the student begin a task.

45. Assess the quality and clarity of directions, explanations, and instructions given to the student.

46. Have the student ask questions about directions, explanations, or instructions not understood.

47. Speak with the student to explain (a) what the student is doing wrong (e.g., not attempting a new task) and (b) what the student should be doing (e.g., asking for assistance or clarification, following directions, starting on time, etc.).

48. Reinforce the student for attempting a new assignment/task: (a) give the student a tangible reward (e.g., classroom privileges, line leading, passing out materials, five minutes free time, etc.) or (b) give the student an intangible reward (e.g., praise, fist bump, smile, etc.).

49. Reinforce those students in the classroom who attempt a new assignment/task.

50. Write a contract with the student specifying what behavior is expected (e.g., attempting a new assignment/task) and what reinforcement will be made available when the terms of the contract have been met.

51. Reinforce the student for attempting a new assignment/task within the length of time he/she can be successful. As the student demonstrates success, gradually decrease the amount of time to begin the task to be reinforced.

52. Evaluate the appropriateness of the task to determine (a) if the task is too easy, (b) if the task is too difficult, and (c) if the length of time scheduled to complete the task is adequate.

53. Communicate with parents (e.g., notes home, phone calls, etc.) to share information about the student's progress. The parents may reinforce the student at home for attempting a new assignment/task at school.

108 Requires repeated drill and practice to learn what other students master easily

1. Have the student practice a new concept independently, with an aide, teacher, or a peer before attempting it with the entire group or being graded on it.

2. Have the student teach concepts just learned to another student.

3. Reduce the emphasis on competition. Competitive activities may increase the student's anxiety and reduce the student's ability to remember information.

4. Initiate a *Learn a Concept a Day* program with the student. Incorporate the concept into the assigned activities for the day.

5. Provide practice of new concepts with a computer software program or a hand-held educational device that gives immediate feedback to the student.

6. Give the student fewer concepts to learn at one time. Spend as much time as needed on each concept for the student to understand it.

7. Recognize quality work (e.g., display the student's work, congratulate the student, etc.).

8. Provide the student with new information in the most direct manner possible (e.g., a list of facts, a summary of important points, outline of important events, etc.).

9. Develop crossword puzzles which contain only the student's spelling words and have him/her complete them.

10. Underline, circle, or highlight important information from any material the student is to learn (e.g., science, math, geography, etc.).

11. Use wall charts to introduce new concepts with visual images such as pictures for the student to associate with previously learned concepts.

12. Reinforce the student for learning new concepts: (a) give the student a tangible reward (e.g., classroom privileges, line leading, passing out materials, five minutes free time, etc.) or (b) give the student an intangible reward (e.g., praise, fist bump, smile, etc.).

13. Provide the student with opportunities for drill activities in the most interesting manner possible (e.g., computer, using a calculator, playing educational games, watching a visual, listening to a recording, etc.).

14. Give the student a list of key words, phrases, or main points to learn for each new concept introduced.

15. Write sentences, passages, paragraphs, etc., for the student to read which reinforce new concepts.

16. Have the student review new concepts each day for a short period of time rather than two or three times per week for longer periods of time.

17. Provide the student with opportunities to use new concepts frequently throughout the day.

18. Have the student highlight or underline key words, phrases, and sentences from reading assignments, newspapers, magazines, etc.

19. Have the student quiz others over new concepts (e.g., teacher, aide, peers, etc.).

20. Choose a peer to participate in daily drill activities with the student.

21. Do not require the student to learn more information than he/she is capable of learning at any time.

22. Record important information. The student can replay the recording as often as necessary.

23. Allow the student to use resources to help him/her successfully perform tasks (e.g., calculator, multiplication tables, abacus, dictionary, a peer, etc.).

24. Require the student to use information resources (e.g., encyclopedia, dictionary, etc.) to successfully perform tasks.

25. Provide the student with various times throughout the day when he/she can participate in drill activities with the teacher, aide, peer, etc.

26. Evaluate the appropriateness of the task to determine (a) if the task is too easy, (b) if the task is too difficult, and (c) if the length of time scheduled for the task is adequate.

109 Does not function appropriately in the presence of verbal and physical stimuli in the classroom

1. Reinforce the student for functioning appropriately in the presence of verbal and physical stimuli in the classroom: (a) give the student a tangible reward (e.g., classroom privileges, line leading, passing out materials, five minutes free time, etc.) or (b) give the student an intangible reward (e.g., praise, fist bump, smile, etc.).

2. Speak to the student to explain (a) what he/she is doing wrong (e.g., failing to attend, getting out of seat, fighting with a peer, talking, etc.) and (b) what he/she should be doing (e.g., maintaining self-control in the presence of verbal and physical stimuli in the classroom).

3. Have the student ask questions about directions, explanations, instructions he/she does not understand.

4. Reinforce those students in the classroom who function appropriately in the presence of verbal and physical stimuli in the classroom.

5. Reinforce the student for functioning appropriately in the presence of verbal and physical stimuli in the classroom based on the length of time the student can be successful. As the student demonstrates success, gradually increase the length of time required for reinforcement.

6. Write a contract with the student specifying what behavior is expected (e.g., maintaining self-control in the presence of verbal and physical stimuli in the classroom) and what reinforcement will be made available when the terms of the contract have been met.

7. Establish classroom rules:
- Concentrate while working.
- Work quietly.
- Remain in your seat.
- Finish task.
- Meet task requirements.

Review rules often. Reinforce the student for following the rules.

8. Communicate with parents (e.g., notes home, phone calls, etc.) to share information about the student's progress. The parents may reinforce the student at home for functioning appropriately in the presence of verbal and physical stimuli in the classroom.

9. Choose a peer to model functioning appropriately in the presence of verbal and physical stimuli in the classroom for the student.

10. Evaluate the verbal and physical stimuli in the classroom to determine the level of stimuli the student can respond to appropriately.

11. Reduce verbal and physical stimuli to a level at which the student can successfully function. As the student demonstrates that he/she can successfully tolerate the increased levels, gradually allow verbal and physical stimuli to increase.

12. Seat the student so that he/she experiences the least amount of verbal and physical stimuli possible.

13. Provide the student with a quiet place in which to work, where verbal and physical stimuli are reduced. This is used to reduce distracting stimuli and not as a form of punishment.

14. Place the student away from those peers in the classroom who create the most verbal and physical stimuli.

15. Reward the student for being productive in the presence of verbal and physical stimuli for short periods of time. As he/she becomes successful, gradually increase the length of time the student is required to be productive.

16. Make sure that all verbal and physical stimuli in the classroom are reduced as much as possible for all learners.

17. Provide the student with the opportunity to move to a quiet place in the classroom any time verbal and physical stimuli interfere with his/her ability to function successfully.

18. Have the student practice a new skill or assignment alone, with an aide, the teacher, or a peer before the entire group attempts the activity or before performing for a grade.

19. Remove the student from an activity in the classroom if he/she is unable to function appropriately in the presence of the verbal and physical stimuli involved in the activity.

20. Teach the student appropriate ways to respond to verbal and physical stimuli in the classroom (e.g., moving to another part of the room, asking others to be quiet, leaving the group, etc.).

21. Provide the student with shorter tasks which do not require extended attention to be successful. As the student demonstrates he/she can be successful in the presence of verbal and physical stimuli, gradually increase the length of the tasks.

22. Have the student participate in small-group activities (e.g., free time, math, reading, etc.) to reduce the level of verbal and physical stimuli in the group. As the student can function successfully in the presence of verbal and physical stimuli, gradually increase the size of the group.

23. Model appropriate behavior in the presence of verbal and physical stimuli in the classroom (e.g., continuing to work, asking for quiet, moving to a quieter part of the classroom, etc.).

24. Allow the student to close the door or windows to reduce verbal and physical stimuli from outside of the classroom.

25. Provide the student with headphones to wear if verbal stimuli interfere with his/her ability to function. As the student can function more successfully in the presence of verbal stimuli, gradually reduce the use of the headphones.

26. Provide the student with a carrel or divider at his/her desk to reduce verbal and physical stimuli.

1. Communicate with parents (e.g., notes home, phone calls, etc.) to share information about the student's progress. The parents may reinforce the student at home for improving the quality of his/her handwriting at school.

2. Provide the student with self-checking materials, requiring correction before turning in assignments.

3. Assess the appropriateness of assigning homework to the student.

4. Maintain consistency in assignment format and expectations.

5. Make sure the assignments measure knowledge of content and not related skills such as reading or writing.

6. Teach the student note-taking skills.

7. Have the student practice an assignment with the teacher, an aide, or a peer before completing the assignment for a grade.

8. Reinforce conscientiousness in improving handwriting (e.g., double checking spelling, proper positioning of letters, spacing, etc.): (a) give the student a tangible reward (e.g., classroom privileges, line leading, passing out materials, five minutes free time, etc.) or (b) give the student an intangible reward (e.g., praise, fist bump, smile, etc.).

9. Teach the student direction-following skills: (a) listen carefully, (b) ask questions, (c) use environmental cues, and (d) rely on examples provided, etc.

10. Provide parents with information regarding appropriate ways in which to help their child with homework (e.g., read directions with the student, work a few problems together, answer questions, check the completed assignment, etc.).

11. Provide frequent interactions and encouragement to support the student's confidence and optimism for success (e.g., make statements such as, "You're doing great." "Keep up the good work." "I'm really proud of you.").

12. Establish classroom rules:
- Concentrate while working.
- Work quietly.
- Remain in your seat.
- Finish task.
- Meet task expectations.

Review rules often. Reinforce students for following the rules.

13. Reinforce conscientiousness in improving accuracy and quality of assignments (e.g., double checking spelling, proper positioning of letters, adequate spacing, etc.): (a) give the student a tangible reward (e.g., classroom privileges, line leading, passing out materials, five minutes free time, etc.) or (b) give the student an intangible reward (e.g., praise, fist bump, smile, etc.).

14. Attach a number line and alphabet strip to the student's desk to use as a reference for the correct formation of letters and numbers.

15. Establish levels of expectations for accuracy and quality of assignments. Require the student to correct or redo assignments until the expectations are met.

16. Deliver reinforcement for any and all measures of improvement.

17. Record the assignments and allow the student to listen to questions as often as necessary.

18. Ask parents to set aside an established length of time each evening (e.g., 45 minutes, one hour, etc.) for homework rather than allowing the student to watch TV or play as soon as his/her homework is finished.

19. Use horizontally and vertically lined paper (e.g., | | | |) to teach the student appropriate spacing skills (e.g., K | a | t | h | y).

20. Allow the student to put an assignment away and return to it at a later time when he/she might be more successful.

21. Along with a directive, provide an incentive statement (e.g., "When you finish your work neatly, you may have free time.").

22. Provide the student with an appropriate model of handwriting (e.g., other students' work, teacher samples, commercial samples, etc.) to use at his/her desk.

23. Teach the student to practice basic study skills (e.g., reading for the main idea, note taking, summarizing, highlighting, studying in a good environment, using time wisely, etc.).

24. Have the student maintain a chart representing the number of tasks completed and the accuracy rate of each task.

25. Reinforce those students in the classroom who turn in assignments which are legible.

26. Reinforce those students in the classroom who turn in assignments which are accurate and of high quality.

27. Reduce the emphasis on competition. Competitive activities may cause the student to rush through work. Students who compete academically and fail to succeed may cease to try to do well and do far less than they are able.

28. If the student does not complete his/her work according to teacher directions and expectations, it must be completed during recreational or break time.

29. Provide the student with evaluative feedback for assignments completed (i.e., identify what the student did successfully, what errors were made, and what should be done to correct the errors).

30. Provide a time during the day when the student can receive assistance at school if he/she has difficulty completing homework assignments with minimal accuracy

31. Modify instructions to include more concrete examples to facilitate student learning.

32. Assess quality and clarity of directions, explanations, and instructions given to the student.

33. Have the student ask questions about directions, explanations, and instructions not understood.

34. Recognize accuracy and quality (e.g., display the student's work, congratulate the student, etc.).

35. Use adhesive material (e.g., tape, Dycem® material, etc.) to keep paper positioned appropriately for handwriting.

36. Monitor student performance to detect errors and determine where learning problems exist.

37. Speak with the student to explain (a) what the student is doing wrong (e.g., turning in work which has spelling errors or spacing errors, work that is illegible, etc.) and (b) what he/she should be doing (e.g., taking time to check for spelling, spacing errors, etc.).

38. Provide the student with opportunities to review his/her work prior to grading assignments.

39. Do not grade every assignment performed by the student. Assignments may be used to evaluate student ability or knowledge and provide feedback. Grades may not need to be assigned until mastery/minimal accuracy has been attained.

40. Provide older students with functional handwriting opportunities (e.g., job application forms, reinforcer surveys, order forms, check writing, etc.).

41. Monitor the first problem or part of the assignment to make sure the student knows what is expected.

42. Teach the student procedures for improving accuracy and quality of work (e.g., listen to directions, make sure directions are understood, work at an acceptable pace, check for errors, correct for neatness, copy the work over, etc.).

43. Provide instruction and task format in a variety of ways (e.g., verbal instructions, written instructions, demonstrations, simulations, manipulative, drill activities with peers, etc.).

44. Gradually reduce the space between lines as the student's handwriting improves.

45. Allow/require the student to make corrections after assignments have been checked the first time.

46. Provide the student with materials (e.g., pencil with eraser, paper, dictionary, handwriting sample, etc.) to neatly perform assignments.

47. Have the student trace handwriting models. Fade the model as the student develops the skill.

48. Have the student chart the number of times his/her handwriting is acceptable during a given week.

49. Provide the student with samples of work which may serve as models for acceptable levels of accuracy and quality (e.g., the student is to match the quality of the sample before turning in the assignment).

50. Work the first few problems of an assignment with the student to make sure that he/she knows what to do, how to complete the assignment, etc.

51. Provide a wide variety of handwriting opportunities for the student to practice handwriting skills (e.g., writing letters to sports and entertainment figures, relatives, friends; writing for free information on a topic in which the student is interested, etc.).

52. Provide the student with ample opportunity to master handwriting skills (e.g., instruction in letter positioning, direction, spacing, etc.).

53. Have the student read/review school work with the teacher to become aware of the quality of his/her work.

54. Build varying degrees of difficulty into assignments to facilitate the student's self-confidence and at the same time provide a challenge (e.g., easier problems are intermingled with problems designed to measure knowledge gained).

55. Establish levels of expectations for quality handwriting performance, and require the student to correct or repeat assignments until the expectations are met.

56. Allow the student to perform school work in a quiet place (e.g., study carrel, library, resource room, etc.) to reduce distractions.

57. Provide the student with a variety of assignments. Have him/her to choose a minimum number from the total amount to complete (e.g., present the student with 10 academic tasks from which 6 must be finished that day).

58. Supervise the student while he/she is performing school work to monitor accuracy and quality.

59. Provide the student with clearly stated step-by-step directions for homework so someone at home may be able to provide assistance.

60. Provide the student with clearly stated criteria for acceptable work.

61. Provide multiple opportunities for the student to learn information covered by assignments (e.g., visuals, visitors, community resources, etc.).

62. Arrange a time for the student to study with a peer tutor before completing a graded assignment.

63. Write a contract with the student specifying what behavior is expected (e.g., improving the accuracy and quality of assignments) and what reinforcement will be made available when the terms of the contract have been met.

64. Modify academic tasks (e.g., format, requirements, length, etc.).

65. Make sure that comments made to the student take the form of constructive criticism rather than criticism that can be perceived as personal, threatening, etc., (e.g., instead of saying, "You always make the same mistake." say, "A better way to do that might be . . .").

66. Evaluate the appropriateness of the task to determine (a) if the task is too easy, (b) if the task is too difficult, and (c) if the length of time scheduled to complete the task is adequate.

67. Provide the student with shorter tasks, but more of them throughout the day (e.g., 4 assignments of 5 problems each rather than one assignment of 20 problems).

68. Have the student verbally respond to tasks.

69. Make sure the student understands that work not done neatly must be redone until it is neat.

70. Use handwriting models with arrows that indicate the direction in which the student should correctly form the letters.

71. Check the student's grip on the pencil to make sure that he/she is holding the pencil correctly.

72. Reduce distracting stimuli (e.g., place the student in the front row, provide a carrel or office space away from distractions, etc.). This is to be used as a means of reducing distracting stimuli and not as a form of punishment.

73. Conduct a preliminary evaluation of the student's assignment. Require him/her to make necessary corrections before final grading.

74. Provide time at school for the completion of homework if homework assigned has not been completed or has resulted in failure. (The student's failure to complete homework assignments may be the result of variables in the home over which he/she has no control.)

75. Allow the student to respond to alternative assignment questions (e.g., more generalized questions that represent global understanding).

76. Reinforce the student for improving the accuracy and quality of his/her work based on ability. As the student demonstrates success, gradually increase the amount of improvement expected for reinforcement.

77. Identify resource personnel from whom the student may receive additional assistance (e.g., librarian, special education teacher, other personnel with expertise or time to help, etc.).

78. Use primary paper to assist the student in sizing upper-case and lower-case letters. Use standard lined paper when the student's skills improve.

79. Make sure that homework relates to concepts already taught rather than introducing a new concept.

80. Give shorter assignments, but give them more frequently. As the student demonstrates success, increase the length of the assignments and decrease the frequency.

81. Have the student use a pencil grip (e.g., three-sided, foam rubber, etc.) to provide assistance in appropriate positioning of the pencil or pen.

82. Provide the student with additional time to perform school work to facilitate quality.

83. Model appropriate handwriting at all times.

84. Evaluate the appropriateness of tasks assigned if the student consistently fails to complete assignments with minimal accuracy.

85. Interact frequently with the student to monitor task performance.

86. Structure the environment to provide the student with increased opportunities for help or assistance on academic or homework tasks (e.g., peer tutors, seat the student near the teacher or aide, etc.).

87. Assess student performance in a variety of ways (e.g., have the student give verbal explanations, simulations, physical demonstrations, etc.).

88. Provide adequate repetition and drill to assure minimal accuracy of assignments (i.e., require mastery/minimal accuracy before moving to the next skill level).

89. Make sure that all educators who work with the student maintain consistent expectations of accuracy and quality.

90. Assign the student shorter tasks while increasing accuracy and quality expectations.

91. Choose a peer to work with the student to provide an acceptable model for the student.

92. Do not expect mastery too soon after introducing new information, skills, etc.

1. Interact frequently with the student to help him/her make appropriate use of study time.

2. Deliver directions verbally to increase the probability of the student's understanding of class assignments.

3. Allow the student the option of performing assignments during another study time (e.g., earlier in the day, later, on another day, or at home).

4. Allow the student to work with a peer who uses study time appropriately.

5. Along with a directive, provide an incentive statement (e.g., "If you make appropriate use of study time, you may have free time.").

6. Assess the degree of task difficulty in relation to the student's ability to perform the task.

7. Encourage the student to define his/her goals. Have the student develop specific strategies to achieve his/her goals and follow through on those strategies.

8. Assess the degree of task difficulty to determine whether or not the student will require additional information, time, assistance, etc., before beginning a task.

9. Assess the quality and clarity of directions, explanations, and instructions given to the student.

10. Choose a peer to help the student with class assignments during study time.

11. Allow the student additional time to complete class assignments.

12. Assign short-term projects that can be quickly completed.

13. Encourage the student to be self-determining by identifying tasks and completing assignments independently.

14. Assign the student shorter tasks (e.g., modify a 20-problem math activity to 4 activities of 5 problems each, to be done at various times during the day). As the student demonstrates success, gradually increase the number of problems over time.

15. Chart those assignments with the student that have been completed during study time.

16. Communicate clearly with the student the length of time he/she has to complete an assignment and when the assignment is due. The student may want to use a timer to complete the tasks within the given period of time.

17. Allow the student to perform alternative assignments during study time. As the student demonstrates success, gradually introduce more components of the regular assignments until those assignments are routinely performed.

18. Communicate with parents (e.g., notes home, phone calls, etc.) to share information about the student's progress. The parents may reinforce the student at home for completing assignments at school.

19. Encourage the student to develop a 30 second definition of his/her goal to help him/her stay on task and focused (e.g., study five vocabulary terms before taking a break).

20. Have the student use a timer to complete the tasks within a given period of time.

21. Help the student develop an awareness of the consequences of his/her behavior by writing down or talking through problems which may occur due to his/her procrastination (e.g., incomplete assignments, low test scores, lack of credit).

22. Encourage the student to manage his/her daily performance as if he/she were self-employed. This should increase his/her motivation to use study time effectively and fulfill his/her responsibilities.

23. Have the student ask for immediate clarification of the directions.

24. Encourage the student to reward himself/herself (e.g., take a ten minute break, speak briefly with a relative, phone a friend, etc.) for completing an assignment within the amount of time allotted.

25. Establish assignment rules (e.g., listen to directions, wait until all directions have been given, ask questions about anything you do not understand, make sure you have all the necessary materials, begin assignment only when you are certain about what you are supposed to do, etc.).

26. Establish classroom rules:
- Concentrate while working.
- Work quietly.
- Remain in your seat.
- Finish task.
- Meet task requirements.

Review rules often. Reinforce students for following the rules.

27. Have the student keep a chart or graph representing the number of class assignments completed during study time.

28. Evaluate the appropriateness of the task to determine (a) if the task is too easy, (b) if the task is too difficult, and (c) if the length of time scheduled to complete the task is adequate.

29. Explain to the student that work not done during study time will have to be done during other times (e.g., break time, recreational time, after school, etc.).

30. Follow a less desirable task with a highly desirable task. Make the following of verbal directions and completion of the first task necessary to perform the second task.

31. Give directions in a variety of ways to facilitate the student's understanding (e.g., if the student does not understand verbal directions, present them in written form).

32. Have reference materials readily available in the classroom (e.g., dictionary, thesaurus, list of frequently misspelled words, etc.).

33. Have the student anticipate future tasks/assignments and develop plans for addressing them.

34. Have the student ask for help when he/she needs it.

35. Have the student assemble all the materials necessary to work on a project, assignment, etc., to reduce the need to search for materials.

36. Have the student complete assignments in a private place (e.g., carrel, office, quiet study area, etc.) to reduce the anxiety of public failure.

37. Have the student develop a checklist/chart to follow which will allow him/her to complete specific assignments during study time.

38. Have the student explain to the teacher what should be done to complete the assignments.

39. Establish times when it is permissible for the student to be out of his/her seat (e.g., leave his/her seat only to get a book, to ask a question of the study supervisor, etc.).

40. Have the student list five qualities of a productive worker. Have the student choose one of those qualities to work on each week for five weeks.

41. Maintain visibility to and from the student to make sure the student is attending. The teacher should be able to see the student and the student should be able to see the teacher. Make eye contact possible at all times.

42. Have the student organize assignments by dividing them into small segments. Set deadlines and provide the student with a reward after completing each segment of the assignment.

43. Interact frequently with the student to maintain his/her involvement with class assignments (e.g., ask the student questions, ask the student's opinion, stand in close proximity to the student, seat the student near the teacher's desk, etc.).

44. Have the student prioritize tasks by importance (e.g., task A must be done today, task B can be done today, and task C can wait until tomorrow).

45. Supervise the student during study time to maintain on-task behavior.

46. Take proactive steps to deal with a student's refusal to perform an assignment to prevent contagion in the classroom (e.g., refrain from arguing with the student, place the student at a carrel or other quiet place to work, remove the student from the group or classroom, etc.).

47. Have the student ask questions about directions, explanations, and instructions not understood.

48. Provide the student with a schedule of daily events so he/she knows exactly what and how much there is to do in a day.

49. Have the student repeat the directions verbally to the teacher.

50. Choose a classmate to model appropriate use of study time for the student.

51. Maintain sample letters, reports, forms, etc., as references for written communication.

52. Choose a peer to model appropriate completion of assignments for the student.

53. Designate a specific period of time (e.g., the last 5 minutes of study time, after completing a task, etc.) when it is permissible for the student to talk with his/her peers.

54. Encourage the student to ask for clarification of the directions for classroom assignments to be completed during study time.

55. Interact frequently with the student to help him/her follow directions for the assignments.

56. Allow the student access to pencils, pens, etc., only after directions have been given.

57. Maintain a consistent daily routine.

58. Maintain consistent expectations within the ability level of the student.

59. Make sure that the student is attending to the teacher when directions are given (e.g., making eye contact, hands free of writing materials, looking at assignment, etc.).

60. Make sure that comments made to the student take the form of constructive criticism rather than perceived as personal, threatening, etc., (e.g., instead of saying, "You always make the same mistake," say, "A better way to do that might be . . .").

61. Make sure the student achieves success when following directions.

62. Make sure the student has assignments to work on during study time.

63. Make sure the student understands the natural consequences of not completing assignments during study time (e.g., students who do not finish their work will not be allowed to do more desirable activities).

64. Have the student time his/her assignments to monitor personal behavior and accept time limits.

65. Provide an incentive statement along with a directive (e.g., "If you make appropriate use of study time, you may have free time.").

66. Structure time limits so the student knows exactly how much time is available to work and when work should be finished.

67. Provide study guides with questions presented in sequential order to facilitate attention to the reading material presented in the student's content area textbooks (e.g., American history, biology, health, etc.).

68. Reinforce the student for attempting and completing assignments based on the amount of work the student successfully completes. As the student demonstrates success, gradually increase the amount of work required for reinforcement.

69. Provide the student with more than enough time to finish an activity. As the student demonstrates success, gradually decrease the amount of time provided to finish an activity.

70. Work a few problems of the assignment with the student to serve as a model and help the student begin a task prior to independent study time.

71. Provide the student with shorter tasks given more frequently.

72. Provide the student with step-by-step written directions for doing assignments during study time.

73. Provide the student with the opportunity to perform assignments/activities in a variety of ways (e.g., recorded, with a calculator, verbally, etc.).

74. Give directions in steps (e.g., give the student each additional step after completion of the previous step).

75. Reduce distracting stimuli (e.g., place the student in the front row, provide a carrel or quiet place away from distractions). This is used as a means of reducing stimuli and not as a form of punishment.

76. Reduce the emphasis on early completion. Hurrying to complete assignments may cause the student to fail to follow directions.

77. Provide clearly stated directions in written or verbal form (i.e., make the directions as simple and concrete as possible).

78. Reinforce the student for attempting and completing class assignments during study time: (a) give the student a tangible reward (e.g., classroom privileges, line leading, passing out materials, five minutes free time, etc.) or (b) give the student an intangible reward (e.g., praise, fist bump, smile, etc.).

79. Reinforce the student for beginning, staying on, and completing assignments during study time.

80. Present one assignment at a time. As each assignment is completed, deliver reinforcement along with the presentation of the next assignment.

81. Prevent the student from becoming over-stimulated by an activity (e.g., frustrated, angry, excited, etc.).

82. Provide alternatives for the traditional format of directions (e.g., record directions, summarize directions, directions given by peers, etc.).

83. Reinforce those students in the classroom who attempt and complete assignments during study time.

84. Move objects used for tactile stimulation (e.g., pens, paper clips, loose change, etc.) away from the student's reach.

85. Practice direction-following skills on nonacademic tasks.

86. Present assignments in the most attractive and interesting manner possible.

87. Repeat directions to increase the probability of understanding.

88. Require the student to begin each assignment within a specified period of time (e.g., three minutes, five minutes, etc.).

89. Set time limits so that the student knows exactly how much time is available to work and when work should be finished.

90. Structure the environment to provide the student with increased opportunities for help or assistance.

91. Provide the student with a variety of assignments. Have him/her to choose a minimum number from the total amount to complete (e.g., present the student with three academic tasks from which two must be completed during study time).

92. Rewrite directions at a lower reading level.

93. Teach the student time-management skills. Have the student make a daily plan and follow it. Encourage the student to avoid becoming distracted by events, impulses, and moods.

94. With the student, chart those assignments that have been completed in a given period of time.

95. Speak with the student to explain (a) what he/she is doing wrong (e.g., not working during study time) and (b) what he/she should be doing (e.g., completing assignments during study time, studying, etc.).

96. Write a contract with the student specifying what behavior is expected (e.g., working on class assignments during study time) and what reinforcement will be made available when the terms of the contract have been met.

97. Specify exactly what is to be done for the completion of an assignment (e.g., indicate definite starting and stopping points, indicate the minimum requirements, etc.).

98. Structure the environment to reduce distracting stimuli (e.g., place the student on or near the front row, provide a carrel or quiet place away from distractions, etc.). This is to be used as a means of reducing distracting stimuli and not as a form of punishment.

99. Use a timer to help the student monitor how much time he/she has to study.

100. Reduce emphasis on academic and social competition. Fear of failure may cause the student to not want to complete assignments in a given period of time.

112 Begins an assignment or activity before receiving or reading complete directions or instructions or fails to follow directions or instructions

1. Practice direction-following skills on nonacademic tasks.

2. Establish classroom rules:
   - Concentrate while working.
   - Work quietly.
   - Remain in your seat.
   - Finish task.
   - Meet task expectations.

Review rules often. Reinforce students for following the rules.

3. Speak with the student to explain (a) what he/she is doing wrong (e.g., not following directions when performing academic tasks) and (b) what he/she should be doing (e.g., listening to directions, asking for clarification if not understood, taking notes, following one step at a time, etc.).

4. Follow a less desirable task with a highly desirable task. Make the completion of the first task necessary to perform the second task.

5. Rewrite directions for the student at a lower reading level.

6. Clarify instructions/directions/expectations before assigning a task.

7. Have the student maintain a record (e.g., chart or graph) of performance in attempting new assignments/activities.

8. Post needed information in a readily accessible location (e.g., bulletin board, desktop, dictation slide, etc.).

9. Reduce the emphasis on competition. Competitive activities may cause the student to hurry to begin the assignment without following the directions.

10. Have the student time his/her activities to monitor personal behavior and accept time limits.

11. Start with a single problem and add more problems to the task over time.

12. Reinforce the student for beginning assignments after receiving directions or instructions: (a) give the student a tangible reward (e.g., classroom privileges, passing out materials, five minutes free time, etc.) or (b) give the student an intangible reward (e.g., praise, fist bump, smile, etc.).

13. Communicate with the student's parents (e.g., notes home, phone calls, etc.) to share information about their child's progress. The parents may reinforce the student at home for beginning assignments after receiving directions at school.

14. Relate the importance of waiting for and following directions as skills required for success on the job site.

15. Assess the quality and clarity of directions, explanations, and instructions given to the student.

16. Require that assignments done incorrectly, for any reason, be redone.

17. Require the student to begin each assignment within a specified period of time (e.g., three minutes, five minutes, etc.).

18. Have the student attempt the new assignment/activity in a private place (e.g., carrel, office, quiet study area, etc.) to reduce the fear of public failure.

19. Have the student develop a flow chart of the steps necessary to complete a task.

20. Allow the student to perform new assignments/activities in a variety of places in the building (e.g., resource room, library, learning center, etc.).

21. Maintain mobility to provide assistance to the student.

22. Reduce the number of directions given at one time (i.e., give the student each additional step after completion of the previous step).

23. Make instructions meaningful to the student. Attempt to relate instructions to future experiences on the job site.

24. Establish assignment rules (e.g., listen to directions, wait until all verbal directions have been given, ask questions about anything not understood, make sure you have all of the necessary materials, and begin the assignment when you are certain about what you are supposed to do, etc.).

25. Make sure that the student is attending to the teacher (e.g., making eye contact, hands free of writing materials, looking at assignment, etc.) before directions are given.

26. Help the student develop an awareness of the consequences of his/her behavior by writing down or talking through problems which may occur due to his/her failure to receive/read directions (e.g., if you don't read the directions before beginning the assignment, you will waste time and possibly have to redo the assignment).

27. Provide directions/instructions on a one-to-one basis before assigning a task.

28. Tell the student that directions will be given only once.

29. Reinforce those students who receive directions before beginning a new task.

30. Teach the student to follow graphic charts and diagrams closely when reading directions.

31. Prevent the student from beginning something before being given directions or instructions (e.g., sit next to him/her, give out materials when it is time to begin the task, etc.).

32. Prevent the student from becoming over-stimulated by an activity (e.g., frustrated, angry, etc.).

33. Do not require the student to complete the assignment/activity in one sitting.

34. Encourage the student to understand the consequences of impulsive behavior (e.g., if you begin a work assignment before all directions are given, you may do things incorrectly).

35. Make sure that the student has all materials needed to complete the assignment/activity.

36. Specify exactly what is to be done for the completion of a task (e.g., make definite starting and stopping points, identify a minimum requirement, etc.).

37. Explain to the student that work done incorrectly during class time will have to be made up at other times (e.g., during homeroom, before/after school, during lunchtime, etc.).

38. Provide the student with more than enough time to finish an activity. As the student demonstrates success, gradually decrease the amount of time provided to finish an activity.

39. Communicate with the student's cooperative work experience/vocational education teacher to consistently reinforce receiving directions prior to beginning a task.

40. Have the student ask questions about directions, explanations, or instructions not understood before beginning a task to reinforce comprehension.

41. Provide the student with a variety of assignments, requiring him/her to choose a minimum number from the total to complete (e.g., present the student with 10 academic tasks from which 6 must be finished that day).

42. Have the student verbally repeat directions, explanations, or instructions after they have been given to reinforce retention.

43. Help the student with the first few items on a task. As the student demonstrates success, gradually reduce the amount of help over time.

44. Provide alternatives to the traditional format for directions (e.g., record directions, summarize directions, peers give directions, etc.).

45. Choose different people (e.g., peer, paraprofessional, friend, etc.) to reinforce the student when he/she receives/reads instructions before beginning a task.

46. Require the student to ask permission from the teacher to begin an assignment.

47. Provide the student with shorter tasks given more frequently.

48. Teach the student direction-following skills (e.g., listen carefully, write down important points, ask for clarification, wait until all directions are received before beginning).

49. Stand next to the student when giving directions.

50. Teach the student to recognize when he/she is becoming overanxious and beginning things before receiving directions or instructions.

51. Choose a peer or volunteer to help the student begin a task.

52. Encourage the student to manage his/her daily performance as if he/she were self-employed. This should increase his/her motivation to successfully complete projects.

53. Have the student outline, underline, or highlight important information in printed materials.

54. Teach and have the student practice listening for key information when he/she is being given directions or receiving information (e.g., write down main points, ideas, step-by-step instructions, etc.).

55. Have the student proofread all of his/her work before submitting it.

56. Have the student highlight important information in written directions prior to beginning an assignment.

57. Present assignments in the most interesting and attractive manner possible.

58. Provide the student with self-checking materials to check work privately, reducing the fear of public failure.

59. Set a positive example by dealing in a socially-acceptable way with situations which require you to sit through directions or instructions.

60. Along with a directive, provide an incentive statement (e.g., "If you wait to begin your work, I will come around to help you with the first problem.").

61. Communicate clearly to the student when it is time to begin.

62. Structure time limits so the student knows exactly how long to work and when to be finished.

63. Provide clearly-stated directions, written or verbal. Make the directions as simple and concrete as possible.

64. Reinforce the student for beginning assignments after receiving directions, instructions, etc., based on the length of time the student can be successful. As the student demonstrates success, gradually decrease the amount of time to begin the task for the student to be reinforced.

65. Provide the student with a schedule of activities so he/she will know exactly what and how much there is to do in a day.

66. Provide the student with a sample of the assignment/activity which has been partially completed by a peer or teacher (e.g., book reports, projects).

67. Interact frequently with the student to help him/her follow directions for the activity.

68. Deliver directions and instructions before handing out materials.

69. Do not allow the student to participate in a situation unless he/she can demonstrate self-control and listen to directions or instructions before beginning.

70. Allow the student access to pencils, pens, etc., only after directions have been given.

71. Reduce distracting stimuli (e.g., place the student in the front row, provide a carrel or office space away from distractions, etc.). This is used as a means of reducing distracting stimuli and not as a form of punishment.

72. Write a contract with the student specifying what behavior is expected (e.g., beginning assignments after listening to directions) and what reinforcement will be made available when the terms of the contract have been met.

73. Provide the student the opportunity to complete the assignment/activity in a variety of ways (e.g., recorded, with a calculator, verbally, etc.).

74. Allow the student the option of performing the assignment at another time (e.g., earlier in the day, later, on another day).

75. Provide directions/instructions in the student's preferred learning style (e.g., visual, auditory, etc.).

76. Choose a peer, paraprofessional, friend, etc., to quiz the student on directions/instructions before he/she begins a task.

77. Have the student imagine the steps required to complete a task before beginning that task.

78. Provide the student with a predetermined signal (e.g., turning lights off and on, hand signals, etc.) when he/she is not beginning a task.

79. Immediately remove the student from a situation when he/she begins doing things before receiving directions or instructions.

80. Organize assignments by dividing them into small segments. Set deadlines and provide the student with a reward after completing each segment of the assignment.

81. Seat the student close to the source of information to maintain attention (e.g., in the front row or near the speaker in a group activity).

82. Require the student to wait until other students begin the task.

83. Have the student practice a new skill (e.g., jumping rope, dribbling a basketball) alone, with a peer, or with the teacher before the entire group attempts the activity.

84. Structure the environment to provide the student with increased opportunities for help or assistance (e.g., peer tutoring, directions for work sent home, frequent interactions, etc.).

85. Maintain visibility to and from the student to keep his/her attention when verbal questions/directions are being delivered. The teacher should be able to see the student and the student should be able to see the teacher. Make eye contact possible at all times.

86. Write down verbal directions. Instruct the student to cross each step off as it is completed.

87. Have the student explain to the teacher what is to be done to complete the assignment.

88. Have the student demonstrate attention to the source of information by maintaining eye contact, keeping hands free from other materials, and practicing attending posture.

89. Require the student to wait until the teacher gives a signal to begin (e.g., hand signal, ringing of bell, etc.).

90. Inform individuals who will be spending time with the student (e.g., substitute teachers, coaches, activity sponsors, etc.) about his/her tendency to begin things before receiving directions or instructions.

91. Give a signal (e.g., clapping hands, turning lights off and on, etc.) before giving verbal directions.

92. Make necessary adjustments in the environment (e.g., give out materials after delivering directions or instructions) to prevent the student from becoming overly excited or anxious.

93. Make sure the student achieves success when following directions.

94. Have the student read directions aloud to ensure directions/instructions are read prior to beginning a task.

95. Give directions in a variety of ways to facilitate the student's understanding (i.e., if the student does not understand verbal directions, present them in written form).

96. Evaluate the appropriateness of the task to determine (a) if the task is too difficult and (b) if the length of time scheduled to complete the task is adequate.

97. Assess the degree of task difficulty to determine whether or not the student will require additional information, time, assistance, etc., before beginning a task.

1. Communicate with parents (e.g., notes home, phone calls, etc.) to share information about their child's progress. The parents may reinforce the student at home for appropriately changing from one activity to another at school.

2. Allow natural consequences to occur due to the student's failure to finish a task (e.g., failing to finish an assignment will result in having to give up a recreational activity to complete an unfinished task).

3. Establish rules for changing activities (e.g., finish one activity before moving on to another, put things away where they belong, return borrowed items in the same or better condition, complete cleanup on time, etc.). These rules should be consistent and followed by everyone in the class. Talk about the rules often.

4. Have the student develop a checklist/chart to follow which will allow him/her to complete all assignments.

5. Reinforce the student for demonstrating acceptable behavior based on the length of time the student can be successful. As the student demonstrates success, gradually increase the length of time required for reinforcement.

6. Use more interesting or stimulating activities as a reward for completing less interesting activities (e.g., complete paperwork before working on the computer)

7. Reduce the student's involvement in activities which prove too stimulating for him/her.

8. Require the student to put all materials away before moving on to a new activity.

9. Establish a timeline for completing an assignment.

10. Require the student to finish an activity unless it will be disruptive to the schedule.

11. Assign the student shorter activities. As the student demonstrates success, gradually increase the length of the activities.

12. Assign short-term projects that can be quickly completed.

13. Establish rules that are to be followed in various parts of the school building (e.g., lunchroom, music room, art room, gymnasium, library, playground, etc.) relating to appropriate transition between activities.

14. Maintain consistent expectations within the ability level of the student.

15. Reinforce those students in the classroom who change from one activity to another without difficulty.

16. Provide the student with a clearly understood list of consequences for inappropriate behavior.

17. Reduce the emphasis on competition. Competitive activities may cause the student to become impatient and leave activities incomplete.

18. Maintain consistency in the classroom's daily routines.

19. Make sure there is a designated place for all items in the classroom.

20. Assess the degree of task difficulty to determine whether or not the student will require additional information, time, assistance, etc., before beginning a task.

21. Schedule recreational activities at the end of the day. Make participation in these activities dependent upon completion of class responsibilities.

22. Set aside time at the end of each class period to complete assignments.

23. Inform the student that work not completed in one sitting can be completed later. Provide the student with enough time to complete earlier assignments to guarantee closure.

24. Provide the student with clearly stated expectations for all situations.

25. Speak to the student to explain (a) what he/she is doing wrong (e.g., failing to complete an activity before beginning another) and (b) what he/she should be doing (e.g., completing an activity before changing to another).

26. Demonstrate to the student how to finish one activity before moving on to another (e.g., return things to their proper places, return borrowed items in the same or better condition, etc.) before expecting the student to perform the responsibilities on his/her own.

27. Establish classroom routines and procedures for transitioning from one activity to the next.

28. Establish rules for organization (i.e., everything has a place and everything should be in its place). Enforce these rules consistently in the classroom.

29. Reinforce the student for changing from one activity to another without difficulty: (a) give the student a tangible reward (e.g., classroom privileges, passing out materials, five minutes free time, etc.) or (b) give the student an intangible reward (e.g., praise, fist bump, smile, etc.).

30. Schedule activities so the student has more than enough time to finish an activity if he/she works consistently.

31. Follow a less desirable task with a more desirable task. Make completion of the first task necessary to perform the second task.

32. Have the student ask for help when he/she needs it.

33. Encourage the student to manage his/her daily performance as if he/she were self-employed. This should increase his/her motivation to successfully complete projects.

34. Assign an activity that involves immediate, short-term tasks.

35. Have the student time activities to monitor his/her behavior and time limits.

36. Identify the expectations of different environments and help the student develop the skills to be successful in those environments.

37. Establish classroom rules:
- Concentrate while working.
- Work quietly.
- Remain in your seat.
- Finish task.
- Meet task requirements.

Review rules often. Reinforce the student for following the rules.

38. Collect the student's materials (e.g., pencil, paper, textbook, workbook, etc.) when it is time to change from one activity to another.

39. Designate a time during each class period to put away materials.

40. In conjunction with other school personnel, create as much consistency across the various environments as possible (e.g., rules, criteria for success, behavioral expectations, consequences, etc.).

41. Provide the student with established time limits before an activity begins.

42. Assist the student in performing his/her responsibilities. As the student demonstrates success in performing responsibilities, gradually decrease assistance and require the student to independently assume more responsibility.

43. Be clear when giving directions to transition from one activity to the next.

44. Write a contract with the student specifying what behavior is expected (e.g., putting materials away and getting ready for another activity) and what reinforcement will be made available when the terms of the contract have been met.

45. Choose a peer to model finishing an activity and putting materials away for the student.

46. Provide the student with more than enough time to finish an activity. As the student demonstrates success, decrease the amount of time provided to finish an activity.

47. Set time limits so that the student knows exactly how long he/she has to work and when he/she must be finished.

48. Provide adequate transition time for the student to finish an activity and get ready for the next activity.

49. Use a timer to help the student know when it is time to change to a new activity.

50. Teach time-management skills. Have the student make a daily plan and follow it. Encourage the student to avoid becoming distracted by events, impulses, and moods.

51. Discuss the student's responsibilities at the beginning of each class period so he/she knows what is expected.

52. Limit the student's use of those items he/she has been irresponsible in putting away, returning, etc.

53. Explain to the student when he/she does not put things away, exactly what he/she is doing wrong, what he/she is supposed to be doing, and why.

54. Make sure that responsibilities given to the student are appropriate for his/her level of development and ability.

55. Employ a signal technique (e.g., turning the lights off and on) to warn that the end of an activity is near and it is time to finish and put materials away.

56. Be consistent in expecting the student to change from one activity to another (e.g., do not allow the student to change activities without putting materials away one time and not the next).

57. Provide an incentive statement along with a directive (e.g., "You may listen to your music after you finish your assignment and put away all materials.").

58. Evaluate the appropriateness of the task to determine (a) if the task is too easy, (b) if the task is too difficult, and (c) if the length of time scheduled to complete the task is adequate.

114 Does not begin assignments after receiving directions, instructions, etc.

1. Structure the environment to provide the student with increased opportunities for help or assistance.

2. Reduce distracting stimuli (e.g., place the student on the front row, provide a carrel or office space away from distractions, etc.). This is used as a means of reducing distracting stimuli and not as a form of punishment.

3. Have the student maintain a record (e.g., chart or graph) of his/her performance in attempting new assignments/activities.

4. Communicate clearly to the student when it is time to begin.

5. Have the student time activities to monitor his/her behavior and time limits.

6. Present the task in the most interesting and attractive manner possible.

7. Maintain mobility to provide assistance to the student.

8. Structure time limits so the student knows exactly how long he/she has to work and when the work must be finished.

9. Provide the student with more than enough time to finish an activity. As the student demonstrates success, gradually decrease the amount of time provided to finish an activity.

10. Give directions in a variety of ways to facilitate the student's understanding (e.g., if the student does not understand verbal directions, present them in written form).

11. Have the student repeat the directions verbally to the teacher.

12. Structure the environment to provide the student with increased opportunity for help or assistance on academic tasks (e.g., peer tutoring, directions for work sent home, frequent interactions, etc.).

13. Give a signal (e.g., clapping hands, turning lights off and on, etc.) before giving verbal directions.

14. Provide the student with a predetermined signal (e.g., turning lights off and on, hand signals, etc.) when he/she is not beginning a task.

15. Tell the student that directions will only be given once.

16. Rewrite directions at a lower reading level.

17. Help the student with the first few items on a task. As the student demonstrates success, gradually reduce the amount of help over time.

18. Reinforce the student for beginning assignments after receiving directions, instructions, etc., based on the length of time the student can be successful. As the student demonstrates success, gradually decrease the amount of time to begin the task to be reinforced.

19. Follow a less desirable task with a highly desirable task. Make completion of the first task necessary to perform the second.

20. Provide the student with a schedule of activities so that he/she knows exactly what and how much there is to do in a day.

21. Prevent the student from becoming overstimulated by an activity (e.g., frustrated, angry, etc.).

22. Specify exactly what is to be done for the completion of a task (e.g., make definite starting and stopping points, identify a minimum requirement, etc.).

23. Require the student to begin each assignment within a specified period of time (e.g., three minutes, five minutes, etc.).

24. Provide the student with shorter tasks given more frequently.

25. Provide the student with a variety of assignments, requiring the student to choose a minimum number from the total to complete (e.g., present the student with ten academic tasks from which six must be finished).

26. Start with a single problem and add more problems to the task over time.

27. Reduce emphasis on competition (e.g., academic or social). Fear of failure may cause the student to refuse to attempt new assignments/activities.

28. Provide the student with self-checking materials so that he/she may check work privately, reducing the fear of public failure.

29. Have the student attempt a new assignment/activity in a private place (e.g., carrel, office, quiet study area, etc.) to reduce the fear of public failure.

30. Have the student practice a new skill (e.g., jumping rope, dribbling a basketball, etc.) alone, with a peer, or with the teacher before the entire group attempts the activity.

31. Provide the student with the opportunity to perform the assignment/activity in a variety of ways (e.g., recorded, with a calculator, verbally, etc.).

32. Allow the student to perform new assignments/activities in a variety of places in the building (e.g., resource room, library, learning center, etc.).

33. Provide the student with a sample of the assignment/activity which has been partially completed by a peer or teacher (e.g., book reports, projects, etc.).

34. Do not require the student to complete the assignment/activity in one sitting.

35. Make sure that the student has all the materials needed to perform the assignment/task.

36. Allow the student the option of performing the assignment at another time (e.g., earlier in the day, later, on another day, etc.).

37. Deliver directions/instructions before handing out materials.

38. Make sure the student achieves success when following directions.

39. Have the student explain to the teacher what he/she thinks should be done to complete the assignment/activity.

40. Explain to the student that work not done during work time will have to be made up at other times (e.g., at recess, before school, after school, during lunchtime, break time, etc.).

41. Teach the student direction-following skills (e.g., listen carefully, write down important points, ask for clarification, and wait until all directions are received before beginning).

42. Provide clearly stated directions, written or verbal (e.g., make the directions as simple and concrete as possible).

43. Interact frequently with the student to help him/her follow directions for the activity.

44. Provide alternatives to the traditional format for directions (e.g., record directions, summarize directions, directions given by peers, etc.).

45. Practice direction-following skills on non-academic tasks.

46. Evaluate the appropriateness of the task to determine (a) if the task is too easy, (b) if the task is too difficult, and (c) if the length of time scheduled to complete the task is adequate.

47. Require that assignments done incorrectly, for any reason, be redone.

48. Establish assignment rules (e.g., listen to directions, wait until all directions have been given, ask questions about anything you do not understand, begin assignment only when you are certain about what is required, make sure you have all necessary materials, etc.).

49. Reduce the emphasis on competition. Competitive academic activities may cause the student to hurry and begin the assignment without following the directions.

50. Write a contract with the student specifying what behavior is expected (e.g., begin assignments after listening to directions) and what reinforcement will be made available when the terms of the contract have been met.

51. Stand next to the student when giving directions.

52. Require the student to ask permission from the teacher to begin.

53. Maintain visibility to and from the student. The teacher should be able to see the student and the student should be able to see the teacher. Make eye contact possible at all times to make sure the student is attending.

54. Along with a directive, provide an incentive statement (e.g., "When you begin your work, I will come around to see if you have questions.").

55. Use a timer to help the student monitor how much time he/she has to follow through with directions.

56. Choose a peer or volunteer to help the student begin a task.

57. Assess the quality and clarity of directions, explanations, and instructions given to the student.

58. Have the student ask questions about directions, explanations, and instructions not understood.

59. Reduce the number of directions given at one time (i.e., give the student each additional step after completion of the previous step).

60. Communicate with the parents (e.g., notes home, phone calls, etc.) to share information about the student's progress. The parents may reinforce the student at home for beginning assignments after receiving directions, instructions, etc., at school.

61. Establish classroom rules:
- Concentrate while working.
- Remain in your seat.
- Finish task.
- Meet task expectations.
- Raise your hand.

Review rules often. Reinforce students for following the rules.

62. Speak to the student to explain (a) what the student is doing wrong (e.g., not beginning assignments after receiving directions, instructions, etc.) and (b) what the student should be doing (e.g., listening to directions, asking for clarification if directions are not understood, taking notes, following one step at a time, etc.).

63. Reinforce the student for beginning assignments after receiving directions, instructions, etc.: (a) give the student a tangible reward (e.g., classroom privileges, line leading, passing out materials, five minutes free time, etc.) or (b) give the student an intangible reward (e.g., praise, fist bump, smile, etc.).

64. Make sure that the student is attending to the teacher (e.g., making eye contact, hands free of writing materials, looking at assignments, etc.) before directions are given.

115 Does not complete assignments after receiving directions, instructions, etc.

1. Structure the environment to provide the student with increased opportunities for help or assistance.

2. Reduce distracting stimuli (e.g., place the student on the front row, provide a carrel or office space away from distractions, etc.). This is used as a means of reducing distracting stimuli and not as a form of punishment.

3. Have the student maintain a record (e.g., chart or graph) of his/her performance in completing assignments.

4. Communicate clearly to the student the length of time he/she has to complete an assignment.

5. Have the student time assignments to monitor personal behavior and accept time limits.

6. Present the task in the most interesting and attractive manner possible.

7. Maintain mobility to provide assistance to the student.

8. Structure time limits so the student knows exactly how long he/she has to work and when the work must be finished.

9. Provide the student with more than enough time to finish an activity. As the student demonstrates success, gradually decrease the amount of time provided to finish an activity.

10. Give directions in a variety of ways to facilitate the student's understanding (e.g., if the student does not understand verbal directions, present them in written form).

11. Have the student repeat the directions verbally to the teacher.

12. Rewrite directions at a lower reading level.

13. Deliver verbal directions in a more basic manner.

14. Provide the student with shorter tasks given more frequently.

15. Provide the student with a schedule of activities so he/she knows exactly what and how much there is to do in a day.

16. Prevent the student from becoming over-stimulated by an activity (e.g., frustrated, angry, etc.).

17. Specify exactly what is to be done for the completion of a task (e.g., indicate definite starting and stopping points, indicate a minimum requirement, etc.).

18. Require the student to begin each assignment within a specified period of time (e.g., three minutes, five minutes, etc.).

19. Follow a less desirable task with a highly desirable task, making the completion of the first necessary to perform the second.

20. Provide the student with a variety of assignments, requiring the student to choose a minimum number from the total to complete (e.g., present the student with ten academic tasks from which six must be finished that day).

21. Provide the student with a certain number of problems to do on an assignment, requiring the student to choose a minimum number from the total to complete (e.g., present the student with ten math problems from which six must be completed).

22. Along with a directive, provide an incentive statement (e.g., "After your work is finished, you may play a game.").

23. Use a timer to help the student monitor how much time he/she has to finish an assignment.

24. Reinforce those students in the classroom who complete assignments after receiving directions, instructions, etc.

25. Assess the quality and clarity of directions, explanations, and instructions the student does not understand.

26. Have the student ask questions about directions, explanations, and instructions not understood.

27. Choose a peer to model appropriate completion of assignments after receiving directions, instructions, etc., for the student.

28. Communicate with the parents (e.g., notes home, phone calls, etc.) to share information about the student's progress. The parents may reinforce the student at home for completing assignments after receiving directions, instructions, etc., at school.

29. Write a contract with the student specifying what behavior is expected (e.g., following directions, meeting task expectations, completing assignments, etc.) and what reinforcement will be made available when the terms of the contract have been met.

30. Reinforce the student for completing assignments after receiving directions, instructions, etc., based on the length of time the student can be successful. As the student demonstrates success, gradually decrease the length of time required for completing assignments for reinforcement.

31. Choose a peer to work with the student and aid him/her in completing an assignment.

32. Establish classroom rules:
- Concentrate while working.
- Work quietly.
- Remain in your seat.
- Finish task.
- Meet task requirements.

Review rules often. Reinforce the student for following the rules.

33. Speak to the student to explain (a) what the student is doing wrong (e.g., not following directions when performing academic tasks) and (b) what the student should be doing (e.g., listening to directions, asking for clarification, taking notes, following one step at a time, etc.).

34. Reinforce the student for completing assignments after receiving directions, instructions, etc: (a) give the student a tangible reward (e.g., classroom privileges, line leading, passing out materials, five minutes free time, etc.) or (b) give the student an intangible reward (e.g., praise, fist bump, smile, etc.).

35. Evaluate the appropriateness of the task to determine (a) if the task is too easy, (b) if the task is too difficult, and (c) if the length of time scheduled to complete the task is adequate.

I. Interpersonal Relationships

Behavior Number

116 Makes inappropriate comments or unnecessary noises in the classroom

1. Communicate with the student's parents (e.g., notes home, phone calls, etc.) to share information about their student's progress. The parents may reinforce the student at home for making comments when appropriate at school.

2. Allow natural consequences to occur due to the student making unnecessary comments or noises in the classroom (e.g., making noises and inappropriate comments during class time will cause the student to have to make up the work during recreational time).

3. Teach the student behaviors that promote self-control (e.g., placing hands on desk, sitting with feet on the floor, making eye contact with the person who is talking, etc.).

4. Give adequate opportunities to respond (i.e., enthusiastic students need many opportunities to contribute).

5. Instruct the student to carry a notepad with him/her at all times and to write information down to help him/her remember.

6. Encourage the student to recite a mantra to himself/herself when entering a situation where he/she may be tempted to make unnecessary comments or noises (e.g., be quiet, be quiet, be quiet).

7. Structure the environment to limit opportunities for inappropriate behaviors (e.g., keep the student engaged in activities, have the student seated near the teacher, etc.).

8. Educate yourself and others about ADHD to increase understanding and accommodation of interruptive behavior.

9. Help the student develop an awareness of himself/herself and those around him/her. Have the student periodically step back and ask himself/herself, "Am I bothering or disturbing others?"

10. Help the student develop an awareness of himself/herself and those around him/her. Have the student periodically step back and ask himself/herself, "Am I talking too loudly or making unnecessary comments or noises?"

11. Encourage the student to pause and consider his/her thoughts before speaking.

12. Educate the student about ADHD and the need to self monitor behavior.

13. Teach the student to recognize and make appropriate comments (e.g., comments within the context of the situation, comments that are a follow-up to what has just been said, etc.).

14. Provide constant, positive reinforcement for appropriate behavior. Ignore as many inappropriate behaviors as possible.

15. Reinforce the student for making appropriate comments in the classroom: (a) give the student a tangible reward (e.g., classroom privileges, passing out materials, five minutes free time, etc.) or (b) give the student an intangible reward (e.g., praise, fist bump, smile, etc.).

16. Reinforce the student for making appropriate comments based on the length of time the student can be successful. As the student demonstrates success, gradually increase the length of time required for reinforcement.

17. Help the student develop an awareness of the consequences of his/her behavior by writing down or talking through problems which may occur due to disturbing others (e.g., perceived as unmannerly, avoided, etc.).

18. Encourage the student to monitor behavior by asking himself/herself questions: *What should I be doing right now?*, *Is what I have to say relevant to this topic?*, and *Is this a good time for me to comment?*

19. Reinforce those students in the classroom who make appropriate comments.

20. Try various groupings in the classroom to determine the situation in which the student is most comfortable.

21. Remove the student from the group or activity until he/she can demonstrate appropriate behavior and self-control.

22. Make sure that the student understands the relationship between inappropriate behavior and the consequences which follow (e.g., making unnecessary noise will cause others to not want to be around him/her).

23. Reduce the emphasis on competition. Competitive activities may cause the student to become anxious and excessively noisy.

24. Teach the student to take cues from others (e.g., if he/she blurts out comments with no response from others, stop talking; when there is silence in class, it is not necessary to fill the silence with comments; etc.)

25. Assess the degree of task difficulty to determine whether or not the student will require additional information, time, assistance, etc., to avoid becoming frustrated and making unnecessary comments and noises.

26. Have the student ask questions about directions, explanations, or instructions he/she does not understand.

27. Schedule recreational activities at the end of the day. Make participation in these activities dependent upon completion of daily responsibilities and appropriate classroom behavior.

28. Speak with the student to explain (a) what he/she is doing wrong (e.g., making unnecessary comments or noises) and (b) what he/she should be doing (e.g., waiting until it is appropriate to speak, thinking of comments which relate to the situation, etc.).

29. Make sure that the student's feelings are considered when it is necessary to discuss his/her inappropriate comments (i.e., handle comments so that the student's enthusiasm for participation is not diminished).

30. Have the student practice waiting for a turn to speak for short periods of time. As the student demonstrates success, gradually increase the length of time required for a turn to speak.

31. Provide the student with a clearly understood list of consequences for inappropriate behavior.

32. Explain to the student that he/she may be trying too hard to fit in and that he/she should relax and make more appropriate comments.

33. Have the student put himself/herself in someone else's place (e.g., ask the student to think about how he/she would feel if someone called him/her dumb or stupid).

34. Reinforce the student for raising his/her hand to be recognized.

35. Encourage the student to review his/her thoughts before speaking and Make sure his/her thoughts have not already been expressed by someone else, the same question asked, etc.

36. Encourage the student to avoid ingesting any substance (e.g., drugs, alcohol, cold remedies, etc.) that might further alter his/her ability to maintain self-control.

37. Make sure that the student is individually supervised if he/she continues to make unnecessary noise.

38. Help the student understand why it is important to work quietly (e.g., if you are making unnecessary noise you may not hear what is being said, others will not listen to you, etc.).

39. Have the student be the leader of a small group activity if he/she possesses mastery of skills or an interest in that area.

40. Have the student make a list of consequences associated with frequently occurring behaviors (e.g., by disrupting others, I will be perceived as unmannerly; by making unnecessary noises, people will avoid me.).

41. Make sure that reinforcement is not inadvertently given for inappropriate behavior (e.g., making unnecessary comments or noises).

42. Provide the student with a predetermined signal if he/she begins to make inappropriate comments or unnecessary noises.

43. Explain to the student the reasons why making unnecessary comments and noise is not acceptable (e.g., impolite, might hurt others' feelings, etc.).

44. Remove the student from the situation until he/she can demonstrate appropriate behavior.

45. Help the student identify the situations in which he/she is most likely to talk beyond what is expected or at inappropriate times. After he/she has identified these situations, have him/her think of ways to minimize their occurrences.

46. Help the student identify the situations in which he/she is most likely to make unnecessary noise. After he/she has identified these situations, have him/her think of ways to minimize their occurrences.

47. Help the student improve concentration skills (e.g., listening to the speaker, taking notes, preparing comments in advance, making comments in the appropriate context, etc.).

48. Teach and practice effective communication skills. These skills include: listening, maintaining eye contact, and positive body language.

49. Have the student work in small groups in which he/she will have frequent opportunities to speak. As the student learns to wait longer for a turn to speak, gradually increase the size of the group.

50. Provide the student with many opportunities for social and academic successes.

51. Assess the appropriateness of the social situation in relation to the student's ability to function successfully.

52. Have a peer cue the student when he/she makes unnecessary noise (e.g., the person can touch the student's arm or desk as a signal that he/she is making unnecessary noise).

53. Write a contract with the student specifying what behavior is expected (e.g., making appropriate comments) and what reinforcement will be made available when the terms of the contract have been met.

54. Do not inadvertently reinforce the student's inappropriate behavior by laughing when he/she is silly, rude, etc.

55. Evaluate the appropriateness of the task to determine (a) if the task is too easy, (b) if the task is too difficult, and (c) if the length of time scheduled for the task is adequate.

56. Encourage the student to model the behavior of peers who are successful at not interrupting.

57. Explain to the student, after telling him/her to stop talking, the reason why he/she should not be talking.

58. Establish classroom rules:
- Concentrate while working.
- Work quietly.
- Remain in your seat.
- Finish task.
- Meet task requirements.

Review rules often. Reinforce the student for following the rules.

59. Teach the student acceptable ways to communicate displeasure, anger, frustration, etc.

60. Make the student aware of the number of times he/she makes unnecessary comments and noises.

61. Maintain visibility to and from the student to keep his/her attention when verbal questions/directions are being delivered. The teacher should be able to see the student and the student should be able to see the teacher. Make eye contact possible at all times.

62. Attempt to provide equal attention to all students in the classroom.

63. Reduce activities which might threaten the student (e.g., announcing test score ranges or test scores aloud, making students read aloud in class, emphasizing the success of a particular student or students, etc.).

64. Make the necessary adjustments in the environment to prevent the student from experiencing stress, frustration, or anger (e.g., reduce peer pressure, academic failure, teasing, etc.) which may result in unnecessary comments or noises.

65. Teach the student to use techniques such as crossing his/her arms and legs, clenching his/her fists, and intertwining his/her fingers when making noise is inappropriate.

66. Interact frequently with the student to reduce the need for him/her to make inappropriate comments or unnecessary noises.

67. Make sure the student understands the relationship between his/her behavior and the consequences which may follow (e.g., failing to listen to directions and making distracting noises will cause the student to not understand what to do).

68. Reduce the occurrence of activities that you know will stimulate the student to make unnecessary comments.

69. Teach active listening skills. Listen to what the other person is saying and respond based on information received.

1. Teach the student problem-solving skills: (a) identify the problem, (b) identify goals and objectives, (c) develop strategies, (d) develop a plan of action, and (e) carry out the plan.

2. Provide the student with positive feedback which indicates he/she is successful, important, respected, etc.

3. Structure the environment (e.g., seating arrangement, supervision, etc.) to reduce opportunities for the student to become physically aggressive toward other students.

4. Maintain visibility to and from the student. The teacher should be able to see the student and the student should be able to see the teacher. Make eye contact possible at all times.

5. Maintain supervision. Do not leave the student alone with other students.

6. Reduce activities which might be threatening to the student (e.g., announcing test score ranges or test scores aloud, making students read aloud in class, emphasizing the success of a particular student(s), etc.).

7. Try various groupings to determine the situation in which the student is most likely to succeed socially.

8. Make the necessary adjustments in the environment that will prevent the student from becoming overstimulated by peers.

9. Reduce the emphasis on competition and perfection. Repeated failure and frustration may cause outbursts of physical aggression.

10. Teach the student alternative ways to deal with situations which make him/her feel frustrated or angry (e.g., withdrawing, talking, etc.).

11. Facilitate on-task behavior by providing a full schedule of activities. Prevent lag time from occurring when the student would be free to participate in inappropriate behavior.

12. Be mobile to be frequently near the student.

13. Provide the student with as many high-interest activities as possible to keep him/her from becoming physically aggressive toward other students.

14. Provide the student with many opportunities for social and academic success.

15. Make sure that all school personnel are aware of the student's tendency to become physically aggressive so they will monitor the student's behavior.

16. Maintain supervision of the student. As the student demonstrates appropriate behavior, gradually decrease supervision.

17. Provide a quiet place for the student to work independently, away from peer interactions. This is not to be used as a form of punishment but rather as an opportunity to increase the student's success in his/her environment.

18. Place reinforcement emphasis on academic productivity and accuracy to reduce the likelihood of the student becoming physically aggressive (i.e., increased productivity and accuracy should reduce the likelihood of inappropriate behavior).

19. Reduce or remove any stimulus in the environment (e.g., possessions, competition, teasing, etc.) which leads to the student's physically aggressive behavior.

20. Make sure the student understands the natural consequences of hurting other students (e.g., less freedom, more restrictive environment, assault charges, etc.).

21. Prevent the student from receiving too much stimulation (e.g., monitor or supervise student behavior to limit overexcitement in physical activities, games, parties, etc.).

22. Limit the student's opportunity to enter areas of the school environment where he/she is more likely to be physically aggressive.

23. Separate the student from the peer(s) who may be encouraging or stimulating the student's inappropriate behavior.

24. Do not force the student to interact or remain in a group when he/she is physically aggressive (e.g., daily reading group, physical education group, etc.).

25. Limit the student's independent movement in the school environment.

26. Intervene early when there is a problem with fighting to prevent more serious problems from occurring.

27. Encourage the student to tell you about problems that occur with other peers at school.

28. Make sure there will always be adult supervision where the student will be.

29. Do not force the student to play with other students with whom he/she is not completely comfortable.

30. Make sure the student does not become involved in overstimulating activities.

31. Talk with the student about individual differences, and discuss strengths and weaknesses of individuals the student knows. Stress that the student does not have to do the same things everyone else does.

32. Choose a peer who will be a good influence (e.g., someone younger/older, of the same gender, of the opposite gender, etc.).

33. Have the student put himself/herself in someone else's place (e.g., ask the student to think about how he/she would feel if someone called him/her dumb or stupid).

34. Do not leave the student alone with other students when he/she is upset or angry.

35. Do not force the student to interact with individuals with whom he/she is not completely comfortable.

36. Before beginning an activity or game, make sure the student knows the rules, is familiar with the activity or game, and will be compatible with the other individuals who will be playing.

37. Teach the student to ask for things in a positive manner. Teach key words and phrases (e.g., "May I borrow your pencil?" "Do you mind if I play the game with you?" etc.).

38. Do not leave a lot of unstructured time for the student.

39. Teach the student to think before acting by asking himself/herself question: *What is happening? What am I doing? What should I do? What will be best for me?*

40. Have the student practice appropriate verbal exchanges which should be made when typical physical exchanges take place (e.g., *Excuse me. I'm sorry.*).

41. Allow the student to voice his/her opinion in situations to avoid becoming angry or upset.

42. Talk to the student about ways of handling conflict situations successfully (e.g., walk away from a situation, change to another activity, ask for help, etc.).

43. Prevent frustrating or anxiety-producing situations from occurring (e.g., give the student tasks only on his/her ability level, give the student only the number of tasks that he/she can tolerate in one sitting, reduce social interactions which stimulate the student to become physically aggressive, etc.).

44. Explain to the student that it is natural for conflict situations to occur. What is important is how he/she reacts to the situation.

45. Communicate with parents (e.g., notes home, phone calls, etc.) to share information about the student's progress. The parents may reinforce the student at home for respecting the norms of physical proximity at school.

46. Write a contract with the student specifying what behavior is expected (e.g., respecting the norms of physical proximity) and what reinforcement will be made available when the terms of the contract have been met.

47. Remove the student from the group or activity until he/she can demonstrate appropriate behavior and self-control.

48. Reinforce the student for demonstrating appropriate behavior based on the length of time the student can be successful. As the student demonstrates success, gradually increase the length of time required for reinforcement.

49. Reinforce those students in the classroom who demonstrate appropriate behavior when interacting with other students.

50. Establish classroom rules:
- Concentrate while working.
- Work quietly.
- Remain in your seat.
- Finish task.
- Meet task requirements.

Review rules often. Reinforce the student for following the rules.

51. Speak with the student to explain (a) what the student is doing wrong (e.g., scratching, hitting, pulling hair, etc.) and (b) what the student should be doing (e.g., following the rules, interacting in appropriate ways, dealing with anger and frustration in appropriate ways, etc.).

52. Reinforce the student for demonstrating appropriate behavior: (a) give the student a tangible reward (e.g., classroom privileges, line leading, passing out materials, five minutes free time, etc.) or (b) give the student an intangible reward (e.g., praise, fist bump, smile, etc.).

53. Evaluate the appropriateness of the task to determine (a) if the task is too easy, (b) if the task is too difficult, and (c) if the length of time scheduled to complete the task is adequate.

54. When the student has responded inappropriately to a conflict situation, take time to explore with him/her appropriate solutions which could have been used in dealing with the problem.

1. Prevent frustrating or anxiety-producing situations from occurring (e.g., give the student tasks only on his/her ability level, give the student only the number of tasks that can be tolerated in one sitting, reduce social interactions which stimulate the student to become physically aggressive, etc.).

2. Teach the student problem-solving skills: (a) identify the problem, (b) identify goals and objectives, (c) develop strategies, (d) develop a plan for action, and (e) carry out the plan.

3. Provide the student with positive feedback which indicates he/she is successful, important, respected, etc.

4. Structure the environment to prevent opportunities for the student to become physically aggressive toward teachers (e.g., interact frequently with the student to prevent him/her from becoming frustrated).

5. Maintain supervision of the student. As the student demonstrates appropriate behavior, gradually decrease supervision.

6. Maintain visibility to and from the student. The teacher should be able to see the student, and the student should be able to see the teacher. Make eye contact possible at all times.

7. Reduce activities which might be threatening to the student (e.g., announcing test score ranges or test scores aloud, making students read aloud in class, emphasizing the success of particular student(s), etc.).

8. Be mobile to be frequently near the student.

9. Try various groupings to determine the situation in which the student is most successful.

10. Reduce the emphasis on competition and perfection. Repeated failure and frustration may cause outbursts of physical aggression.

11. Make the necessary adjustments in the environment to prevent the student from becoming overstimulated by peers, which in turn would make it necessary for the teacher to intervene.

12. Teach the student alternative ways to deal with situations which make him/her frustrated or angry (e.g., withdrawing, talking, etc.).

13. Facilitate on-task behavior by providing a full schedule of activities. Prevent lag time from occurring when the student would be free to participate in inappropriate behavior.

14. Provide the student with as many high-interest activities as possible to keep him/her from becoming physically aggressive toward teachers.

15. Provide the student with opportunities for social and academic success.

16. Make sure that all school personnel are aware of the student's tendency to become physically aggressive so they may monitor his/her behavior.

17. Avoid arguing with the student (e.g., calmly deliver consequences without reacting to the student's remarks).

18. Provide a quiet place for the student to work independently, away from peer interactions. This is not to be used as punishment but as an opportunity to increase the student's success in his/her environment.

19. Place reinforcement emphasis on academic productivity and accuracy to reduce the likelihood of the student becoming physically aggressive toward teachers (i.e., increased productivity and accuracy should reduce the likelihood of inappropriate behavior).

20. Reduce or remove any stimulus in the environment (e.g., possessions, competition, teasing, etc.) which leads to the student's physically aggressive behavior.

21. Make sure the student understands the natural consequences of becoming physically aggressive toward a teacher (e.g., less freedom, more restrictive environment, assault charges, etc.).

22. Prevent the student from receiving too much stimulation (e.g., monitor or supervise student behavior to limit overexcitement in physical activities, games, parties, etc.).

23. Limit the student's opportunity to enter areas of the school environment in which he/she is more likely to be physically aggressive.

24. Do not force the student to interact or remain in a group when he/she is physically aggressive (e.g., daily reading group, physical education group, etc.).

25. Always provide the student with behavioral options (e.g., sitting out of an activity, going to a quiet place in the room, performing another activity, etc.).

26. Maintain consistent behavioral expectations and consequences to reduce the likelihood of the student becoming upset by what he/she considers unfair treatment.

27. Limit the student's independent movement in the school environment.

28. Avoid physical contact with the student who is likely to become physically aggressive.

29. Maintain an appropriate physical distance from the student when interacting with him/her to avoid stimulation of aggressive behavior.

30. Use language that is pleasant and calming when speaking with the student to avoid stimulation of aggressive behavior.

31. Deliver directions in a supportive rather than a threatening manner (e.g., "Please finish your math assignment before going to recess." rather than "You had better turn in your math or else!").

32. Do not criticize when correcting the student, be honest yet supportive. Never cause the student to feel negatively about himself/herself.

33. Intervene early when there is a problem to prevent more serious problems from occurring.

34. Do not embarrass the student by giving him/her orders, demands, etc., in front of others.

35. Teach the student appropriate ways to communicate displeasure, anger, frustration, etc.

36. Have the student put himself/herself in someone else's place (e.g., ask the student to think about how he/she would feel if someone called him/her dumb or stupid).

37. Do not force the student to interact with individuals with whom he/she is not completely comfortable.

38. Teach the student to think before acting by asking himself/herself question: *What is happening? What am I doing? What should I do? What will be best for me?*

39. Have the student practice appropriate verbal exchanges which should be made when typical physical exchanges take place (e.g., *Excuse me. I'm sorry.*).

40. Allow the student to voice his/her opinion in a situation to avoid becoming angry or upset.

41. Evaluate the appropriateness of the task to determine (a) if the task is too easy, (b) if the task is too difficult, and (c) if the length of time scheduled to complete the task is adequate.

42. Reinforce those students in the classroom who demonstrate appropriate behavior when interacting with teachers.

43. Remove the student from the group or activity until he/she can demonstrate appropriate behavior and self-control.

44. Write a contract with the student specifying what behavior is expected (e.g., respecting the norms of physical proximity) and what reinforcement will be made available when the terms of the contract have been met.

45. Reinforce the student for demonstrating appropriate behavior based on the length of time the student can be successful. As the student demonstrates success, gradually increase the length of time required for reinforcement.

46. Establish classroom rules:
- Concentrate while working.
- Remain in your seat.
- Finish task.
- Meet task expectations.
- Raise your hand.

Review rules often. Reinforce students for following the rules.

47. Communicate with parents (e.g., notes home, phone calls, etc.) to share information about the student's progress. The parents may reinforce the student at home for respecting the norms of physical proximity at school.

48. Speak to the student to explain (a) what the student is doing wrong (e.g., pushing, pulling away, grabbing, etc.) and (b) what the student should be doing (e.g., following the rules, interacting in appropriate ways, dealing with anger and frustration in appropriate ways, etc.).

49. Reinforce the student for demonstrating appropriate behavior: (a) give the student a tangible reward (e.g., classroom privileges, line leading, passing out materials, five minutes free time, etc.) or (b) give the student an intangible reward (e.g., praise, fist bump, smile, etc.).

1. Acknowledge the student when he/she seeks attention verbally instead of making it necessary for the student to gain attention through physical contact.

2. Give the student your full attention when communicating with him/her to prevent the student's need for physical contact.

3. Allow natural consequences to occur as a result of the student's inappropriate behavior (e.g., excessive physical contact may cause people to stay away from the student or may result in pushing, shoving, etc.).

4. Encourage faculty/staff members with whom the student interacts to reinforce appropriate physical contact.

5. Avoid inadvertently stimulating the student's unnecessary physical contact (e.g., attire, language used, physical proximity, etc.).

6. Communicate with parents (e.g., notes home, phone calls, etc.) to share information about the student's progress. The parents may reinforce the student at home for respecting the norms of physical proximity at school.

7. Explain to the student what kinds of physical contact are appropriate and acceptable on the student's job site.

8. Make sure the student sees the relationship between his/her behavior and the consequences which may follow (e.g., touching and hugging people all of the time may result in others not wanting to be around him/her).

9. Establish classroom rules:
- Concentrate while working.
- Work quietly.
- Remain in your seat.
- Finish task.
- Meet task requirements.

Review rules often. Reinforce the student for following the rules.

10. Provide the student with many opportunities for social and academic successes.

11. Choose a peer who will be a good influence (e.g., someone younger/older, of the same gender, of the opposite gender, etc.) to play with the student.

12. Speak with the student to explain (a) what the student is doing wrong (e.g., touching, hugging, etc.) and (b) what the student should be doing (e.g., talking, exchanging greetings, etc.). Discuss appropriate ways to seek attention.

13. Model socially acceptable physical contact for the student (e.g., fist bump, pat on the back, etc.)

14. Prevent the student from becoming overstimulated by an activity (e.g., monitor or supervise student behavior to limit overexcitement in physical activities, games, parties, etc.).

15. Provide the student with social interaction in place of physical interaction (e.g., call the student by name, speak to the student, praise, congratulate, etc.).

16. Provide the student with verbal recognition and reinforcement for social and academic successes.

17. Reduce the opportunity for the student to participate in inappropriate physical contact (e.g., stand an appropriate distance from the student when interacting).

18. Try various groupings to find a situation in which the student's need for physical attention can be satisfied by socially acceptable interactions (e.g., holding hands while dancing in an extracurricular activity, a hug for an accomplishment, fist bump or "high five" in sports, etc.).

19. Teach the student appropriate ways to interact with others (e.g., verbal and physical introductions, interactions, etc.).

20. Use natural consequences when the student touches others as they walk by (e.g., move the student to another location in the room, have others walk away from the student, etc.).

21. Work directly with the student only in the presence of others.

22. Reinforce the student for respecting the norms of physical proximity based on the length of time he/she can be successful. As the student demonstrates success, gradually increase the length of time required for reinforcement.

23. Reinforce those students in the classroom who interact appropriately with other students or teachers.

24. Write a contract with the student specifying what behavior is expected (e.g., shaking hands rather than hugging) and what reinforcement will be made available when the terms of the contract have been met.

25. Remove the student from the group or activity until the student can demonstrate appropriate behavior and self-control.

26. Separate the student from the person who is the primary focus of the student's attempts to gain frequent physical contact.

27. Prevent frustrating or anxiety-producing situations from occurring (e.g., give the student tasks only on his/her ability level, give the student only the number of tasks that can be tolerated in one sitting, reduce social interactions which stimulate the student to become physically abusive, etc.).

28. Indicate to the student that public displays of frequent physical contact are inappropriate.

29. Make sure that reinforcement is not inadvertently given for inappropriate behavior (e.g., attending to the student only when he/she makes unnecessary physical contact).

30. Encourage faculty/staff members with whom the student interacts to reinforce appropriate physical contact.

31. Reinforce the student for respecting norms of physical proximity: (a) give the student a tangible reward (e.g., classroom privileges, line leading, passing out materials, five minutes free time, etc.) or (b) give the student an intangible reward (e.g., praise, fist bump, smile, etc.).

32. Provide the student with high-interest activities (e.g., academic activities which are inherently interesting, activities during free time, etc.).

120 Makes inappropriate comments to teachers

1. Teach the student appropriate ways to communicate displeasure, anger, etc.

2. Reduce stimuli which contribute to the student's derogatory comments or inappropriate gestures.

3. Provide the student with a quiet place to work. This is to be used as a means of reducing distracting stimuli and not as punishment.

4. Provide the student with the opportunity to work with a peer who will model communicating in an appropriate manner.

5. Make sure the student understands the natural consequences of his/her inappropriate behavior (e.g., teachers choose not to interact with him/her, exclusion from activities, etc.).

6. Require that the student identify alternative appropriate behaviors following an instance of derogatory comments or inappropriate gestures.

7. Facilitate on-task behavior by providing a full schedule of activities. Prevent lag time from occurring when the student would be free to participate in inappropriate behavior.

8. Reduce the emphasis on competition. Competitive activities may increase the student's anxiety and result in anger and frustration which may take the form of derogatory comments or inappropriate behavior.

9. Emphasize individual success or progress rather than winning or beating other students.

10. Modify or adjust situations which contribute to the student's use of obscene or profane language (i.e., if an assignment causes the student to become upset, modify the assignment to a level at which the student can be successful).

11. Interact frequently with the student to monitor language used.

12. Try various groupings to determine the group in which the student is most successful.

13. Maintain visibility to and from the student. The teacher should be able to see the student, and the student should be able to see the teacher. Make eye contact possible at all times.

14. Prevent frustrating or anxiety-producing situations from occurring (e.g., giving the student tasks only on his/her ability level, give the student only the number of tasks that can be successfully managed in one sitting, reduce social interactions which stimulate the student's use of obscene language, etc.).

15. Reduce activities which might threaten the student (e.g., announcing test score ranges or test scores aloud, making students read aloud in class, emphasizing the success of a particular student(s), etc.).

16. Discuss with the student ways to deal with unpleasant experiences which would typically cause him/her to use obscene language (e.g., talk to the teacher, go to a quiet area in the room, visit a counselor, etc.).

17. Make sure that positive reinforcement is not inadvertently given for inappropriate language (e.g., attending to the student only when he/she is using profane or obscene language).

18. Deliver a predetermined signal (e.g., hand signal, verbal cue, etc.) when the student begins to use inappropriate language.

19. Deal with the student in a calm and deliberate manner rather than in a manner that would show evidence of shock and surprise.

20. Model using appropriate language at all times (e.g., use appropriate language to convey disappointment, unhappiness, surprise, etc.).

21. Teach the student appropriate words or phrases to use in situations of anger, stress, frustration, etc.

22. Have the student ask questions about directions, explanations, or instructions he/she does not understand.

23. Intervene early when inappropriate behavior occurs to prevent the behavior from becoming more serious. Deliberate interventions may prevent future problems.

24. Avoid arguing with the student.

25. Do not embarrass the student by giving him/her orders, demands, etc., in front of others.

26. Treat the student with respect. Talk to the student in an objective and professional manner at all times.

27. Do not ignore the student's inappropriate behavior. Ignored behavior may increase in frequency and may lead to contagion on the part of other students.

28. Avoid confrontations with the student which lead to inappropriate behavior on the part of the student (e.g., give the student options for alternative tasks, other times to perform assignments, assistance in performing assignments, etc.).

29. Develop a routine schedule of activities and tasks for the student so he/she knows what to expect at all times.

30. Evaluate the appropriateness of the task in relation to the student's ability to perform the task.

31. Avoid physical contact with the student who is likely to become verbally abusive (e.g., a pat on the back may cause the student to argue, threaten, call names, curse, etc.).

32. Maintain an appropriate physical distance from the student when interacting with him/her to avoid stimulating the student to make inappropriate comments.

33. Use language that is pleasant and calming when speaking with the student to avoid stimulating the student to make inappropriate comments.

34. Do not criticize. When correcting the student, be honest yet supportive. Never cause the student to feel negatively about himself/herself.

35. Deliver directions in a supportive rather than a threatening manner (e.g., "Please finish your math paper before going to recess." rather than "You had better finish your math paper or else!").

36. Treat the student with respect. Talk in an objective manner at all times.

37. Be consistent in expectations and consequences of behavior.

38. Teach the student appropriate ways to communicate displeasure, anger, frustration, etc.

39. Have the student put himself/herself in someone else's place (e.g., ask the student to think about how he/she would feel if someone called him/her dumb or stupid).

40. Make sure that your comments to the student take the form of constructive criticism rather than criticism that can be perceived as personal, threatening, etc., (e.g., instead of saying, "You always make the same mistake." say, "A better way to do that might be . . .").

41. Reinforce those students in the classroom who communicate in an appropriate manner with teachers.

42. Teach the student to think before acting by asking himself/herself question: *What is happening? What am I doing? What should I do? What will be best for me?*

43. Allow the student to voice his/her opinion in a situation to avoid becoming angry or upset.

44. Speak with the student to explain (a) what the student is doing wrong (e.g., arguing, threatening, calling names, etc.) and (b) what the student should be doing (e.g., following the rules, staying on task, attending to his/her responsibilities, etc.).

45. Communicate with parents (e.g., notes home, phone calls, etc.) to share information about the student's progress. The parents may reinforce the student at home for communicating in an appropriate manner at school.

46. Remove the student from the group or activity until he/she can demonstrate appropriate behavior.

47. Write a contract with the student specifying what behavior is expected (e.g., using appropriate language) and what reinforcement will be made available when the terms of the contract have been met.

48. Reinforce the student for communicating in an appropriate manner based on the length of time the student can be successful. As the student demonstrates success, gradually increase the length of time required for reinforcement.

49. Evaluate the appropriateness of the task to determine (a) if the task is too easy, (b) if the task is too difficult, and (c) if the length of time scheduled for the task is adequate.

50. Establish classroom rules:
- Concentrate while working.
- Work quietly.
- Remain in your seat.
- Finish task.
- Meet task requirements.

Review rules often. Reinforce the student for following the rules.

51. Express your feelings in a socially acceptable manner.

52. Reinforce the student for communicating in an appropriate manner with teachers: (a) give the student a tangible reward (e.g., classroom privileges, line leading, passing out materials, five minutes free time, etc.) or (b) give the student an intangible reward (e.g., praise, fist bump, smile, etc.).

121 Responds inappropriately to praise or recognition from other students or teachers

1. Model appropriate ways to respond to interactions with other students or teachers.

2. Praise or recognize the student when he/she will most likely be able to demonstrate an appropriate response (e.g., when the student is not being singled out in a group).

3. Praise or recognize the student in private. The public aspect of praise or recognition is often the cause of the inappropriate response.

4. Provide the student with many opportunities for social and academic successes so he/she may learn how to respond appropriately.

5. Assess the appropriateness of the social situation in relation to the student's ability to function successfully.

6. Distribute praise and recognition equally to all members of the class.

7. Provide praise or recognition for smaller increments of success so that the student may gradually become accustomed to the recognition.

8. Provide praise and recognition as a natural consequence for appropriate behavior.

9. Try various groupings to determine the group in which the student is most comfortable.

10. Make sure that reinforcement is not inadvertently given for inappropriate behavior (e.g., attending to the student only when he/she responds inappropriately to praise or recognition).

11. Use alternative forms of praise or recognition which are not threatening to the student (e.g., written notes, phone calls to parents, display of work done well, etc.).

12. Present praise with a matter-of-fact delivery and avoid exaggerated exclamations of success.

13. Use feedback related to performance (e.g., test scores, grades, etc.) in place of praise or recognition. As the student becomes more capable of accepting praise and recognition, gradually deliver verbal praise and recognition.

14. Rather than emphasizing winning or beating other students in competition, encourage individual success or progress which may be enjoyed privately rather than publicly.

15. Treat the student with respect. Talk in an objective manner at all times.

16. Maintain trust and confidentiality with the student at all times.

17. Make sure that other teachers and school personnel who work with the student know that the student does not respond appropriately to praise and recognition.

18. Reinforce those students in the classroom who respond appropriately to praise or recognition.

19. Teach the student acceptable ways to communicate displeasure, anger, frustration, etc.

20. Reinforce the student for responding appropriately to praise or recognition: (a) give the student a tangible reward (e.g., classroom privileges, line leading, passing out materials, five minutes free time, etc.) or (b) give the student an intangible reward (e.g., praise, fist bump, smile, etc.).

21. Write a contract with the student specifying what behavior is expected (e.g., saying thank you when given praise or recognition) and what reinforcement will be made available when the terms of the contract have been met.

22. Reinforce the student for responding appropriately to praise or recognition based on the number of times the student can be successful. As the student demonstrates success, gradually increase the number of times required for reinforcement.

23. Speak with the student to explain (a) what the student is doing wrong (e.g., behaving inappropriately when recognized by others) and (b) what the student should be doing (e.g., saying thank you, smiling, etc.).

24. Express your feelings in a socially acceptable way.

25. Communicate with the parents (e.g., notes home, phone calls, etc.) to share information about the student's progress. The parents may reinforce the student at home for responding appropriately to praise or recognition at school.

Reminder: Do not punish a student for his/ her inability to respond appropriately to praise or recognition.

1. Allow the student to take a break to re-group when he/she is becoming angry, annoyed, or upset.

2. Teach and encourage the student to use problem-solving skills: (a) identify the problem, (b) identify goals and objectives, (c) develop strategies, (d) develop a plan of action, and (e) carry out the plan.

3. Teach the student decision-making steps: think about how others may be influenced, think about consequences, consider carefully the unique situation, think of different courses of action which are possible, think about what is ultimately best, etc.

4. Maintain a positive/calm environment (e.g., positive comments, acknowledgment of successes, quiet communications, etc.).

5. Look for the warning signs (e.g., arguing, loud voices, etc.) that the student is getting upset or angry. Intervene to change the activity to prevent more serious problems from occurring.

6. Communicate with the student's parents (e.g., notes home, phone calls, etc.) to share information about their student's progress. The parents may reinforce the student at home for demonstrating self-control at school.

7. Maintain consistent expectations.

8. Talk with the student's family, a school official, a social worker, etc., about the student's behavior if it is causing him/her to have problems getting along with others.

9. Remove the student immediately from a situation when he/she begins to be angry, annoyed, or upset.

10. Facilitate appropriate behavior by providing a full schedule of daily events. Prevent lag time from occurring when the student would be likely to become involved in activities which would cause him/her to be angry, annoyed, or upset.

11. Evaluate the appropriateness of the academic task to determine (a) if the task is too easy, (b) if the task is too difficult, and (c) if the length of time scheduled to complete the task is adequate.

12. Provide the student with alternative activities, games, etc., in case some activities prove upsetting.

13. Educate yourself and others about ADHD to increase understanding and accommodation of impulsive behavior.

14. Communicate with the student's parents, agencies, or the appropriate parties to inform them of the student's problem, determine the cause of the problem, and consider possible solutions to the problem.

15. Teach behaviors that promote self-control. Allow the student to gain his/her composure before continuing an activity (e.g., placing hands on desk, sitting with feet on the floor, making eye contact with the person who is talking, etc.).

16. Allow the student to voice his/her opinion in a situation to avoid becoming angry or upset.

17. Help the student develop an awareness of himself/herself and those around him/her. Have the student periodically step back and ask himself/herself, "Am I behaving too aggressively?"

18. Reduce the emphasis on competition. Repeated failure and frustration may cause the student to become angry, annoyed, or upset.

19. Educate the student about ADHD and the need to self monitor behavior.

20. Make sure that all teachers and staff who have contact with the student understand the importance of maintaining consistency in the discipline of the student.

21. Encourage the student to pause and consider his/her thoughts before acting on them.

22. Provide constant, positive reinforcement for appropriate behavior. Ignore as many inappropriate behaviors as possible.

23. Have the student anticipate future tasks/assignments and develop plans for addressing them.

24. Have the student develop an awareness of the consequences of his/her behavior by writing down or talking through problems which may occur due to his/her inability to adjust his/her behavior to different situations (e.g., perceived as unmannerly, avoided, etc.).

25. Help the student learn to be satisfied with his/her best effort rather than some arbitrary measure of success. Success is measured individually according to ability level. Progress of any kind is a measure of success.

26. Be mobile to be frequently near the student.

27. Teach the student to think before acting by asking himself/herself question: *What is happening? What am I doing? What should I do? What will be best for me?*

28. Reinforce those students in the classroom who demonstrate self-control.

29. Provide the student with a clearly understood list of consequences for inappropriate behavior.

30. Remind the student of the consequences of getting angry, annoyed, or upset before going into a store, going to a friend's house, having friends over, etc., to reinforce the need for the student to develop self-monitoring skills.

31. Discuss with the student the consequences of becoming easily angered, annoyed, or upset on the job site (e.g., fired, not viewed as mature enough for the job, loss of respect of co-workers, etc.).

32. Have the student review the consequences of his/her behavior with someone he/she trusts. Have him/her consider different choices that could have been made and the different outcomes.

33. Maintain a consistent daily classroom routine.

34. Allow flexibility in completing assignments when the student becomes angry, annoyed, or upset (e.g., allow more time, modify assignments, provide help with assignments, etc.).

35. Choose a peer to model self-control for the student.

36. Assess the degree of task difficulty to determine whether or not the student will require additional information, time, assistance, etc., to avoid becoming frustrated.

37. Discuss the student's behavior with him/her in private rather than in front of others.

38. Schedule recreational activities at the end of the day. Make participation in these activities dependent upon completion of daily responsibilities and appropriate behavior.

39. Delegate assignments on group projects. Equally distribute the work load to reduce frustration for group members.

40. Speak to the student to explain (a) what he/she is doing wrong (e.g., hitting, arguing, throwing things, etc.) and (b) what he/she should be doing (e.g., moving away from the situation, asking for assistance from the teacher, etc.).

41. Provide the student with positive feedback which indicates he/she is successful, important, respected, etc.

42. Provide the student with opportunities for social and academic success.

43. Prevent frustrating or anxiety-producing situations from occurring (e.g., give the student tasks only on his/her ability level, give the student only the number of tasks that can be tolerated in one sitting, reduce social interactions which stimulate the student to become physically abusive, etc.).

44. Teach the student ways to gain self-control (e.g., count to ten, walk away, talk with someone, etc.).

45. Set a good example for the student by dealing in a socially acceptable way with situations that may be upsetting.

46. Remove the student from the group or activity until he/she can demonstrate self-control.

47. Do not let the student have his/her way when he/she gets angry.

48. Consider consulting with a mental health provider about the student's failure to control his/her anger.

49. Have the student ask for help when he/she needs it.

50. Have the student ask questions about directions, explanations, or instructions he/she does not understand.

51. Encourage the student to remove himself/herself from a situation when he/she needs to gain self-control.

52. Encourage the student to ask himself/herself questions to avoid impulsive behavior (e.g., "What should I be doing?" "How do I want to be perceived?").

53. Teach the student to verbalize his/her feelings before losing control (e.g., "I'm getting tired of waiting." "I'm getting bored standing here.").

54. Teach the student to verbalize his/her feelings when he/she becomes frustrated (e.g., "I'm getting frustrated with this project." "I'm feeling pressured to get this task accomplished.").

55. Discourage the student from engaging in those activities that cause him/her to become easily angered, annoyed, or upset.

56. Encourage the student to participate in quiet, calming activities (e.g., listen to music, read, etc.) when feeling frustrated.

57. Involve the student in activities in which he/she can be successful and that will help him/her feel good about himself/herself. Repeated failures result in frustration and impatience.

58. Allow the student to participate in mild exercise such as walking up/downstairs, take a message to the office, etc., when he/she is feeling frustrated.

59. Encourage the student to avoid ingesting any substance (e.g., drugs, alcohol, cold remedies, etc.) that might further alter his/her ability to maintain self-control.

60. Do not assume the student is being treated nicely by others. Peers may be stimulating inappropriate behavior.

61. Clarify for the student that it is his/her behavior which determines whether consequences are positive or negative.

62. Have the student make a list of consequences associated with becoming easily angered, annoyed, or upset (e.g., by disrupting others, I will be perceived as unmannerly; by behaving aggressively, people will avoid me.).

63. Provide the student with as many high-interest activities as possible.

64. Avoid topics, situations, etc., that may cause the student to become easily angered, annoyed, or upset (e.g., divorce, death, unemployment, alcoholism, etc.).

65. Maintain a routine that will minimize erratic or impulsive behavior which may result in negative consequences.

66. Teach the student techniques to monitor and maintain awareness of his/her stress and frustration levels (e.g., for immediate control: stop, count to ten using slow deep breaths, and try to relax. If needed, remove him/herself from the situation.).

67. Make sure the student does not become involved in overstimulating activities which cause him/her to become angry, annoyed, or upset.

68. Do not place an emphasis on perfection. If the student feels he/she must live up to your expectations and cannot do so, he/she may become angry, annoyed, or upset.

69. Closely supervise the student to monitor his/her behavior at all times.

70. Teach the student to verbalize his/her feelings before losing self-control (e.g., "The work is hard." "Please leave me alone; you're making me angry.").

71. Separate the student from the peer that stimulates his/her inappropriate behavior.

72. Have the student list the pros and cons of an action. Encourage the student to determine if the pros outweigh the cons before he/she takes action.

73. Have the student list five qualities of a patient and respectful person and choose one to practice. Over the next five weeks, have the student choose an additional one of those qualities to work on each week. At the end of five weeks, he/she will be practicing all five qualities.

74. Deliver directives in a supportive rather than a threatening manner (e.g., "Please finish your math assignment before going to lunch," rather than, "You had better finish your math or else!").

75. Provide the student with a selection of activities that can be performed if he/she becomes angry, annoyed, or upset.

76. Reinforce the student for demonstrating self-control based on the length of time the student can be successful. As the student demonstrates increased self-control, gradually increase the length of time required for reinforcement.

77. Reinforce the student for demonstrating self-control in those situations in which he/she is likely to become angry, annoyed, or upset: (a) give the student a tangible reward (e.g., classroom privileges, passing out materials, five minutes free time, etc.) or (b) give the student an intangible reward (e.g., praise, fist bump, smile, etc.).

78. Reward the student (e.g., cafeteria, gym, hallway, etc.) for maintaining self-control in a particular situation.

79. Have the student identify the situations in which he/she is most easily frustrated. After he/she has identified these situations, have him/her think of ways to minimize their occurrences.

80. Allow the student to attempt something new in private before doing so in front of others.

81. Inform individuals who will be spending time with the student (e.g., substitute teachers, coaches, activity sponsors, etc.) about his/her tendency to become easily angered, annoyed, or upset.

82. Evaluate the visual and auditory stimuli in the classroom. Determine the amount of stimuli the student can tolerate. Remove extraneous stimuli from the environment.

83. Ask the student why he/she becomes easily angered, annoyed, or upset. The student may have the most accurate perception as to why he/she becomes easily angered, annoyed, or upset.

84. Write a contract with the student specifying what behavior is expected (e.g., problem solving, moving away from the situation, asking for assistance from the teacher, etc.) and what reinforcement will be made available when the terms of the contract have been met.

85. Maintain supervision of the student. As the student demonstrates self-control, gradually decrease supervision.

86. Monitor the behavior of other students in the class to make sure they are not teasing or otherwise stimulating the student to become angry, annoyed, or upset.

87. Make sure that comments made to the student take the form of constructive criticism rather than perceived as personal, threatening, etc., (e.g., instead of saying, "You always make the same mistake," say, "A better way to do that might be . . .").

88. Treat the student with respect. Talk in an objective manner at all times.

89. Allow the student some movement while performing tasks. Monitor and limit the amount of movement.

90. Analyze daily, weekly, and monthly tasks at school. Determine which tasks stimulate impatience. Organize activities so a pleasurable activity follows one that stimulates impatience.

91. Make sure the student understands that total fairness is impossible. Sometimes people have to do more than others do or do things they do not want to do simply because they have to be done.

92. Make sure the student understands that for appropriate behavior he/she may earn those things which he/she gets angry, annoyed, or upset about. Those things will not be given to him/her but must be earned with appropriate behavior.

93. Encourage the student to realize that all behavior has negative or positive consequences. Encourage the student to practice behaviors that will lead to positive consequences.

94. Teach the student acceptable ways to communicate displeasure, anger, frustration, etc.

95. Make the necessary adjustments in the environment to prevent the student from experiencing stress, frustration, and anger.

96. Maintain visibility to and from the student to keep his/her attention when verbal questions/directions are being delivered. The teacher should be able to see the student and the student should be able to see the teacher. Make eye contact possible at all times.

97. Maintain supervision. Do not leave the student alone with other students.

98. Make the student aware of the natural consequences for becoming easily angered, annoyed, or upset (e.g., loss of friendships, injury, more restrictive environment, legal action, etc.).

99. Encourage the student to consider the consequences of his/her behavior before engaging in any activity.

100. Reduce activities which might threaten the student (e.g., announcing test score ranges or test scores aloud, making students read aloud in class, emphasizing the success of a particular student or students, etc.).

101. Provide a designated area for the student when he/she becomes frustrated with a situation (e.g., counselor's office, study carrel, resource room, etc.).

102. Help the student to recognize the signs of becoming agitated. Explain the appropriate action to gain self-control.

103. Do not embarrass the student by giving him/her orders, making demands, etc., in front of others.

104. Make other personnel aware of the student's tendency to become easily angered, annoyed, or upset.

105. Do not criticize when correcting the student; be honest yet supportive. Never cause the student to feel negatively about himself/herself.

106. Have the student identify the situations in which he/she is most likely to fail to consider the consequences.

107. Remove the student immediately from the presence of others when he/she gets angered, annoyed, or upset.

108. Provide a quiet place away from peer interactions for the student to work independently. This is not to be used as a form of punishment but as an opportunity to increase the student's success in his/her environment.

109. Explain to the student the reason why he/she cannot have or do something.

110. Try to reduce or prevent things from happening which cause the student to become easily angered, annoyed, or upset.

111. Establish classroom rules:
- Concentrate while working.
- Work quietly.
- Remain in your seat.
- Finish task.
- Meet task requirements.

Review rules often. Reinforce the student for following the rules.

112. Teach the student alternative ways to communicate his/her unhappiness (e.g., talking about a problem, asking for help, etc.).

113. Do not allow the student to use ADHD as an excuse. Hold the student responsible for his/her actions. However, understand and accept problems that ADHD brings into the student's life while he/she is learning to make accommodations.

114. Try various groupings in the classroom to determine the situation in which the student is most successful.

115. Do not allow the student to participate in a situation unless he/she can demonstrate self-control.

116. Do not force the student to interact or remain in a group if he/she is likely to become angry, annoyed, or upset.

117. Make sure that the student understands the relationship between inappropriate behavior and the consequences which follow (e.g., being avoided by others, not being able to participate in special activities, etc.).

118. Talk to the student about ways of successfully handling situations without conflict (e.g., walk away from the situation, change to another activity, ask for help, etc.).

119. Teach the student to recognize when he/she is becoming angry, annoyed, or upset and ways in which to deal with his/her feelings.

120. Encourage the student to associate with peers with whom he/she gets along well to prevent him/her from getting angry, annoyed, or upset.

121. Encourage the student to talk with a trusted adult when he/she is angry, annoyed, or upset.

122. Choose a peer who will be a good influence (e.g., someone younger/older, of the same gender, of the opposite gender, etc.) to work with the student .

123. Be consistent. Handle the student's behavior in a manner that is as fair as possible.

124. Do not force the student to interact with individuals with whom he/she is not completely comfortable.

125. Teach the student alternative ways to deal with situations which make him/her frustrated, angry, etc., (e.g., withdrawing, talking, etc.).

123 Agitates and provokes peers to a level of verbal or physical assault

1. Teach the student acceptable ways to communicate displeasure, anger, etc.

2. Reduce the stimuli that contribute to the student's derogatory comments or inappropriate gestures.

3. Provide the student with a quiet place to work (e.g., study carrel, private office, etc.). This is used as a means of reducing distracting stimuli and not as a form of punishment.

4. Provide the student with the opportunity to work with a peer who will be an appropriate model.

5. Separate the student from the peer(s) who is the primary stimulus or focus of the derogatory comments or inappropriate gestures.

6. Make sure the student understands the natural consequences of inappropriate behavior (e.g., peers choosing not to interact with him/her, exclusion from activities, etc.).

7. Require the student to identify alternative appropriate behaviors following an instance of derogatory comments or inappropriate gestures.

8. Facilitate on-task behavior by providing a full schedule of daily events. Prevent lag time from occurring when the student would be free to participate in inappropriate behavior.

9. Reduce the emphasis on competition. Repeated failure may result in anger and frustration that may take the form of derogatory comments or inappropriate gestures.

10. Emphasize individual success or progress rather than winning or beating other students.

11. Intervene early when the student begins to agitate or provoke peers.

12. Treat the student with respect. Talk in an objective manner at all times.

13. Remove the student from the classroom if he/she is unable to demonstrate self-control. The student should not be allowed to remain in the classroom and be abusive to peers.

14. Maintain visibility to and from the student. The teacher should be able to see the student and the student should be able to see the teacher. Make eye contact possible at all times.

15. Inform others (e.g., teachers, school personnel, etc.) of the behavior expected of the student so they will encourage appropriate behavior from the student.

16. Remove the student from the group or activity until he/she can demonstrate appropriate behavior.

17. Do not embarrass the student by giving him/her orders, demands, etc., in front of others.

18. Have the student put himself/herself in someone else's place (e.g., ask the student to think about how he/she would feel if someone called him/her dumb or stupid).

19. Reinforce those students in the classroom who communicate in an appropriate manner.

20. Encourage the student to use problem-solving skills: (a) identify the problem, (b) identify goals and objectives, (c) develop strategies, (d) develop a plan of action, and (e) carry out the plan.

21. Do not leave a lot of unstructured time for the student.

22. Teach the student to think before acting by asking himself/herself question: *What is happening? What am I doing? What should I do? What will be best for me?*

23. Allow the student to voice his/her opinion in a situation to avoid becoming angry or upset.

24. Evaluate the appropriateness of the task to determine (a) if the task is too easy, (b) if the task is too difficult, and (c) if the length of time scheduled for the task is adequate.

25. Communicate with parents (e.g., notes home, phone calls, etc.) to share information about the student's progress. The parents may reinforce the student at home for demonstrating appropriate behavior at school.

26. Write a contract with the student specifying what behavior is expected (e.g., communicating with peers in a positive manner) and what reinforcement will be made available when the terms of the contract have been met.

27. Make sure there will always be adult supervision where the student will be (e.g., lunch, recess, P.E., etc.).

28. Reinforce the student for communicating in an appropriate manner based on the length of time the student can be successful. As the student demonstrates success, gradually increase the length of time required for reinforcement.

29. Do not force the student to interact with individuals with whom he/she is not completely comfortable.

30. Do not leave the student alone with other students when he/she is upset or angry.

31. Establish classroom rules:
- Concentrate while working.
- Work quietly.
- Remain in your seat.
- Finish task.
- Meet task requirements.

Review rules often. Reinforce the student for following the rules.

32. Speak with the student to explain (a) what the student is doing wrong (e.g., calling names, making inappropriate gestures, etc.) and (b) what the student should be doing (e.g., following the rules, staying on task, attending to his/her responsibilities, etc.).

33. Reinforce the student for communicating in an appropriate manner with peers: (a) give the student a tangible reward (e.g., classroom privileges, line leading, passing out materials, five minutes free time, etc.) or (b) give the student an intangible reward (e.g., praise, fist bump, smile, etc.).

34. Avoid discussion of topics that are sensitive to the student (e.g., divorce, unemployment, alcoholism, etc.).

1. Give the student the responsibility of being a teacher's assistant for an activity (e.g., holding up flash cards, demonstrating the use of equipment, etc.).

2. Give the student the responsibility of tutoring another student.

3. Greet or acknowledge the student as often as possible (e.g., greet in the hallways or cafeteria, welcome to class, acknowledge a job well done, call the student by name, etc.).

4. Ask the student to be the leader of a small group activity if he/she possesses mastery of skills or an interest in that area.

5. Have the student run errands which will require interactions with teachers (e.g., delivering attendance reports, taking messages to other teachers, etc.).

6. Interact with the student from a distance. Gradually decrease the distance until a close proximity is achieved.

7. Make sure that directions, explanations, and instructions are delivered on the student's ability level.

8. Use an alternative form of communication (e.g., puppet).

9. Provide the student with many opportunities for social and academic successes.

10. Create situations in which the student must interact (e.g., handing completed assignments to the teacher, delivering a message to a teacher, etc.).

11. Choose a peer to model appropriate interaction with teachers for the student.

12. Encourage the student to question any directions, explanations, and instructions not understood.

13. Evaluate the appropriateness of expecting the student to communicate needs to teachers.

14. Maintain mobility throughout the classroom to monitor the student's needs.

15. Offer the student assistance frequently throughout the day.

16. Arrange for one-to-one, teacher/student interactions.

17. Structure the environment so the student is not required to communicate all needs to teachers (e.g., make sure the student's tasks are on his/her ability level, be sure instructions are clear, and maintain frequent interactions with the student to facilitate success).

18. To understand the student's needs, communicate with the student as often as opportunities permit.

19. Model appropriate positive verbal greetings, requests, and indications of disagreement for the student.

20. Communicate to the student that he/she is a worthwhile individual.

21. Call on the student often to encourage communication.

22. Teach the student communication skills (e.g., hand raising, expressing needs in written and/or verbal form, etc.).

23. Encourage the student to communicate needs to other personnel in the educational environment (e.g., school counselor, school psychologist, principal, etc.).

24. Communicate with parents, agencies, or the appropriate parties to inform them of the problem, determine the cause of the problem, and consider possible solutions to the problem.

25. Recognize the student's attempts to communicate needs (e.g., facial expressions, gestures, inactivity, self-deprecating comments, etc.).

26. Teach the student appropriate positive verbal greetings (e.g., Hi, how are you doing?, Good to see you., and Haven't seen you in a long time.).

27. Teach the student appropriate positive verbal requests (e.g., Please pass the paper., May I please be excused?, and Will you please help me?).

28. Teach the student positive ways to verbally indicate disagreement (e.g., I'm sorry, but I don't think that's correct.).

29. Demonstrate accepting behavior and interest in the student's needs (e.g., willingness to help others, making criticisms constructive and positive, demonstrating confidentiality in personal matters, etc.).

30. Teach the student appropriate communication skills for problem resolution (e.g., Let's talk about it., Let's compromise., Let's see what would be fair for both of us.).

31. Have the student practice positive verbal communications with an identified number of teachers throughout the school day.

32. Make sure that all teachers interact with the student on a regular basis and use positive verbal communications when speaking to him/her.

33. Encourage the student to interact with several adults (e.g., run errands, request materials, etc.) to increase the opportunities for communication with adults.

34. Teach the student appropriate ways to communicate to teachers that a problem exists (e.g., "I don't understand the directions." "I couldn't complete my assignment." "I can't find all of my materials.").

35. Identify teachers with whom the student most often interacts to make sure that they model appropriate verbal communications for the student.

36. Spend some time each day talking with the student on an individual basis about his/her interests.

37. Teach the student skills in maintaining positive conversations with teachers (e.g., asking questions, listening while the other person speaks, making eye contact, head nodding, making comments which relate to what the other person has said, etc.).

38. Help the student become aware of his/her tone of voice when greeting, requesting, and/or disagreeing by calling attention to inappropriate voice inflections for the situation.

39. Determine an individual(s) in the school environment with whom the student would most want to engage in a conversation (e.g., custodian, librarian, resource teacher, principal, older student, etc.). Allow the student to spend time with the individual(s) each day.

40. Reinforce those students in the classroom who interact appropriately with teachers.

41. Deliver directions in a supportive rather than a threatening manner (e.g., "Please finish your math paper before going to recess." rather than "You had better finish your math paper or else!").

42. Do not criticize. When correcting the student, be honest yet supportive. Never cause the student to feel negatively about himself/herself.

43. Treat the student with respect. Talk in an objective manner at all times.

44. Do not embarrass the student by giving him/her orders, demands, etc., in front of others.

45. Have the student practice appropriate interactions with the teacher(s) in classroom activities (e.g., simulations, role-playing, etc.).

46. Spend individual time with the student. Do not give more attention to students who are more outgoing.

47. Communicate with parents (e.g., notes home, phone calls, etc.) to share information about the student's progress. The parents may reinforce the student at home for interacting with teachers at school.

48. Do not force the student to interact.

49. Write a contract with the student specifying what behavior is expected (e.g., sitting near the teacher, talking to the teacher, etc.) and what reinforcement will be made available when the terms of the contract have been met.

50. Reinforce the student for interacting with teachers based on the length of time the student can be successful. As the student demonstrates success, gradually increase the length of time required for reinforcement.

51. Pair the student with an outgoing student who engages in conversation with teachers on a frequent basis.

52. Establish classroom rules:
- Concentrate while working.
- Work quietly.
- Remain in your seat.
- Finish task.
- Meet task expectations.

Review rules often. Reinforce students for following the rules.

53. Speak with the student to explain (a) what the student is doing wrong (e.g., not talking, not making eye contact, etc.) and (b) what the student should be doing (e.g., talking, looking at the teacher, etc.).

54. Reinforce the student for interacting with teachers: (a) give the student a tangible reward (e.g., classroom privileges, line leading, passing out materials, five minutes free time, etc.) or (b) give the student an intangible reward (e.g., praise, fist bump, smile, etc.).

55. Maintain trust and confidentiality with the student at all times.

Reminder: Do not force the student to interact with teachers.

125 Has little or no interaction with peers

1. Choose a peer to sit/work directly with the student (e.g., in different settings or activities such as art, music, P.E., on the bus, tutoring, group projects, running errands in the building, recess, etc.). As the student becomes comfortable working with another student, gradually increase the size of the group.

2. Encourage or reward others for interacting with the student.

3. Give the student the responsibility of being a teacher's aide for an activity (e.g., holding up flash cards, demonstrating the use of equipment, etc.).

4. Give the student the responsibility of tutoring a peer.

5. Ask the student to choose a peer to work with on a specific assignment. If the student has difficulty choosing someone, determine the student's preference by other means such as a class survey.

6. Choose a peer to model appropriate interactions with peers for the student.

7. Try various groupings to determine the group in which the student is most comfortable.

8. Assess the appropriateness of the social setting in relation to the student's ability to interact with peers.

9. Provide the student with many opportunities for social and academic successes.

10. Assign the student to work with one or two peers on a long-term project (e.g., mural, bulletin board, report, etc.).

11. Create situations in which the student must interact (e.g., returning completed assignments to students, proofreading other students' work, etc.).

12. Have the student work with a peer who is younger or smaller (e.g., choose a peer who would be the least threatening).

13. Establish social rules:
- Share materials.
- Use a quiet voice in the building.
- Walk indoors.
- Use care in handling materials.

Review rules often. Reinforce students for following the rules.

14. Ask the student to be the leader of a small group activity if he/she possesses mastery of skills or an interest in that area.

15. Determine the peer(s) with whom the student would prefer to interact and facilitate this interaction.

16. Choose an outgoing, nonthreatening peer to help the student interact more appropriately with peers.

17. Structure the environment so that the student has many opportunities to interact with peers.

18. Have the student run errands with a peer to facilitate interaction.

19. Conduct a sociometric activity with the class to determine the peer who would most prefer to interact with the student.

20. Make sure the student understands that interacting with a peer is contingent upon appropriate interactions.

21. Teach the student appropriate ways to interact with another student (e.g., how to greet another student, suggest activities, share materials, problem-solve, take turns, talk, etc.).

22. Supervise interaction closely so the peer with whom the student interacts does not stimulate the student's inappropriate behavior.

23. Make sure that the interaction is not so stimulating as to make successful interaction with another student difficult.

24. Involve the student in extracurricular activities to encourage interactions with peers.

25. Choose an older peer with desirable social skills to interact with the student (e.g., in the play area, cafeteria, hallways, etc.).

26. Reduce the emphasis on competition. Failure may cause the student to be reluctant to interact with peers.

27. Teach the student problem-solving skills so he/she may better deal with problems that occur in interactions with another peer (e.g., talking, walking away, calling upon an arbitrator, compromising, etc.).

28. Choose a peer with whom the student is most likely to be able to interact successfully (e.g., a student with similar interests, background, classes, behavior patterns, nonacademic schedule, etc.).

29. Structure interactions (e.g., establish rules, limit the stimulation of the activity, limit the length of the activity, consider time of day, etc.) according to the needs/abilities of the student.

30. Limit opportunities for interaction on those occasions when the student is not likely to be successful (e.g., when the student has experienced academic or social failure prior to the scheduled nonacademic activity).

31. Select nonacademic activities designed to facilitate appropriate interaction of the student and a peer (e.g., board games, model building, coloring, etc.).

32. Through interviews with other students and observations, determine those characteristics of the student which interfere with successful interactions to determine skills or behaviors the student needs to develop.

33. Have the student practice appropriate interactions with the teacher(s).

34. Make sure the student understands that not interacting appropriately with a peer may result in removal from the activity and/or loss of participation in future activities.

35. Encourage the student to interact with others.

36. Have the student interact with a peer for short periods of time to facilitate success. As the student demonstrates success, gradually increase the length of time the student interacts.

37. Do not force the student to interact with someone with whom he/she is not completely comfortable.

38. Communicate with parents (e.g., notes home, phone calls, etc.) to share information about the student's progress. The parents may reinforce the student at home for interacting with peers at school.

39. Write a contract with the student specifying what behavior is expected (e.g., sitting near another student, talking to another student, etc.) and what reinforcement will be made available when the terms of the contract have been met.

40. Reinforce the student for interacting with peers based on the length of time he/she can be successful. As the student demonstrates success, gradually increase the length of time required for reinforcement.

41. Have peers invite the student to participate in school or extracurricular activities.

42. Facilitate the development of friendships with peers (e.g., assign activities for the student involving peers, give the student and a peer joint responsibilities, etc.).

43. Speak with the student to explain (a) what he/she is doing wrong (e.g., not talking, sharing, etc.) and (b) what he/she should be doing (e.g., talking, sharing, etc.).

44. Reinforce the student for interacting with peers: (a) give the student a tangible reward (e.g., classroom privileges, line leading, passing out materials, five minutes free time, etc.) or (b) give the student an intangible reward (e.g., praise, fist bump, smile, etc.).

45. Provide organized activities for the student to participate in before, during, and after school (e.g., board games, softball, four square, tether ball, jump rope, flash cards, etc.).

46. Provide the student with the opportunity to work with a peer who will be an appropriate model for interacting with other students.

47. Encourage the student's peers to include him/her in free time activities.

48. Reinforce those students in the classroom who interact appropriately with peers.

49. Encourage the student to become involved in athletic activities.

50. Establish classroom rules:
- Concentrate while working.
- Work quietly.
- Remain in your seat.
- Finish task.
- Meet task expectations.

Review rules often. Reinforce students for following the rules.

Reminder: Do not force the student to interact with peers.

126 Makes inappropriate comments to other students

1. Model using appropriate language at all times (e.g., use appropriate language to convey disappointment, unhappiness, surprise, etc.).

2. Write a contract with the student specifying what behavior is expected (e.g., communicating with other students in an appropriate manner) and what reinforcement will be made available when the terms of the contract have been met.

3. Teach the student to respect others and their belongings by respecting the student and his/her belongings.

4. Avoid arguing with the student.

5. Have the student put himself/herself in the other student's place (e.g., "How would you feel if someone called you dumb or stupid?").

6. Avoid confrontations with the student which lead to inappropriate behavior on the part of the student (e.g., give the student options for alternative tasks, other times to perform assignments, assistance in performing assignments, etc.).

7. Avoid physical contact with the student who is likely to become verbally abusive (e.g., a pat on the back may cause the student to argue, threaten, call names, curse, etc.).

8. Do not embarrass the student by giving him/her orders, demands, etc., in front of others.

9. Maintain visibility to and from the student. The teacher should be able to see the student; the student should be able to see the teacher. Make eye contact possible at all times.

10. Communicate with parents (e.g., notes home, phone calls, etc.) to share information about the student's progress. The parents may reinforce the student at home for communicating in an appropriate manner with other peers at school.

11. Explain to the student why making inappropriate comments and unnecessary noises is not acceptable (e.g., impolite, might hurt others' feelings, etc.).

12. Be consistent in expectations and consequences of behavior.

13. Deliver directions in a supportive rather than a threatening manner (e.g., "Please finish your math paper before going to recess." rather than "You had better finish your math paper or else!").

14. Have the student ask questions about directions, explanations, and instructions not understood.

15. Discuss with the student ways he/she could deal with unpleasant experiences which would typically cause him/her to use obscene language (e.g., talk to the teacher, go to a quiet area in the school, talk with a counselor, etc.).

16. Avoid ignoring the student's inappropriate behavior. Ignored behavior may increase in frequency and may lead to contagion on the part of other students.

17. Do not criticize. When correcting the student, be honest yet supportive. Never cause the student to feel negatively about himself/herself.

18. Emphasize individual success or progress rather than winning or beating other students.

19. Establish classroom rules:
- Concentrate while working.
- Work quietly.
- Remain in your seat.
- Finish task.
- Meet task requirements.

Review rules often. Reinforce the student for following the rules.

20. Teach the student appropriate ways to communicate displeasure, anger, frustration, etc.

21. Evaluate the appropriateness of the task to determine (a) if the task is too easy, (b) if the task is too difficult, and (c) the length of time scheduled for the task is adequate.

22. Deal with the student in a calm and deliberate manner rather than in a manner that would show evidence of shock and surprise.

23. Facilitate on-task behavior by providing a full schedule of daily events. Prevent lag time from occurring when the student would be free to participate in inappropriate behavior.

24. Have the student practice appropriate verbal exchanges which should be made (e.g., *Excuse me. I'm sorry.*).

25. Provide the student with the opportunity to work with a peer who will be an appropriate model for interacting with other students.

26. Avoid discussion of topics that are sensitive to the student (e.g., divorce, unemployment, alcoholism, etc.).

27. Interact frequently with the student to monitor language used.

28. Intervene early when the student begins to make inappropriate comments to other students to help prevent the student from losing control.

29. Develop a routine schedule of activities and tasks for the student so he/she knows what to expect at all times.

30. Maintain an appropriate physical distance from the student when interacting with him/her to avoid stimulating the student to make inappropriate comments.

31. Encourage the student to interact with others.

32. Make sure that your comments to the student take the form of constructive criticism rather than criticism that can be perceived as personal, threatening, etc., (e.g., instead of saying, "You always make the same mistake." say, "A better way to do that might be . . .").

33. Allow the student to voice his/her opinion in a situation to avoid becoming angry or upset.

34. Provide the student with a quiet place to work. This is used as a means of reducing distracting stimuli and not as a form of punishment.

35. Make sure the student recognizes inappropriate comments (e.g., call attention to the comments when they occur, record each instance, terminate the activity when the comment occurs, etc.).

36. Reinforce the student for communicating in an appropriate manner with other students: (a) give the student a tangible reward (e.g., classroom privileges, line leading, passing out materials, five minutes free time, etc.) or (b) give the student an intangible reward (e.g., praise, fist bump, smile, etc.).

37. Make the student aware of the number of times he/she makes inappropriate comments and unnecessary noises.

38. Teach the student appropriate words or phrases to use in situations of anger, stress, frustration, etc.

39. Modify or adjust situations which contribute to the student's use of obscene or profane language (e.g., if an assignment causes the student to become upset, modify the assignment to a level at which the student can be successful).

40. Prevent frustrating or anxiety producing situations from occurring (e.g., give the student tasks only on his/her ability level, give the student only the number of tasks that he/she can successfully manage in one sitting, reduce social interactions which stimulate the student's use of obscene language, etc.).

41. Provide frequent opportunities for the student to meet new people.

42. Try various groupings to determine the group in which the student is most successful.

43. Reinforce those students in the classroom who communicate in an appropriate manner with teachers and other students.

44. Deliver a predetermined signal (e.g., hand signal, verbal cue, etc.) when the student begins to use inappropriate language.

45. Make sure that positive reinforcement is not inadvertently given for inappropriate language (e.g., attending to the student only when he/she is using profane or obscene language).

46. Provide the student with the opportunity to work with a peer who will model communicating in an appropriate manner.

47. Do not force the student to interact with other students with whom he/she is not completely comfortable.

48. Reduce stimuli which contribute to the student's derogatory comments, inappropriate gestures, arguing, calling names, cursing, etc.

49. Make sure the student understands the natural consequences of his/her inappropriate behavior (e.g., peers will choose not to interact with him/her, exclusion from activities, etc.).

50. Reduce the emphasis on competition. Repeated failure may result in anger and frustration which may take the form of inappropriate comments.

51. Teach the student problem-solving skills: (a) identify the problem, (b) identify goals and objectives, (c) develop strategies, (d) develop a plan for action, and (e) carry out the plan.

52. Reinforce the student for communicating in an appropriate manner based on the length of time the student can be successful. As the student demonstrates success, gradually increase the length of time required for reinforcement.

53. Remove the student from the group or activity until he/she can demonstrate appropriate behavior.

54. Prevent the student from becoming over-stimulated by an activity (i.e., monitor or supervise student behavior to limit overexcitement).

55. Make sure the student knows which comments will not be tolerated at school.

56. Separate the student from the student(s) who is the primary stimulus or focus of the inappropriate comments.

57. Express your feelings in a socially acceptable manner.

58. Use language that is pleasant and calming when speaking with the student to avoid stimulating the student to make inappropriate comments.

59. Require that the student identify alternative, appropriate behaviors following an instance of inappropriate comments (e.g., walking away from the peer, seeking teacher intervention, etc.).

60. Teach the student positive ways to interact with other students.

61. Teach the student to think before acting by asking himself/herself question: *What is happening? What am I doing? What should I do? What will be best for me?*

62. Assess the appropriateness of the social situation in relation to the student's ability to function successfully.

63. Treat the student with respect. Talk to the student in an objective and professional manner at all times.

64. Make sure the student will have adult supervision (e.g., at P.E., lunch, break time, etc.).

65. Reduce activities which might threaten the student (e.g., announcing test score ranges or test scores aloud, making students read aloud in class, emphasizing the success of a particular student, etc.).

66. Speak with the student to explain (a) what the student is doing wrong (e.g., arguing, threatening, calling names, etc.) and (b) what the student should be doing (e.g., following the rules, staying on task, attending to his/her responsibilities, etc.).

127 Responds inappropriately to typical physical exchanges with peers

1. Avoid placing the student in crowded situations where he/she might feel uncomfortable.

2. Choose a peer to accompany the student in congested areas of the school to reduce typical physical exchanges and/or intercede should problems occur.

3. Have the student practice appropriate verbal exchanges which should be made when typical physical exchanges take place (e.g., *Excuse me. I'm sorry.*).

4. Communicate with parents (e.g., notes home, phone calls, etc.) to share information about the student's progress. The parents may reinforce the student at home for responding appropriately to typical physical exchanges with other peers at school.

5. Do not force the student to interact with individuals with whom he/she is not completely comfortable.

6. Have the student practice dealing with typical physical exchanges in the classroom (e.g., peers bumping against his/her desk, bumping into others when forming a line, etc.).

7. Point out the natural consequences of failing to respond appropriately to typical physical exchanges with others (e.g., other students will avoid him/her, loss of friendships, loss of opportunity to interact with peers, etc.).

8. Call attention to those times when the student accidentally bumps, touches, or brushes against other students. Help the student realize that those physical exchanges were typical and accidental.

9. Have the student lead the line, walk beside the line, walk at the end of the line, etc., to avoid or reduce typical physical exchanges with other students.

10. Reinforce those students in the classroom who respond appropriately to typical physical exchanges with other students.

11. Have the student walk on the right hand side of the hallways, stairways, etc.

12. Choose a peer to model the appropriate way to respond to typical physical exchanges with other students.

13. Establish classroom rules:
- Concentrate while working.
- Work quietly.
- Remain in your seat.
- Finish task.
- Meet task requirements.

Review rules often. Reinforce the student for following the rules.

14. Have the student avoid crowded areas. As the student develops the ability to deal with typical physical exchanges with other students in an appropriate manner, gradually allow the student access to crowded areas.

15. Speak to the student to explain (a) what he/she is doing wrong (e.g., hitting others) and (b) what he/she should be doing (e.g., accepting typical physical exchanges in an appropriate manner).

16. Teach the student to avoid typical physical exchanges by giving others room to pass, taking turns, watching the movement of others around him/her, etc.

17. Intervene early when there is a problem to prevent more serious problems from occurring.

18. Make sure that others are not purposely bumping, touching, or brushing against the student.

19. Practice role-playing which involves typical physical exchanges (e.g., being bumped, touched, brushed against, etc.).

20. Teach the student acceptable ways to communicate displeasure, anger, frustration, etc.

21. Reinforce the student for responding appropriately to typical physical exchanges with others: (a) give the student a tangible reward (e.g., classroom privileges, line leading, passing out materials, five minutes free time, etc.) or (b) give the student an intangible reward (e.g., praise, fist bump, smile, etc.).

22. Reinforce the student for responding appropriately to typical physical exchanges with others based on the length of time the student can be successful. As the student demonstrates success, gradually increase the length of time required for reinforcement.

23. Make sure the student will have adult supervision (e.g., at P.E., lunch, recess, break time, etc.).

24. Write a contract with the student specifying what behavior is expected (e.g., responding appropriately to typical physical exchanges with other students) and what reinforcement will be made available when the terms of the contract have been met.

25. Teach the student to think before acting by asking himself/herself questions: *What is happening?, What am I doing?, What should I do?, What will be best for me?*

26. Seat the student away from classroom movement to reduce typical physical exchanges with other students.

1. Model friendly teasing by joking with the students and laughing when they tease you.

2. Speak to the student to explain (a) what he/she is doing wrong (e.g., becoming upset, fighting, etc.) and (b) what he/she should be doing (e.g., laughing, joking in return, etc.).

3. Talk with the student about choosing friends who are friendly and sincere.

4. Allow the student to attempt something new in private before doing so in front of others.

5. Communicate with parents (e.g., notes home, phone calls, etc.) to share information about the student's progress. The parents may reinforce the student at home for responding appropriately to friendly teasing at school.

6. Explain to the student that friendly teasing is a positive means by which people demonstrate that they like other people and enjoy their company.

7. Discuss with the student's peers his/her sensitivity and difficulty in dealing with friendly teasing so they may adjust their behavior accordingly.

8. Allow the student to voice his/her opinion in a situation to avoid becoming angry or upset.

9. Teach the student appropriate ways in which to respond to friendly teasing (e.g., laugh, joke in reply, etc.).

10. Discuss with the students those topics which are not appropriate for friendly teasing (e.g., death, disease, handicaps, poverty, etc.).

11. Do not force the student to interact with others with whom the student is not completely comfortable.

12. Help the student recognize the difference between friendly teasing and unkind, rude remarks so the student can accept and appreciate friendly teasing.

13. Choose a peer to model appropriate responses to friendly teasing for the student.

14. Intervene early when there is a problem to prevent more serious problems from occurring.

15. Point out to the student, when he/she is teasing others, that no harm is meant and that the same holds true when others tease him/her.

16. Teach the student acceptable ways to communicate displeasure, anger, frustration, etc.

17. Encourage others to compliment the student.

18. Express your feelings in a socially acceptable way.

19. Write a contract with the student specifying what behavior is expected (e.g., laughing, joking in return, etc.) and what reinforcement will be made available when the terms of the contract have been met.

20. Help the student learn to deal with teasing which upsets him/her by having the student avoid the teasing, walk away from the situation, move to another location, etc.

21. Help the student understand that if he/she cannot accept friendly teasing, it would be best to avoid those situations where teasing may occur.

22. Reinforce the student for responding appropriately to friendly teasing: (a) give the student a tangible reward (e.g., classroom privileges, line leading, passing out materials, five minutes free time, etc.) or (b) give the student an intangible reward (e.g., praise, fist bump, smile, etc.).

23. Reinforce those students in the classroom who respond appropriately to friendly teasing.

24. Evaluate the interaction to determine (a) if the interaction is appropriate, (b) if the timing of the interaction is appropriate, and (c) if the student is able to handle the interaction successfully.

25. Reinforce the student for responding appropriately to friendly teasing based on the number of times he/she can be successful. As the student demonstrates success, gradually increase the number of times required for reinforcement.

26. Treat the student with respect. Talk in an objective manner at all times.

1. Allow the student more decision-making opportunities relative to class activities and assignments.

2. Do not force the student to interact with others with whom he/she is not completely comfortable.

3. Assess the social situation in relation to the student's ability to function successfully (e.g., number of students in the group, behavior of students in the group, etc.).

4. Avoid competition. Failure may cause the student to ignore consequences of his/her behavior.

5. Call on the student when he/she can answer successfully.

6. Clarify for the student that it is his/her behavior which determines consequences (e.g., positive or negative).

7. Communicate with parents (e.g., notes home, phone calls, etc.) to share information about the student's progress. The parents may reinforce the student at home for appropriately interacting with other peers at school.

8. Do not criticize. When correcting the student, be honest yet supportive. Never cause the student to feel negatively about himself/herself.

9. Encourage and assist the student in joining extracurricular activities, clubs, etc.

10. Encourage the student to further develop any ability or skill he/she may have so peers may view the student in a positive way.

11. Allow the student to attempt something new in private before doing it in front of others.

12. Maintain trust and confidentiality with the student at all times.

13. Encourage the student to tell you about problems that occur with peers (e.g., being "bullied," teased by others, etc.).

14. Make the consequence of a behavior obvious by identifying the consequence as it occurs and discussing alternative behavior which would have prevented the particular consequence.

15. Establish classroom rules:
- Concentrate while working.
- Work quietly.
- Remain in your seat.
- Finish task.
- Meet task requirements.

Review rules often. Reinforce the student for following the rules.

16. Evaluate the appropriateness of the task to determine (a) if the task is too easy, (b) if the task is too difficult, and (c) if the length of time scheduled to complete the task is adequate.

17. Prevent the student from becoming overstimulated by an activity (e.g., monitor or supervise student behavior to limit overexcitement in physical activities, games, parties, etc.).

18. Do not force the student to interact with individuals with whom he/she is not completely comfortable.

19. Deliver a predetermined signal (e.g., hand signal, verbal cue, etc.) when the student begins to exhibit inappropriate behavior(s).

20. Give the student responsibilities in group situations so peers may view the student in a more positive way.

21. Have the student be the leader of a small group activity if he/she possesses mastery of skills or an interest in that area.

22. Reinforce those students in the classroom who appropriately interact with the student.

23. Help the student to identify inappropriate behaviors and teach him/her ways to change those behaviors.

24. Inform others who will be working with the student (e.g., teachers, the principal, clerks, etc.) about the student's tendency to ignore consequences of his/her behaviors.

25. Intervene early when there is a problem to prevent more serious problems from occurring.

26. Provide the student with natural consequences for inappropriate behavior (e.g., for disturbing others during group activities, the student will have to leave the activity).

27. Make sure the student does not become involved in overstimulating activities.

28. Speak with the student to explain that he/she may be trying too hard to fit in and should relax and allow friendships to develop naturally.

29. Model appropriate social behavior for the student at all times.

30. Modify or adjust situations that cause the student to demonstrate behaviors that are different or extreme.

31. Teach the student to be satisfied with his/her best effort and not on perfection.

32. Point out the consequences of other students' behavior as they occur (e.g., take the opportunity to point out that consequences occur for all behavior and for all persons).

33. Give the student the responsibility of tutoring a peer if he/she possesses the necessary skills.

34. Present tasks in the most attractive, interesting manner possible.

35. Prevent peers from engaging in those behaviors which would cause the student to fail to consider or regard consequences of his/her behavior (e.g., keep other students from upsetting the student).

36. Provide a learning experience which emphasizes the cause-and-effect relationship between behavior and the consequence (e.g., both negative and positive consequences).

37. Reinforce those students in the classroom who demonstrate appropriate behavior.

38. Provide the student with a clearly identified list of consequences for inappropriate behavior.

39. Maintain supervision of the student's interactions and gradually decrease the amount of supervision over time.

40. Give the student responsibilities in the classroom (e.g., teacher assistant, peer tutor, group leader, etc.).

41. Provide the student with as many academic and social successes as possible so peers may view the student in a more positive way.

42. Reduce the emphasis on competition. Social interactions may be inhibited if the student's abilities are constantly made public and compared to others.

43. Reinforce the student for appropriately interacting with other students: (a) give the student a tangible reward (e.g., classroom privileges, line leading, passing out materials, five minutes free time, etc.) or (b) give the student an intangible reward (e.g., praise, fist bump, smile, etc.).

44. Reinforce the student for demonstrating appropriate behavior based on the length of time the student can be successful. As the student demonstrates success, gradually increase the length of time required for reinforcement.

45. Try various groupings to determine the group in which the student is most comfortable.

46. Remove the student from the group or activity until he/she can demonstrate appropriate behavior and self-control.

47. Use role-play to simulate various situations the student might be involved with, and to teach the student how to interact appropriately (e.g., how to have an appropriate conversation at the lunch table, how to ask to play a game with others, etc.).

48. Treat the student with respect. Talk in an objective manner at all times.

49. Show an interest in the student (e.g., acknowledge the student, ask the student's opinion, spend time working one-to-one with the student, etc.).

50. Speak with the student to explain (a) what the student is doing wrong (e.g., taking action before thinking about what he/she is doing) and (b) what the student should be doing (e.g., considering consequences, thinking about the correct response, considering other persons, etc.).

51. Help the student develop a friendship by pairing him/her with another student for activities. As the student demonstrates success, gradually increase the number of students in the group.

52. Teach the student problem-solving skills: (a) identify the problem, (b) identify goals and objectives, (c) develop strategies, (d) develop a plan for action, and (e) carry out the plan.

53. Teach the student to think before acting by asking himself/herself questions: *What is happening?, What am I doing?, What should I do?, What will be best for me?*

54. Allow the student to voice his/her opinion in a situation to avoid becoming upset or angry.

55. Write a contract with the student specifying what behavior is expected (e.g., sitting near a student, talking to a student, etc.) and what reinforcement will be made available when the terms of the contract have been met.

56. Supervise the student closely in situations in which he/she is likely to act impulsively (e.g., maintain close physical proximity, maintain eye contact, communicate frequently with the student, etc.).

57. Structure the environment to limit opportunities for inappropriate behavior (e.g., keep the student participating in activities, have the student seated near the teacher, maintain visibility to and from the student, etc.).

58. Make sure that consequences are delivered consistently for behavior demonstrated (i.e., appropriate behavior results in positive consequences and inappropriate behavior results in negative consequences).

1. Interact frequently with the student to reduce his/her need to talk to other students.

2. Allow the student to take a break to regroup when he/she is disturbing others.

3. Arrange for individual assignments when the group setting is overly distracting.

4. Write a contract with the student specifying what behavior is expected (e.g., working quietly) and what reinforcement will be made available when the terms of the contract have been met.

5. Ask the student if he/she needs to talk with you or needs to ask any questions before assigning a task, activity, etc., that will be time consuming.

6. Assess the appropriateness of the social situation in relation to the student's ability to function successfully.

7. Assist the student in identifying the situations in which he/she is most likely to talk beyond what is expected or at inappropriate times. After he/she has identified these situations, have him/her think of ways to minimize their occurrences.

8. Avoid seating the student near people with whom he/she may be tempted to talk during lectures, seminars, group projects, etc.

9. Call on the student when he/she is most likely to be able to respond correctly.

10. Communicate with parents (e.g., notes home, phone calls, etc.) to share information about the student's progress. The parents may reinforce the student at home for demonstrating appropriate behavior at school.

11. Consider carefully the student's ability level before expecting him/her not to intrude on others when they are talking, working, reading, etc.

12. Encourage the student to consider the consequences of his/her behavior before engaging in any activity.

13. Deliver directions, explanations, and instructions in a clear and concise manner to reduce the student's need to ask other students for information.

14. Encourage the student to model the behavior of peers who are successful at not talking to others during quiet activity periods.

15. Designate a specific period of time (e.g., each hour on the hour, break time, after completing a task, etc.) when it is permissible for the student to talk with his/her peers.

16. Encourage the student to reduce impulsivity to increase work productivity and general happiness.

17. Discuss with the student the need to reduce impulsive behavior to increase work productivity and general happiness.

18. Teach the student to recognize appropriate times to talk to other students (e.g., between activities, during breaks, at recess, etc.).

19. Hold the student responsible for his/her actions. Do not allow the student to use ADHD as an excuse. However, understand and accept problems ADHD brings into the student's life while he/she is learning to make accommodations.

20. Do not leave a lot of unstructured time for the student.

21. Educate the student about ADHD and the need to self monitor behavior.

22. Educate yourself and others about ADHD to increase understanding and accommodation of impulsive behavior.

23. Educate yourself and others about ADHD to increase understanding and accommodation of excessive talking.

24. Encourage the student to avoid ingesting any substance (e.g., drugs, alcohol, cold remedies, etc.) that might further alter his/her ability to maintain self-control.

25. Create challenges in assigned tasks to increase interest and motivation.

26. Help the student develop an awareness of himself/herself and those around him/her. Have the student periodically step back and ask himself/herself, "Am I bothering others?"

27. Reinforce the student for demonstrating appropriate behavior based on the length of time he/she can be successful. As the student demonstrates success, gradually increase the length of time required for reinforcement.

28. Encourage the student to monitor his/her impulsivity. Awareness should reduce impulsive behaviors.

29. Establish classroom rules:
• Concentrate while working.
• Work quietly.
• Remain in your seat.
• Finish task.
• Meet task requirements.
Review rules often. Reinforce the student for following the rules.

30. Evaluate the appropriateness of the task to determine (a) if the task is too easy, (b) if the task is too difficult, and (c) if the length of time scheduled to complete the task is adequate.

31. Explain to the student after telling him/her to stop talking the reason why he/she should not be talking.

32. Reduce distracting stimuli (e.g., place the student on the front row, provide a carrel or office away from distractions, etc.). This is used as a means of reducing distracting stimuli and not as a form of punishment.

33. Explain to the student that he/she may be trying too hard to fit in and should relax and wait until more appropriate times to interact.

34. Explain to the student why it is important not to intrude on others. Help him/her understand that it is impolite, that he/she might hurt someone's feelings, etc.

35. Give the student adequate opportunities to speak in the classroom, talk to other students, etc. Enthusiastic students need many opportunities to contribute.

36. Have all the necessary materials assembled to work on a project, assignment, etc., to reduce the need to ask for materials.

37. Have the student be the leader of a small group activity if he/she possesses mastery of skills or an interest in that area.

38. Schedule important activities at times when the student is most likely to maintain attention (e.g., one hour after medication, 45 minutes after lunch, first thing in the morning, etc.).

39. Choose a peer to model appropriate behavior for the student.

40. Have the student ask questions about directions, explanations, or instructions before beginning a task to reinforce comprehension and avoid interrupting peers later to ask questions.

41. Have the student review the consequences of his/her behavior with someone he/she trusts. Have him/her consider different choices that could have been made and the different outcomes.

42. Reinforce those students in the classroom who demonstrate appropriate behavior.

43. Have the student work in small groups in which there are frequent opportunities to speak. As the student learns to wait longer for a turn to speak, gradually increase the size of the group.

44. Help the student improve concentration skills (e.g., listening to the speaker, taking notes, preparing comments in advance, making comments in the appropriate context, etc.).

45. Choose a peer who should be a good influence on the student to interact with him/her (e.g., someone younger/older, of the same/opposite gender, etc.).

46. Give the student responsibilities in the classroom (e.g., running errands, opportunities to help the teacher, etc.).

47. Identify the situations in which the student is most likely to bother other students. After you have identified these situations, think of ways to minimize their occurrences.

48. Interact frequently with the student to maintain his/her involvement in the activity (e.g., ask the student questions, ask the student's opinion, stand close to the student, seat the student near the teacher's desk, etc.).

49. After telling the student why he/she should not be talking, explain the reason.

50. Intervene early when there is a problem to prevent a more serious problem from occurring.

51. Maintain visibility to and from the student to keep his/her attention when verbal questions/directions are being delivered. The teacher should be able to see the student and the student should be able to see the teacher. Make eye contact possible at all times.

52. Reinforce those students in the classroom who work quietly.

53. Make sure that the student's feelings are considered when it is necessary to discuss his/her talking to other students (i.e., handle comments in such a way as to not diminish the student's enthusiasm for participation).

54. Teach the student to differentiate between spur-of-the-moment and important information that needs to be conveyed.

55. Make sure the student knows when it is acceptable to interact with other students.

56. Reinforce the student for working quietly based on the length of time the student can be successful. As the student demonstrates success, gradually increase the length of time required for reinforcement.

57. Reduce the emphasis on competition. Competitive activities may cause the student to become anxious and interrupt others.

58. Make sure the student realizes that all behavior has negative or positive consequences. Encourage the student to practice behaviors that will lead to positive consequences.

59. Help the student develop an awareness of the consequences of his/her behavior by writing down or talking through problems which may occur due to interrupting others (e.g., perceived as unmannerly, avoided, etc.).

60. Make the necessary adjustments in the environment to prevent the student from experiencing stress, frustration or anger (e.g., reduce peer pressure, academic failure, teasing, etc.).

61. Provide constant, positive reinforcement for appropriate behavior. Ignore as many inappropriate behaviors as possible.

62. Make sure that reinforcement is not inadvertently given for inappropriate behavior (e.g., making inappropriate comments, talking to others during quiet activity periods, etc.).

63. Provide the student with a clearly understood list of consequences for inappropriate behavior.

64. Have the student make a list of consequences associated with frequently occurring behaviors (e.g., Perceived as unmannerly, avoided by people, etc.).

65. Deliver a predetermined signal (e.g., hand signal, verbal cue, etc.) if the student begins to talk to other students during quiet activity periods.

66. Deliver a predetermined signal (e.g., hand signal, verbal cue, etc.) when the student begins to display inappropriate behavior.

67. Provide the student with frequent opportunities to participate, share, etc.

68. Seat the student away from those students he/she is most likely to bother.

69. Teach the student to use techniques such as crossing his/her arms and legs, clenching his/her fists, and intertwining his/her fingers when he/she feels the urge to speak to others during quiet activity periods.

70. Present activities which allow the student to be highly active and talkative.

71. Reinforce the student for demonstrating appropriate behavior: (a) give the student a tangible reward (e.g., classroom privileges, passing out materials, five minutes free time, etc.) or (b) give the student an intangible reward (e.g., praise, fist bump, smile, etc.).

72. Reinforce the student for raising his/her hand to be recognized.

73. Provide a full schedule of activities. Prevent lag time from occurring when the student can bother other students.

74. Reinforce the student for working quietly: (a) give the student a tangible reward (e.g., classroom privileges, line leading, passing out materials, five minutes free time, etc.) or (b) give the student an intangible reward (e.g., praise, fist bump, smile, etc.).

75. Provide the student with enjoyable activities to perform when he/she completes a task early.

76. Reinforce those students in the classroom who demonstrate on-task behavior.

77. Provide the student with many opportunities for social and academic successes.

78. Schedule recreational activities at the end of the day. Make participation in these activities dependent upon appropriate behavior during quiet activity periods.

79. Remove the student from the group or activity until he/she can demonstrate appropriate behavior and self-control.

80. Provide students with frequent opportunities to interact with one another (e.g., before and after school, between activities, etc.).

81. Reduce activities which might threaten the student (e.g., announcing test score ranges or test scores aloud, making students read aloud in class, emphasizing the success of a particular student or students, etc.).

82. Structure the environment to limit opportunities for talking to other students during quiet activity periods (e.g., keep the student engaged in activities, have the student seated near the teacher, etc.).

83. Teach appropriate social rituals (e.g., excuse yourself before interrupting, wait until someone stops speaking to begin talking, etc.).

84. Try various groupings to determine the group in which the student is most comfortable.

85. Teach problem-solving skills:
- Identify the problem.
- Identify the goals and objectives.
- Develop a strategy/plan for action.
- Carry out the plan.
- Evaluate the results.

86. Teach the student appropriate ways to communicate his/her needs to others (e.g., waiting a turn, raising his/her hand, etc.).

87. Assess the degree of task difficulty to determine whether or not the student will require additional information, time, assistance, etc., before assigning a task.

88. Make sure that the student understands the relationship between inappropriate behavior and the consequences which follow (e.g., others ignoring him/her, disrupting the learning of others, etc.).

89. Seat the student near the teacher.

90. Speak to the student to explain (a) what he/she is doing wrong (e.g., bothering other students who are trying to work, listen, etc.) and (b) what he/she should be doing (e.g., demonstrating appropriate behavior).

131 Responds inappropriately to others' attempts to be friendly, complimentary, sympathetic, etc.

1. Allow the student to be a member of a group without requiring active participation.

2. Teach the student social interaction skills (e.g., ways in which to appropriately respond to others' attempts to be friendly, complimentary, sympathetic, etc.).

3. Choose a peer to sit/work directly with the student (e.g., in different settings or activities such as art, music, P.E.; on the bus; tutoring; group projects; running errands in the building; break time; etc.). As the student becomes comfortable working with one other student, gradually increase the size of the group.

4. Model appropriate ways to respond to others who are friendly, complimentary, sympathetic, etc.

5. Communicate with parents (e.g., notes home, phone calls, etc.) to share information about the student's progress. The parents may reinforce the student at home for responding appropriately to praise or recognition at school.

6. Distribute praise and recognition equally to the members of the class.

7. Provide the student with many opportunities for social and academic successes.

8. Encourage others to compliment the student.

9. Reduce stimuli which contribute to the student's inappropriate responses to others' attempts to interact.

10. Intervene early to prevent the student from losing self-control.

11. Reinforce other students for responding appropriately to interactions with students or teachers.

12. Limit interactions with the peer(s) who is the primary focus of the student's inappropriate responses.

13. Provide the student with frequent opportunities to meet new people.

14. Make sure that reinforcement is not inadvertently given for inappropriate behavior (e.g., attending to the student only when he/she responds inappropriately to praise or recognition).

15. Praise or recognize the student when he/she will most likely be able to demonstrate an appropriate response (e.g., when the student is not being singled out in a group).

16. Encourage the student to interact with others.

17. Express your feelings in a socially acceptable way.

18. Model appropriate ways to respond to interactions with other students or teachers.

19. Use feedback related to performance (e.g., test scores, grades, etc.) in place of praise or recognition. As the student becomes more capable of accepting praise and recognition, gradually deliver verbal praise and recognition.

20. Reinforce the student for responding appropriately to praise or recognition based on the number of times he/she can be successful. As the student demonstrates success, gradually increase the number of times required for reinforcement.

21. Reinforce those students in the classroom who respond appropriately to praise or recognition.

22. Praise or recognize the student in private. The public aspect of praise or recognition is often the cause of the inappropriate response.

23. Assess the appropriateness of the social situation in relation to the student's ability to be successful.

24. Provide opportunities for appropriate interactions within the classroom (e.g., peer models engaged in appropriate interactions).

25. Treat the student with respect. Talk in an objective manner at all times.

26. Provide praise or recognition for smaller increments of success so that the student may become gradually accustomed to the recognition.

27. Provide the student with positive feedback which indicates he/she is important.

28. Rather than emphasizing winning or beating other students in competition, encourage individual success or progress which may be enjoyed privately rather than publicly.

29. Reinforce the student for responding appropriately to others' attempts to be friendly, complimentary, sympathetic, etc.: (a) give the student a tangible reward (e.g., classroom privileges, line leading, passing out materials, five minutes free time, etc.) or (b) give the student an intangible reward (e.g., praise, fist bump, smile, etc.).

30. Speak with the student to explain (a) what he/she is doing wrong (e.g., using inappropriate language, responding negatively, calling names, making inappropriate gestures, etc.) and (b) what he/she should be doing (e.g., being positive in response to others).

31. Help the student develop social awareness (e.g., people may be embarrassed by what you say, feelings can be hurt by comments, tact is the best policy, remember interactions which have made you feel good and treat others in the same manner, etc.).

32. Present praise with a matter-of-fact delivery and avoid exaggerated exclamations of success.

33. Use alternative forms of praise or recognition which are not threatening to the student (e.g., written notes, phone calls to parents, display work done well, etc.).

34. Respect the student's right to a reasonable amount of privacy.

35. Try various groupings to determine the group in which the student is most comfortable.

36. Provide praise and recognition as a natural consequence for appropriate behavior.

37. Write a contract stating appropriate ways to respond to others and identify what reinforcement will be made available when the terms of the contract have been met.

Reminder: Do not punish a student for his/ her inability to respond appropriately to praise or recognition.

1. Assess the appropriateness of the task or social situation in relation to the student's ability to perform successfully.

2. Encourage sharing by giving assignments which require sharing to complete the activity (e.g., making murals, bulletin boards, maps, art projects, etc.).

3. Encourage peers to share with the student.

4. Teach the student the concept of sharing by having the student borrow from others or loan things to others.

5. Have the student work directly with a peer to model sharing. As the student demonstrates success, gradually increase the size of the group.

6. Reduce competitiveness in the school environment (e.g., avoid situations where refusing to share contributes to winning; situations where winning or beating someone else becomes the primary objective of a game, activity, or academic exercise; etc.).

7. Create and reinforce activities (e.g., school bulletin board, class project, bake sale, etc.) in which students work together for a common goal rather than individual success or recognition. Point out that larger accomplishments are realized through group effort rather than by individual effort.

8. Put the student in charge of communal school items (e.g., rulers, pencils, crayons, etc.) to experience sharing.

9. Allow the student to have many turns and enough materials to satisfy his/her immediate needs. As the student demonstrates success, gradually require sharing and taking turns.

10. Provide special activities for the entire class at the end of the day which are contingent upon sharing throughout the day.

11. Provide enough materials, activities, etc., so sharing will not always be necessary.

12. Structure the classroom environment to take advantage of natural sharing opportunities (e.g., allowing more group activities, pointing out natural consequences when a student shares, etc.).

13. Take advantage of opportunities for the students to share and help (e.g., when there is a spill, assign students different responsibilities for cleaning it up; when a new student enters the classroom, assign students responsibilities for his/her orientation; etc.).

14. Do not allow students to bring unnecessary personal possessions to school.

15. Model sharing behavior by allowing students to use your materials contingent upon return of the items.

16. Provide the student with many opportunities to both borrow and lend to help the student learn the concept of sharing.

17. Make sure that every student gets to use materials, take a turn, etc., and that there is no opportunity for selfishness.

18. Point out to the student the natural rewards of sharing (e.g., personal satisfaction, friendships, having people share in return, etc.).

19. Make sure that those students who are willing to share are not taken advantage of by their peers.

20. Make sure that other students are sharing with the student so a reciprocal relationship can be achieved.

21. Maintain a realistic level of expectation for sharing.

22. Practice sharing by having each student work with a particular school material for an established length of time. At the end of the time period (e.g., ten minutes), have each student pass his/her material to another student.

23. Provide students with adequate time to complete activities requiring sharing, so the selfish use of school materials is not necessary for success. Students are less likely to share if sharing reduces the likelihood of finishing on time, being successful, etc.

24. Reduce the demands for the student to make verbal exchanges when sharing (e.g., shyness may inhibit sharing if the student is required to verbally communicate with others). Materials should be placed in a central location when not in use so they can be obtained by the students. This will facilitate the aspect of sharing which makes materials available to others when not in use.

25. Do not force the student to interact with other students with whom he/she is not completely comfortable.

26. Establish rules for sharing school materials:
- Ask for materials you wish to use.
- Exchange materials carefully.
- Return materials when not in use.
- Offer to share materials with others.
- Take care of shared materials.
- Call attention to materials that need repair.

Review rules often. Reinforce students for following the rules.

27. Intervene early when there is a problem to prevent more serious problems from occurring.

28. Teach the student to respect others' belongings by respecting the student's belongings.

29. Model sharing (e.g., by loaning pencils, paper, etc.).

30. Teach the student to take turns sharing materials (e.g., each student may use the colored pencils for 15 minutes, one student cuts while the other student uses the glue, etc.).

31. Do not allow the student to bring items to school that he/she is not willing to share (e.g., games, toys, etc.).

32. Make sure the student is not expected to share everything (e.g., do not punish the student for not sharing a hat, gloves, personal items, etc.). Everyone has things they would prefer not to share with others.

33. Communicate with parents (e.g., notes home, phone calls, etc.) to share information about the student's progress. The parents may reinforce the student at home for sharing at school.

34. Write a contract with the student specifying what behavior is expected (e.g., sharing) and what reinforcement will be made available when the terms of the contract have been met.

35. Reinforce those students in the classroom who share.

36. Speak with the student to explain (a) what the student is doing wrong (e.g., failing to give others opportunities to use things) and (b) what the student should be doing (e.g., sharing materials).

37. Provide the student with enough materials to satisfy his/her immediate needs (e.g., one of everything). As the student demonstrates success, gradually reduce the number of materials and require the student to share the available materials.

38. Make sure that shared materials are returned to the student so he/she will develop a positive concept of sharing.

39. Students who cannot share with one another because of their personal dislike for each other should not be placed in the same group when sharing is required. If a student prefers not to share with one specific person, it does not mean that he/she does not have the ability to share.

40. Provide the student with many experiences to share with others and have materials returned. When the student learns that shared materials will be returned, the student will be more likely to share in the future.

41. Make sure the student understands that if shared materials are used up, worn out, broken under normal use, etc., they will be replaced.

42. In group situations, provide the student with necessary materials for the activity so sharing problems do not disrupt the learning experience.

43. Do not expect the student to share all materials. Students need to collect some materials (e.g., jewelry, clothing, etc.).

44. Maintain a realistic level of expectation for sharing school materials based on the student's age level and ability to share.

45. Reinforce the student for sharing: (a) give the student a tangible reward (e.g., classroom privileges, line leading, passing out materials, five minutes free time, etc.) or (b) give the student an intangible reward (e.g., praise, fist bump, smile, etc.).

133 Does not allow others to take their turn or participate in activities or games, etc.

1. Assess the appropriateness of the task or social situation in relation to the student's ability to perform successfully.

2. Encourage group participation by giving students assignments which require working together to complete the activity (e.g., making murals, bulletin boards, maps, art projects, etc.).

3. Encourage peers to take turns with the student.

4. Have the student work directly with a peer to model taking turns. Gradually increase the size of the group over time.

5. Reduce competitiveness in the school environment (e.g., avoid situations where refusing to take turns contributes to winning; situations where winning or beating someone else becomes the primary objective of a game, activity, or academic exercise; etc.).

6. Create and reinforce activities in which students work together for a common goal rather than individual success or recognition (e.g., school bulletin board, class project, bake sale, etc.). Point out that larger accomplishments are realized through group effort than by individual effort.

7. Choose an outgoing, nonthreatening peer to interact with the student.

8. Provide special activities for the entire class at the end of the day which are contingent upon taking turns throughout the day.

9. Structure the classroom environment to take advantage of natural opportunities to take turns (e.g., allow more group activities, point out natural consequences when a student takes turns, etc.).

10. Take advantage of opportunities for the students to work together (e.g., when there is a spill, assign students different responsibilities for cleaning it up; when a new student enters the classroom, assign different students responsibilities for his/her orientation; etc.).

11. Have the student practice waiting to take a turn if he/she is unwilling to do so.

12. Provide enough materials, activities, etc., so taking turns will not always be necessary.

13. Provide the student with many opportunities to take turns to help the student learn the concept of taking turns.

14. Make sure that every student gets to use materials, take a turn, etc., and that there is no opportunity for selfishness.

15. Point out to the student the natural rewards of taking turns (e.g., personal satisfaction, friendships, companionship, etc.).

16. Make sure that those students who are willing to take turns are not taken advantage of by their peers.

17. Make sure that other students are taking turns with the student so a reciprocal relationship can be achieved.

18. Maintain a realistic level of expectation for taking turns.

19. Have the student participate in an activity with one peer. As the student demonstrates success, gradually increase the size of the group.

20. Determine the peers with whom the student would most prefer to interact and facilitate the interaction.

21. Allow the student to have many turns and enough materials to satisfy his/her immediate needs, and gradually require sharing and taking turns.

22. Assign the student to interact with younger peers.

23. Assign the student to participate in activities in which he/she is likely to interact successfully with peers.

24. Make sure the student understands that interacting with peers is contingent upon appropriate behavior.

25. Teach the student appropriate ways to interact with peers in group games (e.g., suggest activities, share materials, problem-solve, take turns, follow game rules, etc.).

26. Supervise activities closely so the peer(s) with whom the student interacts does not stimulate inappropriate behavior.

27. Make sure that activities are not so stimulating as to make successful interactions with peers difficult.

28. Involve the student in extracurricular activities to encourage appropriate interaction with peers.

29. Find the peer with whom the student is most likely to be able to successfully interact (e.g., a student with similar interests, background, classes, behavior patterns, nonacademic schedule, etc.).

30. Make sure, beforehand, that the student is able to successfully participate in the activity (e.g., the student understands the rules, the student is familiar with the game, the student will be compatible with the other students playing the game, etc.).

31. Make sure the student understands that not interacting appropriately with peers during activities may result in termination of the game and/or loss of future opportunities to participate in activities.

32. Design activities in which each student takes short turns. Increase the length of each student's turn as the student demonstrates success at taking turns.

33. Establish a set of rules for group games:
- Follow rules of the game.
- Take turns.
- Make positive comments.
- Work as a team member.
- Be a good sport.

Review rules often. Reinforce students for following the rules.

34. Allow natural consequences to occur when the student does not take turns (e.g., other students will not want to interact with him/her, other students will not be willing to take turns, etc.).

35. Talk to the student before playing a game and remind him/her of the importance of taking turns.

36. Provide the student with a predetermined signal when he/she begins to display inappropriate behaviors.

37. Make sure there is adult supervision when the student is playing games with others.

38. Do not force the student to interact with someone with whom he/she is not completely comfortable.

39. Make sure the student does not become involved in overstimulating activities in which he/she gets excited and cannot settle down.

40. Treat the student with respect. Talk in an objective manner at all times.

41. Intervene early when there is a problem to prevent more serious problems from occurring.

42. Teach the student to take turns (e.g., each student may use the colored pencils for 15 minutes, each student may have three turns, etc.).

43. Communicate with the parents (e.g., note home, phone calls, etc.) to share information about the student's progress. The parents may reinforce the student at home for taking turns at school.

44. Write a contract with the student specifying what behavior is expected (e.g., taking turns) and what reinforcement will be made available when the terms of the contract have been met.

45. Reinforce those students in the classroom who take turns.

46. Speak with the student to explain (a) what the student is doing wrong (e.g., failing to give others opportunities to have a turn) and (b) what the student should be doing (e.g., allowing others to have a turn).

47. Reinforce the student for taking turns: (a) give the student a tangible reward (e.g., classroom privileges, line leading, passing out materials, five minutes free time, etc.) or (b) give the student an intangible reward (e.g., praise, fist bump, smile, etc.).

134 Does not demonstrate the ability to resolve conflict situations

1. Reinforce the student for demonstrating the ability to appropriately solve problems in conflict situations: (a) give the student a tangible reward (e.g., classroom privileges, line leading, passing out materials, five minutes free time, etc.) or (b) give the student an intangible reward (e.g., praise, fist bump, smile, etc.).

2. Speak to the student to explain (a) what he/she is doing wrong (e.g., fighting, name calling, etc.) and (b) what he/she should be doing (e.g., withdrawing from conflict situations, reasoning, etc.).

3. Teach the student a variety of ways to solve problems in conflict situations (e.g., withdrawing, reasoning, calling upon an arbitrator, apologizing, compromising, allowing others the benefit of the doubt, etc.).

4. Reinforce the student for demonstrating the ability to appropriately solve problems in conflict situations based on the number of times the student can be successful. As the student demonstrates success, gradually increase the number of times required for reinforcement.

5. Write a contract with the student specifying what behavior is expected (e.g., withdrawing from conflict situations, reasoning, etc.) and what reinforcement will be made available when the terms of the contract have been met.

6. Communicate with parents (e.g., notes home, phone calls, etc.) to share information about the student's progress. The parents may reinforce the student at home for demonstrating the ability to appropriately solve problems in conflict situations at school.

7. Choose a peer to model appropriately solving problems in conflict situations for the student.

8. Have the student ask questions about directions, explanations, instructions he/she does not understand.

9. Evaluate the student's problem-solving ability. Limit his/her exposure to conflict situations at a level with which he/she can participate appropriately.

10. Reinforce those students in the classroom who demonstrate the ability to appropriately solve problems in conflict situations.

11. Model for the student a variety of ways to solve problems in conflict situations (e.g., withdrawing, reasoning, apologizing, compromising, etc.).

12. Provide the student with hypothetical conflict situations and ask him/her to suggest appropriate solutions to the situations.

13. Have the student role-play ways to solve problems in conflict situations with peers and adults (e.g., withdrawing, reasoning, calling upon an arbitrator, apologizing, compromising, allowing others the benefit of the doubt, etc.).

14. Make sure the student understands that natural consequences may occur if he/she reacts inappropriately in conflict situations (e.g., peers may not want to interact, teachers may have to intervene, etc.)

15. Teach the student to solve problems in conflict situations before the situation becomes too difficult for him/her to solve.

16. Teach the student to avoid becoming involved in conflict situations (e.g., move away from the situation, change his/her behavior, etc.).

17. Explain to the student that it is natural for conflict situations to occur. What is important is how he/she reacts to the situation.

18. Discuss typical conflict situations with the student and appropriate solutions to specific situations (e.g., peers taking things from him/her, peers hitting or grabbing, peers not following the rules, etc.).

19. If the student has responded inappropriately to a conflict situation, take time to explore with the student appropriate solutions which could have been used in solving the problem.

20. Maintain mobility throughout the classroom to supervise student interactions and intervene in conflict situations in which the student is unable to successfully solve the problem.

21. Intervene early when there is a problem to prevent more serious problems from occurring.

22. Do not force the student to interact with someone with whom he/she is not completely comfortable.

23. Make sure the student does not become involved in overstimulating activities which may cause a conflict situation.

24. Treat the student with respect. Talk in an objective manner at all times.

25. Teach the student acceptable ways to communicate displeasure, anger, frustration, etc.

26. Have the student put himself/herself in someone else's place (e.g., ask the student to think about how he/she would feel if someone called him/her dumb or stupid).

27. Do not assume that the student is being treated nicely by others. Peers may be stimulating the inappropriate behavior of the student.

28. Encourage the student to interact with others.

29. Do not force the student to interact with individuals with whom he/she is not completely comfortable.

30. Make sure you express your feelings in a socially acceptable way.

31. Teach the student to think before acting by asking himself/herself questions: *What is happening?, What am I doing?, What should I do?, What will be best for me?*

32. Make sure the student is allowed to voice an opinion in a situation to avoid becoming angry or upset.

135 Does not make appropriate use of free time

1. Make sure that assignments are scheduled to minimize free time.

2. Choose a peer for the student to interact with during free time.

3. Communicate with parents (e.g., notes home, phone calls, etc.) to share information about the student's progress. The parents may reinforce the student at home for making appropriate use of free time at school.

4. Develop, with the student, a list of high-interest free time activities that require various amounts of time to perform.

5. Do not leave a lot of unstructured time for the student.

6. Encourage the student to assist younger peers in free time activities.

7. Encourage the student to plan the use of free time in advance.

8. Encourage the student's peers to include him/her in free time activities.

9. Establish centers of high-interest activities at appropriate levels of difficulty for the student's use during free time.

10. Establish free time rules:
- Find an activity.
- Spend time quietly.
- Remain in assigned areas.
- Put materials away when free time is over.

Review rules often. Reinforce students for following the rules.

11. Evaluate the appropriateness of free time activities to determine whether or not the student can be successful with the activity and the length of time scheduled.

12. Find educationally related free time activities for the student to perform (e.g., flash card activities with peers; math, reading, or spelling board games; etc.).

13. Give the student a special responsibility during free time (e.g., grading papers, straightening books, feeding pets, etc.).

14. Provide a quiet, reasonably private area where the student can do nothing during free time.

15. Give the student an individual schedule to follow so that when an activity is finished he/she knows what to do next.

16. Have the student be a peer tutor during free time.

17. Have the student act as a teacher assistant during free time.

18. Have the student begin an ongoing project during free time that will be a regular free time activity.

19. Have the student ask questions about directions, explanations, or instructions not understood.

20. Choose a peer to model appropriate use of free time for the student.

21. Identify a specific activity for the student to participate in during free time.

22. Intervene early when there is a problem to prevent more serious problems from occurring.

23. Allow the student to go to other classrooms for specified activities during free time (e.g., typing, home economics, industrial arts, etc.).

24. Make sure that free time is contingent upon academic productivity and accuracy (e.g., the student must finish three activities with 80 percent accuracy before participating in free time).

25. Make sure that the free time activity does not overstimulate and cause the student to demonstrate inappropriate behavior.

26. Make sure the student does not become involved in overstimulating activities.

27. Make sure the student is able to successfully participate in the free time activity (e.g., the student understands the rules, the student is familiar with the activity, the student will be compatible with other students engaged in the activity, etc.).

28. Make sure the student understands that failing to make appropriate use of free time may result in termination of free time and/or loss of opportunity to earn free time.

29. Separate the student from the peer(s) who stimulates the student's inappropriate use of free time.

30. Reinforce the student for making appropriate use of free time: (a) give the student a tangible reward (e.g., classroom privileges, line leading, passing out materials, five minutes free time, etc.) or (b) give the student an intangible reward (e.g., praise, fist bump, smile, etc.).

31. Make sure the student understands that failure to conclude activities and return to assignments may result in the loss of opportunity to earn free time.

32. Participate in free time activities with the student to model appropriate use of free time.

33. Place free time materials (e.g., paper, pencil, glue, crayons, games, etc.) in a location where the student can access them on his/her own.

34. Provide high interest free time activities for completion of assignments (e.g., listening to music, reading, socializing, going to another part of the building, etc.).

35. Provide sign-up sheets for free time activities.

36. Provide supervision of free time activities to monitor the student's appropriate use of free time.

37. Provide the student with a list of quiet activities to participate in when he/she finishes assignments early.

38. Provide the student with frequent short-term, free time activities so he/she can learn to finish free time projects at another time and be willing to go back to assignments.

39. Provide items of interest for the student during free time (e.g., headphones, coloring books, reading material, etc.).

40. Reinforce the student for making appropriate use of free time based on the length of time the student can be successful. As the student demonstrates success, gradually increase the length of time required for reinforcement.

41. Make sure the student is aware of the length of free time available when beginning an activity.

42. Reinforce those students in the classroom who make appropriate use of free time.

43. Speak to the student to explain (a) what the student is doing wrong (e.g., talking loudly, getting out of seat, etc.) and (b) what he/she should be doing (e.g., talking quietly, sitting quietly, etc.).

44. Write a contract with the student specifying what behavior is expected (e.g., talking quietly, sitting quietly, studying, etc.) and what reinforcement will be made available when the terms of the contract have been met.

1. Reinforce the student for working appropriately with peers in a tutoring situation: (a) give the student a tangible reward (e.g., classroom privileges, line leading, passing out materials, five minutes free time, etc.) or (b) give the student an intangible reward (e.g., praise, fist bump, smile, etc.).

2. Speak to the student to explain (a) what he/she is doing wrong (e.g., not attending to the tutor, arguing with peers, etc.) and (b) what he/she should be doing (e.g., attending to the tutor, doing his/her own work, etc.).

3. Establish tutoring rules:
- Concentrate while working.
- Work quietly.
- Remain in your seat.
- Finish task.
- Meet task expectations.

Review rules often. Reinforce students for following the rules.

4. Reinforce those student in the classroom who work appropriately with peers in a tutoring situation.

5. Reinforce the student for working appropriately with peers in a tutoring situation based on the length of time he/she can be successful. As the student demonstrates success, gradually increase the length of time required for reinforcement.

6. Write a contract with the student specifying what behavior is expected (e.g., attending to the tutor, taking turns, sharing materials, etc.) and what reinforcement will be made available when the terms of the contract have been met.

7. Communicate with parents (e.g., notes home, phone calls, etc.) to share information about the student's progress. The parents may reinforce the student at home for working appropriately with peers in a tutoring situation at school.

8. Evaluate the appropriateness of the task to determine (a) if the task is too easy, (b) if the task is too difficult, and (c) if the length of time scheduled for the task is adequate.

9. Choose a peer to model working appropriately with peers in a tutoring situation for the student.

10. Have the student ask questions about directions, explanations, and instructions he/she does not understand.

11. Make sure that the student and peer tutor are compatible (e.g., the student accepts his/her role in the tutoring situation, the student and peer tutor are accepting of one another, the peer tutor has skills and knowledge to share, etc.).

12. Be sure that the opportunity to work with a peer tutor is contingent upon appropriate behavior prior to and during the tutoring situation.

13. Make sure that the students being tutored together are on the same ability level.

14. Teach the student appropriate behavior for peer tutoring situations (e.g., follow directions, work quietly, etc.).

15. Supervise tutoring situations closely to make sure that the student's behavior is appropriate, the task is appropriate, he/she is learning from the situation, etc.

16. Make sure the tutoring activity involves practice, drill, or repetition of information or skills previously presented.

17. Determine the peers with whom the student would most prefer to interact in tutoring situations and attempt to group these students together for peer tutoring.

18. Choose outgoing, nonthreatening peers to be tutors.

19. Structure the environment so the student has many opportunities for success in tutoring situations.

20. Assign the student to tutoring situations in which he/she is likely to interact successfully with peers being tutored.

21. Conduct a sociometric activity with the class to determine those peers who would most prefer to interact with the student in tutoring situations.

22. Make sure that the student demonstrates appropriate behavior in tutoring situations prior to pairing him/her with a peer.

23. Make sure the student understands that interacting with peers in tutoring situations is contingent upon appropriate behavior.

24. Supervise tutoring situations closely so peers with whom the student interacts do not stimulate inappropriate behavior.

25. Make sure that the tutoring situation is not so stimulating it makes successful interactions with peers difficult.

26. Reduce the emphasis on competition. Failure may stimulate inappropriate behavior in tutoring situations.

27. Teach the student problem-solving skills so he/she may better handle problems that may occur in interactions with peers in tutoring situations (e.g., talking, walking away, calling upon an arbitrator, compromising, etc.).

28. Find the peer with whom the student is most likely to be able to successfully interact in tutoring situations (e.g., a student with similar interests, background, classes, behavior patterns, non-academic schedule, etc.).

29. Through interviews with other students and observation, determine those characteristics of the student which interfere with successful interactions during tutoring situations. Determine skills or behaviors the student needs to develop for successful interactions.

30. Structure the activities of the tutoring situation according to the needs/abilities of the student (e.g., establish rules, limit the stimulation of the activity, limit the length of the activity, consider the time of day, etc.).

31. Limit opportunities for interaction in tutoring situations on those occasions in which the student is not likely to be successful (e.g., the student has experienced academic or social failure prior to the scheduled tutoring activity).

32. Select nonacademic activities (e.g., board games, model building, coloring, etc.) designed to facilitate appropriate interaction between the student and peers.

33. Have the student practice appropriate interactions with the teacher in tutoring situations.

34. Make sure the student is able to successfully participate in the tutoring activity (e.g., the student understands the rules, the student is familiar with the activity, the student will be compatible with the other students engaged in the free-time activity, etc.).

35. Make sure the student understands that not interacting appropriately with peers during tutoring activities may result in removal from the activity and/or loss of future opportunities to participate.

36. Have the student participate in the tutoring situation with peers for short periods of time. As the student demonstrates success, gradually increase the length of time.

37. Provide an appropriate location for the tutoring situation (e.g., quiet corner of the classroom, near the teacher's desk, etc.).

38. Intervene early when there is a problem to prevent more serious problems from occurring.

39. Do not force the student to work in a tutoring situation with a peer with whom he/she is not completely comfortable.

40. Provide the student with a predetermined signal when he/she begins to display inappropriate behaviors in a tutoring situation with peers.

41. Allow the student to attempt something new in private before doing so in a tutoring situation with peers.

1. Reinforce the student for working through his/her difficulties with others without resorting to revenge: (a) give the student a tangible reward (e.g., line leader status, five minutes free time, classroom privileges, etc.) or (b) give the student an intangible behavior (e.g., praise, fist bump, smile, etc.).

2. Write a contract specifying expected behavior (e.g., refraining from hurting others, destroying their property, etc., when he/she feels someone has wronged him/her) and what reinforcement will be available when the terms of the contract have been met.

3. Communicate with parents (e.g., notes home, phone calls, etc.) regarding the student's progress with social and communication skills to replace retributional behavior. Encourage parents to reinforce the student for the use of positive social skills at school, at home, and in community environments.

4. Provide the student with positive role models who do not use revenge to problem-solve.

5. The student who expresses and/or acts upon thoughts of revenge may be needing additional services and supports (e.g., counseling).

6. Use role-play to explore situations in which someone tries to repay "a wrong with a wrong." Discuss the situation, and arrive at positive alternatives which could occur rather than revenge. Explore the benefits the "wronged person" may realize by choosing positive responses rather than revenge.

7. The student may not know how to actively, positively self-advocate. Provide the student with information and training through problem-solving techniques (e.g., identify the problem, generate positive solutions, implement a solution, evaluate effectiveness of the problem-solving plan, and modify if necessary).

8. Role model problem-solving techniques to replace attempts at revenge.

9. Provide outlets for the student who expresses and/or acts upon thoughts of revenge (e.g., art work, diary writing or self-recording, etc.).

10. Maintain close supervision of the student who expresses or attempts to act upon thoughts of revenge.

11. When a dispute occurs, meet with both parties separately and privately to hear each side of the story. Help each party to identify positive alternatives to problem-solve. Working together, determine a positive course of action which would eliminate the need for revenge by anyone.

12. When working with a student who maintains he/she is being slighted or wronged by another, always listen and respond as objectively as possible. Do not indicate to the student that you think he/she is lying about another, because he/she may then "shut you out" and not meaningfully participate in problem solving with you.

13. Let the student know you care about his/her thoughts and feelings. When reality is not consistent with the student's thoughts, feelings, or perceptions, introduce the inconsistency by saying something like "I know this is how you think and feel about the situation, but this is what other people saw . . . ."

14. The student who is undergoing personal stress may be more likely to express and/or act upon thoughts of revenge. Provide the student information and instruction on stress-management techniques.

15. The student may not know how to form friendships. Provide the student with closely supervised opportunities to meet others in recreational and social functions.

16. When incidents occur during the course of a day in which someone could have behaved in a revengeful fashion but chose a positive alternative instead, reinforce that student for his/her choice.

17. Assist the student in actively implementing his/her reasonable, positive alternative to revenge, but make sure the student
  (a) is calm (e.g., no longer feeling hostile),
  (b) has developed his/her thoughts and plans in the event the positive alternative doesn't work (e.g., will use coping skills and positive forms of self-expression, etc.),
  (c) has developed a "Plan B" which consists of another chosen positive alternative to try, and
  (d) will evaluate the effectiveness of his/her approach with the teacher after this has been attempted.

18. The student may associate "bad feelings" with "being bad." Encourage the student to instead view himself/herself as good, and to accept feelings. Encourage the student to view the choices he/she makes as either acceptable or unacceptable, poor/good, etc.

19. Avoid inadvertently reinforcing a student for his/her expressed aggressive thoughts, such as thoughts about "paying someone back." Provide the student with more verbal response for positive actions you would like to see again to prevent or discourage the student from expressing and attempting to act upon aggressive thoughts for attention.

20. In the interests of individual and group safety, never assume a student will not carry out expressed plans for revenge. Always provide the student and any potential victims with close monitoring.

21. Encourage the student to think through the idea of "getting back" at others:
  (a) Think about the thoughts and feelings of others (e.g., the person who is the focus of the "get even" reaction, family members and friends of both parties, classmates, school administration, etc.) if revenge occurred;
  (b) think about the potential consequences to himself/herself if revenge occurred;
  (c) identify positive alternatives to revenge;
  (d) identify thoughts/feelings of others should the positive alternative be attempted; and
  (e) identify thoughts/feelings of himself/herself should the positive alternatives be attempted.

22. Provide the student with a clear chain of command he/she and others in the environment need to use to process complaints, grievances, etc. Practice each communication link, and praise the student for resorting to the chain of command.

23. Working with the student, arrive at coping techniques tailored to individual preferences and abilities (e.g., taking two slow, deep breaths; moving to another part of the classroom to calm down; head on table or desk for 20 seconds; etc.).

24. Provide the student the opportunity to communicate with role models from the community who have success stories to relate. Enlist these community heroes in identifying revengeful behavior as damaging and undesirable.

25. Provide positive activities to
  (a) give the student matters of interest to focus upon, think through, and act upon other than revenge,
  (b) give the student opportunities to experience success (this may help decrease stress related to frustration), and
  (c) give the student positive, structured opportunities to work with others to encourage productive teamwork and hopefully render vengeful thoughts/behaviors counterproductive.

26. Provide the student with focus for his/her actions and behaviors by developing with him/her a daily schedule. Reinforce the student for
  (a) initiating schedule development,
  (b) beginning scheduled activities independently,
  (c) following his/her schedule,
  (d) completing scheduled activities, and
  (e) all positive attempts at working on the schedule and on scheduled activities.

27. Provide the student with frequent, natural opportunities to feel successful on a daily basis.

28. Competition may stimulate inappropriate behavior. Allow the student the chance to work in small groups or teams on activities, but structure team learning opportunities so these are not competitive by establishing sincere ways of providing merit for each group's efforts.

29. The student who is sensitive to failure and who may voice or attempt retribution needs careful monitoring. Offer positive alternative activities instead of ongoing activities when the student indicates signs of frustration or overstimulation.

30. Once a schedule has been created with student involvement, make sure the student receives assistance to achieve success the first few days. As the student demonstrates success, gradually decrease assistance.

31. When providing the student with the opportunity to work with others, try to assure his/her opportunity to complement the group based upon the unique interests and skills he/she will contribute. Avoid grouping students totally by ability, and provide small groups structure and monitoring.

1. Provide a full schedule of daily events. Prevent lag time from occurring when the student can participate in writing and passing notes.

2. Seat the student near the teacher.

3. Maintain visibility to and from the student. The teacher should be able to see the student; the student should be able to see the teacher. Make eye contact possible at all times.

4. Interact frequently with the student to monitor his/her behavior.

5. Remove the student from peers with whom he/she is writing and passing notes.

6. Provide students with frequent opportunities to interact with one another (e.g., before and after school, between activities, etc.).

7. Use "note writing" as a language arts activity each day.

8. Make sure the student understands the consequences of writing and passing notes.

9. Be consistent when delivering consequences to those students who write and pass notes.

10. Set aside time each day when the student is permitted to write notes to other students.

11. Make sure the student understands that passing notes when someone else is talking or giving directions is rude.

12. Do not leave a lot of unstructured time for the student.

13. Choose a peer to model appropriate behavior for the student.

14. Communicate with parents (e.g., notes home, phone calls, etc.) to share information about the student's progress. The parents may reinforce the student at home for not writing and passing notes at school.

15. Write a contract with the student specifying what behavior is expected (e.g., not writing and passing notes) and what reinforcement will be made available when the terms of the contract have been met.

16. Reinforce the student for not writing and passing notes based on the length of time the student can be successful. As the student demonstrates success, gradually increase the length of time required for reinforcement.

17. Reinforce those students in the classroom who do not write and pass notes.

18. Establish classroom rules:
- Concentrate while working.
- Remain in your seat.
- Finish task.
- Meet task expectations.
- Raise your hand.

Review rules often. Reinforce students for following the rules.

19. Speak to the student to explain (a) what the student is doing wrong (e.g., writing and passing notes) and (b) what the student should be doing (e.g., working quietly).

20. Reinforce the student for demonstrating appropriate behavior: (a) give the student a tangible reward (e.g., classroom privileges, line leading, passing out materials, five minutes free time, etc.) or (b) give the student an intangible reward (e.g., praise, fist bump, smile, etc.).

1. Make sure the student knows what information is appropriate to report (e.g., peers' emergencies, injuries, fighting, etc.).

2. Make sure the student knows what information is not appropriate to report (e.g., peers whispering, not working, copying, wasting time, etc.).

3. Maintain mobility to prevent the student's need to tattle. If you see behavior occur, it will not be necessary for the students to call attention to it.

4. Do not inadvertently reinforce tattling by overreacting.

5. Make decisions based on what you observe rather than what is reported to you to maintain objectivity.

6. Model appropriate behavior for the student. Publicly praise and privately redirect student behavior.

7. Reduce the emphasis on competition. A highly competitive environment may increase the likelihood of tattling.

8. Explain the natural consequences of tattling to the student (e.g., peers may not want to interact with him/her, peers may retaliate, etc.).

9. Teach the student appropriate ways to communicate displeasure, anger, frustration, etc.

10. When the student comes to you to tattle, stop and ask the student, "Is this something that is so important that you need to come to me?" "Is someone hurt?" "Is this something you can solve without me?" etc.

11. Encourage the student to use problem-solving skills: (a) identify the problem, (b) identify goals and objectives, (c) develop strategies, (d) develop a plan for action, and (e) carry out the plan.

12. Refuse to listen to the student. Immediately stop the student when tattling begins.

13. Make sure the student does not go to another adult when you won't respond to his/her tattling.

14. Reduce the opportunity for the student to be in competitive activities that may cause tattling.

15. Immediately remove the student from interacting with others when tattling begins.

16. Be consistent in dealing with tattling. Do not allow tattling one time and expect appropriate behavior the next time.

17. Make a list of the number of times each day the student tattles. Make the student aware of the number of times each day he/she comes to you to tattle.

18. If the student has difficulty playing nicely with others, do not allow him/her to have playtime.

19. Make sure that others are friendly and cooperative when interacting with the student.

20. Encourage the student to play with peers who do not tattle.

21. Remind the student before interacting with others of which situations are important enough to involve an adult and which situations are considered tattling.

22. Do not force the student to play with other children. Allow the student to pick his/her own friends.

23. Determine what the student most frequently tattles about (e.g., not playing a certain game fairly, someone calling names, someone playing with a certain toy, etc.), and remove whatever it is from the student's situation (e.g., take the game away, do not have the student interact with someone who calls him/her names, remove the toy that always causes problems, etc.).

24. Determine if there is a legitimate reason for the student to report the behavior of others (another student may be playing too roughly, breaking toys, etc.).

25. Talk to the student about ways of handling situations successfully without tattling (e.g., walk away from the situation, change to another activity, ask for help, etc.).

26. Make sure there are enough materials for all students so that sharing is not a problem.

27. Choose a peer to model appropriate behavior for the student.

28. Communicate with parents (e.g., notes home, phone calls, etc.) to share information about the student's progress. The parents may reinforce the student at home for not tattling.

29. Write a contract with the student specifying what behavior is expected (e.g., not tattling) and what reinforcement will be made available when the terms of the contract have been met.

30. Reinforce the student for demonstrating appropriate behavior based on the length of time the student can be successful. As the student demonstrates success, gradually increase the length of time required for reinforcement.

31. Reinforce those students in the classroom who do not tattle.

32. Establish classroom rules:
- Concentrate while working.
- Remain in your seat.
- Finish task.
- Meet task expectations.
- Raise your hand.

Review rules often. Reinforce students for following the rules.

33. Speak to the student to explain (a) what the student is doing wrong (e.g., tattling) and (b) what the student should be doing (e.g., attending to his/her own activities).

34. Reinforce the student for demonstrating appropriate behavior: (a) give the student a tangible reward (e.g., classroom privileges, line leading, passing out materials, five minutes free time, etc.) or (b) give the student an intangible reward (e.g., praise, fist bump, smile, etc.).

1. Structure the environment to limit opportunities for inappropriate behaviors (e.g., keep the student engaged in activities, have the student seated near the teacher, etc.).

2. Teach the student the concept of sharing by having the student loan items and requiring him/her to return items taken from others.

3. Identify those things the student has been grabbing from others and provide the student with those items as reinforcers for appropriate behavior.

4. Reduce the opportunity to take things from other students by restricting students from bringing unnecessary items to school.

5. Maintain visibility to and from the student. The teacher should be able to see the student; the student should be able to see the teacher. Make eye contact possible at all times.

6. Supervise the student to monitor behavior.

7. Encourage all students to monitor their own belongings.

8. Make sure the student has his/her own necessary school-related items (e.g., pencil, ruler, paper, etc.).

9. Use a permanent marker to label all property brought to school by students and teachers.

10. Secure all school items of value (e.g., recorded material, lab materials, industrial arts and home economics supplies, etc.).

11. Make sure the student understands the natural consequences of inappropriate behavior (e.g., the student must make restitution for taking things which belong to others).

12. Communicate with the student's family to establish procedures whereby the student may earn those things he/she would otherwise take from other students.

13. Teach the student to share (e.g., schedule activities daily which require sharing).

14. Help the student build or create a prized possession to satisfy the need for ownership (e.g., this can be done in art, home economics, industrial arts, etc.).

15. Deal with the grabbing of belongings privately rather than publicly.

16. Provide multiples of the items which are being taken to have enough for all or most students to use (e.g., pencils, erasers, rulers, etc.).

17. Intervene early when there is a problem to prevent more serious problems from occurring.

18. Teach the student to respect others and their belongings by respecting the student's belongings.

19. Make sure the student does not become involved in overstimulating activities when playing with others.

20. Choose a peer who will be a good influence (e.g., someone younger/older, of the same gender, of the opposite gender, etc.).

21. Teach the student acceptable ways to communicate displeasure, anger, frustration, etc.

22. Do not assume the student is being treated nicely by others. Peers may be stimulating inappropriate behavior.

23. Teach the student to ask for things in a positive manner. Teach key words and phrases (e.g., "May I borrow your pencil?" "Do you mind if I play with your ball?" etc.).

24. Teach the student the concept of sharing by having the student borrow from others. Require him/her to ask permission before doing so.

25. Teach the student to take turns sharing possessions (e.g., each child may use the markers for 15 minutes, one child bats while the other throws the ball then players change places after three hits, etc.).

26. Provide the student with enough items that sharing will not be necessary. As the student learns to share, gradually reduce the number of items.

27. Teach the student to think before acting by asking himself/herself questions: *What is happening?, What am I doing?, What should I do?, What will be best for me?*

28. Write a contract with the student specifying what behavior is expected (e.g., not grabbing things away from others) and what reinforcement will be made available when the terms of the contract have been met.

29. Reinforce those students in the classroom who demonstrate appropriate behavior in reference to others' belongings.

30. Remove the student from the group or activity until he/she can demonstrate appropriate behavior and self-control.

31. Reinforce the student for demonstrating appropriate behavior based on the length of time the student can be successful. As the student demonstrates success, gradually increase the length of time required for reinforcement.

32. Establish classroom rules:
- Concentrate while working.
- Work quietly.
- Remain in your seat.
- Finish task.
- Meet task requirements.

Review rules often. Reinforce the student for following the rules.

33. Communicate with the parents (e.g., notes home, phone calls, etc.) to share information about the student's appropriate behavior . The parents may reinforce the student at home for appropriate use or consideration of others' belongings at school.

34. Speak with the student to explain (a) what the student is doing wrong (e.g., grabbing things from others) and (b) what the student should be doing (e.g., asking to use things, borrowing, sharing, returning, etc.).

35. Reinforce the student for demonstrating appropriate behavior: (a) give the student a tangible reward (e.g., classroom privileges, line leading, passing out materials, five minutes free time, etc.) or (b) give the student an intangible reward (e.g., praise, fist bump, smile, etc.).

1. Communicate with the parents (e.g., notes home, phone calls, etc.) to share information about their child's appropriate behavior. The parents may reinforce the student at home for waiting his/her turn to speak at school.

2. Give adequate opportunities to respond (i.e., enthusiastic students need many opportunities to contribute).

3. Structure the environment to limit opportunities for interrupting the teacher (e.g., keep the student engaged in activities, have the student seated near the teacher, etc.).

4. Instruct the student to carry a notepad with him/her at all times and to write information down to help him/her remember.

5. Maintain a full schedule of activities. Keeping the student occupied should prevent interruptive behavior from occurring.

6. Educate yourself and others about ADHD to increase understanding and accommodation of interruptive behavior.

7. Help the student develop an awareness of himself/herself and those around him/her. Have the student periodically step back and ask himself/herself, "Am I interrupting others?"

8. Educate the student about ADHD and the need for developing skills to self monitor behavior.

9. Provide constant, positive reinforcement for appropriate behavior. Ignore as many inappropriate behaviors as possible.

10. Teach the student to use techniques such as crossing his/her arms and legs, clenching his/her fists, and intertwining his/her fingers when he/she feels the urge to interrupt.

11. Explain to the student when he/she interrupts that you are talking now and he/she may talk to you in a few moments.

12. Talk to the student before beginning an activity and remind him/her of the importance of listening and not interrupting.

13. Reinforce those students in the classroom who wait their turn to speak.

14. Provide the student with a clearly understood list of consequences for inappropriate behavior.

15. Reduce the emphasis on competition. Competitive activities may cause the student to become overexcited and interrupt others.

16. Choose a peer, paraprofessional, friend, etc., to cue the student when he/she interrupts others (e.g., the person can touch the student's arm as a signal that he/she is interrupting).

17. Speak with the student to explain (a) what he/she is doing wrong (e.g., interrupting the teacher) and (b) what he/she should be doing (e.g., waiting until it is appropriate to speak, waiting to be called on, etc.).

18. Make sure that the student's feelings are considered when it is necessary to discuss his/her interruptions (i.e., use comments that do not diminish the student's enthusiasm for participation).

19. Reinforce the student for waiting for a turn to speak based on the length of time the student can be successful. As the student demonstrates success, gradually increase the length of time required for reinforcement.

20. Reinforce the student for waiting for a turn to speak: (a) give the student a tangible reward (e.g., classroom privileges, passing out materials, five minutes free time, etc.) or (b) give the student an intangible reward (e.g., praise, fist bump, smile, etc.).

21. Have the student practice waiting for short periods of time for a turn to speak. As the student demonstrates success, gradually increase the length of time required for a turn to speak.

22. Remove the student from the group or activity until he/she can demonstrate appropriate behavior and self-control.

23. Call on the student when he/she is most likely to be able to respond correctly.

24. Encourage the student to remind himself/herself to wait when he/she feels the need to interrupt (e.g., "Stop. Count to ten.").

25. Teach appropriate social rituals (e.g., excuse yourself before interrupting, wait until someone stops speaking to begin talking, etc.).

26. Deliver directions, explanations, and instructions in a clear, concise manner to reduce the student's need to ask questions.

27. Instruct the student on how to interrupt for an emergency. Make sure he/she does it in a way which conveys the urgency (e.g., "I'm sorry for interrupting." "May I stop you for a minute?" etc.).

28. Explain to the student why it is inappropriate to interrupt the teacher (e.g., impolite, unfair to other students, others cannot hear what the teacher is saying, etc.).

29. Have the student make a list of consequences associated with frequently occurring behaviors (e.g., by disrupting others, I will be perceived as unmannerly; by behaving aggressively, people will avoid me.).

30. Make sure that reinforcement is not inadvertently given for inappropriate behavior (e.g., the teacher responds to the student after he/she has interrupted).

31. Make sure that you do not interrupt others. If you interrupt others, the student will continue to do so.

32. Acknowledge the student's presence and/or need to talk with you (e.g., by saying, "Just a minute"; putting your arm around the student; smiling and nodding your head; etc.).

33. Establish rules for conversing with others (e.g., wait your turn to talk, stand quietly by the person with whom you want to talk until you are acknowledged, excuse yourself when you interrupt others, etc.). These rules should be consistent and followed by everyone in the class. Talk about the rules often.

34. Provide the student with a predetermined signal if he/she begins to interrupt.

35. Reinforce the student for raising his/her hand to be recognized.

36. Have the student identify the situations in which he/she is most likely to interrupt. After he/she has identified these situations, have him/her think of ways to minimize their occurrences.

37. Help the student improve concentration skills (e.g., listening to the speaker, taking notes, preparing comments in advance, making comments in the appropriate context, etc.).

38. Be consistent in expecting the student to behave appropriately during class lectures. Do not allow the student to interrupt one time and expect him/her not to interrupt the next time.

39. Write a contract with the student specifying what behavior is expected (e.g., waiting for a turn to speak) and what reinforcement will be made available when the terms of the contract have been met.

40. Treat the student with respect. Talk in an objective manner at all times.

41. Encourage the student to realize that all behavior has negative or positive consequences. Encourage the student to practice behaviors that will lead to positive consequences.

42. Maintain visibility to and from the student to keep his/her attention when verbal questions/directions are being delivered. The teacher should be able to see the student and the student should be able to see the teacher. Make eye contact possible at all times.

43. Reduce activities which might cause the student to interrupt or talk out (e.g., announcing test score ranges or test scores aloud, emphasizing the success of a particular student or students, etc.).

44. Teach the student to recognize the appropriate time to speak (e.g., when the teacher has finished speaking, after raising his/her hand, to make comments within the context of the situation, to make comments that are a follow-up to what has just been said, etc.).

45. Do not reinforce the student's behavior by letting him/her talk to you at the time he/she interrupts. Tell the student that he/she will need to wait until you are finished talking. Allowing the student to talk after interrupting reinforces the behavior and may increase the number of times he/she interrupts others.

46. Do not criticize when correcting the student; be honest yet supportive. Never cause the student to feel negatively about himself/herself.

47. Make the student aware of the number of times he/she interrupts the teacher.

48. Encourage the student to model the behavior of peers who are successful at not interrupting the teacher.

49. Give the student frequent opportunities to join in conversations with others by allowing him/her time to talk, asking him/her to restate an experience, etc.

50. Interact frequently with the student to reduce the need for him/her to interrupt.

51. Attempt to provide equal attention to all students in the classroom.

52. Make sure that the student understands the relationship between inappropriate behavior and the consequences which follow (e.g., others ignoring him/her, hurting others' feelings, etc.).

53. Demonstrate to the student the appropriate way to get someone's attention without interrupting.

54. Do not interrupt the student when he/she is doing something, talking to someone, etc.

55. Make the necessary adjustments in the environment (e.g., reduce peer pressure, academic failure, teasing, etc.) to prevent the student from experiencing stress, frustration, or anger.

56. Hold the student responsible for his/her actions. Do not allow the student to use ADHD as an excuse. However, understand and accept problems ADHD brings into the student's life while he/she is learning to make accommodations.

57. Make sure the student knows when it is acceptable to interrupt others (e.g., in an emergency).

J. Depression/Motivation

142 Has unexcused absences

1. Communicate with parents, agencies, or the appropriate parties to inform them of the problem, determine the cause of the problem, and consider possible solutions to the problem.

2. Have the student document personal attendance at the end of each school day (e.g., have the student maintain a record of attendance in the library, office, etc., and fill in the data at the end of each day).

3. Begin the day or class with a success-oriented activity which is likely to be highly reinforcing for the student.

4. Give the student a responsibility to be performed at the beginning of each day or each class (e.g., feeding the classroom pet, helping to get the classroom ready for the day, etc.).

5. Reinforce the student for getting on the bus or leaving home on time.

6. Assess the degree of task difficulty in comparison with the student's ability to perform the task successfully.

7. Provide the student with as many high-interest activities as possible.

8. Involve the student in extracurricular activities.

9. Provide the student with many opportunities for social and academic successes.

10. Provide the student with academic activities presented in the most attractive and interesting manner possible.

11. Require the student's attendance to be documented by his/her teachers (e.g., have teachers sign an attendance card).

12. Interact frequently with the student in a positive manner throughout the day.

13. Collect anecdotal information on the student's absences/tardies. If a trend can be determined, remove the student from the situation, modify the situation, or help the student develop the skills to be more successful in the situation.

14. Have the parent bring the student to school.

15. Choose a responsible peer to accompany the student to school/activities.

16. Establish a time for the student to leave his/her home in the morning.

17. Require that time spent away from class/school be made up at recess, during lunch, or after school.

18. Make sure the student is appropriately placed according to ability level in those classes in which he/she is enrolled (e.g., the class is not too difficult, the class is not too easy).

19. Reduce the emphasis on competition. Repeated failure may cause the student to be absent to avoid competitive situations.

20. Help the student develop friendships which may encourage his/her attendance in school/class.

21. Maintain open communication with the student's family to make sure that the student is leaving for school at the designated time.

22. Do not force the student to interact with others or do things that make him/her uncomfortable and would cause the student to want to be absent.

23. Make sure the student and parents are aware of the laws involving attendance in school.

24. Communicate with the parents (e.g., notes home, phone calls, etc.) to share information about the student's progress. The parents may reinforce the student at home for school attendance.

25. Write a contract with the student specifying what behavior is expected (e.g., being in attendance) and what reinforcement will be made available when the terms of the contract have been met.

26. Reinforce those students who attend school/class.

27. Reinforce the student for coming to school/class or arriving at an activity at the specified time: (a) give the student a tangible reward (e.g., classroom privileges, line leading, passing out materials, five minutes free time, etc.) or (b) give the student an intangible reward (e.g., praise, fist bump, smile, etc.).

28. Establish classroom rules:
- Concentrate while working.
- Work quietly.
- Remain in your seat.
- Finish task.
- Meet task requirements.

Review rules often. Reinforce the student for following the rules.

29. Speak with the student to explain (a) what the student is doing wrong (e.g., being absent from school/class and (b) what the student should be doing (e.g., being in attendance).

1. Provide the student with a schedule of daily events so he/she will know which activities to attend and at what times.

2. Make sure that the student's daily schedule follows an established routine.

3. Limit the number of interruptions in the student's schedule.

4. Make sure the student has adequate time to get to an activity.

5. Make sure that the student knows how to get from one activity to another.

6. Use a timer to help the student get to activities at specified times.

7. Give the student a responsibility to be performed at the beginning of each day or each class (e.g., feeding the classroom pet, helping to get the classroom ready for the day, etc.).

8. Provide the student with verbal cues when it is time to change activities (e.g., "It is time for the red group to have reading." "Now it is time for the red group to put away materials and move to the next activity.").

9. Determine why the student is not arriving at activities at the specified times.

10. Ask the student the reason for not arriving at activities at the specified times. The student may have the most accurate explanation as to why he/she is absent/tardy.

11. Help the student understand that it is permissible to leave work unfinished and return to it at a later time.

12. Determine if there are aspects of activities that the student dislikes. Remove, reduce, or modify the unpleasant aspects of activities to encourage the student to be on time for and participate in activities.

13. Make the student responsible for time missed (e.g., if the student misses five minutes of an activity, he/she must make up the time during recess, lunch, or other desired activities).

14. Choose a responsible peer to accompany the student to school/activities.

15. Make sure that the student is successful in school-related activities. The student will be more likely to be present/prompt if he/she experiences success.

16. Make the student a leader of the activity or group.

17. Make sure that other students do not make it unpleasant for the student to attend activities.

18. Make sure the student has all the necessary materials for activities.

19. Record or chart attendance/promptness with the student.

20. Begin the day or class with a success-oriented activity which is likely to be highly reinforcing for the student.

21. Provide the student with as many high-interest activities as possible.

22. Provide the student with many opportunities for social and academic successes.

23. Provide the student with academic activities presented in the most attractive and interesting manner possible.

24. Give the student a schedule of daily events to be signed by each teacher to document promptness.

25. Collect anecdotal information on the student's absences/tardies. If a trend can be determined, remove the student from the situation, modify the situation, or help the student develop the skills to be more successful in the situation.

26. Have the student document personal attendance at the end of each activity.

27. Make sure the student is appropriately placed according to ability level in those classes in which he/she is enrolled (e.g., the class is not too difficult, the class is not too easy).

28. Reduce the emphasis on competition. Repeated failure may cause the student to be tardy or absent to avoid competitive situations.

29. Involve the student in extracurricular activities.

30. Interact frequently with the student in a positive manner throughout the day.

31. Give the student a responsibility to be performed at the beginning of each activity.

32. Maintain open communication with the student's family to make sure that the student is leaving for school at the designated time.

33. Do not force the student to interact with others or do things that make him/her uncomfortable and would cause the student to want to be absent/tardy.

34. Begin each day with a fun activity which should cause the student to want to attend and be on time for class.

35. Communicate with the parents (e.g., notes home, phone calls, etc.) to share information about the student's progress. The parents may reinforce the student at home for school attendance/promptness.

36. Write a contract with the student specifying what behavior is expected (e.g., coming to school/class on time) and what reinforcement will be made available when the terms of the contract have been met.

37. Reinforce the student for arriving at an activity within a given period of time. As the student becomes more successful at being punctual, gradually reduce the length of time the student has to arrive at an activity.

38. Reinforce those students in the classroom who come to an activity at the specified time.

39. Establish classroom rules:
- Concentrate while working.
- Work quietly.
- Remain in your seat.
- Finish task.
- Meet task requirements.

Review rules often. Reinforce the student for following the rules.

40. Speak with the student to explain (a) what the student is doing wrong (e.g., coming late to an activity) and (b) what the student should be doing (e.g., arriving at an activity at the specified time).

41. Reinforce the student for arriving at an activity at the specified time: (a) give the student a tangible reward (e.g., classroom privileges, line leading, passing out materials, five minutes free time, etc.) or (b) give the student an intangible reward (e.g., praise, fist bump, smile, etc.).

42. Choose a peer to model arriving at an activity at the specified time for the student.

144 Blames other persons or materials to avoid taking responsibility for his/her mistakes or failures

1. Structure the environment for the student to reduce interference from peers (e.g., remove the opportunity to blame others).

2. Teach the student problem-solving skills: (a) identify the problem, (b) identify goals and objectives, (c) develop strategies, (d) develop a plan of action, and (e) carry out the plan.

3. Provide the student with many opportunities for social and academic successes.

4. Make the necessary adjustments in the environment to prevent the student from experiencing stress, frustration, anger, etc.

5. Provide the student with positive feedback which indicates he/she is successful, competent, important, valuable, etc.

6. Make sure that excuses are not accepted in place of meeting responsibility.

7. Make sure that all materials are appropriate and in good working order.

8. Be sure to assist the student when he/she indicates a need for help.

9. Provide the student with all the necessary information prior to an activity to facilitate the likelihood of success.

10. Reduce stimuli in the environment which may contribute to the student's failures or difficulties.

11. Provide the student with a quiet place to work. This is used as a form of reducing distracting stimuli and not as a form of punishment.

12. Give assignments which will ensure initial success. As the student's ability and responsibility increases, gradually increase the level of difficulty of assignments.

13. Make sure that instructions and expectations are clearly stated.

14. Reduce the emphasis on competition. Repeated failure may result in the student blaming someone or something for his/her own failure.

15. Encourage the student to begin assignments early to have time to deal with problems which may arise.

16. Provide the student with a schedule of daily events to plan his/her time accordingly.

17. When the student blames others for his/her behavior, calmly present the student with the facts. Encourage an open and honest line of communication. Do not make the student fearful of telling the truth even though you may not be happy about the behavior.

18. Help the student to feel comfortable coming to you for assistance with a problem by listening and helping with a solution to the problem.

19. Be consistent with the student. Do not discipline for misbehavior one time and ignore misbehavior the next time.

20. The student must understand that, regardless of the reason, it is necessary to take responsibility for not turning in assignments, losing pencils, etc.

21. Do not put the student in a situation where the student feels that he/she must blame others for his/her mistakes.

22. Evaluate the appropriateness of the task to determine (a) if the task is too easy, (b) if the task is too difficult, and (c) if the length of time scheduled to complete the task is adequate.

23. Avoid arguing with the student concerning whether or not he/she is making excuses; simply explain that he/she is not being completely honest about a situation.

24. Make sure that consequences delivered for inappropriate behavior are not extreme and are directly related to the inappropriate behavior (e.g., things that are destroyed must be replaced, work not done during work time has to be made up during recreational time, etc.).

25. Avoid arguing with the student concerning whether or not he/she is telling the truth. If you do not have proof, it is better to avoid blaming someone who might be innocent.

26. Always determine the accuracy of the student's claim that someone or something caused him/her to have a problem or to fail. In some cases someone or something may legitimately be causing the student to experience problems or failure.

27. Make sure the student understands that not being honest when confronted will result in more negative consequences than telling the truth. Be sure to be very consistent in this approach.

28. Explain to the student that he/she should be satisfied with personal best effort rather than perfection.

29. Attempt to have an open, honest relationship with the student. Encourage the student to tell the truth, and do not use threats to make him/her tell the truth (e.g., "You had better tell the truth or else!").

30. Reinforce those students in the classroom who accept responsibility for their own behavior.

31. Communicate with parents (e.g., notes home, phone calls, etc.) to share information about the student's progress. The parents may reinforce the student at home for accepting the responsibility for his/her behavior at school.

32. Write a contract with the student specifying what behavior is expected (e.g., accepting responsibility for his/her own mistakes) and what reinforcement will be made available when the terms of the contract have been met.

33. Reinforce the student for accepting responsibility for his/her own behavior based on the length of time the student can be successful. As the student demonstrates success, gradually increase the length of time required for reinforcement.

34. Establish classroom rules:
- Concentrate while working.
- Work quietly.
- Remain in your seat.
- Finish task.
- Meet task requirements.

Review rules often. Reinforce the student for following the rules.

35. Speak with the student to explain (a) what the student is doing wrong (e.g., failing to take responsibility for his/her behavior, blaming other persons or materials, etc.) and (b) what the student should be doing (e.g., accepting responsibility for his/her own behavior, accepting outcomes, etc.).

36. Reinforce the student for accepting responsibility for his/her own behavior: (a) give the student a tangible reward (e.g., classroom privileges, line leading, passing out materials, five minutes free time, etc.) or (b) give the student an intangible reward (e.g., praise, fist bump, smile, etc.).

37. Remove the student from the group or activity until the student can accept responsibility for his/her behavior.

145 Does not participate or demonstrate an interest in classroom activities or special events that are interesting to other students

1. Encourage or reward others for participation in group or special activities.

2. Give the student the responsibility of helping another student in the group.

3. Give the student responsibilities in a group so others might view him/her in a positive way.

4. Ask the student questions that cannot be answered yes or no.

5. Call on the student when he/she is most likely to be able to respond successfully (e.g., when discussing something in which the student is interested, when the teacher is sure the student knows the answer, etc.).

6. Try various groupings to determine the situation in which the student is most successful.

7. Have peers invite the student to participate in school or extracurricular activities.

8. Ask the student to be the leader of a small group activity if he/she possesses mastery or an interest in the activity.

9. Allow the student to observe group activities without requiring active participation.

10. Reduce the emphasis on competition. Frequent or continuous failure is likely to result in embarrassment which may cause reluctance to participate.

11. Demonstrate respect for the student's opinions, responses, suggestions, etc.

12. Provide the student with many opportunities for social and academic successes.

13. Provide the student with positive feedback which indicates he/she is successful.

14. Present tasks in the most attractive and interesting manner possible.

15. Determine the student's interests so activities which require participation might be presented through his/her interests.

16. Have the student choose a special event or interesting activity for the class.

17. Provide the student with success-oriented special events or activities so he/she may develop an interest in them.

18. Modify or adjust situations that cause the student to be reluctant to participate (e.g., degree of difficulty, competition, fear of failure, threat of embarrassment, etc.).

19. Emphasize individual success or progress rather than winning or beating other students.

20. Provide the student with opportunities for small-group participation as opposed to large-group participation.

21. Encourage the student to participate in small groups. As the student demonstrates success, gradually increase the size of the group.

22. Encourage the student to share things of special interest with other members of the class.

23. Choose a peer to model appropriate interactions in classroom activities for the student.

24. Have the student ask question about directions, explanations, and instructions not understood.

25. Have the student choose a group of peers with whom he/she feels comfortable.

26. Determine the peers the student would most prefer to interact with in classroom activities and facilitate the interaction.

27. Choose outgoing, nonthreatening peers to help the student participate in classroom activities.

28. Structure the environment so the student has many opportunities to interact with other peers in classroom activities.

29. Assign the student to classroom activities in which he/she is likely to interact successfully with peers.

30. Conduct a sociometric activity with the class to determine those peers who would most prefer to interact with the student in classroom activities.

31. Teach the student appropriate ways to interact with peers in classroom activities (e.g., share materials, problem solving, take turns, talk, etc.).

32. Supervise classroom activities closely so peers with whom the student interacts do not stimulate inappropriate behavior.

33. Make sure that the classroom activity is not so stimulating as to make successful interactions with peers difficult.

34. Teach the student problem-solving skills to better deal with problems that may occur in interactions with peers in classroom activities (e.g., talking, walking away, calling upon an arbitrator, compromising, etc.).

35. Limit opportunities for interaction in classroom activities on those occasions when the student is not likely to be successful (e.g., when the student has experienced academic or social failure prior to the scheduled classroom activity).

36. Select nonacademic activities designed to facilitate appropriate social interaction between the student and peers during classroom activities (e.g., board games, model building, coloring, etc.).

37. Treat the student with respect. Talk in an objective manner at all times.

38. Through interviews with other students and observations, determine those characteristics of the student which interfere with successful interactions during classroom activities. Use the information gained to determine skills or behaviors the student needs to develop for successful interactions.

39. Have the student practice appropriate interactions with the teacher(s) in classroom activities (e.g., simulations, role-playing, etc.).

40. Make sure, beforehand, that the student is able to successfully participate in the classroom activity (e.g., the student understands the rules, is familiar with the activity, will be compatible with peers engaged in the activity, etc.).

41. Make sure the student has the necessary materials for the classroom activity.

42. Assign the student responsibilities to perform during classroom activities to facilitate peer interaction (e.g., being a leader, passing out materials, being a peer tutor, etc.).

43. Make sure the student knows how to use all materials for the classroom activity.

44. Do not punish the student for not participating in classroom activities or special events.

45. Do not force the student to interact with someone with whom he/she is not completely comfortable.

46. Do not embarrass the student by giving him/her orders, demands, etc., in front of others.

47. Make positive comments about participating in school and special events.

48. Do not force the student to interact with individuals with whom he/she is not completely comfortable.

49. Go with the student or have someone else accompany the student to those activities in which he/she may not want to participate. Gradually decrease the length of time you or someone else stays with the student.

50. Carefully consider those activities the student avoids. If something unpleasant is causing the student not to participate, try to modify the situation.

51. Reinforce other students in the classroom for participating in group activities or special events.

52. Choose a peer to sit/work directly with the student (e.g., in different settings or activities such as art, music, P.E., tutoring, group projects, recess, etc.). When the student has become comfortable working with one other student, gradually increase the size of the group.

53. Evaluate the appropriateness of the task to determine (a) if the task is too easy, (b) if the task is too difficult, and (c) if the length of time scheduled to complete the task is adequate.

54. Communicate with parents (e.g., notes home, phone calls, etc.) to share information about the student's progress. The parents may reinforce the student at home for participating in classroom activities or special events at school.

55. Write a contract with the student specifying what behavior is expected (e.g., taking part in classroom activities) and what reinforcement will be made available when the terms of the contract have been met.

56. Give the student the opportunity to pick a topic or activity for the group to work on together.

57. Speak with the student to explain (a) what the student is doing wrong (e.g., failing to take part) and (b) what the student should be doing (e.g., talking, taking turns, playing, sharing, etc.).

58. Reinforce the student for participating in group activities or special events: (a) give the student a tangible reward (e.g., classroom privileges, line leading, passing out materials, five minutes free time, etc.) or (b) give the student an intangible reward (e.g., praise, fist bump, smile, etc.).

59. Establish classroom rules:
- Concentrate while working.
- Work quietly.
- Remain in your seat.
- Finish task.
- Meet task requirements.

Review rules often. Reinforce the student for following the rules.

60. Give the student the opportunity to choose a group activity and the group members (e.g., along with the teacher decide what the activity will be, decide what individual group members will do, etc.).

61. Have the student participate in activities which require minimal participation. As he/she becomes more comfortable, gradually increase the student's participation.

Reminder: Do not force the student to take part in any activity or special event.

1. Explain to the student that he/she should be happy with his/her best effort rather than perfection.

2. Reinforce the student for taking responsibilities for errors that he/she makes.

3. Speak with the student to explain (a) what he/she is doing wrong (e.g., being overly critical of himself/herself) and (b) what he/she should be doing (e.g., being more constructive in self-criticism when evaluating himself/herself).

4. Reward others for taking responsibilities for errors they make.

5. Write a contract with the student specifying what behavior is expected (e.g., accepting his/her best effort) and what reinforcement will be made available when the terms of the contract have been met.

6. Evaluate the appropriateness of the task to determine (a) if the task is too easy, (b) if the task is too difficult, and (c) if the length of time scheduled for the task is adequate.

7. Reinforce the student for improvement rather than expecting excellence.

8. Acknowledge the student often and in various settings (e.g., hallways, cafeteria, etc.).

9. Provide the student with positive feedback which indicates he/she is successful, competent, important, valuable, etc.

10. Provide the student with success-oriented tasks (i.e., the expectation is that success will result in more positive attitudes and perceptions toward self and environment).

11. Provide the student with many opportunities for social and academic successes.

12. Make the necessary adjustments in the environment to prevent the student from experiencing stress, frustration, etc.

13. Choose a peer to help the student with class assignments, homework, etc.

14. Emphasize individual differences and that everyone has strengths and weaknesses.

15. Reduce the emphasis on competition and perfection. Repeated failure may result in unwarranted self-blame or self-criticism.

16. Encourage the student to refrain from comparing his/her performance to other students' performances and emphasize personal improvement (e.g., maintain records of own progress rather than comparing work to others).

17. Provide the student with evidence of his/her ability so that he/she might better understand that self-blame/criticism is unwarranted.

18. Deliver praise and constructive criticism consistently to all students.

19. Reduce activities which might threaten the student (e.g., announcing test score ranges or test scores aloud, making students read aloud in class, emphasizing the success of a particular student(s), etc.).

20. Call on the student when he/she will most likely be able to answer correctly.

21. Have the student regularly record his/her own progress to have tangible evidence of success.

22. Encourage the student to be a peer tutor so he/she may recognize his/her own strengths and abilities.

23. When accidents occur, make cleanup a group responsibility to convey the idea that we all make mistakes and accidents are common to all of us.

Reminder: Make sure that the self-blame or self-criticism is in fact unwarranted.

147 Expresses concerns or worries about school, home, or personal situations through words or pictures

1. Discuss concerns with other professionals to determine if further investigation is warranted (e.g., abuse or neglect).

2. Record or chart the number of times the student writes about fears or concerns regarding school, home, or personal situations to make the student aware of the frequency of his/her behavior.

3. Take the time to listen so the student realizes that your concern is genuine.

4. Explain that fears and concerns are not unusual for students (e.g., everyone worries about tests, grades, etc.).

5. Identify persons the student may contact with his/her fears and concerns (e.g., guidance counselor, school nurse, social worker, school psychologist, etc.).

6. Discuss ways in which to practice self-improvement.

7. Provide the student with opportunities for social and academic success.

8. Separate the student from a peer who may be encouraging or stimulating fears or concerns about school, home, or personal situations.

9. Reduce the emphasis on competition. Repeated failure may result in anxiety about performance at school, home, and in personal situations.

10. Provide parents with necessary information to help the student with homework and study activities at home.

11. Make the necessary adjustments in the environment to prevent the student from experiencing stress, frustration, anxiety, etc.

12. Structure the environment so time does not permit opportunities for the student to dwell on fears or concerns.

13. Provide the student with alternative approaches to testing (e.g., test the student verbally, make the tests shorter, allow the student to respond verbally, allow the student to take the test in the resource room, etc.).

14. Have peers invite the student to participate in extracurricular activities.

15. Emphasize individual differences and that everybody has strengths and weaknesses.

16. Reduce activities which might threaten the student (e.g., announcing test score ranges or test scores aloud in class, emphasizing the success of a particular student(s), etc.).

17. Provide the student with positive feedback which indicates he/she is successful, competent, important, valuable, etc.

18. Seek assistance from the school counselor, the principal, other teachers, etc., to help the student deal with fears and concerns about school, home, and personal problems so he/she can concentrate at school.

19. Encourage the student to use problem-solving skills: (a) identify the problem, (b) identify goals and objectives, (c) develop strategies, (d) develop a plan of action, and (e) carry out the plan.

20. Provide praise and recognition as often as possible.

21. Call attention to the student's accomplishments (e.g., publicly or privately depending on which is more appropriate).

22. Encourage participation in school and extracurricular activities.

23. Try various groupings to determine the situation in which the student is most successful.

24. Demonstrate respect for the student's opinions, responses, suggestions, etc.

25. Avoid discussion of topics sensitive to the student (e.g., divorce, death, unemployment, alcoholism, etc.).

26. Provide the student with opportunities for special project responsibilities, leadership, etc.

27. Provide the student with as many enjoyable and interesting activities as possible.

28. Reinforce the student for improvement rather than expecting excellence.

29. Treat the student with respect. Talk in an objective manner at all times.

30. Maintain trust and confidentiality with the student at all times.

31. Encourage participation in school and extracurricular activities.

32. Provide opportunities for tutoring from peers or a teacher.

33. Choose a peer to sit/work directly with the student.

1. Conduct a reinforcer survey with the student to determine his/her reinforcer preferences.

2. Communicate with parents to determine what the student finds reinforcing at home.

3. Present tasks in the most attractive, interesting manner possible.

4. Write a contract with the student so he/she can earn reinforcement at home for appropriate behavior at school.

5. Make sure that the student can be successful at school to earn reinforcement.

6. Provide a wide variety of reinforcers for the student at school (e.g., eating lunch with the teacher; one-to-one time with the teacher, principal's assistant, assistant to the custodian; extra time in a favorite class, etc.).

7. Reinforce or praise the student in private. Public reinforcement might embarrass the student.

8. Make an agreement with the parents that access to enjoyable activities at home (e.g., watching television, riding bike, visiting with friends, etc.) will be contingent upon appropriate behavior at school.

9. Communicate with parents, agencies, or the appropriate parties to inform them of the problem, determine the cause of the problem, and consider possible solutions to the problem.

10. Provide reinforcers that are social in nature (e.g., extracurricular activities, clubs, community organizations such as 4-H, scouting, YMCA, YWCA, etc.).

11. Help the student develop an interest in a hobby which can be used as a reinforcer at school (e.g., stamp collecting, rock collecting, model building, photography, art, reading, sewing, cooking, etc.).

12. Have the student make a list of reinforcements for which he/she is willing to work.

149 Responds inappropriately to constructive criticism or comments from others

1. Reinforce the student for responding in an appropriate manner to constructive criticism based on the number of times the student can be successful. As the student demonstrates success, gradually increase the number of appropriate responses required for reinforcement.

2. Remove the student from the group or activity until he/she can demonstrate appropriate behavior or self-control.

3. Write a contract with the student specifying what behavior is expected (e.g., responding appropriately to constructive criticism) and what reinforcement will be made available when the terms of the contract have been met.

4. Communicate with the parents (e.g., notes home, phone calls, etc.) to share information about the student's progress. The parents may reinforce the student at home for responding in an appropriate manner to constructive criticism or comments at school.

5. Evaluate the appropriateness of the task to determine (a) if the task is too easy, (b) if the task is too difficult, and (c) if the length of time scheduled for the task is adequate.

6. Demonstrate appropriate ways to respond to constructive criticism.

7. Try various groupings to determine the group in which the student is most comfortable.

8. Provide the student with positive feedback which indicates he/she is successful, competent, important, valuable, etc.

9. Provide the student with many opportunities for social and academic successes.

10. Assess the appropriateness of the social situation in relation to the student's ability to function successfully.

11. Structure the environment so that the teacher is the only one providing constructive criticism. As the student learns to accept constructive criticism from the teacher, allow input from others.

12. Provide constructive criticism in private.

13. Provide constructive criticism equally to all members of the class.

14. Provide constructive criticism when the student is most likely to demonstrate an appropriate response.

15. Make sure that positive reinforcement is not inadvertently given for inappropriate responses (e.g., lowering expectations because the student becomes upset when constructive criticism is delivered).

16. Make sure the student receives adequate, positive reinforcement whenever he/she is responding in an appropriate manner.

17. Assess criticism to make sure it is constructive and positive.

18. Have the student ask questions about anything he/she does not understand while performing assignments.

19. Encourage the student to check and correct his/her own work.

20. Explain to the student that constructive criticism is meant to be helpful, not threatening.

21. Reduce the emphasis on competition and perfection. A highly competitive atmosphere or repeated failure may cause the student to react in inappropriate ways to constructive criticism from others.

22. Make the necessary adjustments in the environment to prevent the student from experiencing stress, frustration, anger, etc.

23. Provide the student with academic tasks which can be self-checked.

24. Supervise the student while he/she is performing tasks to monitor quality.

25. Provide the student with clearly stated criteria for acceptable work.

26. Make sure that constructive criticism is tactfully conveyed.

27. Offer assistance at the same time constructive criticism is delivered.

28. Require a demonstration of ability rather than having the student perform the entire assignment or activity again (e.g., work a few problems correctly rather than repeating the entire assignment).

29. Choose a peer to model appropriate responses to constructive criticism for the student.

30. Have the student ask questions about directions, explanations, and instructions not understood.

31. Allow natural consequences to occur when the student does not respond appropriately to constructive criticism (e.g., make highly reinforcing activities contingent upon responding appropriately to redirection in academic and social situations).

32. Make sure that attention is not inadvertently given to the student for failing to respond appropriately to constructive criticism (i.e., remove attention from the student when he/she fails to respond appropriately to redirection in academic and social situations if the attention is reinforcing his/her inappropriate behavior).

33. Provide adequate time for the student to respond appropriately to constructive criticism.

34. Deliver instructions in a clear and concise manner.

35. Assist the student in responding appropriately to constructive criticism (e.g., help the student correct one or two items to get him/her started).

36. Develop subsequent tasks to be performed the next day based on errors the student makes rather than requiring immediate correction of work done incorrectly.

37. Do not criticize when correcting the student; be honest yet supportive. Never cause the student to feel negatively about himself/herself.

38. Intervene early when there is a problem to prevent more serious problems from occurring.

39. Treat the student with respect. Talk in an objective manner at all times.

40. Do not embarrass the student by giving him/her orders, demands, etc., in front of others.

41. Make sure that comments made to the student take the form of constructive criticism rather than criticism that can be perceived as personal, threatening, etc., (e.g., instead of saying, "You always make the same mistakes." say, "A better way to do that might be . . .").

42. Reinforce those students in the classroom who respond appropriately to constructive criticism.

43. Establish classroom rules:
- Concentrate while working.
- Work quietly.
- Remain in your seat.
- Finish task.
- Meet task requirements.

Review rules often. Reinforce the student for following the rules.

44. Speak with the student to explain (a) what the student is doing wrong (e.g., yelling, cursing, making derogatory comments, crying, etc.) and (b) what the student should be doing (e.g., asking for directions, help, clarification, etc.).

45. Reward others for taking responsibilities for errors they make.

46. Allow the student to attempt something new in private before doing so in front of others.

47. Provide constructive criticism in a private setting rather than in front of others.

48. Reinforce the student for responding in an appropriate manner to constructive criticism: (a) give the student a tangible reward (e.g., classroom privileges, line leading, passing out materials, five minutes free time, etc.) or (b) give the student an intangible reward (e.g., praise, hand-shake, smile, etc.).

150 Tries to avoid situations, assignments, responsibilities

1. Choose a peer to model appropriate participation, performance of assignments, or acceptance of responsibilities for the student.

2. Have the student ask questions about directions, explanations, or instructions not understood.

3. Give the student assignments and responsibilities he/she will enjoy performing (e.g., teacher assistant, line leading, chores in the classroom, etc.). As the student demonstrates success, gradually introduce less desirable assignments and responsibilities.

4. Follow a less desirable activity with a more desirable activity, requiring the student to complete the first to perform the second.

5. Make sure the student understands that leaving the classroom may only be done at regularly scheduled intervals (e.g., during recess, break time, lunch, class changes, etc.).

6. Provide the student with many opportunities for academic and social successes.

7. Assess the appropriateness of the social setting in relation to the student's ability to function successfully (i.e., do not place the student with peers who are threatening to him/her).

8. Plan alternative activities for the student to perform or participate in if he/she has difficulty performing assigned activities. As the student demonstrates success, gradually remove the alternative activities.

9. Allow the student to leave the classroom to get materials from his/her locker, use the restroom, go to the nurse's office, go to the counselor's office, etc., after assignments are completed or responsibilities are performed.

10. Provide the student with positive feedback that indicates he/she is successful, competent, important, valuable, etc.

11. Have the student record and chart his/her own appropriate behavior (e.g., participating in classroom activities, performing assignments, taking responsibilities, etc.).

12. Make sure that reinforcement is not inadvertently given for complaints of physical discomfort (e.g., allowing the student to leave the room, avoid assignments, leave school, etc.).

13. Seek student input in planning the curriculum, extracurricular activities, etc.

14. Reduce the emphasis on competition. Competitive activities may increase the student's anxiety and reduce the student's ability to remember information.

15. Provide the student with a variety of assignments and require the student to choose a minimum number from the total amount to complete (e.g., present the student with ten academic tasks from which six must be finished each day).

16. Explain to the student that work not done during work time must be done during other times (e.g., recreational time, break time, after school, etc.).

17. Give the student a responsibility to be performed at various times throughout the day.

18. Present assignments and responsibilities in the most attractive and interesting manner possible.

19. Interact frequently with the student to maintain his/her involvement in assignments, responsibilities, etc.

20. Make the necessary adjustments in the environment to prevent the student from experiencing stress, frustration, anger, etc., as much as possible.

21. Allow the student to attempt something new in private before doing so in front of others.

22. Identify variables in the environment which cause the student to avoid situations, assignments, or responsibilities; reduce or remove these variables from the environment.

23. Vary the student's assignments and responsibilities so the student does not get tired of doing the same things.

24. Limit the number of assignments and responsibilities for which the student is responsible. As the student demonstrates the ability to complete responsibilities on time, gradually increase the number of assignments and responsibilities.

25. Make sure the student has all the necessary materials to get assignments and responsibilities done on time.

26. Do not accept excuses. The student must understand that, regardless of the reasons, it is necessary that he/she take responsibility for not turning in an assignment, losing pencils, etc.

27. Carefully consider those things the student may be trying to avoid. If something unpleasant is causing the student to pretend to be sick, do all you can to eliminate or reduce the cause.

28. Give the student a special job for assignments (e.g., collecting math papers, passing out materials, sharpening pencils, etc.) to do when the student completes his/her work.

29. Deliver directions in a supportive rather than threatening manner (e.g., "Please turn in your math paper." rather than "You had better turn in your math paper or else!").

30. Sit down with the student and discuss a list of assignments, responsibilities, etc., that he/she needs to do.

31. Assist the student in performing responsibilities. As the student demonstrates success, gradually require him/her to independently assume more responsibility.

32. Schedule the student's work and responsibilities around highly enjoyable activities (e.g., the student may go to recess after the math assignment is finished).

33. Go with the student or have someone else accompany the student to those things he/she may be trying to avoid. As the student demonstrates success, gradually decrease the length of time you or someone else stays with the student.

34. Make positive comments about school and the importance of school.

35. Reinforce those students in the classroom who are participating, performing assignments, or taking responsibilities.

36. Evaluate the appropriateness of the task to determine (a) if the task is too difficult and (b) if the length of time scheduled to complete the task is adequate.

37. Communicate with parents, agencies, or the appropriate parties to inform them of the problem, determine the cause of the problem, and consider possible solutions to the problem.

38. Communicate with parents (e.g., notes home, phone calls, etc.) to share information about the student's progress. The parents may reinforce the student at home for appropriate behavior at school.

39. Write a contract with the student specifying what behavior is expected (e.g., participating, performing assignments, or taking responsibilities) and what reinforcement will be made available when the terms of the contract have been met.

40. Reinforce the student for participating, performing assignments, or taking responsibilities based on the length of time the student can be successful. As the student demonstrates success, gradually increase the length of time required for reinforcement.

41. Set aside time each day for everyone in the classroom to care for belongings.

42. Speak to the student to explain (a) what he/she is doing wrong (e.g., complaining, asking to leave the room, etc.) and (b) what he/she should be doing (e.g., reporting legitimate discomfort or needs).

43. Establish classroom rules:
- Concentrate while working.
- Work quietly.
- Remain in your seat.
- Finish task.
- Meet task requirements.

Review rules often. Reinforce the student for following the rules.

44. Determine if physical discomfort is being used as an excuse to avoid situations and is not the result of a medical problem, neglect, or abuse.

45. Reinforce the student for participating, performing assignments, or taking responsibilities: (a) give the student a tangible reward (e.g., classroom privileges, line leading, passing out materials, five minutes free time, etc.) or (b) give the student an intangible reward (e.g., praise, fist bump, smile, etc.).

Reminder: Do not force the student to participate in any activity.

151 Demonstrates self-destructive behavior

1. Remove the student from the group or activity until he/she can demonstrate appropriate behavior and self-control.

2. Write a contract with the student specifying what behavior is expected (e.g., not engaging in self-destructive behavior) and what reinforcement will be made available when the terms of the contract have been met.

3. Communicate with parents (e.g., notes home, phone calls, etc.) to share information about the student's progress. The parents may reinforce the student at home for appropriate behavior at school.

4. Evaluate the appropriateness of the task to determine (a) if the task is too easy, (b) if the task is too difficult, and (c) if the length of time scheduled to complete the task is adequate.

5. Prevent frustrating or anxiety-producing situations from occurring (e.g., give the student tasks on his/her ability level, give the student the number of tasks that can be tolerated in one sitting, stop social situations which stimulate the student to become self-destructive, etc.).

6. Interact frequently with the student to prevent self-destructive behavior by meeting the student's needs as they occur.

7. Maintain visibility to and from the student. The teacher should be able to see the student, and the student should be able to see the teacher. Make eye contact possible at all times.

8. Facilitate on-task behavior by providing a full schedule of daily events. Prevent lag time from occurring when the student will be free to participate in self-destructive behavior.

9. Remove from the environment any object which the student may use to hurt himself/herself.

10. Provide the student with a quiet place to work (e.g., carrel or study area).

11. Provide the student with positive feedback which indicates he/she is successful, important, respected, etc.

12. Teach the student appropriate ways to communicate displeasure, anger, frustrations, etc.

13. Maintain a positive/calm environment (e.g., deliver positive comments, acknowledgment of successes, quiet communications, etc.).

14. Reduce the emphasis on competition. Repeated failure may result in anger and frustration which may cause the student to try to hurt himself/herself.

15. Talk to the student about ways of handling situations successfully without conflict (e.g., walk away from a situation, change to another activity, ask for help, etc.).

16. Allow the student to have an input relative to making decisions (e.g., changing activities, choosing activities, deciding length of activities, etc.).

17. Provide the student with a selection of optional activities to be performed (e.g., if an activity results in self-destructive behaviors, an optional activity can be substituted).

18. Teach the student appropriate ways to deal with anxiety, frustration, and anger (e.g., move away from the stimulus, verbalize unhappiness, choose another activity, etc.).

19. Teach the student problem-solving skills: (a) identify the problem, (b) identify goals and objectives, (c) develop strategies, (d) develop a plan for action, and (e) carry out the plan.

20. Maintain a consistent daily routine.

21. Avoid discussions or prevent stimuli in the environment which remind the student of unpleasant experiences/sensitive topics (e.g., divorce, death, unemployment, alcoholism, etc.).

22. Do not criticize. When correcting the student, be honest yet supportive. Never cause the student to feel negatively about himself/herself.

23. Intervene early when there is a problem to prevent more serious problems from occurring.

24. Make sure the student does not become involved in overstimulating activities.

25. Treat the student with respect. Talk in an objective manner at all times.

26. Express your feelings in a socially acceptable way.

27. Teach the student to think before acting by asking himself/herself questions: *What is happening?, What am I doing?, What should I do?, What will be best for me?*

28. Allow the student to voice his/her opinion in a situation to avoid becoming angry or upset.

29. Maintain consistent expectations to reduce the likelihood of the student hurting himself/herself.

30. Reinforce the student for demonstrating appropriate behavior based on the length of time the student can be successful. As the student demonstrates success, gradually increase the amount of time required for reinforcement.

31. Reinforce those students in the classroom who participate in appropriate behaviors.

32. Establish classroom rules:
- Concentrate while working.
- Work quietly.
- Remain in your seat.
- Finish task.
- Meet task requirements.

Review rules often. Reinforce the student for following the rules.

33. Speak with the student to explain (a) what the student is doing wrong (e.g., hurting self) and (b) what the student should be doing (e.g., talking about the situation, demonstrating self-control, problem solving, etc.).

34. Reinforce the student for engaging in appropriate behavior: (a) give the student a tangible reward (e.g., classroom privileges, line leading, passing out materials, five minutes free time, etc.) or (b) give the student an intangible reward (e.g., praise, fist bump, smile, etc.).

Note: Help the student accept the fact that self-improvement is more important than getting the highest grade in the class, making all A's, being the first one done with an assignment, etc., by reinforcing and grading on the basis of self-improvement.

1. Remove the student from the group or activity until he/she can demonstrate appropriate behavior and self-control.

2. Communicate with parents (e.g., notes home, phone calls, etc.) to share information about the student's progress. The parents may reinforce the student at home for appropriate behavior at school.

3. Evaluate the appropriateness of the task to determine (a) if the task is too easy, (b) if the task is too difficult, and (c) if the length of time scheduled to complete the task is adequate.

4. Prevent frustrating or anxiety-producing situations from occurring (e.g., give the student tasks on his/her ability level, give the student only the number of tasks that can be tolerated in one sitting, stop social interactions that stimulate the student to threaten self-harm, etc.).

5. Interact frequently with the student to prevent self-abusive behavior by meeting the student's needs as they occur.

6. Maintain visibility to and from the student. The teacher should be able to see the student and the student should be able to see the teacher. Make eye contact possible at all times.

7. Facilitate on-task behavior by providing a full schedule of daily events. Prevent lag time from occurring when the student will be free to participate in self-abusive behavior.

8. Remove from the environment any object that the student may use to hurt himself/herself.

9. Provide the student with positive feedback that indicates he/she is successful, important, respected, etc.

10. Maintain a positive/calm environment (e.g., positive comments, acknowledgment of successes, quiet communications, etc.).

11. Provide the student with a quiet place to work (e.g., carrel, study area).

12. Reduce the emphasis on competition. Repeated failure may result in anger and frustration that may cause the student to try to hurt himself/herself.

13. Maintain consistent expectations.

14. Allow the student to have input relative to making decisions (e.g., changing activities, choosing activities, deciding length of activities, etc.).

15. Provide the student with a selection of optional activities to be performed (e.g., if an activity results in harmful behaviors, an optional activity can be substituted).

16. Teach the student appropriate ways to deal with anxiety, frustration, and anger (e.g., move away from the stimulus, verbalize unhappiness, choose another activity, etc.).

17. Teach the student problem-solving skills: (a) identify the problem, (b) identify goals and objectives, (c) develop strategies, (d) develop a plan of action, and (e) carry out the plan.

18. Maintain a consistent daily routine.

19. Do not allow the student to be unsupervised anywhere in the school environment.

20. Avoid discussions or prevent stimuli in the environment that remind the student of unpleasant experiences/sensitive topics (e.g., divorce, death, unemployment, alcoholism, etc.).

21. Do not criticize. When correcting the student, be honest yet supportive. Never cause the student to feel negatively about himself/herself.

22. Intervene early when there is a problem to prevent more serious problems from occurring.

23. Treat the student with respect. Talk in an objective manner at all times.

24. Maintain trust and confidentiality with the student at all times.

25. Allow the student to voice his/her opinion in a situation to avoid becoming angry or upset.

26. Talk to the student about ways of handling situations successfully without conflict (e.g., walk away from a situation, change to another activity, ask for help, etc.).

27. Reinforce the student for demonstrating appropriate behavior based on the length of time the student can be successful. As the student demonstrates success, gradually increase the amount of time required for reinforcement.

28. Reinforce those students in the classroom who participate in appropriate behavior.

29. Establish classroom rules:
- Concentrate while working.
- Work quietly.
- Remain in your seat.
- Finish task.
- Meet task requirements.

Review rules often. Reinforce the student for following the rules.

30. Speak with the student to explain (a) what the student is doing wrong (e.g., threatening to hurt self) and (b) what the student should be doing (e.g., talking about the situation, demonstrating self-control, problem solving, etc.).

31. Reinforce the student for engaging in appropriate behavior: (a) give the student a tangible reward (e.g., classroom privileges, line leading, passing out materials, five minutes free time, etc.) or (b) give the student an intangible reward (e.g., praise, fist bump, smile, etc.).

32. Share concerns with administration and seek referral to an agency for investigation of abuse or neglect.

33. Investigate the possibility of the student being involved in the use of drugs or alcohol.

34. Be a resource for parents by providing information on agencies, counseling programs, etc.

35. Structure the environment so the student does not have time to dwell on real or imagined problems.

Note: All references to suicide should be considered serious, and steps should be taken to respond to the situation.

153 Indicates that no one likes him/her, no one cares about him/her, etc.

1. Provide the student with as many academic and social successes as possible so peers may view him/her in a more positive way.

2. Make the necessary adjustments in the environment to prevent the student from experiencing stress, frustration, anger, etc.

3. Give the student additional responsibilities (e.g., chores, errands, etc.) to give him/her a feeling of success or accomplishment.

4. Structure the environment so the student does not have time to dwell on real or imagined problems.

5. Take the time to listen so the student realizes your concern and interest.

6. Identify for the student more appropriate ways to express his/her feelings.

7. Reduce stimuli that contribute to the student's verbal expression of unhappiness (e.g., seek input from the student as to what upsets him/her).

8. Separate the student from the peer(s) who stimulates the verbal expression of unhappiness.

9. Reinforce those students in the classroom who deal with unhappiness in an appropriate manner.

10. Try various groupings to determine the situation in which the student is most comfortable.

11. Encourage the student to participate in extracurricular activities that will help develop those skills necessary to interact appropriately with others at school.

12. Make sure that verbal expressions of unhappiness are not inadvertently reinforced (e.g., attention, getting his/her way, etc.).

13. Provide the student with alternative activities to perform in case some activities prove upsetting.

14. Reduce the emphasis on competition. Repeated failure may cause the student to feel that others do not like or care about him/her.

15. Encourage and help the student to make friends (e.g., pair the student with a peer; when that relationship is successful, introduce other students).

16. When natural consequences occur as a result of the student's displays of unhappiness, point them out to him/her (e.g., peers prefer not to interact with the student).

17. Provide the student with as many positive interactions as possible (e.g., recognize the student, greet the student, compliment attire, etc.).

18. Discourage the student from engaging in those activities that cause him/her unhappiness.

19. Help the student identify things he/she wishes were in the environment and work with the student toward those goals.

20. Teach the student alternative ways to deal with unpleasant social interactions during the school-age experience (e.g., deal with problems when they arise, practice self-control at all times, share problems or concerns with others, etc.).

21. Teach the student alternative ways to communicate unhappiness (e.g., written, spoken, etc.).

22. Speak with the student to explain that he/she may be trying too hard to fit in and that he/she should relax and allow friendships to develop naturally.

23. Reinforce those students in the classroom who appropriately interact with other students.

24. Have the student be the leader of a small-group activity if he/she possesses mastery of skills or an interest in that area.

25. Give the student the responsibility of tutoring a peer if he/she possesses the skills to be shared.

26. Provide the student with a predetermined signal (e.g., verbal cue, hand signal, etc.) when he/she begins to demonstrate inappropriate behaviors when interacting with others (e.g., whining, fighting, throwing objects, refusing to share, etc.).

27. Maintain supervision of the student's interaction and gradually decrease the amount of supervision over time.

28. Give the student responsibilities in group situations so peers may view the student in a more positive way.

29. Encourage the student to further develop any ability or skill he/she may have so peers may view the student in a more positive way.

30. Help the student to identify his/her inappropriate behaviors and teach the student ways to change those behaviors.

31. Ask the student to choose a peer to work with on a specific assignment. Encourage the student and peer to interact with each other in nonacademic areas (e.g., recess, lunch, break time, etc.).

32. Do not criticize. When correcting the student, be honest yet supportive. Never cause the student to feel negatively about himself/herself.

33. Do not force the student to interact with students with whom he/she is not completely comfortable.

34. Treat the student with respect. Talk in an objective manner at all times.

35. Allow the student to attempt something new in private before doing so in front of others.

36. Do not assume that the student is being treated nicely by other students. Others may be stimulating inappropriate behavior on the part of the student.

37. Encourage the student to interact with others.

38. Provide the student with frequent opportunities to meet new people.

39. Do not force the student to interact with individuals with whom he/she is not completely comfortable.

40. Make sure the student is not demonstrating a lack of confidence to get the attention of others.

41. Teach the student problem-solving skills: (a) identify the problem, (b) identify goals and objectives, (c) develop strategies, (d) develop a plan for action, and (e) carry out the plan.

42. Record or chart the number of times the student verbally expresses that others do not like or care about him/her to make the student aware of the frequency.

43. Communicate with parents (e.g., notes home, phone calls, etc.) to share information about the student's progress. The parents may reinforce the student at home for interacting appropriately with others at school.

44. Write a contract with the student specifying what behavior is expected (e.g., interacting appropriately with others) and what reinforcement will be made available when the terms of the contract have been met.

45. Remove the student from the group until he/she can interact appropriately with others.

46. Communicate to the student that he/she is a worthwhile individual.

47. Establish classroom rules:
- Concentrate while working.
- Work quietly.
- Remain in your seat.
- Finish task.
- Meet task requirements.

Review rules often. Reinforce the student for following the rules.

48. Reinforce those students in the classroom who make positive, supportive comments to the student.

49. Reinforce the student for interacting with others: (a) give the student a tangible reward (e.g., classroom privileges, line leading, passing out materials, five minutes free time, etc.) or (b) give the student an intangible reward (e.g., praise, fist bump, smile, etc.).

50. Identify individuals the student may contact with his/her concerns (e.g., guidance counselor, school nurse, social worker, school psychologist, etc.).

51. Reinforce the student for interacting with others based on the length of time the student can be successful. As the student demonstrates success, gradually increase the length of time required for reinforcement.

Reminder: Do not force the student to interact with others with whom he/she is uncomfortable.

154 Ignores consequences of his/her behavior

1. Communicate with parents (e.g., notes home, phone calls, etc.) to share information about the student's progress. The parents may reinforce the student at home for engaging in appropriate behaviors at school.

2. Inform others who will be working with the student (e.g., teachers, principal, clerks, etc.) about the student's tendency to ignore the consequences of his/her behaviors.

3. Allow natural consequences to occur (e.g., hitting others will result in suspension, stealing will result in being fined, etc.) due to the student's failure to consider the consequences of his/her behavior.

4. Intervene early when there is a problem to prevent a more serious problem from occurring.

5. Talk with the student's family, a school official, a social worker, a mental health worker, etc., about the student's failure to consider the consequences of his/her behavior.

6. Structure the environment to limit opportunities for inappropriate behavior (e.g., keep the student engaged in activities, have the student seated near the teacher, maintain visibility to and from the student, etc.).

7. Educate the student about ADHD and the need to self monitor behavior.

8. Help the student realize that all behavior has negative or positive consequences. Encourage the student to practice behaviors that will lead to positive consequences.

9. Consider carefully the student's age and ability level before expecting him/her to always think before acting.

10. Remind the student to stop and think when he/she begins to do something without thinking first.

11. Teach the student to stop and think about the consequences of his/her behavior before behaving in a certain manner.

12. Encourage the student to pause and consider his/her thoughts before acting on them.

13. Educate yourself and others about ADHD to increase understanding and accommodation of impulsive behavior.

14. Provide constant, positive reinforcement for appropriate behavior. Ignore as many inappropriate behaviors as possible.

15. Reinforce the student for demonstrating appropriate behavior based on the length of time the student can be successful. As the student demonstrates success, gradually increase the length of time required for reinforcement.

16. Help the student develop an awareness of the consequences of his/her behavior by writing down or talking through problems which may occur due to his/her failure to consider the consequences of his/her behavior.

17. Teach the student to think before acting by asking himself/herself question: *What is happening? What am I doing? What should I do? What will be best for me?*

18. Teach problem-solving skills:
   • Identify the problem.
   • Identify the goals and objectives.
   • Develop a strategy/plan for action.
   • Carry out the plan.
   • Evaluate the results.

19. Discuss consequences with the student before he/she begins an activity (e.g., cheating in a game will result in the game ending and people not playing again).

20. Immediately stop the student from behaving inappropriately and discuss the consequences of the behavior with him/her.

21. Make the consequence of a behavior obvious by identifying the consequence as it occurs and discussing alternative behavior which would have prevented the particular consequence.

22. Reinforce those students in the classroom who participate in appropriate behavior.

23. Provide the student with a clearly understood list of consequences for inappropriate behavior.

24. Make sure that the student understands the relationship between inappropriate behavior and the consequences which follow.

25. Have the student review the consequences of his/her behavior with someone he/she trusts. Have him/her consider different choices that could have been made and the different outcomes.

26. Have the student make a list of consequences associated with frequently occurring behaviors (e.g., by disrupting others, he/she will be perceived as unmannerly; by behaving aggressively, people will avoid him/her.).

27. Explain to the student when he/she fails to consider the consequences of his/her behavior exactly what he/she did wrong, what he/she should have done, and why.

28. Make sure that consequences are delivered consistently for behavior demonstrated (e.g., appropriate behavior results in positive consequences and inappropriate behavior results in negative consequences).

29. Each time a consequence is delivered, whether it is positive or negative, have the student explain to you why he/she thinks it happened.

30. Provide a learning experience which emphasizes the cause-and-effect relationship between inappropriate behavior and the inevitability of some form of consequence (e.g., both negative and positive behaviors and consequences).

31. Speak with the student to explain (a) what he/she is doing wrong (e.g., taking action before thinking about what he/she is doing) and (b) what he/she should be doing (e.g., considering consequences, thinking about the correct response, considering other persons, etc.).

32. Remove the student from the group or activity until he/she can demonstrate appropriate behavior and self-control.

33. Reinforce the student for engaging in appropriate behavior: (a) give the student a tangible reward (e.g., classroom privileges, passing out materials, five minutes free time, etc.) or (b) give the student an intangible reward (e.g., praise, fist bump, smile, etc.).

34. Encourage the student to avoid ingesting any substance (e.g., drugs, alcohol, cold remedies, etc.) that might further alter his/her ability to maintain self-control.

35. Clarify for the student that it is his/her behavior which determines whether consequences are positive or negative.

36. Provide the student with natural consequences for inappropriate behavior (e.g., for disturbing others during group activities, the student will have to leave the activity).

37. Maintain a routine that will minimize erratic or impulsive behavior which may result in negative consequences.

38. Discuss with the student the need to avoid situations in which he/she may participate in risky behavior (e.g., if he/she is more likely to drive fast when his/her friends are in the car, do not drive with friends in the car; abstain from drinking alcohol during parties, etc.).

39. Make sure the student does not become involved in overstimulating activities.

40. Provide the student with many opportunities for social and academic successes.

41. Be sure to take every opportunity to explain to the student that it is his/her behavior that determines whether consequences are positive or negative.

42. Point out the consequences of other students' behavior as they occur (e.g., take the opportunity to point out that consequences occur for all behavior and for all persons).

43. Prevent the student from becoming overstimulated by an activity (e.g., frustrated, angry, excited, etc.).

44. Establish classroom rules:
- Concentrate while working.
- Work quietly.
- Remain in your seat.
- Finish task.
- Meet task requirements.

Review rules often. Reinforce the student for following the rules.

45. Have the student list the pros and cons of an action and determine if the pros outweigh the cons before he/she takes action.

46. Consult with a mental health provider about the student's failure to consider the consequences of his/her behavior.

47. Help the student identify the situations in which he/she is most likely to fail to consider the consequences of his/her behavior. After he/she has identified these situations, have him/her think of ways to minimize their occurrences.

48. Supervise the student closely in situations in which he/she is likely to act impulsively and without considering the consequences (e.g., maintain close physical proximity, maintain eye contact, communicate frequently with the student, etc.).

49. Allow the student more decision-making opportunities relative to class activities and assignments.

50. Write a contract with the student specifying what behavior is expected (e.g., acting in a deliberate and responsible manner) and what reinforcement will be made available when the terms of the contract have been met.

51. Show an interest in the student (e.g., acknowledge the student, ask the student's opinion, spend time working one-to-one with the student, etc.).

52. Make it possible for the student to earn those things he/she wants or needs so that he/she will not participate in inappropriate behavior to get them (e.g., lying or stealing to get something important to him/her).

53. Make sure the student understands that consequences naturally follow behavior. You do not make the consequence happen; it is his/her behavior that makes the consequence occur.

54. Give the student responsibilities in the classroom (e.g., teacher assistant, peer tutor, group leader, etc.).

55. Avoid competition. Failure may cause the student to ignore the consequences of his/her behavior.

56. Encourage the student to consider the consequences of his/her behavior before engaging in any activity.

57. Deliver natural consequences to help the student learn that his/her behavior determines the consequences which follow (e.g., work not done during work time has to be made up during recreational time, what he/she wastes or destroys has to be replaced by him/her, etc.).

58. Prevent peers from engaging in those behaviors which would cause the student to fail to consider or regard the consequences of his/her behavior (e.g., keep other students from upsetting the student).

59. Do not allow the student to use ADHD as an excuse. Hold the student responsible for his/her actions. However, understand and accept problems that ADHD brings into the student's life while he/she is learning to make accommodations.

1. Present tasks in the most attractive and interesting manner possible.

2. Determine those activities the student prefers and provide them often.

3. Reduce or discontinue competitive activities. Repeated failure reduces enjoyment of the activity.

4. Make every attempt to create a positive atmosphere in the classroom (e.g., cooperative group activities, positive motivation strategies, positive communications, etc.).

5. Provide the student with many opportunities for social and academic successes.

6. Include the student in classroom/group activities (e.g., invite the student to join a group, assign the student a part or responsibility in an activity, etc.).

7. Indicate a need for the student's involvement in an activity (e.g., the student is a part of the class/activities, is valued and needed, etc.).

8. Include fun and enjoyable activities as a part of the daily curriculum.

9. Speak to the student to explain (a) that you recognize he/she is unhappy and (b) appropriate ways to deal with unhappiness.

10. Avoid discussions of topics sensitive to the student (e.g., divorce, death, unemployment, alcoholism, etc.).

11. Greet or acknowledge the student as often as possible (e.g., greet in hallways or the cafeteria, welcome to class, acknowledge a job well done, etc.).

12. Call attention to the student's accomplishments (e.g., publicly or privately, depending on which is most appropriate).

13. Interact frequently with the student.

14. Try various groupings to determine the situation in which the student is most comfortable.

15. Make sure that interactions with the student are natural and not contrived.

16. Help the student develop a friendship by assigning him/her to work with a peer on an activity, project, etc.

17. Have the student complete a reinforcer survey to determine his/her interests, favorite activities, what is rewarding to the student, etc., and use the information obtained to create a pleasant atmosphere at school for the student.

18. Have peers invite the student to participate in school and extracurricular activities.

19. Reinforce those students in the classroom who deal with unhappiness in an appropriate manner.

20. Take time to talk with the student so the student realizes that the teacher's interest in him/her is genuine.

21. Make sure that reinforcement is not inadvertently given when the student does not smile, laugh, or demonstrate happiness (e.g., attending to the student only when he/she demonstrates unhappiness).

22. Discourage the student from engaging in those activities which cause him/her unhappiness.

23. Give the student additional responsibilities (e.g., chores, errands, etc.) to give him/her a feeling of success or accomplishment.

24. Help the student identify things he/she wishes were in the environment and work with the student toward these goals.

25. Treat the student with respect. Talk in an objective manner at all times.

26. Allow the student to attempt something new in private before doing so in front of others.

27. Encourage the student to interact with others.

28. Provide the student with frequent opportunities to meet new people.

29. Do not force the student to interact with individuals with whom he/she is not completely comfortable.

30. Express your feelings in a socially acceptable way.

31. Evaluate the appropriateness of the task to determine (a) if the task is too difficult and (b) if the length of time scheduled to complete the task is appropriate.

32. Communicate with parents, agencies, or the appropriate parties to inform them of the problem, determine the cause of the problem, and consider possible solutions to the problem.

33. Reinforce those students in the classroom who participate in classroom activities or special events.

34. Encourage the student to participate in classroom activities or special events.

35. Reinforce the student for demonstrating happiness when appropriate: (a) give the student a tangible reward (e.g., classroom privileges, line leading, passing out materials, five minutes free time, etc.) or (b) give the student an intangible reward (e.g., praise, fist bump, smile, etc.).

1. Have the student ask questions about directions, explanations, or instructions not understood.

2. Review prior to administering tests and quizzes to better prepare the student.

3. Reduce the emphasis on test and quiz scores by grading the student's daily performances.

4. Maintain mobility to frequently be near the student when he/she takes tests or quizzes or performs daily assignments.

5. Reduce the emphasis on competition. Fear of failure may cause the student to resort to cheating or copying others' work to be successful.

6. Seat the student away from others if he/she is prone to cheating and/or copying others' work.

7. Seat the student near the teacher when taking tests or quizzes.

8. Make sure that other students do not allow the student to look at their work during tests and quizzes and while performing assignments.

9. Make sure the student is aware of the consequences for cheating and/or copying others' work (e.g., assignments will be taken away, failing grades will be recorded, etc.).

10. Arrange to have a peer help the student study for tests and quizzes and perform daily assignments.

11. Evaluate the level of difficulty in relation to the student's ability to perform the task.

12. Make sure the student understands all directions, explanations, and instructions prior to taking tests or quizzes and performing assignments.

13. Make sure the student knows that questions can be asked when taking tests and quizzes or performing assigned activities.

14. Communicate with parents or guardians so they may help the student study for tests and quizzes (e.g., send home directions, explanations, instructions relating to content covered on tests and quizzes, material to review, etc.).

15. Have the student take tests and quizzes elsewhere in the building under the individual supervision of an instructor (e.g., library, resource room, counselor's office, etc.).

16. Check the student for obvious attempts to cheat prior to taking a test or quiz (e.g., cheat sheet, answers written on hands or cuffs, etc.).

17. Help the student accept the fact that self-improvement is more important than getting the highest grade in the class, making all A's, being the first one done with an assignment, etc., by reinforcing and grading on the basis of self-improvement.

18. Teach the student to ask for help, stop playing, etc., when he/she feels like cheating.

19. Help the student improve skills in activities in which he/she has cheated to reduce the need to cheat.

20. Do not put an emphasis on perfection or winning. If the student feels that perfection or winning is the most important thing, he/she may resort to cheating to reach perfection or win.

21. Limit the student's participation in competitive activities.

22. Teach the student appropriate ways in which to deal with anger, frustration, etc., so the student does not feel the need to cheat.

23. Help the student accept the fact that self-improvement is more important than being the best, winning, beating someone else, etc., (e.g., improving his/her own best time in swimming is better than always trying to beat someone else, etc.).

24. Before beginning a game or assignment, make sure the student knows the rules, is familiar with the game, understands directions, etc.

25. Encourage the student to participate in less competitive activities (e.g., reading, clubs, scouts, student council, etc.).

26. Help the student to have self-confidence and satisfaction in personal self-worth and successes by pointing out strengths, emphasizing positive aspects, etc.

27. Deal with the student's behavior consistently each time there is a problem with cheating (e.g., when the student cheats remove him/her from the situation and do not allow him/her to return, etc.).

28. Deal with the student's cheating privately rather than in public.

29. Reinforce those students in the classroom who do their own work.

30. Do not take action unless you are certain that the student is cheating.

31. Choose a peer to model performing his/her own work for the student.

32. Communicate with parents (e.g., notes home, phone calls, etc.) to share information about the student's progress. The parents may reinforce the student at home for doing his/her own work at school.

33. Write a contract with the student specifying what behavior is expected (e.g., doing his/her own work) and what reinforcement will be made available when the terms of the contract have been met.

34. Reinforce the student for doing his/her own work based on the length of time the student can be successful. As the student demonstrates success, gradually increase the length of time required for reinforcement.

35. Establish classroom rules:
- Concentrate while working.
- Remain in your seat.
- Finish task.
- Meet task expectations.
- Raise your hand.

Review rules often. Reinforce students for following the rules.

36. Speak to the student to explain (a) what the student is doing wrong (e.g., cheating, copying, etc.) and (b) what the student should be doing (i.e., his/her own work).

37. Evaluate the appropriateness of the task to determine (a) if the task is too difficult and (b) if the length of time scheduled to complete the task is adequate.

38. Reinforce the student for doing his/her own work: (a) give the student a tangible reward (e.g., classroom privileges, line leading, passing out materials, five minutes free time, etc.) or (b) give the student an intangible reward (e.g., praise, fist bump, smile, etc.).

157 Throws temper tantrums

1. Assess the situations in which the student throws temper tantrums. Based on these observations, determine ways to prevent situations from stimulating the student to throw temper tantrums.

2. Try various groupings to determine the situation in which the student is most comfortable.

3. Provide the student with many opportunities for social and academic successes.

4. Take the time to talk with the student so the student realizes that your interest in him/her is genuine.

5. Teach/demonstrate methods for dealing with problems early to prevent problems from becoming overwhelming.

6. Encourage and help the student to make friends (e.g., pair the student with a peer and when that relationship is successful introduce other peers).

7. Explain to the student that feelings of unhappiness are natural, but there is an appropriate length of time for public display of that emotion.

8. When natural consequences occur as a result of the student's throwing temper tantrums, point them out to the student (e.g., peers prefer not to interact with him/her; property is damaged or destroyed, resulting in loss of use or costly replacement; etc.).

9. Provide the student with as many positive interactions as possible (e.g., recognize the student, greet the student, compliment his/her attire, etc.).

10. Provide the student with preferred responsibilities throughout the school environment.

11. Teach and encourage the student to use problem-solving skills: (a) identify the problem, (b) identify goals and objectives, (c) develop strategies, (d) develop a plan for action, and (e) carry out the plan.

12. Make sure that reinforcement is not inadvertently given for inappropriate behavior (i.e., attending to the student only when he/she throws a temper tantrum).

13. Make sure that consequences for both appropriate and inappropriate behavior are consistent.

14. Encourage and assist the student in joining extracurricular activities, clubs, etc.

15. Move the student away from the peer(s) who may be causing his/her unhappiness.

16. Discourage the student from engaging in those activities which cause him/her unhappiness.

17. Provide the student with positive feedback which indicates he/she is successful, competent, important, respected, etc.

18. Identify individuals the student may contact concerning his/her unhappiness (e.g., guidance counselor, school nurse, social worker, school psychologist, etc.).

19. Give the student additional responsibilities (e.g., chores, errands, etc.) to give him/her a feeling of success or accomplishment.

20. Structure the environment so the student does not have time to dwell on real or imagined problems.

21. Help the student identify how he/she wishes things were in the environment and work with the student toward those goals.

22. Teach the student alternative ways to deal with demands, challenges, and pressures of the school-age experience (e.g., deal with problems when they arise, practice self-control at all times, share problems or concerns with others, etc.).

23. Help the student identify when he/she is getting upset so something can be done to help him/her calm down (e.g., walk away, talk about feelings in a socially acceptable way, seek help from an adult, etc.).

24. Teach the student alternative ways to communicate unhappiness (e.g., communicate in writing, verbally, etc.).

25. Avoid topics, situations, etc., which remind the student of unpleasant experiences or problems (e.g., divorce, death, unemployment, alcoholism, etc.).

26. Follow less desirable activities with more desirable activities.

27. Remove the student from the group or activity until he/she can demonstrate appropriate behavior and self-control.

28. Give the student some decision making power (e.g., seating assignment, order of tasks, daily schedule, etc.).

29. Reduce the emphasis on competition. Repeated failure may cause the student to throw a temper tantrum.

30. Help the student choose activities that do not cause anger, frustration, anxiety, etc.

31. Ignore the student's temper tantrums. Do not let the student have his/her way when crying.

32. Demonstrate to the student ways to control angry feelings when things do not go his/her way (e.g., count to ten, say the alphabet, etc.).

33. Make sure you do not give into the student's temper tantrums because others are present. Maintain consistency at all times.

34. Write a contract with the student specifying what behavior is expected (e.g., dealing with unhappiness in an appropriate manner) and what reinforcement will be made available when the terms of the contract have been met.

35. Provide the student with alternative activities, games, etc., in case some activities prove upsetting.

36. Communicate with parents, agencies, or the appropriate parties to inform them of the problem, determine the cause of the problem, and consider possible solutions to the problem.

37. Evaluate the appropriateness of the task to determine (a) if the task is too easy, (b) if the task is too difficult, and (c) if the length of time scheduled to complete the task is adequate.

38. Communicate with parents (e.g., notes home, phone calls, etc.) to share information about the student's progress. The parents may reinforce the student at home for dealing with unhappiness in an appropriate manner at school.

39. After telling the student that he/she cannot do or have something, explain the reason.

40. Provide the student with alternative activities to perform in case some activities prove upsetting.

41. Reinforce the student for dealing with unhappiness in an appropriate manner based on the number of times he/she can be successful. As the student demonstrates success, gradually increase the amount of time required for reinforcement.

42. Reinforce those students in the classroom who deal with unhappiness in an appropriate manner.

43. Establish classroom rules:
- Concentrate while working.
- Work quietly.
- Remain in your seat.
- Finish task.
- Meet task requirements.

Review rules often. Reinforce the student for following the rules.

44. Speak with the student to explain (a) that you recognize that he/she is unhappy and (b) appropriate ways to deal with unhappiness.

45. Reinforce the student for dealing with unhappiness in an appropriate manner (e.g., verbally stating his/her unhappiness, problem solving, etc.): (a) give the student a tangible reward (e.g., classroom privileges, line leading, passing out materials, five minutes free time, etc.) or (b) give the student an intangible reward (e.g., praise, fist bump, smile, etc.).

1. Call on the student when he/she can answer successfully.

2. Provide a full schedule of daily events to keep the student actively involved.

3. Allow the student more decision-making opportunities relative to class activities and assignments.

4. Present tasks in the most attractive and interesting manner possible.

5. Give the student responsibilities in the classroom (e.g., teacher assistant, peer tutor, group leader, etc.).

6. Avoid competition. Failure may cause the student to lose interest or not participate in school activities.

7. Provide the student with many opportunities for academic and social successes.

8. Evaluate the appropriateness of the task in relation to the student's ability to perform the task successfully.

9. Determine the student's preferred activities, interests, etc., and incorporate them into the daily schedule, program, etc., at various points throughout the day.

10. Provide the student with real-life experiences from the environment. Have individuals from the work force (e.g., mechanic, draftsman, secretary, etc.) visit the class to relate the importance of school to work experiences that involve math, reading, writing, etc.

11. Write a contract with the student specifying what behavior is expected (e.g., showing an interest and participating in school activities) and what reinforcement will be made available when the terms of the contract have been met.

12. Investigate the possibility of the student being involved in the use of drugs or alcohol.

13. Do not criticize when correcting the student, be honest yet supportive. Never cause the student to feel negatively about himself/herself.

14. Do not embarrass the student by giving the student orders.

15. Treat the student with respect. Talk in an objective manner at all times.

16. Make positive comments about school and the importance of school.

17. Allow the student to attempt something new in private before doing it in front of others.

18. Provide the student with frequent opportunities to meet new people.

19. Evaluate the appropriateness of the task to determine (a) if the task is too easy, (b) if the task is too difficult, and (c) if the length of time scheduled for the task is adequate.

20. Communicate with parents, agencies, or the appropriate parties to inform them of the problem, determine the cause of the problem, and consider possible solutions to the problem.

21. Communicate with parents (e.g., notes home, phone calls, etc.) to share information about the student's progress. The parents may reinforce the student at home for showing an interest in participating in school activities.

22. Show an interest in the student (e.g., acknowledge the student, ask the student's opinion, spend time working one-to-one with the student, etc.).

23. Reinforce the student for showing an interest and participating in school activities based on the length of time he/she can be successful. As the student demonstrates success, gradually increase the length of time required for reinforcement.

24. Establish classroom rules:
   - Concentrate while working.
   - Work quietly.
   - Remain in your seat.
   - Finish task.
   - Meet task requirements.

Review rules often. Reinforce the student for following the rules.

25. Investigate the student's eating habits and the amount of rest he/she is getting outside of school.

26. Reinforce the student for showing an interest and participating in school activities: (a) give the student a tangible reward (e.g., classroom privileges, line leading, passing out materials, five minutes free time, etc.) or (b) give the student an intangible reward (e.g., praise, fist bump, smile, etc.)

27. Speak with the student to explain (a) what the student is doing wrong (e.g., failing to show an interest and participate in school activities) and (b) what the student should be doing (e.g., showing an interest and participating in school activities).

28. Reinforce those students in the classroom who show an interest and participate in school activities.

159 Indicates that he/she does not care or is not concerned about performance, grades, report cards, graduating, consequences of behavior, etc.

1. Communicate with parents, agencies, or the appropriate parties to inform them of the problem, determine the cause of the problem, and consider possible solutions to the problem.

2. Avoid competition. Failure may cause the student to lose interest or not participate in school activities.

3. Call on the student when he/she can answer successfully.

4. Communicate with parents (e.g., notes home, phone calls, etc.) to share information about the student's progress. The parents may reinforce the student at home for showing an interest and participating in school activities.

5. Allow the student more decision-making opportunities relative to class activities and assignments.

6. Determine the student's preferred activities, interests, etc., and incorporate them into his/her daily schedule, program, etc., at various points throughout the day.

7. Establish classroom rules:
   • Concentrate while working.
   • Work quietly.
   • Remain in your seat.
   • Finish task.
   • Meet task requirements.
Review rules often. Reinforce the student for following the rules.

8. Evaluate the appropriateness of the task in relation to the student's ability to perform the task successfully.

9. Evaluate the appropriateness of the task to determine (a) if the task is too easy, (b) if the task is too difficult, and (c) if the length of time scheduled to complete the task is adequate.

10. Give the student responsibilities in the classroom (e.g., teacher assistant, peer tutor, group leader, etc.).

11. Help the student to develop self-confidence and satisfaction in personal self-worth and successes by pointing out strengths, emphasizing positive aspects, etc.

12. Inform others who will be working with the student (e.g., teachers, principals, clerks, etc.) about the student's tendency to ignore consequences of his/her behavior.

13. Intervene early when there is a problem to prevent more serious problems from occurring.

14. Make sure the student does not become involved in overstimulating activities.

15. Present tasks in the most attractive and interesting manner possible.

16. Provide a full schedule of daily events to keep the student actively involved.

17. Reinforce those students in the classroom who show an interest and participate in school activities.

18. Provide the student with many opportunities for academic and social successes as possible.

19. Reinforce the student for showing an interest and participating in school activities based on the length of time he/she can be successful. As the student demonstrates success, gradually increase the length of time required for reinforcement.

20. Reinforce the student for showing an interest and participating in school activities: (a) give the student a tangible reward (e.g., classroom privileges, line leading, passing out materials, five minutes free time, etc.) or (b) give the student an intangible reward (e.g., praise, fist bump, smile, etc.).

21. Write a contract with the student specifying what behavior is expected (e.g., showing an interest and participating in school activities) and what reinforcement will be made available when the terms of the contract have been met.

22. Show an interest in the student (e.g., acknowledge the student, ask the student's opinion, spend time working one-to-one with the student, etc.).

23. Speak with the student to explain (a) what he/she is doing wrong (e.g., failing to show an interest and participate in school activities) and (b) what he/she should be doing (e.g., showing an interest and participating in school activities).

24. Teach the student to think before acting by asking himself/herself questions: *What is happening?, What am I doing?, What should I do?, What will be best for me?*

25. Provide the student with real-life experiences from the environment. Have individuals from the work force (e.g., mechanic, draftsman, secretary, etc.) visit the class to relate the importance of schoolwork to work experiences that involve, math, reading, writing, etc.

160 Is overly critical of self in school-related performance, abilities, personal appearance, etc.

1. Explain to the student that he/she should be happy with personal best effort rather than expecting perfection.

2. Reinforce the student for taking responsibilities for errors that he/she makes.

3. Speak with the student to explain (a) what the student is doing wrong (i.e., being overly critical of himself/herself) and (b) what the student should be doing (i.e., being more constructive in self-criticism when evaluating himself/herself).

4. Reward others for taking responsibilities for errors they make.

5. Write a contract with the student specifying what behavior is expected (e.g., accepting personal best effort) and what reinforcement will be made available when the terms of the contract have been met.

6. Evaluate the appropriateness of the task to determine (a) if the task is too easy, (b) if the task is too difficult, and (c) if the length of time scheduled to complete the task is adequate.

7. Reinforce the student for improvement rather than expecting excellence.

8. Acknowledge the student often and in various settings (e.g., hallways, cafeteria, etc.).

9. Provide the student with positive feedback which indicates he/she is successful, competent, important, valuable, etc.

10. Provide the student with success-oriented tasks. The expectation is that success will result in more positive attitudes and perceptions toward self and environment.

11. Provide the student with many opportunities for social and academic successes.

12. Make the necessary adjustments in the environment to prevent the student from experiencing stress, frustration, etc.

13. Choose a peer to help the student with class assignments, homework, etc.

14. Emphasize individual differences and that everyone has strengths and weaknesses.

15. Reduce emphasis on competition and perfection. Repeated failure may result in unwarranted self-blame or self-criticism.

16. Encourage the student to refrain from comparing personal performance to other students' performance, and emphasize attention to personal improvement (e.g., maintain records of own progress rather than comparing work to others).

17. Provide the student with evidence of his/her ability so that he/she might better understand that self-blame/criticism is unwarranted.

18. Have the student regularly record his/her own progress to have tangible evidence of success.

19. Deliver praise and constructive criticism consistently to all students.

20. Make cleaning up accidents a group responsibility to convey the idea that we all make mistakes and accidents are common to all of us.

21. Call on the student when he/she will most likely be able to answer correctly.

22. Encourage the student to be a peer tutor to recognize his/her own strengths and abilities.

23. Reduce activities which might threaten the student (e.g., announcing test score ranges or test scores aloud, making students read aloud in class, emphasizing the success of a particular student or students, etc.).

24. Help the student learn those skills necessary to improve his/her personal appearance and hygiene.

25. Make sure that comments made to the student take the form of constructive criticism rather than criticism that can be perceived as personal, threatening, etc., (e.g., instead of saying, "You always make that same mistake." say, "A better way to do that might be . . .").

26. Deliver a predetermined signal when the student begins to be overly critical of him/herself.

27. Assess the appropriateness of the social situation and place the student in the group in which he/she will be most successful.

28. Pair the student with a younger or less capable peer to facilitate his/her feelings of success or accomplishment.

29. Deliver praise and recognition privately so that the student is not aware of the performance of others.

30. Encourage all students to be complimentary of each other's performance.

31. Do not criticize when correcting the student, be honest yet supportive. Never cause the student to feel negatively about himself/herself.

32. Talk with the student about individual differences and discuss strengths and weaknesses of individuals the student knows. Stress that the student does not have to do the same things everyone else does.

33. Encourage the student to refrain from comparing himself/herself to others.

1. Share concerns with administration and seek referral to an agency for investigation of abuse or neglect.

2. Communicate your concern to the student.

3. Reinforce the student for engaging in appropriate behavior: (a) give the student a tangible reward (e.g., classroom privileges, line leading, passing out materials, five minutes free time, etc.) or (b) give the student an intangible reward (e.g., praise, fist bump, smile, etc.).

4. Follow less desirable activities with more desirable activities throughout the day to maintain interest and variety.

5. Choose a peer to participate in recreational activities with the student to develop a friendship.

6. Provide the student with positive feedback that indicates that he/she is successful, competent, important, valuable, etc.

7. Give the student additional responsibilities (e.g., chores, errands, etc.) to give him/her a feeling of success or accomplishment.

8. Identify individuals the student may contact with his/her concerns or problems (e.g., guidance counselor, school nurse, social worker, school psychologist, etc.).

9. Create the most positive environment possible.

10. Seek the student's input in planning the curriculum and extracurricular activities, classes, etc., (i.e., attempt to include student preferences and favored activities).

11. Provide the student with success-oriented tasks (i.e., the expectation is that success will result in more positive attitudes and perceptions toward self and environment).

12. Facilitate the development of friendships with peers (e.g., assign activities for the student involving peers, give the student and a peer joint responsibilities, etc.).

13. Reduce the emphasis on competition. Repeated failure will most likely contribute to the student's unhappiness.

14. Teach the student to be satisfied with his/her best effort rather than insisting on perfection (e.g., reduce the emphasis on competition, help the student realize that success is individually defined).

15. De-emphasize arbitrary levels of success (i.e., rather than absolute excellence, progress of any amount should be considered a measure of success).

16. Respect the student's right to privacy when appropriate.

17. Take the time to listen so the student realizes your concern/interest is genuine.

18. Maintain consistent interactions (e.g., do not provide extra attention when the student is demonstrating facial expressions of displeasure).

19. Make sure that reinforcement is not inadvertently given when the student does not smile, laugh or demonstrate happiness (e.g., attending to the student only when he/she demonstrates unhappiness).

20. Communicate with parents, agencies, or the appropriate parties to inform them of the problem, determine the cause of the problem, and consider possible solutions to the problem.

21. Speak to the student to explain (a) that you recognize he/she is unhappy and (b) appropriate ways to deal with unhappiness.

22. Explain to the student that feelings of unhappiness are natural, but there is an appropriate length of time for public display of that emotion.

23. Teach the student alternative ways to communicate unhappiness (e.g., in writing, by talking, etc.).

24. Remove the student from the group or activity until he/she can be more positive.

25. Ask the student why he/she frowns, scowls, looks unhappy during typical classroom situations. The student may have the most accurate perception.

26. Do not punish the student for not participating in classroom activities.

27. Do not force the student to interact with individuals with whom he/she is not completely comfortable.

28. Treat the student with respect. Talk in an objective manner at all times.

29. Do not embarrass the student by giving him/her orders, demands, etc., in front of others.

30. Make positive comments about participating in school and special activities.

31. Have a peer (e.g., a close friend) accompany the student to those activities in which he/she does not want to participate. As the student demonstrates success, gradually decrease the length of time the peer stays with the student.

32. Carefully consider those activities in which the student does not want to participate. If something unpleasant is causing the student to not participate, do all you can to eliminate or reduce the cause.

33. Do not force the student to interact with individuals with whom he/she is not completely comfortable.

162 Needs immediate rewards, reinforcement, or gratification in order to demonstrate appropriate behavior

1. Have the student maintain a chart representing his/her own appropriate behavior so success is recognized.

2. Provide the student with positive feedback which indicates he/she is successful, competent, important, valuable, etc., (e.g., provide social reinforcement in place of tangible reinforcement).

3. Make sure that natural consequences follow appropriate behavior (e.g., recognition from the group for success, compliments, congratulations, etc.).

4. Reduce the emphasis on material rewards and increase the emphasis on intrinsic rewards (e.g., emphasize a job well done, improvement, personal success, etc.).

5. Provide the student with an abundance of tangible reinforcement so it may satisfy his/her need for gratification.

6. Present the task in an attractive and interesting manner with as much success built in as possible (e.g., the task should be inherently reinforcing).

7. Be sure to greet and acknowledge the student as often as possible rather than providing recognition only as a reinforcer.

8. Encourage the student to save tokens, points, etc., over time for delayed reinforcement (e.g., make tangible reinforcement a goal rather than an immediate need).

9. Make sure that reinforcement is not inadvertently given for inappropriate behavior (e.g., responding to the student only when he/she makes errors, responding to the student when he/she misrepresents a need for help, etc.).

10. Interact frequently with the student to replace tangible reinforcement with social reinforcement.

11. Reinforce with tangibles less often as the student experiences more satisfaction with a job well done (i.e., intrinsic satisfaction begins to replace tangibles as reinforcement).

12. Make sure that reinforcement is used as a natural consequence for a job well done or for appropriate behavior.

13. Reinforce those students who can accept extended time periods between reinforcement.

14. Establish classroom rules:
- Concentrate while working.
- Work quietly.
- Remain in your seat.
- Finish task.
- Meet task requirements.

Review rules often. Reinforce the student for following the rules.

15. Speak with the student to explain (a) what the student is doing wrong (e.g., asking for reinforcement as soon as a task is completed) and (b) what the student should be doing (e.g., waiting for reinforcement until the end of the activity or until an established time, saving tokens or points for reinforcement at a later time, etc.).

16. Reinforce the student as often as necessary while gradually increasing the amount of time between reinforcement: (a) give the student a tangible reward (e.g., classroom privileges, line leading, passing out materials, five minutes free time, etc.) or (b) give the student an intangible reward (e.g., praise, fist bump, smile, etc.).

17. Provide reinforcement at routine intervals so the student learns that reinforcement is delayed but forthcoming (e.g., free time, end of the day, Friday afternoon, etc.).

18. Do not criticize. When correcting the student, be honest yet supportive. Never cause the student to feel negatively about himself/herself.

19. Evaluate the appropriateness of the task to determine (a) if the task is too easy, (b) if the task is too difficult, and (c) if the length of time scheduled to complete the task is adequate.

20. Communicate with parents (e.g., notes home, phone calls, etc.) to share information about the student's progress. The parents may reinforce the student at home for tolerating extended time periods between reinforcement at school.

21. Write a contract with the student specifying what behavior is expected (e.g., working five minutes without asking for reinforcement) and what reinforcement will be available when the terms of the contract have been met.

163 Does not care for personal appearance

Note: Evidence of inappropriate care for personal appearance would include such things as dirt on body and under fingernails, dirty hair, body odor, unbrushed teeth, offensive breath, failure to use a handkerchief appropriately, and toileting accidents.

1. Choose a peer to model appropriate hygiene (e.g., wearing clean clothing, washing hair, cleaning fingernails, etc.) for the student.

2. Have the student ask questions about hygiene expectations he/she does not understand.

3. Establish hygiene rules:
- Bathe regularly.
- Brush teeth.
- Wash hair.
- Launder clothing after wearing.
- Clean and trim nails.
- Maintain personal cleanliness after using restroom.
- Use a handkerchief.

Review rules often. Reinforce students for following the rules.

4. Evaluate the demands of the responsibility on the student for personal hygiene to determine if the expectations are too high. If expectations are too difficult for the student, assistance should be provided.

5. Have the student keep a change of clean clothing at school.

6. Provide the student with training in the use of personal grooming and related materials (e.g., washcloth, soap, shampoo, toothbrush, toothpaste, hairbrush, comb, nail clippers, toilet paper, handkerchief, etc.).

7. Allow the student to attend to personal hygiene needs at school if the opportunity is not available elsewhere (e.g., launder clothing, bathe, wash hair, etc.).

8. Maintain personal hygiene materials at school for the student's use.

9. Provide a comprehensive unit of information and instruction on personal hygiene. The unit should include health and appearance aspects. Classroom visitors can include a dentist, nurse, doctor, cosmetologist, etc.

10. Communicate with parents, agencies, or the appropriate parties to inform them of the problem, determine the cause of the problem, and consider possible solutions to the problem.

11. Encourage the student to maintain a daily routine of grooming and attending to personal hygiene at school.

12. Designate one adult in the educational environment to work directly with the student to help him/her care for personal appearance.

13. As part of instruction on interviewing and job placement, emphasize the importance of personal hygiene and grooming (e.g., have a representative of business or industry visit the class to make a presentation on the importance of personal appearance).

14. Provide the student with a checklist of personal hygiene activities for him/her to complete daily.

15. Provide visual reminders of personal hygiene in appropriate locations (e.g., picture of washing hands and brushing teeth at sink, picture of deodorant in restroom, etc.).

16. Teach the student how to launder clothing.

17. Reinforce the student for gradually improving personal hygiene over time rather than expecting total mastery of personal hygiene skills immediately.

18. Make sure that all communications with the student concerning personal hygiene are conducted in a private manner.

19. Provide the student with scheduled times during the day to attend to personal hygiene needs.

20. Allow the student to arrive early at school to care for his/her personal appearance.

21. Do not criticize when correcting the student; be honest yet supportive. Never cause the student to feel negatively about himself/herself.

22. Communicate with parents (e.g., notes home, phone calls, etc.) to share information about the student's progress. The parents may reinforce the student at home for caring for his/her personal appearance.

23. Write a contract with the student specifying what behavior is expected (e.g., wearing clean clothing, washing hair, cleaning fingernails, etc.) and what reinforcement will be made available when the terms of the contract have been met.

24. Reinforce the student for caring for personal appearance based on the length of time the student can be successful. As the student demonstrates success, gradually increase the length of time required for reinforcement.

25. Reinforce those students in the classroom who care for their personal appearance.

26. Speak to the student to explain (a) what the student is doing wrong (e.g., wearing dirty clothing, failing to wash hair or clean fingernails, etc.) and (b) what the student should be doing (e.g., wearing clean clothing, washing hair, cleaning fingernails, etc.).

27. Reinforce the student for caring for personal appearance: (a) give the student a tangible reward (e.g., classroom privileges, line leading, passing out materials, five minutes free time, etc.) or (b) give the student an intangible reward (e.g., praise, fist bump, smile, etc.).

28. Carefully consider the student's age and experience before expecting him/her to care for personal hygiene independently.

29. Make sure that the student sees the relationship between his/her behavior and the consequences which follow (e.g., offending others, being avoided by others, not being able to participate in special activities, etc.).

30. Set an example for the student by caring about your personal appearance (e.g., combing your hair, bathing daily, etc.).

31. Encourage the student to take a home economics class, a health class, etc., to learn the importance of personal hygiene.

32. Make sure that the student understands that others might make fun of him/her if the student does not comb hair, zip pants, tie shoes, etc.

33. Compliment the student for being neat, clean, etc.

34. Set aside time to practice hair combing, putting on makeup, shaving, using deodorant, etc.

35. Stress to the student the social importance of brushing teeth, washing hair, bathing, etc. Not only is inadequate hygiene offensive, but other children can be cruel with the comments about the student's hygiene.

36. Provide the student with instruction on fastening articles of clothing.

37. Teach the student how to fasten articles of clothing when buttons are missing, zippers are broken, etc., (e.g., sewing a button back in place, using a safety pin, etc.).

38. Guide the student's hands through the activity of zipping, buttoning, and snapping his/her own clothing.

39. Help the student learn those skills necessary to improve his/her personal appearance and hygiene.

40. Provide the student with verbal reminders to fasten his/her articles of clothing.

41. Fasten articles of clothing for the student if he/she is incapable of fastening.

42. Reinforce the student for gradually improving his/her ability to fasten articles of clothing over time rather than expecting total mastery immediately.

43. Reinforce the student at regular intervals throughout the day for having articles of clothing fastened.

44. Provide the student with time to practice fastening his/her articles of clothing while wearing them.

45. Place visual reminders to fasten articles of clothing inside of restrooms and on the classroom door (e.g., pictures of zipping, buttoning, and snapping).

46. Do not embarrass the student by asking him/her to fasten articles of clothing in front of peers.

47. Place a full-length mirror in the classroom for the student to make sure that all of his/her articles of clothing are fastened.

48. Provide the student with a checklist of articles of clothing to fasten (e.g., shirt, pants, shoes, coat, etc.). Have the student complete the checklist routinely throughout the day.

49. Have the student practice fastening articles of clothing with oversized zippers, buttons, and snaps. As the student demonstrates success, gradually reduce the size of the fasteners.

1. Communicate with parents, agencies, or the appropriate parties to inform them of the problem, determine the cause of the problem, and consider possible solutions to the problem.

2. Evaluate the appropriateness of the task to determine (a) if the task is too easy, (b) if the task is too difficult, and (c) if the length of time scheduled to complete the task is adequate.

3. Choose a peer to model positive reactions to situations for the student.

4. Have the student ask questions about directions, explanations, or instructions not understood.

5. Remove the student from the group or activity until he/she can be more positive.

6. Provide the student with many opportunities for social and academic successes.

7. Modify the environment to reduce situations which cause the student to be pessimistic (e.g., determine those activities the student dislikes and avoid forcing the student to participate in those activities).

8. Encourage the student to participate in those activities in which he/she is successful.

9. Provide the student with positive feedback which indicates he/she is successful, competent, important, respected, etc.

10. Identify individuals the student may contact concerning his/her unhappiness (e.g., guidance counselor, school nurse, social worker, school psychologist, etc.).

11. Encourage and help the student to make friends (e.g., pair the student with a peer; when that relationship is successful introduce other peers).

12. Explain to the student that feelings of pessimism are natural, but public display of that emotion should be limited.

13. Make the student aware of natural consequences that occur due to the student's displays of pessimism (e.g., others prefer not to interact with the student, he/she will not be chosen by peers to join in activities, etc.).

14. Provide the student with as many positive interactions as possible (e.g., recognize the student, greet the student, compliment his/her attire, etc.).

15. Require the student to make at least one positive comment about himself/herself on a daily basis. As the student demonstrates success, gradually increase the number of positive comments required.

16. Encourage and assist the student in joining extracurricular activities, clubs, etc.

17. Give the student additional responsibilities (e.g., chores, errands, etc.) to give him/her a feeling of success or accomplishment.

18. Help the student identify how he/she wishes things were in the environment and work with the student toward those goals.

19. Take time to talk with the student so the student realizes your interest in him/her is genuine.

20. Conduct a reinforcer survey with the student to determine his/her reinforcer preferences.

21. Communicate with parents to determine what the student finds reinforcing at home.

22. Help the student to be satisfied with personal best effort rather than insisting on perfection.

23. Identify the words or phrases the student uses to indicate his/her pessimism. Help the student recognize and in turn limit the statements.

24. Give the student a predetermined signal when he/she begins to be pessimistic.

25. Along with a directive, provide an incentive statement (e.g., "When you finish your math, you may have free time." "You may play a game when your desk is cleaned up.").

26. Do not criticize when correcting the student, be honest yet supportive. Never cause the student to feel negatively about himself/herself.

27. Make positive comments about school and the student.

28. Teach the student appropriate ways to communicate displeasure, anger, frustration, etc.

29. Teach the student to think before acting by asking himself/herself questions: *What is happening?, What am I doing?, What should I do?, What will be best for me?*

30. Communicate with parents (e.g., notes home, phone calls, etc.) to share information about the student's progress. The parents may reinforce the student at home for being more positive at school.

31. Speak to the student to explain (a) what the student is doing wrong (e.g., complaining, not taking part, reacting negatively, etc.) and (b) what the student should be doing (e.g., taking part, being enthusiastic, etc.).

32. Write a contract with the student specifying what behavior is expected (e.g., making positive comments) and what reinforcement will be made available when the terms of the contract have been met.

33. Reinforce the student for being more positive based on the length of time the student can be successful. As the student demonstrates success, gradually increase the length of time required for reinforcement.

34. Reinforce those students in the classroom who are positive in reacting to situations.

35. Establish classroom rules:
- Concentrate while working.
- Work quietly.
- Remain in your seat.
- Finish task.
- Meet task requirements.

Review rules often. Reinforce the student for following the rules.

36. Model respecting others by respecting the student.

37. Treat the student with respect. Talk in an objective manner at all times.

38. Reinforce the student for being more positive in reacting to situations (e.g., attempting a task, making a positive comment about an activity, etc.): (a) give the student a tangible reward (e.g., classroom privileges, line leading, passing out materials, five minutes free time, etc.) or (b) give the student an intangible reward (e.g., praise, fist bump, smile, etc.)

39. Allow the student to voice his/her opinion in a situation to avoid becoming angry or upset.

165 Physically runs away from personal or school experiences

1. Structure the environment (e.g., change seating, increase supervision, reduce stimuli which contribute to running away, etc.) to reduce opportunities to run away from the school/classroom.

2. Maintain supervision of the student at all times and in all parts of the school.

3. Maintain visibility to and from the student. The teacher should be able to see the student and the student should be able to see the teacher. Make eye contact possible at all times.

4. Provide the student with many opportunities for academic and social successes.

5. Record or chart attendance with the student.

6. Give the student a responsibility to be performed at various times throughout the day.

7. Present tasks in the most attractive and interesting manner possible.

8. Interact frequently with the student to maintain involvement in the activity (e.g., ask the student questions, ask the student's opinion, stand close to the student, seat the student near your desk, etc.).

9. Make the necessary adjustments in the environment to prevent the student from experiencing stress, frustration, anger, etc., as much as possible.

10. Make sure all school personnel are aware of the student's tendency to run away.

11. Limit the student's independent movement in the school environment.

12. Discuss with the student ways to deal with unpleasant experiences which would typically cause him/her to run away (e.g., talk to a teacher, visit with a counselor, go to a quiet area in the school, etc.).

13. Identify variables in the environment which cause the student to become upset, and reduce or remove those variables.

14. Do not provide the student with additional opportunities to run away by seating the student in the hallway, sending him from class, etc.

15. Consider alternative forms of negative consequences if current consequences cause the student to run away. Do not use negative consequences which contribute to a worsening of the situation.

16. Intervene early to prevent the student from becoming upset enough to run away.

17. Provide the student with a quiet place as an alternative to running away. This can be a place where the student elects to go as a form of self-control instead of running away.

18. Identify the student's favorite activities and provide as many of these as possible throughout the day.

19. Do not criticize when correcting the student; be honest yet supportive. Never cause the student to feel negatively about himself/herself.

20. Intervene early when there is a problem to prevent more serious problems from occurring.

21. Make sure there will be adult supervision at all times for the student (e.g., during P.E., recess, lunch, etc.).

22. Treat the student with respect. Talk in an objective manner at all times.

23. Do not embarrass the student by giving him/her orders, demands, etc., in front of others.

24. Teach the student acceptable ways to communicate displeasure, anger, frustration, etc.

25. Remove the student from the group or activity until he/she can demonstrate appropriate behavior and self-control.

26. Teach the student to think before acting by asking himself/herself questions: *What is happening?, What am I doing?, What should I do?, What will be best for me?*.

27. Talk to the student about ways of handling situations successfully without conflict (e.g., walk away from a situation, change to another activity, ask for help, etc.).

28. Evaluate the appropriateness of the task to determine (a) if the task is too easy, (b) if the task is too difficult, and (c) if the length of time scheduled to complete the task is adequate.

29. Communicate with the parents (e.g., notes home, phone calls, etc.) to share information about the student's progress. The parents may reinforce the student at home for dealing with problems in appropriate ways at school.

30. Encourage the student to use problem-solving skills: (a) identify the problem, (b) identify goals and objectives, (c) develop strategies, (d) develop a plan for action, and (e) carry out the plan.

31. Write a contract with the student specifying what behavior is expected (e.g., asking for help) and what reinforcement will be made available when the terms of the contract have been met.

32. Reinforce the student for dealing with problems in appropriate ways based on the length of time the student can be successful. As the student demonstrates success, gradually increase the length of time required for reinforcement.

33. Reinforce those students in the classroom who deal with problems in appropriate ways.

34. Establish classroom rules:
- Concentrate while working.
- Work quietly.
- Remain in your seat.
- Finish task.
- Meet task requirements.

Review rules often. Reinforce the student for following the rules.

35. Allow the student to voice his/her opinion in a situation to avoid becoming angry or upset.

36. Speak with the student to explain (a) what the student is doing wrong (e.g., running away from situations, running out of the room, running away from school, etc.) and (b) what the student should be doing (e.g., asking for help, calling attention to the problem, practicing problem-solving skills, using self-control, etc.).

37. Reinforce the student for dealing with problems in appropriate ways: (a) give the student a tangible reward (e.g., classroom privileges, line leading, passing out materials, five minutes free time, etc.) or (b) give the student an intangible reward (e.g., praise, fist bump, smile, etc.).

38. Inform others (e.g., teachers, aides, lunchroom clerks, etc.) of the student's tendency to run away to avoid problems.

166 Cries in response to personal or school situations

1. Modify the environment to reduce situations which cause the student to be unhappy (e.g., if the student is upset by losing in competitive activities, reduce the number of competitive activities).

2. Share concerns with the administration and seek referral to an agency for investigation of possible abuse or neglect.

3. Try various groupings to determine the group in which the student is most comfortable.

4. Provide the student with many opportunities for social and academic successes.

5. Take time to talk with the student so the student realizes your interest in him/her is genuine.

6. Teach/demonstrate methods for dealing with problems early to prevent problems from becoming overwhelming.

7. Explain to the student that feelings of unhappiness are natural, but that there is an appropriate length of time for public displays of that emotion.

8. Teach the student to be satisfied with his/her best effort rather than perfection.

9. When natural consequences occur as the result of the student's display of unhappiness, point them out to the student (e.g., peers prefer not to interact with him/her).

10. Provide the student with as many positive interactions as possible (e.g., recognize the student, call the student by name, compliment his/her attire, etc.).

11. Make sure that positive reinforcement is not inadvertently given for inappropriate behavior.

12. Make sure that consequences for inappropriate behavior are consistent.

13. Encourage and assist the student in joining extracurricular activities, clubs, etc.

14. Remove the student from the peer(s) who is causing his/her unhappiness.

15. Discourage the student from engaging in those activities which cause his/her unhappiness.

16. Give the student additional responsibilities (e.g., chores, errands, etc.) to give him/her a feeling of success or accomplishment.

17. Encourage the student to use problem-solving skills: (a) identify the problem, (b) identify goals and objectives, (c) develop strategies, (d) develop a plan for action, and (e) carry out the plan.

18. Identify individuals the student may contact concerning his/her unhappiness (e.g., guidance counselor, school nurse, social worker, school psychologist, etc.).

19. Structure the environment so the student does not have time to dwell on real or imagined problems.

20. Maintain anecdotal records of the student's behavior to check for patterns or changes in behavior.

21. Teach the student alternative ways to express his/her unhappiness (e.g., talking, writing, creating, etc.).

22. Provide the student with a quiet place to relax when becoming upset. This is not to be used as a form of punishment but as an opportunity to function more successfully in the environment.

23. Do not criticize. When correcting the student, be honest yet supportive. Never cause the student to feel negatively about himself/herself.

24. Treat the student with respect. Talk in an objective manner at all times.

25. Do not embarrass the student by giving orders, demands, etc., in front of other students.

26. Make positive comments about school and the student.

27. Teach the student acceptable ways to communicate displeasure, anger, frustration, etc.

28. Make sure you express your feelings in a socially acceptable way.

29. Allow the student to voice his/her opinion in a situation to avoid becoming angry or upset.

30. Communicate with parents, agencies, or the appropriate parties to inform them of the problem, determine the cause of the problem, and consider possible solutions to the problem.

31. Evaluate the appropriateness of the task to determine (a) if the task is too easy, (b) if the task is too difficult, and (c) if the length of time scheduled to complete the task is adequate.

32. Communicate with the parents (e.g., notes home, phone calls, etc.) to share information about the student's progress. The parents may reinforce the student at home for dealing with unhappiness in an appropriate manner at school.

33. Speak with the student to explain (a) that you recognize he/she is unhappy and (b) appropriate ways for dealing with his/her unhappiness (e.g., by talking, problem solving, etc.).

34. Remove the student from the group or activity until he/she can demonstrate appropriate behavior and self-control.

35. Reinforce the student for dealing with unhappiness in an appropriate manner based on the length of time the student can be successful. As the student demonstrates success, gradually increase the amount of time required for reinforcement.

36. Reinforce those students in the classroom who deal with unhappiness in an appropriate manner.

37. Establish classroom rules:
- Concentrate while working.
- Remain in your seat.
- Finish task.
- Meet task expectations.
- Raise your hand.

Review rules often. Reinforce students for following the rules.

38. Reinforce the student for demonstrating appropriate behavior in response to unpleasant situations (e.g., failure, peer pressure, disappointment, losing in competition, etc.): (a) give the student a tangible reward (e.g., classroom privileges, line leading, passing out materials, five minutes free time, etc.) or (b) give the student an intangible reward (e.g., praise, fist bump, smile, etc.).

39. Write a contract with the student specifying what behavior is expected (e.g., dealing with unhappiness in an appropriate manner) and what reinforcement will be made available when the terms of the contract have been met.

K. Inappropriate Behavior Under Normal Circumstances

167 Behaves inappropriately when others do well or receive praise or attention

1. Make sure to help the student achieve a level of success in an activity so he/she will do well and receive praise or attention.

2. Make sure that the student is assigned a role in an activity in which he/she can be successful as a participant and enjoy the activity (e.g., banker in Monopoly®, scorekeeper in a game, teacher assistant, note taker in discussions, etc.).

3. Make sure that some attention is given to the student when others do well or receive praise or attention. As he/she demonstrates appropriate behavior when others do well or receive praise or attention, gradually reduce the attention given to the student.

4. Deliver praise or attention as privately as possible to reduce the likelihood of upsetting any students in the classroom.

5. Reduce the emphasis on competition. Encourage and reinforce participation, team work, good sportsmanship, personal improvement, etc.

6. Reinforce the student for behaving appropriately when others receive praise. As the student demonstrates success, gradually reduce the amount of reinforcement.

7. Make sure that the student succeeds or receives attention often enough to create a balance with those times when other students succeed or receive praise or attention.

8. Make sure that the teacher is a good role model by participating in games, demonstrating good sportsmanship, complimenting others, etc.

9. Establish rules and go over them at the beginning of an activity to reduce the likelihood of misunderstanding.

10. Encourage the student to leave situations which may cause him/her to become upset, angry, embarrassed, etc.

11. Encourage an atmosphere of students helping one another, congratulating each other, finding something about each other to compliment, etc.

12. Have the student take part in activities with students who are appropriate models for behavior when others do well or receive praise or attention.

13. If the student becomes frustrated or upset by the task or activity, remove him/her from the situation, stop the activity, or provide an alternative activity.

14. Make sure that the student understands that an inability to behave appropriately during a game or activity will result in the termination of the activity.

15. Be sure to provide close supervision of the student in tasks and activities to intervene early and provide problem-solving alternatives should inappropriate behaviors occur.

16. Help the student find activities (e.g., reading, creating, peer tutoring, etc.) in which he/she can achieve personal satisfaction and success.

17. Do not require the student to participate in games and activities which may be threatening or cause him/her to demonstrate inappropriate behavior.

18. Make sure the student does not participate in activities with another student(s) who is likely to stimulate inappropriate behavior.

19. Provide the student with several activities throughout the day in which he/she can do well and receive praise and attention.

20. Be aware of the student's strengths and limitations. Have the student participate in activities in which he/she will succeed rather than fail.

21. Have the student participate in games or activities with a younger student with whom he/she will not have a competitive relationship. As the student demonstrates appropriate behavior, gradually have the student participate in games or activities with older, more skilled peers.

22. Call on the student when he/she is most likely to be able to respond correctly (e.g., when discussing something in which the student is interested, when the teacher is sure he/she knows the answer, etc.).

23. Carefully consider the student's age and experience before expecting him/her to behave appropriately when others do well or receive praise or attention.

24. Model respecting others by respecting the student.

25. Encourage the student to refrain from comparing himself/herself to others.

26. Express your feelings in a socially acceptable way.

27. Reinforce the student for behaving appropriately when others do well or receive praise or attention: (a) give the student a tangible reward (e.g., classroom privileges, line leading, passing out materials, five minutes free time, etc.) or (b) give the student an intangible reward (e.g., praise, fist bump, smile, etc.).

28. Do not allow the student to participate if the task or situation is too stimulating.

29. Praise and recognize equally all members of the class.

30. Evaluate the appropriateness of the task or situation to determine (a) if the task is too easy, (b) if the task is too difficult, and (c) if the length of time scheduled to complete the task is adequate.

31. Communicate with parents (e.g., notes home, phone calls, etc.) to share information about the student's progress. The parents may reinforce the student at home for behaving appropriately at school.

32. Write a contract with the student specifying what behavior is expected (e.g., making a positive comment) and what reinforcement will be made available when the terms of the contract have been met.

33. Reinforce the student for behaving appropriately based on the length of time the student can be successful. As the student demonstrates success, gradually increase the length of time required for reinforcement.

34. Reinforce those students in the classroom who behave appropriately when others do well or receive praise or attention.

35. Speak to the student to explain (a) what the student is doing wrong (e.g., getting angry, having a tantrum, etc.) and (b) what the student should be doing (e.g., making positive comments, continuing to participate appropriately, etc.).

36. Establish a set of rules for group games:
- Follow rules of the game.
- Take turns.
- Make positive comments.
- Work as a team member.
- Be a good sport.

Review rules often. Reinforce students for following the rules.

37. Choose a peer to model behaving appropriately when others do well or receive praise or attention for the student.

38. Have the student ask questions about directions, explanations, or instructions not understood.

168 Does not behave in a manner appropriate for the situation

1. Evaluate the appropriateness of the task to determine (a) if the task is too easy, (b) if the task is too difficult, and (c) if the length of time scheduled to complete the task is adequate.

2. Reduce stimuli which would contribute to unrelated or inappropriate behavior (e.g., testing situations, peers, physical activities, etc.).

3. Interact frequently with the student to maintain involvement.

4. Structure the environment so that time does not permit unrelated or inappropriate behavior from occurring.

5. Give the student responsibilities to keep him/her actively involved in the activity.

6. Modify or adjust situations which cause the student to demonstrate unrelated or inappropriate behavior (e.g., keep the student from becoming overstimulated in activities).

7. Make the necessary adjustments in the environment to prevent the student from experiencing stress, frustration, anger, etc., as much as possible.

8. Reduce distracting stimuli (e.g., place the student in the front row, provide a carrel or quiet place away from distractions, etc.). This is used as a means of reducing distracting stimuli and not as punishment.

9. Choose a peer to model on-task behavior for the student.

10. Interact frequently with the student to maintain his/her attention to the activity (e.g., ask the student questions, ask the student's opinions, stand close to the student, seat the student near the teacher's desk, etc.).

11. Model socially acceptable behavior for the student (e.g., pat on the back, fist bump, etc.).

12. Maintain a consistent routine.

13. Make sure that reinforcement is not inadvertently given for the student's inappropriate comments or behaviors (e.g., attending to the student only when he/she demonstrates behaviors which are inappropriate to the situation).

14. Prevent the student from becoming overstimulated by an activity (e.g., monitor or supervise student behavior to limit overstimulation in physical activities, games, parties, etc.).

15. Help the student develop attention-maintaining behaviors (e.g., maintain eye contact, take notes on the subject, ask questions related to the subject, etc.).

16. Try various groupings to determine the situations in which the student demonstrates appropriate behavior.

17. Reduce the emphasis on competition. Repeated failure may result in behaviors which are inappropriate for the situation.

18. Make the student aware of activities or events well in advance so he/she may prepare for them.

19. Remove the student from the group or activity until he/she can demonstrate appropriate behavior and self-control.

20. Do not criticize. When correcting the student, be honest yet supportive. Never cause the student to feel negatively about himself/herself.

21. Intervene early when there is a problem to prevent a more serious problem from occurring.

22. Teach the student to think before acting by asking himself/herself questions: *What is happening?, What am I doing?, What should I do?, What will be best for me?*

23. Talk to the student about ways of handling situations successfully without conflict (e.g., walk away from the situation, change to another activity, ask for help, etc.).

24. Communicate with parents (e.g., notes home, phone calls, etc.) to share information about the student's progress. The parents may reinforce the student at home for demonstrating appropriate behaviors related to situations at school.

25. Write a contract with the student specifying what behavior is expected (e.g., demonstrating appropriate behavior related to the situation) and what reinforcement will be made available when the terms of the contract have been met.

26. Speak with the student to explain (a) what the student is doing wrong (e.g., laughing when a peer gets hurt) and (b) what the student should be doing (e.g., helping the peer).

27. Reinforce the student for demonstrating appropriate behaviors related to the situation based on the length of time the student can be successful. As the student demonstrates success, gradually increase the length of time required for reinforcement.

28. Reinforce those students in the classroom who demonstrate appropriate behaviors related to the situation.

29. Establish classroom rules:
• Concentrate while working.
• Work quietly.
• Remain in your seat.
• Finish task.
• Meet task requirements.
Review rules often. Reinforce the student for following the rules.

30. Deliver a predetermined signal (e.g., hand signal, verbal cue, etc.) when the student begins to display behaviors which are inappropriate for the situation.

31. Make sure the student does not become involved in overstimulating activities.

32. Reinforce the student for demonstrating appropriate behaviors related to the situation: (a) give the student a tangible reward (e.g., classroom privileges, line leading, passing out materials, five minutes free time, etc.) or (b) give the student an intangible reward (e.g., praise, fist bump, smile, etc.).

Reminder: Do not force the student to participate in any activity he/she finds unpleasant, embarrassing, etc.

169 Acts impulsively without apparent self-control

1. Reduce the opportunity to act impulsively by limiting decision making. As the student demonstrates success, gradually increase opportunities for decision making.

2. Provide the student with a routine to be followed when making decisions (e.g., place a list of decision-making strategies to the student's desk).

3. Maintain visibility to and from the student. The teacher should be able to see the student and the student should be able to see the teacher. Make eye contact possible at all times.

4. Be mobile to be frequently near the student.

5. Assign additional responsibilities to the student (e.g., chores, errands, etc.) to give him/her a feeling of success or accomplishment.

6. Prevent the student from becoming over-stimulated by an activity (e.g., monitor or supervise student behavior to limit overexcitement in physical activities, games, parties, etc.).

7. Provide the student with adequate time to perform activities to reduce his/her impulsive behavior.

8. Maintain supervision at all times and in all areas of the school environment.

9. Explain to the student that he/she should be satisfied with personal best effort rather than expecting perfection.

10. Provide the student with clear, simply stated explanations, instructions, and directions so that he/she knows exactly what is expected.

11. Assist the student in beginning each task to reduce impulsive responses.

12. Have a peer work with the student to model deliberate and responsible behavior in academic and social settings.

13. Reduce distracting stimuli (e.g., place the student on the front row, provide a carrel or quiet place away from distractions, etc.). This is used as a means of reducing distracting stimuli and not as a form of punishment.

14. Reduce the emphasis on competition. Competition may result in impulsive behavior to win or be first.

15. Teach the student decision-making steps: (a) think about how other persons may be influenced, (b) think about consequences, (c) carefully consider the unique situation, (d) think of different courses of action which are possible, and (e) think about what is ultimately best for him/her.

16. Make the student aware of the reasons we all must practice responsibility (e.g., others' rights are not infringed upon, others are not hurt, order is not lost, property is not damaged or destroyed, etc.).

17. Emphasize individual success or progress rather than winning or beating other students.

18. To determine if the student heard a direction, have the student repeat it.

19. Allow natural consequences to occur so the student can learn that persons who take turns and act in a deliberate fashion are more successful than those who act impulsively (e.g., if you begin an activity before understanding the directions, you will finish early; but you may complete the assignment incorrectly and receive a failing grade; you may have to repeat the assignment, etc.).

20. Deliver a predetermined signal (e.g., hand signal, verbal cue, etc.) when the student begins to demonstrate impulsive behaviors.

21. Make sure the student does not become involved in overstimulating activities on the playground, during P.E., during lunch, etc.

22. Make sure the student has an adequate amount or number of activities scheduled to prevent the likelihood of impulsively engaging in unplanned activities.

23. Assign the student to an area of the classroom where he/she is to remain at any one time.

24. Maintain a consistent routine of daily activities.

25. Make sure the student knows which areas in the classroom are off limits to him/her.

26. Make sure that all students get equal opportunities to participate in activities (e.g., students take turns, everyone has an equal opportunity to be first, etc.).

27. Do not criticize the student. When correcting the student, be honest yet supportive. Never cause the student to feel negatively about himself/herself.

28. Reinforce those students in the classroom who act in a deliberate and responsible manner.

29. Intervene early when there is a problem to prevent a more serious problem from occurring.

30. Teach the student to think before acting by asking himself/herself questions: *What is happening?, What am I doing?, What should I do?, What will be best for me?*

31. Evaluate the appropriateness of the task to determine (a) if the task is too easy, (b) if the task is too difficult, and (c) if the length of time scheduled to complete the task is adequate.

32. Write a contract with the student specifying what behavior is expected (e.g., acting in a deliberate and responsible manner) and what reinforcement will be made available when the terms of the contract have been met.

33. Remove the student from the group or activity until he/she can demonstrate appropriate behavior and self-control.

34. Reinforce the student for demonstrating appropriate behavior based on the length of time the student can be successful. As the student demonstrates success, gradually increase the length of time required for reinforcement.

35. Reinforce the student for acting in a deliberate and responsible manner: (a) give the student a tangible reward (e.g., classroom privileges, line leading, passing out materials, five minutes free time, etc.) or (b) give the student an intangible reward (e.g., praise, fist bump, smile, etc.).

36. Speak with the student to explain (a) what the student is doing wrong (e.g., taking action before thinking about what he/she is doing) and (b) what the student should be doing (e.g., considering consequences, thinking about the correct response, considering others, etc.).

37. Do not leave a lot of unstructured time for the student.

38. Establish classroom rules:
- Concentrate while working.
- Work quietly.
- Remain in your seat.
- Finish task.
- Meet task requirements.

Review rules often. Reinforce the student for following the rules.

39. Communicate with parents (e.g., notes home, phone calls, etc.) to share information about the student's progress. The parents may reinforce the student at home for acting in a deliberate and responsible manner at school.

Reminder: Do not confuse impulsive behavior with enthusiasm. Impulsive behavior should be controlled while enthusiasm should be encouraged.

1. Provide the student with many opportunities for social and academic successes.

2. Inform the student in advance when a change at school is going to occur (e.g., change in routine, special events, end of one activity and beginning of another, etc.).

3. Provide a consistent routine for the student to facilitate stability.

4. Try various groupings to determine the group in which the student is most comfortable.

5. Allow flexibility in completing assignments when the student demonstrates sudden or dramatic mood changes (e.g., allow more time, modify assignments, provide help with assignments, etc.).

6. Separate the student from the peer who stimulates the sudden or dramatic mood changes.

7. Teach the student problem-solving skills: (a) identify the problem, (b) identify goals and objectives, (c) develop strategies, (d) develop a plan for action, and (e) carry out the plan.

8. Teach the student to recognize a mood change so he/she may deal with it appropriately.

9. Provide a pleasant/calm atmosphere which would lessen the possibility of sudden or dramatic mood changes.

10. Make the necessary adjustments in the environment to prevent the student from experiencing stress, frustration, anger, etc.

11. Give the student adequate time to make adjustments to activity changes, situations, etc., (e.g., provide the student with several minutes to move from one activity to another).

12. Do not criticize. When correcting the student, be honest yet supportive. Never cause the student to feel negatively about himself/herself.

13. Prevent the occurrence of specific stimuli that cause the student to demonstrate sudden or dramatic mood changes (e.g., demanding situations, interruptions, competition, announcing test scores, abrupt changes, etc.).

14. Avoid discussions or prevent stimuli in the environment that remind the student of unpleasant experiences/sensitive topics (e.g., divorce, death, unemployment, alcoholism, etc.).

15. Intervene early when there is a problem to prevent a more serious problem from occurring.

16. Make sure the student does not become involved in overstimulating activities that would cause him/her to have mood changes.

17. Do not embarrass the student by giving him/her orders, demands, etc., in front of others.

18. Teach the student appropriate ways to communicate displeasure, anger, frustration, etc.

19. Express your feelings in a socially acceptable way.

20. Teach the student to think before acting by asking himself/herself questions: *What is happening?, What am I doing?, What should I do?, What will be best for me?*.

21. Talk to the student about ways of handling situations successfully without conflict (e.g., walk away from a situation, change to another activity, ask for help, etc.).

22. Communicate with parents, agencies, or the appropriate parties to inform them of the problem, determine the cause of the problem, and consider possible solutions to the problem.

23. Evaluate the appropriateness of the task to determine (a) if the task is too easy, (b) if the task is too difficult, and (c) if the time scheduled to complete the task is adequate.

24. Reinforce the student for demonstrating consistent and appropriate behavior: (a) give the student a tangible reward (e.g., classroom privileges, line leading, passing out materials, five minutes free time, etc.) or (b) give the student an intangible reward (e.g., praise, fist bump, smile, etc.).

25. Communicate with parents (e.g., notes home, phone calls, etc.) to share information about the student's progress. The parents may reinforce the student at home for demonstrating consistent and appropriate behavior at school.

26. Write a contract with the student specifying what behavior is expected (e.g., consistent and appropriate behavior) and what reinforcement will be made available when the terms of the contract have been met.

27. Establish classroom rules:
- Concentrate while working.
- Work quietly.
- Remain in your seat.
- Finish task.
- Meet task expectations.

Review rules often. Reinforce students for following the rules.

28. Speak with the student to explain (a) what the student is doing wrong (e.g., becoming angry or upset easily, etc.) and (b) what the student should be doing (e.g., following the rules, considering others, controlling impulsive behavior, etc.).

29. Reinforce the student for demonstrating appropriate behavior (academic or social) based on the length of time he/she can be successful. As the student demonstrates success, gradually increase the length of time required for reinforcement.

1. Reduce stimuli which would contribute to unrelated or inappropriate behavior (e.g., testing situations, peers, physical activities, etc.).

2. Modify or adjust situations that cause the student to demonstrate unrelated or inappropriate behavior (e.g., keep the student from becoming overstimulated in activities).

3. Make the necessary adjustments in the environment to prevent the student from experiencing stress, frustration, anger, etc., as much as possible.

4. Reduce distracting stimuli (e.g., place the student in the front row, provide a carrel or quiet place away from distractions, etc.). This is used as a means of reducing distracting stimuli and not as a form or punishment.

5. Try various groupings to determine the situation in which the student demonstrates appropriate behavior.

6. Model socially acceptable behavior for the student (e.g., pat on the back, fist bump, etc.).

7. Make sure that reinforcement is not inadvertently given for inappropriate comments or behaviors.

8. Prevent the student from becoming overstimulated by an activity (i.e., monitor or supervise student behavior to limit overstimulation in physical activities, games, parties, etc.).

9. Choose a peer to work with the student to model appropriate behavior.

10. Reduce the emphasis on competition. Repeated failure may result in unpredictable behavior.

11. Make the student aware of activities or events well in advance so he/she may prepare for them.

12. Discuss concerns with other professionals to determine if further investigation is warranted (e.g., abuse or neglect).

13. Explain that some concerns or worries are not unusual for students (e.g., everyone worries about tests, grades, etc.).

14. Provide the student with opportunities for social and academic success.

15. Separate the student from the peer(s) who may be encouraging or stimulating the inappropriate behavior.

16. Provide praise and recognition of appropriate behavior as often as possible.

17. Teach the student to think before acting by asking himself/herself question: *What is happening? What am I doing? What should I do? What will be best for me?*

18. Do not leave a lot of unstructured time for the student.

19. Structure the environment so time does not permit opportunities for the student to demonstrate inappropriate behavior.

20. Provide the student with alternative approaches to testing (e.g., test the student verbally, make tests shorter, let the student respond verbally, let the student take the test in the resource room, etc.).

21. Avoid discussion of topics sensitive to the student (e.g., divorce, death, unemployment, alcoholism, etc.).

22. Provide as many enjoyable and interesting activities as possible.

23. Provide a consistent routine for the student to facilitate stability.

24. Allow flexibility in completing assignments when the student demonstrates sudden or dramatic mood changes (e.g., allow more time, modify assignments, provide help with assignments).

25. Teach the student to recognize sudden or dramatic changes in behavior so he/she may deal with it appropriately.

26. Inform the student in advance when a change at school is going to occur (e.g., change in routine, special events, end of one activity and beginning of another, etc.).

27. Give the student adequate time to make adjustments to activity changes, new situations, etc., (e.g., provide the student with several minutes to move from one activity to another).

28. Prevent the occurrence of specific stimuli that cause the student to demonstrate sudden or dramatic changes in behavior (e.g., demanding situations, interruptions, competition, abrupt changes, etc.).

29. Provide the student with a variety of assignments and require the student to choose a minimum number from the total amount to complete (e.g., present the student with ten academic tasks from which six must be finished that day).

30. Provide the student with a schedule of daily events so the student will know what is expected of him/her.

31. Deliver a predetermined signal (e.g., quiet sign, hand signal, verbal cue, etc.) when the student begins to demonstrate an inappropriate behavior.

32. Provide a pleasant/calm atmosphere which would lessen the possibility of sudden or dramatic changes in behavior.

33. Reduce distracting stimuli (e.g., place the student in the front row, provide a carrel or quiet place away from distractions, etc.). This is used as a means of reducing stimuli and not as punishment.

34. Do not criticize. When correcting the student, be honest yet supportive. Never cause the student to feel negatively about himself/herself.

35. Treat the student with respect. Talk in an objective manner at all times.

36. Intervene early when there is a problem to prevent more serious problems from occurring.

37. Do not embarrass the student by giving him/her orders, demands, etc., in front of others.

38. Teach the student appropriate ways to communicate displeasure, anger, frustration, etc.

39. Encourage the student to use problem-solving skills: (a) identify the problem, (b) identify goals and objectives, (c) develop strategies, (d) develop a plan for action, and (e) carry out the plan.

40. Evaluate the appropriateness of the task to determine (a) if the task is too easy, (b) if the task is too difficult, and (c) if the length of time scheduled to complete the task is adequate.

41. Communicate with parents (e.g., notes home, phone calls, etc.) to share information about the student's progress. The parents may reinforce the student at home for demonstrating appropriate behaviors related to situations at school.

42. Write a contract with the student specifying what behavior is expected (e.g., demonstrating appropriate behavior related to the situation) and what reinforcement will be made available when the terms of the contract have been met.

43. Remove the student from the group or activity until he/she can demonstrate appropriate behavior and self-control.

44. Speak with the student to explain (a) what the student is doing wrong and (b) what the student should be doing.

45. Reinforce the student for demonstrating appropriate behavior: (a) give the student a tangible reward (e.g., classroom privileges, line leading, passing out materials, five minutes free time, etc.) or (b) give the student an intangible reward (e.g., praise, fist bump, smile, etc.).

46. Establish classroom rules:
- Concentrate while working.
- Work quietly.
- Remain in your seat.
- Finish task.
- Meet task requirements.

Review rules often. Reinforce the student for following the rules.

47. Reinforce the student for demonstrating appropriate behavior related to the situation based on the length of time the student can be successful.

48. Reinforce those students in the classroom who demonstrate appropriate behavior related to the situation.

Reminder: Do not force the student to participate in any activity he/she finds unpleasant, embarrassing, etc.

172 Makes sexually related comments or engages in inappropriate behavior with sexual overtones

1. Indicate to the student that public displays of sexually related behavior are inappropriate.

2. Supervise the student closely to prevent inappropriate sexually related behaviors from occurring.

3. Structure the environment so that time does not permit the student to participate in inappropriate behavior (e.g., maintain a full schedule of activities).

4. Seat the student close to the teacher to provide more direct supervision.

5. Maintain visibility to and from the student. The teacher should be able to see the student, and the student should be able to see the teacher. Make eye contact possible at all times.

6. Be mobile to be frequently near the student.

7. Do not allow the student to be left alone or unsupervised with other students.

8. Make sure the student understands the natural consequences of his/her inappropriate behavior (e.g., peers may not want to interact with him/her, removal from the group may be necessary, etc.).

9. Model socially acceptable behavior for the student (e.g., pat on the back, appropriate verbal communications, fist bump, etc.).

10. Separate the student from the peer(s) who stimulates the inappropriate sexually related behavior.

11. Make sure the student knows exactly which sexually related behaviors are unacceptable at school (e.g., words, gestures, comments, touching, exposing, etc.).

12. Intervene early when there is a problem to prevent more serious problems from occurring.

13. Do not inadvertently reinforce the student for demonstrating sexually related behaviors (e.g., attending to the student only when he/she demonstrates sexually related behaviors, demonstrating shock, etc.).

14. Maintain a professional relationship with students at all times and in all settings, making certain that your behavior does not stimulate sexually related behaviors.

15. Teach the student appropriate ways to communicate displeasure, anger, frustration, etc.

16. Teach the student to think before acting by asking himself/herself question: *What is happening? What am I doing? What should I do? What will be best for me?*

17. Communicate with parents, agencies, or the appropriate parties to inform them of the problem, determine the cause of the problem, and consider possible solutions to the problem.

18. Establish classroom rules:
- Concentrate while working.
- Work quietly.
- Remain in your seat.
- Finish task.
- Meet task expectations.
- Raise your hand.

Review rules often. Reinforce students for following the rules.

19. Communicate with the parents (e.g., notes home, phone calls, etc.) to share information about the student's progress. The parents may reinforce the student at home for engaging in appropriate behavior at school.

20. Write a contract with the student specifying what behavior is expected (e.g., communicating with others in an appropriate manner) and what reinforcement will be made available when the terms of the contract have been met.

21. Do not force the student to interact with individuals with whom he/she is not completely comfortable.

22. Remove the student from the group or activity until he/she can demonstrate appropriate behavior and self-control.

23. Reinforce the student for demonstrating appropriate behavior based on the length of time the student can be successful. As the student demonstrates success, gradually increase the length of time required for reinforcement.

24. Reinforce those students in the classroom who participate in appropriate behavior.

25. Speak with the student to explain (a) what the student is doing wrong (e.g., making sexual references, touching others, making gestures, etc.) and (b) what the student should be doing (e.g., following the rules, working on task, attending to responsibilities, etc.).

26. Reinforce the student for engaging in socially appropriate individual or group behavior: (a) give the student a tangible reward (e.g., classroom privileges, line leading, passing out materials, five minutes free time, etc.) or (b) give the student an intangible reward (e.g., praise, fist bump, smile, etc.).

1. Communicate with parents (e.g., notes home, phone calls, etc.) to share information about their child's progress. The parents may reinforce the student at home for demonstrating physical self-control at school.

2. Give the student additional responsibilities (e.g., chores, errands, etc.) to keep him/her actively involved and give him/her a feeling of success or accomplishment.

3. Facilitate on-task behavior by providing a full schedule of daily events. Prevent lag time when the student would be free to participate in excessive and unnecessary body movements.

4. Intervene early when there is a problem to prevent a more serious problem from occurring.

5. Maintain a full schedule of activities. Keeping the student occupied should prevent unnecessary movement.

6. Make sure the student has all the materials necessary to perform a task to reduce the need to leave his/her seat.

7. Remove the student immediately from an activity when he/she is moving about unnecessarily until he/she can participate appropriately.

8. Maintain supervision at all times and in all parts of the school environment.

9. Help the student develop an awareness of himself/herself and those around him/her. Have the student periodically step back and ask himself/herself "Am I fidgeting and being overactive?"

10. Provide constant, positive reinforcement for appropriate behavior. Ignore as many inappropriate behaviors as possible.

11. Reinforce the student for demonstrating appropriate behavior based on the length of time the student can be successful. As the student demonstrates success, gradually increase the length of time required for reinforcement.

12. Choose a peer to model staying in his/her seat for the student.

13. Consider carefully the student's age before expecting him/her to sit quietly for a period of time. Middle school students need frequent opportunities for movement.

14. Provide the student with a calm, quiet environment in which to work.

15. Reinforce those students in the classroom who demonstrate physical self-control.

16. Provide the student with a clearly understood list of consequences for inappropriate behavior.

17. Reduce the emphasis on competition. Competitive activities may cause the student to become anxious and move about unnecessarily.

18. Schedule recreational activities at the end of the day. Make participation in these activities dependent upon completion of daily responsibilities and appropriate behavior.

19. Speak with the student to explain (a) what he/she is doing wrong (e.g., moving in seat, moving about the room, running, etc.) and (b) what he/she should be doing (e.g., practicing self-control, following the rules, etc.).

20. Remove the student from the group or activity until he/she can demonstrate appropriate behavior and refrain from moving about unnecessarily.

21. Encourage the student to participate in high-energy activities after school that allow him/her to release excess energy (e.g., racquetball, soccer, etc.).

22. Interact frequently with the student to maintain his/her attention to the activity (e.g., ask the student questions, ask the student's opinion, stand close to the student, seat the student near the teacher's desk, etc.).

23. Encourage the student to avoid ingesting any substance (e.g., drugs, alcohol, cold remedies, etc.) that might further alter his/her ability to maintain self-control.

24. Have the student chart the length of time he/she is able to remain in his/her seat without moving about unnecessarily.

25. Establish classroom rules:
- Concentrate while working.
- Work quietly.
- Remain in your seat.
- Finish task.
- Meet task requirements.

Review rules often. Reinforce the student for following the rules.

26. Establish times when it is permissible for the student to be out of his/her seat (e.g., leave his/her seat only to get a book, a drink of water, etc.).

27. Provide the student with the most attractive and interesting activities possible.

28. Remain calm when the student moves about unnecessarily. Calm behavior should have a calming effect on the student.

29. Make sure the student does not become involved in activities which may be overstimulating and cause the student to move about unnecessarily.

30. Make sure that reinforcement is not inadvertently given for inappropriate behavior (e.g., attending to the student only when he/she engages in excessive/unnecessary body movements).

31. Make sure the student does not have a lot of unstructured time.

32. Provide the student with frequent opportunities to participate, take turns, etc., to keep him/her involved in the activity.

33. Separate the student from the peer who stimulates his/her inappropriate behavior.

34. Increase supervision (e.g., by teacher, peer, paraprofessional, etc.) of the student when he/she is involved in activities that tend to cause him/her to move about unnecessarily.

35. Reinforce the student for demonstrating physical self-control: (a) give the student a tangible reward (e.g., classroom privileges, passing out materials, five minutes free time, etc.) or (b) give the student an intangible reward (e.g., praise, fist bump, smile, etc.).

36. Provide the student with a predetermined signal when he/she begins to leave his/her seat without permission.

37. Be proactive. Work with the school counselor to create a schedule to facilitate the student's success (e.g., physical education scheduled the last period of the day, intersperse electives which allow greater freedom of movement with classes requiring extended periods of concentration, etc.).

38. Modify or eliminate situations at school which cause the student to experience stress or frustration and may contribute to the student moving about unnecessarily.

39. Give the student a special signal when he/she is moving about unnecessarily (e.g., a secret word, a hand signal, etc.).

40. Avoid placing the student in situations that require sitting for an extended directions, announcements, seminars, etc. Provide the information for the student through a recording or lecture notes.

41. Evaluate the appropriateness of the task to determine (a) if the task is too easy, (b) if the task is too difficult, and (c) if the length of time scheduled to complete the task is adequate.

42. Evaluate the visual and auditory stimuli in the classroom. Determine the amount of stimuli the student can tolerate. Remove extraneous stimuli which contributes to the student's unnecessary or excessive movement from the classroom environment.

43. Be consistent in expecting the student to sit quietly without moving about unnecessarily. Do not allow the student to move about unnecessarily one day and expect him/her to sit quietly the next day.

44. Schedule short activities for the student to perform while seated. As the student demonstrates success staying in his/her seat, gradually increase the length of the activities.

45. Write a contract with the student specifying what behavior is expected (e.g., demonstrating physical self-control) and what reinforcement will be made available when the terms of the contract have been met.

46. Have a peer cue the student when he/she moves about unnecessarily (e.g., the person can touch the student's arm as a signal that he/she is moving about unnecessarily).

47. Be consistent in having the student leave a situation when he/she begins to move about unnecessarily (e.g., send the student to a study carrel for 10 minutes, have him/her sit in a chair for 5 minutes, etc.).

48. Move objects used for tactile stimulation (e.g., pens, paper clips, loose change, etc.) away from the student's reach.

49. Seat the student near the teacher.

50. Make the necessary adjustments in the environment to prevent the student from experiencing stress, frustration, anger, etc., as much as possible.

51. Arrange for individual assignments when the group setting is overly distracting.

52. Maintain visibility to and from the student to keep his/her attention when verbal questions/directions are being delivered. The teacher should be able to see the student and the student should be able to see the teacher. Make eye contact possible at all times.

53. Have the student assemble all the materials necessary to work on a project, assignment, etc., to reduce the need to search for materials.

54. Establish an environmental setting for the classroom that promotes optimal individual performance (e.g., quiet room, background music, fresh air, etc.).

55. Interact frequently with the student to prevent excessive or unnecessary body movements.

56. Do not allow the student to participate in activities that cause him/her to become so excited that he/she moves about unnecessarily.

57. Supervise the student to prevent him/her from not sitting quietly and moving around unnecessarily.

58. Teach the student to use techniques to gain self-control when he/she is moving about unnecessarily (e.g., count to ten, say the alphabet, sit in a chair, leave the situation, etc.).

59. Give the student frequent opportunities to leave his/her seat for appropriate reasons (e.g., getting materials, running errands, assisting the teacher, etc.).

60. Allow the student some movement while performing tasks. Monitor and limit the amount of movement.

1. Communicate with parents (e.g., notes home, phone calls, etc.) to share information about their child's progress. The parents may reinforce the student at home for demonstrating self-control in the presence of visual and auditory stimuli at school.

2. Intervene early when there is a problem to prevent a more serious problem from occurring.

3. Remove the student from an activity in the classroom if he/she is unable to demonstrate self-control in the presence of visual and auditory stimuli involved with the activity.

4. Educate yourself and others about ADHD to increase understanding and accommodation of overexcited behavior.

5. Remove the student immediately from an activity when he/she becomes too excited and does not calm down.

6. Help the student develop an awareness of himself/herself and those around him/her. Have the student periodically step back and ask himself/herself "Am I too excited?"

7. Educate the student about ADHD and the need to self monitor behavior.

8. Help the student develop an awareness of the consequences of his/her behavior by writing down or talking through problems which may occur due to his/her becoming overexcited (e.g., perceived as unmannerly, avoided, etc.).

9. Reduce all visual and auditory stimuli in the classroom as much as possible for all learners.

10. Teach behaviors that promote self-control. Allow the student to gain his/her composure before continuing an activity (e.g., placing hands on desk, sitting with feet on the floor, making eye contact with the person who is talking, etc.).

11. Encourage the student to pause and consider his/her actions when becoming overexcited.

12. Have the student participate in another activity until he/she can settle down and gain control of his/her behavior.

13. Provide constant, positive reinforcement for appropriate behavior. Ignore as many inappropriate behaviors as possible.

14. Have the student take a break to regroup when he/she is becoming overexcited.

15. Choose a classmate to model demonstrating self-control in the presence of visual and auditory stimuli in the classroom for the student.

16. Remain calm when the student becomes overexcited. Calm behavior should have a calming effect on the student.

17. Teach the student to think before acting by asking himself/herself question: *What is happening? What am I doing? What should I do? What will be best for me?*

18. Model for the student appropriate behavior in the presence of visual and auditory stimuli in the classroom (e.g., continuing to work, asking for quiet, moving to a quieter part of the classroom, etc.).

19. Encourage the student to play games, sports, etc., with friends who do not stimulate him/her to become overexcited.

20. Reinforce those students in the classroom who demonstrate self-control.

21. Provide the student with a clearly understood list of consequences for inappropriate behavior.

22. Reduce the emphasis on competition. Competitive activities may cause the student to become overexcited.

23. Allow flexibility in completing assignments when the student becomes overexcited (e.g., allow more time, modify assignments, provide help with assignments, etc.).

24. Establish classroom rules:
- Concentrate while working.
- Work quietly.
- Remain in your seat.
- Finish task.
- Meet task requirements.

Review rules often. Reinforce the student for following the rules.

25. Assess the degree of task difficulty to determine whether or not the student will require additional information, time, assistance, etc., to avoid becoming overexcited.

26. Explain to the student when he/she does not calm down exactly what he/she is doing wrong, what he/she is supposed to be doing, and why.

27. Do not let the student participate in exciting activities for long periods of time.

28. Speak to the student to explain (a) what he/she is doing wrong (e.g., becoming overexcited or upset) and (b) what he/she should be doing (e.g., following the rules, considering others, controlling impulsive behavior, etc.).

29. Provide the student with a carrel or divider at his/her desk to reduce visual and auditory stimuli.

30. Avoid discussion or prevent stimuli in the environment which reminds the student of unpleasant experiences/sensitive topics (e.g., divorce, death, unemployment, alcoholism, etc.) which might cause the student to become overexcited.

31. Encourage the student to participate in quiet, calming activities (e.g., listen to music, read, etc.) when feeling overexcited.

32. Encourage the student to avoid ingesting any substance (e.g., drugs, alcohol, cold remedies, etc.) that might further alter his/her ability to maintain self-control.

33. Have the student make a list of consequences associated with overexcitement (e.g., break something, hurt someone, embarrass self or others, etc.).

34. Make sure the student does not become involved in overstimulating activities.

35. Provide the student with the opportunity to move to a quiet place in the classroom whenever visual and auditory stimuli interfere with his/her ability to function successfully.

36. Increase supervision (e.g., by teacher, peer, paraprofessional, etc.) of the student when he/she is involved in activities that tend to overexcite him/her.

37. Separate the student from the peer that stimulates his/her inappropriate behavior.

38. Provide the student with a predetermined signal when he/she begins to display inappropriate behavior.

39. Provide the student with a quiet place in which to work where visual and auditory stimuli are reduced. This is used to reduce distracting stimuli and not as a form of punishment.

40. Reinforce the student for demonstrating self-control: (a) give the student a tangible reward (e.g., classroom privileges, passing out materials, five minutes free time, etc.) or (b) give the student an intangible reward (e.g., praise, fist bump, smile, etc.).

41. Allow the student to close the classroom door or windows to reduce visual and auditory stimuli from outside of the classroom.

42. Give the student a special signal when he/she is becoming excited (e.g., a secret word, a hand signal, etc.).

43. Help the student recognize the signs of becoming overexcited. Teach the student appropriate actions to gain self-control.

44. Have the student participate in small-group activities (e.g., free time, math, reading, etc.) to reduce the level of visual and auditory stimuli in the group. As the student successfully functions in the presence of visual and auditory stimuli, gradually increase the size of the group.

45. Prevent the student from becoming so stimulated by an event or activity that he/she cannot control his/her behavior.

46. Evaluate the visual and auditory stimuli in the classroom. Determine the level of stimuli to which the student can respond in an appropriate manner. Remove the extraneous stimuli from the environment.

47. Be consistent in expecting the student to settle down after becoming excited. Do not allow the student to participate until he/she has regained self-control.

48. Be consistent in expecting the student to leave a situation when he/she becomes overexcited (e.g., send the student to the counselor's office, have him/her sit in a chair for 5 minutes, etc.).

49. Designate a specific location the student can go to regain control after becoming overexcited.

50. Provide a consistent routine for the student to facilitate self-control.

51. Encourage the student to consider the consequences of his/her behavior before engaging in any activity.

52. Identify the situations in which the student is most likely to become overexcited. After you have identified these situations, think of ways to minimize their occurrences.

53. Reinforce the student for demonstrating self-control. As the student demonstrates success, gradually increase the length of time required for reinforcement.

54. Teach the student appropriate ways to gain self-control after becoming overexcited (e.g., take slow deep breaths, leave the activity, walk down the hallway to the water fountain, etc.).

55. Do not allow the student to participate in activities that cause him/her to become so excited that he/she cannot settle down.

56. Reduce visual and auditory stimuli to a level at which the student can successfully function. As the student demonstrates that he/she can successfully tolerate the increased levels without becoming overexcited, gradually allow visual and auditory stimuli to increase.

57. Make sure that the student understands the relationship between inappropriate behavior and the consequences which follow (e.g., missing out on special activities, being avoided by peers, etc.).

58. Provide a pleasant/calm atmosphere which will lessen the likelihood of the student becoming overexcited.

59. Write a contract with the student specifying what behavior is expected (e.g., maintaining self-control in the presence of visual and auditory stimuli in the classroom) and what reinforcement will be made available when the terms of the contract have been met.

175 Lies, denies, exaggerates, distorts the truth

1. Explain to the student that he/she should be satisfied with personal best effort rather than expecting perfection.

2. Provide the student with many opportunities for social and academic successes.

3. Provide the student with positive feedback which indicates he/she is successful.

4. Reduce competitiveness in information sharing so the student will not feel compelled to make inaccurate statements about his/her experience.

5. Try various groupings to determine the situation in which the student is most comfortable and does not feel compelled to lie, deny, exaggerate the truth, etc.

6. Provide the student with experiences which can be shared if the absence of such experiences has been causing the student to fabricate information.

7. Reduce or remove punishment for accidents, forgetting, and situations with inadequate evidence. Punishment in these situations often causes students to lie.

8. Treat the student with respect. Talk in an objective manner at all times.

9. Do not punish the student unless you are absolutely sure he/she lied to you.

10. Teach the student that making inaccurate statements does not prevent consequences (e.g., the student has to redo an assignment even though he/she claims the completed assignment was lost).

11. Take no action in situations where conclusive evidence does not exist.

12. Allow natural consequences to occur when the student lies, denies, exaggerates, etc., (e.g., work not completed must be completed, lying to others will cause them not to believe you, etc.).

13. Help the student learn that telling the truth as soon as possible prevents future problems (e.g., admitting that he/she made a mistake, forgot, etc., means that the necessary steps can be taken to correct the situation instead of waiting until the truth is determined in some other way).

14. Help the student to understand that by exaggerating the truth he/she may even come to believe what he/she exaggerates and that exaggerating may become a habit.

15. Teach the student to think before acting by asking himself/herself question: *What is happening? What am I doing? What should I do? What will be best for me?*

16. Develop a system of shared responsibility (e.g., instead of trying to determine who is guilty, classmates work together to help clean up, return materials, make repairs, etc.).

17. Supervise the student closely to monitor the accuracy of statements made.

18. Avoid making accusations which would increase the probability of the student making inaccurate statements in response. If it is known that the student is responsible, an admission of guilt is not necessary to deal with the situation.

19. Avoid putting the student in a situation in which he/she has the opportunity to lie, deny, exaggerate, etc., (e.g., highly competitive activities, situations with limited supervision, etc.).

20. Communicate with parents (e.g., notes home, phone calls, etc.) to share information about the student's progress. The parents may reinforce the student at home for making accurate statements at school.

21. Make sure the student understands that not being honest when confronted will result in more negative consequences than telling the truth. Be sure to be very consistent in this approach.

22. Speak with the student to explain (a) what the student is doing wrong (e.g., lying, denying his/her behavior, etc.) and (b) what the student should be doing (e.g., reporting accurately what has occurred or will occur).

23. Reinforce the student for making accurate statements: (a) give the student a tangible reward (e.g., classroom privileges, line leading, passing out materials, five minutes free time, etc.) or (b) give the student an intangible reward (e.g., praise, fist bump, smile, etc.).

24. Attempt to have an open, honest relationship with the student. Encourage the student to tell the truth, and do not use threats to make him/her tell the truth (e.g., "You had better tell the truth or else!").

25. Write a contract with the student specifying what behavior is expected (e.g., making accurate statements) and what reinforcement will be made available when the terms of the contract have been met.

1. Avoid topics, situations, etc., (e.g., death, divorce, unemployment, alcoholism, etc.) which cause the student to speak in an unnatural voice.

2. Choose a peer to model using a natural voice when speaking.

3. Write a contract with the student specifying what behavior is expected (e.g., using a natural voice) and what reinforcement will be made available when the terms of the contract have been met.

4. Communicate with parents, agencies, or the appropriate parties to inform them of the problem, determine the cause of the problem, and consider possible solutions to the problem.

5. Do not force the student to interact with individuals with whom he/she is not completely comfortable.

6. Reinforce those students in the classroom who use a natural voice when speaking.

7. Evaluate the appropriateness of the task to determine (a) if the task is too easy, (b) if the task is too difficult, and (c) if the length of time scheduled to complete the task is adequate.

8. Give the student a predetermined signal when he/she begins to use an unnatural voice.

9. Ignore the student's unnatural voice if it occurs infrequently or only in stimulating situations.

10. Make sure that all adults (e.g., school and home) require the student to speak in a natural voice.

11. Reinforce the student for speaking in a natural voice based on the length of time he/she can be successful. As the student demonstrates success, gradually increase the length of time required for reinforcement.

12. Do not reinforce inappropriate behavior by laughing when the student talks in an unnatural voice.

13. Make sure that the student's unnatural voice is not inadvertently reinforced by over-attending to it (i.e., the student may speak in an unnatural voice because of the constant attention given to him/her).

14. Express your feelings in a socially acceptable way.

15. Place the student in situations in which he/she is comfortable and most likely to use a natural voice.

16. Reinforce the student for speaking in a natural voice: (a) give the student a tangible reward (e.g., classroom privileges, line leading, passing out materials, five minutes free time, etc.) or (b) give the student an intangible reward (e.g., praise, fist bump, smile, etc.).

17. Speak to the student to explain (a) what he/she is doing wrong (e.g., using an unnatural voice) and (b) what he/she should be doing (e.g., using a natural voice).

18. Teach the student appropriate ways to communicate displeasure, anger, frustration, etc.

19. Communicate with parents (e.g., notes home, phone calls, etc.) to share information about the student's progress. The parents may reinforce the student at home for using a natural voice at school.

20. Require the student to use a natural voice at all times in the classroom.

1. Allow the student to speak without being interrupted or hurried.

2. Model speaking in complete statements or thoughts (e.g., speak clearly, slowly, concisely, and in complete sentences, statements, and thoughts) for the student.

3. Have the student identify who he/she thinks is a good speaker and why.

4. Break down the qualities a good speaker possesses (e.g., rate, diction, volume, vocabulary, etc.) and have the student evaluate himself/herself on each quality. Set a goal for improvement in only one or two areas at a time.

5. Demonstrate acceptable and unacceptable speech. Use complete/incomplete statements and thoughts and have the student critique each example.

6. Have the student practice descriptive statements or thoughts he/she can use when speaking.

7. Do not require the student to speak in front of other students if he/she is uncomfortable doing so. Have the student speak to the teacher or another student privately if he/she would be more comfortable.

8. Choose a peer to model speaking in complete statements or thoughts. Assign the students to work together, perform assignments together, etc.

9. When the student has difficulty during a conversation, remind the student that this occasionally happens to everyone and he/she should not become upset.

10. Verbally correct the student when he/she does not use complete sentences or thoughts when speaking so he/she can hear the correct version of what is being said.

11. Do not force the student to interact with individuals with whom he/she is not completely comfortable.

12. Have the student practice techniques for relaxing (e.g., deep breathing, tensing and relaxing muscles, etc.) which the student can employ when he/she starts to become dysfluent.

13. Reinforce those students in the classroom who use complete statements or thoughts when speaking.

14. If the student is speaking too rapidly, remind him/her to slow down and take his/her time. Be sure to give him/her undivided attention so he/she will not feel a need to hurry or compete with others for attention.

15. Write a contract with the student specifying what behavior is expected (e.g., using complete statements or thoughts when speaking) and what reinforcement will be made available when the terms of the contract have been met.

16. Have the student role-play various situations in which speaking well is important (e.g., during a job interview).

17. Make a list of the attributes that are likely to help a person become a good speaker (e.g., takes his/her time, thinks of what to say before starting, etc.).

18. Prepare simple verbal reading passages in written form in which phrases are separated by large spaces (indicating a pause). Have the student practice reading the passages aloud.

19. Teach the student appropriate ways to communicate displeasure, anger, frustration, etc.

20. Have the student keep a list of times and/or situations in which he/she is nervous, anxious, etc., and has more trouble with speech than usual. Help the student identify ways to feel more successful with those situations.

21. When the student does not use complete sentences (e.g., says, "ball," and points to one), elaborate on what he/she said, (e.g., "Do you want to play with the ball?"). This provides a model for more complete statements and thoughts.

22. Have the student read simple passages and record them. Have him/her listen and underline words or phrases that were omitted, added, substituted, or rearranged.

23. Reinforce the student for using complete statements or thoughts when speaking: (a) give the student a tangible reward (e.g., classroom privileges, line leading, passing out materials, five minutes free time, etc.) or (b) give the student an intangible reward (e.g., praise, fist bump, smile, etc.).

24. Record a spontaneous monologue given by the student. Transcribe the student's speech from the recording and have the student listen to what he/she said. Have the student correct errors and practice speaking in more complete statements or thoughts.

25. Make a list of the most common incomplete statements or thoughts the student uses. Spend time with the student practicing how to make these statements or thoughts complete.

26. Reduce the emphasis on competition. Competitive activities may increase the student's anxiety and reduce the student's ability to complete statements or thoughts.

1. Communicate with parents (e.g., notes home, phone calls, etc.) to share information about their child's progress. The parents may reinforce the student at home for not engaging in nervous habits at school.

2. Provide a calm/pleasant atmosphere.

3. Allow the student to squeeze a tennis ball or rolled up towel to decrease engaging in nervous habits.

4. Allow the student to take a break to re-group when he/she is becoming nervous.

5. Avoid discussion of topics that are sensitive to the student (e.g., divorce, death, unemployment, alcoholism, etc.).

6. Maintain a full schedule of activities. Keeping the student occupied should prevent the student from engaging in nervous habits.

7. Allow the student some physical activity while performing tasks.

8. Provide the student with an alternate activity designed to result in productive behavior (e.g., drawing, cutting, using a calculator, working with a peer, etc.).

9. Help the student develop an awareness of himself/herself and those around him/her. Encourage the student to periodically step back and ask himself/herself "Am I fidgeting and being overactive?"

10. Teach behaviors that promote self-control. Allow the student to gain his/her composure before continuing an activity (e.g., placing hands on desk, sitting with feet on the floor, making eye contact with the person who is talking, etc.).

11. Reinforce the student for demonstrating appropriate behavior: (a) give the student a tangible reward (e.g., classroom privileges, passing out materials, five minutes free time, etc.) or (b) give the student an intangible reward (e.g., praise, fist bump, smile, etc.).

12. Reinforce the student for demonstrating appropriate academic/social behavior based on the length of time he/she can be successful. As the student demonstrates success, gradually increase the length of time required for reinforcement.

13. Allow the student to keep a small object in his/her pocket that is appropriate to handle at all times and would not disturb others (e.g., foam, rubber, or fabric ball; buckeye; worry stone; etc.).

14. Have the student develop an awareness of the consequences of his/her behavior by writing down or talking through problems which may occur due to his/her nervous habits (e.g., perceived as unmannerly, avoided, etc.).

15. Try various groupings in the classroom to determine the situation in which the student is most comfortable.

16. Reinforce those students in the classroom who demonstrate appropriate behavior.

17. Prevent situations in which peers contribute to the student's nervous behaviors.

18. Assess the degree of task difficulty to determine whether or not the student will require additional information, time, assistance, etc., to avoid becoming frustrated and engaging in nervous habits.

19. Speak with the student to explain (a) what he/she is doing wrong (e.g., chewing on pencil, nail biting, twirling objects, etc.) and (b) what he/she should be doing (e.g., practicing self-control, working on assignment, performing responsibilities, etc.).

20. Teach the student ways to gain self-control (e.g., count to ten, walk away, talk with someone, etc.).

21. Remove the student from the group or activity when he/she engages in nervous habits.

22. Provide the student with a high-interest activity he/she prefers.

23. Interact frequently with the student to maintain his/her involvement in class assignments.

24. Encourage the student to participate in quiet, calming activities (e.g., listen to music, read, etc.) when feeling restless and engaging in nervous behaviors.

25. Encourage the student to avoid ingesting any substance (e.g., drugs, alcohol, cold remedies, etc.) that might further alter his/her ability to maintain self-control.

26. Provide the student with many opportunities for social and academic successes.

27. Explain to the student the need to develop self-monitoring skills to decrease nervous habits.

28. Encourage the student to reduce nervous behaviors such as nail biting, knuckle cracking, or chewing his/her lip/cheek by replacing them with a competing behavior (e.g., clinch his/her fists together to avoid cracking his/her knuckles, suck on hard candy instead of chewing his/her lip/cheek, etc.).

29. Remove from the environment any object which may be used by the student to participate in nervous habits (e.g., pencils, pens, rubber-bands, paper clips, etc.).

30. Provide the student with a predetermined signal when he/she engages in nervous habits.

31. Reduce the emphasis on competition. Repeated failure and frustration may cause the student to participate in nervous habits.

32. Encourage the student to practice self-control activities designed to allow him/her to gain composure before continuing an activity (e.g., placing hands on desk, sitting with feet on the floor, making eye contact with the instructor, etc.).

33. Move objects used for tactile stimulation (e.g., pens, paper clips, loose change, etc.) away from the student's reach.

34. Write a contract with the student specifying what behavior is expected (e.g., not engaging in nervous habits) and what reinforcement will be made available when the terms of the contract have been met.

35. Evaluate the appropriateness of the task to determine (a) if the task is too easy, (b) if the task is too difficult, and (c) if the length of time scheduled to complete the task is adequate.

36. Teach the student to use techniques such as crossing his/her arms and legs, clenching his/her fists, and intertwining his/her fingers when he/she is engaging in nervous habits.

37. Structure the environment so time does not allow the student the opportunity to participate in nervous habits.

38. Reduce stimuli which may cause the student to participate in nervous habits (e.g., noise, movement, etc.).

39. Make the necessary adjustments in the environment to prevent the student from experiencing stress, frustration, nervousness, etc.

40. Identify the situations in which the student is likely to participate in nervous habits. After you have identified these situations, think of ways to minimize their occurrences.

41. Teach the student to attend to the source of information by maintaining eye contact, keeping hands free from other materials, and reducing other nervous habits.

42. Interact frequently with the student to reduce nervous behavior.

43. Choose a peer tutor to work directly with the student to prevent stress, frustration, anxiety, etc.

44. Reduce situations which may contribute to nervous behavior (e.g., testing situations, timed activities, competition, etc.).

179 Destroys school, teachers', or other students' property

1. Provide time at the beginning of each day to help the student organize the materials that will be used throughout the day.

2. Provide the student with adequate work space (e.g., a large desk or table at which to work).

3. Provide storage space for materials the student is not using at any particular time.

4. Reduce distracting stimuli (e.g., place the student on the front row, provide a carrel or quiet place away from distractions, etc.). Overstimulation may cause the student to misuse others' property.

5. Interact frequently with the student to prompt organizational skills and appropriate use of materials.

6. Assign the student organizational responsibilities in the classroom (e.g., equipment, software materials, etc.).

7. Limit the student's access to materials (e.g., provide the student with only those materials necessary at any given time).

8. Model organization and appropriate use of work materials (e.g., putting materials away before getting other materials out, having a place for all materials, maintaining an organized desk area, following a schedule for the day, etc.).

9. Provide adequate time for the completion of activities. Inadequate time for completion of activities may result in the student's misuse of others' property.

10. Allow natural consequences to occur as the result of the student's inability to appropriately care for and handle others' property (e.g., property not maintained appropriately may be lost or not useable).

11. Assess the quality and clarity of directions, explanations, and instructions given to the student concerning the care and handling of others' property.

12. Assist the student in beginning each task to reduce impulsive behavior.

13. Provide the student with structure for all academic activities (e.g., specific directions, routine format for tasks, time limits, etc.).

14. Give the student a checklist of materials necessary for each activity.

15. Minimize materials needed.

16. Provide an organizer for materials inside the student's desk.

17. Teach the student appropriate care and handling of others' property (e.g., sharpening borrowed pencils, keeping books free of marks and tears, etc.).

18. Make sure that all personal property is labeled with the student's name.

19. Point out to the student that borrowing personal property from others does not reduce his/her responsibility for the property.

20. Teach the student how to conserve rather than waste materials (e.g., amount of glue, tape, etc., to use; putting lids, caps, and tops on such materials as markers, pens, bottles, jars, cans; etc.).

21. Teach the student appropriate ways to deal with anger and frustration rather than destroying others' property (e.g., pencils, pens, workbooks, notebooks, textbooks, etc.).

22. Teach the student to maintain property belonging to others (e.g., keep property with him/her, know where property is at all times, secure property in locker, etc.).

23. Provide the student with an appropriate place to store/secure others' property (e.g., desk, locker, closet, etc.) and require the student to store all property when not in use.

24. Teach the student that the failure to care for others' property will result in the loss of freedom to use others' property.

25. Provide reminders (e.g., a list of property or materials) to help the student maintain and care for school property.

26. Limit the student's freedom to take property from school if he/she is unable to remember to return the items.

27. Limit the student's opportunities to use others' property if the student is unable to care for his/her own personal property.

28. Reduce the number of materials for which the student is responsible. As the student demonstrates appropriate responsibility for property, gradually increase the number of materials for which the student is responsible.

29. Teach the student safety rules in the care and handling of others' property and materials (e.g., pencils, scissors, compass; biology, industrial arts and home economics materials; etc.).

30. Require that lost or damaged property be replaced by the student. If the student cannot replace the property, restitution can be made by working at school.

31. Make sure the student is not inadvertently reinforced for losing or damaging property by providing him/her with new materials. Provide the student with used or damaged materials, copies of the materials, etc., rather than new materials.

32. Teach the student rules for the care and handling of others' property (e.g., always ask to use others' property, treat the property with care, inform the teacher if the property becomes damaged, return the property in the same or better condition, etc.).

33. Do not permit peers to allow the student to use their property if he/she is not able to care for it properly.

34. Remove others' property from the student if he/she is unable to appropriately care for and handle the property.

35. Maintain mobility throughout the classroom to supervise the student's care and handling of others' property.

36. Remove the student from the group or activity until he/she can demonstrate appropriate behavior and self-control.

37. Structure the environment to reduce free or unplanned time which is likely to contribute to the student's inappropriate behavior.

38. Maintain visibility to and from the student. The teacher should be able to see the student and the student should be able to see the teacher. Make eye contact possible at all times.

39. Make the necessary adjustments in the environment to prevent the student from experiencing stress, frustration, anger, etc., as much as possible.

40. Prevent the student from becoming over-stimulated by an activity.

41. Make the student responsible for specific materials (e.g., recorder, overhead projector, microscope, etc.) in the school environment to facilitate a sense of responsibility and obligation to use the materials with care.

42. Teach the student to respect others and their belongings by respecting the student's belongings.

43. Make sure the student is always under adult supervision.

44. Make sure the student is aware of local and federal laws regarding the destruction of others' property.

45. Require the student to replace damaged items when he/she destroys others' property.

46. Teach the student to think before acting by asking himself/herself question: *What is happening? What am I doing? What should I do? What will be best for me?*

47. Have the student ask questions about directions, explanations, and instructions not understood.

48. Talk to the student about ways of handling situations successfully without conflict (e.g., walk away from a situation, change to another activity, ask for help, etc.).

49. Choose a peer to model appropriate care and handling of others' property for the student.

50. Evaluate the appropriateness of the task to determine (a) if the task is too easy, (b) if the task is too difficult, and (c) if the length of time scheduled to complete the task is adequate.

51. Communicate with parents (e.g., notes home, phone calls, etc.) to share information about the student's progress. The parents may reinforce the student at home for demonstrating appropriate care and handling of others' property at school.

52. Write a contract with the student specifying what behavior is expected (e.g., putting property away, returning property, etc.) and what reinforcement will be made available when the terms of the contract have been met.

53. Reinforce the student for demonstrating appropriate care and handling of others' property based on the length of time the student can be successful. As the student demonstrates success, gradually increase the length of time required for reinforcement.

54. Reinforce those students in the classroom who demonstrate appropriate care and handling of others' property.

55. Choose a peer to model appropriate care and handling of others' property for the student.

56. Establish classroom rules:
- Concentrate while working.
- Work quietly.
- Remain in your seat.
- Finish task.
- Meet task requirements.

Review rules often. Reinforce the student for following the rules.

57. Reinforce the student for demonstrating appropriate care and handling of others' property: (a) give the student a tangible reward (e.g., classroom privileges, line leading, passing out materials, five minutes free time, etc.) or (b) give the student an intangible reward (e.g., praise, fist bump, smile, etc.).

58. Speak to the student to explain (a) what the student is doing wrong (e.g., defacing property, destroying property, etc.) and (b) what the student should be doing (e.g., putting property away, returning property, etc.).

180 Does not accept changes in an established routine

1. Have the student work near a peer to follow change in an established routine.

2. Provide the student with a schedule of revised daily events which identifies the activities for the day and the times when they will occur.

3. Attach to the student's desk revisions in the schedule for the day's events. The student may also carry it with him/her throughout the day.

4. Post the revised routine throughout the classroom (e.g., on the student's desk, wall-mounted board, bulletin board, etc.).

5. Limit the number of times that changes must occur in the student's routine.

6. Discuss any necessary changes in the student's routine well in advance of the occurrence of the changes.

7. Teach the student to tell time to facilitate his/her ability to accept change in an established routine.

8. Have the student rely on a predetermined signal (e.g., lights turned off and on, hand signal, etc.) to facilitate the ability to accept change in an established routine.

9. Have the student use a timer to remind him/her of changes in an established routine.

10. Reduce distracting stimuli which might cause the student to be unable to accept change in an established routine (e.g., movement, noise, peers, etc.).

11. Model acceptance of change in an established routine.

12. Have the student rely on environmental cues to remind the student when to change activities in his/her revised routine (e.g., other students changing activities, bells, lights, buses arriving, etc.).

13. Choose a peer to remind the student of changes in routine.

14. Remind the student when it is time to change activities.

15. Choose a peer to accompany the student to other locations in the building when change in an established routine has occurred.

16. Allow the student an appropriate amount of time to accept changes in an established routine.

17. Explain changes in a routine to the student personally.

18. Provide activities similar to those canceled in the student's routine (e.g., if an art activity is canceled due to the art teacher's absence, provide an art activity in the classroom for the student).

19. Provide the student with highly desirable activities to perform when changes in his/her routine are necessary.

20. If change in the student's routine proves too difficult, have the student remain with the established routine (e.g., if an assembly is overstimulating for the student, have the student continue to follow his/her established routine).

21. Initially limit the number/degree of changes in the student's established routine. As the student demonstrates success, gradually increase the number/degree of changes in the routine.

22. Implement environmental changes within the classroom to provide the student with experience in change (e.g., change in seating, instructional delivery, task format, etc.), to help the student accept change in an established routine.

23. Prepare a substitute teacher information packet that includes all information pertaining to the classroom (e.g., student roster, class schedule, class rules, behavior management techniques, class helpers, etc.).

24. Make sure that the student understands that classroom rules and consequences are in effect when a substitute teacher is in the classroom.

25. Indicate the names of several personnel and where they can be located in case the substitute teacher should need some assistance.

26. Inform the substitute teacher of the classroom rules and the consequences if the rules are not followed by the student.

27. Have the student work on practice work (e.g., work that has already been taught to the student and that the student knows how to do) when a substitute teacher is in the classroom to reduce frustration and feelings of failure.

28. Request a substitute teacher who has the skills necessary to handle problem behavior and special needs students.

29. Make sure that the substitute teacher is familiar with the behavioral support system used in the classroom (e.g., rules, point system, reinforcers, etc.).

30. Provide the substitute teacher with detailed information on the activities and assignments.

31. Assign the student specific activities to perform on any day when a substitute teacher may be responsible for the classroom (e.g., assistant to the substitute teacher, errands to run, line leading, class monitor, etc.).

32. Make sure the substitute teacher follows all procedures indicated by the classroom teacher (e.g., academic activities, behavioral support system, etc.).

33. Have special or unique responsibilities performed by other personnel in the building when a substitute teacher is in the classroom (e.g., administering medication, feeding, toileting, etc.).

34. Choose a peer to model appropriate behavior and provide information necessary for success for the student when changes are made in an established routine.

35. If an aide works in the classroom, have the aide monitor the student's behavior; provide reinforcement; deliver instructions; etc.; when a substitute teacher is in the classroom.

36. Provide a quiet place for the student to work.

37. Inform the student in advance when it will be necessary for a substitute teacher to be in the classroom and establish expectations for behavior and academic performance.

38. Let the student know in advance when changes in his/her schedule will occur (e.g., going to P.E. at a different time, going on a field trip, etc.).

39. Teach the student acceptable ways to communicate displeasure, anger, frustration, etc.

40. Have the student ask questions about directions, explanations, instructions not understood concerning the change in an established routine.

41. Choose a peer to model appropriate acceptance of changes in an established routine for the student.

42. Establish classroom rules:
- Concentrate while working.
- Work quietly.
- Remain in your seat.
- Finish task.
- Meet task requirements.

Review rules often. Reinforce the student for following the rules.

43. Write a contract with the student specifying what behavior is expected (e.g., accepting a change in routine) and what reinforcement will be made available when the terms of the contract have been met.

44. Reinforce those students in the classroom who accept changes in an established routine.

45. Reinforce the student for accepting changes in an established routine based on the number of times the student can be successful. As the student demonstrates success, gradually increase the number of times required for reinforcement.

46. Communicate with parents (e.g., notes home, phone calls, etc.) to share information about the student's progress. The parents may reinforce the student at home for accepting changes in an established routine at school.

47. Speak to the student to explain (a) what the student is doing wrong (e.g., having a tantrum, refusing to accept the change, etc.) and (b) what the student should be doing (e.g., accepting the change in routine).

48. Evaluate the appropriateness of the change in routine. Determine if the change is too difficult and if the length of time scheduled is adequate.

49. Reinforce the student for accepting changes in an established routine: (a) give the student a tangible reward (e.g., classroom privileges, line leading, passing out materials, five minutes free time, etc.) or (b) give the student an intangible reward (e.g., praise, fist bump, smile, etc.).

181 Reacts physically in response to excitement, disappointment, surprise, happiness, fear, etc.

1. Make the necessary adjustments in the environment to prevent the student from experiencing stress, frustration, anger, etc., as much as possible.

2. Maintain visibility to and from the student. The teacher should be able to see the student and the student should be able to see the teacher. Make eye contact possible at all times.

3. Facilitate on-task behavior by providing a full schedule of activities. Prevent lag time from occurring when the student would be more likely to participate in involuntary physical behavior.

4. Seat the student close to the teacher.

5. Reduce stimuli that contributes to unnecessary or excessive behavior.

6. Interact frequently with the student to direct his/her attention to the activity (e.g., ask the student questions, ask the student's opinion, stand close to the student, seat the student near the teacher's desk, etc.).

7. Structure the environment so the student does not have time to dwell on problems that are either real or imagined.

8. Prevent the student from becoming overly stimulated by an activity (e.g., monitor or supervise student behavior to limit overexcitement in physical activities, games, parties, etc.).

9. Expose the student to increased stimuli in the environment on a gradual basis after success has been demonstrated.

10. Teach the student appropriate ways to react to personal or school experiences (e.g., calling attention to the problem, practicing problem solving, moving away from the situation if it is threatening, etc.).

11. Provide the student with many opportunities for social and academic successes.

12. Present the task in the most attractive and interesting manner possible.

13. Identify individuals the student may contact with his/her worries or concerns (e.g., guidance counselor, school nurse, social worker, school psychologist, etc.).

14. Maintain supervision at all times and in all parts of the school environment.

15. Prevent frustrating or anxiety-producing situations from occurring (e.g., give the student tasks only on his/her ability level, give the student only the number of tasks that can be tolerated in one sitting, reduce social interactions which stimulate the student to demonstrate involuntary physical reactions, etc.).

16. Be mobile to be frequently near the student.

17. Teach and encourage the student to use problem-solving skills: (a) identify the problem, (b) identify goals and objectives, (c) develop strategies, (d) develop a plan of action, and (c) carry out the plan.

18. Provide an environment which is calm, consistent, and structured.

19. Provide the student with a predetermined signal if he/she begins to exhibit the inappropriate behavior.

20. Make sure that positive reinforcement is not inadvertently given for inappropriate behavior (e.g., responding to the student when errors arc made, responding to the student when he/she feigns a need for help, etc.).

21. Encourage the student to practice self-control activities designed to allow the student to compose himself/herself before continuing an activity (e.g., placing hands on desk, sitting with feet flat on the floor, making eye contact with the instructor, etc.).

22. Provide the student with a quiet place to work when involuntary physical reactions occur. This is not meant as punishment but as a means of helping the student be more successful in the environment.

23. Remove the student from the group or activity until he/she can demonstrate appropriate behavior and self-control.

24. Make sure the student does not become involved in overstimulating activities.

25. Teach the student acceptable ways to communicate displeasure, anger, frustration, etc.

26. Do not force the student to interact with individuals with whom he/she is not completely comfortable.

27. Express your feelings in a socially acceptable way.

28. Allow the student to voice his/her opinion in a situation to avoid becoming angry or upset.

29. Talk to the student about ways of handling situations successfully without conflict (e.g., walk away from a situation, change to another activity, ask for help, etc.).

30. Try various groupings to determine the group in which the student is most comfortable.

31. Evaluate the appropriateness of the task to determine (a) if the task is too easy, (b) if the task is too difficult, and (c) if the length of time scheduled to complete the task is adequate.

32. Communicate with the parents (e.g., notes home, phone calls, etc.) to share information about the student's progress. The parents may reinforce the student at home for demonstrating physical self-control at school.

33. Intervene early when there is a problem to prevent more serious problems from occurring.

34. Write a contract with the student specifying what behavior is expected (e.g., demonstrating physical self-control) and what reinforcement will be made available when the terms of the contract have been met.

35. Reinforce the student for demonstrating physical self-control based on the length of time the student can be successful. As the student demonstrates success, gradually increase the amount of time required for reinforcement.

36. Reinforce those students in the classroom who demonstrate physical self-control.

37. Establish classroom rules:
- Concentrate while working.
- Work quietly.
- Remain in your seat.
- Finish task.
- Meet task requirements.

Review rules often. Reinforce the student for following the rules.

38. Speak with the student to explain (a) what the student is doing wrong (e.g., shaking, flapping hands, etc.) and (b) what the student should be doing (e.g., practicing self-control).

39. Do not allow the student to begin a new activity until he/she has gained self-control.

40. Reinforce the student for demonstrating physical self-control: (a) give the student a tangible reward (e.g., classroom privileges, line leading, passing out materials, five minutes free time, etc.) or (b) give the student an intangible reward (e.g., praise, fist bump, smile, etc.).

41. Teach the student to recognize signs of becoming overexcited so he/she may deal with it appropriately.

42. Assess the appropriateness of the social situation in relation to the student's ability to function successfully.

182 Engages in inappropriate behaviors related to bodily functions

1. Reinforce the student for demonstrating appropriate behavior related to bodily functions: (a) give the student a tangible reward (e.g., classroom privileges, line leading, passing out materials, five minutes free time, etc.) or (b) give the student an intangible reward (e.g., praise, fist bump, smile, etc.).

2. Speak to the student to explain (a) what he/she is doing wrong (e.g., urinating on floor, masturbating, etc.) and (b) what he/she should be doing (e.g., demonstrating appropriate social behavior).

3. Reinforce those students in the classroom who demonstrate appropriate social behavior.

4. Reinforce the student for demonstrating appropriate social behavior based on the length of time he/she can be successful. As the student demonstrates success, gradually increase the length of time required for reinforcement.

5. Write a contract with the student specifying what behavior is expected (e.g., talking about topics which are appropriate for social situations) and what reinforcements will be made available when the terms of the contract have been met.

6. Communicate with parents (e.g., notes home, phone calls, etc.) to share information about the student's progress. The parents may reinforce the student at home for demonstrating appropriate social behavior at school.

7. Communicate with parents, agencies, or the appropriate parties to inform them of the problem, determine the cause of the problem, and consider possible solutions to the problem.

8. Evaluate the appropriateness of the task to determine (a) if the task is too easy, (b) if the task is too difficult, and (c) if the length of time scheduled to complete the task is adequate.

9. Discuss appropriate social behavior with the student and Make sure he/she understands which behaviors are appropriate for public places and which are not.

10. Provide adequate supervision throughout the school environment to prevent the student from talking about bodily functions, masturbating, etc.

11. Make sure that the student is not inadvertently reinforced for participating in inappropriate behavior related to bodily functions (e.g., deal with the problem privately; avoid reacting in a shocked, disgusted or angry manner, etc.).

12. Make sure that natural consequences follow the student's inappropriate behavior related to bodily functions (e.g., others may not want to interact with the student; require the student to clean up urine, feces, etc.).

13. Do not leave the student unsupervised.

14. Remove the student from the group or activity until he/she demonstrates appropriate behavior.

15. Remove the student from the peer or situation which stimulates him/her to participate in inappropriate behavior related to bodily functions.

16. Inform other school personnel to make them aware of the problem.

17. Make sure the student knows how to use restroom facilities appropriately.

18. Provide the student with accurate information regarding bodily functions to answer questions and clear up misunderstandings.

19. Teach the student alternative ways to deal with his/her anger (e.g., talk with the teacher, move away from the situation, talk to other school personnel, etc.).

20. Share concerns with administration and seek referral to an agency for investigation of possible abuse and neglect.

21. Provide the student with a full schedule of daily events to increase active involvement in the environment.

22. Provide the student with a quiet place to work to reduce overstimulation. This is to be used to reduce stimulation and not as a form of punishment.

23. Choose a peer to model appropriate social behavior for the student.

24. Maintain visibility to and from the student. The teacher should be able to see the student; the student should be able to see the teacher. Make eye contact possible at all times.

183 Becomes pale, may vomit, or pass out when anxious or frightened

1. Reinforce the student for eating a nutritional lunch at school.

2. Discuss concerns with other professionals to determine if further investigation is warranted.

3. Take the time to listen so the student realizes your concern and interest in him/her is genuine.

4. Identify individuals the student may contact if his/her symptoms persist (e.g., guidance counselor, school nurse, social worker, school psychologist, parents, etc.).

5. Provide the student with many opportunities for social and academic successes.

6. Prevent frustrating or anxiety-producing situations from occurring (e.g., give the student tasks only on his/her ability level, give the student only those number of tasks which can be tolerated in one sitting, reduce social interactions which stimulate the student to become angry or upset, etc.).

7. Provide the student with success-oriented tasks. The expectation is that success will result in more positive attitudes and perceptions toward self and environment.

8. Provide the student with positive feedback which indicates that he/she is successful, competent, important, valuable, etc.

9. Teach the student problem-solving skills: (a) identify the problem, (b) identify goals and objectives, (c) develop strategies, (d) develop a plan for action, and (e) carry out the plan.

10. Determine which activities the student most enjoys and include those activities as much as possible in the daily routine.

11. Provide the student with opportunities to rest if necessary.

12. Have the parents reinforce the student at home for a balanced program of nutrition, rest, and exercise.

13. Arrange alternative lunches for the student at school (e.g., bring lunch from home, eat off campus, suggest an additional entree from the cafeteria, etc.).

14. Determine that the physical symptom is not the result of a medical problem, neglect, abuse, or drug use.

15. Reduce the emphasis on competition. High levels of competition or repeated failure may result in physical symptoms such as paleness, vomiting, etc.

16. Emphasize individual success or progress rather than comparing performance to other students.

17. Communicate with the parents (e.g., notes home, phone calls, etc.) to share information about the student's progress. The parents may reinforce the student at home for dealing with problems in appropriate ways at school.

18. Encourage the student to identify problems which result in paleness, vomiting, etc., and act on those problems to resolve their influence.

19. Encourage the student to take responsibility for assignments and obligations in an ongoing fashion rather than waiting until the night before or the day the assignment is due.

20. Help the student recognize problems that are within his/her ability to deal with and not to worry needlessly about situations over which the student has no control.

21. Explain that some concerns or worries are not unusual for students (e.g., everyone worries about tests, grades, etc.).

22. Offer to provide extra academic help for the student when he/she experiences a problem that interferes with his/her academic performance.

23. Do not force the student to do something that he/she is not completely comfortable doing.

24. Do not embarrass the student by giving him/her orders, demands, etc., in front of others.

25. Maintain trust and confidentiality with the student at all times.

26. Allow the student to attempt something new in private before doing so in front of others.

27. Go with the student or have someone else accompany the student to an activity the student may be trying to avoid. If something unpleasant is causing the student to pretend to be sick, do all you can to eliminate or reduce the cause.

28. Teach the student appropriate ways to communicate displeasure, anger, frustration, etc.

29. Do not force the student to interact with individuals with whom he/she is not completely comfortable.

30. Express your feelings in a socially acceptable way.

1. Reinforce the student for taking part in activities: (a) give the student a tangible reward (e.g., classroom privileges, line leading, passing out materials, five minutes free time, etc.) or (b) give the student an intangible reward (e.g., praise, fist bump, smile, etc.).

2. Speak to the student to explain (a) what he/she is doing wrong (e.g., avoiding activities) and (b) what he/she should be doing (e.g., taking part in activities).

3. Evaluate the appropriateness of the expectations for taking part in activities based on the student's ability to perform the task.

4. Reinforce the student for taking part in activities based on the length of time he/she can do so comfortably. As the student demonstrates success, gradually increase the number of times required for reinforcement.

5. Write a contract with the student specifying what behavior is expected (e.g., changing clothing for physical education) and what reinforcement will be made available when the terms of the contract have been met.

6. Communicate with parents (e.g., notes home, phone calls, etc.) to share information about the student's progress. The parents may reinforce the student at home for taking part in activities at school.

7. Choose a peer to model taking part in activities for the student.

8. Have the student ask questions about directions, explanations, instructions he/she does not understand.

9. Reinforce those students in the classroom who participate in activities.

10. If necessary, provide the student with a private place in which to change clothing for physical education.

11. Provide a pleasant/calm atmosphere.

12. To the extent necessary, provide assistance to the student for changing his/her clothing for physical education.

13. Have the student participate in activities which require minimal participation. As the student becomes more comfortable, gradually increase the student's participation.

14. Make sure that the physical education clothing the student is expected to wear is appropriate.

15. If the student is reluctant to change clothing for physical education in the presence of others, allow the student to change clothing in private. As the student becomes more comfortable, gradually increase the number of peers in whose presence he/she changes clothing.

16. Be sure the student makes appropriate use of the time provided for activities.

17. If necessary, provide additional time for the student to change clothing for physical education. As the student demonstrates success, gradually reduce the additional time provided.

18. Make sure the student has the necessary clothing for physical education.

19. Prevent peers from making the student uncomfortable when he/she takes part in activities (i.e., prevent other students from making fun, teasing, etc.).

20. When requiring the student to participate in an activity in which he/she is uncomfortable, pair the student with a peer/friend to reduce his/her discomfort.

21. Evaluate the necessity of requiring the student to participate in activities in which he/she is uncomfortable.

22. Provide the student with alternatives to activities which make him/her uncomfortable (e.g., allow the student to write a poem instead of reciting it in front of a group).

23. Make sure the student has adequate time in which to perform activities.

24. Allow the student to be an observer of activities without requiring him/her to be an active participant.

25. Allow the student to perform functions or activities which require little participation (e.g., scorekeeper, note taker, etc.).

26. Ask the student to identify under what circumstances he/she would be willing to participate in activities (i.e., the student may be able to suggest acceptable conditions under which he/she would be comfortable participating in activities).

27. Provide a schedule whereby the student gradually increases the length of time spent at school each day, in the classroom, in a particular class or activity, etc.

28. Communicate with parents, agencies, or the appropriate parties to inform them of the problem, determine the cause of the problem, and consider possible solutions to the problem.

29. If the student is extremely uncomfortable at school, allow a parent, relative, or friend to stay with the student all day if necessary. As the student becomes more comfortable, gradually reduce the length of time the person remains with the student.

Reminder: Do not force the student to participate in any activity which makes him/her uncomfortable.

185 Does not change from one activity to another without difficulty

1. Prevent the student from becoming over-stimulated by an activity. Supervise student behavior to limit overexcitement in physical activities, games, parties, etc.

2. Establish time limits and provide the student with this information before the activity begins.

3. Inform the student that work not completed in one sitting can be completed later. Provide the student with enough time to complete earlier assignments to guarantee closure.

4. Provide the student with more than enough time to finish an activity. As the student demonstrates success, decrease the amount of time provided to finish an activity.

5. Structure time limits so the student knows exactly the amount of time there is to work and when he/she must be finished.

6. Provide a transition period between activities so the student can make adjustments in his/her behavior.

7. Employ a signal technique (e.g., turning the lights off and on) to warn that the end of an activity is near.

8. Have the student time activities to monitor his/her behavior and time limits.

9. Assign the student shorter activities. As the student demonstrates success, gradually increase the length of the activities.

10. Maintain a consistent daily routine.

11. Maintain consistent expectations within the ability level of the student.

12. Allow the student to finish an activity unless it will be disruptive to the schedule.

13. Provide the student with a list of materials needed for each activity (e.g., pencil, paper, textbook, workbook, etc.).

14. Present instructions/directions prior to handing out necessary materials.

15. Collect the student's materials (e.g., pencil, paper, textbook, workbook, etc.) when it is time to change from one activity to another.

16. Provide the student with clearly stated expectations for all situations.

17. Prevent the student from becoming so stimulated by an event or activity that the student cannot control his/her behavior.

18. Establish rules that are to be followed in various parts of the school building (e.g., lunchroom, music room, art room, gymnasium, library, etc.).

19. Identify the expectations of different environments and help the student develop the skills to be successful in those environments.

20. In conjunction with other school personnel, develop as much consistency as possible in the school environment (e.g., rules, criteria for success, behavioral expectations, consequences, etc.).

21. Reduce the student's involvement in activities which prove too stimulating for him/her.

22. Have the student practice transitional activities to reduce the effects of stimulating activities (e.g., put head on desk, listen to the teacher read a story, put headphones on and listen to relaxing music, etc.).

23. Provide the student with more than enough time to adapt or modify his/her behavior to different situations (e.g., have the student stop free time activities five minutes prior to returning to class).

24. Schedule activities so the student has more than enough time to finish the activity if he/she works consistently.

25. Communicate clearly to the student when it is time to begin an activity.

26. Communicate clearly to the student when it is time to stop an activity.

27. Provide the student with a schedule of daily events so he/she will know which activity comes next and can prepare for it.

28. Reduce the emphasis on competition (e.g., academic or social). Fear of failure may cause the student to fail to adapt or modify his/her behavior to different situations.

29. Have the student begin an activity in a private place (e.g., carrel, office, quiet study area, etc.) to reduce the difficulty in adapting or modifying his/her behavior to different situations.

30. Allow the student the option of performing the activity at another time (e.g., earlier in the day, later in the day, another day, etc.).

31. Do not allow the student to begin a new activity until he/she has gained self-control.

32. Evaluate the appropriateness of the situation in relation to the student's ability to successfully adapt or modify his/her behavior.

33. Let the student know in advance when changes in his/her schedule will occur (e.g., a change from class time to break time, when reading class will begin, etc.).

34. Explain to the student that he/she should be satisfied with personal best effort rather than insisting on perfection.

35. Choose a peer to work with the student to model changing from one activity to another without difficulty.

36. Have the student ask questions about directions, explanations, or instructions not understood.

37. Evaluate the appropriateness of the task to determine (a) if the task is too easy, (b) if the task is too difficult, and (c) if the length of time scheduled to complete the task is adequate.

38. Communicate with parents (e.g., notes home, phone calls, etc.) to share information about the student's progress. The parents may reinforce the student at home for changing activities without difficulty at school.

39. Write a contract with the student specifying what behavior is expected (e.g., putting materials away and getting ready for another activity) and what reinforcement will be made available when the terms of the contract have been met.

40. Reinforce the student for demonstrating acceptable behavior based on the length of time the student can be successful. As the student demonstrates success, gradually increase the length of time required for reinforcement.

41. Reinforce those students in the classroom who change their behavior from one situation to another without difficulty.

42. Establish classroom rules:
- Concentrate while working.
- Work quietly.
- Remain in your seat.
- Finish task.
- Meet task requirements.

Review rules often. Reinforce the student for following the rules.

43. Reinforce the student for changing his/her behavior from one situation to another without difficulty: (a) give the student a tangible reward (e.g., classroom privileges, line leading, passing out materials, five minutes free time, etc.) or (b) give the student an intangible reward (e.g., praise, fist bump, smile, etc.).

44. Speak to the student to explain (a) what the student is doing wrong (e.g., failing to stop one activity and begin another) and (b) what the student should be doing (e.g., changing from one activity to another).

186 Cannot fasten articles of clothing

1. Choose a peer to model fastening articles of clothing appropriately for the student.

2. Have the student ask questions about directions, explanations, or instructions he/she does not understand.

3. Provide the student with instruction on fastening articles of clothing.

4. Provide the student with time to practice fastening his/her articles of clothing while wearing them.

5. Provide the student with adequate time to fasten articles of clothing.

6. Provide visual reminders to fasten articles of closing in appropriate locations (e.g., picture of zipping, buttoning, snapping, etc.).

7. Reinforce the student for gradually improving his/her ability to fasten articles of clothing over time rather than expecting total mastery immediately.

8. Provide the student with a checklist of articles of clothing to fasten that he/she can complete daily.

9. Place a full-length mirror in the classroom for the student to make sure that all of his/her articles of clothing are fastened.

10. Teach the student how to fasten articles of clothing when buttons are missing, zippers are broken, etc., (e.g., sewing a button back in place, using a safety pin, etc.).

11. Guide the student's hands through the activity of zipping, buttoning, and snapping his/her own clothing.

12. Have the student practice fastening articles of clothing with oversized zippers, buttons, and snaps. As the student demonstrates success, gradually reduce the size of the fasteners.

13. Provide the student with verbal reminders to fasten his/her articles of clothing.

14. Reinforce the student at regular intervals throughout the day for having articles of clothing fastened.

15. Fasten articles of clothing for the student if he/she is incapable of fastening.

16. Do not embarrass the student by asking him/her to fasten articles of clothing in front of peers.

17. Evaluate the appropriateness of the task to determine (a) if the task is too easy, (b) if the task is too difficult, and (c) if the length of time scheduled to complete the task is adequate.

18. Communicate with parents (e.g., notes home, phone calls, etc.) to share information about the student's progress. The parents may reinforce the student at home for fastening articles of clothing at school.

19. Write a contract with the student specifying what behavior is expected (e.g., fastening clothing) and what reinforcement will be made available when the terms of the contract have been met.

20. Reinforce those students in the classroom who fasten their articles of clothing.

21. Speak to the student to explain (a) what the student is doing wrong (e.g., failing to fasten clothing) and (b) what the student should be doing (e.g., fastening clothing, etc.).

22. Reinforce the student for caring for personal appearance: (a) give the student a tangible reward (e.g., classroom privileges, line leading, passing out materials, five minutes free time, etc.) or (b) give the student an intangible reward (e.g., praise, fist bump, smile, etc.).

1. Evaluate the appropriateness of the task to determine (a) if the task is too easy, (b) if the task is too difficult, and (c) if the length of time scheduled to complete the task is adequate.

2. If necessary, provide the student with a private place in which to change clothing for physical education.

3. Make sure the student has adequate time in which to change clothing for physical education.

4. To the extent necessary, provide assistance to the student for changing clothing for physical education.

5. Have the student participate in physical education activities which require minimal clothing changes.

6. Determine those peers with whom changing clothing for physical education would prove less threatening for the student, and place the student with those peers when he/she changes clothing for physical education.

7. Make sure that the physical education clothing the student is expected to wear is appropriate.

8. If the student is reluctant to change clothing for physical education in the presence of others, allow the student to change in private. As the student demonstrates success, gradually increase the number of peers in whose presence the student changes clothing for physical education.

9. Be sure the student makes appropriate use of the time provided to change clothing for physical education.

10. If necessary, provide additional time for the student to change clothing for physical education. As the student demonstrates success, gradually reduce the additional time provided.

11. Make sure the student has the necessary clothing for physical education.

12. Make sure the physical education clothing fits the student.

13. Prevent peers from making the student uncomfortable when he/she changes clothing for physical education (i.e., prevent other students from making fun, teasing, etc.).

14. Assess the appropriateness of physical education activities to determine if the activities are threatening to the student and cause him/her to be reluctant to change clothing for participation in the activities.

15. Do not criticize when correcting the student; be honest yet supportive. Never cause the student to feel negatively about himself/herself.

16. Do not embarrass the student by forcing him/her to change clothing for physical education in front of others.

17. Have the student ask questions about directions, explanations, or instructions not understood.

18. Choose a peer to model appropriate changing of clothing for physical education for the student.

19. Communicate with parents (e.g., notes home, phone calls, etc.) to share information about the student's progress. The parents may reinforce the student at home for changing clothing for physical education at school.

20. Write a contract with the student specifying what behavior is expected (e.g., changing clothing for physical education) and what reinforcement will be made available when the terms of the contract have been met.

21. Reinforce the student for changing clothing for physical education based on the number of times the student can be successful. As the student demonstrates success, gradually increase the number of times required for reinforcement.

22. Reinforce those students in the classroom who change clothing for physical education.

23. Speak to the student to explain (a) what the student is doing wrong (e.g., failing to change clothing for physical education) and (b) what the student should be doing (e.g., changing clothing for physical education).

24. Reinforce the student for changing clothing for physical education: (a) give the student a tangible reward (e.g., classroom privileges, line leading, passing out materials, five minutes free time, etc.) or (b) give the student an intangible reward (e.g., praise, fist bump, smile, etc.).

188 Does not demonstrate appropriate mealtime behavior

1. Reinforce the student for demonstrating appropriate mealtime behaviors: (a) give the student a tangible reward (e.g., classroom privileges, line leading, passing out materials, five minutes free time, etc.) or (b) give the student an intangible reward (e.g., praise, fist bump, smile, etc.).

2. Speak to the student to explain (a) what he/she is doing wrong (e.g., eating with his/her fingers) and (b) what he/she should be doing (e.g., using a fork).

3. Reinforce those students who demonstrate appropriate mealtime behaviors.

4. Reinforce the student for demonstrating appropriate mealtime behaviors based on the length of time the student can be successful. As the student demonstrates success, gradually increase the length of time required for reinforcement.

5. Write a contract with the student specifying what behavior is expected (e.g., disposing of his/her food in the trash can) and what reinforcement will be made available when the terms of the contract have been met.

6. Communicate with parents (e.g., notes home, phone calls, etc.) to share information about the student's progress. The parents may reinforce the student at home for demonstrating appropriate mealtime behaviors at school.

7. Evaluate the appropriateness of the task to determine (a) if the task is too easy, (b) if the task is too difficult, and (c) if the length of time scheduled to complete the task is adequate.

8. Choose a peer to model appropriate mealtime behaviors for the student.

9. Have the student ask questions about directions, expectations, instructions he/she does not understand.

10. Provide the student with a list of clearly defined mealtime behavioral expectations (e.g., rules for the cafeteria serving line, sitting at tables, remaining seated, use of utensils, disposing of trash, etc.).

11. Reinforce other students for demonstrating appropriate mealtime behaviors.

12. Assess the appropriateness of the student eating with a group of peers. If necessary, have the student eat with one peer and gradually increase the size of the group as the student experiences success.

13. Instruct the student in the appropriate use of eating utensils in both simulation and actual eating situations.

14. Instruct the student in appropriate mealtime conversation (e.g., topics to discuss, asking conversational questions, speaking quietly, etc.).

15. Instruct the student in appropriate mealtime etiquette (e.g., speaking with an empty mouth, eating with mouth closed, chewing quietly, etc.).

16. Instruct the student in selecting an appropriate amount of food, eating an appropriate amount of food, taking appropriately sized bites, etc.

17. Instruct the student in appropriate clean-up activities upon completion of eating (e.g., disposing of trash, putting trays and tableware in appropriate locations, washing hands, etc.).

18. Instruct the student in the appropriate use of napkins (e.g., keep on lap, wipe mouth, clean up spills, etc.).

19. Instruct the student in appropriate line behavior (e.g., waiting quietly, refraining from physical contact, moving with the line, etc.).

20. Make sure the student sits appropriately while eating (e.g., sits close to the table, sits upright, leans forward, etc.).

21. Instruct the student in appropriate behavior when finishing a meal early (e.g., making conversation, remaining in his/her seat, excusing himself/herself, etc.).

22. Instruct the student in appropriate ways to get seconds or additional food (e.g., asking for seconds, going through the cafeteria line a second time, purchasing seconds, etc.).

23. Remove the student from eating with his/her peers if he/she cannot demonstrate appropriate mealtime behaviors.

24. Teach the student appropriate ways to drink liquids (e.g., opening milk cartons and juice containers, using a straw, pouring into a glass, drinking from a glass, etc.).

25. Teach the student appropriate ways to respond to food he/she does not want (e.g., sample everything at least once, leave the food on the plate, offer extra portions to others, etc.).

26. Instruct the student in appropriate ways to clean up spills (e.g., ask for assistance, use paper towels and napkins, etc.).

27. Instruct the student in appropriate ways to clean clothing when accidents occur during mealtime (e.g., immediately go to the restroom, use paper towels and napkins, etc.).

L. Rules and Expectations

1. Immediately remove the student from interacting with others when cursing.

2. Make sure that you do not curse. If you curse, the student will learn to do the same.

3. Establish a rule (e.g., no cursing). This rule should be consistent and followed by everyone in the school environment. Talk about the rule often.

4. Reward other students in the classroom for not cursing.

5. When the student curses, explain exactly what he/she is doing wrong, what should be done and why. For example: You hear the student cursing at another student. Go to the student and say, "William, you are cursing at Kim. You need to use appropriate language when you are angry at someone or you will offend him/her."

6. Allow natural consequences to occur as a result of the student's cursing (e.g., not being able to participate in special activities, being removed from interacting with others, being avoided by others who do not curse, etc.).

7. Make sure that the student sees the relationship between his/her behavior and the consequences which follow (e.g., being removed from activities).

8. Talk to the student in the manner in which you want him/her to talk to you. Treat the student with respect and do not curse at him/her.

9. Teach the student acceptable ways to express anger, frustration, anxiety, etc.

10. Be consistent when the student curses. Decide on an appropriate consequence for cursing (e.g., sitting in a certain chair for five minutes) and use it every time the student curses.

11. Separate the student from those individuals who encourage or stimulate him/her to curse.

12. Make sure that others with whom the student associates do not use inappropriate language.

13. Separate the student from the peer(s) who stimulate inappropriate language.

14. Inform other teachers, school personnel, etc., of the student's use of inappropriate language to make sure they follow through with discipline.

15. Remind the student of the consequences of swearing before participating in activities.

16. Separate the student from other peers who curse.

17. Avoid those situations which are likely to stimulate the student's swearing (e.g., highly competitive activities, extreme disappointment, quarreling with other students, etc.).

18. Teach the student to recognize when he/she is becoming upset or angry and ways, other than cursing, to express feelings.

19. Do not allow the student to participate in a situation unless he/she can demonstrate self-control.

20. Provide the student with a place to go when he/she gets upset or angry (e.g., a quiet chair, a room, a corner, etc.).

21. Make sure you deal in a socially acceptable way with situations that may be upsetting.

22. Teach the student to verbalize feelings before losing control (e.g., "The work is too hard." "Please leave me alone, you're making me angry.").

23. Monitor the behavior of others to make sure they are not teasing or otherwise stimulating the student to become upset or angry.

24. Teach the student ways to deal with conflict situations (e.g., talking, reasoning, asking an adult to intervene, walking away, etc.).

25. Look for the warning signs (e.g., arguing, loud voices, etc.) that the student is getting upset or angry and intervene to change the activity.

26. Make sure you approach the student with words and phrases that offer support rather than stimulating antagonism, anger, etc.

27. Repeat rules and expectations before activities occur which might result in the student becoming upset or angry.

28. Make sure to intervene early when the student does curse, before cursing becomes an established part of his/her speech.

29. Make sure the student knows the consequences of cursing that will be delivered in your class (e.g., loss of privileges, loss of opportunity to associate with those with whom he curses, loss of freedom to be left alone with friends, etc.).

30. Make sure the student understands that other teachers will not stand for cursing, the student should expect to be embarrassed, and may be prevented from interacting with others.

31. Reduce the emphasis on competition. Highly competitive activities may cause the student to become upset, angry, frustrated, etc., and curse.

32. Do not inadvertently reinforce the student's cursing by laughing, smiling, ignoring, etc.

33. Prevent the student from becoming frustrated to the extent that cursing results. Intervene to help the student in those situations which may result in frustration and cursing.

34. If highly competitive activities contribute to the student's cursing, either reduce the student's involvement in those activities or Make sure the student understands that cursing will result in the loss of opportunities to participate in those activities.

35. Point out to the student successful persons who actively participate in a variety of activities without cursing.

36. Make sure the student is taught words which are socially appropriate to use in place of cursing (e.g., *dang, shoot, darn, heck*, etc.).

37. Cursing is not a behavior that should be ignored. By ignoring the student's cursing, you send the message that it is acceptable.

38. Discuss with the student ways to deal with unpleasant experiences which would typically cause him/her to use obscene language (e.g., talk to the teacher, go to a quiet area in the room, visit a counselor, etc.).

39. Model using appropriate language at all times (e.g., use appropriate language to convey disappointment, unhappiness, surprise, etc.).

40. Deal with the student in a calm and deliberate manner rather than in a manner that would show evidence of shock and surprise.

41. Modify or adjust situations which contribute to the student's use of obscene or profane language (e.g., if an assignment causes the student to become upset, modify the assignment to a level at which the student can be successful).

42. Make sure the student has frequent, positive opportunities to define self-expression without using obscene/profane language.

43. Reinforce the student for behaving responsibly and not using obscene/profane language for self-expression by: (a) give the student a tangible reward (e.g., classroom privileges, line leading, passing out materials, five minutes free time, etc.) or (b) give the student an intangible reward (e.g., praise, fist bump, smile, etc.).

44. Define what has been done correctly and what the student needs to do to improve upon his/her ability to communicate without obscene/profane language.

45. Make sure those who are expressing thoughts and feelings without resorting to obscene/profane language are positively reinforced.

46. Deliver your response and consequences to the use of obscene/profane language in a low key manner because the student may be using this kind of language to elicit shock/surprise responses from those sharing the environment.

47. Teach the student to recognize when he/she feels the need to use obscene/profane language and ways to deal with it (e.g., counting to 10, moving to a different location in the classroom, reading, etc.). Give the student structured practice at using coping skills which could be adapted to life beyond the classroom.

48. Write a contract specifying expected behavior (e.g., taking the time to express thoughts/feelings without use of obscene/profane language) and what reinforcement will be made available when the terms of the contract have been met.

49. Communicate with the student's parents (e.g., notes home, phone calls, etc.) to share information about the student's progress. The parents may reinforce students at home for using positive communication techniques at school.

50. Supervise the student who does not consider the consequences of using obscene/profane language.

51. Provide the student with models of the behavioral choices you expect of him/her during times of frustration or stress to avoid the use of obscene/profane language.

52. Interact frequently with the student to monitor language used.

53. Encourage the student to express thoughts and feelings carefully and thoughtfully. Praise the student for self-expression without using obscene/profane language.

54. Teach the student self-reinforcement techniques for positive self-expression (e.g., going to a movie or out to eat after a week of communicating without obscene/profane language, etc.).

55. Prevent task-related stress so student frustration and temptation to use obscene/profane language is decreased by (a) providing clear task expectations and assuring these are understood by the student before he/she receives task materials and before he/she is expected to begin the task, (b) providing the student enough time for task completion, (c) providing the student frequent opportunities for communication to encourage his/her positive self-expression throughout the day, and (d) making certain tasks are appropriate for the student's age and ability.

56. Deliver consequences in a nonthreatening, calm manner.

57. Make sure the student knows the following:
- You are confident that he/she can communicate thoughts/feelings without using obscene/profane language.
- The student will have many more opportunities to earn positive reinforcement by communicating thoughts/feelings without using obscene/profane language.

58. Choose a peer to model expressing thoughts and feelings without resorting to obscene/profane language for the student.

59. Be a consistent, positive authority figure.

60. Consistently act upon the student's antecedent behaviors (e.g., increased restlessness, marked changes in moods, etc.) to teach positive forms of self-expression. He/she can then have the opportunity to identify and describe thoughts, feelings, and/or problems before the situation escalates.

61. Provide learning experiences which emphasize cause and effect links between behavior (e.g., use of obscene/profane language to express one's thoughts and feelings) and consequences (e.g., loss of others' respect, lost communication because the obscene/profane language overshadowed the message, etc.).

62. Structure the environment to encourage opportunities for self-expression without obscene/profane language (e.g., seating the student in front of the classroom for careful monitoring and to prevent task and communication related frustration, etc.).

63. Teach the student ways of working through problems to decrease frustration and stress-related behavior. These include (a) problem identification, (b) goal/objective development, (c) strategy development, (d) plan development, (e) plan implementation, and (f) evaluation of plan effectiveness.

64. Prevent peers from provoking the student into reactive, verbal responses.

65. Show an interest in the student (e.g., acknowledge the student, ask for the student's opinion, work one-to-one with the student).

66. Help the student focus upon positive attempts to communicate thoughts and feelings without use of obscene/profane language. He/she needs to be able to recognize successes and errors for improvement in self-expression.

67. Help the student identify his/her own unique set of antecedents to the use of obscene/profane language. For every antecedent identified, help the student develop positive, alternative actions he/she may take toward problem solving.

68. Offer the student opportunities for creative self-expression (e.g., sculpting, gymnastics, writing, drawing, dancing, acting, etc.). Activities need to be viewed as an avenue of self-expression rather than a way to reinforce, reward, or earn grades.

69. Introduce and maintain positive, consistent class management which incorporates an opportunity to think through consequences before decisions are made.

70. Provide students and parents information about stress. Include positive alternatives to reduce and/or manage stress.

71. Advocate for supports and services to rule out or provide for organic or physical concerns such as Tourette's Disorder according to individual need.

72. The student who is experiencing emotional or behavior disturbances may respond to stressful situations with abusive or profane language. Advocate for support and service.

73. Observe the student for changes in behavior. A student who does not typically use obscene/profane language but has begun to do so may be experiencing other concerns (e.g., personal crisis, substance abuse, etc.).

74. When teaching the student to express thoughts and feelings without using obscene/profane language, provide functional lessons (e.g., interviewing for a job, attempting an introduction to a new person, etc.) so the student can assign practical value to this skill.

75. Address and correct the use of obscene/profane language by talking one-to-one with the student instead of confronting the student in large groups. Do this to minimize embarrassment and decrease the chances a student may have for vicarious reinforcement (e.g., approving statements and actions of peers for using obscene/profane language, etc.).

76. Encourage the student to view himself/herself positively. Make sure the student understands the use of obscene/profane language represents a poor choice, but he/she is a good person. This may help reduce potential crisis situations in which use of obscene/profane language is an antecedent to other undesirable behaviors (e.g., attempts to hurt himself/herself or others, etc.).

190 Does not demonstrate the ability to follow a routine

1. Communicate with the student's parents (e.g., notes home, phone calls, etc.) to share information about their child's progress. The parents may reinforce the student at home for demonstrating the ability to follow a routine at school.

2. Encourage the student to establish a schedule to follow consistently at home (e.g., make the bed before eating breakfast, load the dishwasher before going to school, perform daily chores right after school, clean the kitchen before sitting down to watch TV, etc.). Have the student post the schedule on the refrigerator as a reminder.

3. Encourage the student to develop a 30 second definition of his/her goal to help him/her stay on task and follow a routine (e.g., "I will complete this task to the best of my ability. The better I focus and stay on task, the better job I will do.").

4. Have the student rely on a predetermined signal (e.g., bells, lights, etc.) to facilitate his/her ability to follow a routine.

5. Consider carefully the student's age and maturity level before expecting him/her to follow a routine.

6. Choose a classmate to model the ability to follow a routine for the student.

7. Have the student ask questions about directions, explanations, or instructions he/she does not understand about a routine.

8. Have the student work near a peer to follow the same routine that the peer follows.

9. Make sure that the student consistently follows his/her daily routine.

10. Provide the student with a schedule of daily events which identifies the daily activities and the times at which they occur.

11. Provide the student with a schedule of daily events to be attached to the student's desk and/or carried with the student at all times.

12. Give the student as much structure and consistency in his/her school day as possible.

13. Have the student develop an awareness of the consequences of his/her behavior on the job site by writing down or talking through problems which may occur due to his/her inability to follow a routine (e.g., if you do not establish a routine, you will not finish all your responsibilities then you may not get the raise you want or you could lose your job).

14. Establish a routine to follow before changing activities (e.g., put away materials, assemble materials for the next activity, make a list of what materials need to be replenished, etc.).

15. Reduce distracting stimuli which might cause the student to be unable to follow a routine (e.g., peers, physical activity, etc.).

16. Monitor the student's performance in activities or tasks to make sure the student begins, works on, and completes an assignment to be ready to move to the next activity in his/her routine.

17. Have the student develop a checklist/chart to follow which will allow him/her to follow a specific routine.

18. Maintain consistency in the classroom's daily routine.

19. Allow the student to help decide what his/her routine responsibilities will be.

20. Have the student rely on environmental events to remind him/her when to change activities in his/her routine (e.g., other students changing activities, bells, etc.).

21. Provide the student with structure for all academic activities (e.g., specific directions, routine format for tasks, time limits, etc.).

22. Have the student define his/her goals. Assist the student in developing specific strategies to achieve his/her goals and follow through on those strategies.

23. Have the student ask himself/herself questions (e.g., "What's next?") to keep himself/herself focused on the daily classroom routine.

24. Discuss the student's routine with him/her at the beginning of each day and Make sure that he/she knows the expectations.

25. Allow the student to participate in deciding when changes in his/her routine will occur.

26. Limit the number of changes in the student's established routine. As the student demonstrates success, gradually increase the number of changes in the routine.

27. Remind the student when it is time to change activities to facilitate his/her ability to follow a routine.

28. Make sure that the activities in the student's routine are on his/her ability level.

29. Make sure that the teacher is a model for following a routine.

30. Explain to the student the need to maintain flexibility in following a routine when changes in the routine are required.

31. Make sure the student does not have a lot of unstructured time.

32. Have the student choose a peer who has the ability to follow a routine. Encourage the student to observe that person and try to model the behaviors which allow him/her to follow a routine without becoming distracted.

33. Make it a habit to periodically review the classroom/school routines with the student.

34. Establish classroom routines (e.g., materials ready when class begins, homework turned in before the end of class, etc.).

35. Have the student use electronic reminders to assist him/her in following a routine (e.g., a programmable watch, computer programs, electronic calendar, etc.).

36. Have the student maintain written reminders of task sequences.

37. Have the student establish a routine for himself/herself. Assist the student in developing a weekly schedule and weekend schedule.

38. Have the student imagine the steps required to complete a routine before beginning it.

39. Establish rules for working:
- Work on the task at hand.
- Work quietly.
- Remain in your seat.
- Complete the task.
- Meet task expectations.

Review rules often. Reinforce students for following the rules.

40. Limit interruptions in the student's routine by persons or events in the school (e.g., cancellation of classes or activities such as art, music, physical education; testing; special services; delays; etc.).

41. Provide the student with a limited routine to follow. As the student demonstrates success, gradually increase the activities in the routine as the student experiences success.

42. Provide the student with an alternative routine to follow if he/she encounters difficulty following his/her regular routine.

43. Provide the student with a schedule of daily events so that he/she will know which activity comes next and can prepare for it.

44. Choose different people (e.g., parent, school counselor, peer, etc.) to help the student follow a daily routine.

45. Choose a peer to accompany the student to other locations in the building which are part of the student's routine.

46. Allow the student to contribute to the development of his/her routine to facilitate his/her ability to follow the routine (e.g., have the student determine the order of activities).

47. Choose a peer to remind the student when to change activities according to his/her routine.

48. Be consistent in expecting the student to follow a routine. Do not allow the student to not follow a routine one time and expect him/her to follow a routine the next time.

49. Be personally available for assistance when the student is dealing with changes in his/her routine (e.g., switching semester classes, attending school assembly, etc.).

50. Limit the student's responsibilities to facilitate his/her ability to focus on a routine (e.g., extracurricular activities, part-time job, etc.).

51. Have the student anticipate future tasks/assignments and develop plans for addressing them.

52. Post the classroom routine throughout the classroom (e.g., on the student's desk, wall-mounted board, bulletin board, etc.).

53. Have the student perform the same responsibilities each day, week, etc.

54. Provide the student with a revised schedule of daily events when there is a change in routine which identifies the activities for the day and the times when they will occur (e.g., special assembly schedule, half day schedule, etc.).

55. Discuss any necessary changes in the student's routine well in advance of the occurrence of the changes.

56. Make sure the student is able to tell time to facilitate his/her ability to follow a routine.

57. Reinforce the student for demonstrating the ability to follow a routine: (a) give the student a tangible reward (e.g., classroom privileges, passing out materials, five minutes free time, etc.) or (b) give the student an intangible reward (e.g., praise, fist bump, smile, etc.).

58. Speak to the student to explain (a) what he/she is doing wrong (e.g., failing to come to class on time, failing to follow the schedule of activities, etc.) and (b) what he/she should be doing (e.g., coming to class on time, following the schedule of activities, etc.).

59. Establish classroom rules:
- Concentrate while working.
- Work quietly.
- Remain in your seat.
- Finish task.
- Meet task expectations.

Review rules often. Reinforce students for following the rules.

60. Reinforce those students in the classroom who demonstrate the ability to follow a routine.

61. Reinforce the student for demonstrating the ability to follow a routine based on the length of time the student can be successful. As the student demonstrates success, gradually increase the length of time required for reinforcement.

62. Allow the student to contribute to the development of his/her routine to facilitate his/her ability to follow the routine (e.g., have the student determine the order of activities).

63. Provide the student with a verbal reminder of changes in his/her routine.

64. Have the student use a timer to indicate when to change activities in his/her routine.

65. Determine an expected length of time for each individual activity to help the student follow his/her routine (i.e., make sure the student can finish an activity in an established length of time to help him/her stay within the time restrictions of the routine).

66. Communicate with the student's parents to establish a routine for the student to follow for getting ready for school, doing chores, completing homework, etc. This will help the student remember what is expected.

67. Write a contract with the student specifying what behavior is expected (e.g., following the schedule of activities) and what reinforcement will be made available when the terms of the contract have been met.

68. Make sure that the student's daily routine is consistent.

69. Teach the student to tell time to facilitate his/her ability to follow a routine.

70. Evaluate the appropriateness of the routine to determine (a) if the routine is too easy, (b) if the routine is too difficult, and (c) if the length of time scheduled to complete the routine is adequate.

71. Teach problem-solving skills:
- Identify the problem.
- Identify the goals and objectives.
- Develop a strategy/plan for action.
- Carry out the plan.
- Evaluate the results.

191 Does not take appropriate care of personal property

1. Reinforce the student for appropriate care of personal property: (a) give the student a tangible reward (e.g., classroom privileges, line leading, passing out materials, five minutes free time, etc.) or (b) give the student an intangible reward (e.g., praise, fist bump, smile, etc.).

2. Communicate with parents (e.g., notes home, phone calls, etc.) to share information about the student's progress. The parents may reinforce the student at home for organization and appropriate use of materials at school.

3. Establish classroom rules:
- Concentrate while working.
- Work quietly.
- Remain in your seat.
- Finish task.
- Meet task requirements.

Review rules often. Reinforce the student for following the rules.

4. Reinforce the student for appropriate care of personal property based on the length of time the student can be successful. As the student demonstrates success, gradually increase the length of time required for reinforcement.

5. Write a contract with the student specifying what behavior is expected (e.g., organization and appropriate use of materials) and what reinforcement will be made available when the terms of the contract have been met.

6. Speak to the student to explain (a) what he/she is doing wrong (e.g., failing to maintain organization or use materials appropriately) and (b) what he/she should be doing (e.g., keeping inside of desk organized, organizing materials on top of desk, using materials as instructed, etc.).

7. Provide the student with additional work space (e.g., a larger desk or table at which to work).

8. Choose a peer to work directly with the student to serve as a model for appropriate use and organization of materials.

9. Provide time at the beginning of each day for the student to organize his/her materials.

10. Provide time at various points throughout the day for the student to organize his/her materials (e.g., before school, break time, lunch, at the end of the day, etc.).

11. Evaluate the appropriateness of the task to determine (a) if the task is too easy, (b) if the task is too difficult, and (c) if the length of time scheduled to complete the task is adequate.

12. Provide storage space for materials the student is not using.

13. Reduce distracting stimuli (e.g., place the student on the front row, provide a carrel or quiet place away from distractions, etc.). This is used as a means of reducing distracting stimuli and not as a form of punishment.

14. Interact frequently with the student to encourage organizational skills or appropriate use of materials.

15. Assign the student organizational responsibilities in the classroom (e.g., equipment, software materials, etc.).

16. Limit the student's access to materials (e.g., provide only necessary materials to the student).

17. Model organization and appropriate use of work materials (e.g., putting materials away before getting more out, having a place for all materials, maintaining an organized desk area, following a schedule for the day, etc.).

18. Provide adequate transition time between activities for the student to organize himself/herself.

19. Establish a routine to be followed for organization and appropriate use of work materials (e.g., provide the routine for the student in written form or verbally review often).

20. Provide adequate time for the completion of activities.

21. Supervise the student while he/she is performing schoolwork to monitor appropriate care of materials.

22. Allow natural consequences to occur as the result of the student's inability to organize or use materials appropriately (e.g., materials not maintained appropriately may be lost or not useable).

23. Assess the quality and clarity of directions, explanations, and instructions given to the student.

24. Assist the student in beginning each task to reduce impulsive behavior.

25. Provide the student with structure for all academic activities (e.g., specific directions, routine format for tasks, time limits, etc.).

26. Give the student a checklist of materials necessary for each activity.

27. Minimize materials needed.

28. Provide an organizer inside the student's desk for materials.

29. Provide the student with an organizational checklist (e.g., routine activities and steps to follow).

30. Teach the student appropriate care of personal property (e.g., sharpening pencils, keeping books free of marks and tears, etc.).

31. Make sure that all personal property is labeled with the student's name.

32. Point out to the student that loaning personal property to other students does not reduce his/her responsibility for the property.

33. Provide reminders (e.g., list of property or materials) to help the student maintain and care for personal property.

34. Teach the student how to conserve rather than waste materials (e.g., amount of glue, paper, tape, etc., to use; putting lids, caps, and tops on such materials as markers, pens, bottles, jars, cans; etc.).

35. Teach the student appropriate ways to deal with anger and frustration rather than destroying personal property and school materials (e.g., pencils, pens, workbooks, notebooks, textbooks, etc.).

36. Teach the student to maintain care of personal property and school materials (e.g., keep property with him/her, know where property is at all times, secure property in locker, leave valuable property at home, etc.).

37. Provide the student with an appropriate place to store/secure personal property (e.g., desk, locker, closet, etc.) and require the student to store all property when not in use.

38. Teach the student that failure to care for personal property will result in the loss of freedom to retain property (e.g., if the student cannot care for property, the teacher(s) will store all property).

39. Limit the student's freedom to take property from school if he/she is unable to remember to return the items.

40. Provide the student with verbal reminders of personal property or materials needed for each activity.

41. Limit the student's opportunity to use school materials if he/she is unable to care for his/her own personal property.

42. Make sure that failure to have necessary materials results in losing the opportunity to participate in activities or a failing grade for that day's activity.

43. Reduce the number of materials for which the student is responsible. As the student demonstrates appropriate responsibility for property, increase the number of materials for which the student is responsible.

44. Teach the student the appropriate use of personal property and materials (e.g., scissors; pencils; compass; rulers; and science, industrial arts, and home economic materials; etc.).

45. Require that lost or damaged property be replaced by the student. If the student cannot replace the property, restitution can be made by working at school.

46. Make sure that the student is not inadvertently reinforced for losing or damaging property (e.g., replace lost property with used or damaged materials, copies of materials, etc., rather than new materials).

47. Carefully consider the student's age and experience when expecting him/her to care for personal property.

48. Allow natural consequences to occur due to the student's inability to care for personal property (e.g., having to write with a crayon because the student lost his/her pencil, using free time to make up homework that was not turned in, etc.).

49. Be consistent when expecting the student to care for personal property. Do not allow the student to get out of caring for personal property one time and expect him/her to care for personal property the next time.

50. Make a list of written directions you want the student to follow (e.g., put away pencils and paper, hang up coat, put book bag on the back of your chair, etc.).

51. Have the student do those things that need to be done when it is discussed instead of later (e.g., put the lunchbox up now instead of later so that it will not be missing at lunchtime, etc.).

52. Assist the student in performing responsibilities. As the student demonstrates success, gradually require the student to independently assume more responsibility.

53. Require the student to care for personal property even though he/she forgot to do so at the established time.

54. Do not expect the student to pick up toys, games, materials, etc., that others failed to put away. Encourage everyone to pick up toys, games, materials, etc.

55. Do not put out additional toys, games, materials, etc., for the student if he/she is not able to care for the items he/she is using.

56. Provide shelving, containers, organizers, etc., for the student's personal possessions. Label the storage areas and require the student to keep possessions organized.

57. Limit the use of those things which the student is careless in using.

58. Set aside time each day for everyone in the room to care for personal property.

192 Steals or forcibly takes things from other students, teachers, the school building, etc.

1. Communicate with the student's parents (e.g., notes home, phone calls, etc.) to share information about their child's appropriate behavior. The parents may reinforce the student at home for appropriate use or consideration of others' belongings at school.

2. Intervene early when there is a problem to prevent a more serious problem from occurring.

3. Help the student develop an awareness of the consequences of his/her behavior by writing down or talking through problems which may occur due to his/her impulsivity (e.g., perceived as unmannerly, avoided, etc.).

4. Help the student develop an awareness of himself/herself and those around him/her. Have the student periodically step back and ask himself/herself, "Am I behaving impulsively?"

5. Provide constant, positive reinforcement for appropriate behavior. Ignore as many inappropriate behaviors as possible.

6. Reinforce the student for demonstrating appropriate behavior: (a) give the student a tangible reward (e.g., classroom privileges, passing out materials, five minutes free time, etc.) or (b) give the student an intangible reward (e.g., praise, fist bump, smile, etc.).

7. Reinforce the student for demonstrating appropriate behavior based on the length of time the student can be successful. As the student demonstrates success, gradually increase the length of time required for reinforcement.

8. Establish rules (e.g., be friendly, ask permission to borrow things, share, etc.). These rules should be consistent and followed by everyone in the class. Talk about the rules often.

9. Demonstrate to the student how to ask permission to use something and how to react if he/she is told no.

10. Arrange for the student to be involved in many activities with other students to help him/her learn the skills necessary to interact appropriately with them.

11. Teach the student to think before acting by asking himself/herself questions: *What is happening?, What am I doing?, What should I do?, What will be best for me?*

12. Deal with the grabbing of belongings privately rather than publicly.

13. Reinforce those students in the classroom who demonstrate appropriate behavior in reference to others' belongings.

14. Provide the student with a clearly understood list of consequences for inappropriate behavior.

15. Help the student build or create a prized possession to satisfy the need for ownership (e.g., this can be done in art, home economics, industrial arts, etc.).

16. Make sure that the student does not get away with taking things from others by having him/her immediately return what he/she takes forcibly.

17. Speak with the student to explain (a) what he/she is doing wrong (e.g., grabbing things from others) and (b) what he/she should be doing (e.g., asking to use things, borrowing, sharing, returning, etc.).

18. Teach the student acceptable ways to communicate displeasure, anger, frustration, etc.

19. Supervise the student to monitor behavior.

20. Communicate with the student's family to establish procedures whereby the student may earn those things he/she would otherwise take from other students.

21. Teach the student to ask for things in a positive manner. Teach key words and phrases (e.g., "May I borrow your pencil?" "Do you mind if I use your cellphone?" etc.).

22. Remove the student from the group or activity until he/she can demonstrate appropriate behavior and self-control.

23. Identify those things the student has been grabbing from others and provide the student with those items as reinforcers for appropriate behavior.

24. Encourage the student to ask himself/herself questions to avoid impulsive behavior (e.g., "What should I be doing?" "How do I want to be perceived?").

25. Encourage the student to monitor his/her impulsivity. Awareness should reduce impulsive behaviors.

26. Teach the student to handle his/her anger, frustration, disappointment, etc., by walking away from the situation, talking with an adult, etc.

27. Encourage the student to verbalize his/her feelings before losing control (e.g., "I'm starting to act impulsively. I need to walk away from this situation.").

28. Choose a peer who will be a good influence on the student (e.g., someone younger/older, of the same/opposite gender, etc.) to participate in activities with the student.

29. Remove the student immediately from interacting with others when he/she begins to take things in a forceful manner.

30. Do not assume the student is being treated nicely by others. Peers may be stimulating inappropriate behavior.

31. Use a permanent marker to label all property brought to school by students and teachers.

32. Have the student make a list of consequences associated with grabbing things away from others (e.g., break something, hurt someone, embarrass self or others, etc.).

33. Make sure other students do not take things forcibly from the student. That may result in him/her attempting to forcibly take things from others.

34. Teach the student how to borrow by loaning and requiring the return of those things the student has been taking from others.

35. Teach the student to respect others and their belongings by respecting the student's belongings.

36. Increase supervision (e.g., by teacher, peer, paraprofessional, etc.) of the student and those activities in which he/she is likely to forcibly take things from others.

37. Have the student identify the situations in which he/she is likely to act impulsively. After he/she has identified these situations, have him/her think of ways to minimize their occurrences.

38. Write a contract with the student specifying what behavior is expected (e.g., not grabbing things away from others) and what reinforcement will be made available when the terms of the contract have been met.

39. Make sure the student understands that things he/she breaks, destroys, etc., when taking things forcibly will be replaced by him/her.

40. Make sure the student understands the natural consequences of inappropriate behavior (e.g., the student must make restitution for taking things which belong to others).

41. Teach the student the concept of borrowing by allowing the student to borrow things from you. Require him/her to ask permission before doing so.

42. Encourage the student to consider the consequences of his/her behavior before engaging in any activity.

43. Encourage all students to monitor their own belongings.

44. Reduce the opportunity to take things from other students by restricting students from bringing unnecessary items to school.

45. Give the student suggestions of things to do (e.g., count to 10, say the alphabet to himself/herself, walk away from the situation and then return, etc.) to avoid taking things from others in a forceful manner.

46. Do not allow the student to participate in activities with those students with whom he/she has trouble getting along.

47. Become aware of the times when the student is most impulsive (e.g., in a large group of people, when he/she is angry, etc.) and limit his/her interactions with others during these times.

48. Be consistent. Deal with the student and his/her behavior in a manner that is as consistent as possible by reacting in the same manner each time, using the same consequences, etc.

1. Communicate with the student's parents (e.g., notes home, phone calls, etc.) to share information about the student's progress. The parents may reinforce the student at home for behaving appropriately while seated at school.

2. Intervene early when there is a problem to prevent a more serious problem from occurring.

3. Seat the student next to a peer who behaves appropriately while seated.

4. Maintain a full schedule of activities. Keeping the student engaged in learning should decrease inappropriate behaviors.

5. Choose a peer to model appropriate ways to sit in his/her seat for the student.

6. Provide constant, positive reinforcement for appropriate behavior. Ignore as many inappropriate behaviors as possible.

7. Reinforce the student for behaving appropriately in his/her seat based on the length of time the student can be successful. As the student demonstrates success, gradually increase the length of time required for reinforcement.

8. Reinforce the student for behaving appropriately in his/her seat: (a) give the student a tangible reward (e.g., classroom privileges, passing out materials, five minutes free time, etc.) or (b) give the student an intangible reward (e.g., praise, fist bump, smile, etc.).

9. Help the student develop an awareness of himself/herself and those around him/her. Have the student periodically step back and ask himself/herself, "Am I fidgeting and being overactive?"

10. Have the student make a list of consequences associated with frequently occurring behaviors (e.g., by disrupting others, I will be perceived as unmannerly; by behaving aggressively, people will avoid me.).

11. Make sure the student is aware of the natural consequences that may occur from behaving inappropriately while seated (e.g., injury, damaging property, hurting others, etc.).

12. Teach the student to think before acting by asking himself/herself questions: *What is happening?, What am I doing?, What should I do?, What will be best for me?*

13. Place the student in a carrel to reduce distracting stimuli which may cause the student to behave inappropriately while seated.

14. Reinforce those students in the classroom who behave appropriately while seated.

15. Provide the student with a clearly understood list of consequences for inappropriate behavior.

16. Reduce the emphasis on competition. Competitive activities may cause the student to act inappropriately while seated.

17. Assess the degree of task difficulty to determine whether or not the student will require additional information, time, assistance, etc., to avoid becoming frustrated and engaging in inappropriate behaviors while seated.

18. Establish classroom rules:
- Concentrate while working.
- Work quietly.
- Remain in your seat.
- Finish task.
- Meet task expectations.
- Raise your hand.

Review rules often. Reinforce students for following the rules.

19. Speak to the student to explain (a) what he/she is doing wrong (e.g., tipping chair) and (b) what he/she should be doing (e.g., sitting with all chair legs on the floor).

20. Deliver a predetermined signal (e.g., give a hand signal, ring a bell, etc.) when the student begins to behave inappropriately while seated.

21. Speak with the student to let him/her know exactly what he/she is doing wrong, what he/she should be doing, and what the consequences are for inappropriate behavior.

22. Make sure that the chair or desk the student is assigned is appropriate and/or comfortable for him/her (e.g., the desk is not too high, the chair is not too small, etc.).

23. Choose different people (e.g., peer, paraprofessional, friend, etc.) to reinforce the student when he/she sits still.

24. Choose a peer who has self-control. Encourage the student to observe that person and try to model the behaviors which contribute to self-control.

25. Seat the student away from peers to reduce the likelihood that the student will behave inappropriately while in his/her seat.

26. Avoid seating the student near people with whom he/she may be tempted to talk during assemblies, seminars, group projects, etc.

27. Provide the student with a specific description of appropriate in-seat behavior (e.g., facing forward, feet on floor, back straight, etc.).

28. Move objects used for tactile stimulation (e.g., pens, paper clips, loose change, etc.) away from the student's reach.

29. Write a contract with the student specifying what behavior is expected (e.g., behaving appropriately while seated) and what reinforcement will be made available when the terms of the contract have been met.

30. Seat the student near the teacher.

31. Explain to the student, after telling him/her to stop talking, the reason why he/she should not be talking.

32. Remove any materials which the student uses to make noise while seated.

33. Do not criticize when correcting the student; be honest yet supportive. Never cause the student to feel negatively about himself/herself.

34. Maintain consistent expectations for the student to sit appropriately in his/her seat.

35. Identify the situations in which the student is most likely to participate in inappropriate behavior while seated. After you have identified these situations, think of ways to minimize their occurrences.

36. Evaluate the necessity of having the student sit facing forward, feet on floor, back straight, etc.

37. Provide activities which are interesting to the student to keep the student on task and behaving appropriately while seated.

38. Encourage the student to attend to the source of information by maintaining eye contact, keeping hands free from other materials, and reducing other distractions. This should decrease inappropriate behaviors.

39. Model for the student appropriate ways to sit in a chair or at a desk.

40. Reinforce those students in the classroom who sit appropriately in their seats.

41. Implement logical consequences for students who participate in inappropriate behaviors while seated (e.g., the student will have to sit on the floor, stand next to his/her desk to work, sit in a chair without a desk, etc.).

42. Communicate with the student's cooperative work experience/vocational education teacher to choose a job that allows for a high degree of physical movement (e.g., jobs which allow the student to be on his/her feet, move from room to room, have frequent contact with people, and travel from one job site to another, etc.).

43. Have desks and/or chairs that can be fastened to the floor or which are designed to prevent tipping.

44. Place the student in a carrel to reduce distracting stimuli which may cause the student to sit inappropriately in his/her seat.

45. Structure the environment so that the student remains active and involved in appropriate behavior.

46. Use natural consequences when the student touches others as they walk by (e.g., move the student to another location in the room, have others walk away from the student, etc.).

47. Allow the student some movement while performing tasks. Monitor and limit the amount of movement.

48. Carefully consider the student's age before expecting him/her to sit quietly for a period of time.

49. Facilitate on-task behavior by providing a full schedule of activities. Prevent lag time from occurring when the student would be free to participate in inappropriate behavior.

50. Evaluate the appropriateness of the task to determine (a) if the task is too easy, (b) if the task is too difficult, and (c) if the length of time scheduled to complete the task is adequate.

51. Allow the student some movement while listening to instruction from the teacher. Monitor and limit the amount of movement.

194 Does not follow directives from teachers or other school personnel

1. Structure the environment to reduce free or unplanned time which is likely to contribute to the student's inappropriate behavior.

2. Maintain visibility to and from the student. The teacher should be able to see the student and the student should be able to see the teacher. Make eye contact possible at all times.

3. Give the student a responsibility to be performed at the beginning of each directive.

4. Present the tasks in the most interesting and attractive manner possible.

5. Maintain supervision of the student. As the student is able to successfully follow directives, gradually decrease supervision.

6. Have the student maintain a chart representing the amount of time spent following teacher directives, rules, regulations, expectations, etc., with reinforcement for increasing acceptable behavior.

7. Be mobile to be frequently near the student.

8. Provide the student with many opportunities for social and academic successes.

9. Provide the student with positive feedback that indicates he/she is successful.

10. Post rules in various places (e.g., on the student's desk, in the hallways, etc.).

11. Make sure the student receives the information necessary to perform activities (e.g., written information, verbal directions, reminders, etc.).

12. Teach the student direction-following skills.

13. Maintain a positive and professional relationship with the student (e.g., an adversarial relationship is likely to result in failure to follow directions).

14. Be a consistent authority figure (e.g., be consistent in your relationship with the student).

15. Provide the student with optional courses of action to prevent total refusal to conform to rules, regulations, expectations, laws, etc., (e.g., return to the classroom).

16. Intervene early to prevent the student's behavior from leading to contagion for other students.

17. Deliver directions in a step-by-step sequence.

18. Choose a peer to model following directives for the student.

19. Interact with the student frequently to determine if school rules are being followed.

20. Make sure that all educators maintain consistent enforcement of school rules.

21. Allow natural consequences to occur as a result of the student's inability to follow directives from teachers and other school personnel (e.g., assignments are performed incorrectly, detention will be assigned, etc.).

22. Limit the student's opportunity to participate in activities in which he/she will not follow directives from teachers and other school personnel (e.g., recess, industrial arts activities, field trips, etc.).

23. Do not allow the student to be unsupervised anywhere.

24. Along with a directive, provide an incentive statement (e.g., "When you finish your math, you may go outside." "You may have free time after you finish your work.").

25. Have the student verbally repeat directions.

26. Deliver directions in a supportive rather than a threatening manner (e.g., "Please finish your work." rather than "You had better finish your work or else!").

27. Teach the student to respect others and their belongings by respecting the student's belongings.

28. Teach the student to think before acting by asking himself/herself question: *What is happening? What am I doing? What should I do? What will be best for me?*

29. Allow the student to voice his/her opinion in a situation to avoid becoming angry or upset.

30. Evaluate the appropriateness of the task to determine (a) if the task is too easy, (b) if the task is too difficult, and (c) if the length of time scheduled to complete the task is adequate.

31. Communicate with the parents (e.g., notes home, phone calls, etc.) to share information about the student's progress. The parents may reinforce the student at home for following directives from teachers or other school personnel.

32. Write a contract with the student specifying what behavior is expected (e.g., asking for help) and what reinforcement will be made available when the terms of the contract have been met.

33. Remove the student from the group or activity until he/she can demonstrate appropriate behavior and self-control.

34. Reinforce the student for following the directives of teachers and other school personnel based on the length of time the student can be successful. As the student demonstrates success, gradually increase the length of time required for reinforcement.

35. Reinforce those students in the classroom who follow directives from teachers and other school personnel.

36. Establish classroom rules:
- Concentrate while working.
- Remain in your seat.
- Finish task.
- Meet task expectations.
- Raise your hand.

Review rules often. Reinforce students for following the rules.

37. Speak with the student to explain (a) what the student is doing wrong (e.g., not following directives from teachers or other school personnel, etc.) and (b) what the student should be doing (e.g., asking for help, calling attention to a problem, etc.).

38. Reinforce the student for following directives from teachers or other school personnel: (a) give the student a tangible reward (e.g., classroom privileges, line leading, passing out materials, five minutes free time, etc.) or (b) give the student an intangible reward (e.g., praise, fist bump, smile, etc.).

1. Reinforce the student for demonstrating appropriate behavior: (a) give the student a tangible reward (e.g., classroom privileges, line leading, passing out materials, five minutes free time, etc.) or (b) give the student an intangible reward (e.g., praise, fist bump, smile, etc.).

2. Speak with the student to explain (a) what he/she is doing wrong (e.g., bringing inappropriate or illegal materials to school) and (b) what he/she should be doing (e.g., following an established code of conduct, following the rules, taking care of responsibilities, etc.).

3. Establish classroom rules:
• Concentrate while working.
• Work quietly.
• Remain in your seat.
• Finish task.
• Meet task requirements.
Review rules often. Reinforce the student for following the rules.

4. Reinforce those students in the classroom who demonstrate appropriate behavior.

5. Reinforce the student for demonstrating appropriate behavior based on the length of time he/she can be successful. As the student demonstrates success, gradually increase the length of time required for reinforcement.

6. Remove the student from the group or activity until he/she can demonstrate appropriate behavior and self-control.

7. Write a contract with the student specifying what behavior is expected (e.g., not bringing alcohol to school) and what reinforcement will be made available when the terms of the contract have been met.

8. Communicate with parents (e.g., notes home, phone calls, etc.) to share information about the student's progress. The parents may reinforce the student at home for not bringing inappropriate or illegal materials to school.

9. Encourage the student's parents to be positive and supportive with the student as opposed to being negative and threatening.

10. Provide a drug information program for the individual student, the class, or the student body.

11. Provide information on penalties for possession or use of alcohol and drugs at school.

12. Involve the student in extracurricular activities to help him/her develop appropriate interests.

13. Identify individuals the student may contact with his/her concerns (e.g., guidance counselor, school nurse, social worker, school psychologist, etc.).

14. Share concerns with the administration and seek referral to an agency for investigation of alcohol or drug abuse.

15. Encourage the student to become involved in athletic or extracurricular activities.

16. Assign the student activities which would require interactions with a respected role model (e.g., older student, high school student, college student, community leader, someone held in esteem, etc.).

17. Provide the student with intelligent, accurate information concerning drugs and alcohol rather than sensationalized scare tactic information.

18. Provide many opportunities for social and academic success.

19. Encourage the student to excel in a particular area of interest (e.g., provide information for the student, provide personal and professional support, sponsor the student, etc.).

20. Maintain frequent contact with the student during school hours (e.g., follow up on details of earlier communications, maintain a direction for conversation, etc.).

21. Lead and direct the student. Do not lecture and make demands.

22. When natural consequences from peers occur (e.g., criticism, loss of friendship, etc.) as the result of the use of drugs or alcohol at school bring the consequences to the attention of the student.

23. Communicate with parents, agencies, or the appropriate parties to inform them of the problem, determine the cause of the problem, and consider possible solutions to the problem.

24. Be a resource for parents by providing information on agencies, counseling programs, etc.

25. Reduce the emphasis on competition and help the student realize that success is individually defined.

26. Maintain adequate supervision at all times and in all areas of the school (e.g., hallways, bathrooms, between classes, before and after school, school grounds, etc.).

27. Be willing to take the time to listen, share, and talk with the student.

28. Increase your own professional knowledge of laws and treatment concerning drug or alcohol use and abuse.

29. Maintain anecdotal records of the student's behavior to check patterns or changes in behavior.

30. Provide appropriate reading material (e.g., magazines, novels, etc.) at school, which is of interest to the student, so that he/she will not bring inappropriate reading material to school.

31. Teach the student to be satisfied with his/her best effort rather than perfection.

32. Teach the student alternative ways to deal with demands, challenges, and pressures of the school-age experience (e.g., deal with problems when they arise, practice self-control at all times, share problems or concerns with others, etc.).

196 Responds inappropriately to redirection in academic and social situations

1. Reinforce those students in the classroom who respond appropriately to redirection in academic and social situations.

2. Make sure that communications with the student regarding redirection are appropriate to that student's ability to respond (e.g., match the form in which redirection is delivered to the student's most likely successful response, such as "Would you please go to your seat" rather than "You need to go to your seat immediately.").

3. Establish classroom rules:
- Concentrate while working.
- Work quietly.
- Remain in your seat.
- Finish task.
- Meet task requirements.

Review rules often. Reinforce the student for following the rules.

4. Allow natural consequences to occur when the student does not respond appropriately to redirection in academic and social situations (e.g., make highly reinforcing activities contingent upon responding appropriately to redirection in academic and social situations).

5. Do not criticize when correcting the student; be honest yet supportive. Never cause the student to feel negatively about himself/herself.

6. Assist the student in responding appropriately to redirection in academic situations (e.g., help the student correct one or two items to get him/her started).

7. Deliver instructions in a clear and concise manner.

8. Base expectations for student response to redirection in academic situations on ability level (e.g., one student may be expected to return to his/her seat immediately upon redirection while another student may be given three minutes to respond appropriately).

9. Make sure that an activity does not overstimulate and result in the student's inability to respond appropriately to redirection in academic situations.

10. Be consistent in expectations when redirecting the student in academic situations (e.g., require the student to immediately correct errors after work has been checked, require the student to return to his/her seat within three minutes, etc.).

11. Choose a peer to model responding appropriately to redirection in academic and social situations for the student.

12. Deliver redirection to the student as privately as possible.

13. Reinforce the student for responding appropriately to redirection within a given period of time based on the number of times the student can be successful. As the student demonstrates success, gradually increase the number of times required for reinforcement.

14. Determine the reason for errors made by the student.

15. Develop subsequent tasks based on errors the student makes rather than requiring an immediate correction of work done incorrectly.

16. Evaluate the appropriateness of the task to determine if (a) the task is too easy, (b) the task is too difficult, and (c) the length of time scheduled to complete the task is adequate.

17. Do not allow redirection to become a necessary part of every academic situation in which the student participates.

18. Evaluate the demands made on the student in academic situations to make sure that all expectations are within the student's ability level.

19. Make sure that attention is not inadvertently given to the student for failing to respond appropriately to redirection in academic and social situations (i.e., remove attention from the student if the attention is reinforcing his/her inappropriate behavior).

20. Avoid those circumstances where the student demonstrates difficulty responding appropriately to redirection in academic situations (e.g., highly competitive situations, situations in which the student is embarrassed by his/her errors, etc.).

21. To reduce the need for redirection in academic situations, require the student to check all work for errors prior to handing in assignments.

22. Make sure that redirection in academic and social situations is delivered in the most positive manner possible.

23. Have the student rephrase the directions to make sure the student understands the assignment or activity.

24. Reinforce those students in the classroom who respond appropriately to redirection in academic and social situations.

25. Communicate with parents (e.g., notes home, phone calls, etc.) to share information about the student's progress. The parents may reinforce the student at home for responding appropriately to redirection in academic and social situations at school.

26. Make sure that the student understands that redirection is designed to help him/her succeed rather than as a form of punishment (e.g., use statements such as, "This sentence would be much easier to read if it were written with correct capitalization and punctuation. Please write it again and I'll check it for you.").

27. Reinforce the student for responding appropriately to redirection in academic and social situations: (a) give the student a tangible reward (e.g., classroom privileges, line leading, passing out materials, five minutes free time, etc.) or (b) give the student an intangible reward (e.g., praise, fist bump, smile, etc.).

28. Speak to the student to explain (a) what the student is doing wrong (e.g., not correcting errors on an assignment, failing to return to seat when told to do so, etc.) and (b) what the student should be doing (e.g., correcting errors on an assignment, returning to seat when told to do so, etc.).

29. Have the student ask questions about directions, explanations, instructions not understood.

30. Remove the student from the activity if he/she does not respond appropriately to redirection in academic and social situations.

31. When the student is redirected in academic situations, make sure that an explanation for the redirection is also given (e.g., "You need to return to your seat because we are ready to begin a new activity.").

32. Write a contract with the student specifying what behavior is expected (e.g., returning to seat when told to do so) and what reinforcement will be made available when the terms of the contract have been met.

33. Monitor the student's behavior to provide redirection before the student's errors or inappropriate behavior exceed his/her ability to respond appropriately.

34. Provide adequate time for the student to respond appropriately to redirection in academic and social situations.

1. Be a consistent authority figure (e.g., be consistent in your relationship with the student).

2. Communicate with the student's parents (e.g., notes home, phone calls, etc.) to share information about their child's progress. The parents may reinforce the student at home for following school rules.

3. Choose a peer to model following school rules for the student.

4. Structure the environment so that the student remains active and involved.

5. Intervene early when there is a problem to prevent a more serious problem from occurring.

6. Consult with the school psychologist about the student's failure to consider the consequences of his/her behavior.

7. Make sure the student is actively involved in the environment (i.e., give the student responsibilities, activities, and errands to run to provide purposeful behavior).

8. Educate yourself and others about ADHD to increase understanding and accommodation of impulsive behavior.

9. Help the student develop an awareness of the consequences of his/her behavior by writing down or talking through problems which may occur due to his/her inability to adjust his/her behavior to different situations (e.g., perceived as unmannerly, avoided, etc.).

10. Educate the student about ADHD and the need for developing skills to self monitor behavior.

11. Encourage the student to pause and consider his/her thoughts before acting on them.

12. Provide constant, positive reinforcement for appropriate behavior. Ignore as many inappropriate behaviors as possible.

13. Have the student make a list of consequences associated with frequently occurring behaviors (e.g., perceived as unmannerly, avoided by people, etc.).

14. Teach the student to think before acting by asking himself/herself questions: *What is happening?, What am I doing?, What should I do?, What will be best for me?*.

15. Make sure that rules and behavior expectations are consistent in the classroom and throughout the school.

16. Inform other personnel of any behavior problem that the student may have so that supervision and assistance may be provided.

17. Model those behaviors the student is expected to display in the school environment.

18. Have the student maintain a chart representing the amount of time spent following school rules. Reinforcement should be given for increasing acceptable behavior.

19. Reinforce those students in the classroom who follow school rules.

20. Provide the student with a clearly understood list of consequences for inappropriate behavior.

21. Teach problem-solving skills:
- Identify the problem.
- Identify the goals and objectives.
- Develop a strategy/plan for action.
- Carry out the plan.
- Evaluate the results.

22. Reduce the emphasis on competition. Competitive activities may cause the student to act inappropriately.

23. Be consistent in enforcing the rules and consequences contained in the school discipline plan.

24. Have the student review the consequences of his/her behavior. Have the student consider different choices he/she could have made and the different outcomes.

25. Provide the student with optional courses of action to prevent total refusal to obey school rules (e.g., may return to the classroom).

26. Have the student ask questions about directions, explanations, or instructions he/she does not understand.

27. Reinforce the student for going directly from one location to another.

28. Speak to the student to explain (a) what he/she is doing wrong (e.g., failing to follow school rules) and (b) what he/she should be doing (e.g., following school rules).

29. Hold the student accountable for failing to follow school rules.

30. Provide the student with positive feedback that indicates he/she is successful.

31. Be consistent in applying consequences for behavior (e.g., appropriate behavior receives positive consequences while inappropriate behavior receives negative consequences).

32. Reinforce the student for moving from one place to another in an appropriate length of time.

33. Teach the student ways to gain self-control (e.g., count to ten, walk away, talk with someone, etc.).

34. Encourage the student to play games, sports, etc., with friends who do not encourage him/her to disregard school rules.

35. Reinforce the student for remaining in assigned areas (e.g., student lounge, recreational area, assembly, etc.).

36. Clarify for the student that it is his/her behavior which determines whether consequences are positive or negative.

37. Provide the student with a list of school rules and/or behavior expectations to carry with him/her at all times in the school environment.

38. Make sure that all educators who work with the student consistently enforce school rules.

39. Make sure the student knows the rules before beginning a new activity.

40. Maintain a routine that will minimize erratic or impulsive behavior which may result in negative consequences.

41. Be mobile to be frequently near the student.

42. Separate the student from the peer that stimulates his/her inappropriate behavior.

43. Post school rules in various places (e.g., on the student's desk, in the hallways, etc.).

44. Explain verbally the school discipline plan and consequences to the student on a one-to-one basis.

45. Have the student carry a point card at all times so that he/she can be reinforced anywhere in the school environment for following the rules.

46. Have the student list the pros and cons of an action. Have the student consider if the pros outweigh the cons before he/she takes action.

47. Discuss with the student the role and benefit of rules outside the school setting (e.g., job site, social situation, recreational activities, etc.).

48. Reinforce the student for following school rules based on the length of time the student can be successful. As the student demonstrates success, gradually increase the length of time required for reinforcement.

49. Reinforce the student for following school rules: (a) give the student a tangible reward (e.g., classroom privileges, passing out materials, five minutes free time, etc.) or (b) give the student an intangible reward (e.g., praise, fist bump, smile, etc.).

50. Help the student identify specific school rules he/she has difficulty following and make these rules into goals for behavior improvement.

51. Have the student ask questions about school rules he/she does not understand.

52. Have the student and his/her parents sign a copy of the school discipline plan and consequences for failing to follow school rules.

53. Have the student identify the situations in which he/she is most likely to fail to consider the consequences of his/her behavior. After he/she has identified these situations, have him/her think of ways to minimize their occurrences.

54. Provide the student with many opportunities for social and academic successes.

55. Maintain supervision of the student. As the student is able to successfully follow school rules, gradually decrease supervision.

56. Choose a peer to accompany the student in nonacademic settings.

57. Write a contract with the student specifying what behavior is expected and what reinforcement will be made available when the terms of the contract have been met.

58. Use related consequences for the student's inappropriate behavior (e.g., running in the halls results in having to walk with an adult, throwing food in the cafeteria results in having to sit next to an adult when eating, disruption in the library requires additional adult supervision, etc.).

59. Intervene early to prevent the student's behavior from leading to contagion of other students.

60. Encourage the student to realize that all behavior has negative or positive consequences. Discuss with the student behaviors that will lead to positive consequences.

61. Have the student verbally repeat the school discipline plan and consequences.

62. Require the student to verbalize the school rules at designated times throughout the day (e.g., before school, during recess, at lunch, at the end of the day, etc.).

63. Maintain visibility to and from the student. The teacher should be able to see the student and the student should be able to see the teacher. Make eye contact possible at all times.

64. Do not allow the student to use ADHD as an excuse. Hold the student responsible for his/her actions. However, understand and accept problems that ADHD brings into the student's life while he/she is learning to make accommodations.

65. Interact with the student frequently to determine if school rules are being followed.

66. Make sure that the student understands the relationship between inappropriate behavior and the consequences which follow (e.g., lunch detention, suspension, after school detention, etc.).

67. Establish school rules:
- Walk in halls.
- Arrive for class on time.
- Respect the privacy of others.
- Talk quietly in the halls.

Review rules often. Reinforce students for following the rules.

198 Demonstrates inappropriate behavior on the school grounds before and after school

1. Provide the student with a list of school rules and/or behavior expectations to carry at all times in the school environment.

2. Separate the student from the peer(s) who stimulates his/her inappropriate behavior on the school grounds before and after school.

3. Choose a responsible peer to accompany the student when he/she is on the school grounds before and after school.

4. Make sure the behavioral demands are appropriate for the student's ability level (e.g., interacting with peers, entering the building when appropriate, leaving the building when appropriate, using school equipment with care, etc.).

5. Make sure the student is actively involved in the environment (e.g., give the student responsibilities, activities, and errands to run to provide purposeful behavior).

6. Have the student carry a point card at all times so that he/she can be reinforced anywhere in the school environment for conforming to rules, expectations, laws, etc.

7. Inform other school personnel of any behavior problems the student may have so supervision and assistance may be provided.

8. Be consistent in applying consequences for behavior (e.g., appropriate behavior receives positive consequences, while inappropriate behavior receives negative consequences).

9. Reinforce the student for remaining in assigned areas (e.g., play areas, student lounge, recreational area, etc.).

10. Provide organized activities in which to participate in assigned areas before, during, and after school (e.g., kickball, dodge ball, softball, four square, tether ball, jump rope, foot races, etc.).

11. Allow the student to enter the building early or remain in the building after school to work on assignments or special projects, assist teachers, assist the custodian, etc.

12. Reinforce the student for arriving on the school grounds shortly before school begins (e.g., 5 minutes) and leaving the school grounds shortly after school.

13. Change the student's bus assignment so the student does not arrive early and does not stay late after school.

14. Identify an area of the school grounds to be used as a time-out area when the student demonstrates inappropriate behavior on the school grounds.

15. Have the student be responsible for a younger peer on the school grounds before and after school.

16. Have the student be responsible for organizing and supervising activities and distributing or collecting materials on the school grounds before and after school.

17. Give the student a specific job to perform on the school grounds before and after school (e.g., crosswalk patrol, bus monitor, raising and lowering the flag, picking up litter on the school grounds, etc.).

18. Intervene early when there is a problem to prevent more serious problems from occurring.

19. Teach the student to think before acting by asking himself/herself question: *What is happening? What am I doing? What should I do? What will be best for me?*

20. Have the student ask questions about school ground rules he/she does not understand.

21. Establish rules for the school grounds:
- Remain in assigned areas.
- Share school equipment.
- Use appropriate language.
- Use school property with care.

Review rules often. Reinforce students for following the rules.

22. Choose a peer to model appropriate behavior on the school grounds before and after school for the student.

23. Communicate with parents (e.g., notes home, phone calls, etc.) to share information about the student's progress. The parents may reinforce the student at home for demonstrating appropriate behavior on the school grounds before and after school.

24. Reinforce those students who demonstrate appropriate behavior on the school grounds before and after school.

25. Write a contract with the student specifying what behavior is expected (e.g., playing, sharing school equipment, visiting, etc.) and what reinforcement will be made available when the terms of the contract have been met.

26. Reinforce the student for demonstrating appropriate behavior on the school grounds before and after school based on the length of time he/she can be successful. As the student demonstrates success, gradually increase the length of time required for reinforcement.

27. Speak to the student to explain (a) what the student is doing wrong (e.g., fighting with peers) and (b) what the student should be doing (e.g., playing appropriately, sharing school equipment with peers, visiting, etc.).

28. Reinforce the student for demonstrating appropriate behavior on the school grounds before and after school: (a) give the student a tangible reward (e.g., classroom privileges, line leading, passing out materials, five minutes free time, etc.) or (b) give the student an intangible reward (e.g., praise, fist bump, smile, etc.).

1. Structure the environment so that the student remains active and involved while demonstrating acceptable behavior.

2. Maintain visibility to and from the student. The teacher should be able to see the student, and the student should be able to see the teacher. Make eye contact possible at all times.

3. Be a consistent authority figure (e.g., be consistent in your relationship with the student).

4. Present tasks in the most interesting and attractive manner possible.

5. Have the student maintain a chart representing the amount of time spent following classroom rules, with reinforcement for increasing acceptable behavior.

6. Be mobile to be frequently near the student.

7. Provide the student with many opportunities for social and academic successes.

8. Provide the student with positive feedback that indicates he/she is successful.

9. Post rules in various places (e.g., on the student's desk, etc.).

10. Make sure the student receives the information necessary to perform activities (e.g., written information, verbal directions, reminders, etc.).

11. Teach the student direction-following skills.

12. Maintain a positive and professional relationship with the student (e.g., an adversarial relationship is likely to result in failure to follow directions).

13. Give the student preferred responsibilities.

14. Provide the student with optional courses of action to prevent total refusal to obey teacher directives.

15. Intervene early to prevent the student's behavior from leading to contagion of other students.

16. Have the student ask questions about directions, explanations, or instructions not understood.

17. Require the student to verbalize the classroom rules at designated times throughout the day (e.g., before school, during recess, at break time, at lunch, at the end of the day, etc.).

18. Deliver directions in a step-by-step sequence.

19. Choose a peer to model following the rules of the classroom for the student.

20. Interact with the student frequently to determine if directives are being followed.

21. Maintain consistent rules, routine, and general expectations of conduct and procedure.

22. Remove the student from the group or activity until he/she can demonstrate acceptable behavior and self-control.

23. Help the student identify specific rules he/she has difficulty following and make these areas goals for behavior improvement.

24. Separate the student from the peer(s) who stimulates his/her inappropriate behavior.

25. Make sure that rules and behavior expectations are consistent throughout the school and classrooms.

26. Along with a directive, provide an incentive statement (e.g., "When you finish your math, you may go outside to play." or, "You may have free time after you finish your work.").

27. Intervene early when there is a problem to prevent more serious problems from occurring.

28. Before beginning a new activity, make sure the student knows the classroom rules.

29. Teach the student to think before acting by asking himself/herself questions: *What is happening?, What am I doing?, What should I do?, What will be best for me?*.

30. Evaluate the appropriateness of the assigned task to determine (a) if the task is too easy, (b) if the task is too difficult, and (c) if the length of time scheduled to complete the task is adequate.

31. Communicate with parents (e.g., notes home, phone calls, etc.) to share information about the student's progress. The parents may reinforce the student at home for following the rules of the classroom.

32. Provide the student with a list of rules and/or behavior expectations.

33. Reinforce the student for following the rules of the classroom: (a) give the student a tangible reward (e.g., classroom privileges, line leading, passing out materials, five minutes free time, etc.) or (b) give the student an intangible reward (e.g., praise, fist bump, smile, etc.).

34. Reinforce the student for following the rules of the classroom based on the length of time the student can be successful. As the student demonstrates success, gradually increase the length of time required for reinforcement.

35. Establish classroom rules:
- Concentrate while working.
- Work quietly.
- Remain in your seat.
- Finish task.
- Meet task requirements.

Review rules often. Reinforce the student for following the rules.

36. Speak with the student to explain (a) what the student is doing wrong (e.g., failing to follow classroom rules) and (b) what the student should be doing (e.g., following the rules of the classroom).

37. Write a contract with the student specifying what behavior is expected (e.g., following classroom rules) and what reinforcement will be made available when the terms of the contract have been met.

38. Reinforce those students who follow the rules of the classroom.

200 Does not wait appropriately for an instructor to arrive

1. Choose a peer to model appropriate behavior for the student when a supervisor is detained (e.g., stay in seat or assigned area, remain quiet, work on assigned task, etc.).

2. Have the student ask questions about directions, explanations, or instructions not understood.

3. Choose a peer to supervise the student when an instructor is detained.

4. Provide a list of possible activities for the students to participate in when an instructor is detained (e.g., write a letter to a friend, work on assigned tasks, organize work area, look at a magazine, etc.).

5. Along with a directive, provide an incentive statement (e.g., "If you wait quietly, you can have five minutes of free time.").

6. Make sure the student knows when it is acceptable to get others' attention (e.g., in an emergency).

7. Communicate with parents (e.g., notes home, phone calls, etc.) to share information about the student's progress. The parents may reinforce the student at home for waiting appropriately for a supervisor.

8. Write a contract with the student specifying what behavior is expected (e.g., stay in seat or assigned area, remain quiet, and work on assigned task) and what reinforcement will be made available when the terms of the contract have been met.

9. Deliver directions in a supportive rather than a threatening manner (e.g., "Please wait quietly." rather than "You had better wait quietly or else!").

10. Reinforce the student for waiting appropriately for a supervisor to arrive based on the length of time the student can be successful. As the student demonstrates success, gradually increase the length of time required for reinforcement.

11. Reinforce those students in the classroom who stay in their seat or assigned area, remain quiet, and work on assigned tasks.

12. Establish classroom rules:
- Concentrate while working.
- Remain in your seat.
- Finish task.
- Meet task expectations.
- Raise your hand.

Review rules often. Reinforce students for following the rules.

13. Speak to the student to explain (a) what the student is doing wrong (e.g., leaving seat, talking, making noises, etc.) and (b) what the student should be doing (e.g., sitting in seat or assigned area, remaining quiet, etc.).

14. Reinforce the student for waiting appropriately for a supervisor to arrive: (a) give the student a tangible reward (e.g., classroom privileges, line leading, passing out materials, five minutes free time, etc.) or (b) give the student an intangible reward (e.g., praise, fist bump, smile, etc.).

201 Does not wait appropriately for assistance from an instructor

1. Communicate with the student's parents (e.g., notes home, phone calls, etc.) to share information about their child's progress. The parents may reinforce the student at home for waiting appropriately for assistance from an instructor at school.

2. Evaluate the appropriateness of the task to determine (a) if the task is too easy, (b) if the task is too difficult, and (c) if the length of time scheduled to complete the task is adequate.

3. Tell the student that you will assist him/her as soon as possible (e.g., "Stephen, I'll be with you shortly.") to increase the probability that the student will wait appropriately for assistance.

4. Choose a peer from whom the student may seek assistance.

5. Attempt to provide assistance immediately. As the student demonstrates success, gradually increase the length of time the student must wait for assistance when the instructor is helping another student, instructing, etc.

6. Have the student ask for clarification if he/she does not understand directions that are given verbally or in writing.

7. Reinforce the student for waiting appropriately for assistance from an instructor: (a) give the student a tangible reward (e.g., classroom privileges, passing out materials, five minutes free time, etc.) or (b) give the student an intangible reward (e.g., praise, fist bump, smile, etc.).

8. Speak to the student to explain (a) what he/she is doing wrong (e.g., leaving his/her seat, talking to other students, etc.) and (b) what he/she should be doing (e.g., waiting quietly for assistance, remaining seated, etc.).

9. Establish classroom rules:
- Concentrate while working.
- Work quietly.
- Remain in your seat.
- Finish task.
- Meet task expectations.

Review rules often. Reinforce students for following the rules.

10. Reinforce those students in the classroom who remain seated in assigned areas and remain quiet while waiting for assistance from the instructor.

11. Reinforce the student for waiting appropriately for assistance from an instructor based on the length of time he/she can be successful. As the student demonstrates success, gradually increase the length of time required for reinforcement.

12. Choose a classmate to model appropriate behavior (e.g., remaining in seat or assigned area, remaining quiet, etc.) when waiting for assistance from an instructor for the student.

13. Encourage the student to go to the next problem, go to another part of the assignment, begin a new assignment, etc., when waiting for assistance from an instructor.

14. Provide constant, positive reinforcement for appropriate behavior. Ignore as many inappropriate behaviors as possible.

15. Provide the student with a clearly understood list of consequences for inappropriate behavior.

16. Increase supervision (e.g., by teacher, peer, etc.) of the student to allow intervention to occur before the student exhibits disruptive behavior.

17. Have the student ask questions about directions, explanations, or instructions before beginning a task to reinforce comprehension.

18. Reduce the emphasis on competition. Highly competitive activities may cause the student to feel anxious and have difficulty waiting for assistance from the teacher.

19. Discuss the student's behavior with him/her in private rather than in front of others.

20. Make sure that the activities in which the student engages are not too difficult for him/her.

21. Do not place an emphasis on perfection. If the student feels he/she must live up to your expectations and cannot, it may cause him/her to become impatient while waiting for assistance.

22. Closely supervise the student to monitor his/her behavior at all times.

23. Assess the degree of task difficulty to determine whether or not the student will require additional information, time, assistance, etc., before beginning a task.

24. Post needed information in a readily accessible location (e.g., bulletin board, desktop, etc.), to decrease the student's need for assistance from the instructor.

25. Establish alternative activities for the student to perform when waiting for assistance from an instructor (e.g., check work already completed, look at a magazine, organize work area, begin another task, etc.).

26. Maintain visibility to and from the student while he/she waits until assistance can be provided. The instructor should be able to see the student and the student should be able to see the instructor. Make eye contact possible at all times.

27. Maintain verbal communication with the student until assistance can be provided (e.g., "Thank you for waiting quietly. I'll be there shortly.").

28. Teach the student to use techniques which limit the need for teacher assistance (e.g., refer to previous math problems for models, use reference materials as a source for answers, etc.).

202 Does not demonstrate appropriate use of school-related materials

1. Reinforce the student for demonstrating appropriate use of school-related materials: (a) give the student a tangible reward (e.g., classroom privileges, line leading, passing out materials, five minutes free time, etc.) or (b) give the student an intangible reward (e.g., praise, fist bump, smile, etc.).

2. Speak to the student to explain (a) what he/she is doing wrong (e.g., failing to use school-related materials appropriately) and (b) what he/she should be doing (e.g., using materials as directed).

3. Establish classroom rules:
• Concentrate while working.
• Work quietly.
• Remain in your seat.
• Finish task.
• Meet task requirements.
Review rules often. Reinforce the student for following the rules.

4. Provide time at the beginning of each day to help the student organize his/her school-related materials.

5. Reinforce the student for using school-related materials appropriately based on the length of time the student can be successful. As the student demonstrates success, gradually increase the length of time required for reinforcement.

6. Write a contract with the student specifying what behavior is expected (e.g., appropriate use of school-related materials) and what reinforcement will be made available when the terms of the contract have been met.

7. Communicate with parents (e.g., notes home, phone calls, etc.) to share information about the student's progress. The parents may reinforce the student at home for using school-related materials appropriately at school.

8. Evaluate the appropriateness of the task to determine (a) if the task is too easy, (b) if the task is too difficult, and (c) if the length of time scheduled to complete the task is adequate.

9. Choose a peer to model appropriate use of school-related materials for the student.

10. Have the student ask questions about directions, explanations, instructions he/she does not understand.

11. Reinforce those students in the classroom who use school-related materials appropriately.

12. Provide time at various points throughout the day to help the student organize his/her school-related materials (e.g., before school, break time, lunch, end of the day, etc.).

13. Provide the student with adequate work space (e.g., a larger desk or table at which to work).

14. Provide storage space for school-related materials the student is not using.

15. Reduce distracting stimuli (e.g., place the student on the front row, provide a carrel or quiet place away from distractions, etc.). This is used as a means of reducing distracting stimuli and not as a form of punishment.

16. Interact frequently with the student to prompt organizational skills and appropriate use of school-related materials.

17. Assign the student organizational responsibilities in the classroom (e.g., equipment, software, materials, etc.).

18. Limit the student's use of school-related materials (e.g., provide only necessary school-related materials to the student).

19. Model organization and appropriate use of school-related materials (e.g., putting materials away before getting out other materials, having a place for all materials, maintaining an organized desk area, following a schedule for the day, etc.).

20. Provide adequate transition time between activities for the student to organize himself/herself.

21. Establish a routine to be followed for organization and appropriate use of school-related materials.

22. Provide adequate time for the completion of activities.

23. Require the student to organize his/her work area at regular intervals. It is recommended that this be done at least three times per day or more often if necessary.

24. Supervise the student while he/she is performing schoolwork to monitor quality.

25. Allow natural consequences to occur as the result of the student's inability to organize or use school-related materials appropriately (e.g., materials not maintained appropriately may be lost or not useable).

26. Assess the quality and clarity of directions, explanations, and instructions given to the student.

27. Assist the student in beginning each task to reduce impulsive behavior.

28. Provide the student with structure for all academic activities (e.g., specific directions; routine format for tasks, time limits, etc.).

29. Give the student a checklist of school-related materials necessary for each activity.

30. Minimize the amount of school-related materials needed.

31. Provide an organizer inside the student's desk for school-related materials.

32. Provide the student with an organizational checklist (e.g., routine activities and steps to follow).

33. Teach the student appropriate care of school-related materials (e.g., sharpening pencils, keeping books free of marks and tears, etc.).

34. Make sure that all of the student's school-related materials are labeled with his/her name.

35. Point out to the student that loaning his/her school-related materials to other students does not reduce his/her responsibility for the materials.

36. Teach the student to conserve rather than waste school-related materials (e.g., amount of glue, paper, tape, etc., to use; putting lids, caps, and tops on such materials as markers, pens, bottles, jars, cans, etc.).

37. Teach the student appropriate ways to deal with anger and frustration rather than destroying school-related materials.

38. Teach the student to maintain school-related materials (e.g., keep materials with him/her, know where materials are at all times, secure materials in lockers, etc.).

39. Provide the student with an appropriate place to store/secure school-related materials (e.g., desk, locker, closet, etc.). Require the student to store all materials not in use.

40. Explain to the student that failure to care for school-related materials will result in the loss of their use.

41. Provide reminders (e.g., a list of school-related materials) to help the student maintain and care for school-related materials.

42. Limit the student's freedom to take school-related materials from school if he/she is unable to return such items.

43. Teach the student the appropriate use of school-related materials (e.g., scissors; pencils; compass; rulers; science, industrial arts, and home economics materials; etc.).

44. Provide the student with verbal reminders of school-related materials needed for each activity.

45. Make sure that failure to have necessary school-related materials results in the losing the opportunity to participate in activities or a failing grade for that day's activity.

46. Reduce the number of school-related materials for which the student is responsible. As the student demonstrates appropriate care of materials, increase the number of materials for which the student is responsible.

47. Teach the student safety rules in the handling of school-related materials (e.g., pencils; scissors; compass; science, industrial arts, and home economics materials; etc.).

48. Require that lost or damaged school-related materials be replaced by the student. If the student cannot replace the property, restitution can be made by working at school.

49. Make sure the student is not inadvertently reinforced for losing or damaging school-related materials (e.g., replace lost materials with used or damaged materials, copies of the materials, etc., rather than new materials).

50. Limit the student's opportunity to use school-related materials if he/she is unable to care for his/her own personal property.

203 Does not demonstrate appropriate care and handling of others' property

1. Reinforce the student for demonstrating appropriate care and handling of others' property: (a) give the student a tangible reward (e.g., classroom privileges, line leading, passing out materials, five minutes free time, etc.) or (b) give the student an intangible reward (e.g., praise, fist bump, smile, etc.).

2. Speak to the student to explain (a) what he/she is doing wrong (e.g., losing property, destroying property, etc.) and (b) what he/she should be doing (e.g., putting property away, returning property, etc.).

3. Establish classroom rules:
- Concentrate while working.
- Work quietly.
- Remain in your seat.
- Finish task.
- Meet task requirements.

Review rules often. Reinforce the student for following the rules.

4. Write a contract with the student specifying what behavior is expected (e.g., putting property away, returning property, etc.) and what reinforcement will be made available when the terms of the contract have been met.

5. Reinforce the student for demonstrating appropriate care and handling of others' property based on the length of time the student can be successful. As the student demonstrates success, gradually increase the length of time required for reinforcement.

6. Reinforce those students in the classroom who demonstrate appropriate care and handling of others' property.

7. Communicate with parents (e.g., notes home, phone calls, etc.) to share information about the student's progress. The parents may reinforce the student at home for demonstrating appropriate care and handling of others' property at school.

8. Choose a peer to model appropriate care and handling of others' property for the student.

9. Have the student ask questions about directions, explanations, instructions he/she does not understand.

10. Provide time at the beginning of each day to help the student organize the materials he/she will use throughout the day.

11. Provide time at various points throughout the day to help the student organize materials he/she will use throughout the day (e.g., before school, break time, lunch, end of the day; etc.).

12. Provide the student with structure for all academic activities (e.g., specific directions, routine format for tasks, time limits, etc.).

13. Provide storage space for materials the student is not using.

14. Reduce distracting stimuli (e.g., place the student on the front row, provide a carrel or quiet place away from distractions, etc.). Overstimulation may cause the student to misuse others' property.

15. Interact frequently with the student to prompt organizational skills and appropriate use of materials.

16. Assign the student organizational responsibilities in the classroom (e.g., equipment, software, materials, etc.).

17. Limit the student's access to materials (e.g., provide only necessary materials to the student).

18. Model organization and appropriate use of work materials (e.g., putting materials away before getting out other materials, having a place for all materials, maintaining an organized desk area, following a schedule for the day, etc.).

19. Provide adequate time for the completion of activities. Inadequate time for completion of activities may result in the student's misuse of others' property.

20. Establish a routine to be followed for organization and appropriate use of work materials.

21. Require the student to organize his/her work area at regular intervals.

22. Allow natural consequences to occur as the result of the student's inability to appropriately care for and handle others' property (e.g., property not maintained appropriately may be lost or not useable).

23. Teach the student that failure to care for others' property will result in the loss of freedom to use others' property.

24. Assist the student in beginning each task to reduce impulsive behavior.

25. Provide the student with adequate work space (e.g., a large desk or table at which to work).

26. Give the student a checklist of materials necessary for each activity.

27. Minimize the amount of materials needed.

28. Provide an organizer inside the student's desk for materials.

29. Provide the student with an organizational checklist (e.g., routine activities and materials needed).

30. Teach the student appropriate care and handling of others' property (e.g., sharpening pencils, keeping books free of marks and tears, etc.).

31. Make sure that all personal property is labeled with the students' names.

32. Point out to the student that borrowing personal property from others does not reduce his/her responsibility for the property.

33. Teach the student how to conserve rather than waste materials (e.g., amount of glue, paper, tape, etc., to use; putting lids, caps, and tops on such materials as markers, pens, bottles, jars, cans, etc.).

34. Teach the student appropriate ways to deal with anger and frustration rather than destroying property belonging to others (e.g., pencils, pens, workbooks, notebooks, textbooks, etc.).

35. Teach the student to maintain property belonging to others (e.g., keep property with him/her, know where property is at all times, secure property in locker, etc.).

36. Provide the student with an appropriate place to store/secure others' property (e.g., desk, locker, closet, etc.). Require the student to store all property when not in use.

37. Assess the quality and clarity of directions, explanations, and instructions given to the student for use in the care and handling of others' property.

38. Provide reminders (e.g., a list of property or materials) to help the student maintain and care for school property.

39. Limit the student's freedom to take property from school if he/she is unable to remember to return such items.

40. Limit the student's opportunity to use others' property if he/she is unable to care for his/her own personal property.

41. Do not permit peers to allow the student to use their property if he/she is not able to care for it properly.

42. Teach the student safety rules in the care and handling of others' property and materials (e.g., pencils; scissors; compass; science, industrial arts, and home economics materials; etc.).

43. Require that lost or damaged property be replaced by the student. If the student cannot replace the property, restitution can be made by working at school.

44. Remove others' property from the student if he/she is unable to appropriately care for and handle the property.

45. Make sure the student is not inadvertently reinforced for losing or damaging property (e.g. replace lost property with used or damaged materials, copies of the materials, etc., rather than new materials).

46. Maintain mobility throughout the classroom to supervise the student's care and handling of others' property.

47. Provide adequate transition time between activities for the student to organize himself/herself.

48. Teach the student rules for the care and handling of others' property (e.g., always ask to use others' property, treat the property with care, inform the teacher if the property becomes damaged, return the property in the same or better condition than when it was borrowed, etc.).

49. Reduce the number of materials for which the student is responsible. As the student demonstrates appropriate responsibility for property, increase the number of materials for which the student is responsible.

50. Permit the student to use only the amount of property that he/she can care for and handle appropriately. As the student demonstrates success, gradually increase the amount of property.

204 Does not raise hand when appropriate

1. Evaluate the appropriateness of requiring the student to raise his/her hand. The student may not be capable or developmentally ready for hand raising. Have the student use other appropriate means of gaining attention.

2. Establish rules for hand raising (e.g., raise hand for permission to talk, do not leave seat, etc.). These rules should be consistent and followed by everyone in the class. Talk about the rules often.

3. Allow natural consequences to occur when the student does not raise his/her hand when appropriate (e.g., students who raise their hands will have their needs met, those students who fail to raise their hands will not have their needs met until they raise their hands, etc.).

4. Provide the student with a verbal reminder to raise his/her hand (e.g., at the beginning of the day, at the beginning of the activity, when the student forgets, etc.).

5. Choose a peer to model appropriate hand raising for new students, students who do not raise their hands, etc.

6. Post hand-raising rules in the classroom.

7. Reinforce those students in the classroom who raise their hands when appropriate.

8. Acknowledge the student immediately upon raising his/her hand (e.g., let the student know when you see his/her hand, call upon the student, go to the student, etc.).

9. Be sure to let the student know that you will be with him/her as soon as possible when it is necessary to be detained (e.g., when working with another student, speaking with another teacher, instructing a small group, etc.).

10. Do not grant the student's request until his/her hand is raised.

11. Maintain consistent expectations within the ability level of the student.

12. Provide the student with alternative and appropriate attention-seeking methods (e.g., display a *Help* sign on desk).

13. Maintain mobility to be frequently near the student when he/she displays appropriate attention-seeking behaviors (e.g., hand raising).

14. Make sure the student knows when it is acceptable to interrupt others (e.g., in an emergency).

15. Before beginning an activity, make sure the student knows the rules (e.g., wait quietly until the teacher is able to help, work quietly at your desk, etc.).

16. Have the student raise his/her hand to question any directions, explanations, and instructions he/she does not understand.

17. Choose a peer to model raising his/her hand when appropriate for the student.

18. Communicate with parents (e.g., notes home, phone calls, etc.) to share information about the student's progress. The parents may reinforce the student at home for raising his/her hand when appropriate at school.

19. Write a contract with the student specifying what behavior is expected (e.g., raising his/her hand for teacher assistance) and what reinforcement will be made available when the terms of the contract have been met.

20. Establish classroom rules:
- Concentrate while working.
- Work quietly.
- Request assistance when needed.
- Remain in your seat.
- Finish task.
- Meet task expectations.

Review rules often. Reinforce students for following the rules.

21. Reinforce the student for raising his/her hand when appropriate based on the number of times the student can be successful. As the student demonstrates success, gradually increase the number of times required for reinforcement.

22. Speak to the student to explain (a) what the student is doing wrong (e.g., talking out, engaging in a behavior without raising his/her hand to get permission, etc.) and (b) what the student should be doing (e.g., raising his/her hand for permission to speak, or move about the room, etc.).

23. Make sure that reinforcement is not inadvertently given for inappropriate behavior (e.g., attending to the student only when he/she blurts out answers without being called on).

24. Reinforce the student for raising his/her hand when appropriate: (a) give the student a tangible reward (e.g., classroom privileges, line leading, passing out materials, five minutes free time, etc.) or (b) give the student an intangible reward (e.g., praise, fist bump, smile, etc.).

205 Demonstrates inappropriate behavior going to and from school

1. Evaluate the appropriateness of the task in relation to the student's ability to perform the task successfully.

2. Choose a peer to accompany the student when going to and from school to monitor and encourage appropriate behavior.

3. Accompany the student when going to and from school to teach the student appropriate behavior (e.g., using sidewalks, crossing at crosswalks, taking the most direct route, boarding the bus, sitting quietly, remaining seated, leaving the bus, etc.).

4. Assign the student responsibilities to perform when going to and from school (e.g., act as the bus driver's assistant to monitor behavior, accompany a younger peer to and from school, pick up trash on the way to and from school, etc.).

5. Encourage the student to report problems that occur while going to and from school (e.g., being bullied, approached by strangers, teased by other students, etc.).

6. Allow natural consequences to occur if the student fails to demonstrate appropriate behavior when going to and from school (e.g., parents will have to provide transportation and/or supervision).

7. Make sure the student is seated near the bus driver to prevent inappropriate behavior when riding the bus to and from school.

8. Develop a behavioral contract with the bus driver and the student for appropriate behavior on the bus while riding to and from school.

9. Ask parents in the neighborhood to monitor the student's behavior when going to and from school.

10. Before the student leaves the school, make sure that he/she knows the rules about walking to and from school (e.g., walk on the sidewalk, walk nicely with friends, etc.).

11. Have the student ask questions about directions, explanations, or instructions he/she does not understand.

12. Establish rules for appropriate behavior when going to and from school:
- Sit quietly on the bus.
- Remain seated on the bus.
- Use a quiet voice while on the bus.
- Take the most direct route when walking to and from school.
- Use sidewalks.
- Follow crossing rules at crosswalks.
- Refrain from fighting on the way to and from school.

Review rules often. Reinforce students for following the rules.

13. Choose a peer to model appropriate behavior going to and from school for the student.

14. Communicate with parents (e.g., notes home, phone calls, etc.) to share information about the student's progress. The parents may reinforce the student at home for demonstrating appropriate behavior when going to and from school.

15. Write a contract with the student specifying what behavior is expected (e.g., sitting quietly on the bus) and what reinforcement will be made available when the terms of the contract have been met.

16. Reinforce the student for demonstrating appropriate behavior going to and from school based on the number of times the student can be successful. As the student demonstrates success, gradually increase the number of times required for reinforcement.

17. Reinforce those students in the classroom who demonstrate appropriate behavior going to and from school.

18. Speak to the student to explain (a) what the student is doing wrong (e.g., fighting on the bus, taking an indirect route to and from school, etc.) and (b) what the student should be doing (e.g., sitting quietly on the bus, taking the most direct route to and from school, etc.).

19. Reinforce the student for demonstrating appropriate behavior going to and from school: (a) give the student a tangible reward (e.g., classroom privileges, line leading, passing out materials, five minutes free time, etc.) or (b) give the student an intangible reward (e.g., praise, fist bump, smile, etc.).

1. Reinforce the student for taking notes during class when necessary: (a) give the student a tangible reward (e.g., classroom privileges, line leading, passing out materials, five minutes free time, etc.) or (b) give the student an intangible reward (e.g., praise, fist bump, smile, etc.).

2. Speak to the student to explain (a) what he/she is doing wrong (e.g., failing to take notes) and (b) what he/she should be doing (e.g., taking notes).

3. Establish classroom rules:
- Concentrate while working.
- Work quietly.
- Remain in your seat.
- Finish task.
- Meet task requirements.

Review rules often. Reinforce the student for following the rules.

4. Reinforce those students in the classroom who take notes during class when necessary.

5. Reinforce the student for taking notes during class based on the length of time he/she can be successful. As the student demonstrates success, gradually increase the required length of time for taking notes for reinforcement.

6. Choose a peer to model taking notes during class for the student.

7. Write a contract with the student specifying what behavior is expected (e.g., taking notes) and what reinforcement will be made available when the terms of the contract have been met.

8. Communicate with parents (e.g., notes home, phone calls, etc.) to share information about the student's progress. The parents may reinforce the student at home for taking notes during class when necessary.

9. Have the student ask questions about directions, explanations, instructions, etc., he/she does not understand.

10. Teach the student note-taking skills (e.g., copy main ideas from the board, identify main ideas from lectures, condense statements into a few key words, etc.).

11. Provide a standard format for writing down directions or explanations (e.g., have paper and pencil or pen ready, listen for the steps in directions or explanations, write a shortened form of directions or explanations, ask to have any steps repeated when necessary, etc.).

12. Provide a standard format for taking lecture notes (e.g., have paper and pencil or pen ready, listen for main ideas or important information, write a shortened form of main ideas or important information, ask to have any main ideas or important information repeated when necessary, etc.).

13. Evaluate the appropriateness of note taking to determine (a) if the task is too easy, (b) if the task is too difficult, and (c) if the length of time scheduled to complete the task is adequate.

14. Point out to the student that instructions, directions, lectures, etc., should be written in the form of notes when they are presented.

15. Have the student practice legible manuscript or cursive handwriting during simulated and actual note-taking activities.

16. Have the student keep his/her notes organized in a folder for each subject or activity.

17. Check the student's notes before he/she begins an assignment to determine if they contain adequate information for the assignment.

18. Provide the student with an outline or questions to be completed during the presentation of instructions, directions, lectures, etc.

19. Provide the student with samples of students' notes of classroom instructions, directions, lectures, etc., that have been given so that he/she may learn what information is necessary when taking notes.

20. Make sure the student is in the best location in the classroom to receive information for note taking (e.g., near the board, teacher, or other source of information).

21. Make sure that supervision of the student's note taking can easily be provided.

22. Have the student prepare for tests using the "Who, What, Where, When, How, and Why" method. The teacher should then test this same information.

23. Present instructions, directions, lectures, etc., clearly and loudly enough for the student to hear.

24. Provide the student with both verbal and written instructions.

25. Match the rate of delivery of the instructions, directions, lectures, etc., to the student's ability to take notes.

26. Provide instructions, directions, lectures, etc., in sequential steps to facilitate student note taking.

27. Present information in short segments for the student to take notes. As the student experiences success, gradually increase the length of the segments that are presented.

28. Make sure the vocabulary used in presenting instructions, directions, lectures, etc., is appropriate for the student's ability level.

29. Make sure the student has all the materials necessary for note taking (e.g., paper, pencil, pen, etc.).

30. Make sure the student uses any necessary aids to facilitate note taking (e.g., eyeglasses, hearing aid, etc.).

31. Place the student next to a peer so the student can copy the notes taken by the peer.

32. Make sure the student has adequate surface space on which to write when taking notes (e.g., uncluttered desk top).

33. Reduce distracting stimuli that interferes with the student's note taking (e.g., other students talking, outdoor activities, movement in the classroom, hallway noise, etc.).

34. Present the information in the most interesting manner possible.

35. Have the student record instructions, directions, lectures, etc., as an alternative to written note taking.

36. Summarize the main points of instructions, directions, lectures, etc., for the student.

37. Present directions following the (1) What, (2) How, (3) Materials, and (4) When outline.

38. Maintain visibility to and from the student when delivering instructions, directions, lectures, etc., to facilitate the student's success in note taking.

39. Have the student take notes following the "What, How, Materials, and When" format when directions are being given.

40. Have the student listen and take notes for "Who, What, Where, When, How, and Why" when concepts are presented.

41. Present concepts following the (1) Who, (2) What, (3) Where, (4) When, (5) How, and (6) Why outline.

207 Is preoccupied with drugs or alcohol or possesses or uses drugs or alcohol at school

1. Communicate with parents, agencies, or the appropriate parties to inform them of the problem, determine the cause of the problem, and consider possible solutions to the problem.

2. Provide a drug information program for the individual student, the class, or the student body.

3. Provide information on penalties for possession or use of alcohol and drugs at school.

4. Involve the student in extracurricular activities to help him/her develop appropriate interests.

5. Identify individuals the student may contact with his/her concerns (e.g., guidance counselor, school nurse, social worker, school psychologist, etc.).

6. Share concerns with the administration and seek referral to an agency for investigation of alcohol or drug abuse.

7. Encourage the student to become involved in athletic or extracurricular activities.

8. Assign the student activities which would require interactions with a respected role model (e.g., older student, high school student, college student, community leader, someone held in esteem, etc.).

9. Provide the student with intelligent, accurate information concerning drugs and alcohol rather than sensationalized scare tactic information.

10. Provide the student with many opportunities for social and academic successes.

11. Encourage the student to excel in a particular area of interest (e.g., provide information for the student; provide personal and professional support; sponsor the student; etc.).

12. Maintain frequent contact with the student during school hours (e.g., follow up on details of earlier communications, maintain a direction for conversation, etc.).

13. Lead and direct the student. Do not lecture and make demands.

14. Maintain anecdotal records of the student's behavior to check patterns or changes in behavior.

15. When natural consequences from peers occur (e.g., criticism, loss of friendship, etc.) as the result of the use of drugs or alcohol at school bring, the consequences to the attention of the student.

16. Encourage the student's parents to be positive and supportive with the student as opposed to being negative and threatening.

17. Be a resource for parents by providing information on agencies, counseling programs, etc.

18. Teach the student to be satisfied with his/her personal best effort rather than perfection.

19. Reduce the emphasis on competition and help the student realize that success is individually defined.

20. Be willing to take the time to listen, share, and talk with the student.

21. Increase your own professional knowledge of laws and treatment concerning drug or alcohol use and abuse.

22. Teach the student alternative ways to deal with demands, challenges, and pressures of the school-age experience (e.g., deal with problems when they arise, practice self-control at all times, share problems or concerns with others, etc.).

23. Maintain adequate supervision at all times and in all areas of the school (e.g., hallways, bathrooms, between classes, before and after school, school grounds, etc.).

24. Make sure the student is aware of local, state, and federal laws regarding the possession of inappropriate or illegal materials on school grounds.

25. Communicate with parents (e.g., notes home, phone calls, etc.) to share information about the student's progress. The parents may reinforce the student at home for demonstrating appropriate behavior at school.

26. Write a contract with the student specifying what behavior is expected (e.g., not bringing alcohol to school) and what reinforcement will be made available when the terms of the contract have been met.

27. Remove the student from the group or activity until he/she can demonstrate appropriate behavior and self-control.

28. Reinforce the student for demonstrating appropriate behavior based on the length of time he/she can be successful. As the student demonstrates success, gradually increase the length of time required for reinforcement.

29. Reinforce those students in the classroom who demonstrate appropriate behavior.

30. Establish classroom rules:
- Concentrate while working.
- Work quietly.
- Remain in your seat.
- Finish task.
- Meet task requirements.

Review rules often. Reinforce the student for following the rules.

31. Speak with the student to explain (a) what the student is doing wrong (e.g., bringing inappropriate or illegal materials to school) and (b) what the student should be doing (e.g., following an established code of conduct, following rules, taking care of responsibilities, etc.).

32. Reinforce the student for demonstrating appropriate behavior: (a) give the student a tangible reward (e.g., classroom privileges, line leading, passing out materials, five minutes free time, etc.) or (b) give the student an intangible reward (e.g., praise, fist bump, smile, etc.).

33. Provide the student with personal acknowledgment during school hours (e.g., follow up on details of earlier communications, maintain a direction for conversation, etc.).

34. Intervene early when there is a problem to prevent more serious problems from occurring.

35. Teach the student to think before acting by asking himself/herself questions: *What is happening?, What am I doing?, What should I do?, What will be best for me?*

1. Establish classroom rules:
   - Concentrate while working.
   - Remain in your seat.
   - Finish task.
   - Meet task expectations.
   - Raise your hand.

Review rules often. Reinforce students for following the rules.

2. Communicate with parents (e.g., notes home, phone calls, etc.) to share information about the student's appropriate behavior. The parents may reinforce the student at home for waiting to be called on before speaking.

3. Call on the student frequently to prevent the student from becoming impatient and blurting out answers.

4. Do not criticize when correcting the student; be honest yet supportive. Never cause the student to feel negatively about himself/herself.

5. Do not reinforce the student's behavior by letting him/her talk to you at the time he/she blurts out answers. Tell the student that he/she will need to wait until you are finished talking. Allowing the student to talk after interrupting reinforces the behavior and may increase the number of times he/she blurts out answers.

6. Provide the student with many opportunities for social and academic successes.

7. Do not allow the student to use ADHD as an excuse. Hold the student responsible for his/her actions. However, understand and accept problems that ADHD brings into the student's life while he/she is learning to make accommodations.

8. Call on the student when he/she is most likely to be able to respond correctly.

9. Attempt to provide equal attention to all students in the classroom.

10. Deliver directions, explanations, and instructions in a clear, concise manner to reduce the student's need to ask questions.

11. Reduce activities which might threaten the student (e.g., reduce peer pressure, academic failure, teasing, etc.).

12. Give the student responsibilities in the classroom (e.g., running errands, opportunities to help the teacher, etc.).

13. Have the student be the leader of a small group activity if he/she possesses mastery of a skill or has an interest in that area.

14. Remove the student from the group or activity until he/she can demonstrate appropriate behavior and self-control.

15. Treat the student with respect. Talk in an objective manner at all times.

16. Teach the student to use techniques such as crossing his/her arms and legs, clenching his/her fists, and intertwining his/her fingers when he/she feels the urge to blurt out answers without being called on.

17. Explain to the student the reasons why blurting out answers without being called on is inappropriate (e.g., impolite, hurts others' feelings, etc.).

18. Reinforce the student for waiting to be called on before speaking: (a) give the student a tangible reward (e.g., classroom privileges, line leading, passing out materials, five minutes free time, etc.) or (b) give the student an intangible reward (e.g., praise, fist bump, smile, etc.).

19. Reinforce the student for waiting to be called on before speaking based on the number of times the student can be successful.   As the student demonstrates success, gradually increase the number of times required for reinforcement.

20. Make sure that the student's feelings are considered when it is necessary to discuss inappropriate comments. Handle comments in such a way as to not diminish the student's enthusiasm for participation.

21. Make sure that reinforcement is not inadvertently given for inappropriate behavior (e.g., attending to the student only when he/she blurts out answers without being called on).

22. Reinforce the student for raising his/her hand to be recognized.

23. Explain to the student why he/she has been asked not to talk.

24. Provide the student with a predetermined signal if he/she begins to blurt out answers without being called on.

25. Provide constant, positive reinforcement for appropriate behavior. Ignore as many inappropriate behaviors as possible.

26. Encourage the student to monitor his/her impulsivity. Awareness should reduce impulsive behaviors.

27. Have the student work in small groups in which there are frequent opportunities to speak. As the student learns to wait longer for a turn to speak, gradually increase the size of the group.

28. Assess the appropriateness of the social situation in relation to the student's ability to function successfully.

29. Structure the environment to limit opportunities for inappropriate behaviors (e.g., keep the student engaged in activities, have the student seated near the teacher, allow multiple responses when appropriate, etc.).

30. Educate yourself and others about ADHD to increase understanding and accommodation of impatient behavior.

31. Provide the student with a clearly understood list of consequences for inappropriate behavior.

32. Help the student improve concentration skills (e.g., listening to the speaker, taking notes, preparing comments in advance, making comments in the appropriate context, etc.).

33. Reduce the emphasis on competition. Competitive activities may cause the student to become overexcited and blurt out answers without being called on.

34. Educate the student about ADHD and the need for developing skills to self monitor behavior.

35. Help the student develop an awareness of himself/herself and those around him/her. Have the student periodically step back and ask himself/herself, "Am I blurting out answers and dominating the conversation?"

36. Help the student develop an awareness of the consequences of his/her behavior by writing down or talking through problems which may occur due to his/her impulsivity (e.g., perceived as unmannerly, avoided, etc.).

37. Make the student aware of the number of times he/she blurts out answers without being called on.

38. Instruct the student to carry a notepad with him/her at all times and to write information down to help him/her remember.

39. Make sure the student does not become overstimulated by an activity.

40. Have the student practice waiting for short periods of time for a turn to speak. As the student demonstrates success, gradually increase the length of time required for a turn to speak.

41. Give adequate opportunities to respond (i.e., enthusiastic students need many opportunities to contribute).

42. Provide academic and leisure activities which allow the student to be highly active and talkative.

43. Interact frequently with the student to reduce the need to blurt out answers without being called on.

44. Try various groupings to determine the group in which the student is most comfortable.

45. Choose a peer, paraprofessional, friend, etc., to cue the student when he/she blurts out responses (e.g., the person can touch the student on his/her arm or desk as a signal that he/she is blurting out responses).

46. Teach the student to recognize the appropriate time to speak (e.g., when the teacher has finished speaking, after raising his/her hand, to make comments within the context of the situation, to make comments that are a follow-up to what has just been said, etc.).

47. Make the necessary adjustments in the environment to prevent the student from experiencing stress, frustration or anger (e.g., reduce peer pressure, academic failure, teasing, etc.).

48. Encourage the student to remind himself/herself to wait (e.g., "Stop. Count to ten.") when he/she feels the urge to blurt out responses/answers.

49. Maintain visibility to and from the student to keep his/her attention when verbal questions/directions are being delivered. The teacher should be able to see the student and the student should be able to see the teacher. Make eye contact possible at all times.

50. Establish rules for conversing with others (e.g., wait your turn to talk, stand quietly by the person with whom you want to talk until you are acknowledged, excuse yourself when you interrupt others, etc.). These rules should be consistent and followed by everyone in the class. Talk about the rules often.

51. Reinforce those students in the classroom who wait to be called on before speaking.

52. Speak with the student to explain (a) what the student is doing wrong (e.g., blurting out answers) and (b) what the student should be doing (e.g., waiting until it is appropriate to speak, waiting to be called on before speaking, etc.).

53. Write a contract with the student specifying what behavior is expected (e.g., waiting to be called on before speaking) and what reinforcement will be made available when the terms of the contract have been met.

54. Encourage the student to model the behavior of peers who wait to answer questions.

1. Communicate with the student's parents (e.g., notes home, phone calls, etc.) to share information about the student's appropriate behavior. The parents may reinforce the student at home for not interrupting other peers at school.

2. Encourage the student to recite a mantra to himself/herself when entering a situation where he/she may be inclined to interrupt (e.g., do not interrupt, do not interrupt, do not interrupt).

3. Instruct the student to carry a notepad with him/her at all times and to write information down to help him/her remember.

4. Educate yourself and others about ADHD to increase understanding and accommodation of interruptive behavior.

5. Help the student realize that all behavior has negative or positive consequences. Encourage the student to practice behaviors that will lead to positive consequences.

6. Help the student develop an awareness of himself/herself and those around him/her. Have the student periodically step back and ask himself/herself, "Am I interrupting others?"

7. Help the student develop an awareness of the consequences of his/her behavior by writing down or talking through problems which may occur due to interrupting others (e.g., perceived as unmannerly, avoided, etc.).

8. Consider carefully the student's age and ability level before expecting him/her not to interrupt others when they are talking, working, reading, etc.

9. Educate the student about ADHD and the need to self monitor behavior.

10. Provide constant, positive reinforcement for appropriate behavior. Ignore as many inappropriate behaviors as possible.

11. Reinforce the student for demonstrating appropriate behavior: (a) give the student a tangible reward (e.g., classroom privileges, passing out materials, five minutes free time, etc.) or (b) give the student an intangible reward (e.g., praise, fist bump, smile, etc.).

12. Reinforce the student for demonstrating appropriate behavior (e.g., waiting for a turn to speak, working quietly, etc.) based on the length of time the student can be successful. As the student demonstrates success, gradually increase the length of time required for reinforcement.

13. Choose a peer to model appropriate behavior for the student.

14. Encourage the student to become aware of the times when he/she is most impulsive and likely to interrupt others (e.g., in a large group of people, when he/she is angry, etc.) and limit his/her interactions with others during these times.

15. Talk to the student before beginning an activity and remind him/her of the importance of listening to others.

16. Reinforce those students in the classroom who wait their turn to speak, do not interrupt others, work quietly, etc.

17. Provide the student with a clearly understood list of consequences for inappropriate behavior.

18. Reduce the emphasis on competition. Competitive activities may cause the student to become anxious and interrupt others.

19. Teach the student to take cues from others (e.g., if he/she begins to interrupt a peer and that person continues to talk, realize that he/she is interrupting and stop talking; when there is silence in a class, it is not necessary to fill the silence with comments, etc.).

20. Have the student ask questions about directions, explanations, or instructions before beginning a task to reinforce comprehension and avoid interrupting peers later to ask questions.

21. Speak to the student to explain (a) what he/she is doing wrong (e.g., interrupting other students who are trying to work, listen, etc.) and (b) what he/she should be doing (e.g., waiting for a turn to speak, working quietly, etc.).

22. Remove the student from the group or activity until he/she can demonstrate appropriate behavior and self-control.

23. Teach the student to ask himself/herself questions: *What should I be doing right now?*, *Is what I have to say relevant to this topic?*, and *Is this a good time for me to comment?*

24. Encourage the student to remind himself/ herself to wait when he/she feels the urge to interrupt (e.g., "Stop. Count to ten.").

25. Teach the student to use techniques such as crossing his/her arms and legs, clenching his/ her fists, and intertwining his/her fingers when he/she feels the urge to interrupt.

26. Explain to the student the importance of treating people as he/she wants to be treated (e.g., people will not interrupt you if you do not interrupt them).

27. Interact frequently with the student to maintain his/her involvement in the activity (e.g., ask the student questions, ask the student's opinion, stand close to the student, seat the student near the teacher's desk, etc.).

28. Explain to the student why it is important not to interrupt others. Help him/her understand that it is impolite, that he/she might hurt someone's feelings, etc.

29. Have the student make a list of consequences associated with frequently occurring behaviors (e.g., By disrupting others, he/she will be perceived as unmannerly. By behaving aggressively, people will avoid him/her.).

30. Explain to the student the need to reduce impulsive behavior to increase work productivity and general happiness.

31. Make sure that you do not interrupt others. If you interrupt others, the student will continue to do so.

32. Establish rules for conversing with others (e.g., wait your turn to talk, stand quietly by the person with whom you want to talk until you are acknowledged, excuse yourself when you interrupt others, etc.). These rules should be consistent and followed by everyone in the class. Talk about the rules often.

33. Choose a peer who does not interrupt others. Encourage the student to observe that person and try to model the behaviors which allow him/her to be patient.

34. Deliver a predetermined signal (e.g. hand signal, verbal cue, etc.) when the student begins to display inappropriate behaviors.

35. Reinforce consistently the class rules regarding talking aloud during quiet activity periods.

36. Teach appropriate social rituals (e.g., excuse yourself before interrupting, wait until someone stops speaking to begin talking, etc.).

37. Have the student identify the situations in which he/she is most likely to interrupt. After he/she has identified these situations, have him/her think of ways to minimize their occurrences.

38. Teach and practice effective communication skills. These skills include: listening, maintaining eye contact, and positive body language.

39. Establish classroom rules:
- Concentrate while working.
- Remain in your seat.
- Finish task.
- Meet task expectations.
- Raise your hand.

Review rules often. Reinforce students for following the rules.

40. Have a peer cue the student when he/she is interrupting others (e.g., the peer can touch the student's arm or desk as a signal that he/she is interrupting).

41. Be consistent in expecting the student to behave appropriately. Do not allow the student to interrupt one time and expect him/her not to interrupt the next time.

42. Write a contract with the student specifying what behavior is expected (e.g., waiting for a turn to speak, working quietly, etc.) and what reinforcement will be made available when the terms of the contract have been met.

43. Treat the student with respect. Talk in an objective manner at all times.

44. Explain to the student when he/she interrupts that you are talking now and he/she may talk to you in a few moments.

45. Do not criticize when correcting the student; be honest yet supportive. Never cause the student to feel negatively about himself/herself.

46. Maintain visibility to and from the student to keep his/her attention when verbal questions/directions are being delivered. The teacher should be able to see the student and the student should be able to see the teacher. Make eye contact possible at all times.

47. Seat the student away from those students he/she is most likely to bother.

48. Teach the student appropriate ways to communicate needs to others (e.g., waiting a turn, raising his/her hand, etc.).

49. Hold the student responsible for his/her actions. Do not allow the student to use ADHD as an excuse. However, understand and accept problems ADHD brings into the student's life while he/she is learning to make accommodations.

50. Provide students with frequent opportunities to interact with one another (e.g., before and after school, between activities, etc.).

51. Give the student frequent opportunities to join in conversations with others by allowing him/her time to talk, asking him/her to restate an experience, etc.

52. Make sure that the student understands the relationship between inappropriate behavior and the consequences which follow (e.g., others ignoring him/her, hurting others' feelings, etc.).

53. Demonstrate to the student the appropriate way to get someone's attention without interrupting.

54. Do not interrupt the student when he/she is doing something, talking to someone, etc.

55. Make sure the student knows when it is acceptable to interrupt others (e.g., in an emergency).

56. Seat the student near the teacher.

1. Reinforce the student for working quietly: (a) give the student a tangible reward (e.g., classroom privileges, line leading, passing out materials, five minutes free time, etc.) or (b) give the student an intangible reward (e.g., praise, fist bump, smile, etc.).

2. Speak with the student to explain (a) what the student is doing wrong (e.g., talking to others during quiet activity periods) and (b) what the student should be doing (e.g., waiting until it is appropriate to speak, working quietly, etc.).

3. Establish classroom rules:
• Concentrate while working.
• Work quietly.
• Remain in your seat.
• Finish task.
• Meet task requirements.
Review rules often. Reinforce the student for following the rules.

4. Reinforce those students in the classroom who work quietly during activity periods.

5. Reinforce the student for working quietly based on the length of time the student can be successful. As the student demonstrates success, gradually increase the length of time required for reinforcement.

6. Remove the student from the group or activity until he/she can demonstrate appropriate behavior and self-control.

7. Write a contract with the student specifying what behavior is expected (e.g., working quietly) and what reinforcement will be made available when the terms of the contract have been met.

8. Communicate with parents (e.g., notes home, phone calls, etc.) to share information about the student's appropriate behavior. The parents may reinforce the student at home for working quietly at school.

9. Have the student be the leader of a small group activity if he/she possesses mastery of skills or an interest in that area.

10. Evaluate the appropriateness of the task to determine (a) if the task is too easy, (b) if the task is too difficult, and (c) if the length of time scheduled to complete the task is adequate.

11. Make sure that reinforcement is not inadvertently given for inappropriate behavior (e.g., making inappropriate comments, talking to others during quiet activity periods, etc.).

12. Give the student adequate opportunities to speak in the classroom, talk to other students, etc. Enthusiastic students need many opportunities to contribute.

13. Deliver a predetermined signal (e.g., hand signal, verbal cue, etc.) when the student begins to talk to other students during quiet activity periods.

14. Explain to the student that he/she may be trying too hard to fit in and he/she should relax, talk less, and talk at appropriate times.

15. Structure the environment to limit opportunities for talking to other students during quiet activity periods (e.g., keep the student engaged in activities, have the student seated near the teacher, etc.).

16. Give the student responsibilities in the classroom (e.g., running errands, opportunities to help the teacher, etc.).

17. Reduce activities which might be threatening to the student (e.g., announcing test score ranges or test scores aloud, making students read aloud in class, emphasizing the success of particular student(s), etc.).

18. Provide the student with many opportunities for social and academic success.

19. Make the necessary adjustments in the environment to prevent the student from experiencing stress, frustration, and anger.

20. Interact frequently with the student to reduce the need for him/her to talk to other students.

21. Maintain visibility to and from the student to keep his/her attention when verbal questions/directions are being delivered. The teacher should be able to see the student and the student should be able to see the teacher. Make eye contact possible at all times.

22. Assess the appropriateness of the social situation in relation to the student's ability to function successfully.

23. Try various groupings to determine the group in which the student is most comfortable.

24. Reinforce the student for raising his/her hand to be recognized.

25. Call on the student when he/she is most likely to be able to respond correctly (e.g., when discussing something in which the student is interested, when the teacher is sure he/she knows the answer, etc.).

26. Teach the student to recognize when to speak, to know how much to say, and to make appropriate comments (e.g., brief comments, comments within the context of the situation, comments that are a follow-up to what has just been said, etc.).

27. Have the student work in small groups in which he/she would have frequent opportunities to speak. As the student learns to wait longer for his/her turn to speak, gradually increase the size of the group.

28. Make sure that the student's feelings are considered when it is necessary to discuss his/her talking to other students (i.e., handle comments in such a way as to not diminish the student's enthusiasm for participation).

29. Encourage the student to model the behavior of peers who are successful at not talking to others during quiet activity periods.

30. Help the student improve concentration skills (e.g., listening to the speaker, taking notes, preparing comments in advance, making comments in the appropriate context, etc.).

31. Have the student ask questions about directions, explanations, or instructions he/she does not understand prior to asking other students for information.

32. Deliver directions, explanations, and instructions in a clear, concise manner to reduce the student's need to ask other students for information.

33. Deliver a predetermined signal (e.g., hand signal, verbal cue, etc.) if the student talks to others during quiet activity periods.

34. After telling the student why he/she should not be talking, explain the reason.

35. Do not leave a lot of unstructured time for the student.

211 Leaves seat or assigned area without permission

1. Communicate with the student's parents (e.g., notes home, phone calls, etc.) to share information about their child's appropriate behavior. The parents may reinforce the student at home for staying in his/her seat at school.

2. Allow the student to take a break while working on monotonous assignments to relieve restlessness and improve concentration.

3. Encourage the student to recite a mantra to himself/herself when entering a situation where he/she has to sit for an extended period of time (e.g., be still, be still, be still).

4. Have the student chart the length of time he/she is able to remain in his/her seat.

5. Make sure the student knows when it is acceptable to leave his/her seat (e.g., in an emergency).

6. Require the student to have all the necessary materials assembled prior to beginning a project, assignment, etc., to reduce the need to leave his/her seat.

7. Provide constant, positive reinforcement for appropriate behavior. Ignore as many inappropriate behaviors as possible.

8. Have the student ask questions about directions, explanations, or instructions he/she does not understand.

9. Allow some time for movement between assignments if the student appears to need a break.

10. Try various groupings in the classroom to determine the situation in which the student is most comfortable and remains seated without constant supervision.

11. Make the necessary adjustments in the environment to prevent the student from experiencing stress, frustration, anger, etc., as much as possible, to decrease the student's tendency to leave his/her seat.

12. Reinforce those students in the classroom who stay in their seat, ask permission to leave their seat, etc.

13. Reinforce the student for staying in his/her seat based on the length of time he/she can be successful. As the student demonstrates success, gradually increase the length of time required for reinforcement.

14. Remove the student from the group or activity until he/she can stay in his/her seat.

15. Provide the student with a clearly understood list of consequences for inappropriate behavior.

16. Reduce the emphasis on competition. Competitive activities may cause the student to become overstimulated and leave his/her seat.

17. Choose a peer to model staying in his/her seat for the student.

18. Schedule short activities for the student to perform while seated. As the student demonstrates success staying in his/her seat, gradually increase the length of the activities.

19. Give the student frequent opportunities to leave his/her seat for appropriate reasons (e.g., getting materials, running errands, assisting the teacher, etc.).

20. Speak with the student to explain (a) what he/she is doing wrong (e.g., leaving seat without permission, etc.) and (b) what he/she should be doing (e.g., remaining in his/her seat, asking permission to leave seat, etc.).

21. Establish classroom rules:
- Concentrate while working.
- Work quietly.
- Remain in your seat.
- Finish task.
- Meet task requirements.

Review rules often. Reinforce the student for following the rules.

22. Make sure that the expectation for the student to remain seated is appropriate for his/her level of development and ability.

23. Encourage the student to remind himself/herself to wait when he/she feels the urge to get out of his/her seat (e.g., "Stop. Count to ten.").

24. Encourage the student to monitor his/her behavior to decrease the need for teacher intervention to remain seated.

25. Interact frequently with the student to maintain his/her attention to the activity (e.g., ask the student questions, ask the student's opinions, stand close to the student, seat the student near the teacher's desk, etc.).

26. Remind the student when needed to remain in his/her seat.

27. Reinforce the student for staying in his/her seat: (a) give the student a tangible reward (e.g., classroom privileges, five minutes free time, etc.) or (b) give the student an intangible reward (e.g., praise, fist bump, smile, etc.).

28. Encourage the student to participate in high-energy activities after school that allow him/her to release excess energy (e.g., racquetball, soccer, etc.).

29. Provide the student with frequent opportunities to participate, take a turn, etc., to keep him/her involved in an activity.

30. Prevent the student from becoming overstimulated by an activity (e.g., frustrated, angry, excited, etc.).

31. Seat the student near the teacher.

32. Separate the student from the peer who stimulates his/her inappropriate behavior.

33. Provide the student with the most attractive and interesting activities possible.

34. Provide the student with a calm, quiet environment in which to work.

35. Establish times when it is permissible for the student to be out of his/her seat (e.g., leave his/her seat only to get a book, only after obtaining permission, etc.).

36. Provide the student with a predetermined signal when he/she begins to leave his/her seat.

37. Make sure that reinforcement is not inadvertently given for inappropriate behavior (e.g., attending to the student only when he/she leaves his/her seat).

38. Be proactive. Work with the school counselor to create a schedule to facilitate the student's success (e.g., physical education scheduled the last period of the day, intersperse electives which allow greater freedom of movement with classes requiring extended periods of concentration, etc.).

39. Avoid placing the student in situations that require sitting for an extended directions, announcements, seminars, assemblies, etc. Provide the information for the student through a recording or lecture notes.

40. Evaluate the visual and auditory stimuli in the classroom. Determine the amount of stimuli the student can tolerate. Remove extraneous stimuli from the environment.

41. Interact frequently with the student to prevent the student from leaving his/her seat.

42. Evaluate the appropriateness of tasks to determine (a) if the tasks are too easy, (b) if the tasks are too difficult, and (c) if the length of time scheduled for the tasks is adequate.

43. Be consistent in expecting the student to stay seated. Do not allow him/her to get up and walk around one time and expect him/her to remain seated the next time.

44. Discuss your concerns regarding the student's attention span and inability to remain seated with his/her family, a school official, etc., if it is interfering with his/her progress at school.

45. Have the student perform one task or assignment at a time. Give the student the opportunity for movement between activities.

46. Facilitate on-task behavior by providing a full schedule of daily events. Prevent lag time when the student would be free to leave his/her seat.

47. Teach the student to use techniques such as crossing his/her arms and legs, clenching his/her fists, and intertwining his/her fingers when he/she feels the urge to leave his/her seat.

48. Write a contract with the student specifying what behavior is expected (e.g., staying in his/her seat) and what reinforcement will be made available when the terms of the contract have been met.

49. Maintain visibility to and from the student to keep his/her attention when verbal questions/directions are being delivered. The teacher should be able to see the student and the student should be able to see the teacher. Make eye contact possible at all times.

50. Communicate with the student's cooperative work experience/vocational education teacher to place the student on a job site allowing a high degree of physical movement.

51. Limit the amount of time you expect the student to be seated to perform tasks and assignments. Do not initially give him/her things to do that take more than 10-15 minutes to complete.

52. Identify the situations in which the student is most likely to participate in inappropriate behavior and fail to remain seated. After you have identified these situations, think of ways to minimize their occurrences.

1. Reinforce the student for being ready for an activity at the specified time: (a) give the student a tangible reward (e.g., classroom privileges, line leading, passing out materials, five minutes free time, etc.) or (b) give the student an intangible reward (e.g., praise, fist bump, smile, etc.).

2. Speak to the student to explain (a) what he/she is doing wrong (e.g., coming late/early to an activity) and (b) what he/she should be doing (e.g., arriving at an activity at the specified time).

3. Establish classroom rules:
- Concentrate while working.
- Work quietly.
- Remain in your seat.
- Finish task.
- Meet task requirements.

Review rules often. Reinforce the student for following the rules.

4. Choose a peer to model being ready for an activity at the specified time for the student.

5. Reinforce the student for arriving at an activity within a given period of time. As the student becomes more successful in being punctual, gradually reduce the length of time the student has to arrive at an activity.

6. Write a contract with the student specifying what behavior is expected (e.g., coming to class on time, having necessary materials, etc.) and what reinforcement will be made available when the terms of the contract have been met.

7. Communicate with parents (e.g., notes home, phone calls, etc.) to share information about the student's progress. The parents may reinforce the student at home for being ready for activities at the specified time at school.

8. Evaluate the appropriateness of the task to determine (a) if the task is too easy, (b) if the task is too difficult, and (c) if the length of time scheduled to complete the task is adequate.

9. Give the student a specific responsibility to be performed at the beginning of each activity to encourage him/her to be on time.

10. Choose a peer to accompany the student to activities.

11. Make sure that the student's daily schedule follows an established routine.

12. Limit the number of interruptions in the student's schedule.

13. Make sure the student has adequate time to get to an activity.

14. Make sure that the student knows how to get from one activity to another.

15. Use a timer to help the student get to activities at specified times.

16. Reinforce those students in the classroom who are ready for an activity at the specified time.

17. Provide the student with verbal cues when it is time to change activities (e.g., "It is time for the red group to have reading." "Now it is time for the red group to put away materials and move to the next activity.").

18. Determine why the student is not ready for activities at the specified times.

19. Ask the student why he/she is not ready for activities at the specified times. The student may have the most accurate perception as to why he/she is not ready for activities at the specified times.

20. Help the student understand that it is permissible to leave work unfinished and return to it at a later time.

21. Have the student document his/her attendance at the end of each activity.

22. Determine if there are aspects of activities that the student dislikes. Remove, reduce, or modify the unpleasant aspects of activities to encourage the student to be ready for and participate in activities.

23. Make the student responsible for time missed (e.g., if the student misses five minutes of an activity, he/she must make up the time during recess, lunch, or other desired activities).

24. Provide the student with a schedule of daily events so that he/she will know which activities to attend and their times.

25. Make sure that the student is successful in school-related and social activities. The student will be more likely to be ready for activities in which he/she experiences success.

26. Give the student a schedule of classes that must be signed by every instructor to document his/her promptness.

27. Make sure that other students do not make it unpleasant for the student to attend activities.

28. Make sure the student has all the necessary materials for activities.

29. Record or chart promptness with the student.

30. Begin activities with a task that is highly reinforcing to the student.

31. Assess appropriateness of the level of difficulty of tasks in comparison with the student's ability.

32. Provide the student with many opportunities for high-interest activities as possible.

33. Provide the student academic activities in the most attractive manner possible.

34. Make the student a leader of the activity or group.

35. Collect anecdotal information on the student's tardy behavior. If a trend can be determined, remove the student from the situation and/or help the student be prompt.

36. Make sure the student is appropriately placed according to his/her ability level in those classes in which he/she is enrolled.

37. Reduce the emphasis on competition. Repeated failure may cause the student to avoid being on time for activities which are competitive.

38. Teach the student how to use a calender to become aware of upcoming activities that are not part of the daily routine (e.g., Tuesday at 12:00- field trip to the zoo, etc.).

39. Deliver directions in a supportive rather than a threatening manner (e.g., "Please come to your reading group now." rather than "You had better come to your reading group or else!" etc.).

40. Give the student a special responsibility before the group meets (e.g., sharpening pencils, arranging chairs, passing out books, etc.).

41. Use a timer to help the student monitor how much time he/she has to follow through with directions.

42. Treat the student with respect. Talk in an objective manner at all times.

43. Do not embarrass the student by giving him/her orders, demands, etc., in front of others.

44. Make sure the student knows how to tell time and has an understanding of his/her daily routine.

45. Provide the student with a schedule of events for the day to keep at his/her desk. Make notes of any special materials needed for an activity.

46. Make sure the student has a working watch or clock available to encourage his/her promptness to an activity.

47. Along with a directive, provide an incentive statement (e.g., "When you come to your reading group, you may pass out the books." "Please come to your reading group early to help arrange the chairs.").

48. Allow natural consequences to occur as a result of the student not being ready for an activity at the specified time (e.g., miss an assembly, miss the bus, late for class, etc.).

49. Teach the student organizational skills (e.g., before leaving the classroom, make sure materials are put away; take all the necessary materials along; arrive five minutes early; etc.).

50. Teach the student to use a pocket calender to record specific times, places and activities that need to be remembered.

M. Group Behavior

1. Communicate with parents (e.g., notes home, phone calls, etc.) to share information about their child's progress. The parents may reinforce the student at home for moving appropriately with a group at school.

2. Allow natural consequences to occur as a result of the student's inappropriate behavior (e.g., excessive physical contact may cause people to stay away from the student or may result in pushing, shoving, etc.).

3. Have the student be a line leader, line monitor, etc., when moving with a group.

4. State clearly the expectations for appropriate behavior when moving with a group.

5. Choose a classmate to model appropriate movement with a group for the student.

6. Reinforce the student for demonstrating appropriate behavior when moving with a group: (a) give the student a tangible reward (e.g., classroom privileges, line leading, passing out materials, etc.) or (b) give the student an intangible reward (e.g., praise, fist bump, smile, etc.).

7. Reinforce those students who demonstrate appropriate behavior when moving with a group.

8. Reinforce the student for moving appropriately with a group based on the length of time the student can be successful. As the student demonstrates success, gradually increase the length of time required for reinforcement.

9. Have the student walk with arms crossed, arms against his/her side, hands in pockets, etc., if touching others is a problem.

10. Provide constant, positive reinforcement for appropriate behavior. Ignore as many inappropriate behaviors as possible.

11. Reinforce the student for walking at the same pace as other students when moving with a group.

12. Have the student walk alone, behind the group, beside the teacher, etc., when he/she displays inappropriate behavior when moving with a group.

13. Provide the student with a clearly understood list of consequences for inappropriate behavior when moving with a group.

14. Demonstrate/model for the student moving appropriately with a group.

15. Evaluate the appropriateness of the expectation of moving with a group to determine (a) if the task is too easy, (b) if the task is too difficult, and (c) if the length of time scheduled to complete the task is adequate.

16. Speak to the student to explain (a) what he/she is doing wrong (e.g., running, pushing peers, etc.) and (b) what he/she should be doing (e.g., walking without touching peers).

17. Establish rules for moving appropriately with a group:
- Walk in the halls.
- Go directly from one area to another.
- Talk quietly in the halls.
- Walk on the right side of the hall.
- Use the appropriate stairway.

Review rules often. Reinforce students for following the rules.

18. State clearly the manner in which you expect the student to act before going out in public or to a place where he/she has never been before.

19. Stop the line frequently to facilitate the student's success when moving with a group.

20. Have the students walk in pairs when moving as a group.

21. Separate the student from the peer that stimulates his/her inappropriate behavior.

22. Form a second line or group for those students who move at a slower pace.

23. Write a contract with the student specifying what behavior is expected (e.g., walking appropriately in a group) and what reinforcement will be made available when the terms of the contract have been met.

24. Remind the student before leaving the classroom of the rules for walking in a group (e.g., walk behind the person in front of you, keep hands to yourself, walk quietly, etc.).

214 Behaves more appropriately alone or in small groups than with the whole class or in large group activities

1. Do not force the student to participate in group situations.

2. Choose a peer, paraprofessional, friend, etc., to sit/work directly with the student (e.g., in different settings such as art, music, or P.E.; or different activities such as tutoring, group projects, running errands in the building, recess, etc.).

3. Reward or encourage other students for participation in group situations.

4. Give the student the responsibility of helping a peer in group situations.

5. Give the student responsibilities in group situations so others might view the student in a positive way.

6. Call on the student when he/she is most likely to be able to respond successfully (e.g., when discussing a topic in which the student is interested, when the teacher is sure the student knows the answer, etc.).

7. Try various groupings to determine the group in which the student is most comfortable.

8. Have peers invite the student to participate in school or extracurricular activities.

9. Have the student lead a small group activity when he/she possesses mastery or an interest in the activity.

10. Allow the student to observe group activities without requiring active participation. Require more involvement over time as the student becomes more active in group situations.

11. Reduce the emphasis on competition. Fear of failure may cause the student to be reluctant to participate in group situations.

12. Have the student work with one or two other group members. As the student becomes more comfortable, gradually increase the size of the group.

13. Demonstrate respect for the student's opinions, responses, suggestions, etc.

14. Give the student the opportunity to pick a topic or activity for the group to work on together.

15. Give the student the opportunity to choose a group activity and the group members (e.g., along with the teacher decide what the activity will be, decide what individual group members will do, etc.).

16. Assign the student a role to perform in the group activity which he/she can perform successfully (e.g., secretary, researcher, group behavior monitor, etc.).

17. Make sure the student is productive and accurate in performing individual assignments before placing him/her in a group activity.

18. Go over group rules and expectations at the beginning of each group activity.

19. Make sure that the student can follow classroom rules and expectations independently before placing him/her in a group activity.

20. Help the student learn to be satisfied with his/her best effort rather than some arbitrary measure of success. Success is measured individually according to ability level. Progress of any kind is a measure of success.

21. Make sure the student understands instructions/directions for the group activity (e.g., give instructions in a variety of ways, make sure that the student understands his/her role, go over the rules for group behavior before the activity begins, etc.).

22. Make sure the student has all needed materials to perform his/her role in the group (e.g., paper, pencil, art supplies, reference materials, etc.).

23. Group the student with peers who will be appropriate role models and are likely to facilitate the student's academic and behavioral successes.

24. Group the student with students who are least likely to be threatening (e.g., younger students, students just learning a skill he/she has mastered, etc.).

25. Make sure the student has enough room to work successfully (e.g., distance from other students, room for all materials, etc.).

26. Make sure the student is actively involved in the group situation (e.g., call on the student frequently, assign the student a responsibility such as teacher assistant, have him/her be the group leader, etc.).

27. Remove the student from the group if his/her behavior is inappropriate.

28. Make sure the academic and social demands of the group situation are within the student's ability level.

29. Evaluate the appropriateness of the task to determine (a) if the task is too easy, (b) if the task is too difficult, and (c) if the length of time scheduled for the task is adequate.

30. Help the student get to know group members before requiring group participation (e.g., introduce the students to one another, allow the students unstructured free time together, etc.).

31. Reduce distracting stimuli which could interfere with the student's success in a group activity (e.g., provide enough room for him/her to move without physical contact, keep noise level at a minimum, keep movement in the environment to a minimum, etc.).

32. Schedule group activities as part of the student's daily routine (i.e., group activities should occur on a regularly scheduled basis so the student will be prepared and know what to expect).

33. Schedule group activities so the teacher can spend uninterrupted time with the group.

34. Place the student in those group activities he/she prefers. As the student demonstrates success, gradually require the student to participate in less desirable activities.

35. Provide the student with alternative ways to perform a group assignment and Have the student choose the most desirable (e.g., a written paragraph assignment may be accomplished by writing a note to a friend, writing about a recent experience, describing a favorite pastime, etc.).

36. Allow the student to participate in one group activity he/she prefers. Require the student to participate in more group activities as he/she experiences success.

37. Schedule group activities when the student is most likely to be successful (e.g., before recess rather than immediately after recess, after the first individual assignment of the day has been completed to establish productive behavior, etc.).

38. Plan alternative individual activities if the student is unlikely to be successful (e.g., if the schedule has been changed, if holidays or special events have stimulated the student and make successful group interaction unlikely, etc.).

39. Allow the student to join the group after the activity has begun if he/she is unable to participate appropriately at the beginning of the group activity.

40. Position the student's desk or work area so he/she works near other students but is not visually distracted by them (e.g., turn the student's desk away from other students, etc.).

41. Allow the student to leave a group activity and return to independent work when he/she can no longer be successful in the group activity (e.g., as an alternative to disrupting the group, fighting, etc.).

42. Teach the student to think before acting by asking himself/herself question: *What is happening? What am I doing? What should I do? What will be best for me?*

43. Communicate with parents (e.g., notes home, phone calls, etc.) to share information about the student's progress. The parents may reinforce the student at home for participating in group situations at school.

44. Write a contract with the student specifying what behavior is expected (e.g., making short, appropriate comments and speaking at appropriate times) and what reinforcement will be made available when the terms of the contract have been met.

45. Speak with the student to explain (a) what the student is doing wrong (e.g., failing to take part) and (b) what the student should be doing (e.g., talking, taking turns, playing, sharing, etc.).

46. Establish classroom rules:
- Concentrate while working.
- Remain in your seat.
- Finish task.
- Meet task expectations.
- Raise your hand.

Review rules often. Reinforce students for following the rules.

47. Reinforce the student for working in a group situation: (a) give the student a tangible reward (e.g., classroom privileges, line leading, passing out materials, five minutes free time, etc.) or (b) give the student an intangible reward (e.g., praise, fist bump, smile, etc.).

48. Reinforce other students in the classroom for working appropriately in a group situation.

215 Demonstrates inappropriate behavior in a small academic group setting

1. Do not force the student to participate in group situations.

2. Choose a peer, paraprofessional, friend, etc., to sit/work directly with the student (e.g., in different settings such as art, music, or P.E.; or different activities such as tutoring, group projects, running errands in the building, recess, etc.).

3. Ask the student questions that cannot be answered yes or no.

4. Call on the student when he/she is most likely to be able to respond successfully (e.g., something in which the student is interested, when the teacher is sure the student knows the answer, etc.).

5. Try various groups to determine the situation in which the student is most successful.

6. Have peers invite the student to participate in school or extracurricular activities.

7. Ask the student to be the leader of a small group activity if he/she possesses mastery or an interest in the activity.

8. Allow the student to observe group activities without requiring active participation.

9. Have the student work with one or two other group members. As the student becomes more comfortable, gradually increase the size of the group.

10. Demonstrate respect for the student's opinions, responses, suggestions, etc.

11. Give the student the opportunity to pick a topic or activity for the group to work on together.

12. Go over group rules and expectations at the beginning of each group activity.

13. Give the student the opportunity to choose a group activity and the group members (e.g., along with the teacher decide what the activity will be, decide what individual group members will do, etc.).

14. Assign the student a role to perform in the group activity which he/she can perform successfully (e.g., secretary, researcher, group behavior monitor, etc.).

15. Make sure the student is productive and accurate in performing individual assignments before placing him/her in a small group activity.

16. Make sure that the student can follow classroom rules and expectations independently before placing him/her in a small group activity.

17. Reduce the emphasis on competition. Fear of failure may cause the student to be reluctant to participate in small group situations.

18. Help the student learn to be satisfied with his/her best effort rather than some arbitrary measure of success. Success is measured individually according to ability level. Progress of any kind is a measure of success.

19. Group the student with peers who will be appropriate role models and are likely to facilitate the student's academic and behavioral successes.

20. Group the student with students who are least likely to be threatening (e.g., younger students, students just learning a skill he/she has mastered, etc.).

21. Make sure the student understands instructions/directions for the group activity (e.g., give instructions in a variety of ways, make sure that the student understands his/her role, go over the rules for group behavior before the activity begins, etc.).

22. Remove the student from the group if his/her behavior is inappropriate.

23. Make sure the student has all needed materials to perform his/her role in the group (e.g., paper, pencil, art supplies, reference materials, etc.).

24. Make sure the student has enough room to work successfully (e.g., distance from other students, room for all materials, etc.).

25. Make sure the student is actively involved in the group situation (e.g., call on the student frequently, assign the student a responsibility such as teacher assistant, have him/her be the group leader, etc.).

26. Make sure the academic and social demands of the group situation are within the student's ability level.

27. Help the student get to know group members before requiring group participation (e.g., introduce the students to one another, allow the students unstructured free time together, etc.).

28. Reduce distracting stimuli which could interfere with the student's success in a group activity (e.g., provide enough room for him/her to move without physical contact, keep noise level at a minimum, keep movement in the environment to a minimum, etc.).

29. Schedule group activities so the teacher can spend uninterrupted time with the group.

30. Schedule group activities as part of the student's daily routine (i.e., group activities should occur on a regularly scheduled basis so the student will be prepared and know what to expect).

31. Place the student in those group activities he/she prefers. As the student demonstrates success, gradually require the student to participate in less desirable activities.

32. Provide the student with alternative ways to perform a group assignment and Have the student choose the most desirable (e.g., a written paragraph assignment may be accomplished by writing a note to a friend, writing about a recent experience, describing a favorite pastime, etc.).

33. Allow the student to participate in one group activity he/she prefers. Require the student to participate in more group activities as he/she experiences success.

34. Schedule group activities when the student is most likely to be successful (e.g., before recess rather than immediately after recess, after the first individual assignment of the day has been completed to establish productive behavior, etc.).

35. Plan alternative individual activities if the student is unlikely to be successful (e.g., if the schedule has been changed, if holidays or special events have stimulated the student and make successful group interaction unlikely, etc.).

36. Allow the student to join the group after the activity has begun if he/she is unable to participate appropriately at the beginning of the group activity.

37. Position the student's desk or work area so he/she works near other students but is not visually distracted by them (e.g., turn the student's desk away from other students, etc.).

38. Allow the student to leave a small group activity and return to independent work when he/she can no longer be successful in the group activity (e.g., as an alternative to disrupting the group, fighting, etc.).

39. Teach the student to think before acting by asking himself/herself question: *What is happening? What am I doing? What should I do? What will be best for me?*

40. Have the student ask questions about directions, explanations, or instructions he/she does not understand.

41. Evaluate the appropriateness of the assigned task to determine (a) if the task is too easy, (b) if the task is too difficult, and (c) if the length of time scheduled is adequate.

42. Communicate with parents (e.g., notes home, phone calls, etc.) to share information about the student's progress. The parents may reinforce the student at home for participating in small academic group situations at school.

43. Write a contract with the student specifying what behavior is expected (e.g., working appropriately with peers) and what reinforcement will be made available when the terms of the contract have been met.

44. Speak to the student to explain (a) what the student is doing wrong (e.g., failing to take part) and (b) what the student should be doing (e.g., talking, taking turns, sharing, etc.).

45. Reinforce the student for demonstrating appropriate behavior in a small academic group setting: (a) give the student a tangible reward (e.g., classroom privileges, line leading, passing out materials, five minutes free time, etc.) or (b) give the student an intangible reward (e.g., praise, fist bump, smile, etc.).

46. Establish classroom rules:
- Concentrate while working.
- Remain in your seat.
- Finish task.
- Meet task expectations.
- Raise your hand.

Review rules often. Reinforce students for following the rules.

47. Reinforce those students in the classroom who demonstrate appropriate behavior in a small academic group setting.

48. Reinforce the student for demonstrating appropriate behavior in a small academic group setting based on the length of time he/she can be successful. As the student demonstrates success, gradually increase the length of time required for reinforcement.

216 Does not demonstrate appropriate behavior in the presence of a substitute authority figure

1. Prepare an information packet for a substitute authority figure that includes all information pertaining to the classroom (e.g., student roster, class schedule, class rules, behavior management techniques, class helpers, etc.).

2. Make sure that the student understands that classroom rules and behavioral consequences are in effect when a substitute authority figure is in the classroom.

3. Indicate where all needed materials are located to maintain structure in the classroom.

4. Indicate various activities in which the student can participate after completing his/her work for the day.

5. Indicate the names of several personnel and where they can be located in case the substitute authority figure should need some assistance.

6. Inform the substitute authority figure of the classroom rules and the consequences if the rules are not followed by the student.

7. Express the need for the substitute authority figure to maintain consistent discipline while in and outside of the classroom.

8. Inform the substitute authority figure of all privileges the students have both in and outside of the classroom.

9. Have the student work on practice work (e.g., work that has already been taught to the student and that he/she knows how to do) to reduce frustration and feelings of failure.

10. Set aside 10 minutes at the beginning of the day for the substitute authority figure to develop rapport with the students (e.g., introduce himself/herself to the class, learn the students' names, talk about things the students enjoy doing, etc.).

11. Indicate to the student that the substitute authority figure is in charge of the classroom at all times.

12. Schedule a fun educational activity (e.g., computer game) during the day to provide an incentive for the student to stay on task and behave appropriately.

13. Assign a special job for the student to perform when there is a substitute authority figure in the classroom (e.g., substitute teacher's assistant, line leader, class monitor, etc.). Inform the substitute authority figure of this special job.

14. Have the substitute authority figure present instructions/directions in a variety of ways (e.g., verbally, written, etc.).

15. Request a substitute authority figure who has the skills necessary to handle problem behavior and special needs students.

16. Make sure that the substitute authority figure is familiar with the behavioral support system used in the classroom (e.g., rules, point system, reinforcers, etc.).

17. Communicate directly with the substitute authority figure, if possible, to share information which will contribute to the student's success.

18. Choose a student(s) to be an assistant to the substitute authority figure during the day's activities (e.g., the student(s) provides accurate information about the schedule of activities, behavioral support system, etc.).

19. Provide the substitute authority figure with detailed information on the activities and assignments.

20. Make sure the substitute authority figure follows all procedures indicated by the classroom teacher (e.g., academic activities, behavioral support system, etc.).

21. Have the substitute authority figure provide a written review of the day as feedback for the classroom teacher (e.g., activities completed, student behavior, absences, incidents concerning individual students, etc.).

22. Have special or unique responsibilities performed by other personnel in the building (e.g., administering medication, feeding, toileting, etc.).

23. Have the student record his/her own behavior when a substitute authority figure is in the classroom.

24. Choose a peer to work with the student to model appropriate behavior and to provide information necessary for success for the student.

25. If an aide works in the classroom; have the aide monitor the student's behavior, provide reinforcement, deliver instructions, etc.

26. If there is an aide in the classroom, have the aide work with the student on a one-to-one basis throughout the day.

27. Provide the student with an individualized schedule of daily events. The schedule should be attached to the student's desk or carried with him/her at all times.

28. Instruct the substitute authority figure to interact with the student frequently to provide reinforcement, deliver instructions, provide encouragement, etc.

29. Have the substitute authority figure maintain visibility to and from the student. The substitute authority figure should be able to see the student; the student should be able to see the substitute authority figure. Make eye contact possible at all times.

30. Provide the student with as many high-interest activities as possible.

31. Provide a quiet place for the student to work.

32. Make the student aware of the natural consequences concerning inappropriate behavior in the presence of a substitute authority figure (e.g., removal from the classroom, loss of privileges, etc.).

33. Have a peer deliver instructions to the student.

34. Begin the day or class with an activity which is of high interest to the student.

35. Present activities in the most attractive, interesting manner possible.

36. Do not schedule highly stimulating activities when a substitute authority figure is in the classroom.

37. Structure the environment to reduce the opportunity for inappropriate behavior (e.g., reduce periods of inactivity by having the student actively involved at all times).

38. Provide the substitute authority figure with a seating chart and indicate the student(s) who needs additional supervision.

39. Indicate, for the substitute authority figure, those peers who might be likely to stimulate the student's inappropriate behavior. (It may be necessary to keep the students separated.).

40. Have the substitute authority figure check the student's completed assignments to make sure that work is not carelessly performed.

41. Write a contract with the student or the entire class for reinforcement based on appropriate behavior when a substitute authority figure is present.

42. Have the substitute authority figure maintain mobility to be frequently near the student.

43. Make sure the student receives the necessary information to perform activities (e.g., written information, verbal directions, reminders, etc.).

44. Make sure the substitute authority figure consistently follows the routine established by the classroom teacher (e.g., schedule, delivering instructions, task requirements, reinforcement, negative consequences, etc.).

45. Provide the student with a clearly identified list of consequences for inappropriate behavior in the presence of a substitute authority figure.

46. Have the substitute authority figure help the student begin assignments, check his/her work, provide immediate feedback, etc.

47. Have the student maintain a record of his/her academic performance while a substitute authority figure is in the classroom.

48. Inform the students in advance when it will be necessary for a substitute authority figure to be in the classroom. Establish expectations for behavior and academic performance.

49. Provide the substitute authority figure with instructions for action to be taken if the student becomes abusive or threatening.

50. Teach the student to think before acting by asking himself/herself questions: *What is happening?, What am I doing?, What should I do?, What will be best for me?*

51. Have the student ask questions about directions, explanations, instructions not understood.

52. Evaluate the appropriateness of the task to determine (a) if the task is too easy, (b) if the task is too difficult, and (c) if the length of time scheduled to complete the task is adequate.

53. Communicate with parents (e.g., notes home, phone calls, etc.) to share information about the student's progress. The parents may reinforce the student at home for demonstrating appropriate behavior in the presence of a substitute authority figure.

54. Write a contract with the student specifying what behavior is expected (e.g., following the substitute authority figure's directions) and what reinforcement will be made available when the terms of the contract have been met.

55. Reinforce those students in the classroom who demonstrate appropriate behavior in the presence of a substitute authority figure.

56. Establish classroom rules:
- Concentrate while working.
- Remain in your seat.
- Finish task.
- Meet task expectations.
- Raise your hand.

Review rules often. Reinforce students for following the rules.

57. Speak to the student to explain (a) what the student is doing wrong (e.g., not following the substitute authority figure's directions, not following classroom rules, etc.) and (b) what the student should be doing (e.g., following the substitute authority figure's directions, following classroom rules, etc.).

58. Allow the student to voice his/her opinion in a situation to hear the student's side of the story.

59. Reinforce the student for demonstrating appropriate behavior in the presence of a substitute authority figure: (a) give the student a tangible reward (e.g., classroom privileges, line leading, passing out materials, five minutes free time, etc.) or (b) give the student an intangible reward (e.g., praise, fist bump, smile, etc.).

217 Demonstrates inappropriate behavior in a large academic group setting

1. Choose a peer to sit/work directly with the student (e.g., in different settings such as art, music, P.E.; or different activities such as tutoring; group projects; etc.).

2. Do not force the student to participate in a large academic group setting.

3. Reward or encourage others for participation in the group.

4. Give the student the responsibility of helping another student in the group.

5. Give the student responsibilities in the group so that others might view him/her in a more positive way.

6. Ask the student questions that cannot be answered simply by yes or no.

7. Call on the student when he/she is most likely to be able to respond successfully (e.g., when discussing something in which the student is interested, when you are certain the student knows the answer, etc.).

8. Try various groupings to determine the situation in which the student is most comfortable.

9. Ask the student to be the leader of a large group activity if he/she possesses mastery or an interest in the activity.

10. Allow the student to be present during large group activities without requiring active participation. As the student demonstrates success, require more involvement.

11. Reduce the emphasis on competition. Fear of failure may cause the student to avoid participating in large academic group settings.

12. Have the student work with one or two other group members. As the student becomes more comfortable, gradually increase the size of the group.

13. Demonstrate respect for the student's opinions, responses, suggestions, etc.

14. Give the student the opportunity to pick a topic or activity for the group to work on together.

15. Give the student the opportunity to choose a group activity and choose the group members who will participate (e.g., along with the teacher decide what the activity will be, what individual group members will do, etc.).

16. Assign the student a role to perform in the group activity which he/she can perform successfully (e.g., secretary, researcher, group behavior monitor, etc.).

17. Make sure the student is productive and accurate in performing individual assignments before placing him/her in large group activities.

18. Review group rules/expectations at the beginning of each group activity.

19. Make sure the student can follow classroom rules/expectations independently before placing him/her in a large group activity.

20. Help the student learn to be satisfied with his/her best effort rather than some arbitrary measure of success. Success is measured individually according to ability level. Progress of any kind is a measure of success.

21. Place the student with peers who will be appropriate role models and are likely to facilitate his/her academic and behavioral success.

22. Place the student with group members who are least likely to be threatening to the student (e.g., younger students, students just learning a skill he/she has mastered, etc.).

23. Make sure that the student has all needed materials to perform his/her role in the group (e.g., paper, pencil, art supplies, reference materials, etc.).

24. Make sure that the student understands instructions/directions for the group activity (e.g., give instructions in a variety of ways, make sure that the student understands his/her role, review the rules for group behavior before the activity begins, etc.).

25. Make sure the student has enough room to work successfully (e.g., distance from other students, room for all materials, etc.).

26. Make sure the student is actively involved in the group (e.g., call on the student frequently, assign the student a responsibility such as teacher assistant, have the student be group leader, etc.).

27. Remove the student from the group if he/she behaves inappropriately.

28. Make sure the academic and social demands of the group situation are within the student's ability level.

29. Help the student get to know group members before requiring group participation (e.g., introduce the students to one another; allow the students unstructured free time together; etc.).

30. Reduce distracting stimuli which could interfere with the student's success in a group activity (e.g., provide enough room for him/her to move without physical contact; keep noise level to a minimum; keep movement in the environment to a minimum; etc.).

31. Schedule activities so your time can be spent uninterrupted with the group.

32. Schedule large group activities as part of the student's daily routine (e.g., large group activities should occur on a regularly scheduled basis so that the student will be prepared and know what to expect).

33. Provide the student with alternative ways to perform a group assignment and allow him/her to choose the most desirable (e.g., a written paragraph assignment may be accomplished by writing a note to a friend, writing about a recent experience, describing a favorite pastime, etc.).

34. Allow the student to participate in the large group activity he/she prefers. As the student experiences success, require him/her to participate in more large group activities.

35. Have the student participate in at least one large group activity per day. As the student demonstrates success, gradually require the student to participate in more large group activities.

36. Schedule large group activities when the student is most likely to be successful (e.g., before recess rather than immediately after recess, after the first individual assignment of the day has been completed to establish productive behavior, etc.).

37. Plan alternative individual activities if the student is unlikely to be successful (e.g., if the schedule has been changed; if holidays or special events have stimulated the student, making successful group interactions unlikely; etc.).

38. Allow the student to join the group after the activity has begun if he/she is unable to participate appropriately at the beginning of the activity.

39. Position the student's desk or work so that he/she works near other students but is not visually distracted by them (e.g., turn the student's desk away from other students).

40. Allow the student to leave a group activity and return to independent work when he/she can no longer be successful in the group activity (e.g., as an alternative to disrupting the group, fighting, etc.).

41. Arrange the student's seating so that you can interact with him/her frequently (e.g., near the front of the room, on the perimeter of the group, etc.).

42. Choose a peer to sit/work next to the student to provide assistance.

43. Have the student maintain a list of classroom rules at his/her desk (e.g., attached to the surface of the desk, inside the desk, etc.).

44. Use a time-out area to allow the student to gain self-control if problem behaviors occur during a large academic group activity.

45. Provide a carrel or other quiet study area for the student to use if he/she cannot be successful at his/her seat.

46. Use removal from the group as a natural consequence for inappropriate behavior.

47. Present academic tasks in the most attractive and interesting manner possible.

48. Integrate the student into a large academic group activity only after he/she has had success with one other student, a small group, etc.

49. Integrate the student into a large academic group activity gradually (e.g., short periods of time with the group lead to longer periods of time).

50. Provide the student with the opportunity to work with a peer tutor, volunteer, etc., for enrichment or support of content presented in the large academic group activity.

51. Provide structure so that the large academic group activity does not become overstimulating for the student.

52. Publicly praise the student for appropriate behavior and privately redirect inappropriate behavior.

53. Write group contracts which encourage students to work together for group success.

54. Find related group activities the student can perform successfully (e.g., acting as teacher assistant, giving directions, handing out materials, collecting materials, etc.).

55. Schedule daily activities so that highly desirable activities follow large academic group activities and are contingent upon appropriate behavior in the large academic group activity.

56. Have the student ask questions about directions, explanations, or instructions he/she does not understand.

57. Teach the student to think before acting by asking himself/herself questions: *What is happening?, What am I doing?, What should I do?, What will be best for me?*

58. Make sure that comments made to the student take the form of constructive criticism rather than criticism that can be perceived as personal, threatening, etc., (e.g., instead of saying, "You always make the same mistake." say, "A better way to do that might be . . .").

59. Evaluate the appropriateness of the task to determine (a) if the task is too easy, (b) if the task is too difficult, and (c) if the length of time scheduled to complete the task is adequate.

60. Communicate with parents (e.g., notes home, phone calls, etc.) to share information about the student's progress. The parents may reinforce the student at home for working appropriately in a large academic group setting at school.

61. Write a contract with the student specifying what behavior is expected (e.g., working appropriately with peers) and what reinforcement will be made available when the terms of the contract have been met.

62. Reinforce the student for demonstrating appropriate behavior in a large academic group setting based on the length of time he/she can be successful. As the student demonstrates success, gradually increase the length of time required for reinforcement.

63. Reinforce those students in the classroom who demonstrate appropriate behavior in a large academic group setting.

64. Establish classroom rules:
- Concentrate while working.
- Work quietly.
- Remain in your seat.
- Finish task.
- Meet task expectations.

Review rules often. Reinforce students for following the rules.

65. Speak to the student to explain (a) what he/she is doing wrong (e.g., talking out of turn, failing to take part, etc.) and (b) what he/she should be doing (e.g., talking when appropriate, taking turns, sharing, etc.).

66. Reinforce the student for demonstrating appropriate behavior in a large academic group setting: (a) give the student a tangible reward (e.g., classroom privileges, line leading, passing out materials, five minutes free time, etc.) or (b) give the student an intangible reward (e.g., praise, fist bump, smile, etc.).

218 Has difficulty working effectively in a group situation

1. Reinforce the student for working in a group situation: (a) give the student a tangible reward (e.g., classroom privileges, line leading, passing out materials, five minutes free time, etc.) or (b) give the student an intangible reward (e.g., praise, fist bump, smile, etc.).

2. Speak with the student to explain (a) what the student is doing wrong (e.g., failing to take part) and (b) what the student should be doing (e.g., talking, taking turns, playing, sharing, etc.).

3. Establish classroom rules:
- Concentrate while working.
- Remain in your seat.
- Finish task.
- Meet task expectations.
- Raise your hand.

Review rules often. Reinforce students for following the rules.

4. Reinforce other students in the classroom for working appropriately in a group situation.

5. Write a contract with the student specifying what behavior is expected (e.g., working appropriately with peers) and what reinforcement will be made available when the terms of the contract have been met.

6. Communicate with parents (e.g., notes home, phone calls, etc.) to share information about the student's progress. The parents may reinforce the student at home for participating appropriately in group situations at school.

7. Do not force the student to participate in group situations until he/she can be successful.

8. Choose a peer to sit/work directly with the student (e.g., in different settings such as art, music, P.E., on the bus; or different activities such as tutoring, group projects, running errands in the building, recess, etc.).

9. Reward or encourage other students for participation in group situations.

10. Give the student the responsibility of helping a peer in group situations.

11. Go over group rules and expectations at the beginning of each group activity.

12. Call on the student when he/she is most likely to be able to respond successfully (e.g., when discussing a topic in which the student is interested, when the teacher is sure the student knows the answer, etc.).

13. Try various groupings to determine the situation in which the student is most comfortable.

14. Have peers invite the student to participate in school or extracurricular activities.

15. Have the student lead a small group activity when he/she possesses mastery or an interest in the activity.

16. Allow the student to observe group activities without requiring active participation. Require more involvement over time as the student becomes more active in group situations.

17. Reduce the emphasis on competition. Fear of failure may cause the student to be reluctant to participate in group situations.

18. Have the student work with one or two other group members. As the student becomes more comfortable, gradually increase the size of the group.

19. Demonstrate respect for the student's opinions, responses, suggestions, etc.

20. Give the student the opportunity to pick a topic or activity for the group to work on together.

21. Give the student the opportunity to choose a group activity and the group members (e.g., along with the teacher decide what the activity will be, decide what individual group members will do, etc.).

22. Assign the student a role to perform in the group activity which he/she can perform successfully (e.g., secretary, researcher, group behavior monitor, etc.).

23. Make sure the student is productive and accurate in performing individual assignments before placing him/her in a group activity.

24. Give the student responsibilities in group situations so others might view the student in a positive way.

25. Make sure that the student can follow classroom rules and expectations independently before placing him/her in a group activity.

26. Help the student learn to be satisfied with his/her best effort rather than some arbitrary measure of success. Success is measured individually according to ability level. Progress of any kind is a measure of success.

27. Group the student with peers who will be appropriate role models and are likely to facilitate the student's academic and behavioral successes.

28. Group the student with students who are least likely to be threatening (e.g., younger students, students just learning a skill he/she has mastered, etc.).

29. Make sure the student understands instructions/directions for the group activity (e.g., give instructions in a variety of ways, make sure that the student understands his/her role, go over the rules for group behavior before the activity begins, etc.).

30. Make sure the student has all needed materials to perform his/her role in the group (e.g., paper, pencil, art supplies, reference materials, etc.).

31. Make sure the student has enough room to work successfully (e.g., distance from other students, room for all materials, etc.).

32. Make sure the academic and social demands of the group situation are within the student's ability level.

33. Remove the student from the group if his/her behavior is inappropriate.

34. Make sure the student is actively involved in the group situation (e.g., call on the student frequently, assign the student a responsibility such as teacher assistant, have him/her be the group leader, etc.).

35. Allow the student to join the group after the activity has begun if he/she is unable to participate appropriately at the beginning of the group activity.

36. Help the student get to know group members before requiring group participation (e.g., introduce the students to one another, allow the students unstructured free time together, etc.).

37. Reduce distracting stimuli which could interfere with the student's success in a group activity (e.g., provide enough room for him/her to move without physical contact, keep noise level at a minimum, keep movement in the environment to a minimum, etc.).

38. Schedule group activities so the teacher can spend uninterrupted time with the group.

39. Schedule group activities as part of the student's daily routine (i.e., group activities should occur on a regularly scheduled basis so the student will be prepared and know what to expect).

40. Place the student in those group activities he/she prefers. As the student demonstrates success, gradually require the student to participate in less desirable activities.

41. Provide the student with alternative ways to perform a group assignment and Have the student choose the most desirable (e.g., a written paragraph assignment may be accomplished by writing a note to a friend, writing about a recent experience, describing a favorite pastime, etc.).

42. Allow the student to participate in one group activity he/she prefers. Require the student to participate in more group activities as he/she experiences success.

43. Schedule group activities when the student is most likely to be successful (e.g., before recess rather than immediately after recess, after the first individual assignment of the day has been completed to establish productive behavior, etc.).

44. Plan alternative individual activities if the student is unlikely to be successful (e.g., if the schedule has been changed, if holidays or special events have stimulated the student and make successful group interaction unlikely, etc.).

45. Evaluate the appropriateness of the assigned task to determine (a) if the task is too easy, (b) if the task is too difficult, and (c) if the length of time scheduled is adequate.

46. Position the student's desk or work area so he/she works near other students but is not visually distracted by them (e.g., turn the student's desk away from other students, etc.).

47. Allow the student to leave a group activity and return to independent work when he/she can no longer be successful in the group activity (e.g., as an alternative to disrupting the group, fighting, etc.).

48. Carefully consider the student's age and experience before expecting him/her to get along in a group.

49. Intervene early when there is a problem to prevent more serious problems from occurring.

50. Do not force the student to interact with people with whom he/she is not completely comfortable.

51. Teach the student acceptable ways to communicate displeasure, anger, frustration, etc.

52. Teach the student to think before acting by asking himself/herself question: *What is happening? What am I doing? What should I do? What will be best for me?*

53. Encourage the student to use problem-solving skills: (a) identify the problem, (b) identify goals and objectives, (c) develop strategies, (d) develop a plan for action, (e) carry out the plan.

54. Allow the student to voice his/her opinion in a situation to avoid becoming angry or upset.

55. Talk to the student about ways of handling situations successfully without conflict (e.g., walk away from the situation, change to another activity, ask for help, etc.).

56. Reinforce the student for talking an appropriate length of time and at appropriate times in the classroom: (a) give the student a tangible reward (e.g., classroom privileges, line leading, passing out materials, five minutes free time, etc.) or (b) give the student an intangible reward (e.g., praise, fist bump, smile, etc.).

57. Speak with the student to explain (a) what he/she is doing wrong (e.g., talking more than is necessary or at inappropriate times) and (b) what he/she should be doing (e.g., keeping comments brief, waiting until it is appropriate to speak, thinking of comments which relate to the situation, etc.).

58. Reinforce those students in the classroom who make their comments brief or speak at appropriate times.

59. Reinforce the student for making appropriate comments or speaking at the appropriate time based on the length of time he/she can be successful. As the student demonstrates success, gradually increase the length of time required for reinforcement.

60. Make sure that reinforcement is not inadvertently given for inappropriate behavior (e.g., talking beyond what is expected or at inappropriate times).

61. Give adequate opportunities to respond (i.e., enthusiastic students need many opportunities to contribute).

62. Provide the student with a predetermined signal if he/she begins to talk beyond what is expected or at inappropriate times.

63. Explain to the student that he/she may be trying too hard to fit in and he/she should relax, talk less, and talk at appropriate times.

64. Provide the student with many opportunities for social and academic successes.

65. Make the necessary adjustments in the environment (e.g., reduce peer pressure, academic failure, teasing, etc.) to prevent the student from experiencing stress, frustration, or anger.

66. Maintain visibility to and from the student. The teacher should be able to see the student and the student should be able to see the teacher. Make eye contact possible at all times.

67. Interact frequently with the student to reduce his/her need to talk beyond what is expected or at inappropriate times.

68. Assess the appropriateness of the social situation in relation to the student's ability to function successfully.

69. Reinforce the student for raising his/her hand to be recognized.

70. Teach the student to recognize when to speak, to know how much to say and to make appropriate comments (e.g., brief comments, comments within the context of the situation, comments that are a follow-up to what has just been said, etc.).

71. Have the student work in small groups in which he/she would have frequent opportunities to speak. As the student learns to wait longer for his/her turn to speak, gradually increase the size of the group.

72. Make sure that the student's feelings are considered when it is necessary to discuss his/her inappropriate comments (i.e., use comments that do not diminish the student's enthusiasm for participation).

73. Encourage the student to model the behavior of peers who are successful.

74. Create and reinforce activities (e.g., school bulletin board, class project, bake sale, etc.) in which students work together for a common goal rather than individual success or recognition. Point out that larger accomplishments are realized through group effort rather than by individual effort.

75. Deliver directions, explanations, and instructions in a clear and concise manner to reduce the student's need to ask questions.

76. Have the student practice waiting for short periods of time for his/her turn to speak. As the student demonstrates success, gradually increase the length of time required for reinforcement.

77. Explain to the student the reasons why talking beyond what is expected and at inappropriate times is unacceptable (e.g., is impolite, interrupts others, etc.).

78. Attempt to provide equal attention to all students in the classroom.

79. Make the student aware of the number of times he/she talks beyond what is expected and at inappropriate times.

80. Write group contracts which encourage students to work together for group success.

81. Explain to the student why he/she has been asked no to talk.

82. Have the student participate in small group activities (e.g., free time, math, reading, etc.) to reduce the level of auditory and visual stimuli in the group. As the student can function successfully, gradually increase the size of the group.

83. Help the student improve concentration skills (e.g., listening to the speaker, taking notes, preparing comments in advance, making comments in the appropriate context, etc.

84. Have the student ask questions about directions, explanations, or instructions he/she does not understand.

1. Reinforce the student for demonstrating appropriate behavior in group games: (a) give the student a tangible reward (e.g., classroom privileges, line leading, passing out materials, five minutes free time, etc.) or (b) give the student an intangible reward (e.g., praise, fist bump, smile, etc.).

2. Speak to the student to explain (a) what he/she is doing wrong (e.g., failing to follow rules, cheating, etc.) and (b) what he/she should be doing (e.g., following the rules, playing fairly, etc.).

3. Establish classroom rules:
• Concentrate while working.
• Remain in your seat.
• Finish task.
• Meet task expectations.
• Raise your hand.
Review rules often. Reinforce students for following the rules.

4. Reinforce those students in the classroom who demonstrate appropriate behavior in group games.

5. Reinforce the student for demonstrating appropriate behavior in group games based on the length of time the student can be successful. As the student demonstrates success, gradually increase the length of time required for reinforcement.

6. Write a contract with the student specifying what behavior is expected (e.g., following the rules) and what reinforcement will be made available when the terms of the contract have been met.

7. Communicate with parents (e.g., notes home, phone calls, etc.) to share information about the student's progress. The parents may reinforce the student at home for demonstrating appropriate behavior in group games at school.

8. Evaluate the appropriateness of the group game to determine if the game is too difficult and if the length of time scheduled to complete the game is adequate.

9. Choose a peer to model appropriate behavior in group games for the student.

10. Have the student ask questions about directions, explanations, or instructions he/she does not understand.

11. Evaluate the expectations for participation in group games to determine if the student can be successful in the interaction and for the expected length of time.

12. Have the student choose a group of peers with whom he/she feels comfortable to play group games.

13. Have the student participate in a game activity with one peer. As the student demonstrates success, gradually increase the size of the group.

14. Determine the peers with whom the student would most prefer to interact in group games and facilitate the interaction.

15. Choose outgoing, nonthreatening peers to interact with the student in group games.

16. Structure the environment so the student has many opportunities to interact with peers in group games.

17. Assign the student to interact with younger peers in group games.

18. Choose group games in which the student is likely to interact successfully with peers.

19. Conduct a sociometric activity with the class to determine those peers who would most prefer to interact with the student in group games.

20. Make sure that the student demonstrates appropriate behavior in nonacademic situations prior to placing him/her with peers for group games.

21. Make sure that the student understands that interacting with peers in group games is contingent upon appropriate behavior.

22. Have the student practice appropriate interactions with the teacher(s) in group games.

23. Teach the student appropriate ways to interact with peers in group games (e.g., suggest activities, share materials, problem-solve, take turns, follow game rules, etc.).

24. Supervise group games closely so peers with whom the student interacts do not stimulate inappropriate behavior.

25. Make sure that group games are not so stimulating as to make successful interactions with peers difficult.

26. Assign older peers with desirable social skills to interact with the student in group games.

27. Involve the student in extracurricular activities to encourage interaction with peers in group games.

28. Reduce the emphasis on competition. Failure may stimulate inappropriate behavior in group games.

29. Teach the student problem-solving skills so he/she may better deal with problems that may occur in interactions with peers in group games (e.g., talking, walking away, calling upon an arbitrator, compromising, etc.).

30. Find the peer with whom the student is most likely to be able to successfully interact in group games (e.g., a student with similar interests, background, classes, behavior patterns, nonacademic schedule, etc.).

31. Structure the group games according to the needs/abilities of the student (e.g., establish rules, limit the stimulation of the activities, limit the length of the game, consider the time of day, etc.).

32. Limit opportunities for interaction in group games on those occasions when the student is not likely to be successful (e.g., if the student has experienced academic or social failure prior to the scheduled group game).

33. Select group games designed to facilitate appropriate interaction of the student and peers.

34. Through interviews with other students and observations, determine those characteristics of the student which interfere with successful interactions during group games to determine skills or behaviors the student needs to develop for successful interactions.

35. Make sure beforehand that the student is able to successfully participate in the group game (e.g., the student understands the rules, the student is familiar with the game, the student will be compatible with the other students playing the game, etc.).

36. Make sure the student understands that not interacting appropriately with peers during group games may result in termination of the game and/or loss of future opportunities to participate in group games.

37. Have the student interact with peers for short periods of time to facilitate success. As the student demonstrates success, gradually increase the length of time the student interacts.

38. Have the student study, practice, simulate, etc., the rules for group games before participating.

39. Establish a set of rules for group games (e.g., follow rules of the game, take turns, make positive comments, work as a team member, be a good sport, etc.).

40. Remove the student from group games if he/she is unable to demonstrate appropriate behavior.

41. Play the game with the student before he/she engages in the game with peers to model appropriate behavior, determine the student's ability to play the game, determine the student's ability to follow behavior rules, etc.

42. Have the student participate in group games of short duration. As the student demonstrates success, gradually increase the duration of group games.

43. Teach the student necessary skills needed to successfully participate in particular group games (e.g., volleyball, basketball, football, baseball, etc.).

44. Have the student choose the group games which he/she will play with peers.

45. Carefully consider the student's age and experience before expecting him/her to get along with others when playing group games.

46. Encourage the student to use problem-solving skills: (a) identify the problem, (b) identify goals and objectives, (c) develop strategies, (d) develop a plan for action, and (e) carry out the plan.

47. Make sure the student sees the relationship between his/her behavior and the consequences which may follow (e.g., failing to get along when playing a group game will result in others not wanting to play with him/her).

48. Teach the student acceptable ways to communicate displeasure, anger, frustration, etc.

49. Choose a peer who will be a good influence (e.g., someone younger, older, of the same gender, of the opposite gender, etc.) to play with the student.

50. Teach the student to think before acting by asking himself/herself question: *What is happening? What am I doing? What should I do? What will be best for me?*

51. Allow the student to voice his/her opinion in a situation to avoid becoming angry or upset.

52. Talk to the student about ways of handling situations successfully without conflict (e.g., walk away from a situation, change to another activity, ask for help, etc.).

53. Do not force the student to play games with someone with whom he/she is not completely comfortable.

54. Intervene early when there is a problem to prevent more serious problems from occurring.

N. Social Skills/Communication

1. Provide activities that encourage play (e.g., bubbles, water play, shaving cream, silly string, twister, a large piece of paper on the floor or table where the student can draw/color with others and "create" together, etc.).

2. Have the student choose a special event or interesting activity for the class.

3. Have the student participate in a game activity with one peer. As the student demonstrates success, gradually increase the size of the group.

4. Ask the student to choose a peer to work with on a specific assignment. If the student has difficulty choosing someone, determine the student's preference by other means such as a class survey.

5. Determine the student's interests so activities which require participation might be presented through his/her interests.

6. Find educationally related, leisure/recreational activities for the student to perform (e.g., flash card activities with peers; math, reading, or spelling board games; etc.).

7. Involve the student in extracurricular activities to encourage interaction with peers in group games.

8. Through interviews with other students and observations, determine those characteristics of the student which interfere with successful interactions to determine skills or behaviors the student needs to develop.

9. Use a highly preferred toy as motivation for teaching how to pretend while playing.

10. Carefully consider the student's age and experience before expecting him/her to join others when playing group games.

11. Take advantage of opportunities for the students to share and help (e.g., when there is a spill, assign students different responsibilities for cleaning it up; when a new student enters the classroom, assign students responsibilities for his/her orientation; etc.).

12. Encourage joint attention between you and the student through use of simple things (e.g., make eye contact before gaining another push on the swing; use a single word to express a desire, etc.). Remember to begin on the student's ability level.

13. Choose a peer to model appropriate interactions with one other student in nonacademic situations for the student.

14. Have the student choose a group of peers with whom he/she feels comfortable to play group games.

15. Reinforce the student for interacting appropriately with one other student in nonacademic situations: (a) give the student a tangible reward (e.g., classroom privileges, line leading, passing out materials, five minutes free time, etc.) or (b) give the student an intangible reward (e.g., praise, fist bump, smile, etc.).

16. Make sure that shared materials are returned to the student so he/she will develop a positive concept of sharing.

17. Make the initial imaginative play as concrete as possible. Then add to this play various abstract items/ideas as the student demonstrates success.

18. Use a scripted role-play to assign roles and duties to all students in a play activity.

19. Present tasks in the most attractive and interesting manner possible.

20. Establish a set of rules for group games (e.g., follow rules of the game, take turns, make positive comments, work as a team member, be a good sport, etc.).

21. Model appropriate interactions. Mediate play between the student and others.

22. Have a peer share a book with the student while the book is being read aloud.

23. Ask the student questions that cannot be answered yes or no.

24. Modify or adjust situations that cause the student to be reluctant to interact (e.g., degree of difficulty, competition, fear of failure, threat of embarrassment, etc.).

25. If the student has difficulty choosing a topic to play, use his/her favorite item to initiate play.

26. Reinforce those students in the classroom who participate in group situations or classroom activities.

27. Make sure that redirection is delivered in the most positive manner.

28. Have the student ask questions about directions or expectations he/she does not understand.

29. Maintain a realistic level of expectation for sharing.

30. Provide the student with many experiences to share with others and have materials returned. When the student learns that shared materials will be returned, the student will be more likely to share in the future.

31. Speak to the student to explain (a) what he/she is doing wrong (e.g., not interacting with others) and (b) what he/she should be doing (e.g., talking, taking turns, playing, sharing, etc.).

32. Select nonacademic activities designed to facilitate appropriate social interaction between the student and peers during classroom activities (e.g., board games, model building, coloring, etc.).

33. Establish leisure time rules:
- Find an activity.
- Find someone to work with.
- Remain in assigned areas.
- Put materials away when free time is over.

Review rules often. Reinforce the student for following the rules.

34. Provide the student with opportunities for small group participation as opposed to large group participation.

35. Make sure that every student gets to use materials, take a turn, etc., and that there is no opportunity for selfishness.

36. Have the student participate in group games of short duration. As the student demonstrates success, gradually increase the duration of group games.

37. Deliver a predetermined signal (e.g., hand signal, verbal cue, etc.) when the student begins to withdraw from group activities.

38. For a more experienced student, have him/her play with more than one other student so that he/she must wait for a turn and fit his/her actions to those of others.

39. Teach the student social skills he/she may need to participate in leisure/recreational activities (e.g., team members need to know how to work together, people who are watching a movie in a theater are typically quiet, etc.).

40. Call on the student when he/she is most likely to be able to respond successfully (e.g., something in which the student is interested, when the teacher is sure the student knows the answer, etc.).

41. Explain to the student that his/her best effort is more important than perfection to help decrease frustration with group leisure/recreational time activity.

42. Communicate with parents (e.g., notes home, phone calls, etc.) to share information about the student's progress. The parents may reinforce the student at home for interacting with others at school.

43. Use verbal/physical prompting (hand-over-hand if necessary) to help the student pretend.

44. Encourage the student to participate in small groups. As the student demonstrates success, gradually increase the size of the group.

45. Encourage and assist the student in joining extracurricular activities, clubs, etc.

46. Encourage the student's peers to include him/her in free time activities.

47. Have the student practice appropriate interactions with the teacher(s) in classroom activities (e.g., simulations, role-playing, etc.).

48. Evaluate the expectations for peer interactions to determine if the student can be successful in the interactions and for the expected length of time the student interacts.

49. Structure interactions (e.g., establish rules, limit the stimulation of the activity, limit the length of the activity, consider time of day, etc.) according to the needs/abilities of the student.

50. Establish social rules:
- Share materials.
- Use a quiet voice in the building.
- Walk indoors.
- Use care in handling materials.

Review rules often. Reinforce the student for following the rules.

51. Discuss with the student items needed to play pretend (e.g., play house, dress-up clothes, a place that is the kitchen, a place that is the bedroom, maybe some make-believe cars/tricycles or bikes, etc.).

52. Give the student the responsibility of passing out snacks/materials to the class.

53. Let the student press the on/off button for music in a dance/freeze game with the class.

54. Demonstrate respect for the student's opinions, responses, suggestions, etc.

55. Provide the student with many opportunities to both borrow and lend to help the student learn the concept of sharing.

56. Encourage or reward others for participation in the group situations or classroom activities.

57. Pair the student with a peer who enjoys similar toys and will quietly encourage him/her to join them. A quiet tone of voice is important.

58. Have the student and a peer work on an easel, either side-by-side or on opposite sides, to draw pictures/paint and model comments peers can make to each other.

59. Pair the student with a peer to be a partner for dancing to music.

60. Assign the student responsibilities to perform during activities to facilitate peer interaction (e.g., being a leader, passing out materials, being a peer tutor, etc.).

61. Have a peer and adult play turn taking games with the student to model appropriate behavior.

62. Discuss idea sources for pretend play. Ideas can be found in books, magazines, newspapers, movies or TV programs. Have the student list these ideas in a book to help with the development of ideas for pretend play.

63. Allow the student to observe group activities without requiring active participation.

64. Give the student the responsibility of helping another student in the group.

65. Make costumes to use while pretending (e.g., create face masks and use a mirror; make bear masks and pretend you are in the woods, etc.)

66. Provide sign-up sheets for leisure/recreational activities that involve small groups of students.

67. Teach the student to be satisfied with his/her best effort and not insist on perfection.

68. Create and reinforce activities (e.g., school bulletin board, class project, bake sale, etc.) in which students work together for a common goal rather than individual success or recognition. Point out that larger accomplishments are realized through group effort rather than by individual effort.

69. Provide the student with frequent short-term leisure/recreational activities with other students so he/she can learn to attempt activities with peers.

70. Have the student study, practice, simulate, etc., the rules for group games before participating.

71. Assess the appropriateness of the social setting in relation to the student's ability to interact with peers.

72. Use role-play to simulate various situations the student might be involved with, and to teach the student how to interact appropriately (e.g., how to have an appropriate conversation at the lunch table, how to ask to play a game with others, individualized social story with pictures to demonstrate how to play with others, etc.).

73. Assign the student to nonacademic situations in which he/she is likely to interact successfully with another student.

74. Assign peers with desirable social skills to interact with the student during leisure/recreational activities.

75. Teach the student problem-solving skills so he/she may better deal with problems that occur in interactions with another peer (e.g., talking, walking away, calling upon an arbitrator, compromising, etc.).

76. Establish classroom rules:
• Concentrate while working.
• Remain in your seat.
• Finish task.
• Meet task expectations.
• Raise your hand.
Review rules often. Reinforce the student for following the rules.

77. Reduce the emphasis on competition. Social interactions may be inhibited if the student's abilities are constantly made public and compared to others.

78. Show an interest in the student (e.g., acknowledge the student, ask the student's opinion, spend time working one-to-one with the student, etc.).

79. Make sure, beforehand, that the student is able to successfully participate in the group situation (e.g., the student understands the rules, is familiar with the activity, will be compatible with peers engaged in the activity, etc.).

80. Write a contract with the student specifying what behavior is expected (e.g., interacting appropriately with peers) and what reinforcement will be made available when the terms of the contract have been met.

81. Create situations in which the student must interact (e.g., returning completed assignments to students, proofreading other students' work, group mural, team sports, etc.).

82. Provide organized activities for the student to participate in before, during, and after school (e.g., board games, softball, four square, tether ball, jump rope, flash cards, etc.).

83. Practice sharing by having each student work with a particular school material for an established length of time. At the end of the time period (e.g., ten minutes), have each student pass his/her material to another student.

84. Practice play skills with the student frequently across all environments so he/she can become comfortable with the process of play.

85. Play the game with the student before he/she engages in the game with peers to model appropriate behavior, determine the student's ability to play the game, determine the student's ability to follow behavior rules, etc.

86. Make the play accessible. Many students do not have the initiative to think of play when it is not visibly accessible and set up.

87. Treat the student with respect. Talk in an objective manner at all times.

88. Evaluate the appropriateness of the task to determine (a) if the task is too easy, (b) if the task is too difficult, and (c) if the length of time scheduled to complete the task is adequate.

89. Be open to flexibility in teaching a learning model. Make changes to previously provided lesson plans or expectations to accommodate the student's learning style.

90. Point out to the student the natural rewards of sharing (e.g., personal satisfaction, friendships, having people share in return, etc.).

91. Model appropriate social behavior for the student at all times.

92. Evaluate the demands made on the student in academic and social situations to make sure that expectations are within the student's level of ability.

93. Perform hand-over-hand assistance from behind the student.

94. Avoid competition. Failure may cause the student to avoid interacting with others.

95. Use a visual schedule of the pretend play with events listed in order. For example:
- Little Bear wakes up and is in his bed.
- He goes outside to play.
- He meets a new friend who is a bear named Jake.
- Jake and Little Bear pretend they are going to the moon on a space ship.
- When they are finished, they go home.

96. Ask the student to be the leader of a small group activity if he/she possesses mastery or an interest in the activity.

97. Use video self-modeling to allow the student to see himself/herself playing with other students.

98. Try various groupings to determine the group in which the student is most comfortable.

99. Do not criticize. When correcting the student, be honest yet supportive. Never cause the student to feel negatively about himself/herself.

100. Determine the peers with whom the student would prefer to interact in group situations and facilitate the interaction.

101. Have the student choose the game which he/she will play with peers.

102. Maintain trust and confidentiality with the student at all times.

103. Make sure the student sees the relationship between his/her behavior and the consequences which may follow (e.g., failing to join a group game will result in others not playing with him/her).

104. Talk while playing to assist the student with processing the playing (e.g., "I'm making food for my friend Jenny. I need to cook the food. Now it's time for a plate. Here, Jenny, this is your lunch. Doesn't it look yummy!").

105. Supervise nonacademic situations closely so the peer with whom the student interacts does not stimulate the student's inappropriate behavior.

106. Structure the environment so that the student has many opportunities to interact with peers.

107. Have a person act as the student's shadow to work on interactions, turn taking, sharing items and interactive play (e.g., cooking with toy stove, etc.).

108. Have a person act as the student's shadow to assist the student to take turns. The shadow would help the student to associate his/her hands with the action rather than later presenting his/her hands to perform the action.

109. Choose classroom activities in which the student is likely to interact successfully with peers.

110. Encourage the student to share things of special interest with other members of the class.

111. Limit opportunities for interaction on those occasions when the student is not likely to be successful (e.g., when the student has experienced academic or social failure prior to the scheduled nonacademic activity).

112. Introduce new items to the student, even when he/she avoids such activities. Practice new skills in a "3 times then a break" method.
- Assist the student hand-over-hand to hit the ball off the tee.
- Assist the student to retrieve the ball and put it back on the tee.
- Do this three times and then give the student a break.

113. Teach the student appropriate ways to interact with peers in classroom activities (e.g., share materials, problem solving, take turns, talk, etc.).

114. Choose an outgoing, nonthreatening peer to help the student interact appropriately.

115. Teach the student acceptable ways to communicate displeasure, anger, frustration, etc.

116. Have a peer blow bubbles toward the student to form a connection between them.

117. Teach the student appropriate ways to interact with another student in nonacademic situations (e.g., how to greet another student, suggest activities, share materials, problem-solve, take turns, talk, etc.).

118. Do not force the student to interact with other students with whom he/she is not completely comfortable.

119. Ask each student to take turns placing blocks to create a structure (e.g., a giant tower, etc.).

120. Teach the student to take turns sharing materials (e.g., each student may use the colored pencils for 15 minutes, one student cuts while the other student uses the glue, etc.).

121. Make sure that the student understands that participation in nonacademic situations is contingent upon appropriate behavior.

122. Encourage sharing by giving assignments which require sharing to complete the activity (e.g., making murals, bulletin boards, maps, art projects, etc.).

123. Reinforce the student for interacting with a peer based on the length of time he/she can be successful. As the student demonstrates success, gradually increase the length of time required for reinforcement.

124. Encourage the student to plan with his/her peers the use of leisure/recreational time in advance.

125. Provide one-to-one assistance to help with playing appropriately.

126. Assign the student to interact with a younger student in nonacademic situations (e.g., free time areas, cafeteria, hallways, etc.).

127. Facilitate the development of friendships with peers (e.g., assign activities for the student involving peers, give the student and a peer joint responsibilities, etc.).

128. Have the student work directly with a peer to model sharing. As the student demonstrates success, gradually increase the size of the group.

129. Have the student run errands with a peer to facilitate interaction.

130. Encourage the student to interact with others.

131. Choose a peer to sit/work directly with the student in different settings or activities (e.g., art, music, P.E., on the bus, tutoring, group projects, running errands in the building, recess, etc.). As the student becomes comfortable working with another student, gradually increase the size of the group.

132. Share a piece of bubble wrap with the student and a peer. With hands or feet, each person pops the bubble wrap working toward the middle.

133. Determine the student's level of play. Play develops in stages (e.g., solitary, the student is in a room full of people but he/she is playing alone and does not attend to anyone; parallel, the student may be playing the same game/activity as the other students or the students are playing next to each other but are not talking or doing the same activity; associative, the student is playing the same game as the other students but they are not all working together or connecting with one other; or cooperative, the student is working with other students to play a game).

134. Facilitate the development of friendships with peers (e.g., assign activities for the student involving peers, give the student and a peer joint responsibilities, etc.).

135. If the student will play but will not initiate play, directly teach verbal and nonverbal ways to initiate play with others (e.g., "Want to play?" "Play with me please." Hand another person the toy/game.).

136. Modify or adjust situations that cause the student to be reluctant to participate (e.g., degree of difficulty, competition, fear of failure, threat of embarrassment, etc.).

137. Teach the student appropriate ways to interact with another student (e.g., how to greet another student, suggest activities, share materials, problem-solve, take turns, talk, etc.).

Reminder: Do not force the student to interact with peers.

1. Allow some alone time for the student and schedule time when he/she is to socialize. This participation may be watching the other students or being in the same vicinity as the other students.

2. Explicitly teach age-appropriate leisure skills such as ball skills and board games.

3. Have the student practice social skills and develop regular conversation to use at different times, such as when meeting someone (e.g., "Hi, My name is _____. Would you like to play?" etc.).

4. Choose a peer to play with the student during recess.

5. Engage the student socially while incorporating activities that he/she enjoys playing alone.

6. Use free time tickets to reward friend time. The student may use free time tickets to participate in solitary play.

7. Encourage the parents to invite a peer from the student's class for one-to-one supervised play dates. Choose a peer with similar interests.

8. Implement a weekly social skill into the class curriculum (e.g., this week we are practicing hand shaking, etc.).

9. Encourage the student to enroll in after school activities that are attended by peers (dance class, music class, boy scouts, etc.).

10. Provide increased supervision during recess to facilitate appropriate peer interactions and prevent victimization.

11. Organize a lunch bunch. Choose three to four students to eat lunch together twice a week with a teacher or psychologist to practice skills.

12. Ask the school psychologist to create a weekly social skills group. Follow up by practicing the social skills in the classroom.

13. Provide opportunities for cooperative projects with an aide to assist pairs that include the student.

14. Develop, with the student, a list of high interest, leisure/recreational activities that require various amounts of time to perform and involve other students.

15. Encourage parental input in developing behavioral and activity expectations in community sites to encourage consistency between home and school.

16. Expose the student to a variety of group leisure/recreational resources in his/her home community to help the student make informed decisions about leisure/recreational activities that he/she might enjoy.

17. Allow passive participation as a social choice across learning activities and environments.

18. Help the student establish a daily routine which includes a chosen leisure/recreational activity (e.g., dancing, walking, exercising, etc.) and praise him/her for participating in the activity.

19. Have the student ask questions about directions, explanations, and instructions not understood.

20. Have the student practice appropriate interactions with the teacher(s) in classroom activities (e.g., simulations, role-play, etc.).

21. Encourage the student to assist a younger peer in new leisure time activities.

22. Encourage the student to attempt new things and to play with students who are outgoing.

23. Evaluate the appropriateness of available leisure and recreational activities to determine whether or not the student can be successful with the activity, the length of time scheduled, and the others involved in the activity.

24. Ask the student to be the leader of a small group activity if he/she possesses mastery or an interest in the activity.

25. Have the student choose a group of peers with whom he/she feels comfortable.

26. Ask the student to choose a peer to work with on a specific assignment. Encourage the student and peer to interact with each other in nonacademic areas (e.g., recess, lunch, break time, etc.).

27. Have the student choose a special event or interesting activity for the class.

28. Assign the student to classroom activities in which he/she is likely to interact successfully with peers.

29. Reduce the emphasis on competition. Failure may cause the student to be reluctant to interact with peers.

30. Do not criticize. When correcting the student, be honest yet supportive. Never cause the student to feel negatively about himself/herself.

31. Try various groupings to determine the group in which the student is most likely to succeed socially.

32. Choose a peer to participate in recreational activities with the student to develop a friendship.

33. Have the student run errands with a peer to facilitate interaction.

34. Encourage or reward others for interacting with the student.

35. Encourage or reward others for participation in the group situations or classroom activities.

36. Provide the student with frequent opportunities to meet new people.

37. Provide ample opportunities for friendships to occur.

38. Facilitate the development of friendships with peers (e.g., assign activities for the student involving peers, give the student and a peer joint responsibilities, etc.).

39. Help the student develop friendships by pairing him/her with another student for activities. As the student is socially successful, gradually increase the number of students in the group.

40. Give the student responsibilities in group situations so peers may view the student in a more positive way.

41. Have the student participate in activities which require minimal participation. As he/she becomes more comfortable, gradually increase the student's participation.

42. Communicate with parents (e.g., notes home, phone calls, etc.) to share information about the student's progress. The parents may reinforce the student at home for interacting with peers at school.

43. Establish classroom rules that indicate times when it is acceptable to socialize (e.g., at recess, during class parties, lunchtime, after work is completed at the end of the day, at the beginning of each day before attendance, etc.). Review rules often. Reinforce the student for positive social exchanges.

44. Reinforce the student for interacting with others: (a) give the student a tangible reward (e.g., classroom privileges, line leading, passing out materials, five minutes free time, etc.) or (b) give the student an intangible reward (e.g., praise, fist bump, smile, etc.).

45. Reinforce the student for interacting with others based on the length of time the student can be successful. As the student demonstrates success, gradually increase the length of time required for reinforcement.

46. Consider the student's current interests and abilities in skill-building plans for recreation and leisure.

47. Provide the student with opportunities to learn how to interact in social situations by teaching social mannerisms in role-play.

48. Give the student the opportunity to choose a group activity and the group members (e.g., along with the teacher decide what the activity will be, decide what individual group members will do, etc.).

49. Go with the student or have someone else accompany the student to those activities in which he/she may not want to participate. Gradually decrease the length of time you or someone else stays with the student.

50. Involve the student and parents in developing a list of leisure/recreational activities involving others, from which the student makes his/her choices.

51. Encourage the student to participate in small groups. As the student demonstrates success, gradually increase the size of the group.

52. Provide supervision of leisure/recreational time activities to monitor the student's willingness to try leisure time activities that involve other students.

53. Treat the student with respect. Talk in an objective manner at all times.

54. Model appropriate ways to respond to interactions with other students or teachers.

55. Encourage the student to share things of special interest with others in the class (e.g., special hobbies such as coin collecting, etc.).

56. Choose a peer to sit/work directly with the student in different settings or activities (e.g., art, music, P.E., on the bus, tutoring, group projects, running errands in the building, recess, etc.). As the student becomes comfortable working with one person, gradually increase the size of the group.

57. Determine the student's interests so activities which require participation might be presented through his/her interests.

58. Do not force the student to socialize. It is more important to offer opportunities for positive reinforcement from socialization than to demand display of socialization skills.

59. Do not force the student to interact with individuals with whom he/she is not completely comfortable.

60. Do not push the student too hard when encouraging interaction with others. The student may become frightened.

61. Encourage and assist the student in joining extracurricular activities, clubs, etc.

62. Demonstrate respect for the student's opinions, responses, suggestions, etc.

63. Ask the student questions that cannot be answered with a yes or no. Provide the student with encouragement for his/her attempts at answering these open-ended questions.

64. Structure the environment so that the student has many opportunities to interact with peers.

65. Identify peers with whom the student would prefer to interact and facilitate interaction.

66. Carefully consider those activities the student avoids. If something unpleasant is causing the student not to participate, try to change the situation.

67. Maintain consistent expectations within the ability level of the student.

68. Reinforce those students in the classroom who participate in leisure/recreational activities with others.

69. Allow enough time for the student to prepare for a special event (e.g., talking about how much fun the birthday party will be, how much fun it will be to visit Grandma's, etc.).

70. Modify situations that cause the student to be reluctant to participate (e.g., degree of difficulty, competition, fear of failure, threat of embarrassment, etc.).

71. Encourage friendship building in the classroom (e.g., students may wish to attend extracurricular activities in small groups, etc.).

72. Write a contract with the student specifying what behavior is expected (e.g., engaging in leisure/recreational time activities with others, etc.) and what reinforcement will be made available when the terms of the contract have been met.

73. Provide organized activities for the student to participate in before, during, and after school (e.g., board games, softball, four square, tether ball, jump rope, flash cards, etc.).

74. Reinforce other students in the classroom for participating in group activities or special events.

75. Assess the appropriateness of the social setting in relation to the student's ability to interact with peers.

76. Participate in leisure/recreational time activities with the student to model appropriate use of leisure time.

77. Select nonacademic activities designed to facilitate appropriate social interaction between the student and peers during classroom activities (e.g., board games, model building, coloring, etc.).

78. Assign the student responsibilities to perform during activities to facilitate peer interaction (e.g. being a leader, passing out materials, being a peer tutor, etc.).

79. Conduct a sociometric activity to identify peers who would most prefer to interact with the student in classroom activities.

80. Speak to the student to explain (a) what the student is doing wrong (e.g., working alone) and (b) what he/she should be doing (e.g., participating in an activity with a friend, etc.).

81. Encourage the student to use problem-solving skills: (a) identify the problem, (b) identify goals and objectives, (c) develop strategies, (d) develop a plan of action, and (e) carry out the plan.

82. Assign the student to work with one or two peers on a long-term project (e.g., mural, bulletin board, report, etc.).

83. Teach the student appropriate ways to interact with another student (e.g., how to greet another student, suggest activities, share materials, problem-solve, take turns, talk, etc.).

84. Choose classroom activities in which the student is likely to interact successfully with peers.

85. Determine the peers with whom the student would prefer to interact and facilitate the interaction.

86. Have the student interact with a peer for short periods of time to facilitate success. As the student demonstrates success, gradually increase the length of time the student interacts.

222 Does not exhibit awareness of social "codes of conduct" or does not learn appropriate behavior from observing such behaviors

1. Use visuals (posters) in the classroom or school that remind the student of appropriate simple social skills.

2. Use specially designed programs/books to teach social skills at an age appropriate level.

3. Involve the student in a social skills class or group on a weekly basis.

4. Be a social mediator for the student. Be with the student, but not involved in the play, so that you can give cues to help him/her be more successful.

5. Develop special words or clues to help the student know when he/she needs to pay closer attention to peers' requests.

6. Shadow the student during play. When a social code of conduct has been initiated by someone, assist the student to respond appropriately.

7. Explain social codes of conduct to the student and the importance of appropriate behavior. Make your explanations short and to the point.

8. Teach the student to check in when talking about a subject of great interest. Have the student ask his/her peer/teacher/other person if they would like to hear more. This keeps the student in check when he/she wants to dominate the conversation.

9. Read or discuss social stories before the skill is expected to be used.

10. Have peers model expected behaviors while drawing the student's attention to them.

11. Make a picture representation of what is expected.

12. Provide picture cues at the locations where focus behaviors are expected to occur (in lunch line, by play area, etc.).

13. Provide the student with a written list/description of expected behavior(s). Ask the student to review the list daily (with a peer, an adult, etc.).

14. Have all class members participate in making a class video modeling appropriate behavior(s). The video can then be viewed as a reminder.

15. Make an audio recording of expected behaviors so the student can independently review the expected behaviors.

16. Have all students work in groups to develop comic strip depictions of expectations. Display the comic strip in various locations.

17. Organize structured lessons to teach a specific skill (e.g., a board game with the focus on turn taking, etc.) This should be facilitated by an adult and aided with picture cards.

18. Have the student practice saying what you or another student has said. Teach the student to imitate inflectional patterns and facial expressions as well as to repeat the words. Video record this activity and have the student analyze his/her success at this activity.

19. Pair the student with a peer and have them take turns being interviewed and interviewing. This may be done with the students acting as themselves or pretending to be fictitious characters. Emphasize the appropriate use of ritualistic greetings/closings.

20. Teach the student to take turns (e.g., each student may use the colored pencils for 15 minutes, each student may have three turns, etc.).

21. Use a private signal (e.g., holding up a finger, etc.) to remind the student to use appropriate greetings/closings.

22. Have the student use a play phone to practice greetings/closings.

23. Choose a peer to participate with the student in different activities and model appropriate responses to environmental social cues.

24. Reinforce the student for adjusting his/her behavior to various social cues and expectations from one environment or activity to another.

25. Make sure there is adult supervision when the student is playing games with others.

26. Carefully consider the student's age and experience before expecting him/her to respond appropriately to environmental cues in social situations.

27. Make sure the academic and social demands of the situation are within the student's ability level.

28. Audio record the student and have him/her listen to the recording to determine instances in which he/she is using appropriate/inappropriate greetings/closings.

29. Have the student ask questions about environmental social cues not understood.

30. Practice sharing by having each student work with a particular school material for an established length of time. At the end of the time period (e.g., ten minutes), have each student pass his/her material to another student.

31. Have the student's hearing checked if it has not been recently checked.

32. Model appropriate positive verbal greetings, requests, and indications of disagreement for the student.

33. Point out examples of appropriate verbal and nonverbal language usage involving ritualistic greetings and closings as they occur during the day.

34. Have the student practice appropriate responses to environmental social cues with the teacher(s) in classroom activities (e.g., simulations, role-playing, etc.).

35. Have the student practice appropriate verbal exchanges which should be made (e.g., *Excuse me. I'm sorry.*).

36. Reinforce the student for asking the meaning of environmental social cues not understood (e.g., rules, etc.).

37. Teach the student to be aware of listener response to determine if the meaning of his/her greeting/closing has been received accurately.

38. Talk to the student before playing a game and remind him/her of the importance of taking turns.

39. Provide the student with clearly stated expectations for all situations.

40. Teach the student the concept of sharing by having the student borrow from others or loan things to others.

41. Have the student work directly with a peer to model sharing and taking turns. As the student demonstrates success, gradually increase the size of the group.

42. Design activities in which each student takes short turns. Increase the length of each student's turn as the student demonstrates success at taking turns.

43. Encourage the student to participate in social situations in which he/she is likely to respond successfully to environmental social cues.

44. Prepare the student in advance for environmental and social expectations to facilitate his/her ability to successfully respond.

45. Identify expectations of different environments and help the student develop the skills to be successful in those environments.

46. Provide enough materials, activities, etc., so sharing and taking turns will not always be necessary.

47. Create a communication unit for the entire classroom which includes the basic rules of conversation.

48. Make the student responsible for identifying social cues with his/her peers (e.g., saying please and thank you at lunch and during snack times).

49. Allow the student to have many turns and enough materials to satisfy his/her immediate needs, and gradually require sharing and taking turns.

50. Prompt the student to help him/her use greetings/closings more appropriately (e.g., Teacher says, "How are you?" and the student does not respond. Teacher then says, "I'm fine today. How are you?").

51. Make sure explanations regarding how the student should respond to social cues are delivered in a way the student understands. This can be checked by asking the student to repeat the explanation in his/her own words.

52. Have the student participate in an activity with one peer and gradually increase the size of the group as the student demonstrates success.

53. Give the student responsibilities in school and community environments which promote his/her ability to socially interact in a positive manner.

54. Do not allow students to bring unnecessary personal possessions to school.

55. Encourage appropriate eye contact in all communicative interactions. Say, "Eye contact means you are being attentive and listening. When you do not look at the person talking to you, they think you are being rude, not listening, or ignoring them. It is important to turn to the person's direction, look in their vicinity or at their face when they are talking."

56. Have the student participate in simulated conversational activities with feedback designed to teach conversational skills (e.g., greetings, closings, questions, topics of conversations, etc.).

57. Allow the student to interact with a group of peers with whom he/she feels comfortable to practice appropriate responses to environmental cues.

58. Teach the student social interaction skills (e.g., ways in which to appropriately respond to others when first seeing them or when leaving them, etc.). Be specific about phrases which are appropriate to use and situations in which you would use them.

59. To facilitate success in responding to nonverbal facial cues, have the student observe and imitate the responses of peers to nonverbal facial cues. For example, when the student is learning to interact appropriately as a spectator at a sporting event, he/she can imitate the behavior of peers who display appropriate behavior at the sporting event.

60. Provide the student with many experiences to share with others and have materials returned. When the student learns that shared materials will be returned, the student will be more likely to share in the future.

61. Provide the student with many academic and social successes.

62. As much as possible, match cues to the student's ability to respond (e.g., visual cues are used for students who cannot hear, auditory cues and symbols are used for students who cannot see, etc.).

63. Make sure that shared materials are returned to the student so he/she will develop a positive concept of sharing.

64. Choose a peer to model the use of ritualistic greetings and closings for the student.

65. Communicate with parents (e.g., notes home, phone calls, etc.) to share information about the student's progress. The parents may reinforce the student at home for demonstrating appropriate social interaction skills at school.

66. Maintain a realistic level of expectation for sharing school materials based on the student's age level and/or ability to share.

67. Greet or acknowledge the student as often as possible (e.g., hallways, cafeteria, welcome to class, a job well done, etc.). Encourage him/her to acknowledge you in return.

68. Teach the student conversational phrases (e.g., "How are you?" "I'm fine." "How's it going?" "See you later." etc.) to use when greetings/ closings are appropriate.

69. Teach the student appropriate positive verbal requests (e.g., "Please pass the paper." "May I please be excused?" "Will you please help me?" etc.).

70. Teach the student appropriate positive ways to verbally indicate disagreement (e.g., "Excuse me, I think I was here first." "Pardon me, I need to get to my locker." "I'm sorry, but I don't think that's correct.").

71. Have the student practice waiting to take a turn if he/she is unwilling to do so.

72. Teach the student appropriate positive verbal greetings (e.g., "Hi, how are you doing?" "Good to see you." "Haven't seen you in a long time.").

73. Have the student practice social interaction skills with a specified number of peers throughout the school day.

74. Make sure that positive reinforcement is not inadvertently given for inappropriate social interactions (e.g., attending to the student only when he/she has demonstrated inappropriate social interactions).

75. Treat the student with respect. Talk in an objective manner at all times.

76. Provide repeated practice in responding appropriately to environmental social cues.

77. Establish rules for sharing school materials:
- Ask for materials you wish to use.
- Exchange materials carefully.
- Return materials when not in use.
- Offer to share materials with others.
- Take care of shared materials.
- Call attention to materials that need repair.

Review rules often. Reinforce the student for following the rules.

78. Model sharing (e.g., by loaning pencils, paper, etc.).

79. Reinforce the student for sharing: (a) give the student a tangible reward (e.g., classroom privileges, line leading, passing out materials, five minutes free time, etc.) or (b) give the student an intangible reward (e.g., praise, fist bump, smile, etc.).

80. Provide the student with simulation activities in the classroom to teach successful responses to environmental social cues.

81. Teach the student communication skills (e.g., hand raising, expressing needs in written and/or verbal form, etc.).

82. Make sure that every student gets to use materials, take a turn, etc., and that there is no opportunity for selfishness.

83. Establish a set of rules for group games:
- Follow the rules of the game.
- Take turns.
- Make positive comments.
- Work as a team member.
- Be a good sport.

Review rules often. Reinforce the student for following the rules.

84. Establish cues (e.g., bells, rules, manners, etc.) that the student is expected to follow.

85. Interact frequently with the student to monitor his/her social interactions.

86. Do not force the student to interact with other students with whom he/she is not completely comfortable.

87. Do not allow the student to bring items to school that he/she is not willing to share (e.g., games, toys, etc.).

88. Point out to the student the natural rewards of sharing and taking turns (e.g., personal satisfaction, friendships, companionship, etc.).

89. Make sure that other students are sharing with the student so a reciprocal relationship can be achieved.

90. Have the student practice taking messages to different persons in the school setting (e.g., librarian, school counselor, principal, etc.) and later actually deliver messages. Include ritualistic greetings/closings during the practice.

91. Speak with the student to explain that he/she is not using ritualistic greetings/closings when appropriate. Be specific about the types of interactions the student is using inappropriately and the situation(s) in which they are used.

92. Assess the appropriateness of the social situation in relation to the student's ability to be successful.

93. Teach a unit which is centered around finding examples of language which are appropriate for use in ritualistic greetings and closings.

94. Determine an individual(s) in the school environment with whom the student would most want to engage in a conversation (e.g., custodian, librarian, resource teacher, principal, older student, etc.). Allow the student to spend time carrying on a conversation with the individual(s) each day. Make sure these people model appropriate use of greetings/closings.

95. Role-play various situations with the student to model appropriate social interactions (e.g., appropriate greetings, closings, conversations, etc.).

96. Reinforce other students in the classroom for appropriate use of ritualistic greetings and closings.

97. Write a contract with the student specifying what behavior is expected (e.g., responding appropriately to social cues) and what reinforcement will be made available when the terms of the contract have been met.

98. Maintain consistent expectations within the ability level of the student.

99. Provide students with adequate time to complete activities requiring sharing, so the selfish use of school materials is not necessary for success. Students are less likely to share if sharing reduces the likelihood of finishing on time, being successful, etc.

100. Rephrase the student's words to assist the student in utilizing more appropriate greetings/closings.

101. Speak to the student to explain (a) what the student is doing wrong and (b) what the student should be doing.

102. Make sure the student understands the natural consequences of inappropriate social interactions (e.g., others will choose not to interact with him/her, exclusion from activities, etc.).

103. Pair social cues with verbal explanations and immediate reinforcement for appropriate responses.

104. Reinforce the student for using ritualistic greetings/closings when appropriate: (a) give the student a tangible reward (e.g., classroom privileges, line leading, passing out materials, five minutes free time, etc.) or (b) give the student an intangible reward (e.g., praise, fist bump, smile, etc.).

105. Explain the benefits of trying one's best to follow social cues in the community (e.g., a person would be more welcome to return, a person might acquire positive social regard from other people, etc.).

106. Provide the student with verbal reminders before entering a social situation (e.g., "Remember to shake hands when being introduced." "Say, 'Excuse me,' when you need to leave a conversation.").

107. Use vocabulary that is within the student's level of comprehension when delivering directions, explanations, and information.

108. Take advantage of opportunities for the students to work together (e.g., when there is a spill, assign students different responsibilities for cleaning it up; when a new student enters the classroom, assign different students responsibilities for orientation; etc.).

1. Use videos to teach the student about emotions.

2. Use videos to instruct the student regarding social skills.

3. Involve the student in a social skills group.

4. Use individualized social stories to explain how others feel in a variety of situations.

5. Use written stories/books to teach about actions and feelings.

6. Use the student's past experiences to explain others' actions and feelings associated with the actions. Connect the other person's feelings to a feeling the student has had in the past (e.g., "Remember when you didn't get a tricycle at the playground? That made you angry and sad. Well, Johnny feels like that when you take his crayons.").

7. Act as a shadow behind the student during play. When his/her actions adversely affect another person, assist the student to respond appropriately.

8. Explain how the student's actions affect others and the importance of appropriate behavior. Make your explanations short and to the point.

9. Use one event and explain how many different feelings can result from one event.

10. Praise the student for demonstrating understanding of how his/her actions made someone feel.

11. Determine if the student understands nonverbal cues (e.g., understanding someone's face when it is happy, sad, excited, surprised, mad, etc.).

12. Use pictures of faces to identify various feelings of others.

13. Teach the student to "check in" when talking about a subject of great interest. Have the student ask his/her peer/teacher/other person, "Would you like to hear more?" This keeps the student in check when he/she wants to dominate the conversation.

14. Have the student carry a point card at all times so that he/she can be reinforced anywhere in the school environment for demonstrating appropriate behavior.

15. Deliver a predetermined signal (e.g., hand signal, verbal cue, etc.) when the student begins to display behaviors which are inappropriate for the situation.

16. Maintain a consistent routine.

17. Have the student practice "echoing" what you or another student says. Teach the student to imitate inflectional patterns and facial expressions as well as to repeat the words.

18. Create and reinforce activities (e.g., school bulletin board, class project, bake sale, etc.) in which students work together for a common goal rather than individual success or recognition. Point out that larger accomplishments are realized through group effort rather than by individual effort.

19. Help the student develop a friendship by pairing him/her with another student for activities. As the student demonstrates success, gradually increase the number of students in the group.

20. Have the student make a list of consequences associated with frequently occurring behaviors (e.g., By disrupting others, I will be perceived as unmannerly. By making unnecessary noises, people will avoid me.).

21. Express your feelings in a socially acceptable way.

22. Make the consequence of a behavior obvious by identifying the consequence as it occurs and discussing alternative behavior which would have prevented the particular consequence.

23. Carefully consider the student's age and experience before expecting him/her to get along in a group.

24. Have the student ask questions about directions, explanations, or instructions he/she does not understand.

25. Have the student practice appropriate interactions with the teacher(s) in classroom activities (e.g., simulations, role-playing, etc.).

26. Allow the student to be a member of a group without requiring active participation.

27. Reinforce the student for appropriately interacting with other students: (a) give the student a tangible reward (e.g., classroom privileges, line leading, passing out materials, five minutes free time, etc.) or (b) give the student an intangible reward (e.g., praise, fist bump, smile, etc.).

28. Instruct the student to carry a note pad with him/her at all times and to write information down to help him/her remember.

29. Make sure that consequences are delivered consistently for behavior demonstrated (i.e., appropriate behavior results in positive consequences and inappropriate behavior results in negative consequences).

30. Attempt to provide equal attention to all students in the classroom.

31. Help the student develop attention-maintaining behaviors (e.g., maintain eye contact, take notes on the subject, ask questions related to the subject, etc.).

32. Help the student become aware of his/her tone of voice when greeting, requesting, and/or disagreeing with others by calling attention to voice inflections which are inappropriate for the situation.

33. Inform others who will be working with the student (e.g., teachers, the principal, clerks, etc.) about the student's tendency to ignore consequences of his/her behaviors.

34. Have the student choose a group of peers with whom he/she feels comfortable to play group games.

35. Maintain mobility throughout the classroom to supervise student interactions and intervene in conflict situations in which the student is unable to successfully solve the problem.

36. Make sure that the classroom activity is not so stimulating it makes successful interaction with peers difficult.

37. Teach and practice effective communication skills. These skills include listening, maintaining eye contact, and positive body language.

38. When engaging in verbal communication, be sure to use vocabulary that is within the student's level of comprehension.

39. Make sure that verbal communications are delivered in a nonthreatening manner (e.g., positive voice, facial expressions, language, etc.).

40. Reinforce the student for demonstrating acceptable behavior based on the length of time the student can be successful. As the student demonstrates success, gradually increase the length of time required for reinforcement.

41. Assign older peers with desirable social skills to interact with the student in group games.

42. Try various groups to determine the situation in which the student is most successful.

43. Help the student develop an awareness of himself/herself and those around him/her. Have the student periodically step back and ask himself/herself, "Am I bothering or disturbing others?"

44. Identify the expectations of different environments and help the student develop the skills to be successful in those environments.

45. Write group contracts which encourage students to work together for group success.

46. Evaluate the appropriateness of expectations for the student to demonstrate appropriate social interaction skills.

47. Involve the student in extracurricular activities to encourage interactions with others.

48. Maintain a consistent format for verbal communications with the student.

49. Maintain visibility to and from the student. The teacher should be able to see the student and the student should be able to see the teacher. Make eye contact possible at all times.

50. Acknowledge the student when he/she seeks attention verbally instead of making it necessary for the student to gain attention through physical contact.

51. Have the student put himself/herself in someone else's place (e.g., ask the student to think about how he/she would feel if someone called him/her dumb or stupid).

52. Help the student to identify inappropriate behaviors and teach him/her ways to change those behaviors.

53. Have the student participate in a game activity with one peer. As the student demonstrates success, gradually increase the size of the group.

54. Set up a situation in which the student can "role-play" various emotions. Provide feedback on how effectively the idea was communicated.

55. Have the student participate in group games of short duration. As the student demonstrates success, gradually increase the duration of group games.

56. Have the student practice transitional activities to reduce the effects of stimulating activities (e.g., put head on desk, listen to the teacher read a story, put headphones on and listen to relaxing music, etc.).

57. Have the student participate in simulated social activities with feedback designed to improve behavioral responses to various social situations.

58. Give the student responsibilities in group situations so peers may view the student in a more positive way.

59. Deliver directions, explanations, and instructions in a clear and concise manner to reduce the student's need to ask questions.

60. Make sure the student is aware of the different expectations for different social situations (e.g., rules, schedules, directions, etc.).

61. Intervene early when there is a problem to prevent more serious problems from occurring.

62. Make sure that reinforcement is not inadvertently given for the student's inappropriate comments or behaviors (e.g., attending to the student only when he/she demonstrates behaviors which are inappropriate to the situation).

63. Encourage the student to model the behavior of peers who are successful.

64. Choose a peer to model appropriate adjustment of his/her behavior to the expectations of different social situations for the student.

65. Communicate with parents (e.g., notes home, phone calls, etc.) to share information about the student's progress. The parents may reinforce the student at home for appropriately interacting with other peers at school.

66. Allow natural consequences to occur so the student can learn that persons who adjust behavior to the demands of the social situation are more successful than those who are inflexible in their behavior (e.g., if you are never willing to compromise to acceptable demands, others may avoid being in social situations with you).

67. Establish classroom rules:
- Concentrate while working.
- Remain in your seat.
- Finish task.
- Meet task expectations.
- Raise your hand.

Review rules often. Reinforce the student for following the rules.

68. Evaluate the expectation for peer interaction to determine if the student can be successful in the interactions and for the expected length of time.

69. Group the student with peers who will be appropriate role models and are likely to facilitate the student's academic and behavioral successes.

70. Reduce distracting stimuli (e.g., place the student on the front row, provide a carrel or office away from distractions, etc.). This is used as a means of reducing distracting stimuli and not as a form of punishment.

71. Have the student study, practice, simulate, etc., the rules for competitive activities before participating.

72. Teach the student to recognize appropriate times to talk to other students (e.g., between activities, during breaks, at recess, etc.).

73. Teach the student to recognize the appropriate time to speak (e.g., when the teacher has finished speaking, after raising his/her hand, to make comments within the context of the situation, to make comments that are a follow-up to what has just been said, etc.).

74. Assign the student to situations in which he/she is likely to interact successfully with another person.

75. Make sure the student recognizes inappropriate social interactions (e.g., call attention to the comments when they occur, record each instance, terminate the activity when the comment occurs, etc.).

76. Model appropriate ways to respond to interactions with other students or teachers.

77. If the student has responded inappropriately to a conflict situation, take time to explore with the student appropriate solutions which could have been used in solving the problem.

78. In conjunction with other school personnel, develop as much consistency across the various environments as possible (e.g., rules, criteria for success, behavioral expectations, consequences, etc.).

79. Encourage the student to monitor behavior by asking himself/herself questions: *What should I be doing right now?*, *Is what I have to say relevant to this topic?*, and *Is this a good time for me to comment?*

80. Choose a peer to sit/work directly with the student in different settings or activities (e.g., art, music, P.E.; on the bus; tutoring; group projects; running errands in the building; break time; etc.). As the student becomes comfortable working with one other student, gradually increase the size of the group.

81. Teach the student problem-solving skills: (a) identify the problem, (b) identify goals and objectives, (c) develop strategies, (d) develop a plan of action, and (e) carry out the plan.

82. Establish rules for conversing with others (e.g., wait your turn to talk, stand quietly by the person with whom you want to talk until you are acknowledged, excuse yourself when you interrupt others, etc.). These rules should be consistent and followed by everyone in the class. Talk about the rules often.

83. Establish a set of rules for group games (e.g., follow rules of the game, take turns, make positive comments, work as a team member, be a good sport, etc.).

84. Help the student develop social awareness (e.g., people may be embarrassed by what you say, feelings can be hurt by comments, tact is the best policy, remember interactions which have made you feel good and treat others in the same manner, etc.).

85. Interact frequently with the student to maintain involvement.

86. Make sure that the student understands that participation with others is contingent upon appropriate behavior.

87. Make sure that the student can verbalize the reason for real-life outcomes of behavior (e.g., why the student had to leave the class line on the way to recess, why he/she earned the privilege of being line leader, etc.).

88. Play the game with the student before he/she engages in the game with peers to model appropriate behavior, determine the student's ability to play the game, determine the student's ability to follow behavior rules, etc.

89. Do not criticize the student. When correcting the student, be honest yet supportive. Never cause the student to feel negatively about himself/herself.

90. Through interviews with other students and observations, determine those characteristics of the student which interfere with successful interactions during group games to determine skills or behaviors the student needs to develop for successful interactions.

91. Structure the environment to limit opportunities for inappropriate behavior (e.g., keep the student participating in activities, have the student seated near the teacher, maintain visibility to and from the student, etc.).

92. Teach the student to take cues from others (e.g., if he/she blurts out comments with no response from others, stop talking; when there is silence in class, it is not necessary to fill the silence with comments; etc.)

93. Assess the degree of task difficulty in relation to the student's ability to perform the task successfully.

94. Teach the student behaviors that promote self-control (e.g., placing hands on desk, sitting with feet on the floor, making eye contact with the person who is talking, etc.).

95. Help the student realize that all behavior has negative or positive consequences. Encourage the student to practice behaviors that will lead to positive consequences.

96. Clarify for the student that it is his/her behavior which determines consequences (e.g., positive or negative).

97. Modify or adjust situations that cause the student to demonstrate behaviors that are different or extreme.

98. Do not force the student to interact with individuals with whom he/she is not completely comfortable.

99. Be consistent in expecting the student to behave appropriately. Do not allow the student to interrupt one time and expect him/her not to interrupt the next time.

100. Choose activities in which the student is likely to interact successfully with peers.

101. Make sure beforehand that the student is able to successfully participate in the activity (e.g., the student understands the rules, the student is familiar with the activity, the student will be compatible with the other student engaged in the free time activity, etc.).

102. Remove the student from the situation until he/she can demonstrate appropriate behavior.

103. Role-play various situations with the student to model appropriate social interactions (e.g., appropriate greetings, closings, conversations, etc.).

104. Explain to the student the importance of treating people as he/she wants to be treated (e.g., people will not interrupt you if you do not interrupt them).

105. Write a contract with the student specifying what behavior is expected (e.g., interacting appropriately with peers) and what reinforcement will be made available when the terms of the contract have been met.

106. Maintain consistent expectations within the ability level of the student.

107. Using "sequence cards" have the student place the cards in the appropriate order and explain the sequence; then have the student tell you what might have happened before or after the provided sequence.

108. Assess the appropriateness of the social situation in relation to the student's ability to function successfully.

109. Demonstrate to the student the appropriate way to get someone's attention without interrupting.

110. Explain to the student the reasons why talking beyond what is expected and at inappropriate times is unacceptable (e.g., impolite, interrupts others, etc.).

111. Encourage the student to think of more appropriate ways to have handled the situation.

112. Select nonacademic activities designed to facilitate appropriate interaction between the student and another person (e.g., board games, model building, coloring, etc.).

113. Speak with the student to explain (a) what the student is doing wrong (e.g., taking action before thinking about what he/she is doing) and (b) what the student should be doing (e.g., considering consequences, thinking about the correct response, considering other persons, etc.).

114. Experiment with various groupings to determine the group in which the student is most comfortable in adjusting his/her behavior to the demands of various social situations.

115. Encourage the student to use gestures when necessary to clarify his/her message. Gestures may also facilitate recall of vocabulary the student is having difficulty retrieving.

116. Teach the student a variety of ways to solve problems in conflict situations (e.g., withdrawing, reasoning, calling upon an arbitrator, apologizing, compromising, allowing others the benefit of the doubt, etc.).

117. Use role-play to simulate various situations the student might be involved with, and to teach the student how to interact appropriately (e.g., how to have an appropriate conversation at the lunch table, how to ask to play a game with others, etc.).

118. Teach the student appropriate verbal and nonverbal responses to common everyday situations.

119. Have the student role-play ways to solve problems in conflict situations with peers and adults (e.g., withdrawing, reasoning, calling upon an arbitrator, apologizing, compromising, allowing others the benefit of the doubt, etc.).

120. Determine the peer(s) with whom the student would prefer to interact and facilitate the interaction.

121. Conduct a sociometric activity with the class to determine the peer who would most prefer to interact with the student.

1. Use pictures, mirrors, etc., to teach the student how to identify various emotions.

2. Use personalized social stories to explain the emotions of others and how the student should respond.

3. Create a form of communication if the student is nonverbal (e.g., pictures, assistive communication device, etc.).

4. Explain/teach the purpose of understanding others.

5. Teach simple social skills at the appropriate developmental age of the student.

6. Modify the "If You're Happy and You Know It . . ." song to include other emotions.

7. Use videos to teach the student about emotions, sharing and the need to interact with others.

8. Have the student attend a social skills group.

9. Teach the student simple actions/words that can be used when he/she identifies an emotion expressed by another person.

10. Use social stories to explain what people do when they identify an individual's emotions.

11. Begin on the student's level to teach emotions (e.g., "Oh no, Thomas the Train® has fallen off the track. He is very sad!" "When I see a sad face or tears, I say, 'Are you okay?' and give a pat on the shoulder to feel better.").

12. Act as a shadow behind the student during play. When the individual interacting with the student displays an emotional response, assist the student to respond appropriately (e.g., "I see that Hanna made a frown face. That tells me she is sad. She didn't like it when you took her train. Better give it back and make her smile/happy again.").

13. Gain the student's attention prior to requesting social referencing by removing items that make concentrating difficult.

14. Explain how to read others' emotions and use that information to make the next choice. The student may not understand this type of interaction and may need extra help understanding how to read others' emotional state. Make your explanations short and to the point.

15. Praise the student for any action made that was based on understanding the feelings of others.

16. Use pictures of faces to identify various feelings. Help the student to understand these pictures and feelings.

17. Play *Guess That Feeling* game. Make faces and ask the student what you are feeling.

18. Have the student practice "echoing" what you or another student says. Teach the student to imitate inflectional patterns and facial expressions as well as to repeat the words.

19. Deliver a predetermined signal (e.g., hand signal, verbal cue, etc.) when the student begins to demonstrate inappropriate behavior in his/her immediate environment.

20. Deliver a predetermined signal (e.g., holding up a finger, etc.) to remind the student to give a relevant response.

21. Provide the student with a book without words and have him/her narrate the story.

22. Provide the student with a list of questions involving opinions, feelings, and/or emotions and assist him/her in answering verbally (e.g., "How do you feel when you get an A on a test?" "Do you think recess should be before or after lunch?" "Should people wear seat belts?" etc.).

23. Express your feelings in a socially acceptable way.

24. Allow passive participation as a social choice across learning activities and environments.

25. Have the student illustrate a story about an event which has emotional overtones. Point out the emotions portrayed or involved in the story.

26. Assign responsibilities related to activities (e.g., being a leader, passing out materials, being a peer tutor, etc.) which may facilitate the student's opportunities for interaction.

27. When the student makes an irrelevant response, have him/her rephrase in his/her own words the original question to check for comprehension.

28. Audio record the student and have him/her listen to the recording to determine instances in which he/she makes an irrelevant response.

29. Write a contract stating appropriate ways to respond to others and identify what reinforcement will be made available when the terms of the contract have been met.

30. Have the student practice appropriate verbal interactions with peers and teacher(s).

31. When engaging in verbal communication, be sure to use vocabulary that is within the student's level of comprehension.

32. Make sure that verbal communications are delivered in a nonthreatening manner (e.g., positive voice, facial expressions, language, etc.).

33. Reduce the emphasis on competition. Frequent or continuous failure may result in embarrassment which will cause reluctance to participate.

34. Provide the student with concrete examples of ways to express opinions, feelings and/or emotions (e.g., speaking, writing, gestures, drawing, etc.)

35. Allow the student to be a member of a group without requiring active participation.

36. Do not criticize. When correcting the student, be honest yet supportive. Never cause the student to feel negatively about himself/herself.

37. Reinforce the student for demonstrating appropriate behaviors related to the situation based on the length of time the student can be successful. As the student demonstrates success, gradually increase the length of time required for reinforcement.

38. Reinforce the student for demonstrating appropriate behaviors related to the situation: (a) give the student a tangible reward (e.g., classroom privileges, line leading, passing out materials, five minutes free time, etc.) or (b) give the student an intangible reward (e.g., praise, fist bump, smile, etc.).

39. Try various groupings to determine the group in which the student is most comfortable.

40. Provide the student with direct eye contact and communicate to him/her that you expect him/her to do the same with you.

41. Encourage students to give each other positive feedback for small group contributions and other forms of positive verbal exchange.

42. Make a list of emotions (e.g., sad, scared, happy, etc.) and have the student express them in a sentence.

43. Ask the parents to encourage the student's use of relevant responses at home by praising him/her when these are used.

44. Allow the student to finish responding before you begin talking. Reinforce other students in the classroom for allowing the student to finish responding before they begin talking.

45. Provide praise or recognition for smaller increments of success so that the student may become gradually accustomed to the recognition.

46. Maintain a consistent format for verbal communications with the student.

47. Set up a situation in which the student can role-play various emotions. Provide feedback on how effectively the idea was communicated.

48. Allow the student to interact with peers with whom he/she feels comfortable.

49. Encourage the student to interact with others.

50. Choose a peer to model for the student appropriate interactions during classroom activities.

51. Teach the student social interaction skills (e.g., ways in which to appropriately respond to others' attempts to be friendly, complimentary, sympathetic, etc.). Begin with the most basic skills and move to more complex skills.

52. Provide opportunities for appropriate interactions within the classroom (e.g., peer models engaged in appropriate interactions).

53. Include opportunities for small-group exchanges in social situations (e.g., recess, lunchtime, school parties, dances, etc.).

54. Make sure that reinforcement is not inadvertently given for the student's inappropriate comments or behaviors (e.g., attending to the student only when he/she demonstrates behaviors which are inappropriate to the situation).

55. Ask questions which stimulate language. Avoid questions which can be answered by yes/no or a nod of the head (e.g., "What did you do at recess?" rather than "Did you play on the slide?" or "Tell me about your vacation." rather than "Did you stay home over the holidays?" etc.).

56. Communicate with parents (e.g., notes home, phone calls, etc.) to share information about the student's progress. The parents may reinforce the student at home for interacting appropriately with another person at school.

57. Evaluate the expectation for peer interaction to determine if the student can be successful in the interactions and for the expected length of time.

58. Provide the student with pictures of people who are happy, sad, angry, etc., and have him/her create stories which are based upon the pictures.

59. Create a *Feeling Box*. Place an unseen item in the box and have the student describe what it feels like, while another student tries to guess what it is.

60. Teach the student to recognize and make appropriate comments (e.g., comments within the context of the situation, comments that are a follow-up to what has just been said, etc.).

61. Point out examples of relevant verbal responses as they occur during the day.

62. Model appropriate ways to respond to others who are friendly, complimentary, sympathetic, etc.

63. Choose a peer to sit/work directly with the student in different settings or activities (e.g., art, music, P.E., on the bus, tutoring, group projects, running errands in the building, recess, etc.). As the student becomes comfortable working with one person, gradually increase the size of the group.

64. Teach the student communication skills (e.g., hand raising, expressing needs in written and/or verbal form, etc.). Begin with the most basic skills and move to more complex skills.

65. Help the student develop social awareness (e.g., people may be embarrassed by what you say, feelings can be hurt by comments, tact is the best policy, remember interactions which have made you feel good and treat others in the same manner, etc.).

66. Do not force the student to interact with individuals with whom he/she is not completely comfortable.

67. Each day provide the student with situations which elicit particular emotions and assist the student in expressing those emotions (e.g., "A stranger takes you by the arm in a department store. How do you feel?" "You see smoke coming out of a neighbor's house. Are you happy?" etc.).

68. Make sure that the student's feelings are considered when it is necessary to discuss his/her irrelevant responses (i.e., handle comments in such a way as to not diminish the student's enthusiasm for participation).

69. Routinely record the student's speech and point out irrelevant comments. With each successive taping, reinforce the student as his/her use of relevant responses improves.

70. Assess the appropriateness of the social situation in relation to the student's ability to function successfully.

71. Structure the activities of the situation according to the need/abilities of the student (e.g., establish rules, limit the stimulation of the activities, limit the length of activities, consider time of day, etc.).

72. Modify situations that cause the student to be reluctant to participate (e.g., degree of difficulty, competition, fear of failure, threat of embarrassment, etc.).

73. Identify peers with whom the student would prefer to interact and facilitate interaction.

74. Intervene early to prevent the student's behavior from becoming inappropriate.

75. Reinforce those students in the classroom who express opinions, feelings, and/or emotions.

76. Evaluate the appropriateness of the task to determine (a) if the task is too easy, (b) if the task is too difficult, and (c) if the length of time scheduled to complete the task is adequate.

77. Provide the student with time and encouragement to establish rapport regardless of his/her lack of verbal response. Any major change in behavior, such as a student opting total withdrawal after displaying acceptable and typical age appropriate social behaviors, may warrant the need of additional support for the student.

78. Conduct a sociometric activity to identify peers who would most prefer to interact with the student in classroom activities.

79. Select nonacademic activities designed to facilitate appropriate interaction between the student and another person (e.g., board games, model building, coloring, etc.).

80. Encourage the student to use gestures when necessary to clarify his/her message. Gestures may also facilitate recall of vocabulary the student is having difficulty retrieving.

81. Choose an older peer with desirable social skills to interact with the student.

82. Have the student role-play various situations in which relevant verbal responses are important (e.g., during a job interview).

83. Allow a transition period when changing environments so the student can make adjustments in his/her behavior.

84. Determine the peer(s) with whom the student would prefer to interact and facilitate the interaction.

85. Choose a peer with whom the student is most likely to be able to successfully interact (e.g., a student with similar interests, background, classes, behavior patterns, nonacademic schedule, etc.).

86. Have the student interact with one other person for short periods of time to facilitate success. As the student demonstrates success, gradually increase the length of time the student interacts.

87. Encourage verbal expression in your classroom and listen carefully when the student is trying to express opinions, feelings or emotions about any topic.

88. Maintain consistent expectations within the ability level of the student.

1. Consult with other professionals regarding difficulties (e.g., psychiatrist and/or doctor to determine medical needs, occupational therapist to determine functioning abilities, speech language pathologist to determine language needs, social worker, etc.).

2. Consider the student's need for various types of input. Have the student assessed by an occupational therapist to determine sensory needs. Seeking specific sensory input may explain why the student hangs on others, crashes into others or bumps others.

3. Provide the student with several ways that he/she can interact with others, without invading personal space. One way can be by sitting across the table from others or sitting on carpet squares to define one's space.

4. Teach the student who can be in close proximity of his/her body versus those that should not be close. Use various concentric rings. In the center ring draw a picture of the student. In the center rings also go family members. The next ring out contains good friends to whom one would give a high five. The outer ring contains persons he/she knows in the community but are not good friends. These people would include neighbors, members of his/her religious affiliation or individuals from his/her school. These people would be given a fist bump.

5. Teach the students in the class to give a visual or verbal warning to the "space invader."

6. Determine the student's ability to navigate the classroom. Frequently, those who do not process proprioceptive (i.e., sensory reception) input have poor self-concepts and struggle with body position in space. Consult with an occupational therapist to determine the student's needs.

7. Remove other distracters (e.g., visual, auditory, taste, smell, touch, movement, etc.).

8. Use the student's form of speech for communication (e.g., pictures, single words, single sentences, etc.), to explain personal space.

9. Use videos and songs to teach the student about personal space.

10. Use books that are of special interest to the student. Emphasize the correct use of personal space.

11. Have the student participate in groups that work on practicing appropriate personal space and boundaries. This will provide times when the student can observe others interacting appropriately.

12. Use the student's previous experiences to develop further understanding of personal space and appropriate boundaries of others.

13. Develop opportunities throughout the student's day to practice using appropriate boundaries so he/she practices consistently.

14. Determine the student's level of verbal and nonverbal communication skills. Communicate verbally and nonverbally with the student at his/her level to facilitate appropriate boundaries or personal space.

15. Help the student generalize information by practicing appropriate personal space in a variety of settings.

16. Use personalized social stories to explain personal space in various situations that are specific to the student. Include times where the boundaries are correct and times they are incorrect (provide correction). Review these stories prior to engaging in activities and prior to going home. Have the student repeat some of the information to his/her parents/guardians at home to carryover learned information.

17. Have the student role-play situations where appropriate personal space and personal boundaries are the focus.

18. Determine the student's level of understanding. The student may not be able to understand personal space and boundary rules.

19. Determine the student's level of motivation. The student may not use appropriate boundaries or demonstrate appropriate personal space because he/she is not motivated to do so.

20. Use the student's interests to teach specific rules of personal space.

21. Determine if your expectations are appropriate for the level of the student.

22. Be sure to use appropriate personal space and boundaries in the student's presence.

23. Provide the student with an individual work space.

24. Model the desired behavior by putting your arm up to demonstrate that you are an arms length away when carrying on a conversation with the student.

25. Use tape to mark a space on the floor around desks to identify each student's space. Permission must be obtained before entering another student's space.

26. Use a key word or phrase (e.g., my space or bubble) to indicate that the student is in someone else's personal space.

27. Create social stories which discuss personal space.

28. Create an *Am I too Close?* activity for pairs of students to play.

29. Reward desired behavior when it is maintained for a given period of time or during an activity.

30. Have the student hold a cumbersome object while walking down a hallway.

31. Have the student keep his/her thumbs in his/her pockets when walking down the hallway or when standing in a group.

32. Have the student hold onto the end of a piece of rope or a jump rope that is 2-3 feet long. The teacher holds the other end. The student must keep the rope straight while walking or talking with the teacher. This gives the student a visual idea of personal space.

33. Say, "personal space," when the student gets too close. This is something that can be done at home as well as school.

34. If the student is bumping into others, create a safe place to bump into with permission (e.g., gym mat up against the wall, etc.).

35. Use role-playing with classmates to act out proper behaviors.

36. Teach the student to ask for the teacher/adult's arm or offer his/her arm to a lady. This will help eliminate inappropriate personal space issues.

37. If the student likes to climb/bump into others, ask the gym teacher to choose him/her to demonstrate in the gym. This can be used as a reward for respecting personal space in other settings.

38. Put a hula hoop or string around the student so he/she can visually see personal space. Adjust the size as he/she lessens unwanted behavior.

39. Document activities, persons present, etc., prior to the personal space issue. Review documentation daily/weekly to see if there is a pattern.

40. Provide the student with a predetermined signal when he/she does not respect the personal space of others.

41. Have the student develop an awareness of the consequences of his/her behavior by writing down or talking through problems which may occur due to his/her failure to identify the personal space of others (e.g., perceived as unmannerly, avoided, etc.).

42. Have the student ask questions about part of the activity or the responses you expect of him/her that the student does not understand.

43. Teach the student to avoid typical physical exchanges by giving others room to pass, taking turns, watching the movement of others around him/her, etc.

44. Model socially acceptable physical contact for the student (e.g., fist bump, pat on the back, etc.).

45. Try various groupings to find a situation in which the student's need for physical attention can be satisfied by socially acceptable interactions (e.g., holding hands while dancing in an extracurricular activity; a hug for an accomplishment; fist bump, fist bump, or high five in sports; etc.).

46. Provide constant, positive reinforcement for appropriate behavior. Ignore as many inappropriate behaviors as possible.

47. Give the student your full attention when communicating with him/her to prevent his/her need for physical contact.

48. Acknowledge the student when he/she seeks attention verbally instead of making it necessary for the student to gain attention through physical contact.

49. Require that the student identify alternative appropriate behaviors following an instance of inappropriate social interactions (e.g., shaking hands rather than hugging, asking/answering conversational questions, seeking teacher intervention, etc.).

50. Intervene early when there is a problem to prevent more serious problems from occurring.

51. Provide the student with many opportunities to demonstrate appropriate social interaction skills.

52. Choose a peer to model appropriate social interaction skills (e.g., maintaining appropriate distance from others, greeting others appropriately, etc.) for the student.

53. Make sure attention is not inadvertently given to the student for failing to respond to a social cue (e.g., only responding to the student when he/she demonstrates inappropriate behavior).

54. Communicate with parents (e.g., notes home, phone calls, etc.) to share information about the student's progress. The parents may reinforce the student at home for respecting the norms of physical proximity at school.

55. Allow natural consequences to occur as a result of the student's inappropriate behavior (e.g., excessive physical contact may cause people to stay away from the student or may result in pushing, shoving, etc.).

56. Have the student walk on the right hand side of the hallways, stairways, etc.

57. Reinforce the student for respecting the norms of physical proximity based on the length of time the student can be successful. As the student demonstrates success, gradually increase the length of time required for reinforcement.

58. Reinforce the student for respecting norms of physical proximity: (a) give the student a tangible reward (e.g., classroom privileges, line leading, passing out materials, five minutes free time, etc.) or (b) give the student an intangible reward (e.g., praise, fist bump, smile, etc.).

59. Make sure the student sees the relationship between his/her behavior and the consequences which may follow (e.g., touching and hugging people all of the time may result in others not wanting to be around him/her).

60. Provide the student with social interaction in place of physical interaction (e.g., call the student by name, speak to the student, praise, congratulate, etc.).

61. Help the student develop social awareness (e.g., an acquaintance may be uncomfortable if hugged by someone he/she does not know well, it is not acceptable to reveal personal information to someone you have just met, etc.).

62. Avoid inadvertently stimulating the student's unnecessary physical contact (e.g., attire, language used, physical proximity, etc.).

63. Increase supervision (e.g., by teacher, peer, paraprofessional, etc.) of the student when he/she is involved in activities that tend to overexcite him/her to facilitate the student's ability to adjust behavior to different situations.

64. Indicate to the student that public displays of frequent physical contact are inappropriate. Provide the student with high interest activities (e.g., academic activities which are inherently interesting, activities during free time, etc.).

65. Assess the appropriateness of the social situation in relation to the student's ability to function successfully.

66. Role-play various situations with the student to model appropriate social interactions (e.g., appropriate greetings, closings, conversations, etc.).

67. Determine an individual(s) in the school environment with whom the student would most want to engage in a conversation (e.g., custodian, librarian, resource teacher, principal, older student, etc.). Allow the student to spend time carrying on a conversation with the individual(s) each day. Make sure these people model appropriate physical proximity.

68. Have the student lead the line, walk beside the line, walk at the end of the line, etc., to avoid or reduce the contact with other students.

69. Have a peer accompany the student in congested areas of the school to reduce typical physical exchanges and/or intercede should problems occur.

70. Write a contract with the student specifying what behavior is expected (e.g., shaking hands rather than hugging) and what reinforcement will be made available when the terms of the contract have been met.

71. Speak to the student to explain (a) what he/she is doing wrong (e.g., hugging, climbing on others, standing too close, etc.) and (b) what he/she should be doing (e.g., shaking hands when greeting an acquaintance, respecting personal space, etc.).

72. Explain the benefits of trying one's best to follow social cues in the community (e.g., a person would be more welcome to return, a person might acquire positive social regard from other people, etc.).

73. Practice role-playing which involves typical physical exchanges (e.g., being bumped, touched, brushed against, etc.).

74. Explain to the student what he/she has done correctly, what is expected for total correct response, and what he/she can do to improve toward or reach total correct response.

75. Explain to the student what kinds of physical contact are appropriate and acceptable.

76. Pair social cues with verbal explanations and immediate reinforcement for appropriate responses.

77. Encourage faculty/staff members with whom the student interacts to reinforce appropriate physical contact.

78. Use vocabulary that is within the student's level of comprehension when delivering directions, explanations, and information.

79. Provide opportunities for interactions within the classroom to allow the student to practice determining the appropriate amount of personal space (e.g., peer models engaged in interactions which respect personal space).

1. Reinforce the student for participating in group activities or special events, taking responsibility, etc.: (a) give the student a tangible reward (e.g., classroom privileges, line leading, passing out materials, five minutes free time, etc.) or (b) give the student an intangible reward (e.g., praise, fist bump, smile, etc.).

2. Speak with the student to explain (a) what he/she is doing wrong (e.g., failing to take part) and (b) what he/she should be doing (e.g., participating, taking turns, playing, sharing, remaining involved in an activity or group, etc.).

3. Design group projects (e.g., fundraisers) to create a situation for group cohesiveness and loyalty.

4. Choose a peer to sit/work directly with the student (e.g., in different settings or activities such as art, music, P.E.; on the bus; tutoring; group projects; running errands in the building; etc.). As the student becomes comfortable working with one other student, gradually increase the size of the group. Monitor the student's loyalty to one other student and members of the group as it grows.

5. Encourage or reward others for participation in group or special activities.

6. Write a contract with the student specifying what behavior is expected (e.g., taking part in group activities, being a member of a group, working on a project to its completion, etc.) and what reinforcement will be made available when the terms of the contract have been met.

7. Communicate with parents (e.g., notes home, phone calls, etc.) to share information about the student's progress. The parents may reinforce the student at home for participating in group activities, joining a group, maintaining a friendship, etc.

8. Establish classroom rules:
- Concentrate while working.
- Work quietly.
- Remain in your seat.
- Finish task.
- Meet task expectations.

Review rules often. Reinforce the student for following the rules.

9. Reinforce students in the classroom for participating in group activities or special events, working with a friend, etc.

10. Give the student the responsibility of helping another student in the group.

11. Give the student responsibilities in a group so others might view him/her in a positive light.

12. Assign the student activities to perform with a friend which will require teamwork and dependence on one another.

13. Have the student join a team or group activity which exists for a specific purpose (e.g., sports, community services, etc.).

14. Try various groupings to determine the group in which the student is most successful.

15. Have peers invite the student to participate in school activities, extracurricular activities, groups, etc.

16. Ask the student to be the leader of a small group activity if he/she possesses mastery or an interest in the activity.

17. Allow the student to observe group activities without requiring active participation.

18. Reduce the emphasis on competition. Frequent or continuous failure is likely to result in embarrassment which may cause reluctance to participate.

19. Demonstrate respect for the student's opinions, responses, suggestions, etc.

20. Provide the student with many social and academic successes.

21. Provide the student with positive feedback which indicates he/she is successful in interactions with peers, group membership, etc.

22. Present awards for attendance, contributions made to a group, accomplishments in a group, etc.

23. Determine the student's interests. Present activities which require participation based on his/her interests.

24. Have the student choose a special event or interesting activity for the class.

25. Provide the student with success-oriented special events or activities so he/she may develop an interest in them.

26. Modify or adjust situations that cause the student to be reluctant to participate (e.g., degree of difficulty, competition, fear of failure, threat of embarrassment, etc.).

27. Emphasize individual satisfaction, success, or progress rather than winning or beating other students.

28. Provide the student with opportunities for small group participation as opposed to large group participation to develop close friendships, sharing, mutual dependence, etc.

29. Encourage the student to participate in small groups. As the student demonstrates success, gradually increase the size of the group.

30. Encourage the student to share items of special interest with other members of the class.

31. Choose a peer to model appropriate interactions in classroom activities for the student.

32. Have the student choose a group of peers with whom he/she feels comfortable.

33. Determine the peers with whom the student would most prefer to interact in classroom activities and facilitate the interaction.

34. Choose outgoing, nonthreatening peers to help the student participate in classroom activities.

35. Structure the environment so that the student has many opportunities to interact with other peers in classroom activities.

36. Choose classroom activities in which the student is likely to interact successfully with peers.

37. Conduct a sociometric activity with the class to determine those peers who would most prefer to interact with the student in classroom activities.

38. Teach the student appropriate ways to interact with peers in classroom activities (e.g., share materials, problem solving, take turns, talk, etc.).

39. Supervise classroom activities closely so the peers with whom the student interacts do not stimulate inappropriate behavior.

40. Make sure that the classroom activity is not so stimulating it makes successful interactions with peers difficult.

41. Teach the student appropriate ways to interact with another student (e.g., how to greet another student, suggest activities, share materials, problem-solve, take turns, talk, etc.).

42. Limit opportunities for interaction in classroom activities on those occasions in which the student is not likely to be successful (e.g., when the student has experienced academic or social failure prior to the scheduled classroom activity).

43. Through interviews with other students and observations, determine those characteristics of the student which interfere with successful interactions during classroom activities. Use the information gained to determine skills or behaviors the student needs to develop for successful interactions.

44. Select nonacademic activities designed to facilitate appropriate social interaction between the student and peers during classroom activities (e.g., board games, model building, etc.).

45. Make sure, beforehand, that the student is able to successfully participate in the classroom activity (e.g., the student understands the rules, is familiar with the activity, will be compatible with peers participating in the activity, etc.).

46. Teach the student problem-solving skills so he/she may better handle problems that may occur in interactions with peers in classroom activities (e.g., talking, walking away, calling upon an arbitrator, compromising, etc.).

47. Have the student work with a peer who is younger or smaller (e.g., choose a peer who would require assistance, be less threatening, etc.).

48. Have the student practice appropriate interactions with the teacher in classroom activities (e.g., simulations, role-playing, etc.).

1. Allow the student to place a buzzer (i.e., vibrating toy) on his/her face.

2. Have the student participate in a play that has facial expressions labeled in the dialogue after skills are generalized.

3. Create and review social stories about appropriate facial expressions with the student.

4. Take pictures of the student and his/her peers showing the same emotions. Ask the student to look at the pictures. Help the student make comparisons between the pictures.

5. Ask the student to imitate and label emotions from photographs.

6. Use pictures of the student and his/her peers to illustrate the different facial expressions. Ask the student to group the pictures that show similar facial expressions.

7. Teach scripts to the student and reward him/her for using appropriate scripts in social settings.

8. Reinforce the student for using appropriate facial expressions: (a) give the student a tangible reward (e.g., classroom privileges, line leading, passing out materials, five minutes free time, etc.) or (b) give the student an intangible reward (e.g., praise, fist bump, smile, etc.).

9. Reward the student for using appropriate facial expressions based on a predetermined behavior management plan.

10. Be sure inappropriate facial expressions are not caused by neuropsychological factors.

11. If the student is not aware he/she is making expressions, gently state, "You are making that face again." Model expression back to the student and allow him/her to see it in a mirror.

12. Have the student identify emotions being expressed by others by their facial expressions (e.g., show normal and extreme facial expressions; ask him/her what he/she normally sees when people are happy, sad, angry, etc.).

13. Share all strategies with parents, caregivers, and in-home trainers to ensure generalization of skills and consistency of methods.

14. Determine which events or circumstances cause the student to make inappropriate facial expressions.

15. Have the student use a chart to indicate his/her emotions (e.g., happy face, sad face, etc.).

16. Teach appropriate facial expressions for different situations using social stories with pictures of appropriate facial expressions.

17. Have the student label the emotions expressed in pictures of facial expressions of friends using pre-made labels.

18. Have the student practice identifying emotions when watching television.

19. Massage the student's face.

20. Teach the student appropriate facial expressions for his/her age and grade level.

21. Have the student practice appropriate facial expressions using a mirror.

22. Create a red message card for the student to use rather than displaying odd expressions. The student can hold the card up to gain attention rather than using facial expressions.

23. Have the student compare his/her facial expressions to those of his/her peers.

24. Encourage the student to reward himself/herself when his/her inappropriate expressions have decreased.

25. Explain to the student why his/her expressions are inappropriate.

26. Develop a social story to illustrate how people react when they believe others are making faces at them.

27. Have the student role-play scenarios involving specific emotions with a teacher or an aide.

28. Have the student use a mirror to see how his/her facial expressions change and label each emotion.

29. Have the student self-record incidences of inappropriate facial expressions.

30. Put pictures with multiple emotions on a magnet and have the student move the magnet when his/her emotion changes.

31. Ask the student to draw pictures of how he/she is feeling and label his/her emotions.

32. Play a memory game using pre-labeled cards and pictures of facial expressions.

33. Read a short story or scenario and have the student identify and demonstrate the emotions of the characters.

34. Discuss feelings in class meetings so the students can hear feelings being discussed.

35. Create a chart where the student earns stickers for having appropriate facial expressions. After earning a certain number of stickers, the student may exchange them for a desired item or activity (e.g., computer time, toy, etc.). The student should not lose stickers for inappropriate facial expressions.

36. Use a video of the student to show him/her his/her facial expressions.

37. Have *Silly Day.* Tell the student it is an appropriate time for odd facial expressions. Provide clear and concise rules placed on the student's table.

38. Provide appropriate items for the student to chew on. The student may be moving his/her muscles to the end range to tense them. Chewing may help create the needed tension.

39. Use a signal (touching the student's back or desk) to let the student know when he/she is too animated with his/her facial expressions.

40. Play a game by pairing students and playing *Guess the Emotion.*

41. Have the student watch a television show without the volume. Ask the student to identify the emotions he/she sees.

42. Role-play different emotional scenarios with the student.

43. Use a mirror to show the student his/her facial expressions.

44. Take the student out in the community with a social story book so skills can be applied and generalized.

45. Scaffold skills by first having the student hold up happy, sad, etc., cards and then fading the prompts to verbal cues.

46. Write social stories and ask the student to identify each emotion described.

47. Play games requiring the student to use a variety of facial expressions.

48. Place mirrors around the room to provide visual feedback for the student.

49. Use exaggerated facial expressions (e.g., wide eyes, big smile, etc.) to express emotion.

1. Teach the student the rule of 3's (i.e., say 3 things only, then allow the other person to comment).

2. Teach the student questions that can be asked about the topic.

3. Steer the student back to the focus of the conversation (e.g., "Yes, I understand that, but we are going to talk about this right now," etc.).

4. Use a picture to remind the student of the focus of the conversation.

5. Role-play conversational situations with the teacher and peers.

6. Use a "Don't Say Bag" when the student gets off task or topic or fixates on a single topic. Have the student write out the word that describes the off-task topic and put it in a zip lock storage bag labeled, "Don't Say."

7. Have the student self monitor on-task conversations.

8. Develop an at-home reinforcer for appropriate conversation outside of school.

9. Develop an in-school reinforcer for appropriate conversation in academic settings.

10. Use a "Tap Cue," when the student is off task with conversation. Tell the student ahead of time that a tap on the shoulder will mean to return to meaningful conversation.

11. Have the student watch videos of peers having an appropriate conversation.

12. Have the student complete either in written or verbal form appropriate responses to various introductory greetings.

13. Have the student write a story with conversation between two characters.

14. Use a cue card (e.g., laminated colored card). Place the cue card on the student's desk as a reminder when he/she is not maintaining conversation.

15. Point out examples of appropriate language usage (both verbal and nonverbal) involving topic initiation, maintenance, and/or closure which occur during the day.

16. Have the student practice "echoing" what you or another student says. Teach the student to imitate inflectional patterns as well as to repeat the words. Video record this activity and have the student analyze his/her success at this activity.

17. Audio record the student and have him/her listen to the recording to determine instances in which he/she is using inappropriate greetings or closings or switching topics at an inappropriate time.

18. Use a private signal (e.g., holding up a finger, etc.) to remind the student to continue speaking on the original topic.

19. Use puppets to retell a story or act out an activity. Have the student do the same by following your model.

20. Provide the student with a topic (e.g., rules to follow when riding your bike) and have him/her make up complete sentences about it.

21. Provide the student with a book without words and have him/her narrate the story.

22. Have the student use a play phone to practice topic initiation, maintenance, and/or closure.

23. Choose a topic for a paragraph or story and alternate making up sentences with the student to provide a model of the components of a complete sentence.

24. Pair the student with a peer and have them take turns being interviewed and interviewing. This may be done with the students acting as themselves or pretending to be fictitious characters. Emphasize appropriate topic initiation, maintenance, and closure.

25. Pair the student with an outgoing student who engages in appropriate verbal interactions on a frequent basis.

26. Have the student ask questions about directions, explanations, and instructions he/she does not understand.

27. Reinforce the student for appropriate topic initiation, maintenance, and/or closure: (a) give the student a tangible reward (e.g., classroom privileges, line leading, passing out materials, five minutes free time, etc.), or (b) give the student an intangible reward (e.g., praise, fist bump, smile, etc.).

28. Have the student practice appropriate verbal interactions with peers and teacher(s).

29. Have a sharing time at school. Encourage the student to talk about anything of interest to him/her while emphasizing appropriate topic initiation, maintenance, and closure.

30. Be sure to act as an appropriate model for topic initiation, maintenance, and/or closure.

31. Have the student sequence cartoon strips, after they have been cut apart and rearranged, and explain the logic of the sequence created.

32. Reduce the emphasis on competition. Competitive activities may cause the student to hurry and not initiate, maintain or close a topic appropriately.

33. Choose a peer who demonstrates appropriate topic initiation, maintenance, and closure to act as a model for the student.

34. When the student has difficulty during a conversation, remind him/her that this occasionally happens to everyone and he/she should not become upset.

35. Give the student a factual statement (e.g., some animals are dangerous) and have him/her provide several complete sentences relating to that topic.

36. Create a communication unit for the entire classroom which includes the basic rules of conversation.

37. List the qualities a good speaker possesses (e.g., rate, diction, volume, vocabulary, maintenance of topic, etc.) and have the student evaluate himself/herself on each characteristic. Set a goal for improvement in only one or two areas at a time.

38. Set up fictitious situations in the classroom (e.g., restaurant, gas station, grocery store, etc.) and have the students in the class role-play working in each situation. Have them change roles often and emphasize appropriate topic initiation, maintenance, and closure.

39. Rephrase the student's words to assist the student in topic maintenance (e.g., when student switches topics, the teacher should rephrase his/her statement to redirect the conversation in the appropriate direction).

40. Have the student participate in simulated conversational activities with feedback designed to teach conversational skills (e.g., greetings, closings, questions, topics of conversation, topic maintenance, etc.).

41. Utilizing a topic which is interesting to the student, help him/her to create and act in a short skit which revolves around that topic.

42. Focus on the completeness of the student's thought and not the grammatical accuracy of the statement. Reinforce complete thoughts that include specific vocabulary.

43. Increase the student's awareness of the problem by recording the student while he/she is speaking with another student who maintains a topic of conversation. Play back the recording for the student to see if he/she can identify his/her changes of topic. Have him/her make appropriate modifications.

44. Encourage verbal output. Increase the student's opportunities to communicate verbally to provide him/her with necessary practice.

45. After a field trip or special event, have the student retell the activities which occurred with an emphasis on using descriptive vocabulary and complete sentences.

46. Have the student read short stories without endings. Assist the student in expressing opinions, feelings, and/or emotions about the endings to the stories.

47. Allow the student to show visitors and new students around the school.

48. Allow the student to speak without being interrupted or hurried.

49. Pause often when you speak. This pause time encourages participation in the communication act.

50. Provide opportunities for the student to play games which require taking turns with other students. The turn-taking skills developed in games are very important to conversation.

51. Routinely record the student's speech and point out incomplete statements and nondescript terminology. With each successive taping, reinforce the student as his/her use of complete sentences and specific vocabulary improves.

52. Assess the appropriateness of the social situation in relation to the student's ability to be successful.

53. Teach a unit which is centered around finding examples of language which would be appropriate for topic initiation, maintenance, and/or closure.

54. Reinforce other students in the classroom when they demonstrate appropriate topic initiation, maintenance, and/or closure.

55. Speak with the student to explain that he/she is not demonstrating appropriate topic initiation, maintenance, and/or closure.

56. To understand the student's needs and to provide opportunity for relevant verbal interaction, communicate with the student as often as opportunities permit. Be sure to spend some time talking with the student on an individual basis and include topics which are of interest to the student.

57. Make a list of the attributes which are likely to help a person become a good speaker (e.g., takes his/her time, thinks of what to say before starting, etc.).

58. Determine an individual(s) in the school environment with whom the student would most want to engage in a conversation (e.g., custodian, librarian, resource teacher, principal, older student, etc.). Allow the student to spend time carrying on a conversation with the individual(s) each day.

59. Encourage verbal expression in your classroom and listen carefully when the student is using language as a tool. Try to set up situations where the student can see that his/her attempts at language usage have been successful.

60. Experiment with various groupings to determine the group in which the student is most comfortable initiating and maintaining conversations with peers and adults.

1. Explain the purpose of conversation and how it is important to take turns.

2. Teach the student the rule of 3's (i.e., say 3 things only, then allow the other person to comment).

3. Teach the student to "check in" with the other person. Ask, "Would you like to hear more?"

4. Work on identifying facial expressions (e.g., bored, excited, interested, uninterested, etc.).

5. Set a timer allowing the student to speak about his/her topic of interest for a specified amount of time. When the timer goes off, say, "Ok, now it's my turn to choose what we talk about."

6. Model/mediate appropriate conversation (e.g., "We know you really like dinosaurs, but Johnny just asked you what your favorite sport is. Let's try to talk about that instead.").

7. Establish a set time daily for the student to talk about personal interests.

8. Teach the student to verify whether or not there is an audience for his/her topic.

9. Teach the student to identify when others are ready to change the subject. Use visuals of expressions that demonstrate others being bored or losing interest and use direct quotes people may use when changing the subject.

10. Provide a time limit for the student to discuss a topic of interest with others in conversations.

11. Use a cue card to indicate it is time for a new topic.

12. Teach the student to take turns sharing topics of interest by limiting the number of exchanges in conversation on his/her interest.

13. Teach the student to talk about personal topics of interest with a limited number of sentences on that particular topic.

14. For every sentence the student shares on his/her favorite topic, he/she must listen to the other participant for an equal number of sentences.

15. Choose a peer to work with the student. Give each student green and red circles and a variety of topics to discuss. They must choose a topic to discuss and remain on topic. A green circle is displayed as the students stay on topic. A red circle is shown to remind the students to return to the current topic.

16. Have the student practice "echoing" what you or another student says. Teach the student to imitate inflectional patterns and facial expressions as well as to repeat the words.

17. Use a private signal (e.g., holding up a finger, etc.) to remind the student to continue speaking on the original topic.

18. Reduce the emphasis on competition. Competitive activities may cause the student to hurry and not initiate, maintain or close a topic appropriately.

19. Have the student use a play phone to practice topic initiation, maintenance, and/or closure.

20. Provide the student with a book without words and have him/her narrate the story.

21. Pair the student on a frequent basis with an outgoing student who engages in appropriate verbal interactions.

22. Use puppets to retell a story or act out an activity. Have the student do the same by following your model.

23. Provide the student with a topic (e.g., rules to follow when riding your bike) and have him/her make relevant statements about it.

24. Pair the student with a peer and have them take turns being interviewed and interviewing. This may be done with the students acting as themselves or pretending to be fictitious characters. Emphasize appropriate topic initiation, maintenance, and closure.

25. Audio record the student and have him/her listen to the recording to determine instances in which he/she is using inappropriate greetings or closings or switching topics at an inappropriate time.

26. Have the student ask questions about directions, explanations, and instructions he/she does not understand.

27. Have the student practice appropriate verbal interactions with peers and teacher(s).

28. Reinforce the student for appropriate topic initiation, maintenance, and/or closure: (a) give the student a tangible reward (e.g., classroom privileges, line leading, passing out materials, five minutes free time, etc.), or (b) give the student an intangible reward (e.g., praise, fist bump, smile, etc.).

29. Point out examples of appropriate language usage (both verbal and nonverbal) involving topic initiation, maintenance, and/or closure which occur during the day.

30. Brainstorm words/phrases that are overused in your school to increase the student's awareness of words/phrases.

31. Be sure to act as an appropriate model for topic initiation, maintenance, and/or closure.

32. Have a sharing time at school. Encourage the student to talk about anything of interest to him/her while emphasizing appropriate topic initiation, maintenance, and closure.

33. Teach the student to be aware of listener response to determine if the meaning of his/her greeting/closing has been received accurately or if the intended topic of conversation is being appropriately maintained.

34. Have the student practice being someone else in specific situations (e.g., talking on the phone, being a cashier in a grocery store, etc.). Make sure all responses are relevant to the situation.

35. When engaging in verbal communication, be sure to use vocabulary that is within the student's level of comprehension.

36. Choose a peer who demonstrates appropriate topic initiation, maintenance, and closure to act as a model for the student.

37. When the student has difficulty during a conversation, remind him/her that this occasionally happens to everyone and he/she should not become upset.

38. Identify expectations of different environments and help the student develop the skills to be successful in those environments.

39. Create a communication unit for the entire classroom which includes the basic rules of conversation.

40. Alternating with a peer, have the student take turns adding words in a sentence to create one long sentence. The sentence should be as long as possible without becoming a run-on sentence.

41. Rephrase the student's words to assist the student in topic maintenance (e.g., when student switches topics, the teacher should rephrase his/her statement to redirect the conversation in the appropriate direction).

42. Have the student participate in simulated conversational activities with feedback designed to teach conversational skills (e.g., greetings, closings, questions, topics of conversation, topic maintenance, etc.).

43. Make sure that reinforcement is not inadvertently given for irrelevant responses.

44. Ask questions which stimulate language. Avoid questions which can be answered by yes/no or a nod of the head (e.g., "What did you do at recess?" rather than "Did you play on the slide?" or "Tell me about your vacation." rather than "Did you stay home over the holidays?" etc.).

45. Choose a peer to model relevant responses for the student.

46. Maintain consistent expectations within the ability level of the student.

47. To understand the student's needs and to provide opportunity for relevant verbal interaction, communicate with the student as often as opportunities permit. Spend time talking with the student on an individual basis and include topics which are of interest to the student.

48. After a field trip or special event, have the student retell the activities which occurred with an emphasis on using relevant responses.

49. Provide opportunities for the student to play games which require taking turns with other students. The turn-taking skills developed in games are very important to conversation.

50. Routinely record the student's speech and point out irrelevant comments. With each successive taping, reinforce the student as his/her use of relevant responses improves.

51. Make sure that the student's feelings are considered when it is necessary to discuss his/her irrelevant responses (i.e., handle comments in such a way that the student's enthusiasm for participation is not diminished).

52. To understand the student's needs and to provide opportunity for spontaneous verbal interaction, communicate with the student as often as opportunities permit.

53. Determine an individual(s) in the school environment with whom the student would most want to engage in a conversation (e.g., custodian, librarian, resource teacher, principal, older student, etc.). Allow the student to spend time carrying on a conversation with the individual(s) each day. Make sure these people model appropriate topic initiation, maintenance, and/or closure.

54. Speak with the student to explain that he/she is not demonstrating appropriate topic initiation, maintenance, and/or closure.

55. Experiment with various groupings to determine the group in which the student is most comfortable initiating and maintaining conversations with peers and adults.

56. Provide the student with verbal reminders or prompts when he/she perseverates.

57. Teach a unit which is centered around finding examples of language which would be appropriate for topic initiation, maintenance, and/or closure.

230 Is unable to interpret nonverbal facial cues of others

1. Practice emotions with the student using mirrors to reinforce the facial appearance of each emotion.

2. Use videos to identify emotions.

3. Teach the student to identify emotional states from pictures.

4. If the student has difficulty identifying facial expressions, teach him/her to ask about the emotional state of others.

5. Remind the student to look at the face of the person speaking.

6. Read picture books about emotion and practice making the appropriate faces. Try using a mirror during this exercise.

7. Use real-life interactions (e.g., "Look at Johnny's face. How do you think he feels?" etc.).

8. Examine photo albums and scrapbooks provided by the student's family and discuss the facial expressions and possible feelings that were felt at the time familiar pictures were taken.

9. Look at the daily newspapers and talk about the captions underneath selected pictures. Point out facial expressions in the pictures.

10. Provide the student with a worksheet with large circles and a scenario on it. Have the student draw facial expressions that would be plausible for selected situations (e.g., "Dad just wrecked his car." or "You just got all A's on your report card.").

11. Show the student expression cards. Have the student make up a situation in which this expression might take place.

12. Use various facial expressions for the student to replicate. Ask the student why someone would make a particular facial expression.

13. Use a mirror to view the teacher's reaction to given scenarios.

14. Ask the student to match expression cards and feeling cards.

15. Ask the student to write a description of the facial expression in a picture of a scenario.

16. Pair the student with a peer. Provide facial expression cards or situations for them to play *Charades* or pantomime alternating roles.

17. Communicate with the parents (e.g., notes home, phone calls, etc.) to share information about the student's progress. The parents may reinforce the student at home for responding to nonverbal facial cues at school.

18. Have the student maintain a record (e.g., chart or graph) of his/her performance in adjusting his/her behavior to expectations of different situations.

19. Express your feelings in a socially acceptable way.

20. Help the student develop a friendship by assigning him/her to work with a peer on an activity, project, etc.

21. Have the student ask questions about environmental social cues not understood.

22. Make sure the academic and social demands of the situation are within the student's ability level.

23. Have the student complete a reinforcer survey to determine his/her interests, his/her favorite activities, what is rewarding to him/her, etc.; and use the information obtained to create a pleasant atmosphere at school for the student.

24. Choose a peer to accompany the student as the student engages in different activities, to act as a model in teaching appropriate responses to nonverbal facial cues.

25. Reinforce the student for adjusting his/her behavior to varying nonverbal facial cues and expectations from one environment or activity to another. As the student demonstrates success, gradually increase the time required for reinforcement.

26. Carefully consider the student's age and experience before expecting him/her to respond appropriately to nonverbal facial cues in social situations.

27. Have the student develop an awareness of the consequences of his/her behavior by writing down or talking through problems which may occur due to his/her inability to correctly interpret nonverbal facial cues (e.g., perceived as unmannerly, avoided, etc.).

28. Have the student practice appropriate interactions with the teacher(s).

29. Have the student practice appropriate responses to environmental social cues with the teacher(s) in classroom activities (e.g., simulations, role-playing, etc.).

30. Give a signal (e.g., clapping hands, turning lights off and on, etc.) to indicate the student needs to correctly interpret a nonverbal facial cue.

31. Include the student in classroom/group activities (e.g., invite the student to join a group, assign the student a part or responsibility in an activity, etc.).

32. Have the student run errands with another person to facilitate interaction.

33. Point out the natural consequences of failing to respond appropriately to nonverbal facial cues from other students (e.g., other students will avoid him/her, loss of friendships, misunderstandings, etc.).

34. Make every attempt to create a positive atmosphere in the classroom (e.g., cooperative group activities, positive motivation strategies, positive communications, etc.).

35. Try various groupings to determine the group in which the student is most comfortable.

36. Encourage the student to participate in social situations in which he/she is likely to respond successfully to nonverbal facial cues.

37. Prepare the student in advance for environmental and social expectations to facilitate his/her ability to successfully respond.

38. Identify expectations of different environments and help the student develop the skills to be successful in those environments.

39. Involve the student in extracurricular activities to provide additional opportunities for him/her to practice appropriate responses to nonverbal facial cues.

40. Make sure explanations regarding how the student should respond to social cues are delivered in a way the student understands. This can be checked by asking the student to repeat the explanation in his/her own words.

41. Limit opportunities for interaction in situations on those occasions in which the student is not likely to be successful (e.g., the student has experienced academic or social failure prior to the scheduled activity).

42. Allow natural consequences to occur so the student can learn that persons who adjust behavior to the demands of the social situation are more successful than those who are inflexible in their behavior (e.g., if you do not recognize facial cues, others may avoid being in social situations with you).

43. Have the student participate in simulated social activities with feedback designed to improve his/her ability to correctly interpret nonverbal facial cues.

44. Give the student responsibilities in school and community environments which promote his/her ability to socially interact in a positive manner.

45. Allow the student to interact with a group of peers with whom he/she feels comfortable to practice appropriate responses to nonverbal facial cues.

46. Teach the student social interaction skills (e.g., ways to respond to changing social situations). Be specific about ways of reacting to certain situations.

47. To increase success in learning nonverbal facial cues, have the student observe and imitate the responses of peers to nonverbal facial cues (e.g., as the student is learning to interact appropriately when a spectator at a sporting event, the student can imitate the behavior of peers who participate in appropriate behavior when they are spectators at a sporting event).

48. Choose a peer to model appropriate interactions with one other person for the student.

49. Model appropriate responses to nonverbal facial cues for the student to imitate.

50. Make sure attention is not inadvertently given to the student for failing to respond to a social cue (e.g., only responding to the student when he/she demonstrates inappropriate behavior).

51. Provide the student with simulation activities in the classroom to teach successful responses to nonverbal facial cues.

52. Encourage the student to pause and consider his/her thoughts before acting on them.

53. Choose an outgoing, nonthreatening peer to help the student interact more appropriately.

54. Evaluate the expectation for peer interaction to determine if the student can be successful in the interactions and for the expected length of time.

55. Reinforce the student for responding appropriately to nonverbal facial cues: (a) give the student a tangible reward (e.g., classroom privileges, line leading, passing out materials, five minutes free time, etc.) or (b) give the student an intangible reward (e.g., praise, fist bump, smile, etc.).

56. Provide repeated practice in responding appropriately to nonverbal facial cues.

57. Do not force the student to interact with individuals with whom he/she is not completely comfortable.

58. Do not criticize the student. When correcting the student, be honest yet supportive. Never cause the student to feel negatively about himself/herself.

59. Make sure that other teachers and school personnel who work with the student know that the student does not respond appropriately to nonverbal facial cues.

60. Explain to the student that he/she should be satisfied with his/her best effort rather than perfection.

61. Interact frequently with the student.

62. Structure the environment so that the student has many opportunities to interact successfully with another person.

63. Establish environmental social cues that the student is expected to follow (e.g., when it is appropriate to interact, when it is not appropriate to interact, etc.).

64. Evaluate the appropriateness of the environmental social cues the student is expected to follow to determine (a) if the cue is too difficult and (b) if the length of time required to respond to the cue is adequate.

65. Have the student identify the situations in which he/she does not adjust his/her behavior. After identifying these situations, have the student think of ways to reduce their occurrences.

66. Assess the appropriateness of the social situation in relation to the student's ability to be successful.

67. Provide the opportunity for the student to experience many social and academic successes.

68. Write a contract with the student specifying what behavior is expected (e.g., responding appropriately to nonverbal facial cues) and what reinforcement will be made available when the terms of the contract have been met.

69. Maintain consistent expectations within the ability level of the student.

70. Select nonacademic activities designed to provide the student with social situations during which he/she can respond to nonverbal facial cues appropriately.

71. Speak to the student to explain (a) what the student is doing wrong (e.g., failing to be flexible to changing social situations) and (b) what the student should be doing (e.g., adjusting his/her behavior to the demands of social situations).

72. Explain the benefits of trying one's best to follow social cues in the community (e.g., a person would be more welcome to return, a person might acquire positive social regard from other people, etc.).

73. Provide the student with verbal reminders or prompts when he/she misses a nonverbal facial cue.

74. Teach the student appropriate verbal and nonverbal responses to common everyday situations.

75. Demonstrate accepting behavior (e.g., willingness to help, making criticisms constructive and positive, etc.) to encourage the student to socialize and communicate in learning environments.

76. Pair nonverbal facial cues with verbal explanations and immediate reinforcement for appropriate responses.

77. Conduct a sociometric activity with the class to determine the peer who would most prefer to interact with the student.

78. Have the student interact with one other person for short periods of time to facilitate success. As the student experiences success, gradually increase the length of time the student interacts.

79. Provide opportunities for interactions within the classroom to allow the student to practice adjusting his/her behavior to the demands of various social situations.

80. Choose a peer to work with the student to provide an appropriate model for interpreting nonverbal facial cues.

231 Does not communicate for the purpose of sharing positive affect

1. Create a form of communication for a nonverbal student (e.g., pictures, assistive communication device, etc.).

2. Use every moment with the student as a time to share positive affect with him/her.

3. Explain/teach the purpose of communicating with others.

4. Teach simple social skills at the appropriate developmental age of the student.

5. Encourage the student to interact with others to get items he/she wants or needs.

6. Use videos to teach the student about emotions, sharing, and the need for others.

7. Use social stories to explain how people interact with each other.

8. Use written stories/books to teach about actions and feelings.

9. Use the student's interests to begin an interaction. Begin on his/her playing level to create interest.

10. Act as a shadow behind the student during play. When the individual interacting with the student wants positive affect, provide the affect with hand-over-hand/body assistance, thus assisting the student to respond appropriately.

11. Be sure to be at the student's eye level when interacting.

12. Try to gain the student's attention prior to requesting/sharing positive affects.

13. Explain how to share positive affect with others and how the student's action make others feel. The student may not understand this type of interaction and may need extra help understanding how his/her behavior affects others. Make your explanations short and to the point.

14. Praise the student for sharing positive affect with others.

15. Use pictures of faces to identify various feelings.

16. Determine if the student connects with you on a basic level (e.g., comes to you to get things he/she wants). Build from a basic level to interaction and then feelings.

17. Have the student practice "echoing" what you or another student says. Teach the student to imitate inflectional patterns and facial expressions, as well as to repeat the words. Video record this activity and have the student analyze his/her success at this activity.

18. Use a private signal (e.g., holding up a finger, etc.) to remind the student to use appropriate verbal and/or nonverbal language.

19. Provide the student with a wordless picture book and have him/her narrate the story.

20. Pair the student on a frequent basis with an outgoing student who engages in appropriate verbal interactions.

21. Provide the student with a list of statements/questions which could be used to obtain specific results and assist him/her in using the statements at appropriate times (e.g., "Would you help me move this?" "I would like to get a drink now.").

22. Audio record the student and have him/her listen to the recording to determine instances in which he/she is using inappropriate verbal and/or nonverbal language.

23. Have the student ask questions about directions, explanations, or instructions he/she does not understand.

24. Have the student practice appropriate verbal interactions with peers and teacher(s).

25. Point out examples of appropriate language usage (both verbal and nonverbal) as they occur during the day.

26. Communicate with the student as often as opportunities permit to understand the student's needs and to provide an opportunity for spontaneous verbal interaction.

27. Help the student become aware of his/her tone of voice when greeting, requesting, and/or disagreeing with others by calling attention to voice inflections which are inappropriate for the situation.

28. Teach the student to be aware of listener response to determine if the meaning of a message has been received accurately.

29. Allow the student to be a member of a group without requiring active participation.

30. Provide immediate feedback and cues for the student when his/her message has not been received accurately.

31. Teach the student that he/she must respond differently depending on the person to whom he/she is talking (e.g., "What's happening?" is acceptable for a peer but not for the principal).

32. Try various groupings to determine the group in which the student is most comfortable carrying on a conversation with peers and adults.

33. Provide the student with direct eye contact and communicate to him/her that you expect him/her to do the same with you.

34. Make sure that all educators interact with the student on a regular basis and use positive verbal communication in speaking to him/her.

35. Make a list of emotions (e.g., sad, scared, happy, etc.) and have the student express each of them in a sentence.

36. Make a recording of environmental sounds and have the student identify them. Ask leading questions if necessary.

37. Have the student run errands which will require interactions with teachers, administrators, staff, etc., (e.g., delivering attendance reports to the office, taking messages to other teachers, etc.).

38. Evaluate the appropriateness of expectations for the student to use communication skills to initiate positive interpersonal relationships with others.

39. Be an appropriate model for the student by expressing yourself concisely and by demonstrating that verbal language can be used as a tool to obtain desired results.

40. Encourage or reward others for initiating interactions with the student.

41. Have the student play games which require carrying on conversations with others.

42. Prompt the student to help him/her use more appropriate verbal/nonverbal language (e.g., Teacher says, "How are you?" Student says, "Fred." Teacher says, "How are you feeling, Fred?" or "Your name is Fred. Can you tell me how you are feeling?").

43. Plan for one-to-one teacher-student interactions at various times throughout the school day.

44. Help the student heighten his/her awareness of the differences between fantasy and reality by discussing stories, movies, TV programs, etc., that are familiar to him/her. Point out specific aspects that are realistic and make-believe.

45. Encourage appropriate eye contact in all communicative situations.

46. Have the student participate in simulated conversational activities with feedback designed to teach conversational skills (e.g., greetings, questions, topics of conversations, etc.).

47. Teach the student social interaction skills (e.g., ways in which to appropriately respond to others' attempts to be friendly, complimentary, sympathetic, etc.).

48. Provide the student with many social and academic successes.

49. Provide the student with many opportunities for successful verbal communications with peers.

50. Choose a peer to model appropriate use of communication skills to initiate positive interpersonal relationships with others for the student.

51. Model appropriate verbal and nonverbal language in social situations and in interactions with peers and adults.

52. Communicate with parents (e.g., notes home, phone calls, etc.) to share information about the student's progress. The parents may reinforce the student at home for using communication skills to initiate positive interpersonal relationships with others at school.

53. Place interesting pictures or objects on a table and have the student choose one and describe it in detail. Provide assistance in utilizing originality and variety in the descriptions.

54. Reinforce the student for using communication skills to initiate positive interpersonal relationships with others: (a) give the student a tangible reward (e.g., classroom privileges, line leading, passing out materials, five minutes free time, etc.) or (b) give the student an intangible reward (e.g., praise, fist bump, smile, etc.).

55. Greet or acknowledge the student as often as possible (e.g., hallways, cafeteria, welcome to class, a job done well, etc.). Encourage him/her to acknowledge you in return.

56. Create a *Feeling Box*. Place an unseen item in the box and have the student describe what it feels like, while another student tries to guess what it is.

57. Teach the student appropriate positive verbal greetings (e.g., "Hi, how are you doing?" "Good to see you." "Haven't seen you in a long time.").

58. Teach the student appropriate positive verbal requests (e.g., "Please pass the paper." "May I please be excused?" "Will you please help me?" etc.).

59. Have the student practice positive verbal communications with a specified number of peers throughout the school day.

60. Teach the student conversational questions (e.g., "How are you?" "What have you been up to?" "How is it going?" etc.) to use when speaking to peers and adults.

61. Choose a peer to sit/work with the student (e.g., in different settings or activities such as art, music, P.E.; on the bus; tutoring; group projects; running errands in the building; free time; etc.) to facilitate the student's opportunity to participate in conversation.

62. Teach the student communication skills (e.g., hand raising, expressing needs in written and/or verbal form, etc.).

63. Teach the student positive social communication skills to initiate positive interpersonal relationships with others (e.g., waiting your turn to speak, asking conversational questions, using an appropriate tone of voice, talking about appropriate subjects with others, etc.).

64. Pause often when you speak. This pause encourages participation in the communication act.

65. Communicate to the student that he/she is a worthwhile individual.

66. Each day provide the student with situations in which the student must use verbal language as a tool to obtain desired results (e.g., The student wants to get a drink. Indicate that he should tell you when he wants a drink rather than waiting for you to provide the break.).

67. Have the student practice taking written messages to different persons in the school setting (e.g., librarian, school counselor, principal, etc.) and later delivering the messages verbally.

68. Explain to the student that nonliteral forms of language are used to make communication more interesting, but that they never mean exactly what they say. Identify the concept of "playing" with language through nonliteral forms.

69. Use simple comic strips that focus on absurdities and have the student identify what could or couldn't really happen and why it is funny.

70. Assess the appropriateness of the demands of the social situation to determine an appropriate level of expectation for the student's verbal interaction with others.

71. Reinforce other students in the classroom for appropriate verbal and/or nonverbal interactions.

72. Write a contract with the student specifying what behavior is expected (e.g., carrying on conversations with peers and adults) and what reinforcement will be made available when the terms of the contract have been met.

73. Determine whether or not the student has a limited expressive and/or receptive vocabulary which would influence his/her ability to comprehend absurdities.

74. Determine an individual(s) in the school environment with whom the student would most want to engage in a conversation (e.g., custodian, librarian, resource teacher, principal, older student, etc.). Allow the student to spend time carrying on a conversation with the individual(s) each day.

75. Teach a unit which is centered around finding examples of language which are appropriate for use in various situations.

76. Using "sequence cards," have the student place the cards in the appropriate order and explain the sequence; then have the student tell you what might have happened before or after the provided sequence.

77. Evaluate the appropriateness of the task to determine (a) if the task is too easy, (b) if the task is too difficult, and (c) if the length of time scheduled to complete the task is adequate.

78. Model appropriate responses for the student to imitate.

79. Speak to the student to explain (a) what he/she is doing wrong (e.g., failing to talk with peers and adults) and (b) what he/she should be doing (e.g., carrying on conversations with peers and adults).

80. Always allow the student to finish responding before you begin talking. Reinforce other students in the classroom for allowing the student to finish responding before they begin talking.

81. Experiment with various groupings to determine the groups in which the student is most comfortable carrying on conversations with peers and adults.

82. Recognize the student's attempts to communicate his/her needs (e.g., facial expressions, gestures, inactivity, self-deprecating comments, etc.).

83. Point out that some TV commercials and magazine ads use absurdities to get attention. Have the student identify the absurdities in specific examples.

84. Reinforce the student for using communication skills to initiate positive interpersonal relationships with others based on the number of times the student can be successful. As the student demonstrates success, gradually increase the number of times required for reinforcement.

85. Have the student deliver verbal messages to other staff members to facilitate his/her opportunity to carry on conversations.

86. Encourage the student to verbally recognize the feelings and expressions of others.

87. Encourage verbal expression in your classroom and listen carefully when the student is using language as a tool. Try to set up situations where the student can see that his/her attempts at language usage have been successful.

232 Is unable to participate in conversational turn taking

1. Work with the student to develop self-autonomy. If the student does not comprehend self, it will be difficult for the student to understand the perspective of others.

2. Explain the importance of conversation and how to reply to others.

3. Explain what other students can provide (e.g., obtaining things he/she needs, interacting during play, helping him/her when needed/asked, etc.).

4. Use teachers and other classmates to promote social communication.

5. If the student is nonverbal, develop a form of communication with the use of an assistive device or pictures. Have the student carry this device or keep it near him/her to promote use each time others communicate with him/her. This will reinforce communication.

6. Be consistent in your attempts to have a conversation. Begin with one request and ask all staff members to consistently make the request (e.g., greeting others that say hello/goodbye to the student).

7. Provide hand-over-hand assistance to complete the communication, if the student will accept this form of assistance.

8. Explain conversational turn-taking. Use an interest of the student's to give demonstrations of the skill (e.g., video, cartoon, movies, etc.).

9. Discuss with parents ways the student communicates at home and use this form of communication whenever possible to reinforce his/her communication skills. Build on this communication with higher order communication skills.

10. Use the student's interests when teaching and reinforcing conversation (e.g., if the student is interested in trains; use pictures of trains for communicating, coloring, writing, reading, cutting, etc.).

11. Have the student participate in play groups where the need for reciprocal conversation is used throughout the group.

12. Discuss with the speech language pathologist the appropriate ways to reinforce communication with the student.

13. Provide the student with reciprocal conversations by trying three times and taking a break. Set the conversation up so that the student has three turns then gets a break to do what he/she wants.

14. Promote conversational turn-taking using the student's interests. Ask the student for some form of conversational turn-taking to obtain a favorite toy/item.

15. Look at the student's neurological system and see if he/she needs a specific type of input (e.g., swinging, jumping on a trampoline, etc.) prior to working on conversational turn-taking.

16. Work with an occupational therapist to evaluate the student's sensory-based needs.

17. Develop opportunities in the student's day to perform and follow through with conversational turn-taking, so he/she practices consistently.

18. Determine the student's level of communication skills. Encourage the student to communicate at his/her level when conversational turn-taking is initiated.

19. Use videos to teach the student appropriate forms of conversational turn-taking when others initiate conversation, both verbal and nonverbal.

20. Use songs to reinforce the different forms of conversational turn-taking.

21. Exaggerate different verbal and non-verbal communications with the use of tone and facial expressions to engage the student.

22. Assess the student's auditory processing to determine if the student is hearing accurately.

23. Have the student role-play situations where simple conversational turn-taking would be used when others initiate conversations (e.g., pictures, gestures, nonverbal expression, verbal expressions, etc.).

24. Communicate with parents to reinforce the form of communication used at school to promote continuation at home and in the community. Express the importance of conversational turn-taking.

25. Show the student a preferred item and ask for some form of communication for him/her to obtain the item.

26. Determine if the student is listening by asking questions rather than requiring eye contact. The student may not be able to process multiple sensory inputs at the same time (vision and auditory).

27. Use student drawings, computer program, etc., to write a personalized social story from the student's viewpoint on how he/she should participate.

28. Train one or two (or whole class!) to engage the student and cue him/her on appropriate participation.

29. Play turn-taking games (nonverbal) (e.g., have each player [2-3] copy the previous person's action and add his/her own, copy only the preceding and add actions.). When the students have mastered copying one action and adding one, include a memory component and require copying all actions.

30. Provide the student with an answer after the question is posed and encourage imitation then silence.

31. Provide visual cues for the student to pause/stop or provide verbal responses.

32. Use an object/timer during small group discussions/conversations to cue students to start/stop participation.

33. Do word/song play such as *Cookie Jar* or *Going to the Grocery Store* where short, predictable participation is required.

34. Video or record the student in conversation and analyze it together.

35. Read plays of familiar stories and practice active listening/role-play conversation skills.

36. Have the student self monitor and evaluate after a brief conversation (e.g., Did I stay on subject? Did I let others talk too? Could others keep up with the conversation? etc.).

37. Implement a picture cue card. Only the person whose "talking" card is face-up can talk.

38. Use a game spinner to take turns talking. When your turn is up, you spin to pick the next talker.

39. Use mechanical switch devices. The students hit the switch to take a turn.

40. Implement a point system for appropriate turn-taking. Award points for appropriate behavior and remove points for interrupting. Points may be redeemed at the end of each day.

41. Use a soft, sponge type ball to play *Hot Potato* to select the next speaker.

42. Teach hand signals to cue the student (stop, hold on, almost done, your turn, etc.).

43. Use a cooking timer to end individual talking time and signal another's turn.

44. Learn components of conversation (statement, opinion, question, response, etc.) and practice implementing them successfully.

45. Teach and implement appropriate conversation starters, middles, and endings.

46. Identify nonverbal conversation cues (interest, boredom, avoidance, etc.) in pictures, then in reality, and coach appropriate responses to these cues.

47. Use role-play with low-preferenced topics to allow for others to guide the conversation.

48. Place the student in social groups with typical peers. Participants may participate in games, crafts, and other activities that promote conversations.

49. Incorporate daily classroom conversation into the schedule. Students are given a topic to discuss with a peer or adult.

50. The student and peers take turns reading the scripted lines of a conversation.

51. Have the student practice "echoing" what you or another student say. Teach the student to imitate inflectional patterns and facial expressions as well as to repeat words.

52. Deliver a predetermined signal (e.g., hand signal, verbal cue, etc.) if the student begins to talk beyond what is expected or at inappropriate times.

53. Teach appropriate social rituals (e.g., excuse yourself before interrupting, wait until someone stops speaking to begin talking, etc.).

54. Provide the student with a topic (e.g., rules to follow when riding your bike) and have him/her make relevant statements about it.

55. Consider carefully the student's age and ability level before expecting him/her not to interrupt others when they are talking, working, reading, etc.

56. When the student makes an inappropriate response, immediately rephrase his/her response to make it relevant/appropriate.

57. Acknowledge the student's presence and/or need to talk with you (e.g., by saying, "Just a minute"; putting your arm around the student; smiling and nodding your head; etc.).

58. Audio record the student and have him/her listen to the recording to determine instances in which he/she makes an irrelevant response.

59. Have the student practice appropriate verbal interactions with peers and teacher(s).

60. Make a list of attributes which are likely to help a person become a good speaker (e.g., takes his/her time, thinks of what to say before starting, etc.).

61. Allow the student to be a member of a group without requiring active participation.

62. Instruct the student to carry a notepad with him/her at all times and to write information down to help him/her remember.

63. Have the student choose a group of peers with whom he/she feels comfortable.

64. Rephrase directions, explanations, questions, comments, instructions, etc., to facilitate the likelihood of the student understanding and providing a relevant response.

65. When engaging in verbal communication, be sure to use vocabulary that is within the student's level of comprehension.

66. Teach and practice effective communication skills. These skills include listening, maintaining eye contact, and positive body language.

67. Make sure that verbal communications are delivered in a nonthreatening manner (e.g., positive voice, facial expressions, language, etc.).

68. Reduce the emphasis on competition. Failure may cause the student to be reluctant to respond.

69. Help the student improve concentration skills (e.g., listening to the speaker, taking notes, preparing comments in advance, making comments in the appropriate context, etc.).

70. Reinforce the student for carrying on conversations with peers and adults: (a) give the student a tangible reward (e.g., classroom privileges, line leading, passing out materials, five minutes free time, etc.) or (b) give the student an intangible reward (e.g., praise, fist bump, smile, etc.).

71. Do not criticize when correcting the student; be honest yet supportive. Never cause the student to feel negatively about himself/herself.

72. Encourage the student to differentiate between spur-of-the-moment and important information that needs to be conveyed.

73. Provide the student with direct eye contact and communicate to him/her that you expect him/her to do the same with you.

74. Allow the student to finish responding before you begin talking. Reinforce other students in the classroom for allowing the student to finish responding before they begin talking.

75. Provide constant, positive reinforcement for appropriate behavior. Ignore as many inappropriate behaviors as possible.

76. Maintain a consistent format for verbal communications with the student.

77. Choose a peer, paraprofessional, friend, etc., to cue the student when he/she interrupts others (e.g., the person can touch the student's arm as a signal that he/she is interrupting).

78. Maintain visibility to and from the student to keep his/her attention at times when he/she should not talk. The teacher should be able to see the student and the student should be able to see the teacher. Make eye contact possible at all times.

79. Alternating with a peer, have the student take turns adding words in a sentence to create one long sentence. The sentence should be as long as possible without becoming a run-on sentence. Check to ensure that all additions to the sentence are relevant.

80. Teach the student that he/she must respond differently depending on the person to whom he/she is talking (e.g., "What's happening?" is acceptable for a peer but not for the principal). Discuss how age, position, and/or familiarity can change the form of the greeting/closing used.

81. Have the student participate in simulated conversational activities with feedback designed to teach conversational skills (e.g., greetings, closings, questions, topics of conversation, etc.).

82. Deliver directions, explanations, and instructions in a clear, concise manner to reduce the student's need to ask questions.

83. Plan for one-to-one teacher-student interactions at various times throughout the school day.

84. Make sure the student is attending to the speaker (e.g., making eye contact, hands free of distracting materials, looking at assignment, etc.) before communicating verbally with him/her.

85. Make sure that reinforcement is not inadvertently given for inappropriate behavior (e.g., the teacher responds to the student after he/she has interrupted).

86. Ask questions which stimulate language. Avoid questions which can be answered by yes/no or a nod of the head (e.g., "What did you do at recess?" rather than "Did you play on the slide?" or "Tell me about your vacation." rather than "Did you stay home over the holidays?" etc.).

87. Choose a peer to model appropriate use of communication skills to maintain positive interpersonal relationships with others for the student.

88. To understand the student's needs and to provide opportunity for relevant verbal interaction, communicate with the student as often as opportunities permit. Spend time talking with the student on an individual basis and include topics which are of interest to the student.

89. Communicate with parents (e.g., notes home, phone calls, etc.) to share information about the student's appropriate behavior. The parents may reinforce the student at home for talking when appropriate at school.

90. Maintain a full schedule of activities. Keeping the student occupied should prevent interruptive behavior from occurring.

91. Give the student frequent opportunities to join in conversations with others by allowing him/her time to talk, asking him/her to restate an experience, etc.

92. Provide students with frequent opportunities to interact with one another (e.g., before and after school, between activities, etc.).

93. Evaluate the expectation for peer interaction to determine if the student can be successful in the interactions and for the expected length of time.

94. Teach the student appropriate positive verbal requests (e.g., "Please pass the paper." "May I please be excused?" "Will you please help me?" etc.).

95. Teach the student appropriate positive verbal greetings (e.g., "Hi, how are you doing?" "Good to see you." "Haven't seen you in a long time.").

96. Have the student practice positive verbal communications with a specified number of people throughout the school day.

97. Teach the student to recognize the appropriate time to speak (e.g., when the teacher has finished speaking, after raising his/her hand, to make comments within the context of the situation, to make comments that are a follow-up to what has just been said, etc.).

98. Teach the student to recognize and make appropriate comments (e.g., comments within the context of the situation, comments that are a follow-up to what has just been said, etc.).

99. Choose a peer to sit/work with the student (e.g., in different settings or activities such as art, music, P.E.; on the bus; tutoring; group projects; running errands in the building; free time; etc.) to increase the student's opportunity to participate in conversation.

100. Assign the student to situations in which he/she is likely to interact successfully with another person.

101. Use role-play to demonstrate situations in which the student would need to use positive interactions with others (e.g., interactions with peers at recess, interactions with cafeteria cooks at lunchtime, interaction with P.E. teacher, etc.).

102. Teach the student positive social communication skills to maintain positive interpersonal relationships with others (e.g., waiting your turn to speak, asking conversational questions, using an appropriate tone of voice, talking about appropriate subjects with others, making eye contact, nodding your head, etc.).

103. Pause often when you speak to encourage the student to participate in conversation.

104. Explain to the student the reasons why talking beyond what is expected and at inappropriate times is unacceptable (e.g., impolite, interrupts others, etc.).

105. Write a contract with the student specifying what behavior is expected (e.g., making short, appropriate comments and speaking at appropriate times) and what reinforcement will be made available when the terms of the contract have been met.

106. Demonstrate to the student the appropriate way to get someone's attention without interrupting.

107. Encourage verbal output. Increase the student's opportunities to communicate verbally to provide him/her with necessary practice.

108. Assess the appropriateness of the social situation in relation to the student's ability to function successfully.

109. Reinforce those students in the classroom who use communication skills to maintain positive interpersonal relationships with others.

110. Be consistent in expecting the student to behave appropriately. Do not allow the student to interrupt one time and expect him/her not to interrupt the next time.

111. Select nonacademic activities designed to facilitate appropriate interaction between the student and another person (e.g., board games, model building, coloring, etc.).

112. Recognize the student's attempts to communicate his/her needs (e.g., facial expressions, gestures, inactivity, self-deprecating comments, etc.).

113. Speak to the student to explain (a) what he/she is doing wrong (e.g., failing to take a turn when carrying on conversations with peers and adults) and (b) what he/she should be doing (e.g., taking turns when carrying on conversations with peers and adults).

114. Encourage the student to use gestures when necessary to clarify his/her message. Gestures may also facilitate recall of vocabulary the student is having difficulty retrieving.

115. Have the student deliver verbal messages to other staff members to increase his/her opportunity to carry on conversations.

116. Have the student practice waiting for short periods of time for his/her turn to speak. Gradually increase the length of time required for a turn to speak.

117. Reinforce the student for waiting for a turn to speak based on the length of time the student can be successful. As the student demonstrates success, gradually increase the length of time required for reinforcement.

118. Teach the student appropriate ways to communicate needs to others (e.g., waiting a turn, raising his/her hand, etc.).

119. Discuss with the student what is expected (e.g., making relevant responses).

120. Establish rules for conversing with others (e.g., wait your turn to talk, stand quietly by the person with whom you want to talk until you are acknowledged, excuse yourself when you interrupt others, etc.). These rules should be consistent and followed by everyone in the class. Talk about the rules often.

121. Have the student interact with one other person for short periods of time to facilitate success. As the student experiences success, gradually increase the length of time the student interacts.

122. Through observations and interviews with other students, determine those characteristics of the student which interfere with successful interaction to determine skills or behaviors the student needs to develop for successful interaction.

1. Consult with other professionals regarding difficulties (e.g., psychiatrist and/or doctor to determine medical needs, occupational therapist to determine functioning abilities, speech language pathologist to determine language needs, social worker, etc.).

2. Remove other distracters (e.g., visual, auditory, taste, smell, touch, movement, etc.)

3. Use the student's form of speech for communication (e.g., pictures, single words, single sentences, etc.).

4. Use videos and songs to teach the student appropriate communication skills.

5. Discuss with the parents the use of communication skills and understanding perspectives at home to reinforce correct use both at school and at home for increased follow through.

6. Use the student's interests when teaching him/her to understand other's points of view (e.g., if the student is interested in trains; use pictures, songs, videos of trains to develop this skill, etc.).

7. Use the student's specific experiences to explain the feelings/perspective of others.

8. Use books that are of special interest to the student. Emphasize the perspectives of others in the book and the importance of understanding or considering other's perspectives.

9. Have the student participate in groups that work on understanding the point of view of others. This will provide times when he/she can observe others.

10. Develop opportunities throughout the student's day to practice understanding the point of view of others so he/she practices consistently.

11. Determine the student's level of communication skills and communicate with the student at this level.

12. Have the student practice understanding other's point of view in various settings to help him/her generalize information.

13. Exaggerate the use of understanding the point of view of others. Use speech patterns and gestures; as well as facial expressions to express the importance of other's perspectives.

14. Have the student role-play situations where understanding the point of view of others is emphasized.

15. Use personalized social stories to explain understanding the point of view of others in various situations that are specific to the student. Include times where the view points are understood and times where they are not (provide correction). Review these stories frequently throughout the school year and provide a copy for review at home. Have the student repeat some of the information to his/her parents/guardians at home to carryover learned information.

16. Determine the student's level of motivation. The student may not understand the point of view of others because there was no inherent gain from this knowledge. Develop some form of importance in understanding perspectives of others and emphasize this during teaching.

17. Determine if your expectations are appropriate for the level of the student.

18. Be sure to emphasize others' points of view during communication between staff members to provide the student with examples of the process of interpreting communication of others.

19. Develop a game associated with understanding the point of view of others.

20. Develop short interactions where the purpose of the conversation is to understand perspectives. Allow the student frequent breaks because participation can be difficult for him/her.

21. Begin with students in small groups, 1:1. As the students begin to understand other's points of view, expand the group to three participants.

22. Have the student's family members role-play situations with him/her.

23. Embed the teaching of this behavior throughout the student's home and school life.

24. Explicitly teach facial expressions and the motions they convey using posters that show faces that are happy, sad, surprised, scared, etc.

25. Pair the teaching of this behavior with the practicing of turn-taking during games and turn-taking during conversations (e.g., I talk, the other student listens, then the other student talks and I listen).

26. Pair the teaching of this behavior with something that is of high interest to the student (his/her favorite ice cream is chocolate, but a classmate's is vanilla).

27. Have the student draw, paint, etc., a picture showing two different people/animals/characters having different interests/points of view.

28. Provide/use comic strip stories to illustrate a situation where different points of view are expressed.

29. Use cue cards to signal the student to use appropriate, previously taught scripts.

30. Provide social scripts as visuals for the student during verbal exchanges.

31. Tell a social story that explains tolerance versus acceptance.

32. Use a social skills chart (visual) to teach the student what another point of view looks and sounds like.

33. Give the student 3-5 seconds to process the communication after stating a point of view.

34. Keep conversations simple. Begin with 1-2 sentences at a time. This will help the student understand.

35. Teach nonverbal and body language cues to the student to help him/her understand the context of a viewpoint.

36. Provide opportunities for social interaction in a structured setting to lessen anxiety.

37. Practice social skills through role-play and scripting to give the student skills to accept others' viewpoints.

38. Choose a peer to help the student navigate social situations and let him/her know when he/she is not respecting others' views.

39. Make a circle of friends model for the student while he/she is out of the room. This will make the student feel more included in the class culture.

40. Create play dates for young students to build social skills. Include play therapy sessions which teach social skills.

41. Set up a class case study where a discussion takes place (e.g., an argument between students with the class commenting on how to resolve the issue, etc.).

42. Play games such as board games, checkers, etc., to teach the student to take turns and understand that he/she is not always right.

43. Stage a conversation where the student is required to respond in a give and take manner. The student not only learns to talk in a social setting but also learns to extend his/her sentences on a particular topic.

44. Discuss understanding and accepting other people's views (e.g., raising your hand to speak, listening while others are speaking, etc.).

45. Have the student practice "echoing" what you or another student say. Teach the student to imitate inflectional patterns and facial expressions as well as to repeat words.

46. Create and reinforce activities (e.g., school bulletin board, class project, bake sale, etc.) in which students work together for a common goal rather than individual success or recognition. Point out that larger accomplishments are realized through group effort rather than by individual effort.

47. Use a private signal (e.g., holding up a finger, a wink, thumbs up, etc.) to remind the student to use positive communication skills with others.

48. Provide the student with a routine to be followed when making decisions (e.g., place a list of decision-making strategies on the student's desk).

49. Model for the student a variety of ways to solve problems in conflict situations (e.g., withdrawing, reasoning, apologizing, compromising, etc.).

50. Evaluate the student's problem-solving ability. Limit his/her exposure to conflict situations at a level with which he/she can participate appropriately.

51. Choose a peer to accompany the student as the student engages in different activities, to act as a model in teaching appropriate responses to environmental social cues.

52. Make sure the academic and social demands of the group situation are within the student's ability level.

53. Have the student practice appropriate interactions with the teacher(s).

54. Allow the student to observe group activities without requiring active participation. Require more involvement over time as the student becomes more active in group situations.

55. Maintain mobility throughout the classroom to supervise student interactions and intervene in conflict situations in which the student is unable to successfully solve the problem.

56. Reduce the emphasis on competition (e.g., academic or social). Fear of failure may create anxiety resulting in inappropriate responses to environmental social cues.

57. Point out the natural consequences of failing to respond appropriately to environmental social cues from other students (e.g., other students will avoid him/her, loss of friendships, misunderstandings, etc.).

58. Be mobile to be frequently near the student.

59. Maintain visibility to and from the student. The teacher should be able to see the student and the student should be able to see the teacher. Make eye contact possible at all times.

60. Make sure explanations regarding how the student should respond to social cues are delivered in a way the student understands. This can be checked by asking the student to repeat the explanation in his/her own words.

61. Provide the student with hypothetical conflict situations and ask him/her to suggest appropriate solutions to the situations.

62. Have the student participate in simulated conversational activities with feedback designed to teach conversational skills (e.g., greetings, closings, questions, topics of conversation, etc.).

63. Allow the student to interact with a group of peers with whom he/she feels comfortable to practice appropriate responses to environmental cues.

64. Allow the student to leave a small group activity and return to independent work when the student can no longer be successful in the group activity (e.g., he/she is disrupting the group, fighting, etc.).

65. Encourage the student to model the behavior of peers who are successful.

66. Communicate with parents (e.g., notes home, phone calls, etc.) to share information about the student's progress. The parents may reinforce the student at home for using communication skills to maintain positive interpersonal relationships with others at school.

67. Allow natural consequences to occur when the student does not respond appropriately to constructive criticism (e.g., make highly reinforcing activities contingent upon responding appropriately to redirection in academic and social situations).

68. Make sure that an offer of assistance is made at the same time constructive criticism is delivered.

69. Choose an outgoing, nonthreatening peer to help the student interact more appropriately.

70. Evaluate the expectation for peer interaction to determine if the student can be successful in the interactions and for the expected length of time.

71. Group the student with peers who will be appropriate role models and are likely to facilitate the student's academic and behavioral successes.

72. Teach the student appropriate positive ways to verbally indicate disagreement (e.g., "Excuse me, I think I was here first." "Pardon me, I need to get to my locker." "I'm sorry, but I don't think that's correct.").

73. Make sure the student receives adequate, positive reinforcement whenever he/she is behaving in an appropriate manner.

74. Make sure that positive reinforcement is not inadvertently given for inappropriate social interactions (e.g., attending to the student only when he/she has demonstrated inappropriate social interactions).

75. If the student has responded inappropriately to a conflict situation, take time to explore with the student appropriate solutions which could have been used in solving the problem.

76. In conjunction with other school personnel, develop as much consistency across the various environments as possible (e.g., rules, criteria for success, behavioral expectations, consequences, etc.).

77. Establish social rules (e.g., share materials, use a quiet voice in the building, walk indoors, use care in handling materials). Review rules often and reinforce students for following the rules.

78. Provide the student with simulation activities in the classroom to teach successful responses to environmental social cues.

79. Make sure that the situation is not so stimulating it makes successful interactions with another person difficult.

80. Use role-play to demonstrate situations in which the student would need to use positive interactions with others (e.g., interactions with peers at recess, interactions with cafeteria cooks at lunchtime, interaction with P.E. teacher, etc.).

81. Teach the student problem-solving skills: (a) identify the problem, (b) identify goals and objectives, (c) develop strategies, (d) develop a plan of action, and (e) carry out the plan.

82. Teach the student positive social communication skills to maintain positive interpersonal relationships with others (e.g., waiting your turn to speak, asking conversational questions, using an appropriate tone of voice, talking about appropriate subjects with others, making eye contact, nodding your head, etc.).

83. Make sure that the student understands instructions/directions for the group activity (e.g., give instructions in a variety of ways, make sure that the student understands his/her role, review the rules for group behavior before the activity begins, etc.).

84. Do not criticize the student. When correcting the student, be honest yet supportive. Never cause the student to feel negatively about himself/herself.

85. Make sure that the student's feelings are considered when it is necessary to discuss his/her inappropriate comments (i.e., use comments that do not diminish the student's enthusiasm for participation).

86. Explain to the student that it is natural for conflict situations to occur. What is important is how he/she reacts to the situation.

87. Assess the demands of the social situation to determine an appropriate level of expectation for the student's social interaction skills.

88. Write a contract with the student specifying what behavior is expected (e.g., understanding other's point of view) and what reinforcement will be made available when the terms of the contract have been met.

89. Role-play various situations with the student to model appropriate ways to react to others points of view (e.g., listen carefully, ask for explanations, etc.).

90. Provide the student with the opportunity to work with a peer who will be an appropriate model for social interactions.

91. Assess the appropriateness of the social situation in relation to the student's ability to function successfully.

92. Pair social cues with verbal explanations and immediate reinforcement for appropriate responses.

93. Select nonacademic activities designed to facilitate appropriate interaction between the student and another person (e.g., board games, model building, coloring, etc.).

94. Make sure the student understands that natural consequences may occur if he/she reacts inappropriately in conflict situations (e.g., peers may not want to interact, teachers may have to intervene, etc.)

95. Encourage the student to use problem-solving skills: (a) identify the problem, (b) identify goals and objectives, (c) develop strategies, (d) develop a plan of action, (e) carry out the plan.

96. Reinforce the student for using communication skills to maintain positive interpersonal relationships with others: (a) give the student a tangible reward (e.g., classroom privileges, line leading, passing out materials, five minutes free time, etc.) or (b) give the student an intangible reward (e.g., praise, fist bump, smile, etc.).

97. Reinforce the student for using communication skills to maintain positive interpersonal relationships with others based on the number of times the student can be successful. As the student demonstrates success, gradually increase the number of times required for reinforcement.

98. Teach the student a variety of ways to solve problems in conflict situations (e.g., withdrawing, reasoning, calling upon an arbitrator, apologizing, compromising, allowing others the benefit of the doubt, etc.).

99. Teach the student appropriate verbalizations for problem resolution as an alternative to fighting (e.g., "Let's talk about it." "Let's compromise." "Let's see what would be fair for both of us.").

100. Have the student role-play ways to solve problems in conflict situations with peers and adults (e.g., withdrawing, reasoning, calling upon an arbitrator, apologizing, compromising, allowing others the benefit of the doubt, etc.).

101. Demonstrate accepting behavior (e.g., willingness to help, making criticisms constructive and positive, etc.) to encourage the student to socialize and communicate in learning environments.

102. Use vocabulary that is within the student's level of comprehension when delivering directions, explanations, and information.

103. Encourage the student to think of more appropriate ways to have handled the situation.

1. Use a study carrel to help remove other visual distracters when working on a task.

2. Use sound reducing headphones or ear plugs to decrease the amount of auditory distracters the student hears.

3. Consult with an occupational therapist that specializes in sensory processing. Have the therapist assess the student for use of one of the various auditory programs. These programs focus on auditory processing, including engagement with the environment and others.

4. Educate the student regarding the importance of attending to the environment.

5. Use teachers and other classmates to promote appropriate attending to the environment when performing tasks.

6. If the student is nonverbal, develop a form of communication with the use of an assistive device, pictures, etc. Work with a speech language pathologist to determine communication needs.

7. Discuss with the parents medical treatments/additional professionals that would be helpful for the student (e.g., an assessment done by a physician who specializes in decreased visual attention, distraction, and poor ability to attend to the environment; an assessment done by a pediatric neuropsychologist to determine possible attention difficulties [Attention Deficit Disorder or Attention Deficit/Hyperactivity Disorder]; etc.).

8. Provide the student with frequent breaks when performing activities that require more attention to avoid fatigue.

9. Use the student's strong interests to promote success with attending to the environment.

10. Use various musical compact discs, such as classical, to decrease environmental distracters in the learning environment.

11. Use videos to teach the student about attending to the environment.

12. Look at the student's neurological system and see if there is a type of input that he/she needs (e.g., swinging, jumping on a trampoline, etc.) prior to providing appropriate engagement with you or others.

13. Work with an occupational therapist that specializes in sensory processing to evaluate the student's sensory-based needs.

14. Use songs to teach the student about attending to the environment.

15. Provide an individualized incentive for using appropriate attention to the environment. Be consistent in using the incentive to promote continued learning and success for the student.

16. Consult with other professionals regarding difficulties (e.g., psychiatrist and/or doctor to determine medical needs, occupational therapist to determine functioning abilities, speech language pathologist to determine language needs, social worker, etc.).

17. Remove other distracters (e.g., visual auditory, taste, smell, touch, movement, etc.) when working on the skill.

18. Use books that are of special interest to the student. Emphasize how characters are attending to the environment when observed in the books. Have the student identify times where the character is using appropriate attention.

19. Have the student participate in groups that work on attention. This will provide times when the student can observe others and their ability to use their vision to assist them to complete a task.

20. Develop opportunities throughout the student's day to practice using attention so he/she practices consistently.

21. Practice in all situations in to help the student appropriately generalize information to various situations.

22. Determine the student's level of understanding. He/she may not be able to understand how to attend. Assist the student to develop appropriate skills to facilitate success in all environments.

23. Use personalized social stories to explain how one should attend to the environment in various situations that are specific to the student.

24. Emphasize using appropriate attention throughout the day. Have staff members emphasize this as well to reinforce this skill in various situations.

25. Remove items that are distracters to the student and may limit his/her ability to interact with you versus the item.

26. The student may not be able to process multiple sensory inputs at the same time (vision/eye contact and auditory/listening to directions). Determine if this is a factor in his/her decreased attention.

27. Consult an Irlen specialist (Irlen Syndrome). These professionals develop specialized glasses that assist the eyes to process visual input and thus increase visual attention.

28. Give the student a squeeze ball to use at his/her desk to keep his/her sensory needs activated.

29. Attach the rough side of a loop fastener strip (about two inches) to the edge of the student's desk to allow for sensory stimulation that is not distracting to other students.

30. Place a discreet timer on the student's desk that quietly beeps every minute to allow awareness of time during independent work.

31. Place a textured, inflatable rubber seat cushion on the student's seat for discreet movement at his/her desk.

32. Provide audio books to accompany novels and textbooks (all subjects) to keep the student interacting with the text despite reading struggles.

33. Use picture cues to discreetly redirect the student's attention.

34. Teach skills ahead of time so that the student has a foundation to build upon during lessons to prevent staring due to frustration.

35. Present tasks in shortened amounts/for shorter time-spans with frequent short breaks to keep the student active.

36. Provide frequent and quick rewards for observed on-task behaviors, followed by a quick explanation of the good behavior in 10 words or less.

37. Use active learning opportunities so that the student can participate in activities.

38. Allow for alternate work areas (e.g., standing behind desk, sitting in reading corner, sitting by teacher, etc.) and give the student preferential seating for prompting and redirecting, and a quiet setting to focus.

39. Teach the student to set and self monitor goals in regard to attending with a built-in reward system.

40. Allow choices in learning opportunities to create more student interest in the current activity.

41. Give both verbal and written directions to provide a visual reminder of instructions for the task at hand.

42. Provide immediate feedback to the student.

43. Reduce the number of distractions surrounding the student.

44. Teach the student to self monitor by placing a tally on a desk paper every time he/she is found staring off into space.

45. Call on the student frequently so that he/she must stay focused on the lesson.

46. Change the pitch of your voice and the rhythm of your movement to maintain the student's attention.

47. Observe behavior to determine if it occurs more frequently at certain times and adjust teaching style to include more hands-on activities and games at those times.

48. Deliver a predetermined signal (e.g., hand signal, verbal cue, etc.) when the student begins to stare off into space.

49. Provide the student with a timer to be used to increase the amount of time during which he/she maintains attention (e.g., have the student work on the activity until the timer goes off).

50. Provide the student with a quiet place in which to work where auditory and visual stimuli are reduced. This is used to reduce distracting stimuli and not as a form of punishment.

51. Provide an incentive statement along with a directive (e.g., "When you complete this assignment, you may earn a pass to the water fountain.").

52. Deliver reinforcement for any and all measures of improvement.

53. Reinforce the student for attending to a task based on the length of time he/she can be successful. As the student demonstrates success, gradually increase the length of time required for reinforcement.

54. Reinforce the student for attending to the source of information. Continuous eye contact is not necessary for reinforcement.

55. Help the student develop attention-maintaining behaviors (e.g., maintain eye contact, take notes on the subject, ask questions related to the subject, etc.).

56. Use multiple modalities (e.g., auditory, visual, tactile, etc.) when presenting directions, explanations, and instructional content. Determine which modality is stronger and use the results.

57. Allow the student to close the door or windows to reduce auditory and visual stimuli from outside of the classroom.

58. Reward the student for concentrating on an assignment for a specific length of time (e.g., take a break, get a drink of water, talk briefly with a peer, etc.).

59. Try various groupings to determine the group in which the student is most comfortable.

60. Reduce distracting stimuli which could interfere with the student's ability to remain on task (e.g., provide enough room for him/her to move without physical contact, keep noise level to a minimum, keep movement in the environment to a minimum, etc.).

61. Provide the student with headphones to wear if auditory stimuli interfere with his/her ability to function. As the student functions more successfully in the presence of auditory stimuli, gradually reduce the amount of time the headphones are worn.

62. Stop at various points during the presentation of information to ensure the student is attending and maintaining eye contact.

63. Identify the student's most effective learning mode. Use it consistently to facilitate the student's understanding and remaining on task for longer periods of time.

64. Choose a peer, paraprofessional, etc., to cue the student when he/she is off task (e.g., the person can touch the student's arm as a signal that he/she is not remaining on task).

65. Maintain visibility to and from the student. The teacher should be able to see the student and the student should be able to see the teacher. Make eye contact possible at all times.

66. Have the student chart his/her on-task behavior. Reinforce the student for increasing the amount of time spent on task.

67. Monitor the student's performance in activities or tasks to make sure the student begins, works on, and completes an assignment to be ready to move to the next activity in his/her routine.

68. Reinforce the student for maintaining eye contact: (a) give the student a tangible reward (e.g., classroom privileges, five minutes free time, etc.) or (b) give the student an intangible reward (e.g., praise, fist bump, smile, etc.).

69. Allow the student some movement while performing tasks. Monitor and limit the amount of movement.

70. Have the student take notes when information is verbally presented.

71. Communicate with parents (e.g., notes home, phone calls, etc.) to share information about the student's progress. The parents may reinforce the student at home for staying on task in the classroom.

72. Position the student's desk or work area so that he/she is not visually distracted by others (e.g., turn the student's desk away from other students, etc.).

73. Choose different people (e.g., peer, paraprofessional, counselor, friend, etc.) to help the student maintain eye contact.

74. Place the student with peers who will be appropriate role models and facilitate his/her academic and behavioral success.

75. Have the student verbally repeat directions, explanations, and instructions after they have been given to reinforce retention.

76. Provide the student with shorter tasks which do not require extended attention to be successful. As the student demonstrates success, gradually increase the length of the tasks.

77. Make sure that the student is seated close enough to make eye contact with and hear the teacher when information is being delivered.

78. Interact frequently with the student to maintain involvement in the activity (e.g., ask the student questions, ask the student's opinion, stand close to the student, seat the student near the teacher's desk, etc.).

79. Allow the student to take assignments/tasks to other areas of the school where he/she is most likely to be able to demonstrate on-task behavior (e.g., library, study hall, learning center, etc.).

80. Allow the student to take a break while working on monotonous assignments to relieve restlessness and improve concentration.

81. Follow a less desirable task with a more desirable task. Make completion of the first task necessary to perform the second.

82. Give the student one task to perform at a time. Introduce the next task only when the student has successfully completed the previous task.

83. Assign the student shorter tasks but more of them (e.g., modify a 20-problem math activity to four activities of 5 problems each, to be performed at various times during the day). As the student demonstrates success, gradually increase the number of problems for each activity and decrease the number of activities.

84. Develop a classroom environment that is quiet and uncluttered (e.g., clean, well-lighted, fresh-smelling, and at a comfortable temperature).

85. Evaluate the auditory and visual stimuli in the classroom to determine what level of stimuli the student can respond to in an appropriate manner.

86. Minimize stimulation which interferes with the student's ability to remain on task (e.g., maintain a routine schedule of events, schedule special activities for the end of the day, etc.).

87. Write a contract with the student specifying what behavior is expected (e.g., establish a reasonable length of time to stay on task) and what reinforcement will be made available when the terms of the contract have been met.

88. Teach the student appropriate ways to respond to visual and auditory stimuli in the classroom (e.g., moving to another part of the room, asking others to be quiet, leaving the group, etc.).

235 Does not adjust behavior to the demands of the social situation

1. Prevent the student from becoming over-stimulated by an activity. Supervise student behavior to limit overexcitement in physical activities, games, parties, etc.

2. Provide the student with clearly stated expectations for all situations.

3. Prevent the student from becoming so stimulated by an event or activity that the student cannot control his/her behavior.

4. Identify the expectations of different environments and help the student develop the skills to be successful in those environments.

5. In conjunction with other school personnel, develop as much consistency across the various environments as possible (e.g., rules, criteria for success, behavioral expectations, consequences, etc.).

6. Reduce the student's involvement in activities which prove too stimulating for him/her.

7. Have the student practice transitional activities to reduce the effects of stimulating activities (e.g., put head on desk, listen to the teacher read a story, put headphones on and listen to relaxing music, etc.).

8. Reduce the emphasis on academic and/or social competition. Fear of failure may cause the student to fail to adapt or modify his/her behavior to different social situations.

9. Evaluate the appropriateness of the social situation in relation to the student's ability to successfully adapt or modify his/her behavior.

10. Evaluate the appropriateness of the task to determine (a) if the task is too easy, (b) if the task is too difficult, and (c) if the length of time scheduled to complete the task is adequate.

11. Write a contract with the student specifying what behavior is expected (e.g., compromising to reasonable demands) and what reinforcement will be made available when the terms of the contract have been met.

12. Reinforce those students in the classroom who adjust their behavior from one social situation to another without difficulty.

13. Speak to the student to explain (a) what the student is doing wrong (e.g., failing to be flexible to changing social situations) and (b) what the student should be doing (e.g., adjusting his/her behavior to the demands of social situations).

14. Reinforce the student for adjusting his/her behavior to the demands of the social situation without difficulty: (a) give the student a tangible reward (e.g., classroom privileges, line leading, passing out materials, five minutes free time, etc.) or (b) give the student an intangible reward (e.g., praise, fist bump, smile, etc.).

15. Reinforce those students in the classroom who adjust their behavior to the expectations of different situations.

16. Reinforce the student for adjusting his/her behavior to the expectations of different social situations based on the length of time the student can be successful. As the student demonstrates success, gradually increase the length of time required for reinforcement.

17. Communicate with parents (e.g., notes home, phone calls, etc.) to share information about the student's progress. The parents may reinforce the student at home for adjusting his/her behavior to the expectations of different social situations at school.

18. Choose a peer to model appropriate adjustment of his/her behavior to the expectations of different social situations for the student.

19. Provide a transition period between activities so the student can make adjustments in his/her behavior.

20. Maintain consistent expectations within the ability level demonstrated by the student.

21. Maintain a consistent daily routine.

22. Have the student maintain a record (e.g., chart or graph) of his/her performance in adjusting his/her behavior to expectations of different social situations.

23. Communicate to the student that he/she is a worthwhile individual.

24. Do not criticize the student. When correcting the student, be honest yet supportive. Never cause the student to feel negatively about himself/herself.

25. Pair the student with a peer who demonstrates the ability to adjust his/her behavior to the demands of social situations.

26. Provide opportunities for interactions within the classroom to allow the student to practice adjusting his/her behavior to the demands of various social situations.

27. Assess the appropriateness of the social situation in relation to the student's ability to be successful.

28. Experiment with various groupings to determine the group in which the student is most comfortable in adjusting his/her behavior to the demands of various social situations.

29. Teach the student social interaction skills (e.g., ways to respond to changing social situations). Be specific about ways of reacting to certain situations.

30. Teach the student appropriate verbal and nonverbal responses to common everyday situations.

31. Have the student participate in simulated social activities with feedback designed to improve behavioral responses to various social situations.

32. Allow natural consequences to occur so the student can learn that persons who adjust behavior to the demands of the social situation are more successful than those who are inflexible in their behavior (e.g., if you are never willing to compromise to acceptable demands, others may avoid being in social situations with you).

33. Provide the opportunity for the student to experience many social and academic successes.

34. Intervene early when there is a problem to prevent a more serious problem from occurring.

35. Teach the student to think before acting by asking himself/herself questions: *What is happening?, What am I doing?, What should I do?, What will be best for me?*

36. Make sure the student is aware of the different expectations for different social situations (e.g., rules, schedules, directions, etc.).

37. Teach the student acceptable ways to communicate displeasure, anger, frustration, etc.

38. In conjunction with other school personnel, develop as much consistency across different environments as possible (e.g., rules, criteria for individual success, behavioral expectations, consequences, etc.).

1. Discuss with the speech language pathologist the appropriate ways to reinforce positive communication with the student.

2. Explain the importance of others' perspectives and how this understanding can assist the student in many situations.

3. Discuss with the parents medical treatments/additional professionals that would be helpful for the student (e.g., high levels of metals in the body can lead to poor neurological processing and less connectedness to others, etc.).

4. Determine the student's level of communication skills. Encourage him/her to communicate with others at his/her level when communication is initiated.

5. Work with student to develop an understanding of others' perspectives.

6. Use teachers and other classmates to promote social communication.

7. If the student is nonverbal, develop a form of communication with the use of an assistive device, pictures, etc. Work with a speech language pathologist to determine communication needs.

8. Instruct the student to "check in" with others during play or a conversation. This is done by having the student tell several things about the item/event, and then ask the other person if he/she would like to hear more. If the person says yes, then the student may continue. If the person says no, then the student must discontinue the conversation or transition to a different topic.

9. Teach the student the social skills related to engaging with others and having friends. This includes the give and take of play and conversations. Sometimes, it will be appropriate for the student to dominate the conversation or dictate play, whereas other times it will be necessary for the student to allow his/her peer to do so.

10. If the student uses an augmentative device, have the student carry this device or keep it near him/her to promote use each time others communicate with him/her. This will reinforce communication.

11. Be consistent in your attempts to communicate or assist the student to communicate. Require consistent follow through by all staff members to reinforce communication by the student.

12. Discuss with parents ways the student engages and communicates at home. Build on this engagement and communication with higher order skills. Provide the parents with informational updates and ways they can provide carryover of the skill at home.

13. Use the student's strong interests to promote engaging with others on topics other than personal interest. The student first engages in a preferred activity of a peer and then obtains his/her preferred item from a peer or teacher. Set a timer to indicate when the activity will begin and end to assist the student in knowing when he/she will be able to participate in his/her preferred activity.

14. Look at the student's neurological system and see if he/she needs a specific type of input (e.g., swinging, jumping on a trampoline, etc.) to fulfill his/her need to engage only in activities which focus on his/her personal topics of interest.

15. Work with an occupational therapist that specializes in sensory processing to evaluate the student's sensory-based needs.

16. Use videos to teach the student the appropriate social skills. Include the importance of following others' interests for the purpose of engaging with a peer. Demonstrate both verbal and nonverbal communication.

17. Use songs to reinforce appropriate social skills and rules of engagement.

18. Have the student role-play situations where appropriate engagement with others is the focus.

19. Communicate with parents to encourage use of appropriate social skills and engagement rules at home and in the community.

20. Determine if the student is listening during instruction of appropriate social skills by asking questions rather than requiring eye contact. The student may not be able to process multiple sensory inputs at the same time (vision/eye contact and auditory/listening to directions).

21. Consult with other professionals regarding difficulties (e.g., psychiatrist and/or doctor to determine medical needs, occupational therapist to determine functioning abilities, speech language pathologist to determine language needs, social worker, etc.).

22. Teach the student specific social rules regarding engagement with others.

23. Instruct the student to observe nonverbal cues regarding the other person's level of interest. Watch for a wrinkled brow, wandering eyes, or lack of facial expression which may indicate the participant's boredom.

24. Remove other distracters (e.g., visual, auditory, taste, smell, touch, movement, etc.) that the student may need/seek or to which he/she may have an aversion.

25. Use books that are of special interest to the student. Emphasize the correct use of social skills during various forms of engagement.

26. Teach the student various forms of engagement that are dependent on the individual's age. Engaging with a baby involves making eye contact, silly noises that are soft and quiet which are perceived as safe, playing with simple toys 6-10" from the baby's face. Engaging with school age children involves playing games, role-play and simple skills such as cutting, coloring and pasting. Engagement with adults involves conversations, understanding social rules and appropriate topics.

27. Have the student participate in groups that work on practicing social skills. This will provide times when the student can observe others interacting appropriately.

28. Use the student's previous experiences to develop further understanding of social skills.

29. Develop opportunities throughout the student's day to practice using appropriate social skills related to engagement so he/she practices consistently.

30. Determine the student's level of communication skills. Remember to communicate with the student at this level both verbally and nonverbally to emphasize appropriate social skills related to engagement.

31. Practice in all situations to help the student appropriately generalize information to various situations.

32. Have the student role-play situations where using appropriate social skills is the focus.

33. Use personalized social stories to explain the social skills used during engagement with others in various situations that are specific to the student.

34. Determine the student's level of understanding. He/she may not be able to understand appropriate social skills.

35. Determine the student's level of motivation. The student may not use appropriate social skills because he/she is not motivated to do so.

36. Use the student's interests to teach specific rules of engagement.

37. Determine if your expectations are appropriate for the student's level.

38. Be sure to use appropriate social skills during engagement in the student's presence.

39. Emphasize using correct social skills throughout the day. Ask staff members to emphasize these as well to reinforce skills in various situations.

40. Develop a game associated with using appropriate social skills as a tool and/or generalizing this skill in various situations.

41. Use visuals (e.g., posters) in the classroom or school that remind the student of appropriate, simple social skills.

42. Be a social mediator for the student. Be with the student, but not involved in the play, so that you can give cues to help him/her be more successful.

43. Act as a shadow behind the student during play. When the student is struggling with social communication and other social skills assist him/her to respond appropriately.

44. Remove items that are distracters to the student and may limit his/her ability to interact with you versus the item.

45. Help the student develop social scripts for regular communication sequences (e.g., asking the person he/she is talking to if they want to hear more, paying attention to that person's facial expression and body language, etc.). This will determine the listener's level of interest.

46. Allow the student to participate in the preferred activity at appropriate times by incorporating the interest area into the curriculum.

47. Use tickets/tokens/notecards to limit the number of times the student can participate in or talk about the topic of interest. (e.g., The student has seven tokens [opportunities] that allow him to participate in the activity. When the tokens are gone he can no longer participate in the topic of interest for that day.).

48. Use a first-then strip. First the student completes another activity, then he/she can participate in the preferred activity.

49. Limit the amount of time, but not the number of opportunities, the student can participate in the activity. The student may request the activity as often as he/she wants, but may only participate in the activity for a brief time before returning to another activity.

50. Provide a safe spot for the object of the personal topic of interest. The safe spot might be in a clear plastic box on a highly visible shelf or on his/her desk, etc. The object of interest remains in the safe spot and can be seen, but not used until the appropriate time.

51. Minimize stimulation which interferes with the student's ability to remain on task (e.g., maintain a routine schedule of events, schedule special activities for the end of the day, etc.).

52. Teach the student to participate in other topics/activities.

53. During social conversation/circle time/group time, one student will have an opportunity to talk about a topic of interest to him/her. Every other person must ask the speaker one question about his/her topic.

54. Use a talking stick to show whose turn it is to talk. The person holding the stick is the one whose turn it is to talk.

55. Have the student keep a journal of "things to talk about and/or do with other people." Every page could represent a different person. If available, include a picture of the other person/student. Underneath the picture or name list topics of interest to that person.

56. Use a topic stick to visually show the topic under discussion. All students must make comments about the designated topic.

57. Give the student a choice between the topic of interest (A) with another tolerated topic (B). Continue to give the same choices for an extended time while you also teach topic B. Then remove topic A and give the student a choice between topic (B), the known topic, and a new topic (C).

58. Use personal interests of the student to reinforce appropriate behavior and social skills.

59. Have instructional materials in the classroom that cover the student's personal interests (e.g., books, magazines, manipulatives, etc.).

60. Provide a visual daily classroom schedule for the student.

61. Use general education peer helpers to assist the student during unstructured times such as lunch, recess, and physical education.

62. Put the student's desk on a rug or inside a circle drawn on the floor to establish boundaries.

63. Use verbal praise when the student is working on assigned tasks.

64. Develop an IEP plan and a behavior plan for the student with appropriate staff (e.g., behavior, speech, or occupational therapist, etc.).

65. Use cooperative learning to help develop social skills.

66. The student may use the computer with a peer helper to reinforce learning a task that is not a personal interest.

67. Use time out as a consequence for inappropriate behavior. Use a visual clock where the time is indicated in red which disappears as the time ticks down or an audible timer that signals the student may return to his/her seat when the time has expired.

68. Employ a signal technique (e.g., turning the lights off and on) to warn that the end of an activity is near and it is time to finish and put materials away.

69. Deliver a predetermined signal (e.g., turning lights off and on, hand signals, etc.) when the student is not beginning a task.

70. Provide the student with a timer to be used to increase the amount of time during which he/she maintains attention (e.g., have the student work on the activity until the timer goes off).

71. Provide the student with a schedule of daily events so he/she will know which activity comes next and can prepare for it.

72. Have the student develop a checklist/chart to follow which will allow him/her to follow a specific routine.

73. Have the student time activities to monitor his/her behavior and time limits.

74. Assign the student shorter activities. As the student demonstrates success, gradually increase the length of the activities.

75. Provide the student with adequate transition time between activities to increase on-task behavior after activities have begun (e.g., after break time, lunch, special activities, etc.).

76. Provide an incentive statement along with a directive (e.g., "When you complete this assignment, you may earn a pass to the water fountain.").

77. Deliver reinforcement for any and all measures of improvement.

78. Have the student practice appropriate interactions with the teacher(s) in classroom activities (e.g., simulations, role-playing, etc.).

79. Reinforce the student for attending to a task based on the length of time he/she can be successful. As the student demonstrates success, gradually increase the length of time required for reinforcement.

80. Help the student develop attention-maintaining behaviors (e.g., maintain eye contact, ask questions related to the subject, etc.).

81. Provide a transition period between activities so the student can make adjustments in his/her behavior.

82. Limit the number of changes in the student's established routine. As the student demonstrates success, gradually increase the number of changes in the routine.

83. Provide the student with clearly stated expectations for all situations (e.g., rules, schedules, directions, etc.).

84. Set time limits for completing assignments.

85. Schedule highly desirable activities contingent upon staying on task a required amount of time (i.e., staying on task for a required amount of time earns the student the opportunity to participate in a desirable activity).

86. Allow the student to contribute to the development of his/her routine to facilitate his/her ability to follow the routine (e.g., have the student determine the order of activities).

87. Attach to the student's desk revisions in the schedule for the day's events. The student may also carry it with him/her throughout the day.

88. Make sure the student does not have a lot of unstructured time.

89. Provide the student with established time limits before an activity begins.

90. Choose a peer, paraprofessional, etc., to cue the student when he/she is off task (e.g., the person can touch the student's arm as a signal that he/she is not remaining on task).

91. Establish a routine to follow before changing activities (e.g., put away materials, assemble materials for the next activity, make a list of what materials need to be replenished, etc.).

92. Maintain visibility to and from the student. The teacher should be able to see the student and the student should be able to see the teacher. Make eye contact possible at all times.

93. Have the student chart his/her on-task behavior. Reinforce the student for increasing the amount of time spent on task.

94. Provide assignments that involve immediate, short-term tasks.

95. Have the student practice transitional activities to reduce the effects of stimulating activities (e.g., put head on desk, put headphones on and listen to relaxing music, etc.).

96. Monitor the student's performance in activities or tasks to make sure the student begins, works on, and completes an assignment to be ready to move to the next activity in his/her routine.

97. Make sure the student is able to tell time to facilitate his/her ability to follow a routine.

98. Make sure that reinforcement is not inadvertently given for inappropriate behavior (e.g., attending to the student only when he/she is off task, etc.).

99. Remind the student when it is time to change activities.

100. Make sure the student knows what to do when he/she cannot successfully perform assignments (e.g., raise hand, ask for assistance, go to the teacher, etc.).

101. Choose a peer to model appropriate behavior (e.g., sitting still during a lecture, staying with a task until it is completed, etc.) for the student.

102. Choose a peer to model on-task behavior for the student.

103. Provide the student with more than enough time to finish an activity. As the student demonstrates success, gradually decrease the time provided to finish an activity.

104. Communicate with parents (e.g., notes home, phone calls, etc.) to share information about the student's progress. The parents may reinforce the student at home for staying on task in the classroom.

105. Determine an expected length of time for each individual activity to help the student follow his/her routine (i.e., make sure the student can finish an activity in an established length of time to help him/her stay within the time restrictions of the routine).

106. Evaluate the demands made on the student in academic situations to make sure that all expectations are within the student's ability level.

107. Establish classroom rules:
- Concentrate while working.
- Work quietly.
- Remain in your seat.
- Finish task.
- Meet task expectations.

Review rules often. Reinforce the student for following the rules.

108. Use a timer (visual or audible) to help the student monitor how much time he/she has to follow through with directions.

109. In conjunction with other school personnel, create as much consistency across the various environments as possible (e.g., rules, criteria for success, behavioral expectations, consequences, etc.).

110. Place the student with peers who will be appropriate role models and facilitate his/her academic and behavioral success.

111. Allow the student to perform new assignments/activities in a variety of places in the building (e.g., resource room, library, learning center, etc.).

112. Assist the student in performing certain activities. As he/she demonstrates success, gradually reduce the amount of assistance provided.

113. Along with a directive, provide an incentive statement (e.g., "When you begin your work, I will come around to see if you have questions.").

114. Structure the environment to reduce the opportunity for off-task behavior. Reduce lag time by providing the student with enough activities to maintain productivity.

115. Reinforce the student for remaining on task: (a) give the student a tangible reward (e.g., classroom privileges, line leading, passing out materials, etc.) or (b) give the student an intangible reward (e.g., praise, pat on the back, smile, etc.).

116. Base expectations for student response to redirection in academic situations on ability level (e.g., one student may be expected to return to his/her seat immediately upon redirection while another student may be given three minutes to respond appropriately).

117. In conjunction with other school personnel, develop as much consistency across different environments as possible (e.g., rules, criteria for individual success, behavioral expectations, consequences, etc.).

118. Encourage the student to monitor himself/herself. Encourage the student to take a break to regroup when he/she is acting inappropriately.

119. Provide the student with shorter tasks given more frequently.

120. Provide the student with structure for all academic activities (e.g., specific directions, routine format for tasks, time limits, etc.).

121. Communicate clearly with the student the length of time he/she has to complete an assignment. The student may want to use a timer to complete the tasks within the given period of time.

122. Communicate clearly to the student when it is time to stop an activity and prepare for a new activity or situation.

123. Interact frequently with the student to maintain involvement in the activity (e.g., ask the student questions, ask the student's opinion, stand close to the student, seat the student near the teacher's desk, etc.).

124. Assess the degree of task difficulty in relation to the student's ability to successfully perform the task.

125. Follow a less desirable task with a highly desirable task, making the completion of the first task necessary to perform the second task.

126. Give the student one task to perform at a time. Introduce the next task only when the student has successfully completed the previous task.

127. Teach the student to tell time to facilitate his/her ability to follow a routine.

128. Seat the student so that he/she experiences the least amount of auditory and visual stimuli.

129. Evaluate the appropriateness of the task to determine (a) if the task is too easy, (b) if the task is too difficult, and (c) if the length of time scheduled for the task is adequate.

130. Be consistent when expecting the student to remain on task. Do not allow the student to not attend to a task one time and expect him/her to attend to a task the next time.

131. Reinforce those students in the classroom who demonstrate on-task behavior.

132. Model for the student the appropriate way to stay on task (e.g., listening quietly as a student shares information, finishing a task in class, etc.).

133. Explain to the student the need to maintain flexibility in following a routine when changes in the routine are required.

134. Write a contract with the student specifying what behavior is expected (establish a reasonable length of time to stay on task) and what reinforcement will be made available when the terms of the contract have been met.

135. Specify exactly what is to be done for the completion of a task (e.g., indicate definite starting and stopping points, indicate the minimum requirements, etc.).

136. Make sure the student understands the instructions/directions for the task (e.g., present instructions in a variety of ways, have the student verbalize what he/she is to do to perform the activity, etc.).

137. Evaluate the auditory and visual stimuli in the classroom to determine what level of stimuli the student can respond to in an appropriate manner.

138. Choose a peer to work with the student to model adjusting his/her behavior.

139. Have the student maintain written reminders of task sequences.

237 Responds inappropriately to environmental social cues

1. Choose a peer to model appropriate responses to environmental social cues for the student.

2. Have the student ask questions about environmental social cues not understood.

3. Establish environmental social cues that the student is expected to follow (e.g., when it is appropriate to interact, when it is not appropriate to interact, etc.).

4. Provide repeated practice in responding appropriately to environmental social cues.

5. Pair social cues with verbal explanations and immediate reinforcement for appropriate responses.

6. Model appropriate responses to environmental social cues for the student to imitate.

7. To facilitate success in responding to nonverbal facial cues, have the student observe and imitate the responses of peers to nonverbal facial cues. For example, when the student is learning to interact appropriately as a spectator at a sporting event, he/she can imitate the behavior of peers who display appropriate behavior at the sporting event.

8. Choose a peer to accompany the student as the student engages in different activities, to act as a model in teaching appropriate responses to environmental social cues.

9. Provide the student with simulation activities in the classroom to teach successful responses to environmental social cues.

10. Reinforce the student for asking the meaning of environmental social cues not understood (e.g., rules, etc.).

11. Provide the student with verbal reminders or prompts when he/she misses environmental social cues.

12. Use vocabulary that is within the student's level of comprehension when delivering directions, explanations, and information.

13. Evaluate the appropriateness of the environmental social cues the student is expected to follow to determine (a) if the cue is too difficult and (b) if the length of time required to respond to the cue is adequate.

14. Communicate with the parents (e.g., notes home, phone calls, etc.) to share information about the student's progress. The parents may reinforce the student at home for responding to environmental social cues at school.

15. Write a contract with the student specifying what behavior is expected (e.g., responding appropriately to social cues) and what reinforcement will be made available when the terms of the contract have been met.

16. Reinforce the student for responding appropriately to environmental social cues based on the number of environmental social cues the student can successfully follow. As the student demonstrates success, gradually increase the number of environmental social cues required for reinforcement.

17. Reinforce those students in the classroom who respond appropriately to environmental social cues.

18. Speak to the student to explain (a) what the student is doing wrong and (b) what the student should be doing.

19. Reinforce the student for responding appropriately to environmental social cues: (a) give the student a tangible reward (e.g., classroom privileges, line leading, passing out materials, five minutes free time, etc.) or (b) give the student an intangible reward (e.g., praise, fist bump, smile, etc.).

20. Allow the student to interact with a group of peers with whom he/she feels comfortable to practice appropriate responses to environmental cues.

21. Structure the environment so that the student has many opportunities to interact with other peers in classroom activities.

22. Encourage the student to participate in social situations in which he/she is likely to respond successfully to environmental social cues.

23. Involve the student in extracurricular activities to provide additional opportunities for him/her to practice appropriate responses to environmental social cues.

24. Identify expectations of different environments and help the student develop the skills to be successful in those environments.

25. Point out the natural consequences of failing to respond appropriately to environmental social cues from other students (e.g., other students will avoid him/her, loss of friendships, misunderstandings, etc.).

26. Make sure the academic and social demands of the situation are within the student's ability level.

27. Through interviews with other students and observations, determine those characteristics of the student which interfere with successful interactions in social situations. Use the information gained to determine skills or behaviors the student needs to develop for successful interactions.

28. Model for the student appropriate responses to environmental cues in social situations.

29. Make sure that other teachers and school personnel who work with the student know that the student does not respond appropriately to environmental social cues.

30. Have the student practice appropriate responses to environmental social cues with the teacher(s) in classroom activities (e.g., simulations, role-playing, etc.).

31. Carefully consider the student's age and experience before expecting him/her to respond appropriately to environmental cues in social situations.

32. Prevent the student from becoming over-stimulated by an activity. Supervise student behavior to limit overexcitement in physical activities, games, parties, etc.

33. Maintain consistent expectations within the ability level of the student.

34. Provide the student with clearly stated expectations for all situations.

35. Prevent the student from becoming so stimulated by an event or activity that the student cannot control his/her behavior.

36. Select nonacademic activities designed to provide the student with social situations during which he/she can respond to environmental social cues appropriately.

37. In conjunction with other school personnel, develop as much consistency across the various environments as possible (e.g., rules, criteria for success, behavioral expectations, consequences, etc.).

38. Prepare the student for environmental and social expectations in advance to facilitate his/her ability to successfully respond.

39. Reduce the emphasis on competition (e.g., academic or social). Fear of failure may create anxiety resulting in inappropriate responses to environmental social cues.

40. Explain to the student what he/she has done correctly, what is expected for total correct response, and what he/she can do to improve toward or reach total correct response.

41. Establish cues (e.g., bells, rules, manners, etc.) that the student is expected to follow.

42. Reinforce the student for adjusting his/her behavior to various social cues and expectations from one environment or activity to another.

43. Have the student ask questions about part of the activity or the responses you expect of him/her that the student does not understand.

44. Explain to the student that he/she should be satisfied with his/her best efforts rather than perfection.

45. Identify the expectations of different environments and help the student develop skills needed for success in all environments.

46. Explain the benefits of trying one's best to follow social cues in the community (e.g., a person would be more welcome to return, a person might acquire positive social regard from other people, etc.).

47. Provide the student with social cues commonly found across environments (e.g., signs to be quiet, signs to wait before being seated, bathroom signs, etc.).

48. Provide the student with more than enough time to adapt or modify his/her behavior to different situations (e.g., have the student stop recess activities five minutes prior to coming into the building).

49. As much as possible, match cues to the student's ability to respond (e.g., visual cues are used for students who cannot hear, auditory cues and symbols are used for students who cannot see, etc.).

50. Make sure attention is not inadvertently given to the student for failing to respond to a social cue (e.g., only responding to the student when he/she demonstrates inappropriate behavior).

51. Make sure explanations regarding how the student should respond to social cues are delivered in a way the student understands. This can be checked by asking the student to repeat the explanation in his/her own words.

52. Demonstrate accepting behavior (e.g., willingness to help, making criticisms constructive and positive, etc.) to encourage the student to socialize and communicate in learning environments.

53. Teach the student to communicate his/her needs in an appropriate manner (e.g., raise hand, use normal tone of voice when speaking, use soft tones of voice when speaking in a restaurant, etc.).

54. Give the student responsibilities in school and community environments which promote his/her ability to socially interact in a positive manner.

55. Make the student responsible for identifying social cues with his/her peers (e.g., saying please and thank you at lunch and during snack times).

238 Lacks spontaneity, originality, and/or variety in verbal interactions

1. Have the student's hearing checked if it has not been recently checked.

2. Evaluate the appropriateness of the task to determine if the task is too difficult.

3. Reinforce the student for verbal interactions which are spontaneous, original and contain variety: (a) give the student a tangible reward (e.g., classroom privileges, line leading, passing out materials, five minutes free time, etc.) or (b) give the student an intangible reward (e.g., praise, fist bump, smile, etc.).

4. Reinforce other students in the classroom for spontaneous verbal interactions which are original and contain variety.

5. Be sure to act as an appropriate model, including spontaneous statements which contain originality and variety in your verbal interactions.

6. Choose a peer to act as an appropriate model for the student. The peer should exhibit verbal interactions which are spontaneous and which include sufficient originality and variety.

7. Reinforce the student for using new or more difficult words when speaking.

8. Give the student a list of words and have him/her provide antonyms, synonyms, and/or associated words as appropriate.

9. Have the student make up sentences or stories using new words he/she has learned.

10. Explain to the student where he/she can go to find word meanings in the classroom library (e.g., dictionary, thesaurus, encyclopedia, etc.).

11. Recognize the student's attempts to communicate his/her needs (e.g., facial expressions, gestures, inactivity, self-deprecating comments, etc.).

12. Communicate to the student that he/she is a worthwhile individual.

13. To understand the student's needs and to provide opportunity for spontaneous verbal interaction, communicate with the student as often as opportunities permit.

14. Teach the student communication skills (e.g., hand raising, expressing needs in written and/or verbal form, etc.).

15. Pair the student on a frequent basis with an outgoing student who engages in appropriate verbal interactions.

16. Determine an individual(s) in the school environment with whom the student would most want to engage in a conversation (e.g., custodian, librarian, resource teacher, principal, older student, etc.). Allow the student to spend time carrying on a conversation with the individual(s) each day.

17. Spend some time talking with the student on an individual basis about his/her interests.

18. Provide the student with many academic and social successes.

19. Explain to the student that overused words/phrases limit the meaning of what he/she is trying to say and that together you will work on reducing the times these words/phrases are used. Teach the student appropriate alternatives for the overused words/phrases.

20. Use a private signal (e.g., holding up a finger, etc.) to remind the student to limit the number of overused words/phrases.

21. Brainstorm words/phrases that are overused in your school to increase the student's awareness of words/phrases.

22. Brainstorm different ways to replace overused words/phrases.

23. Audio record the student and have him/her listen to the recording to determine those words/phrases he/she is overusing.

24. Expand upon the student's limited vocabulary to assist him/her in utilizing more elaborate verbal interactions (e.g., Student says, "That's ugly." Teacher says, "That's the most unattractive animal I've ever seen.").

25. Prompt the student to help him/her create more interesting verbal interactions (e.g., Student says, "That thing." Teacher says, "What thing, what is it doing?" etc.).

26. Teach a unit which is centered around finding examples of language which are spontaneous and which include originality and variety.

27. Point out examples of elaborative language as they occur during the day.

28. Make a list of emotions (e.g., sad, scared, happy, etc.) and have the student express them in a sentence.

29. Play word games, such as *Twenty Questions,* in which you provide clues to clarify questions (e.g., Is it edible? Is it alive?) and then gradually fade the clues.

30. Encourage the whole class to wait quietly for any student to respond to a question.

31. Create a *Feeling Box.* Place an unseen item in the box and have the student describe what it feels like, while another student tries to guess what it is.

32. Make a recording of environmental sounds and have the student attempt to identify them. Ask leading questions if necessary.

33. Create a group activity in which students are to create rules for a fictitious society.

34. Alternating with a peer, have the student take turns adding words in a sentence to create one long sentence. The sentence should be as long as possible without becoming a run-on sentence.

35. Place interesting pictures or objects on a table and have the student choose one and describe it in detail. Provide assistance in utilizing originality and variety in the descriptions.

36. Use puppets to retell a story or act out an activity. Have the student do the same by following your model.

37. Utilizing a topic which is interesting to the student, help him/her to create and act in a short skit which revolves around that topic.

38. Have the student practice being someone else in specific situations (e.g., talking on the phone, being a cashier in a grocery store, etc.).

39. Have the student watch a video or television program and then tell you what he/she thinks might have happened before or after the story.

40. Have the student practice taking messages to different persons in the school setting (e.g., librarian, school counselor, principal, etc.) and later actually deliver messages.

41. Have the student practice saying what you or another student has said. Teach the student to imitate inflectional patterns and facial expressions as well as to repeat the words. Video record this activity and have the student analyze his/her success at this activity.

42. Ask the student to provide pictures of himself/herself at various ages and then help the student to explain what his/her reactions to certain situations would have been at those particular ages; then ask the student to speculate on what his/her reaction would be ten years later.

43. Use pictures/cartoons with captions removed and have the student develop his/her own captions.

44. Have the student draw a picture of himself/herself and then narrate a story in which he/she is the main character.

45. Using sequence cards, have the student place the cards in the appropriate order and explain the sequence; then have the student tell you what might have happened before or after the provided sequence.

46. Set up fictitious situations in the classroom (e.g., restaurant, gas station, grocery store, etc.) and have the student role-play working in each situation; have him/her change roles often.

47. Provide the student with a book without words and have him/her narrate the story.

48. Pair the student with a peer and have them take turns being interviewed and interviewing. This may be done with the students acting as themselves or pretending to be another person or fictitious character.

49. Have the student give answers to what if questions (e.g., "What if you were ten feet tall?" "What if dinosaurs still roamed the earth?").

1. Have the student's hearing checked if it has not been recently checked.

2. Evaluate the appropriateness of the task to determine if it is too difficult.

3. Reinforce the student for responding quickly and with relevant responses: (a) give the student a tangible reward (e.g., classroom privileges, line leading, passing out materials, five minutes free time, etc.) or (b) give the student an intangible reward (e.g., praise, fist bump, smile, etc.).

4. Reinforce other students in the classroom who respond quickly and in a relevant manner.

5. Discuss with the student what is expected (e.g., responding more quickly and with relevant responses).

6. Act as a model for appropriate responses.

7. Choose a peer to act as an appropriate model for relevant responses.

8. Give the student a list of words and have him/her provide antonyms, synonyms, and/or associated words.

9. Provide the student with direct eye contact and communicate to him/her that you expect him/her to do the same with you.

10. Always allow the student to finish responding before you begin talking. Reinforce other students in the classroom for allowing the student to finish responding before they begin talking.

11. When the student is slow to respond or makes an irrelevant response, have him/her rephrase in his/her own words your original question to check for comprehension.

12. Pause often when you speak. This pause time encourages participation in the communication act.

13. Make sure the rate of speech you are using is appropriate for the situation.

14. Obtain the student's attention before giving instructions or asking a question.

15. Have the student make up sentences or stories using new words he/she has learned.

16. Explain to the student where he/she can go to find word meanings in the classroom library (e.g., dictionary, thesaurus, encyclopedia, etc.).

17. Communicate to the student that he/she is a worthwhile individual.

18. To understand the student's needs and to provide opportunity for relevant verbal interaction, communicate with the student as often as opportunities permit. Be sure to spend some time talking with the student on an individual basis and include topics which are of interest to the student.

19. Teach the student communication skills (e.g., hand raising, expressing needs in written and/or verbal form, etc.).

20. Provide the student with many academic and social successes.

21. Reduce the emphasis on competition. Failure may cause the student to be reluctant to respond.

22. Have the student practice appropriate verbal interactions with peers and teacher(s).

23. Determine an individual(s) in the school environment with whom the student would most want to engage in a conversation (e.g., custodian, librarian, resource teacher, principal, older student, etc.). Allow the student to spend time carrying on a conversation with the individual(s) each day.

24. Pair the student with an outgoing peer who engages in relevant verbal interactions on a frequent basis.

25. Use a private signal (e.g., holding up a finger, etc.) to remind the student to respond quickly and/or with a relevant response.

26. Audio record the student and have him/her listen to the recording to determine instances in which he/she responds slowly and/or makes an irrelevant response.

27. When the student makes an inappropriate response, immediately rephrase his/her response to make it relevant/appropriate.

28. Prompt the student to help him/her respond more quickly and with relevant verbal responses (e.g., Student says, "That thing." Teacher says, "What thing, what is it doing?" etc.).

29. Point out examples of relevant verbal responses as they occur during the day.

30. Encourage the whole class to wait quietly for any student to respond to a question.

31. Make a list of emotions (e.g., sad, scared, happy, etc.) and have the student express them in a sentence.

32. Play word games, such as *Twenty Questions*, in which you provide clues to clarify questions (e.g., Is it edible? Is it alive?) and then gradually fade the clues.

33. Create a *Feeling Box*. Place an unseen item in the box and have the student describe what it feels like, while another student tries to guess what it is.

34. Make a recording of environmental sounds and have the student identify them. Ask leading questions if necessary.

35. Alternating with a peer, have the student take turns adding words in a sentence create one long sentence. The sentence should be as long as possible without becoming a run-on sentence. Check to ensure that all additions to the sentence are relevant.

36. Place interesting pictures or objects on a table and have the student choose one and describe it in detail. Encourage the student to respond quickly and provide assistance in formulating relevant responses in these descriptions.

37. Have the student practice being someone else in specific situations (e.g., talking on the phone, being a cashier in a grocery store, etc.). Make sure all responses are relevant to the situation.

38. Have the student watch a video or television program and then tell you what he/she thinks might have happened before or after the story.

39. Have the student practice taking messages to different persons in the school setting (e.g., librarian, school counselor, principal, etc.) and later actually deliver messages.

40. Have the student practice saying what you or another student has said. Teach the student to imitate inflectional patterns and facial expressions as well as to repeat the words. Video record this activity and have the student analyze his/her success at this activity.

41. Ask the student to provide pictures of himself/herself at various ages and then help the student to explain what his/her reactions to certain situations would have been at those particular ages; then ask the student to speculate on what his/her reaction would be ten years later.

42. Use pictures/cartoons with captions removed and have the student develop his/her own captions.

43. Using sequence cards, have the student place the cards in the appropriate order and explain the sequence; then have the student tell you what might have happened before or after the provided sequence.

44. Provide the student with a book without words and have him/her narrate the story.

45. Set up fictitious situations in the classroom (e.g., restaurant, gas station, grocery store, etc.) and have the student role-play working in each situation; have him/her change roles often.

46. Pair the student with a peer and have them take turns being interviewed and interviewing. This may be done with the students acting as themselves or pretending to be another person or a fictitious character.

47. Have the student give answers to what if questions (e.g., "What if you were ten feet tall?" "What if dinosaurs still roamed the earth?").

48. Have the student compete against himself/herself by timing how fast he/she can name a series of pictured objects. Have the student try to increase his/her speed as proficiency increases.

240 Uses inappropriate verbal and/or nonverbal language in social situations or interactions with peers and/or adults

1. Have the student's hearing checked if it has not been recently checked.

2. Reinforce the student for using appropriate verbal and/or nonverbal language in social situations or interactions with peers and/or adults: (a) give the student a tangible reward (e.g., classroom privileges, line leading, passing out materials, five minutes free time, etc.) or (b) give the student an intangible reward (e.g., praise, fist bump, smile, etc.).

3. Reinforce other students in the classroom for appropriate verbal and/or nonverbal interactions.

4. Be sure to act as an appropriate model for verbal and nonverbal language in social situations and in interactions with peers and adults.

5. Speak with the student to explain that he/she is using inappropriate verbal and/or nonverbal language. Be specific about the types of language the student is using and the situation(s) in which they are occurring.

6. Choose a peer to act as an appropriate model for verbal and nonverbal language in social situations and in interactions with peers and adults.

7. Recognize the student's attempts to communicate his/her needs (e.g., facial expressions, gestures, inactivity, self-deprecating comments, etc.).

8. Communicate to the student that he is a worthwhile individual.

9. Encourage appropriate eye contact in all communicative situations.

10. To understand the student's needs and to provide opportunities for appropriate verbal interactions, communicate with the student as often as opportunities permit.

11. Provide the student with many academic and social successes.

12. Determine an individual(s) in the school environment with whom the student would most want to engage in a conversation (e.g., custodian, librarian, resource teacher, principal, older student, etc.). Allow the student to spend time carrying on a conversation with the individual(s) each day.

13. Spend some time talking with the student on an individual basis about his/her interest.

14. Pair the student with an outgoing student who engages in appropriate verbal interactions on a frequent basis.

15. Provide opportunities for appropriate interactions within the classroom.

16. Reduce stimuli which contribute to the student's inappropriate language.

17. Allow the student to be a member of a group without requiring active participation.

18. Allow the student to show visitors and new students around the school.

19. Greet or acknowledge the student as often as possible (e.g., greet him/her in the hallways or cafeteria, welcome him/her to class, acknowledge a job done well, etc.). Encourage him/her to recognize you in return.

20. Have the student run errands which will require verbal and/or nonverbal interactions with other students, teachers, administrators, etc.

21. Experiment with various groupings to determine the groups in which the student is most comfortable carrying on conversations with peers and adults.

22. Have the student play games which require carrying on conversations with others.

23. Teach the student social interaction skills (e.g., ways in which to appropriately respond to others' attempts to be friendly, complimentary, sympathetic, etc.).

24. Teach the student conversational phrases (e.g., "How are you?" "I'm fine." "How's it going?" "See you later." etc.) to use when speaking to peers and adults.

25. Teach the student conversational rules (e.g., explain that it is appropriate to greet a person when you're seeing him/her for the first time of the day but not when it's been only five minutes since the last encounter).

26. Teach the student appropriate verbal and nonverbal responses to common everyday situations.

27. Teach the student appropriate body language and explain the different effects it can have on communication.

28. Explain to the student that prosody (e.g., inflectional patterns, loudness, pitch, rate) can influence the communicative message. Have the student practice different statements while varying these parameters, then discuss the resulting influence on meaning.

29. Teach the student that he/she must respond differently depending on the person to whom he/she is talking (e.g., "What's happening?" is acceptable for a peer but not for the principal).

30. Have the student participate in simulated conversational activities with feedback designed to teach conversational skills (e.g., greetings, questions, topics of conversations, etc.).

31. Help the student develop social awareness (e.g., people may be embarrassed by what you say, feelings can be hurt by comments, tact is the best policy, remember interactions which have made you feel good and treat others in the same manner, etc.).

32. Use a private signal (e.g., holding up a finger, etc.) to remind the student to use appropriate verbal and/or nonverbal language.

33. Audio record the student and have him/her listen to the recording to determine instances in which he/she is using inappropriate verbal and/or nonverbal language.

34. Rephrase the student's words to assist him/her in utilizing more appropriate verbal interactions.

35. Prompt the student to help him/her utilize more appropriate verbal/nonverbal language (e.g., Teacher says, "How are you?" Student says, "Fred." Teacher says, "How are you feeling, Fred?" or "Your name is Fred. Can you tell me how you are feeling?").

36. Teach a unit which is centered around finding examples of language which are appropriate for use in various situations.

37. Point out examples of appropriate language usage (both verbal and nonverbal) as they occur during the day.

38. Encourage the whole class to wait quietly for any student to respond to a question.

39. Make a list of emotions (e.g., sad, scared, happy, etc.) and have the student express them in a sentence.

40. Create a *Feeling Box*. Place an unseen item in the box and have the student describe what it feels like, while another student tries to guess what it is.

41. Use puppets to retell a story or act out an activity. Have the student do the same by following your model.

42. Utilizing a topic which is interesting to the student, help him/her to create and act in a short skit which revolves around that topic.

43. Have the student practice being someone else in a specific situation (e.g., talking on the phone, being a cashier in a grocery store, etc.).

44. Have the student watch a video or television program and then tell you what he/she thinks might have happened before or after the story.

45. Have the student practice taking messages to different persons in the school setting (e.g., librarian, school counselor, principal, etc.) and later actually deliver messages.

46. Have the student practice saying what you or another student has said. Teach the student to imitate inflectional patterns and facial expressions as well as to repeat the words. Video record this activity and have the student analyze his/her success at this activity.

47. Have a peer deliberately make mistakes while conveying a message (e.g., leaving out the place or time when a date is being made). Have the student identify the errors and ask for clarification.

48. Teach the student to be aware of listener response to determine if the meaning of a message has been received accurately.

49. Ask the student to provide pictures of himself/herself at various ages and then help the student to explain what his/her reactions to certain situations would have been at those particular ages; then ask the student to speculate on what his/her reaction would be ten years later.

50. Provide immediate feedback and cues for the student when his/her message has not been received accurately.

51. Have the student draw a picture of himself/herself and then narrate a story in which he/she is the main character.

52. Set up fictitious situations in the classroom (e.g., restaurant, gas station, grocery store, etc.) and have the student role-play working in each situation; have him/her change roles often.

53. Provide the student with a book without words and have him/her narrate the story.

54. Pair the student with a peer and have them take turns being interviewed and interviewing. This may be done with the students acting as themselves or pretending to be another person or a fictitious character.

241 Demonstrates difficulty expressing logical and reasonable responses to questions

1. Have the student's hearing checked if it has not been recently checked.

2. Evaluate the appropriateness of the task to determine if the task is too difficult.

3. Reinforce the student for appropriate decision making: (a) give the student a tangible reward (e.g., classroom privileges, line leading, passing out materials, five minutes free time, etc.) or (b) give the student an intangible reward (e.g., praise, fist bump, smile, etc.).

4. Reinforce those students in the classroom who demonstrate logical thinking (e.g., making appropriate decisions, solving problems, making inferences, etc.).

5. Give the student responsibilities that require logical thinking (e.g., assign the student to water plants and provide him/her with a watering can and a glass telling him/her to use the most appropriate container).

6. Have the student ask questions about directions, explanations, and instructions he/she does not understand.

7. Each day provide the student with problem-solving situations which require logical thinking (e.g., "A stranger takes you by the arm in a department store. What do you do?" "You see smoke coming out of a neighbor's house and no one is home. What do you do?" etc.). Help the student role-play these situations.

8. Make sure the student experiences the consequences of his/her behavior (e.g., appropriate behavior results in positive consequences while inappropriate behavior results in negative consequences).

9. Provide the student with a list of questions involving logic, which he/she answers verbally (e.g., "Why do we post wet paint signs?" "Why do we have stop signs at intersections?" "Why do we wear seat belts?" etc.).

10. When something is broken, lost, etc., have the student identify what could have been done to prevent the situation. Have the student discuss the value of keeping materials organized, maintained, and serviceable.

11. Have the student explain outcomes, consequences, etc. (e.g., when the student earns a reward or privilege, make sure he/she can explain that the reward was the result of hard work and accomplishment).

12. Have the student respond to what if questions (e.g., "What if it rained for forth days and forty nights?" "What if there were no rules and laws?" etc.).

13. Be sure to relate what the student has learned in one setting or situation to other situations (e.g., vocabulary words learned should be pointed out in reading selections, math word problems, story writing, etc.).

14. Call attention to situations in the classroom which will generalize to future real-life situations (e.g., being on time for class is the same as being on time for work; school work not done during work time has to be made up before school, after school, or during recreational time, just as responsibilities at places of employment would have to be completed at night or on weekends if not completed on the job; etc.).

15. Have the student read stories involving a moral (e.g., *The Tortoise and the Hare*, *The Boy Who Cried Wolf*, etc.) and explain the reason for the outcome of the story.

16. Have the student read short stories without endings. Have the student develop logical endings for the stories.

17. Give the student situations/pictures and have him/her explain what variables are related (e.g., "Snow is falling, and the wind is blowing. Is the temperature hot or cold? What should you wear outdoors?").

18. Give the student fill-in-the-blank statements requiring an appropriate response from multiple choice possibilities (e.g., The boy's dog was dirty so the boy decided to give his dog a _____ [dog biscuit, bath, toy].).

19. Have the student sequence cartoon strips, after they have been cut apart and rearranged, and explain the logic of the sequence created.

20. Use a variety of instructional approaches to help the student generalize knowledge gained to real-life situations (e.g., after studying the judicial system, provide a simulated courtroom trial).

21. Teach the student to define words/concepts in his/her own words. This skill builds comprehension and aids in generalization and decision making skills.

22. Show the student pictures of dangerous situations and have him/her explain why they are dangerous (e.g., a child running into the street between parked cars, a child riding a bicycle without using his/her hands, etc.).

23. Use cause-and-effect relationships as they apply to nature and people. Discuss what led up to a specific situation in a story or picture, what could happen next, etc.

24. Make sure that the student can verbalize the reason for real-life outcomes of behavior (e.g., why the student had to leave the class line on the way to recess, why he/she earned the privilege of being line leader, etc.).

25. Have the student make up rules and explain why each rule would be necessary.

26. Have the student identify appropriate consequences for rules (e.g., consequences for following rules and consequences for not following rules). Have the student explain the choice of consequences he/she identified.

27. Have the student answer such questions as "Why do we have rules?" "Why do you have to be a certain age before you can drive a car?" etc.

28. Have the student answer a series of *who, what, when, where, why, how, how many,* or *how much* questions which gradually increase in complexity. Use material from the student's textbooks, workbooks, readers, etc., as well as questions which reflect the student's interests.

29. Have the student answer analogy situations (e.g., a garage is to a car as a house is to a _____).

30. In problem solving, the student must be able to ask himself/herself questions. Have the student ask questions related to his/her daily work and/or the daily schedule.

31. Set aside time each day for a problem-solving game, analogies, decision making activities, assigned responsibilities, etc.

32. Encourage the student to think out loud when planning. Model it as you plan your teaching activities.

33. Create a problem-solving unit for the whole classroom, placing the student in a small group which will allow him/her to have ample opportunity for participation.

34. Have the student(s) approach problem solving using the scientific approach: state the problem, form a hypothesis, test the hypothesis, evaluate, and draw conclusions.

35. Have the student brainstorm several solutions to a problem.

36. Teach for comprehension by telling the student what he/she is going to learn. Check for understanding over several days' time.

37. Have the student practice new concepts/words several times over a period of weeks.

38. Have a scavenger hunt which contains riddles/clues. Place the student in a group which contains classmates who are able to problem-solve and who will include the student in their attempt to decipher the clues.

39. Have the student list the steps that he/she must follow in to solve a particular problem.

40. Have the student list the equipment/information he/she will need to solve a particular problem.

41. Ask the parents to encourage the student's decision making skills at home.

242 Has difficulty expressing opinions, feelings, and/or emotions

1. Have the student's hearing checked if it has not been recently checked.

2. Evaluate the appropriateness of the task to determine if it is too difficult.

3. Reinforce the student for expressing opinions, feelings, and/or emotions: (a) give the student a tangible reward (e.g., classroom privileges, line leading, passing out materials, five minutes free time, etc.) or (b) give the student an intangible reward (e.g., praise, fist bump, smile, etc.).

4. Reinforce those students in the classroom who express opinions, feelings, and/or emotions.

5. Be an appropriate model for the student by expressing your own opinions, feelings, and/or emotions. Attempt to clearly identify each when you do express them.

6. Each day provide the student with situations which elicit particular emotions and assist the student in expressing those emotions (e.g., "A stranger takes you by the arm in a department store. How do you feel?" "You see smoke coming out of a neighbor's house. Are you happy?" etc.).

7. Have the student read stories involving a moral (e.g., *The Tortoise and the Hare*, *The Boy Who Cried Wolf*, etc.) and state his/her opinions about the outcome of the stories.

8. Provide the student with a list of questions involving opinions, feelings, and/or emotions and assist him/her in answering verbally (e.g., "How do you feel when you get an A on a test?" "Do you think recess should be before or after lunch?" "Should people wear seat belts?" etc.).

9. Have the student explain outcomes, consequences, etc. (e.g., when the student earns a reward or privilege, make sure he/she can explain that the reward was the result of hard work and accomplishment and that he/she should feel proud).

10. Have the student respond to what if questions (e.g., "What if it rained for forty days and forty nights?" "What if there were no rules and laws?" etc.) to encourage the expression of opinions and/or feelings.

11. Have the student read short stories without endings. Assist the student in expressing opinions, feelings and/or emotions about possible endings to the stories.

12. Show the student pictures of dangerous situations and have him/her explain why they are dangerous (e.g., a child running into the street between parked cars, a child riding a bicycle without using his/her hands, etc.).

13. Use cause-and-effect relationships as they apply to nature and people. Discuss what led to a specific situation in a story or picture, what could happen next, etc.

14. Make sure that the student can verbalize the reason for real-life outcomes of behavior (e.g., why the student had to leave the class line on the way to recess, why he/she earned the privilege of being line leader, etc.).

15. Have the student make up rules and explain why each rule is necessary.

16. Have the student identify appropriate consequences for rules (e.g., consequences for following rules and consequences for not following rules). Have the student explain the choices of consequences he/she identified.

17. Have the student illustrate a story about an event which has emotional overtones. Point out the emotions portrayed or involved in the story.

18. Provide the student with concrete examples of ways to express opinions, feelings and/or emotions (e.g., speaking, writing, gestures, drawing, etc.).

19. When the student displays anger, take the time to listen and respond not only to what he/she is saying, but also to what the student might be feeling.

20. Provide the student with pictures of people who are happy, sad, angry, etc., and have him/her create stories which are based upon the pictures.

21. Set up a situation in which the student can role-play various emotions. Provide feedback on how effectively the idea was communicated.

22. Pair the student with a peer who is effective in expressing opinions, feelings and/or emotions. Have them participate in a simple debate on a current topic of controversy.

23. Have the student take a poll of classmates concerning their feelings about particular TV shows, rock groups, movies, foods, etc.

24. Encourage verbal expression in your classroom and listen carefully when the student is trying to express opinions, feelings or emotions about any topic.

243 Has difficulty using ritualistic greetings/closings when appropriate

1. Have the student's hearing checked if it has not been recently checked.

2. Reinforce the student for using ritualistic greetings/closings when appropriate: (a) give the student a tangible reward (e.g., classroom privileges, line leading, passing out materials, five minutes free time, etc.) or (b) give the student an intangible reward (e.g., praise, fist bump, smile, etc.).

3. Reinforce other students in the classroom for appropriate use of ritualistic greetings and closings.

4. Be sure to act as a model for appropriate use of ritualistic greetings and/or closings.

5. Speak with the student to explain that he/she is not using ritualistic greetings/closings when appropriate. Be specific about the types of interactions the student is using inappropriately and the situation(s) in which they are used.

6. Choose a peer to act as an appropriate model for the use of ritualistic greetings and closings.

7. Communicate to the student that he/she is a worthwhile individual.

8. Encourage appropriate eye contact in all communicative interactions.

9. Teach the student communication skills (e.g., hand raising, expressing needs in written and/or verbal form, etc.).

10. Provide the student with many academic and social successes.

11. Determine an individual(s) in the school environment with whom the student would most want to engage in a conversation (e.g., custodian, librarian, resource teacher, principal, older student, etc.). Allow the student to spend time carrying on a conversation with the individual(s) each day. Make sure these people model appropriate use of greetings/ closings.

12. Pair the student with an outgoing student who engages in appropriate verbal interactions on a frequent basis.

13. Provide opportunities for appropriate interactions within the classroom.

14. Assess the appropriateness of the social situation in relation to the student's ability to be successful.

15. Allow the student to show visitors and new students around the school.

16. Greet or acknowledge the student as often as possible (e.g., hallways, cafeteria, welcome to class, a job well done, etc.). Encourage him/her to acknowledge you in return.

17. Have the student run errands which will require verbal and/or nonverbal interactions with other students, teachers, administrators, etc.

18. Experiment with various groupings to determine the group in which the student is most comfortable carrying on conversations with peers and adults.

19. Teach the student social interaction skills (e.g., ways in which to appropriately respond to others when first seeing them or when leaving them, etc.). Be specific about phrases which are appropriate to use and situations in which you would use them.

20. Teach the student conversational rules (e.g., explain that it is appropriate to greet a person when you're seeing him/her for the first time of the day but not when it's been only five minutes since the last encounter.

21. Teach the student appropriate verbal and nonverbal responses to common everyday situations.

22. Teach the student appropriate body language and explain the different effects it can have on communication.

23. Teach the student that he/she must respond differently depending on the person to whom he/she is talking (e.g., "What's happening?" is acceptable for a peer but not for the principal). Discuss how age, position, and/or familiarity can change the form of the greeting/closing used.

24. Have the student participate in simulated conversational activities with feedback designed to teach conversational skills (e.g., greetings, closings, questions, topics of conversations, etc.).

25. Teach the student conversational phrases (e.g., "How are you?" "I'm fine." "How's it going?" "See you later." etc.) to use when greetings/closings are appropriate.

26. Help the student develop social awareness (e.g., people may be embarrassed by what you say, feelings can be hurt by comments, tact is the best policy, remember interactions which have made you feel good and treat others in the same manner, etc.).

27. Create a communication unit for the entire classroom which includes the basic rules of conversation.

28. Use a private signal (e.g., holding up a finger, etc.) to remind the student to use appropriate greetings/closings.

29. Audio record the student and have him/her listen to the recording to determine instances in which he/she is using appropriate/inappropriate greetings/closings.

30. Rephrase the student's words to assist the student in utilizing more appropriate greetings/closings.

31. Prompt the student to help him/her utilize greetings/closings more appropriately (e.g., Teacher says, "How are you?" Student says nothing. Teacher says, "I'm fine today. How are you?").

32. Teach a unit which is centered around finding examples of language which are appropriate for use in ritualistic greetings and closings.

33. Point out examples of appropriate verbal and nonverbal language usage involving ritualistic greetings and closings as they occur during the day.

34. Have the student use a play phone to practice greetings/closings.

35. Have the student practice taking messages to different persons in the school setting (e.g., librarian, school counselor, principal, etc.) and later actually deliver messages. Include ritualistic greetings/closings in the practice.

36. Have the student practice saying what you or another student has said. Teach the student to imitate inflectional patterns and facial expressions as well as to repeat the words. Video record this activity and have the student analyze his/her success at this activity.

37. Teach the student to be aware of listener response to determine if the meaning of his/her greeting/closing has been received accurately.

38. Set up fictitious situations in the classroom (e.g., restaurant, gas station, grocery store, etc.) and have the students in the class role-play working in each situation. Have them change roles often and emphasize the use of ritualistic greetings and closings in the role-play situation.

39. Pair the student with a peer and have them take turns being interviewed and interviewing. This may be done with the students acting as themselves or pretending to be fictitious characters. Emphasize the appropriate use of ritualistic greetings/closings.

244 Exhibits difficulty using verbal language as a tool to obtain desired results

1. Have the student's hearing checked if it has not been recently checked.

2. Evaluate the appropriateness of the task to determine if it is too difficult.

3. Reinforce the student when he/she uses language effectively and is able to obtain the desired results: (a) give the student a tangible reward (e.g., classroom privileges, line leading, passing out materials, five minutes free time, etc.) or (b) give the student an intangible reward (e.g., praise, fist bump, smile, etc.).

4. Reinforce students in the classroom who appropriately use verbal language as a tool to obtain desired results.

5. Be an appropriate model for the student by expressing yourself concisely and by demonstrating that verbal language can be used as a tool to obtain desired results.

6. Have the student read short stories without endings. Assist the student in expressing opinions, feelings, and/or emotions about the endings to the stories.

7. Each day provide the student with situations in which the student must use verbal language as a tool to obtain desired results (e.g., The student wants to get a drink. Indicate that he should tell you when he wants a drink rather than waiting for you to provide the break.).

8. Provide the student with a list of statements/questions which could be used to obtain specific results and assist him/her in using the statements at appropriate times (e.g., "Would you help me move this?" "I would like to get a drink now.").

9. Have the student explain outcomes, consequences, etc. (e.g., when the student earns a reward or privilege, make sure he/she can explain that the reward was the result of hard work and accomplishment and that he/she should feel proud).

10. Use cause-and-effect relationships as they apply to nature and people. Discuss what led up to a specific situation in a story or picture, what could happen next, etc.

11. Make sure that the student can verbalize the reason for real-life outcomes of behavior (e.g., why the student had to leave the class line on the way to recess, why he/she earned the privilege of being line leader, etc.).

12. Have the student make up rules and explain why each is necessary.

13. Pair the student with a peer who is effective in using verbal language as a tool to obtain desired results.

14. Have the student identify appropriate consequences for rules (e.g., consequences for following rules and consequences for not following rules). Have the student explain the choice of consequences he/she identified.

15. Encourage verbal expression in your classroom and listen carefully when the student is using language as a tool. Try to set up situations where the student can see that his/her attempts at language usage have been successful.

245 Can only speak in short, simple sentences which lack complexity

1. Have the student's hearing checked if it has not been recently checked.

2. Ascertain the type of verbal model to which the student is exposed at home. Without placing negative connotations on his/her parent's language skills, explain the purpose of using elaborated sentences.

3. Reinforce the student for using more complex sentences: (a) give the student a tangible reward (e.g., classroom privileges, line leading, passing out materials, five minutes free time, etc.) or (b) give the student an intangible reward (e.g., praise, fist bump, smile, etc.).

4. Encourage verbal output. Generally, students who use very short sentences also talk less than most students. Increasing their opportunities to communicate verbally will provide them with necessary practice.

5. Make sure the student understands that sentences express thoughts about a subject and what that subject is or does. Explain that complex thoughts require complex sentences which include descriptive words and connecting words.

6. Be sure that the student understands more complex sentences by asking questions to ascertain his/her comprehension (e.g., after saying "Before you get a drink of water, finish your social studies." ask "What should you do first?").

7. Reinforce those students in the classroom who use various types of complex sentences.

8. When the student uses short, simple sentences which lack complexity, provide him/her with models of expansion and conjoining using his/her sentences as a foundation.

9. Provide the student with an elaborated sentence and have him/her identify the descriptive vocabulary used. If necessary, ask the student questions to elicit the appropriate information.

10. Use gestural and/or verbal prompts to remind the student to expand his/her sentences (e.g., use a gesture to indicate "more" while asking the student to "tell me more," or point to specific parts of a picture or object he/she is describing to elicit specific descriptive vocabulary).

11. Begin sentences with compound subjects and have the student complete the thought (e.g., The bear and the frog _____.). This activity can be expanded by providing verb phrases without subjects.

12. During the day, write down some of the student's simple sentences. Read the sentences to the student and ask him/her questions requiring additional descriptive vocabulary to expand the sentences (e.g., Student says: "My dog can run." Teacher says: "What color is your dog? What size is your dog? How fast can your dog run?" Encourage the student to use these words to make his/her original sentence longer. Student says: "My big, black dog can run fast." Accept any additional expansions the student incorporates into his/her sentences without expecting all the descriptors to be used initially.).

13. Have the student use conjunctions to expand sentences containing opposites (e.g., "A man is big, but a boy is little.").

14. Ask questions which stimulate language. Avoid those which can be answered by yes/no or a nod of the head (e.g., "What did you do at recess?" instead of "Did you play on the slide?" or "Tell me about your vacation." instead of "Did you stay home over the holidays?").

15. Have the student make up sentences. Encourage the use of descriptive words and phrases where appropriate.

16. Have the student assist in adding descriptive words and phrases to other students' simple sentences.

17. Ask the parents to help encourage the student's use of more complex sentences at home by praising him/her when longer sentences are used.

18. Video the student and his/her classmates performing various actions. Play back the recording with the sound turned off and have the student describe what is happening. Encourage the use of descriptive words and phrases where appropriate. (This activity could be modified by using a prerecorded video.)

19. Give the student a list of transition words (e.g., therefore, although, because, etc.) and have him/her make sentences using each word.

20. Give the student several short sentences and have him/her combine them to make one longer sentence (e.g., "The dog is big. The dog is brown. The dog is mine." becomes "The big, brown dog is mine.").

21. Provide the student with conjunctions to be used in sentence expansion, including sentence combining, compound subjects and verbs, etc.

22. Give the student a group of related words (e.g., "author," "read," "love," "best-seller," etc.) and have him/her make up sentences including all the words.

23. Make groups of cards containing subjects, verbs, adjectives, etc. Have the student combine the cards in various ways to construct sentences which are appropriate in complexity.

24. Build lists by providing nouns that go with a specific adjective (e.g., red could be followed by apple, car, book, etc.). Then have the student select one of the nouns and build a list of appropriate adjectives (e.g., car could be followed by big, metal, expensive, etc.). Have the student use this information to formulate complex sentences.

25. Using books without words, have the student tell the story, encouraging the use of longer, more complex sentences.

246 Has difficulty understanding directions and/or carrying out instructions and often requires repetition or rephrasing

1. Have the student's hearing checked if it has not been recently checked.

2. Evaluate the appropriateness of the task to determine (a) if the directions provided are too long and/or difficult or (b) if the length of time required for the student to remember is unacceptable (e.g., presentation of information was too brief or time lapse between presentation of material and request for recall was too long).

3. Explain the importance of understanding directions and/or carrying out instructions.

4. Discuss with the student what behavior is expected (e.g., following one-step directions, etc.).

5. Write a contract with the student specifying what behavior is expected (e.g., following directions without repetition or with one cue, etc.) and what reinforcement will be made available when the terms of the contract have been met.

6. Reinforce the student for following directions and/or carrying out instructions: (a) give the student a tangible reward (e.g., classroom privileges, line leading, passing out materials, five minutes free time, etc.) or (b) give the student an intangible reward (e.g., praise, fist bump, smile, etc.).

7. Reduce distracting stimuli when directions are being presented. Move the student away from other students who may interfere with his/her ability to attend to directions, explanations or instructions.

8. Seat the student near the teacher and away from noisy or visually distracting areas.

9. Make sure that directions, explanations, or instructions are delivered loudly enough to be heard by the student.

10. Stand close to or directly in front of the student when delivering verbal instructions.

11. Maintain mobility to provide assistance to the student.

12. Draw the student's attention to key aspects of auditory communications as they occur (e.g., repeat important points, call the student by name, tell the student which information is particularly important, etc.).

13. Teach the student to recognize key words and phrases related to directions/instructions to facilitate his/her ability to follow directions accurately.

14. Make sure the student is attending to the source of information (e.g., eye contact is being made, hands are free of materials, student is looking at assignment, etc.).

15. Informally assess the student's auditory and visual short-term memory skills to determine which is the stronger. Utilize the results when presenting directions, explanations, and instructional content.

16. When the student is required to recall information, provide him/her with auditory cues to help him/her remember the information previously presented (e.g., say, "Remember yesterday when I said . . .").

17. Reduce abstractions by giving concrete examples and firsthand experiences. Use simple demonstrations.

18. Have the student audio record directions, explanations, and instructions so that he/she may replay needed information.

19. Provide visual information to support information the student receives auditorily (e.g., wall-mounted board, pictures, projections, gestures, etc.).

20. Provide the student with written directions and instructions to supplement verbal directions and instructions.

21. Deliver information in both verbal and written form.

22. Write stories, directions, etc., so the student may read along as he/she listens.

23. Teach the student to visualize the instructions as if they were a movie, then play it back (e.g., The student sees himself/herself opening an English book, then sees himself/herself turning to page 212, etc.).

24. Use multiple modalities (e.g., auditory, visual, tactile, etc.) when presenting directions, explanations, and instructional content.

25. Establish a routine for the student to follow in performing activities, assignments, etc. (e.g., listen to the person speaking to you, wait until directions are given before starting the assignment, make sure you have all needed materials, etc.).

26. Have the student follow directions as soon as they are given to minimize the impact of irrelevant and distracting information on his/her ability to carry out the instructions.

27. Teach the student how to organize information into smaller units or segments (e.g., break the number sequence 132563 into units of 13, 25, 63, and point out that phone numbers are learned as 573, then 581, then 0000).

28. Tell the student what to listen for before delivering auditory information.

29. Use a predetermined signal prior to delivering verbal questions and directions (e.g., clap hands, turn lights off and on, call the student by name, etc.).

30. Have the student read ahead on a subject to be discussed in class so that he/she is familiar with new vocabulary and concepts that will be used during instructional periods. (If the student cannot read, have a peer/parent/sibling read the information to him/her or record the material, with emphasis on the vocabulary.)

31. Deliver directions, explanations, and instructional content in a clear manner and at an appropriate pace.

32. Deliver verbal directions prior to handing out materials.

33. Stop at key points when delivering directions, explanations, and instructions to determine student comprehension. Ask questions about what he/she needs to do.

34. Deliver information to the student on a one-to-one basis. Gradually include more students in the group with the student as he/she demonstrates the ability to listen successfully.

35. Decrease the steps and/or stages involved in a series of directions until the student meets with success. As the student demonstrates proficiency, gradually increase expectations.

36. Give the student one task to perform at a time. Introduce the next task only when the student has successfully completed the previous task.

37. Establish assignment rules (e.g., listen to directions, wait until all verbal directions have been given, ask questions about anything you do not understand, begin the assignment only when you are certain about what you are to do, make sure you have all necessary materials, etc.).

38. Have the student ask questions about directions, explanations, and instructions he/she does not understand.

39. Reinforce those students in the classroom who follow directions appropriately.

40. Choose a peer who follows directions to act as a model for the student.

41. Choose a peer to deliver and/or repeat verbal questions and directions.

42. Review the schedule of the morning or afternoon activities with the student and have him/her repeat the sequence. Increase the length of the sequence as the student demonstrates success.

43. Provide the student with a schedule of daily events for each day's activities at school.

44. Print the day's schedule on the board and refer to it frequently.

45. Have the student physically perform directions (e.g., have the student go to the door and then stand near the teacher, etc.).

46. Have the student practice following directions by engaging in sequential activities which are purposeful to him/her (e.g., operating equipment, following recipes, opening a combination lock, etc.).

47. At the end of the school day, have the student recall three activities in which he/she was engaged during the day. As the student demonstrates success, gradually increase the number of activities he/she is expected to recall.

48. After a field trip or special event, have the student sequence the activities which occurred.

49. Use the calendar every day and discuss what the student did yesterday, is doing today, or will do tomorrow.

50. Provide the student with environmental cues and prompts designed to facilitate his/her success in the classroom (e.g., posted rules, schedule of daily events, steps for performing tasks, etc.).

51. Teach the student to make reminders for himself/herself (e.g., notes, lists, etc.).

52. Have the student practice making notes for specific information and directions he/she wants and/or needs to remember. Encourage him/her to use these notes as a checklist to make sure that he/she has completed all the steps.

53. Teach the student information-gathering skills (e.g., listen carefully, write down important points, ask for clarification, wait until all information is received before beginning, etc.).

54. Provide the student with written lists of things to do, materials he/she will need, etc.

55. Make sure the student is not engaged in activities that interfere with listening to directions, explanations, and instructions (e.g., looking at other materials, putting away materials, talking to others, etc.).

56. Teach the student to use associative memory clues.

57. Have the student practice repetition of information to increase short-term memory skills (e.g., repeating names, phone numbers, dates of events, etc.).

58. Have the student repeat/paraphrase directions, explanations, and instructions as soon as possible after hearing them.

59. Reduce the emphasis on competition. Competitive activities may cause the student to hurry and begin without listening carefully.

60. Have the student pretend he/she is a waiter/waitress. Have the student recall the items from an order given to him/her.

61. Have the student play "barrier" games, where a screen is placed between two students so they can hear but cannot see each other's paper, objects, etc. Have one student give the other one directions (e.g., Mark an "x" below an "o."). Have them check after the directions are given to see how accurately the instructions were followed.

62. Have the student act as a classroom messenger. Give the student a verbal message to deliver to another teacher, secretary, administrator, etc. Increase the length of the messages as the student demonstrates success.

247 Has limited expressive and/or receptive vocabulary

1. Have the student's hearing checked if it has not been recently checked.

2. Explain the importance of expanding one's receptive and expressive vocabulary (i.e., comprehension and communication are based on the knowledge and use of appropriate/accurate vocabulary).

3. Reinforce the student for expanding his/her receptive and/or expressive vocabulary: (a) give the student a tangible reward (e.g., classroom privileges, line leading, passing out materials, five minutes free time, etc.) or (b) give the student an intangible reward (e.g., praise, fist bump, smile, etc.).

4. Have the student label all the objects, persons, places, etc., in the environment that he/she can. Then have him/her point to items in the environment as you label the ones he/she was unable to name. The items he/she is unable to label will comprise a foundation for new vocabulary to be learned. Activities to foster expansion of expressive vocabulary should focus on the items he/she could point to but could not label.

5. Have the student divide cards that label objects, persons, places, etc., in the environment into different categories (e.g., function, color, size, use, composition, etc.). Point out the similarities and differences between items as they change categories (e.g., a ball and an apple may both be red, round, and smooth; but you can only eat the apple).

6. Ascertain the type of language model the student has at home. Without placing negative connotations on the language model in his/her home, explain the difference between language which is rich in meaning and that which includes a limited repertoire of vocabulary.

7. Explain to the student how to classify new words as to category, function, antonym and synonym, etc., so he/she will have a way of "filing" the words in his/her memory.

8. In addition to labeling objects, persons, places, etc., have the student provide verbs that could be used with each (e.g., "book" - read, browse through, skim, etc.).

9. In addition to identifying objects, persons, actions, etc., have the student provide places where each could be seen (e.g., "actor" - TV, theater, stage, etc.).

10. In addition to labeling objects, have the student state the uses of each (e.g., "knife" - cut, spread, slice, etc.).

11. Have the student provide as many adjectives as possible to go with a given noun. Then have him/her choose one of the adjectives and produce as many nouns as possible to go with it.

12. Have the student provide as many adverbs as possible to go with a given verb. Then have him/her choose one of the adverbs and produce as many verbs as possible to go with it.

13. Have the student list all the vocabulary he/she can think of that goes with a specific word (e.g., "space" - astronaut, lunar rover, rocket, shuttle, launch, etc.).

14. Give the student a picture of a specific location (e.g., grocery story) and have him/her name as many objects, actions, persons, etc., as he/she can think of that can be found there.

15. Reinforce those students in the classroom who use an expanded speaking vocabulary.

16. Choose a peer who demonstrates comprehension and use of an expanded vocabulary to work with the student to improve his/her comprehension of vocabulary and act as a model to expand the student's speaking vocabulary.

17. Use "hands-on" activities to teach vocabulary by constructing objects and/or organizing manipulatives.

18. Teach the student to use context clues and known vocabulary to determine the meaning of unknown vocabulary.

19. Explain to the student how to use context clues to determine the meaning of words he/she hears or sees (e.g., listening to or looking at the surrounding words and determining what type of word would be appropriate).

20. Explain to the student where he/she can go to find word meanings in the classroom library (e.g., dictionary, thesaurus, encyclopedia, etc.).

21. Have the student maintain a vocabulary notebook with definitions of words whose meanings he/she does not know.

22. Prepare a list of new words which the student will encounter while reading a given assignment. Help him/her (or have a peer help him/her) look up each word and practice saying it and using it in a sentence before reading the given assignment.

23. Select relevant and appropriate reading material and have the student underline each unfamiliar word. Make a list of these words and review their meanings with the student until he/she can use them when speaking.

24. Use a multisensory approach to facilitate retention when teaching new vocabulary (e.g., the scent of fragrant flowers or freshly baked spice cake in the room will facilitate retention of the vocabulary word "aroma").

25. Use visual aids whenever possible when introducing new vocabulary.

26. Use a large, old purse, box, bag, etc., with objects inside. Have the student reach into the container and try to determine what the item is based on the way it feels before he/she is allowed to see it.

27. Take advantage of unusual or unique situations to teach new vocabulary. Typically, a student will retain information learned in a novel situation better than that learned during a regular routine. The uniqueness of the situation will also facilitate the student's memory skills when you provide a reminder to help the student recall the vocabulary (e.g., "Remember yesterday during the fire drill when we talked about _____.").

28. Make up or use games to teach comprehension and expression of new vocabulary. (Research has shown that novel situations help students to learn new information.)

29. To reinforce new vocabulary, write the new word on an envelope and put pictures inside that do and do not go with it (e.g., "arctic" - polar bears, snow, parrots, palm trees, etc.). Have the student remove the inappropriate vocabulary and explain why it doesn't belong.

30. Have the student paste a picture from a magazine on one side of a piece of paper and list all of the vocabulary that could be associated with it on the other side (including verbs). Have him/her dictate or write a story about the picture using the vocabulary.

31. Refer to previously presented information that is related to the topic when presenting new vocabulary.

32. Teach new vocabulary within the context of known information (e.g., category, associations, etc.).

33. Have the student act out verbs and label actions performed by classmates.

34. Have the student demonstrate and identify different verbs of the same class (e.g., walk, creep, slither, saunter, march, etc.).

35. Have the students apply new vocabulary to his/her personal experiences in written and verbal work.

36. Include new vocabulary in daily conversation as often as possible.

37. Have the student participate in role-play to foster use of new vocabulary (e.g., set up an imaginary restaurant and have the student and his/her peers play the various roles of customers, waiter/waitress, cook, etc., varying the time of day and the occasion.

38. Record the student's spontaneous speech, noting specific words he/she uses; then have the student make a list of other words (synonyms) which could be substituted for these words.

39. Give the student a list of words and ask him/her to tell the opposite of each word.

40. Have the student make up sentences or stories using new words he/she has learned.

41. Name a category and have the student identify all the things within the category. Introduce new words which belong in the same group.

42. Give the student a series of words or pictures and have him/her name the category in which they belong (e.g., objects, persons, places, etc.).

43. Describe objects, persons, places, etc., and have the student name the items described.

44. Discuss with parents the ways in which they can help the student develop an expanded speaking vocabulary (e.g., encouraging the student to read the newspaper, novels, magazines, or other materials for enjoyment). Emphasize to parents that they can set a good example by reading with the student.

45. Send home new vocabulary words and encourage parents to use them in activities and general conversation.

46. Give the student a "word of the day" which is to be incorporated into conversations. Reinforce the student each time he/she uses the word.

47. During conversation repeat phrases used by the student, revising the vocabulary to include additional words (e.g., The student says, "The TV show was good." Repeat by saying, "I'm glad the TV show was so entertaining.").

48. Use new words in a sentence completion activity. Have the student explain how the use of different words changes the meaning of the sentence (e.g., I like Jerry because he is _____ sincere/humorous/competitive.).

49. Point out words that have a variety of meanings and use them appropriately in different contexts.

50. Have the student provide associations for given words (e.g., "circus" - clown, elephant, trapeze, tent, lion tamer, etc.).

248 Has difficulty understanding nonliteral forms of speech such as idioms, proverbs, similes, metaphors, jokes, puns, and riddles

1. Have the student's hearing checked if it has not been recently checked.

2. Reinforce the student for demonstrating comprehension of figurative language: (a) give the student a tangible reward (e.g., classroom privileges, line leading, passing out materials, five minutes free time, etc.) or (b) give the student an intangible reward (e.g., praise, fist bump, smile, etc.).

3. Explain to the student that nonliteral forms of language are used to make communication more interesting, but that they never mean exactly what they say. Identify the concept of "playing" with language through nonliteral forms.

4. Reinforce those students in the classroom who demonstrate comprehension of nonliteral forms of language.

5. Choose a peer who demonstrates comprehension of figurative language to work with the student to improve his/her comprehension of nonliteral forms of language.

6. Develop a unit on figurative language. Have the student choose the more interesting of sentence pairs (e.g., "Joe talks too much." vs. "Joe is always shooting off his mouth.").

7. Have the student keep a vocabulary or figurative language notebook in which he/she can list new vocabulary and nonliteral forms of language accompanied by definitions for reference.

8. Point out idioms, similes, metaphors, etc., that are contained in the student's everyday reading materials. Help him/her determine the meaning from context by providing two or three choices, including the literal translation.

9. Have the student identify idioms, similes, metaphors, etc., in his/her everyday reading material and determine the meaning from context. Provide choices of definitions, including the literal translation, when necessary.

10. Point out to the student that a simile uses as or like and a metaphor does not. Emphasize that neither form of figurative language is meant to be interpreted literally.

11. Have the student list things which possess a specific quality (e.g., blue things: October sky, cornflower, sapphire; hot things: oven, sun, firecracker; etc.). Then have him/her complete a statement with an appropriate simile or metaphor (e.g., "Her eyes were as blue as _____." or "On a summer day, the front seat of the car _____.").

12. Have the student match idioms, similes, metaphors, etc., to their definitions.

13. Have the student choose an idiom, simile, metaphor, etc., from a list to complete a sentence, paragraph, story, etc.

14. Have the student illustrate the literal translation and true meaning of an idiom, simile, metaphor, etc. (e.g., raining cats and dogs, mad as a hornet, feeling blue, etc.).

15. Draw attention to idioms, similes, metaphors, etc., used throughout the day and have the student explain his/her interpretation of their meanings.

16. Divide the class into teams and have one team illustrate an idiom, simile, metaphor, etc., according to its literal translation while the other team guesses what it is and uses it appropriately in a sentence.

17. Have the class design greeting cards, posters, ads, bulletin boards, etc., using idioms, similes, metaphors, etc.

18. Point out that some TV commercials and magazine/TV ads use figurative language to get attention. Have the student identify idioms, similes, puns, etc., in specific commercials or ads.

19. Have the students ask parents/grandparents to provide examples of figurative language used when they were younger (e.g., out of sight, far out, etc.).

20. Post an *Idiom for the Day* and have the class use it in as many contexts as possible to reinforce its meaning (e.g., seeing eye to eye, clear as mud, etc.). Similes and metaphors could be posted and used in the same way.

21. Point out proverbs in context, as in *Aesop's Fables*, *Poor Richard's Almanac*, etc. Have the student use the context of the story to help him/her choose an appropriate moral from two options.

22. Have the student find matches for proverbs that have been cut into two parts (e.g., money burns a hole/in your pocket; don't kill the goose that lays/the golden egg; etc.).

23. Have the student match a list of proverbs with their definitions.

24. Post a "proverb for the day" and use it throughout the day. Have the class identify its meaning whenever it is used.

25. Point out that nonverbal communication can serve as a cue that a joke is being made (e.g., smile, wink, nudge, etc.).

26. Have the student choose a punch line for a riddle (e.g., What has four wheels and flies? - a car, an airplane, or a garbage truck).

27. Have the student illustrate both meanings of proverbs, puns, etc.

28. Have the class design greeting cards, bulletin boards, posters, advertisements, etc., using proverbs, puns, etc.

1. Determine the student's level of communication skills and communicate with the student at this level.

2. Determine the student's level of understanding. It may be that the student has used the comment as a general form of communication.

3. Develop a form of communication appropriate for the student (e.g., words, picture exchange, use of an assistive device, etc.).

4. Discuss with parents ways the student communicates with them and use these whenever possible to reinforce the student's communication (e.g., short phrases, comments, regular body language, etc.)

5. Use the student's interests when teaching concepts and reinforcing communication (e.g., if the student is interested in trains, use pictures of trains for communicating, coloring, writing, reading, cutting, etc.), to explain the use of communication.

6. Determine if your expectations are appropriate for the student's level.

7. Have the student participate in play groups where his/her type of communication is used as well as other forms of communication to provide times where the student can observe others communicating.

8. Be sure to use appropriate language in the student's presence.

9. Avoid using slang or abstract phrases during communication with the student.

10. Assist the student hand-over-hand/hand-on-body so that he/she can successfully communicate.

11. Explain to staff members your expectations for the student so there is carryover throughout the day (e.g., if you are working on sentences and the student tends to use single word requests, instruct the staff member to prompt him/her for a sentence).

12. Discuss with the speech language pathologist the appropriate way to communicate with the student.

13. Consider the literal meaning of the word/phrase that has been used. Many students with this diagnosis are very literal and concrete in their communication.

14. Promote communication using the student's interests. Ask the student for some form of communication to obtain a favorite toy/item.

15. Look at the student's neurological system and see if he/she needs a specific type of input (e.g., swinging, jumping on a trampoline, etc.) prior to working on communication.

16. Work with an occupational therapist to evaluate the student's sensory-based needs.

17. Develop opportunities in the student's day to perform the appropriate communication so he/she practices consistently.

18. Determine the student's level of communication skills and communicate with the student at this level.

19. Use videos to teach the student the correct way to use communication, both verbal and nonverbal.

20. Use songs to reinforce the correct forms of communication.

21. Exaggerate different verbal and nonverbal communications with the use of tone and facial expressions.

22. Assess the student's auditory processing to determine if he/she is hearing or processing accurately.

23. Have the student role-play situations where simple communication would be used (e.g., pictures, gestures, nonverbal expression, verbal expressions, etc.).

24. Communicate with parents to reinforce the form of communication used at school to promote continuation at home and in the community.

25. Show the student a preferred item and ask for some form of communication.

26. Have the student practice saying what you or another student has said. Teach the student to imitate inflectional patterns and facial expressions as well as to repeat the words. Video record this activity and have the student analyze his/her success at this activity.

27. Use a private signal (e.g., holding up a finger, etc.) to remind the student to use appropriate verbal and/or nonverbal language.

28. Have the student keep a notebook of words encountered each day which are difficult for him/her to accurately produce. These can be practiced by the student with teacher or peer assistance.

29. Pair the student on a frequent basis with an outgoing student who engages in appropriate verbal interactions.

30. Have the student use a carrier phrase combined with targeted words (e.g., "I like _____." "I see a _____.").

31. Provide the student with a wordless picture book and have him/her narrate the story.

32. Audio record the student and have him/her listen to the recording to determine instances in which he/she is using inappropriate verbal and/or nonverbal language.

33. Provide the student with a list of statements/questions which could be used to obtain specific results and assist him/her in using the statements at appropriate times (e.g., "Would you help me move this?" "I would like to get a drink now.").

34. Have the student identify and correct errors after listening to examples of sentences containing incorrect word order.

35. Point out examples of appropriate language usage (both verbal and nonverbal) as they occur during the day.

36. Teach the student to be aware of listener response to determine if the meaning of a message has been received accurately.

37. Reinforce students in the classroom who appropriately use verbal language as a tool to obtain desired results.

38. Reduce the emphasis on competition. Competitive activities may cause the student to hurry and not use correct word order when speaking.

39. Provide immediate feedback and cues for the student when his/her message has not been received accurately.

40. Have the student practice descriptive statements or thoughts containing correct word order which he/she can use when speaking (e.g., describe an object, picture, activity, etc., using correct word order).

41. During the day, write down examples of the student's incorrect word order. Read the sentences to the student and have him/her make appropriate corrections verbally.

42. Make a list of emotions (e.g., sad, scared, happy, etc.) and have the student express each of them in a sentence.

43. Ask the parents to encourage the student's use of correct word order at home by praising him/her for using grammatically correct sentences.

44. Be an appropriate model for the student by expressing yourself concisely and by demonstrating that verbal language can be used as a tool to obtain desired results.

45. Alternating with a peer, have the student take turns adding words in a sentence to create one long sentence. The sentence should be as long as possible without becoming a run-on sentence.

46. Prompt the student to help him/her use more appropriate verbal/nonverbal language (e.g., Teacher says, "How are you?" and the student says, "Fred." Teacher then says, "How are you feeling, Fred?" or "Your name is Fred. Can you tell me how you are feeling?").

47. Have the student participate in simulated conversational activities with feedback designed to teach conversational skills (e.g., greetings, questions, topics of conversations, etc.).

48. Expand upon the student's limited vocabulary to assist the student in utilizing more elaborate verbal interactions (e.g., student says, "That's ugly." and the teacher responds, "That's the most unattractive animal I've ever seen.").

49. Give the student a list of words and have him/her provide antonyms, synonyms, and/or associated words as appropriate.

50. If the student has little or no intelligible speech, provide an augmentative communication board which contains pictures representing daily needs. This can be used to communicate toileting needs, hunger, etc., and can be expanded or changed as appropriate.

51. Choose a peer to model appropriate verbal and nonverbal language in social situations and in interactions with peers and adults for the student.

52. Model appropriate verbal and nonverbal language in social situations and in interactions with peers and adults.

53. Place interesting pictures or objects on a table and have the student choose one and describe it in detail. Provide assistance in utilizing originality and variety in the descriptions.

54. Greet or acknowledge the student as often as possible (e.g., hallways, cafeteria, welcome to class, a job done well, etc.). Encourage him/her to acknowledge you in return.

55. Have the student cut out pictures of items depicting targeted words. Display them where they can be practiced each day.

56. Ask the student to provide pictures of himself/herself at various ages. Help the student to explain what his/her reactions to certain situations would have been at those particular ages and to speculate on what his/her reaction might be ten years from his/her current age.

57. Create a *Feeling Box*. Place an unseen item in the box and have the student describe what it feels like, while another student tries to guess what it is.

58. Evaluate the appropriateness of requiring the student to accurately produce certain sounds (e.g., developmentally, certain sounds may not be produced accurately until the age of 8 or 9). This may naturally interfere with daily communication in some instances.

59. Have the student read short stories without endings and assist the student in expressing opinions, feelings, and/or emotions about the endings to the stories.

60. Teach the student communication skills (e.g., hand raising, expressing needs in written and/or verbal form, etc.).

61. Use pictures of similar sounding words and have the student name each picture as the teacher points to it (e.g., run and one, or bat and back).

62. Each day provide the student with situations in which the student must use verbal language as a tool to obtain desired results (e.g., The student wants to get a drink. Indicate that he should tell you when he wants a drink rather than waiting for you to provide the break.).

63. Routinely record the student's speech and point out inappropriate word order in sentences. With each successive taping, reinforce the student as his/her use of correct word order improves.

64. After recording the student's speech, have him/her identify instances of incorrect word order in sentences and make appropriate modifications.

65. Use a board game that requires the student to describe pictures utilizing intelligible speech. The student needs to use accurate speech production before he/she can move on the game board. (This activity can be simplified or expanded based on the level of expertise of the student.)

66. Make a list of the attributes which are likely to help a person become a good speaker (e.g., takes his/her time, thinks of what to say before starting, etc.).

67. Make a list of the student's most common errors in word order. Spend time with the student practicing how to correct the word order when speaking.

68. Determine an individual(s) in the school environment with whom the student would most want to engage in a conversation (e.g., custodian, librarian, resource teacher, principal, older student, etc.). Allow the student to spend time carrying on a conversation with the individual(s) each day.

69. Using "sequence cards," have the student place the cards in the appropriate order and explain the sequence; then have the student tell you what might have happened before or after the provided sequence.

70. To understand the student's needs and to provide opportunities for appropriate verbal interactions, communicate with the student as often as opportunities permit.

71. Teach the student ways to restate or rephrase a misunderstood message rather than continuing to repeat the original message with the same error pattern.

72. Rephrase the student's words to assist the student in utilizing more appropriate verbal interactions.

73. Recognize the student's attempts to communicate his/her needs (e.g., facial expressions, gestures, inactivity, self-deprecating comments, etc.).

74. Experiment with various groupings to determine the groups in which the student is most comfortable carrying on conversations with peers and adults.

75. Make sure the student understands that sentences express thoughts about a subject and what the subject is or does.

76. Teach the student the components of a complete sentence (i.e., subject, verb, and an object). Point out the components using objects, pictures, sentences, etc., depending on the student's abilities.

77. Explain to the student where he/she can go to find word meanings in the classroom library (e.g., dictionary, thesaurus, encyclopedia, etc.).

78. Have the student make up sentences or stories using new words he/she has learned.

79. Reinforce the student for using appropriate verbal and/or nonverbal language in social situations or interactions with peers and/or adults: (a) give the student a tangible reward (e.g., classroom privileges, line leading, passing out materials, five minutes free time, etc.) or (b) give the student an intangible reward (e.g., praise, fist bump, smile, etc.).

80. Reinforce the student for using new or more difficult words when speaking.

81. Encourage verbal expression in your classroom and listen carefully when the student is using language as a tool. Try to set up situations where the student can see that his/her attempts at language usage have been successful.

1. Determine the sensory expectations in each environment. Consider if the student is able to perform in each environment with the sensory expectations.

2. Discuss with parents ways the student communicates with them and determine the specific difficulties.

3. Request information from the student in different locations to determine the actual difficulty.

4. Use the student's interests when teaching concepts and reinforcing communication (e.g., if the student is interested in trains, use pictures of trains for communicating, coloring, writing, reading, cutting, etc.).

5. Have the student participate in play groups where other students are expected to produce information in various environments or situations to provide times when he/she can observe others communicating.

6. Assist the student hand-over-hand/hand-on-body so that he/she can successfully communicate.

7. Discuss with the speech language pathologist the appropriate ways to reinforce communication with the student.

8. Use speech the student does have and work to reproduce this in various environments or situations.

9. Promote communication using the student's interests. Ask the student for some form of communication to obtain a favorite toy/item.

10. Look at the student's neurological system and see if he/she needs a specific type of input (e.g., swinging, jumping on a trampoline, etc.) prior to working on communication.

11. Work with an occupational therapist to evaluate the student's sensory-based needs.

12. Develop opportunities in the student's day to produce the information so he/she practices consistently.

13. Determine the student's level of communication skills and communicate with the student at this level.

14. Use videos to teach the student appropriate forms of communication, both verbal and nonverbal.

15. Use songs to reinforce the different forms of communication.

16. Exaggerate different verbal and nonverbal communications with the use of tone and facial expressions.

17. Assess the student's auditory processing to determine if he/she is hearing accurately.

18. Have the student role-play situations where simple communication would be used in specific situations (e.g., pictures, gestures, nonverbal expression, verbal expressions, etc.).

19. Communicate with parents to reinforce the form of communication used at school and promote continuation at home and in the community.

20. Show the student a preferred item and ask for some form of communication.

21. Use personalized social stories to describe things that have happened in the day. Review these stories prior to going home. Have the student provide some of the information to his/her parents/guardians at home.

22. Have the student use a Schedule of Daily Events to recall assignments to be reviewed.

23. Have the student read a story. Provide statements out of sequence which reflect the main points of the story. Have the student arrange the statements in the correct order to demonstrate comprehension.

24. If the context of a word which the student is having difficulty generalizing appears too difficult, introduce the word by using an alternate text written at a lower reading level.

25. Have the student keep a list of words that he/she is having difficulty generalizing. Provide opportunities for the student to use these words frequently to facilitate generalization.

26. Have the student develop a series of responses representing his/her ability to generalize information to common situations in the environment (e.g., "We should drive no more than 55 miles per hour on our highways because . . ." Appropriate responses could include safety, conservation of fuel, care of vehicle, and fines for speeding.).

27. Have the student be a classroom messenger. Give the student a verbal message to deliver to another teacher, secretary, administrator, etc. As the student demonstrates success, increase the length of the messages.

28. Assign one task at a time. Give the student adequate time to complete it.

29. Identify concepts related to a topic and explain to the student how a person can generalize from one to another (e.g., numbers to money, fuel to energy, words to sentences, etc.).

30. Provide the student with a list of questions involving logic, which he/she answers verbally (e.g., "Why do we post wet paint signs?" "Why do we have stop signs at intersections?" "Why do we wear seat belts?" etc.).

31. Consider carefully the student's ability level and experience when assigning responsibilities for him/her to complete.

32. Review the morning and afternoon schedule of activities with the student and have him/her repeat the sequence. As the student is successful, increase the length of the sequence.

33. Have the student listen and take notes following the "Who, What, Where, When, How, and Why" format when concepts are presented.

34. Reduce distracting stimuli (noise and motion) around the student (e.g., place the student on the front row; provide a carrel or quiet place away from distractions; etc.). This is used as a means of reducing distracting stimuli and not as a form of punishment.

35. Make sure the student applies a newly learned skill to a real-life situation as soon as possible to facilitate generalization (e.g., when he/she learns to count by fives have him/her practice adding nickels).

36. Informally assess the student's auditory and visual short-term memory skills to determine which one is stronger. Use the results when presenting directions, explanations, and instructional content.

37. Use multiple modalities (e.g., auditory, visual, tactile, etc.) when presenting instructional content.

38. Give the student a choice of answers (e.g., more than one possible answer, multiple-choice on a worksheet, etc.) to facilitate his/her ability to recognize the correct answer.

39. Initiate a *Learn a Concept a Day* program with the student and incorporate the new concept into the assigned activities for the day.

40. Provide practice for new concepts by using a computer software program or a handheld educational device that gives the student immediate feedback.

41. Give the student fewer concepts to learn at one time. Spend additional time on each concept until the student has mastered it.

42. Review daily those skills, concepts, tasks, etc., which have been previously introduced to help the student remember information previously presented.

43. Set aside time each day for problem-solving games, analogies, decision making activities, assigned responsibilities, etc. Show the student an object or a picture of an object for a few seconds. Ask the student to recall specific attributes of the object (e.g., color, size, shape, etc.).

44. Reinforce the student for demonstrating short-term or long-term memory skills based on the length of time the student can be successful. As the student demonstrates success, gradually increase the length of time required for reinforcement.

45. Reinforce the student for demonstrating short or long-term memory skills: (a) give the student a tangible reward (e.g., classroom privileges, five minutes free time, etc.) or (b) give the student an intangible reward (e.g., praise, fist bump, smile, etc.).

46. Use sentence dictation to develop the student's short-term memory skills. Begin with three-word sentences. As the student demonstrates success, increase the length of the sentences.

47. Instruct the student to develop a checklist/chart to follow to facilitate him/her in completing all assignments. Assist the student in developing the checklist/chart if appropriate.

48. Ask the parents to encourage the student to generalize concepts learned at school to everyday situations.

49. Help the student develop an awareness of himself/herself and the environment. Instruct the student to periodically step back and ask himself/herself, "Am I on task and paying attention?" "What could I do to remember this information?"

50. Stop at various points during the presentation of directions, explanations, or instructions to check for the student's comprehension of the information presented.

51. Provide reminders throughout the educational environment to help the student be more successful in remembering information (e.g., rules, lists, schedules, etc.).

52. Identify the student's most effective learning mode. Use it consistently to facilitate the student's understanding (e.g., if the student does not understand directions or information given verbally, present it in written form; if the student has difficulty understanding written information or directions, present it verbally; etc.).

53. Describe objects, persons, places, etc., to the student and have him/her name the items described.

54. Label objects, persons, places, etc., in the environment to facilitate the student's ability to recall their names.

55. Deliver instructions by using examples of relationships (e.g., rely on what has already been learned, use examples from the student's environment, etc.).

56. Record important information for the student to replay as often as necessary.

57. Have the student look for story elements when reading a selection (e.g., setting, characters, plot, ending).

58. Record reading material for the student to listen to as he/she reads along. Have the student stop at various points to retell/summarize the selection.

59. Establish a regular routine for the student to follow in performing activities, assignments, etc. (e.g., listen to the person speaking to you, wait until directions are completed, make sure you have all the materials necessary, etc.).

60. Name a category or group and ask the student to identify as many things as possible which belong in the group. Begin with large categories (e.g., living things) and move to more specific categories (e.g., things which are green).

61. Have the student look for shapes in the environment when teaching shapes (e.g., find all the circles in the room).

62. Provide a demonstration and hands-on learning when teaching new skills.

63. Make sure the student has mastery of concepts at each level before introducing a new skill.

64. Make sure the student has adequate opportunities for repetition of information through different experiences to facilitate memory.

65. After reading a selection, have the student complete a semantic map answering the questions "Who, What, Where, When, How, and Why."

66. Provide auditory cues to help the student recall information (e.g., key words, a brief verbal description to clue the student, etc.).

67. Encourage the student and his/her parents to establish a regular daily routine to follow to help him/her remember to take care of responsibilities. For example: 6:30 a.m. - get up, make bed, get dressed 7:00 a.m. - eat breakfast 7:30 a.m. - leave for school 3:30 p.m. - return from school 4:00 p.m. - feed pets 5:00 p.m. - set the table for dinner 5:30 p.m. - eat dinner 7:00 p.m. - do homework 8:00 p.m. - go to bed. Post the schedule in a central location (e.g., on the refrigerator, in the student's room, etc.) to remind the student of what to do and when to do it.

68. Reward the student (e.g., homework pass, visit briefly with a peer, etc.) for remembering information for a specific length of time.

69. Actively involve the student in learning to remember sequences by having the student physically perform sequential activities (e.g., operating equipment, following recipes, solving math problems, etc.).

70. Evaluate the sensory stimuli in the classroom and remove or reduce extraneous environmental stimuli (i.e., visual, auditory, smell, taste, proprioceptive [sensation in the muscles and joints-tells us where our body is in relation to its parts], and vestibular [movement]).

71. Underline, circle, or highlight important information from any material the student is to learn (e.g., science, math, geography, etc.).

72. Call attention to situations in the classroom which generalize to more global situations (e.g., being on time for class is the same as being on time for work; school work not done during work time has to be made up before school, after school, or during recreational time, just as responsibilities at places of employment would have to be completed at night or weekends if not completed on the job; etc.).

73. Have the student participate in memory game activities with a limited number of symbols. As the student demonstrates success, gradually increase the number of symbols.

74. When presenting explanations and information, be sure to use vocabulary that is within the student's level of comprehension.

75. Write down verbal directions. Instruct the student to mark each step off as it is completed.

76. Instruct the student to keep needed information in a readily accessible location (e.g., bookbag, wallet, folder, locker, etc.).

77. Instruct the student to keep necessary materials for specified activities together (e.g., gym clothes in a gym bag in the car, backpack with all school-related materials by the door, etc.).

78. Teach concepts through associative learning (i.e., build new concepts based on previous learning).

79. Give the student pairs of objects and ask him/her to name the ways in which they are alike and the ways they are different. Proceed from concrete objects which can be seen and touched to abstract ideas which cannot be seen or touched.

80. Have the student write letters, fill out applications, etc., to see the generalization of handwriting, spelling, grammar, sentence structure, etc., to real-life situations.

81. Give the student a list of key words, phrases, or main points to learn for each new concept introduced.

82. Cut out pictures from magazines and newspapers and have the student match captions to them. This activity could be varied by having one student write a caption while another student determines if it is appropriate.

83. Have the student practice making notes for specific information he/she wants and/or needs to remember.

84. Assess how meaningful the material is to the student. He/she is more likely to remember the material if he/she can relate it to real experiences.

85. Help the student use memory aids or mnemonic devices to recall words (e.g., a name might be linked to another word, for example, Mr. Green is a very colorful person.).

86. Have the student review new concepts each day for a short period of time rather than two or three times per week for longer periods of time.

87. Have the student make notes, lists, etc., of important information to carry with him/her at all times.

88. Provide the student with opportunities for drill activities in the most interesting manner possible (e.g., working with a computer, using a calculator, playing educational games, watching a visual, listening to a recording, etc.).

89. After a field trip or special event have the student recall and sequence the activities which occurred.

90. Choose a peer to participate in memory activities with the student (e.g., memory games, flash cards, math facts, etc.).

91. Choose different people (e.g., peer, counselor, paraprofessional, etc.) to help the student improve his/her memory.

92. Give the student situations/pictures and have him/her explain what variables are related (e.g., "Snow is falling; the wind is blowing. Is the temperature hot or cold? What should you wear outdoors?").

93. Encourage the student to play word games such as Hangman®, Scrabble®, Password™, etc.

94. Make it pleasant and positive for the student to ask questions about things not understood.

95. Teach the student to recognize key words and phrases related to information to facilitate short-term or long-term memory skills.

96. Have the student record important information he/she should remember.

97. Assist the student in remembering responsibilities. As the student demonstrates success, gradually decrease the assistance and require the student to independently assume responsibilities.

98. Have the student practice repetition of information to facilitate short-term memory skills (e.g., repeating names, phone numbers, dates of events, etc.).

99. When the student is required to recall information, remind him/her of the situation in which the material was originally presented (e.g., "Remember yesterday when we talked about . . ." "Remember when we were outside and I told you about the . . .").

100. When the student is required to generalize knowledge from one situation to another, provide him/her with visual and/or auditory cues to help him/her remember information previously presented (e.g., repeat key words, expose part of a picture, etc.).

101. Prior to reading a selection, prepare an outline for the student to reference and add details to while reading the selection.

102. Have the student practice short-term memory skills by engaging in activities which are purposeful to him/her (e.g., delivering messages, being in charge of room clean up, acting as custodian's helper, operating equipment, etc.).

103. Teach and practice information-gathering skills (e.g., listen carefully, write down important points, ask for clarification, wait until all information is presented before beginning a task, etc.).

104. Reduce the amount of stimulation in the room (e.g., visual input from the walls, auditory input from the surrounding environment, etc) if it is distracting to the student.

105. Teach and practice different strategies to remember information: repetition, mnemonic, acronym, and association.

106. Make sure that the student is provided with an explanation of "why" he/she is learning particular information or skills (e.g., we learn to spell, read, and write to be able to communicate; we learn to solve math problems to be able to make purchases, use a checking account, measure, and cook; etc.).

107. Each day provide the student with problem-solving situations which require logical thinking (e.g., "A stranger takes you by the arm in a department store. What do you do?" "You see smoke coming out of a neighbor's house and no one is home. What do you do?" etc.).

108. Do not require the student to learn more information than he/she is capable of remembering at any time.

109. Record a message. Have the student write down the message after he/she has listened to it. As the student demonstrates success, increase the length of the message.

110. Determine whether or not the student can make inferences, predictions, determine cause-effect, etc., in everyday experiences. Teach these skills in contexts that are meaningful to the student to facilitate the ability to employ these concepts when reading.

111. At the end of the school day, ask the student to recall three activities in which he/she participated during the day. As he/she demonstrates success, gradually increase the number of activities the student is required to recall.

112. Have the student match vocabulary words with pictures representing the words.

113. Have the student memorize the first sentence or a line of a poem, song, etc. As the student experiences success, require him/her to memorize more lines at a time.

114. When reading verbally with the student, pause at various points to discuss material read up to that point. Have the student predict what will happen next before proceeding.

115. Evaluate the appropriateness of the information to be recalled to determine (a) if the task is too difficult and (b) if the length of time scheduled to complete the task is adequate.

116. Demonstrate for the student the correct way to perform a task. Assist the student in performing the task several times before having him/her perform the task independently.

117. Use cause-and-effect relationships as they apply to nature and people. Discuss what led up to a specific situation in a story or a picture, what could happen next, etc.

118. Give the student sufficient time to read a selection, emphasizing comprehension not speed.

119. Use daily drill activities to help the student memorize flash cards with math facts, sight words, etc.

120. Do not give directions to the student from across the classroom. Go to the student, get his/her undivided attention, and tell the student what he/she is to do.

121. Evaluate the responsibilities given to the student and make sure they are appropriate for his/her level of development and ability.

122. Teach the student how to organize information into smaller units (e.g., divide the number sequence 132563 into units of 13, 25, 63).

123. Encourage the student to use visual reminders (e.g., attach a note to a backpack, place a self-adhesive note on the inside of his/her locker, etc.).

124. Allow the student to use resources to help him/her successfully perform tasks (e.g., calculator, multiplication tables, abacus, dictionary, etc.).

125. Encourage the student to use an electronic pocket organizer to record the day's homework assignments, general reminders, and messages.

126. Provide the student with various times throughout the day when he/she can participate in drill activities with the teacher, an aide, a peer, etc.

127. Provide the student with written one-step, two-step, and three-step direction-following activities (e.g., sharpen your pencil, open your text to page 121, etc.).

128. Have the student role-play various real-life situations to facilitate generalization.

III. Appendix

CONTRACT

I, _____,

HEREBY DECLARE THAT I WILL _____

_____

_____.

THIS JOB WILL BE CONSIDERED SUCCESSFUL _____

_____.

NAME: _____,

FOR THE SUCCESSFUL COMPLETION OF THE ABOVE JOB,

YOU MAY _____

_____

DATE SIGNED: _____

DATE COMPLETED: _____

_____
SIGNED

Outline Form

Subject: _____

Topic: _____

	General	Specific

Who:

What:

Where:

When:

How:

Why:

Vocabulary:

Outline Form (Alternative)

Subject: _____

Topic: _____

	General	**Specific**

What:

Why:

How:

Vocabulary:

Example:

Mapping Form

```
          ┌─────────┐
┌──────┐  │         │  ┌──────┐
│ WHO  │──│  TOPIC  │──│ WHY  │
└──────┘  │         │  └──────┘
┌──────┐  └─────────┘  ┌──────┐
│ WHAT │    ╱     ╲    │ HOW  │
└──────┘   ╱       ╲   └──────┘
      ┌────────┐ ┌────────┐
      │ WHERE  │ │  WHEN  │
      └────────┘ └────────┘
```

Double-Column Form

Subject: _____

Who:	
What:	
Where:	
When:	
How:	
Why:	

Assignment Form

Subject: _____

	General	Specific
What:		
How:		
Materials:		
When:		

Subject: _____

	General	Specific
What:		
How:		
Materials:		
When:		

Assignment Sheet

ASSIGNMENT SHEET

DATE _____

SUBJECT	ASSIGNMENT	DUE DATE	TEACHER INITIALS

Comments:

_____

PARENT SIGNATURE

ASSIGNMENT SHEET

DATE _____

SUBJECT	ASSIGNMENT	DUE DATE	TEACHER INITIALS

Comments:

_____

PARENT SIGNATURE

2-Week Project Outline

DAY 1   **Determine the exact assignment**
- Identify due date

DAY 2-4   **Project preparation**
- Read assigned materials
- Research related materials
- Gather necessary materials

DAY 5   **Summarize reading material**
- Answer: Who, What, Where, When, How, Why

DAY 6   **Preliminary project construction**
- Make sketches, determine scale, make revisions

DAY 7-11   **Project construction**
- Lay out all materials
- Prepare materials to scale
- Draw/color
- Cut
- Glue
- Paint

DAY 12   **Touch up work**
- Label, check that all items are secure, etc.

DAY 13   **Write paragraph from summary (Day 5)**

DAY 14   **Turn in!**

Test-Taking Skills

1. Survey entire test for the kinds of items that are included (e.g., true-false, multiple-choice, fill-in-the-blank, etc.).

2. Read all directions.

3. Underline or circle all key words or phrases in the directions (e.g., locate, write, choose the best answer, identify the main idea, etc.).

4. Do not answer any items until the directions are thoroughly understood (i.e., ask the teacher for clarification if directions are not thoroughly understood).

5. Respond to all items for which the answer is known; skip remaining items to answer later.

6. For those items which are difficult to answer, underline the key words (e.g., who, what, where, when, how, why) and then respond.

7. For those items still not understood, ask the teacher for clarification.

8. Go back and check all answers for accuracy (e.g., followed directions, proper use of math operations, no careless errors).

ADDITIONAL SUGGESTIONS

- In order for a statement to be true, all of the statement must be true (e.g., note words such as all, never, always, etc.).

- When matching, first answer items that are known. Cross off answers that are used; then go back to remaining items and make the best choice.

- Some items may provide clues or reminders for items that could not be answered the first time through the test.

- When writing an essay answer, construct the answer around Who, What, Where, When, How, and Why.

- On multiple-choice items, read all choices before responding. If any of the choices look new or different, they are probably not the correct answer.

- If a true-false item looks new or different, it is probably false.

Studying for a Test

1. Identify the information to be covered on the test.

2. Identify and collect all necessary materials (e.g., textbook, notebook, etc.).

3. Identify major topics.

4. Under each topic, identify major headings.

5. Under each heading, use the Outline Form to identify Who, What, Where, When, How, and Why or underline/highlight.

6. Make study aids such as flash cards. (See Forms.)

7. Memorize information using the Outline Form and/or mnemonic strategies.

ADDITIONAL SUGGESTIONS

● Study with a friend.

● Write practice questions from the Outline Form and answer the questions.

● If study questions are provided, answer all questions.

● Make sure that all information in the summary is thoroughly understood.

Flash Card Study Aid

Topic: _____

Who:

What:

Where:

When:

How:

Why:

Topic: _____

Who:

What:

Where:

When:

How:

Why:

Fiction Frame

Title: _____

Author: _____

This story takes place _____.

An important character in this story is _____

who _____.

A problem occurs when _____

_____.

Next, _____

_____.

The problem is solved when _____

_____

_____.

At the end of the story, _____

_____

_____.

Parent Letter Sample

Dear Parent(s):

    Your child will be bringing home an assignment sheet each day. This assignment sheet will indicate the assignments that are to be completed at home and when they are due.

    Please check for this sheet every day in order to monitor homework completion. After all assignments are completed, please sign the sheet and return it to school with your child. Thank you for your support.

        Sincerely,

Note Taking

- **Outline Form**
  (e.g., Who, What, Where, When, How, Why)

- **Mapping Form**
  (e.g., Who, What, Where, When, How, Why)

- **Double-Column Form**
  (e.g., Who, What, Where, When, How, Why)

- **Assignment Form**
  (e.g., What, How, Materials, When)

- **Assignment Sheet**

- **2-Week Project Outline**

Selected Abbreviations and Symbols

ab.	about		qt.	quart
addn.	addition		rd.	road
bk.	book		rep.	representative
bldg.	building		Rev.	Reverend
c/o	in care of		s.s.	social studies
cap.	capital		S.S.#	social security number
cent.	century		sc.	science
ch., chap.	chapter		sch.	school
cm	centimeter		sig.	signature
co.	company		sp.	spelling
cont.	continent		sq.	square
cont.	continued		subj.	subject
corp.	corporation		subt.	subtraction
D.O.B.	date of birth		syn.	synonym
DB	database		T	ton
dept.	department		temp.	temporary
dict.	dictionary		treas.	treasurer
doz.	dozen		univ.	university
educ.	education		US, USA	United States of America
enc.	encyclopedia		v.	verb
Eng.	English		VP	vice president
etc.	et cetera, and so forth		vs.	versus
fig.	figure		w/	with
g	gram		wk.	week
geog.	geography		wt.	weight
gov., govt.	government		yd.	yard
hist.	history		yr.	year
ht., hgt.	height		&	and
ill., illus.	illustration		@	at
in.	inch		¢	cents
intro.	introduction		$	dollars
lab.	laboratory		#	number or pound
lang.	language		☠	poison
lat.	latitude		♻	recycle
lb.	pound
leg.	legislature
lib.	library
liq.	liquid
max.	maximum
meas.	measure
mi.	mile
min.	minute
misc.	miscellaneous
mo.	month
natl.	national
no.	number
oz.	ounce
p., pg.	page
par.	paragraph
PC	personal computer
pd.	paid
pop.	population
Pres.	president
pt.	pint

The above list only serves as an example. The student should further develop his/her own list.

References:

Cormier, R.A. (1995). *Error-free writing: A lifetime guide to flawless business writing.* Englewood Cliffs, NJ: Prentice-Hall.

Merriam-Webster's collegiate dictionary (11th ed.). (2003). Springfield, MA: Merriam-Webster.

The new york public library™ desk reference (4th ed.). (2002) New York, NY: Hyperion.

University of Chicago Press. (2003). *The chicago manual of style (15th ed.).* Chicago: Author.

Typical Methods of Modifying Academic Tasks

- Reduce the number of problems on a page (e.g., five problems to a page; the student may be required to do four pages of five problems on each page throughout the day if necessary).

- Use a highlight marker to identify key words, phrases, or sentences for the student to read.

- Remove pages from workbooks or reading material and present these to the student one at a time rather than allowing the student to become anxious with workbooks or texts.

- Outline reading material for the student at his/her reading level, emphasizing main ideas.

- Record material for the student to listen to as he/she reads along.

- Read tests/quizzes aloud for the student.

- Record tests/quizzes for the student.

- Make a bright construction paper border for the student to place around reading material to maintain his/her attention to the task.

- Make a reading window from construction paper which the student places over sentences or paragraphs to maintain attention.

- Provide manipulative objects for the student to use in solving math problems.

- Rearrange problems on a page (e.g., if crowded, create more space between the problems).

- Use graph paper for math problems, handwriting, etc.

- Rewrite directions at an appropriate reading level.

- Record directions.

- Have peers deliver directions or explanations.

- Allow more time to take tests or quizzes.

Preventing Behavior Problems

- Determine reinforcer preferences.

- Determine academic ability levels.

- Determine social interaction skills.

- Determine ability to remain on task.

- Determine group behavior.

- Monitor and limit contemporary determinants of inappropriate behavior such as having to wait, task length, task difficulty, peer involvement, etc.

- Base seating arrangements on behavior.

- Base group involvement on behavior.

- Maintain teacher mobility in the classroom.

- Maintain teacher/student contact: visual, verbal, and physical.

- Use criteria for expectations based on observed behavior and performance.

- Use shaping, fading, and imitation procedures to gradually change behavior.

- Maintain variety in reinforcers.

- Use the *Premack Principle* in arranging the schedule (i.e., a more desirable task can be used to reinforce the completion of a less desirable task).

- Use curriculum as reinforcement.

- Use rules, point cards, and schedules of daily events as discriminative stimuli.

- Use contracting to individualize, specify expected behavior, and identify reinforcers.

- Arrange seating so all students have visibility to and from the teacher, and the teacher can scan the entire class.

- Maintain a full schedule of activities.

- Use language that is positive and firm, not demeaning, insulting, or harassing.

- Intervene early when any form of conflict occurs.

- Do not ignore behavior as an excuse for not intervening.

- Use time-out to help the student resolve problem behavior.

- Use removal to prevent contagion, destruction of property, and danger to others.

- Communicate and coordinate with other teachers.

- Communicate with home to prevent students playing one adult against another.

Elementary Reinforcer Survey

Name: _____ Age: _____ Date: _____

1. The things I like to do after school are _____
   _____

2. If I had ten dollars, I would _____
   _____

3. My favorite TV programs are _____
   _____

4. My favorite game at school is _____
   _____

5. My best friends are _____
   _____

6. My favorite time of day is _____
   _____

7. My favorite toys are _____
   _____

8. My favorite music is _____
   _____

9. My favorite subject at school is _____
   _____

10. I like to read about _____
    _____

11. The places I like to go in town are _____
    _____

12. My favorite foods are _____
    _____

13. My favorite inside activities are _____
    _____

14. My favorite outside activities are _____
    _____

15. My hobbies are _____
    _____

16. My favorite animals are _____
    _____

17. The three things I like to do most are _____
    _____

The Reinforcer Survey may be given to one student or a group of students. If the students cannot read, the survey is read to them. If they cannot write their answers, the answers are given verbally.